Advancing Higher Education with Mobile Learning Technologies:

Cases, Trends, and Inquiry-Based Methods

Jared Keengwe
University of North Dakota, USA

Marian B. Maxfield
Ashland University, USA

A volume in the Advances in Higher Education and Professional Development (AHEPD) Book Series

Information Science
REFERENCE
An Imprint of IGI Global

Managing Director: Lindsay Johnston
Production Editor: Jennifer Yoder
Development Editor: Austin DeMarco
Acquisitions Editor: Kayla Wolfe
Typesetter: Kaitlyn Kulp
Cover Design: Jason Mull

Published in the United States of America by
Information Science Reference (an imprint of IGI Global)
701 E. Chocolate Avenue
Hershey PA, USA 17033
Tel: 717-533-8845
Fax: 717-533-8661
E-mail: cust@igi-global.com
Web site: http://www.igi-global.com

Copyright © 2015 by IGI Global. All rights reserved. No part of this publication may be reproduced, stored or distributed in any form or by any means, electronic or mechanical, including photocopying, without written permission from the publisher. Product or company names used in this set are for identification purposes only. Inclusion of the names of the products or companies does not indicate a claim of ownership by IGI Global of the trademark or registered trademark.
    Library of Congress Cataloging-in-Publication Data

Advancing higher education with mobile learning technologies : cases, trends, and inquiry-based methods / Jared Keengwe and Marian B. Maxfield, editors.
    pages cm
  Includes bibliographical references and index.
  ISBN 978-1-4666-6284-1 (hardcover) -- ISBN 978-1-4666-6285-8 (ebook) -- ISBN 978-1-4666-6287-2 (print & perpetual access) 1. Education, Higher--Computer-assisted instruction. 2. Education, Higher--Effect of technological innovations on. 3. Educational technology. I. Keengwe, Jared, 1973- II. Maxfield, Marian B., 1979-
  LB2395.7.A377 2015
  378.1'758--dc23
                                                            2014017267

This book is published in the IGI Global book series Advances in Higher Education and Professional Development (AHEPD) (ISSN: 2327-6983; eISSN: 2327-6991)

British Cataloguing in Publication Data
A Cataloguing in Publication record for this book is available from the British Library.

All work contributed to this book is new, previously-unpublished material. The views expressed in this book are those of the authors, but not necessarily of the publisher.

For electronic access to this publication, please contact: eresources@igi-global.com.

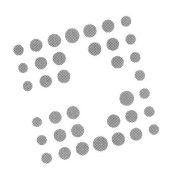

Advances in Higher Education and Professional Development (AHEPD) Book Series

Jared Keengwe
University of North Dakota, USA

ISSN: 2327-6983
EISSN: 2327-6991

Mission

As world economies continue to shift and change in response to global financial situations, job markets have begun to demand a more highly-skilled workforce. In many industries a college degree is the minimum requirement and further educational development is expected to advance. With these current trends in mind, the **Advances in Higher Education & Professional Development (AHEPD) Book Series** provides an outlet for researchers and academics to publish their research in these areas and to distribute these works to practitioners and other researchers.

AHEPD encompasses all research dealing with higher education pedagogy, development, and curriculum design, as well as all areas of professional development, regardless of focus.

Coverage

- Adult Education
- Assessment in Higher Education
- Career Training
- Coaching and Mentoring
- Continuing Professional Development
- Governance in Higher Education
- Higher Education Policy
- Pedagogy of Teaching Higher Education
- Vocational Education

IGI Global is currently accepting manuscripts for publication within this series. To submit a proposal for a volume in this series, please contact our Acquisition Editors at Acquisitions@igi-global.com or visit: http://www.igi-global.com/publish/.

The Advances in Higher Education and Professional Development (AHEPD) Book Series (ISSN 2327-6983) is published by IGI Global, 701 E. Chocolate Avenue, Hershey, PA 17033-1240, USA, www.igi-global.com. This series is composed of titles available for purchase individually; each title is edited to be contextually exclusive from any other title within the series. For pricing and ordering information please visit http://www.igi-global.com/book-series/advances-higher-education-professional-development/73681. Postmaster: Send all address changes to above address. Copyright © 2015 IGI Global. All rights, including translation in other languages reserved by the publisher. No part of this series may be reproduced or used in any form or by any means – graphics, electronic, or mechanical, including photocopying, recording, taping, or information and retrieval systems – without written permission from the publisher, except for non commercial, educational use, including classroom teaching purposes. The views expressed in this series are those of the authors, but not necessarily of IGI Global.

Titles in this Series

For a list of additional titles in this series, please visit: www.igi-global.com

Handbook of Research on Higher Education in the MENA Region Policy and Practice
Neeta Baporikar (Ministry of Higher Education, Oman)
Information Science Reference • copyright 2014 • 527pp • H/C (ISBN: 9781466661981) • US $315.00 (our price)

Advancing Knowledge in Higher Education Universities in Turbulent Times
Tanya Fitzgerald (La Trobe University, Australia)
Information Science Reference • copyright 2014 • 337pp • H/C (ISBN: 9781466662025) • US $195.00 (our price)

Cases on Teacher Identity, Diversity, and Cognition in Higher Education
Paul Breen (Greenwich School of Management, UK)
Information Science Reference • copyright 2014 • 437pp • H/C (ISBN: 9781466659902) • US $195.00 (our price)

Handbook of Research on Trends in European Higher Education Convergence
Alina Mihaela Dima (Bucharest Academy of Economic Studies, Romania)
Information Science Reference • copyright 2014 • 516pp • H/C (ISBN: 9781466659988) • US $315.00 (our price)

Overcoming Challenges in Software Engineering Education Delivering Non-Technical Knowledge and Skills
Liguo Yu (Indiana University South Bend, USA)
Engineering Science Reference • copyright 2014 • 556pp • H/C (ISBN: 9781466658004) • US $235.00 (our price)

Multicultural Awareness and Technology in Higher Education Global Perspectives
Tomayess Issa (Curtin University, Australia) Pedro Isaias (Universidade Aberta (Portuguese Open University), Portugal) and Piet Kommers (University of Twente, The Netherlands)
Information Science Reference • copyright 2014 • 449pp • H/C (ISBN: 9781466658769) • US $215.00 (our price)

Cutting-Edge Technologies and Social Media Use in Higher Education
Vladlena Benson (Kingston University, UK) and Stephanie Morgan (Kingston University, UK)
Information Science Reference • copyright 2014 • 436pp • H/C (ISBN: 9781466651746) • US $215.00 (our price)

Building Online Communities in Higher Education Institutions Creating Collaborative Experience
Carolyn N. Stevenson (Kaplan University, USA) and Joanna C. Bauer (Kaplan University, USA)
Information Science Reference • copyright 2014 • 473pp • H/C (ISBN: 9781466651784) • US $205.00 (our price)

Using Technology Tools to Innovate Assessment, Reporting, and Teaching Practices in Engineering Education
Firoz Alam (RMIT University, Australia)
Engineering Science Reference • copyright 2014 • 409pp • H/C (ISBN: 9781466650114) • US $215.00 (our price)

www.igi-global.com

701 E. Chocolate Ave., Hershey, PA 17033
Order online at www.igi-global.com or call 717-533-8845 x100
To place a standing order for titles released in this series, contact: cust@igi-global.com
Mon-Fri 8:00 am - 5:00 pm (est) or fax 24 hours a day 717-533-8661

Editorial Advisory Board

Emmanuel Adjei-Boateng, *University of North Dakota, USA*
Joachim Agamba, *Idaho State University, USA*
Steven Grubaugh, *University of Nevada, USA*
Afra Hersi, *Loyola University, USA*
Fred Iraki, *United States International University, Kenya*
Kenneth Kungu, *Tennessee State University, USA*
Lydia Kyei-Blankson, *Illinois State University, USA*
Dianna L. Newman, *University at Albany (SUNY), USA*
Esther Ntuli, *Idaho State University, USA*
Grace Onchwari, *University of North Dakota, USA*
Elijah Onsomu, *Winston Salem State University, USA*
John Rugutt, *Illinois State University, USA*
Joseph Rugutt, *Missouri State University – West Plains, USA*
Gary Schnellert, *University of North Dakota, USA*
Peggy Semingson, *University of Texas – Arlington, USA*

Table of Contents

Foreword xv

Preface xvii

Acknowledgment xxi

Chapter 1
Mobile Social Media as a Catalyst for Collaborative Curriculum Redesign 1
    Thomas Cochrane, Auckland University of Technology, New Zealand
    Matthew Guinibert, Auckland University of Technology, New Zealand
    Clinton Simeti, Auckland University of Technology, New Zealand
    Ross Brannigan, Auckland University of Technology, New Zealand
    Abhishek Kala, Auckland University of Technology, New Zealand

Chapter 2
Developing Faculty to Effectively Use Mobile Learning Technologies in Collegiate Classes: A
Guide for Department Chairs 22
    Richard E. Newman, University of Arkansas, USA
    Michael T. Miller, University of Arkansas, USA
    Kenda S. Grover, University of Arkansas, USA

Chapter 3
A Case Study of Developing Suitable Mobile Learning Technology for a Distance Learning
Masters Programme 35
    Tracey Dodman, University of Leicester, UK
    Terese Bird, University of Leicester, UK
    David Hopkins, University of Leicester, UK

Chapter 4
Mobile Learning: Trends, Issues, and Challenges in Teaching and Learning 60
    Chien Yu, Mississippi State University, USA
    Sang Joon Lee, Mississippi State University, USA
    Carlos Ewing, Mississippi State University, USA

Chapter 5
Teacher Development, Support, and Training with Mobile Technologies 88
    Nance S. Wilson, State University of New York at Cortland, USA
    Vassiliki (Vicky) I. Zygouris-Coe, University of Central Florida, USA
    Victoria M. Cardullo, Auburn University, USA

Chapter 6
Using Mobile Technology for Student Teaching Observations of Special Education Candidates 114
    Josh Harrower, California State University – Monterey Bay, USA
    Cathi Draper Rodríguez, California State University – Monterey Bay, USA

Chapter 7
Mobile Technology in Higher Education: Patterns of Replication and Transferability 128
    Meghan Morris Deyoe, University at Albany (SUNY), USA
    Dianna L. Newman, University at Albany (SUNY), USA
    Jessica M. Lamendola, University at Albany (SUNY), USA

Chapter 8
Improving the Work Integrated Learning Experience through Mobile Technologies 154
    Chris Dann, The University of the Sunshine Coast, Australia
    Tony Richardson, The University of the Sunshine Coast, Australia

Chapter 9
Opportunities and Challenges of Mobile Technologies in Higher Education Pedagogy in Africa:
A Case Study 170
    Frederick Kang'ethe Iraki, United States International University, Kenya

Chapter 10
Promoting Strategic Reading Using the iBooks Author Application 179
    Natalia Auer, University of Leicester, UK

Chapter 11
Using Mobile Technologies to Co-Construct TPACK in Teacher Education 195
    Cornelis de Groot, University of Rhode Island, USA
    Jay Fogleman, University of Rhode Island, USA
    Diane Kern, University of Rhode Island, USA

Chapter 12
Reconceptualizing Learning Designs in Higher Education: Using Mobile Devices to Engage
Students in Authentic Tasks 220
    Nathaniel Ostashewski, Curtin University, Australia
    Sonia Dickinson-Delaporte, Curtin University, Australia
    Romana Martin, Curtin University, Australia

Chapter 13
Framing Mobile Learning: Investigating the Framework for the Rationale Analysis of Mobile Education 238
    Kim A. Hosler, University of Denver, USA

Chapter 14
Integrating Mobile Technologies in Multicultural Multilingual Multimedia Projects 254
    Melda N. Yildiz, Kean University, USA
    Kristine Scharaldi, Independent Scholar, USA

Chapter 15
Web 2.0 Technology Use by Students in Higher Education: A Case of Kenyan Universities 278
    Rhoda K. Gitonga, Kenyatta University, Kenya
    Catherine G. Murungi, Kenyatta University, Kenya

Related References 288

Compilation of References 319

About the Contributors 353

Index 362

Detailed Table of Contents

Foreword xv

Preface xvii

Acknowledgment xxi

Chapter 1
Mobile Social Media as a Catalyst for Collaborative Curriculum Redesign 1
  Thomas Cochrane, Auckland University of Technology, New Zealand
  Matthew Guinibert, Auckland University of Technology, New Zealand
  Clinton Simeti, Auckland University of Technology, New Zealand
  Ross Brannigan, Auckland University of Technology, New Zealand
  Abhishek Kala, Auckland University of Technology, New Zealand

This chapter illustrates the potential of mobile social media to be used as a catalyst for collaborative curriculum redesign. The authors critique a case study implementing a mobile social media framework for creative pedagogies and draw out the implications of this framework for wider educational contexts. They conclude that an effective mobile social media framework for collaborative curriculum redesign must meet three goals: model the building of learning communities, explore the unique affordances of mobile social media to enable new pedagogies, and establish a supporting technology infrastructure.

Chapter 2
Developing Faculty to Effectively Use Mobile Learning Technologies in Collegiate Classes: A Guide for Department Chairs 22
  Richard E. Newman, University of Arkansas, USA
  Michael T. Miller, University of Arkansas, USA
  Kenda S. Grover, University of Arkansas, USA

Mobile devices have become a common accessory for many college students, and with the habits and tendencies that have formed from frequent use, colleges have begun to incorporate mobile devices into the delivery of education. As mobile learning has grown as a teaching strategy, some faculty have found it difficult to adapt to open access to computing, and others have simply attempted to ignore the new reliance on technology. Department chairs are uniquely situated to bridge the world of technology and the contemporary campus, and through strategic and intentional faculty development, they have the potential to successfully bring mobile learning to higher education. Throughout the chapter, strategies outline how to use adult learning to build faculty development programs that encourage the effective use of m-learning as an instructional strategy.

Chapter 3
A Case Study of Developing Suitable Mobile Learning Technology for a Distance Learning Masters Programme 35

Tracey Dodman, University of Leicester, UK
Terese Bird, University of Leicester, UK
David Hopkins, University of Leicester, UK

In 2012, following some development work, the Department of Criminology launched a new distance-learning course: the MSc Security, Conflict, and International Development (SCID). The target profile for students looking to enroll in this course were living or working in and around conflict regions; they may be forces personnel or professional staff stationed in areas of conflict or recent conflict. Therefore, reliable Internet connection (broadband or cellular) is often rare or intermittent. The course was designed to give learners a rich learning experience in such a way that their learning could remain largely uninterrupted when they experienced loss of Internet connection. Learners in this course were sent an Apple iPad as part of their course fees and given instructions to download a Course App comprising multimedia-rich learning resources. The programme enabled students to study and learn whilst on the move and provided an opportunity for study where otherwise it would have been very difficult, if not impossible for some. The authors believe they have widened participation and enhanced learning capacity through the innovative programme design. This programme is explored in this chapter.

Chapter 4
Mobile Learning: Trends, Issues, and Challenges in Teaching and Learning 60

Chien Yu, Mississippi State University, USA
Sang Joon Lee, Mississippi State University, USA
Carlos Ewing, Mississippi State University, USA

The purpose of this chapter is to provide the readers with an overview of the association between mobile learning technologies and the nature of teaching and learning. In addition to the benefits of using mobile learning, the current educational and strategic uses of the mobile technology are discussed. Based on a review of scholarly publications, the chapter delineates the current trends and issues pertinent to the development of mobile learning or e-learning at large. By outlining some fundamental issues and considerations, the chapter further presents some challenges and impacts of mobile learning in teaching and training as well. Additional examples drawn from literature are included to explore the use of mobile learning in education and the strategies of effective mobile learning applications.

Chapter 5
Teacher Development, Support, and Training with Mobile Technologies 88

Nance S. Wilson, State University of New York at Cortland, USA
Vassiliki (Vicky) I. Zygouris-Coe, University of Central Florida, USA
Victoria M. Cardullo, Auburn University, USA

Preparing teachers to integrate iPads into the classroom requires designing professional development that supports teacher knowledge development as well as the development of a teacher as metacognitive. In this chapter, the authors describe training and support that builds teachers' development of a Metacognitive Technological Pedagogical Framework (M-TPACK) for integrating iPads. The professional development emphasizes the metacognitive teacher with positive dispositions towards technology integration as a key factor in ensuring that teachers implement knowledge of content, technology, pedagogy, and students. Finally, this chapter presents authentic and relevant examples for teacher development with mobile technologies.

Chapter 6
Using Mobile Technology for Student Teaching Observations of Special Education Candidates.....114
    Josh Harrower, California State University – Monterey Bay, USA
    Cathi Draper Rodríguez, California State University – Monterey Bay, USA

Student teacher supervision has been an important part of teacher preparation almost since the inception of teacher education programs. The goal of this type of supervision is to strengthen the skills of the pre-service teacher. Providing this type of observation can be difficult for teacher preparation programs and university faculty. Many factors, including large numbers of students in teacher education programs and student placements in remote schools, contribute to this. In order to make the most effective use of faculty and pre-service teacher time, other options for providing this support need to be explored. The rapidly developing field of mobile technology (e.g., iPads, iPhones, Smart Phones) can be used to facilitate student teaching observations. This chapter discusses how teacher preparation programs can implement candidate field supervision using video conferencing via mobile technology to increase the ability to conduct observations in schools and in a more efficient manner. It also explores the security of video conferencing applications and the issues related to using video conferencing in special education classrooms, where student confidentiality is heightened.

Chapter 7
Mobile Technology in Higher Education: Patterns of Replication and Transferability......................128
    Meghan Morris Deyoe, University at Albany (SUNY), USA
    Dianna L. Newman, University at Albany (SUNY), USA
    Jessica M. Lamendola, University at Albany (SUNY), USA

Innovative instructional strategies and approaches are in high demand in STEM higher education. Currently, interest lies in the integration of mobile technology within these settings to provide learning opportunities that are flexible and feasible enough to increase student understanding using critical inquiry. Although the positive impact of the use of mobile technology in many pilot settings is known, there are still numerous questions left unanswered in relation to the effectiveness of the use of mobile technology as it is replicated from developer across enthusiastic replicator use to required use. This chapter examines the replication and transferability patterns related to the use of a mobile technology device within and across multiple instructors, settings, context, and content areas. Key variables explored relate to student and instructor prior use and experience with the mobile technology, pedagogical goals, and similarly, content and context to original use.

Chapter 8
Improving the Work Integrated Learning Experience through Mobile Technologies........................154
    Chris Dann, The University of the Sunshine Coast, Australia
    Tony Richardson, The University of the Sunshine Coast, Australia

The inclusion of technological solutions in higher education has led to a vast array of options for educators. An educational problem has driven each solution and the associated research into defining the effectiveness of those solutions. This chapter describes some of the problems faced by a teacher education program, triggered by the use of Work Integrated Learning (WIL), to connect theory taught in universities to the realities of a teacher's life. The underlying beliefs of the authors are that there needs to be critical discourse about the teaching and learning models used to engage students in the art of workplace learning, that this critical discourse needs to be based on facilitating a teaching and learning environment that is highly effective, and that the nexus is that the student's Work Integrated Learning (WIL) experience will not be counterproductive. This chapter highlights a concrete example of how one university implemented these beliefs in a structured and proactive manner.

Chapter 9
Opportunities and Challenges of Mobile Technologies in Higher Education Pedagogy in Africa:
A Case Study...170
    Frederick Kang'ethe Iraki, United States International University, Kenya

Since the late 1990s, Kenya has undergone a real technological revolution, especially in the domain of mobile telephony and Internet connectivity. From a negligible number of handsets in the hands of the political elites, today almost every adult Kenyan has a mobile phone, or access to one. This is thanks to reduced costs following expansion and diversification of the market niche. Despite this remarkable progress, research has shown that cell phones are used mainly for financial transactions, social communication, and entertainment, but hardly for learning purposes. This means that despite the impressive number of smartphone owners in the university, for example, the devices are not used for enhancing student learning or teaching. In Kenya, more than 60% of the population employs mobile banking, thus underscoring the immense potential that the cell phones have for education. This chapter explores the benefits and challenges in employing mobile telephony to improve the quality of teaching and learning.

Chapter 10
Promoting Strategic Reading Using the iBooks Author Application 179
    Natalia Auer, University of Leicester, UK

Students are increasingly bringing their own mobile devices into the classroom. However, they do not take advantage of the various features that technology offers for supporting learning. The focus of the chapter is on digital reading in learning and particularly in foreign language learning with tablets. The author reviews the literature on digital reading and discusses briefly the use of reading strategies to promote reading comprehension. This is followed by a discussion of how the application iBooks Author was used in a research project in September 2012 in an Adult Education Centre in Denmark. The aim of the project was to determine to what extent students employ reading strategies when using tablets and which functions in the tablets support reading comprehension. Using a theoretical framework for learning strategies, the author discusses the design of digital material embedding reading strategies. The chapter concludes with practical suggestions for teachers and educational designers for promoting strategic reading using the iBooks Author application.

Chapter 11
Using Mobile Technologies to Co-Construct TPACK in Teacher Education....................................195
    Cornelis de Groot, University of Rhode Island, USA
    Jay Fogleman, University of Rhode Island, USA
    Diane Kern, University of Rhode Island, USA

How student teachers might benefit from using their mobile technologies during teaching experiences is a timely question for teacher educators. This chapter describes efforts to use the TPACK framework (Mishra & Koehler, 2006) to investigate how students use iPad computers during their student teaching and design appropriate supports. A design-based approach (Sandoval & Bell, 2004) was used over two years with two cohorts of student teachers (N=60). Descriptions of the use of the TPACK framework in this endeavor and findings from surveys and field notes about how and to what degree mobile technology can facilitate activities and interactions in planning, teaching, reflecting, and sharing are included. The case is made for co-learning and co-constructing by student teachers and teacher educators of the various TPACK domains of teacher knowledge in the context of mobile technology. Implications for developing supportive learning environments for 21st century student teachers are also discussed.

Chapter 12
Reconceptualizing Learning Designs in Higher Education: Using Mobile Devices to Engage
Students in Authentic Tasks 220
    Nathaniel Ostashewski, Curtin University, Australia
    Sonia Dickinson-Delaporte, Curtin University, Australia
    Romana Martin, Curtin University, Australia

This goal of this chapter is to provide a design and development roadmap for the adaptation of traditional classroom activities into engaging iPad-based digital learning activities. Reporting on an ongoing longitudinal case study, the chapter provides an overview of rationale and design considerations of the authentic iPad learning design implementation project, and the outcomes and improvements made over time. The iPad activities described provide further details of the approach taken and adaptations made. Since implementing iPad activities into this higher education environment several terms ago, the lecturer reports significantly higher levels of student engagement. Additionally, students report that the classroom activities in the post-graduate marketing course are authentic, transferrable, and are more engaging due the use of the iPad-based activities.

Chapter 13
Framing Mobile Learning: Investigating the Framework for the Rationale Analysis of Mobile
Education 238
    Kim A. Hosler, University of Denver, USA

The purpose of this chapter is to introduce faculty and instructors, and those interested in using mobile technologies to support teaching and learning, to the Framework for the Rationale Analysis of Mobile Education (FRAME; Koole, 2009). This chapter discusses how mobile or handheld devices can be used to promote inquiry-based learning and constructivist and authentic pedagogies. Additionally, the chapter discusses Koole's (2009) FRAME model as a scaffold for guiding "the development of learning materials, and the design of teaching and learning strategies for mobile education" (p. 25). Lastly, the FRAME model is used to guide the implementation of an inquiry-based instructional unit incorporating mobile or handheld devices.

Chapter 14
Integrating Mobile Technologies in Multicultural Multilingual Multimedia Projects 254
   Melda N. Yildiz, Kean University, USA
   Kristine Scharaldi, Independent Scholar, USA

This chapter explores the role of mobile technologies, such as Global Positioning System (GPS) and cell phones and tablet PC technologies, in higher education and professional development; offers creative strategies and possibilities for integrating GPS and mobile technologies into the curriculum with limited resources; outlines participants' projects and digital stories; and demonstrates examples that integrates Maps, Mathematics, and Media Education using cell phones, tablet PCs, and GPS devices in a gallery walk. The study explores a wide range of meanings participants associated with experiential project-based learning activities; the impact of mobile technologies in developing multicultural and multilingual curriculum that promotes inclusive and differentiated instruction; the ways in which participants integrated math, maps, and media into their learning; and how they gained alternative points of view on global education and renewed interest and commitment to community service and socially responsible teaching. This chapter will benefit teacher candidates and teacher educators who seek innovative and cost-effective strategies and tools in higher education.

Chapter 15
Web 2.0 Technology Use by Students in Higher Education: A Case of Kenyan Universities............ 278
   Rhoda K. Gitonga, Kenyatta University, Kenya
   Catherine G. Murungi, Kenyatta University, Kenya

Web 2.0 technologies are technologies on the Internet such as blogs, wikis, and online forums that allow people to create, share, collaborate, and communicate their ideas. Blogs are known to enhance team cooperation and foster a learning community within the class. Wikis have been used to promote group work. Online discussion forums assist with problem-based learning. Facebook/Twitter have the potential to support social learning through community networking services such as wall pasting, chatting, content-sharing, and tagging. Despite the enormous potential and apparent cost effectiveness of new learning media for facilitating social-networked learning, problem-based learning, and promoting group work, its application by institutions of higher learning in developing African countries is low. The purpose of the study was to investigate the use of Web 2.0 technologies in teaching and learning in Kenyan universities. The researchers used surveys to collect data for this study. The findings reveal that the use of Web 2.0 technologies by students in Kenyan universities was quite low. Finally, other implications need to be explored in the context of the study, including the learners and the Web 2.0 technology resources available.

Related References 288

Compilation of References 319

About the Contributors 353

Index 362

Foreword

Where is the knowledge we have lost in information? – T.S. Eliot, 1934, Choruses from the Rock.

Mobile computing is ubiquitous computing. Whether it is a laptop, tablet, smartphone or even Google Glass, the tools are available to bring content and information to learners wherever they are. This immense access to information does not guarantee learning or an increase in knowledge (or wisdom if we consider more of T.S. Eliot's poem). So how do institutions of higher learning transcend the challenge of the ubiquity of a technology, and therefore information, while at the same time ensuring that the technology helps transform content into increased knowledge?

A beginning point is to understand the true penetration level and therefore, potential of mobile computing for college students. In September 2013, EDUCAUSE released the 2013 edition of the ECAR Study of Undergraduate Students and Information Technology. Seventy-five percent of undergraduate students responded that they agree or strongly agree that technology is important for their preparation and to achieve their academic goals. At the same time, mobile computing ownership is at all time high levels. Nine out of ten students own at least two devices and the more devices they own, the more likely they are to believe that these devices are critical for their academic success. One third of all students have identified that the ultimate mobile technology, the smartphone, could be used as an effective learning tool during class.

While student access to mobile technologies is critical, it is only part of the equation of the learning process. A critical variable in the complex formula is the faculty. The ECAR results indicate that students desire to learn about the use and application of their technology from their instructors, and they prefer that this training occur during their regularly offered classes. Fortunately, a slight majority of students indicate that their instructors provide adequate technology training, have adequate skills, use technology effectively, and are using the right kinds of technology.

Unfortunately, despite students' readiness to use mobile technology, few students report that they are encouraged, much less required, to use these tools in the classroom (EDUCAUSE, 2013). Instructors place the most restrictions on smartphone use, with the use of them often banned. While students do recognize that they can be distracted by their mobile devices, using them for social networking or entertainment, others express a desire to be able to use their technologies to record lectures and research class content for greater learning gains.

In *Advancing Higher Education with Mobile Learning Technologies: Cases, Trends, and Inquiry-Based Methods,* Keengwe and Maxfield have compiled a volume that explores how to maximize the saturation of mobile technologies to help students achieve their academic goals as they desire. The chapters explore the critical issues of instructor development and the supports that are needed to help faculty effectively use the tools available. These supports include curriculum, administration, appropriate and accessible learning resources, and assessment. The contributing authors also appropriately examine ways to help students not only learn from mobile learning technologies in higher education settings, but discover their potential as a life-long learner.

Oblinger (2012) labels information technology as a game changer. She also correctly points out that an effective learning experience is also a game changes for students. There is synergy behind these two truths; mobile technologies bring together convenience and collaborative tools to engage students in authentic, quality learning experiences. It is through these interactions that higher education will be advanced. This edited volume explores the multiple concepts of building a bridge from information to knowledge through mobile technology tools.

Susan M. Powers
Indiana State University, USA

Susan Powers *serves as Associate Vice President of Academic Affairs for Curriculum and Faculty at Indiana State University and is a Professor of Education Technology. Dr. Powers earned her doctorate at the University of Virginia. She has been involved with distance learning since 1997 and co-chaired Indiana State University's move to adopt a laptop requirement for all students. She has over 18 years of experience with teacher training grants for educational technologies, and has authored a book, papers, and presentations on the effective integration of technology for teaching and learning. She is also the author and co-chair of institutional and programmatic accreditation reports.*

REFERENCES

Dahlstrom, E., Walker, J. D., & Dziuban, C. (2013). ECAR Study of undergraduate students and information technology, 2013 (Research Report). Louisville, CO: EDUCAUSE Center for Analysis and Research; Available from http://www.educause.edu/ecar

Oblinger, D. G. (2012). IT as a game changer. In D.G. Oblinger (Ed.), *Game changers: Education and information technologies.* EDUCAUSE. Available from http://www.educause.edu/research-and-publications/books

Preface

Many educators agree that mobile technology has great potential not only to improve our educational practices but also to change traditional learning platforms and classroom learning environments. There are also many advantages to integrating mobile technologies into the 21st century classrooms to support teaching and learning. Mobile technology tools such as iPads, iPad minis, mobile applications, tablets, palm devices, e-readers, and smartphones are becoming real-world tools that should be integrated into modern intructional practices to support digital learners and to promote meaningful learning. Educators are harnessing mobile devices within and beyond the classroom due to the flexibility, portability, affordability, and popularity of those devices.

Similarly, educators are looking at implementing mobile technologies within faculty development, pre-service teacher training, and in K-12 to assist with student achievement and meaningful learning, and to reach students in remote places that might not be able to have access to education otherwise (Gronn, Romeo, McNamara, & Teo, 2013; Martin & Ertzberger, 2013). There is also evidence to suggest positive results when Mobile Learning (M-Learning) best-practices and trends are implemented into the teaching and learning process to engage the digital natives and promote real-world learning and to further the professional development of K-20 teachers (Merchant, 2012). Mobile devices (and appropriate instructional practices, such as inquiry-based learning) have the capability to help motivate students, encourage persistence on challenging tasks and real-world problems, allow students to be self-directed, and create a personal learning environment suited to each learner (Jones, Scanlon, & Clough, 2013).

In most cases, traditional learning pedagogies have changed to reflect an authentic and real-world approach to learning and teaching with a focus on inquiry-based learning and technnology integration. Additionally, although there is great promise to integrate mobile technology as a learning tool, there are several issues, challenges, and concerns to be addressed. Some of the main concerns are practicality and sustainability within educational environments. There are also concerns that the multiple functions available could inhibit or distract from learning (Wood, Zivcakova, Gentile, Archer, De Pasquale, & Nosko, 2011).

The emergence of technologies in the real-world and in education reflect the need for professional development required by teachers in this area to prepare the next generation of learners for the 21st century. To this end, *Advancing Higher Education with Mobile Learning Technologies: Cases, Trends, and Inquiry-Based Methods* brings together researchers who study and professionals who utilize mobile technologies in educational settings for meaningful learning to share paradigms, perspectives, insights, best practices, challenges, and effective models. Further, the book explores the effectiveness of mobile technologies within 21st century classrooms and the constructivist or inquiry-based learning environments on the teaching and learning processes and outcomes.

Chapter 1 examines the potential of mobile social media to be used as a catalyst for collaborative curriculum redesign. A case study is critiqued for implementing a mobile social media framework for creative pedagogies and the implications of this framework are drawn out for wider educational contexts. An effective mobile social media framework for collaborative curriculum redesign must meet three goals: model the building of learning communities, explore the unique affordances of mobile social media to enable new pedagogies, and establish a supporting technology infrastructure.

Chapter 2 examines how department chairs are uniquely situated to bridge the world of technology and the contemporary campus, and through strategic and intentional faculty development, they have the potential to successfully bring mobile learning to higher education. Throughout the chapter, strategies outline how to use adult learning to build faculty development programs that encourage the effective use of m-learning as an instructional strategy.

Chapter 3 discusses a program that was designed to provide rich learning experiences with the use of Apple iPads that would be reliable with intermittent Internet connections. This program allows students to learn while on the move and provides opportunity for studying when it might be otherwise difficult or impossible.

Chapter 4 provides an overview between mobile learning technologies and the nature of teaching and learning. It specifically reviews the current trends, strategies, and issues related to the development of mobile learning and outlines the current challenges and impacts within teaching and training.

Chapter 5 discusses the professional development that prepares teachers to implement iPads into the classroom. It describes the training and support that builds teachers' development of a Metacognitive Technological Pedagogical Framework (M-TPACK) for integrating iPads. It focuses on the positive dispositions towards technology integration as a key factor in ensuring that teachers implement knowledge of content, technology, pedagogy, and students. This chapter also presents authentic and relevant examples for teacher development with mobile technologies.

Chapter 6 discusses how teacher preparation programs can be implemented into candidate field supervision using video conferencing via mobile technology to increase the ability to conduct observations in schools and in a more efficient manner. It also explores the security of video conferencing applications and the issues related to using video conferencing in special education classrooms, where student confidentiality is of high importance.

Chapter 7 explores the integration of mobile technology within STEM educational settings to provide learning opportunities that are flexible and feasible enough to increase student understanding using critical inquiry. This chapter also examines the replication and transferability patterns related to the use of a mobile technology devices within and across multiple instructors, settings, context, and content areas.

Chapter 8 describes some of the problems faced by a teacher education program, triggered by the use of Work Integrated Learning (WIL), to connect theory taught in universities to the realities of a teacher's life. The authors explain their belief that there needs to be critical discourse about the teaching and learning models used to engage students in the art of workplace learning; that this critical discourse needs to be based on facilitating a teaching and learning environment that is highly effective; and that the nexus is that the student's Work Integrated Learning (WIL) experience will not be counterproductive. A concrete example is highlighted by how one university implemented these beliefs in a structured and proactive manner.

Chapter 9 examines the benefits and challenges in employing mobile telephony to improve the quality of teaching and learning. The chapter explores challenges including cultural inhibitions and at times oral language cognitive costs, and the ethical issues relating to the "privacy" of a cell phone.

Chapter 10 addresses the theme of Mobile Learning Technologies and Applications in Education, specifically regarding digital reading in learning, and particularly in foreign language learning with tablets. Practical suggestions for teachers and educational designers for promoting strategic reading using the iBooks Author application are also discussed.

Chapter 11 describes efforts to use the TPACK framework (Mishra & Koehler, 2006) to investigate how students use iPad computers during their student teaching and design appropriate supports. Implications for developing supportive learning environments for 21st century student teachers are also discussed.

Chapter 12 describes a design and development roadmap for the adaptation of traditional higher education classroom activities into engaging iPad-based digital learning activities. The chapter provides an overview of rationale and design considerations of the authentic iPad learning design implementation project and the positive outcomes and improvements (made over time) related to this project.

Chapter 13 discusses how mobile or handheld devices can be used to promote inquiry-based learning and constructivist and authentic pedagogies. Additionally, the chapter discusses Koole's FRAME model, which is also used to guide the implementation of an inquiry-based instructional unit incorporating mobile or handheld devices.

Chapter 14 explores the role of mobile technologies such as Global Positioning System (GPS) and cell phones and tablet PC technologies in higher education and professional development. It offers creative strategies and possibilities for integrating GPS and mobile technologies into the curriculum with limited resources, outlines participants' projects, and demonstrates examples that integrate Maps, Mathematics, and Media Education using cell phones, tablet PCs, and GPS devices in a gallery walk.

Chapter 15 investigates the use of Web 2.0 technologies in learning in Kenyan universities. Web 2.0 technologies are technologies on the Internet such as blogs, wikis, and online forums that allow people to create, share, collaborate, and communicate their ideas. Despite the enormous potential and apparent cost effectiveness of new learning media for facilitating social-networked learning, problem-based learning, and promoting group work, its application by institutions of higher learning in developing African countries is low. The study findings reveal that Web 2.0 technology use by students in Kenyan universities was quite low. Finally, other implications need to be explored in the context of the study, including the learners and the Web 2.0 technology resources available.

Our hope is that the research and information presented in this book will further the agenda and advance the discussion on the implementation of mobile technology within the field of education in accordance with inquiry-based and authentic learning settings. Furthermore, it is our hope that the book becomes an excellent reference resource for professionals working in the field, including faculty, teachers, school administrators, technology staff, directors of teaching and learning centers, and other educational and technology stakeholders.

Jared Keengwe
University of North Dakota, USA

Marian Maxfield
Ashland University, USA

REFERENCES

Gronn, D., Romeo, G., McNamara, S., & Teo, Y. H. (2013). Web conferencing of pre-service teachers' practicum in remote schools. *Journal of Technology and Teacher Education, 21*(2), 247–271.

Jones, A. C., Scanlon, E., & Clough, G. (2013). Mobile learning: Two case studies of supporting inquiry learning in informal and semiformal settings. *Computers & Education, 61*, 21–32. doi:10.1016/j.compedu.2012.08.008

Martin, F., & Ertzberger, J. (2013). Here and now mobile learning: An experimental study on the use of mobile technology. *Computers & Education, 68*, 76–85. doi:10.1016/j.compedu.2013.04.021

Wood, E., Zivcakova, L., Gentile, P., Archer, K., De Pasquale, D., & Nosko, A. (2011). Examining the impact of off-task multi-tasking with technology on real-time classroom learning. *Computers & Education, 58*(1), 365–374. doi:10.1016/j.compedu.2011.08.029

Acknowledgment

I would like to express my sincere gratitude to my colleague and co-editor, Dr. Marian Maxfield (Ashland University). Thank you Marian, for your assistance drafting both the book proposal and the preface and for your assistance coordinating the Editorial Advisory Board (EAB) review process and activities.

I am forever indebted to my close family members who continue to inspire me to laugh often and write. Specifically, I appreciate that YOU BELIEVE IN ME—your belief that I can ALWAYS successfully accomplish any—yes, any writing project if I just tried.

Thanks to the wonderful staff at IGI Global who participated in the overall development and successful completion of this great project. Finally, I am very grateful to the Editorial Advisory Board (EAB) team.

Jared Keengwe
University of North Dakota, USA

Chapter 1
Mobile Social Media as a Catalyst for Collaborative Curriculum Redesign

Thomas Cochrane
Auckland University of Technology, New Zealand

Clinton Simeti
Auckland University of Technology, New Zealand

Matthew Guinibert
Auckland University of Technology, New Zealand

Ross Brannigan
Auckland University of Technology, New Zealand

Abhishek Kala
Auckland University of Technology, New Zealand

ABSTRACT

This chapter illustrates the potential of mobile social media to be used as a catalyst for collaborative curriculum redesign. The authors critique a case study implementing a mobile social media framework for creative pedagogies and draw out the implications of this framework for wider educational contexts. They conclude that an effective mobile social media framework for collaborative curriculum redesign must meet three goals: model the building of learning communities, explore the unique affordances of mobile social media to enable new pedagogies, and establish a supporting technology infrastructure.

INTRODUCTION

Balsamo (2011) argues that higher education needs a "reboot" in order to engage with new pedagogies relevant to today's learners and their prospective professions. Such a reboot requires curriculum redesign, and Laurillard et al., (2011) argue that curriculum design should be a collaborative process, and should be regarded as a valid design science (Laurillard, 2012). The challenge of innovation in curriculum design is enabling lecturers to think differently or creatively about pedagogy, content delivery, and assessment, this effectively involves a culture change or ontological shift (Chi & Hausmann, 2003) where the role of the teacher, the learner, and technology are reconceptualised. Hase and Kenyon (2007) note that "people only change in response to a very

DOI: 10.4018/978-1-4666-6284-1.ch001

clear need. This usually involves distress such as confusion, dissonance, and fear or a more positive motive such as intense desire". Thus some form of catalyst is required to bring about pedagogical change. We argue that mobile social media is such a catalyst (Kukulska-Hulme, 2010) that enables a pedagogical refocus from teacher-directed content delivery to student-generated content and student-generated learning contexts. This refocus can be viewed as part of a continuum of pedagogical change enabled by new and emerging technologies, and the emergence of mobile social media in particular. We illustrate this continuum in Table 1.

We call this pedagogical change timeline the post web 2.0 continuum to reflect the technological developments and their pedagogical affordances from the rise of the Internet, web 2.0, and the virtually ubiquitous uptake of mobile devices such as cellphones. This project was also informed by the researcher's six critical success factors for maximising the potential of mobile social media for higher education (Cochrane, 2014):

1. The pedagogical integration of the technology into the course and assessment.
2. Lecturer modelling of the pedagogical use of the tools.
3. Creating a supportive learning community.
4. Appropriate choice of mobile devices and Web 2.0 social software.
5. Technological and pedagogical support.
6. Creating sustained interaction that facilitates the development of ontological shifts, both for the lecturers and the students.

Smartphones and tablets are powerful computing devices with unique affordances that enable student learning in multiple contexts. These mobile devices facilitate rich-media recording of student activity in the form of images, video, audio, and geolocation data. With multiple built-in sensors and ubiquitous connectivity these mobile devices can be used to rethink collaboration and develop the potential for enhanced engagement and learning outcomes. Large-scale mobile learning research projects in the UK (Attewell, Savill-Smith, Douch, & Parker, 2010) and Europe (Unterfrauner & Marschalek, 2010) have demonstrated that mlearning empowers marginalized learners, and Australian research has shown mlearning is a catalyst for enabling authentic learning (Herrington, Herrington, Mantei, Olney, & Ferry, 2009).

However, while mobile learning (mlearning) is an established field of research (Pachler, Bachmair, & Cook, 2010; Parsons, 2013; Sharples, 2009) there are two significant gaps in current knowledge. Firstly it is increasingly clear that 'net-generation' learners do not automatically apply the functionality of their devices to the attainment of deep learning outcomes (Kennedy, et al., 2007; Sheely, 2008; White & Le Cornu, 2011). More knowledge is required about how to achieve the shifts in conceptions of learning that are necessary for effective use of mobile devices. Secondly there is a lack of studies on integration of findings from mlearning research into sustainable change in curriculum, policy and infrastructure (Traxler, 2010, 2011). The project aimed to address these gaps by implementing a framework for enhanced

Table 1. Post Web 2.0 continuum

1995	2005	2013
• Web 1.0. • Teacher. • LMS. • Content delivery.	• Web 2.0. • Student. • ePortfolio. • Student-generated content.	• Mobile. • Collaboration. • Connectivism. • Creativity. • Student-generated contexts.

learning and institutional change across different disciplines and institutions. The project aims to generate a range of practical strategies for students, teachers and leaders to utilise the affordances of mobile devices for pedagogical transformation and empowering learners.

Thus we argue that the power of mobile learning is in the potential to change entrenched pedagogical cultures rather than focus upon developing mobile accessible content that does not necessarily result in pedagogical change (Cochrane, 2013). Based upon this we have developed a mobile social media framework that was implemented within the communications studies course at the researcher's university (Table 2).

This framework is focused upon cultivating creative pedagogies within the context of the curriculum. The framework is essentially a mashup of several interrelated learning frameworks. The frameworks include: the Pedaogogy-Andragogy-Heutagogy continuum (Luckin, et al., 2010), Puentedura's (2006) SAMR model (Substitution, Augmentation, Modification, Redefinition) of educational technology transformation. and Sternberg, Kaufman and Pretz's (2002) view of creativity involving incrementation (or modification of a current idea) followed by reinitiation (or redefinition). Aligning these frameworks with the unique affordances of mobile social media provides an overall framework for designing new course activities and assessments that leverage new pedagogies. The goal of this framework is to produce graduates "who can think creatively and become active participants of the community of practitioners associated with their chosen field of design" (Cochrane & Antonczak, 2013a,

Table 2. A framework for using mobile social media to enable creative pedagogies (modified from Luckin, et al., (2010))

	Pedagogy	**Andragogy**	**Heutagogy**
Activity Types	• Content delivery. • Digital assessment. • Teacher delivered content. • Teacher defined projects.	• Teacher as guide. • Digital identity. • Student-generated content. • Student negotiated teams.	• Teacher as co-learner. • Digital presence. • Student-generated contexts. • Student negotiated projects.
Locus of control	Teacher	Student	Student
Cognition	Cognitive	Meta-cognitive	Epistemic
SAMR (Puentedura, 2006)	Substitution & Augmentation: • Portfolio to eportfolio. • PowerPoint on iPad. • Focus on productivity. • Mobile device as personal digital assistant and consumption tool.	Modification: • Reflection as VODCast. • Prezi on iPad. • New forms of collaboration. • Mobile device as content creation and curation tool.	Redefinition: • In situ reflections. • Presentations as dialogue with source material. • Community building. • Mobile device as collaborative tool.
Creativity (Sternberg, Kaufman & Pretz, 2002)	Reproduction	Incrementation	Reinitiation
Knowledge production	Subject understanding: lecturers introduce and model the use of a range of mobile social media tools appropriate to the learning context	Process negotiation: students negotiate a choice of mobile social media tools to establish an eportfolio based upon user-generated content	Context shaping: students create project teams that investigate and critique user-generated content within the context of their discipline. These are then shared, curated, and peer-reviewed in an authentic COP

p. 1). This involves an ontological shift, reconceptualizing the role of mobile social media in education, and reconceptualizing the roles of the teachers and learners – moving away from a teacher-focused content delivery mode towards a student-directed learning paradigm (heutagogy). In this process students move from passive receptors of knowledge to become active participants within authentic professional communities. Our framework resonates closely with a recent manifesto of teaching and learning for the modern age by Ihanainen and Gallagher (2013) as part of a call for vision papers for higher education by the European Commission:

We believe that the greatest learning we can provide is learning that empowers learners to make sense of their own interactions, to compile learning into collages or other assemblies of meaning, to consistently and confidently interact with their peers to negotiate meaning. We believe that the role of teachers is to facilitate trust and authenticity in learning, to help learners create metaphorical constructs to filter meaning, to become comfortable in the use and analysis of multimedia, and to become accustomed to consistent meaning-making. (p127)

Thus the project was driven by a reconception of pedagogy rather than technological determinism. Mobile social media provided the tools for this pedagogical reconception.

METHODOLOGY

The project followed a three-stage approach, including: establishing a lecturer community of practice (COP), creating a supporting technology infrastructure, and collaborative redesign of curriculum processes, activities and assessments to focus upon the development of student-generated mobile social media eportfolios.

A participatory action research methodology (Swantz, 2008) was used to inform the iterative development of the collaborative curriculum redesign. We worked closely with the institution's IT department to establish an appropriate wireless infrastructure to support the use of mobile devices as collaborative tools. This involved not only the provision of adequate wifi coverage but also the development of Mobile Airplay Screens (MOAs) to enable small screen personal devices such as the iPad and iPhone to become collaborative tools by wirelessly mirroring the screen of these devices to a large (50 inch) moveable screen. These moveable screens could be used by small groups of students or lecturers anywhere on campus that the WiFi network extended to and a mains power connection was accessible. The MOAs were developed in semester 1 of 2013 before the implementation of the Communications studies project (Cochrane, Munn, & Antonczak, 2013).

The lecturer COP was supported by a weekly face-to-face meeting as well as the establishment of a range of mobile social media tools as the basis for the development of personal eportfolios (including: Wordpress blogs and Twitter), and collaboration (including: Google Docs, and a Google Plus Community). These tools also provided a record of the COP activity and were the primary source of data for analysis of the project progress and outcomes.

Research Questions

We were primarily interested in investigating two questions through the project:

1. Could we establish a community of practice of lecturers within the department that would facilitate collaborative curriculum redesign?
2. How can mobile social media be used as a catalyst to introduce new pedagogies and assessment strategies into the curriculum?

Figure 1. Mobile Airplay Screen (MOAs)

CASE STUDY

The communications studies lecturer COP was launched before the beginning of semester 1 with the loaning of iPad minis to each of the participating lecturers, the loan of two MOAs to be shared across the four courses, and a workshop facilitated by the researcher overviewing the use of mobile augmented reality as a basis for student projects. Following this introduction, a weekly community of practice meeting was established at a local coffee shop where there was good coffee and free wifi access allowing the lecturers to connect and collaborate using their iPad minis. A Google Plus virtual community was established (http://bit.ly/GA4kQW) to support the face-to-face COP and curate the outcomes of the project, including linking to the participants' Twitter activity and Wordpress blogs. Figure 2 illustrates the range of mobile social media tools utilised in the project.

Figure 2. Mobile social media portfolio apps

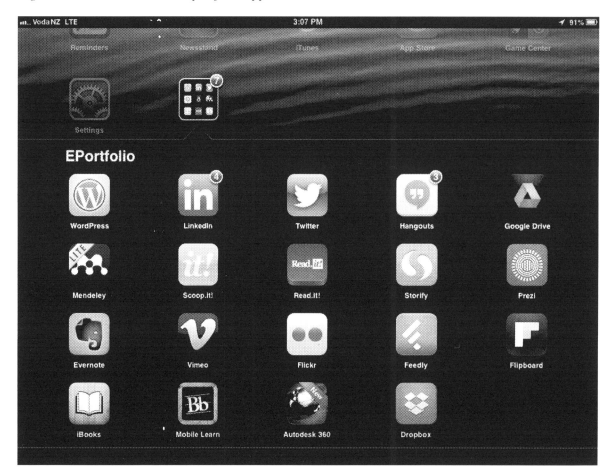

These tools were chosen as examples of a range of collaborative tools including:

1. GMail which provided access to the Google suite of collaborative tools.
2. Wordpress as a reflective space.
3. Twitter to facilitate an asynchronous community.
4. Google Plus Hangouts for synchronous community building.
5. Feedly for collating social media.
6. LinkedIn as a professional portfolio.
7. ResearchGate to create a research portfolio.
8. ScoopIt for curating social media.
9. http://www.autodesk.com/mobile-apps a suite of mobile 3D modelling Apps.

The formation of a lecturer COP exploring mobile social media within the Communications Department focused upon the following outcomes:

- Innovation in teaching and learning enabled by technology, in particular a focus upon student-owned devices to enable the establishment of student eportfolios as a core platform for the Department.

- Exploring the development of collaborative student-generated augmented reality games in an international team-based context.
- The COP also explored the affordances of mobile social media technologies to act as a catalyst for pedagogical change and curriculum design as the Communications.
- The creation of a new eportfolio-based submission system to update or replace the antiquated sFTP system presently in use. The new system enables the use of mobile devices and web 2.0 technologies to enable:
  - Students to provide online feedback on work in progress/summative submissions.
  - Student forums for sharing research and resources.
  - Using social media as tool for documenting and reporting beyond the classroom.
  - Building publicly available portfolios alongside the submission process, to replace the physical end of year show and present an alternative "online exhibition" that invites stakeholders to comment on student work and directions for work before graduation, opening employment opportunities.
- New approaches to classroom interaction - for example the use of MOAs (MObile Airplay screens) for enhancing student collaboration via their mobile devices.
- New pedagogies that are appropriate to a 21st Century Post Web 2.0 communications education.

The contexts covered by the project within the School of Communications' Digital Media department and additional papers included: Creative Practice, 3D animation, Honours, Masters in Communication Studies, and Performance Communication. Each of these are outlined in the following sections. While the Communications courses in general utilized a high level of computing technologies the teaching approaches employed prior to the project were located at the Web 1.0 end of the Post Web 2.0 continuum. For example there was no integration of social media within the courses.

Creative Practice

Creative practice is the core Digital Media paper in the Postgraduate Diploma in Communication studies. Two equally weighted assignments were redesigned in line with our research's intended outcomes. The first assignment involved student team development of a m-learning application. The course assessment requirements were redesigned from focusing upon the submission of a written Word report on the development process to the establishment of a team-based project eportfolio using mobile social media such as Google Plus Communities, Blogs and Google Drive. Students were able to use large screen displays or Mobile Airplay Screens (MOAs) in class to collaborate on their App development and preview their development directly from their mobile devices, rather than asking the lecturers permission to use the lectern to present over a class projector using emulation software as they had previously. As the students didn't need the use of the lectern they could take charge of their own learning within the classes as they worked through their assignment. Table 3 shows a comparison of an example of one previous assessment outline and the redesigned outline based upon our mobile social media framework.

Table 4 shows a comparison of the change in curriculum activities and assessments, with the original assessment approach situated firmly within a teacher-directed pedagogy, while the redesigned assessment activities move towards student-directed heutagogy.

Students were encouraged to establish their own Wordpress blogs as reflective journals for their semester 2 2013 course, to establish Google

Table 3. Assessment criteria for an educational mobile web app

Previous Assessment Criteria	Redesigned Assessment Criteria
• Your research on the topic you selected to be taught within a folder named "YOURINITIALS_Research". • A diagram of your mobile web app as a .pdf named "Diagram". • A Mockup of your mobile apps pages as .jpgs or .pdfs named "Wireframe". • Your completed mobile web app and all its components contained in a folder named "WebApp". • Your individual contribution as a .doc names "INITIALS_Contribution" . • Your references as a .doc named "References". • Ensure all files are named correctly and contained within a folder labeled "TeamName_Brief4". Due date for submission of material is the 30th August 2013 no later than 4pm.	• Your research and media for the project must be uploaded to your Wordpress blog and external media embedded or linked to your blog. • Make at least a weekly project progress summary blog post, and attach/embed supporting media to this post. • Use the hashtag #148302a3 to filter blog posts and media for this assignment. • Create a Google Plus Group for scheduling and recording your group meetings and activity. • Create a shared Mendeley library of your references, using APA formatting, and link this to a blog post named "References". • Your final blog post will be a reflection on the project, including a summary of the team and your specific contribution to the team project - this can include a short 1 minute VODCast uploaded to either YouTube or Vimeo and embedded in your blog post. • Due date for the final submission is 30th August, 4pm.

Table 4. Mobile social media in the Communications curriculum

	Pedagogy	Andragogy	Heutagogy
Activity Types	• Teacher defined projects: course requirements, Project scope. • Teacher delivered examples. • Assignments descriptive. • Assignment submission via Word reports and PowerPoint.	• Teacher as guide. • Digital identity: Wordpress journals. • Student-generated content using smartphones. • Student negotiated teams in Google Plus Communities.	• Teacher modelling use of mobile social media within collaborative curriculum redesign team. • Student-generated contexts: Authentic mobile App design and development.
Creativity	Reproduction	Incrementation	Reinitiation

Plus Communities for their team-based projects, and share documents via Google Drive. Students then invited their lecturers as viewers and commentators on these sites. This represented a significant reconception of the role of social media for online learning, from a focus upon lecturer created forums on the institution's LMS (Learning Management System) to student-owned social media spaces that the lecturers were then invited into.

One student team extended the use of Wordpress beyond a reflective journal to capture and present all the research and decisions made throughout the assignment. They nominated a team member to capture all the information flowing through the various social media streams and class discussions, then edit and consolidate it into blog posts. The blog was made public so the rest of the team could review and amend posts. The result was a professionally presented, clear and concise report of all research and decisions conducted by the team that they used as part of their submission.

The use of a Google Plus Community (for example see Figure 3) was particularly important to one of the student teams where one of the team members participated remotely on the project updating their progress, sharing project resources with the rest of the team, and scheduling synchronous Google Plus Hangouts while on holiday in Spain during the majority of the project. This team of 4 students generated 42 posts and 92 comments over the six weeks of the project.

Google drive's ability to be integrated tightly with Google Plus proved beneficial over other cloud based storage services in this project. As the teams were coding their app there were many

Figure 3. Example G+ Community post

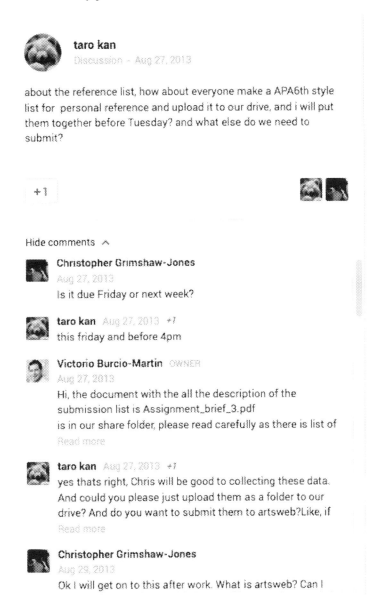

assets that needed to be brought together, managed correctly, and updated in consultation with the team. As files were changed they could be linked back into the Google Plus Community allowing for discussion of file changes and then flagging of issues early. In the case of errors created as a result of these changes beyond the expertise of the students a lecturer could be flagged in the discussion and have a record of previous changes that may have lead to the problem.

The Mobile airplay screens did not work as intended within the computer lab setting. The labs narrow paths between desks and the amount of chairs in the room made it very difficult to move the Mobile Airplay Screens. This often saw them become fixed features within the computer labs at the front of the class where there was adequate room, much like one would expect a class projector to work. As each lab is equipped with a projector a similar result could be achieved simply by connecting an Apple TV unit to the lectern. This defeated the mobile aspect of the device, which was disappointing in this particular scenario. The lack of physical flexibility of the room layout limited the deployment of the MOAs, which were better suited to flexible spaces enabling team collaboration.

The student interaction through the MOAs was weighted heavily towards those with Apple devices such as iPhones and iPads due to the hardware requirements for screen mirroring. The immaturity of Android hardware for collaborative screen-mirroring of mobile devices created a rift or divide in the class as those without Apple devices became passive observers or partnered with an iOS mobile device owning student.

3D Animation

A Google Plus community was established to provide a forum for discussion and peer support for the semester 2 animation paper. This was the lecturer's first experience of using social media as part of the course, and thus an initially conservative approach was taken to the accessibility of the Google Plus community.

This is a community for sharing ideas about projects, concepts and posting any questions you have about various topics that you have covered in class. Either myself or one of the main lecturers can help to answer any queries you may have. Feel free to help each other out and give your own opinions on topics that may arise either during class or within this community. This is a private community and will only consist of students in your class as well as myself and both main lecturers. (Google Plus comment, 2013)

Figure 4 shows an extract from a typical post and comments on the 3D Animation Google Plus community.

Reflecting on the experience (http://bit.ly/1eRX55M) the lecturer noted that while there was significant buy in from the students and a lot of activity generated on the non-compulsory Google Plus Community, students defaulted to using the community to ask their lecturer questions in a virtual help-desk fashion. Although student peers often replied to each other's posts and comments, they were reticent to initiate peer to peer conversations on the community. Strategies for encouraging a more peer to peer support and collaboration culture around the use of a Google Plus Community for the course in the future include: beginning by establishing social interaction online via sharing information about the participants, lecturers modelling this culture on the community, and assigning an assessment percentage to peer commenting and collaboration to the Google Plus Community participation. One of the limitations of the use of a Google Plus Community within the course is the inability to upload and share 3D models directly within posts, however posts can include links to any web-based content or another repository for students' 3D files. This will be investigated further for the second iteration of using a Google Plus Community within the course.

Performance

The 2013 performance course was relocated into a new building space that incorporated state of the art performance facilities for drama, dance, and live theatre, but no thought had been given to providing an infrastructure to enable presentation and collaboration technologies within this space. Hence the use of three MOAs and iPad minis for the course lecturers enabled this space to be used for students to record their performances, play them back on the MOAs, critique their performance, and view and discuss supporting material in the performance space rather than in a separate classroom space. This project also resulted in the development of a guide to the use of the MOAs that was shared between all of the projects (http://goo.gl/8xkuU0). Example lecturer reflections on

Figure 4. Google Plus Community screen shot

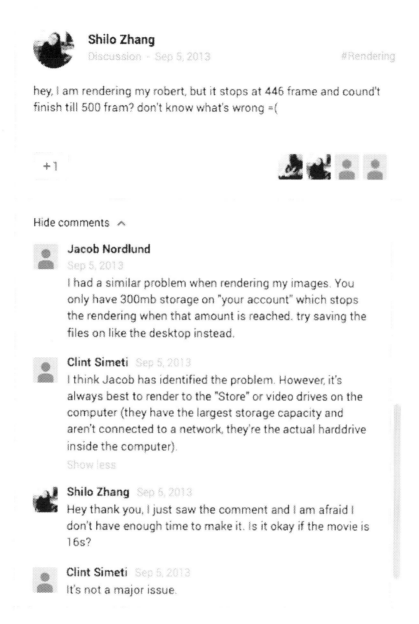

the use of the MOAs can be viewed at http://youtu.be/5-CFUufVyU8. Lecturers quickly evaluated the benefits of utilising wireless mobile devices and the MOAs for screen-mirroring. They recognised the need to think differently about their teaching processes and the types of assessment activities utilised in the curriculum.

We've been using the MOA and the iPad minis in our teaching. Initially we were using it as a presentation device, which has limitations and it is difficult to transfer files to the iPad. For example PowerPoint on the iPad messes up fonts and layouts and embedded videos do not play. However there are other applications of the devices that are quite useful, for example showing videos using GoodReader, and being able to immediately show student videos straight after they are recorded is great. So part of the relevance for our context of performance for screen is that students can use the technology to film themselves doing things and then immediately show the rest of the class and form the basis for a discussion. We are also looking at ways of creating online communities where students can discuss things amongst themselves and present assessments less as written activities than as video blogs of their performance - we're teaching them performance, so rather than writing it down as a journal entry they can express their performance as a combination of written and video reflections. (Lecturer 1, 2013)

I teach a performance communications paper and I've been using the iPad mini and the MOA in my classroom teaching, and it's been fantastic for recording performances and then I could take the iPad mini home and review the performances. My students have also used the MOA for presenting their projects in class. It's also been useful for presenting interviews and discussing these in class. I'm not confident with new technology, but once I had a few practices of connecting wirelessly and knew what I was doing I found it really exciting and I'm now much more confident with it. (Lecturer 2, 2013)

We established regular brainstorming sessions between the researcher and the performance lecturers to cover both technical implementation issues and ideas for new assessment strategies. One of the main technical issues revolved around the wireless connectivity design of the MOAs. The lecturers were used to connecting video cameras via HDMI cables to projectors to record and review student performances. Troubleshooting wireless connectivity issues was initially difficult for the lecturers to conceptualize when there were no wires involved to see how the devices were connected.

Masters and Honours Students

A Google Plus community was formed for students conducting research with an interest in Digital Media as a means of providing a forum for discussion and peer support to try to overcome the isolation students often feel when writing a thesis or dissertation. We believed that the community would need little input to thrive, as students desired interaction with each other. Students where also encouraged to start blogs to document their progress and share it with other students. This was an interesting experiment in that participation was entirely optional and students invited were not tied to any particular class or supervisor as with the other social media communities.

The Google Plus community experienced limited discussion or active participation. Without any common mechanism such as assessment integration, or participating in common classes the cohort saw little reason to participate in dialogues using social media. This saw the majority of posts written by a supervisor. This was met with mixed reactions. Many of the students surprisingly reported the community beneficial as the majority of posts contained helpful information on conducting research. Because there was little interaction the knowledge was only flowing one way and the Community served more as a weekly newsletter than a collaborative environment one would expect of a social media platform.

The Google Plus community did have an unexpected positive outcome as both a support tool for students considering enrolment and a marketing tool. New students (Honours or Masters) looking for both supervisors and information on where to start were given invites to the Google Plus community. This allowed for a channel of communication to be opened up with potential students before they chose to enrol. Knowledge on topics such as how to start research, the insecurities we feel as beginner researchers, and links to a few students' blogs documenting their journey were covered in the community. This allowed supervision staff to aid potential students with minimum of effort by simply directing questions to community posts dealing with the subject. This helped secure enrolments in two ways. First potential students felt more confident in enrolling. Secondly students commented they felt the staff were engaged with their ideas before even enrolling, which they perceived as high motivation and competency levels from the academic staff.

A small portion of students reported the Google Plus community as a pointless activity, one even light heartedly posted a meme of a dog using a computer with sarcastic captions. When these students were asked why they felt negatively or indifferently, many responded that they had enough social media in the form of Facebook, Twitter, or similar and did not feel any desire to participate in another social network. Of the students expressing indifferent or negative responses it was noted that they were all coming to the end of their research projects, while those who valued the community still had a considerable amount of time remaining.

Wordpress's adoption among this eclectic cohort of students conducting research experienced limited use and very little interaction. The general consensus among students was one of doubtful questioning about the benefit of an additional blog to the material being written and presented regularly to a supervisor. Students were advised maintaining a blog would allow other students to comment and provide another avenue of feedback, however this was met with scepticism. Students believed that no one would read their blogs, and even if they did they would not receive feedback.

One student decided to try Wordpress and regularly posted her research's progression. As part of an agreement she has with her employer, regular updates on her research are required. This provided a strong motivating force to start a blog as a means of evidencing progress. The blog had many unexpected positive outcomes for this student. It allowed many stakeholders including businesses in the field, researchers with similar interests and potential interview participants an open and honest portal into her research. In total 80 people now follow her blog. Through this stakeholders can submit feedback and help refine her research. The process of reporting her progress to an audience has also provided motivation to keep a steady and regular pace with her work.

DISCUSSION

The communications study project led to the development of several new pedagogical and assessment strategies for the curriculum that will be applied in 2014. These include:

- Establishing a student Blog as the core element of an eportfolio within one of the compulsory first year papers
- Introducing Google Plus communities as supporting student discussion forums
- Purchasing iPad minis for the lecturers
- Purchasing a set of MOAs for the performance space
- Providing students with a recommended minimum specification for purchasing their own mobile devices

The COP also established the beginnings of a culture of scholarship and reflective research around teaching and learning within the department (Cochrane, Antonczak, Guinibert, & Mulrennan, 2014; Cochrane, Antonczak, et al., 2013).

SAMR and Heutagogy

As has been found with many mobile learning projects, the biggest impact of the first iteration of a project was with the lecturers' personal productivity.

The iPad has allowed me to make more productive use of my down time (particularly when sitting on public transport for a couple of hours each day). I've been able to monitor student problems and progress via the Google+ app. I've been able to review/re-write lecture notes and to view video tutorials whilst on the move. Although I haven't incorporated apps like Layar (augmented reality) and Autodesk 360 (collaborative 3d design) into my teaching, seeing them or at least even knowing about them (via the iPad/Apps Store) opens up the possibility that I may be able to incorporate them into my work in some way in the future. (Lecturer G+ Post, 2013)

I love how the iPad and social media tools enabled me to interact with my class any time from anywhere. Rather than being tied down to office hours or class times, I could answer questions or initiate discussions on a more frequent basis using tools like Google+. I especially liked how I could do this on the bus on the way to work. It reclaimed an hour or two of my day (depending on traffic) that was unproductive, that I can now spend on other areas like research. I also quite enjoy the iPads portability when combined with online learning services like lynda.com or technology news feeds through Google+ or Scoop. it. Being a lecturer of digital media you have to always keep up with the new developments in this rapidly changing field or be left behind. The iPad combined with these services provided a way of getting daily doses of this information in times that were often spent unproductively, such as commercial breaks, waiting for meetings to start, waiting for the bus, etc. (Lecturer, 2013)

This equates to substitution and augmentation of current practice on the SAMR framework scale. However there was also evidence of modification and redefinition of process and practice achieved through the project, illustrated by the integration of Google Plus communities for supporting collaboration and coordination of student team projects, facilitating responsive formative feedback from their lecturers on project progress, and the use of mobile devices and MOAs within the performance courses facilitating live recording and feedback upon student performance and technique. The integration of mobile social media into the courses also enabled a conceptual shift from a focus upon teacher-delivered content towards more flexible student negotiated projects and student-generated content.

The outcomes of the project illustrated three major factors impacting the success of the integration of mobile social media within the curriculum: modelling the building of learning communities, exploring the unique affordances of mobile social media to enable new pedagogies, and establishing a supporting technology infrastructure.

Modelling the Building of Learning Communities

The project provided lecturers with several new experiences that modelled the establishment of learning communities: 1. A weekly face-to-face discussion at a local café where the participants utilised their wireless mobile devices to collaborate, 2. The use of Wordpress.com blogs as learning journals and 3. The establishment of a virtual Google Plus community. The use of student-owned Wordpress.com blogs and Google Plus communities were consequently integrated into two of the three courses in the project, resulting in a simple yet effective strategy for building learning communities for these courses.

Using WordPress to capture student progress worked very well. In the group context it provided a forum where the students could collect their ideas, thoughts, and progress... In future we will be rolling this out in a number of classes. I can see the creation and maintenance of a word press site by students could easily replace activities like class presentations and provide a space for not only practicing critique but receiving it too. (Lecturer blog post, 2013)

As a tool in class I was very impressed by Google+. It was implemented in Creative Practice and provided a great digital meeting spot. Both teams used it extensively with very little encouragement needed. Both teams seemed to enjoy Google+ as it afforded them a simple way to keep in touch. A great example of this is one student was not present for a month of classes. He was able to keep in touch with his team in the class and ensure that his team was on track and contribute. For the other students they used this ability to delegate tasks and both ask for and give feedback throughout the week, rather than having to wait for class to roll round. Also as a lecturer this was a handy tool for distributing knowledge quickly. (Lecturer blog post, 2013)

Creating a refocus upon building learning communities throughout the courses required a significant change of culture, which was easier established in undergraduate students rather than with post graduate students. For supporting teamwork in undergraduate classes it worked very well, however as an informal meeting space for grouping postgraduate researchers it did not work as well. Thus we established that building a new culture within the curriculum requires staging and scaffolding across the length of the course, and must start in the first year of the course and be built upon in the subsequent years of the course. Consequently the curriculum is being rewritten to implement the establishment of student eportfolios using student-owned Wordpress.com blogs as an assessed activity within the first year of the course, followed by the exploration of student-generated content using mobile devices in second year, and the use of Google Plus communities to support student negotiated team projects in the third year of the course. This culture will then flow on to postgraduate students, as many follow on from the undergraduate course.

Exploring the Unique Affordances of Mobile Social Media to Enable New Pedagogies

The project focused upon implementing collaborative curriculum redesign and development of technical expertise within communities of practice, facilitated by an expert 'technology steward/academic advisor' (Cochrane, 2013). In this process the teaching staff were equipped with mobile devices and learnt how to use them effectively while re-thinking and re-conceptualising pedagogy and assessment strategies within their own specific teaching contexts (see for example: (Cochrane, Sissons, & Mulrennan, 2012)). Providing the lecturers with iPad mini's and MOAs to experience and use throughout a semester provided them with an experience as a learner using these tools. Previously their experience of mobile social media had been limited by their experience of the relatively immature Android and Windows Mobile tablet ecosystems (at the time of the project). The integrated infrastructure developed around the use of iOS devices, MOAs, and the depth of iOS social media Apps provided the lecturers with a broader realisation of what was possible to achieve using mobile social media.

Establishing a Supporting Technology Infrastructure

We collaborated with IT services to develop an appropriate infrastructure that enables personal mobile devices to become collaborative tools. This involved establishing a robust and speedy campus wireless network, along with more flexible protocols for access and widespread availability, as these requirements are critical success factors for m-learning. The framework has highlighted the importance of a collaborative approach, where the pedagogical aspects drive the development of infrastructure (Salmon & Angood, 2013). Working with ICT Services we have enabled the existing network to be more 'mobile friendly' in terms of supporting different devices and operating systems. We have also designed and produced mobile presentation and screen-sharing MOAs that can be used in a variety of formal and informal learning spaces to promote collaborative uses of mobile devices by teachers and students. While we attempted to be platform agnostic and produce a framework utilising mobile social media that could be implemented on either iOS, Android or Windows mobile devices, in reality a robust wireless mobile screen-mirroring solution is still hardware dependent. After experimenting with the current capabilities of iOS, Android and Windows mobile devices we chose to support the more mature iOS ecosystem when developing the MOAs. However while iOS devices can seamlessly screen-mirror to our MOA (Airplay) infrastructure, it is still possible for Android devices to stream media wirelessly to the MOAs via Airplay, and Windows 8 devices can screen mirror via Airplay using third party solutions such as Air Parrot. While the lecturers were initially pro Android for its user-configurability, they "ate humble pie" and became convinced of the affordances of iOS devices for usability and collaboration via a robust screen-mirroring infrastructure that could not be matched by Android devices.

Both the tablets [iOS and Android] came with devices to wireless connect them to either the classes projector or the Mobile Airplay Screens (MOAs) we had on loan. These were the apple TV and a Sharecast dongle Both devices connected with ease and I never had any problems with the connections dropping on either. The problems with both devices connecting was highlighted when students wanted to connect. The all share cast works on a pairing system that takes a minute or two to setup initially. Once a device is paired all it needs is to be plugged in and a switch flicked on the Samsung tablet and the device connects.

This system made it so much easier to connect than apple devices so long as you only ever want to use one device. The pain with this system is that as soon as someone else wants to connect it requires the device to be paired to their device which is slow. It also does not remember previously paired devices so you need to constantly be pairing it. This hindered the class joining in with their own devices. In comparison the Apple TV was much better for collaboration as once setup on a students device they could jump on or off as they pleased. The problem with the airplay was it involved checking you were on the right WiFi network and sometimes required telling the device to "forget" other WiFi networks in order to work. Of the two I felt Apple provided the best solution for collaborative classroom sharing of mobile devices by a significant margin. (Lecturer blog post, 2013)

Beyond screen mirroring, we made sure that the social media tools that we chose were supported by Apps across all three major mobile OS's.

FUTURE RESEARCH DIRECTIONS

We have presented the application of our mobile social media framework for creative pedagogies within the context of transforming a communications studies curriculum. In order to test the transferability of this framework into other contexts we have also been implementing this framework in a number of related contexts within our University (Cochrane & Antonczak, 2013b; Cochrane & Rhodes, 2013; Cochrane, Sissons, Mulrennan, & Pamatatau, 2013; Cochrane & Withell, 2013). In the future we would like to explore the transferability of this framework in other higher education institutions.

One of our identified keys to supporting this framework is developing an appropriate technology infrastructure, which raises the issue of cost. While providing a robust and adequate wifi infrastructure to support the increasing demand of wireless mobile devices is now part of institutional IT budgets, providing cost effective solutions for enabling collaborative learning environments around student-owned mobile devices is often neglected. We achieved this by the development of MOAs. This was an in-house designed system driven mainly because of needing a more cost-effective and agile solution than commercially available systems. Our MOA stands were designed by one of our Product Design students at a cost of $500NZ per stand, and by specifying a fifty-inch plasma full HD screen connected via an AppleTV and audio via optical connection to a mounted iHome iW1 audio system kept the total price per MOA under $3000NZ, which was significantly cheaper than any commercially available system.

While we did explore offering Android wireless mirroring capability to the MOAs, the immaturity of available Android screen-mirroring solutions made this impractical. In the future we will continue to explore alternative cross-platform mobile wireless mirroring technologies, such as the emerging Chromecast from Google, and Crestron's development of AirMedia. As mobile devices represent a rapidly developing and changing technology the implementation of our mobile social media framework will require constant redesign of activities and assessments enabled by the affordances of new mobile social media technologies. In particular the developing arena of wearable computing such as Google Glasses and smart-watches represent the potential for new and innovative pedagogical strategies and activities.

CONCLUSION

Here we draw out the key principles identified by the communications case study supporting the development of a mobile social media framework for collaborative curriculum design. In summary the case study illustrates that an effective mobile social media framework for collaborative curriculum redesign must meet three goals: model the building of learning communities, explore the unique affordances of mobile social media to enable new pedagogies, and establish a supporting technology infrastructure. Our framework (Table 2) maps a pedagogical shift from teacher-directed content to student-directed learning onto the types of activities and assessments that can be facilitated by mobile social media to realise this pedagogical reconception. By utilising the relatively simple SAMR technology adoption framework we can scaffold lecturers and students in moving from merely substitution of current practice onto new technologies towards redefining practice with mobile social media. This is a unique journey for every different educational context, which can be supported by the establishment of communities of practice of lecturers and academic developers enabling collaborative curriculum redesign. As in the communications studies case, this is an on-going journey of discovery by all of the participants.

REFERENCES

Attewell, J., Savill-Smith, C., Douch, R., & Parker, G. (2010). *Modernising education and training: Mobilising technology for learning.* Available from http://www.talpalink.co.uk/resources/Modernising+education+and+training$2C+mobilising+technology+for+learning.pdf

Balsamo, A. (2011). *Designing Culture: The Technological Imagination at Work*. Duke University Press. doi:10.1215/9780822392149

Chi, M., & Hausmann, R. (2003). Do radical discoveries require ontological shifts? In L. Shavinina, & R. Sternberg (Eds.), *International Handbook on Innovation* (Vol. 3, pp. 430–444). New York: Elsevier Science Ltd. doi:10.1016/B978-008044198-6/50030-9

Cochrane, T. (2013). Mlearning as a catalyst for pedagogical change. In Z. Berge, & L. Muilenburg (Eds.), *Handbook of mobile learning* (pp. 247–258). Routledge.

Cochrane, T., & Antonczak, L. (2013a, September 18). *Mobile Social Media as a Catalyst For Creative Pedagogy*. Paper presented at the EC-TEL 2013 Eigth European conference on technology enhanced learning: Scaling up learning for sustained impact. Paphos, Cyprus.

Cochrane, T., & Antonczak, L. (2013b). Post Web 2.0 Media: Mobile Social Media. *QScience Proceedings,* (3), 2.

Cochrane, T., Antonczak, L., Guinibert, M., & Mulrennan, D. (2014). *Developing a mobile social media framework for creative pedagogies*. Paper presented at the 10th International Conference on Mobile Learning. Retrieved from http://www.mlearning-conf.org

Cochrane, T., Antonczak, L., Guinibert, M., Withell, A., Mulrennan, D., Mountfort, P., et al. (2013). *Collaboration unplugged: Herding a flock of MOAs*. Paper presented at the Electric Dreams: 30th Ascilite Conference. Sydney, Australia.

Cochrane, T., Munn, J., & Antonczak, L. (2013). *Design thinking for mlearning: Herding a flock of MOAs*. Paper presented at the 3rd Mobile Creativity and Innovation Symposium. Auckland, New Zealand.

Cochrane, T., & Rhodes, D. (2013). iArchi[tech]ture: Developing a mobile social media framework for pedagogical transformation. *Australasian Journal of Educational Technology, 29*(3), 372–386.

Cochrane, T., Sissons, H., & Mulrennan, D. (2012). Journalism 2.0: Exploring the impact of Mobile and Social Media on Journalism Education. In I. A. Sánchez & P. Isaias (Eds.), *Proceedings of the IADIS International Conference on Mobile Learning 2012* (pp. 165-172). Berlin, Germany: IADIS International Association for Development of the Information Society.

Cochrane, T., Sissons, H., Mulrennan, D., & Pamatatau, R. (2013). Journalism 2.0: Exploring the impact of Mobile and Social Media on Journalism Education. *International Journal of Mobile and Blended Learning, 5*(2), 22–38. doi:10.4018/jmbl.2013040102

Cochrane, T., & Withell, A. (2013). Augmenting design education with mobile social media: A transferable framework. *Journal of the NUS Teaching Academy, 3*(4), 150-168.

Cochrane, T. D. (2014). Critical success factors for transforming pedagogy with mobile Web 2.0. *British Journal of Educational Technology, 45*(1), 65–82. doi:10.1111/j.1467-8535.2012.01384.x

Hase, S., & Kenyon, C. (2007). Heutagogy: A child of complexity theory. *Complicity: An International Journal of Complexity and Education, 4*(1), 111–118.

Herrington, J., Herrington, A., Mantei, J., Olney, I., & Ferry, B. (Eds.). (2009). *New technologies, new pedagogies: Mobile learning in higher education*. Wollongong: Faculty of Education, University of Wollongong.

Ihanainen, P., & Gallagher, M. S. (2013). Pedagogy supporting the simultaneous learning processes of open education: Pedagogy of Simultaneity (PoS). In I. Garcilaso (Ed.), Open Education 2030. JRC-IPTS call for vision papers. (Seville, Spain: European Commission, Joint Research Centre, Institute for Prospective Technological Studies.

Kennedy, G., Dalgarno, B., Gray, K., Judd, T., Waycott, J., & Bennett, S. et al. (2007). The net generation are not big users of Web 2.0 technologies: Preliminary findings. In R. J. Atkinson, C. McBeath, S. K. A. Song, & C. Cheers (Eds.), *Proceedings of Ascilite 2007, ICT: Providing choices for learners and learning* (pp. 517–525). Singapore: Centre for Educational Development, Nanyang Technological University.

Kukulska-Hulme, A. (2010). Mobile learning as a catalyst for change. *Open Learning: The Journal of Open and Distance Learning, 25*(3), 181–185. doi:10.1080/02680513.2010.511945

Laurillard, D. (2012). *Teaching as a design science: Building pedagogical patterns for learning and technology*. New York: Routledge.

Laurillard, D., Charlton, P., Craft, B., Dimakopoulos, D., Ljubojevic, D., Magoulas, G., et al. (2011). A constructionist learning environment for teachers to model learning designs. *Journal of Computer Assisted Learning, Pre-Publication*. Retrieved from. doi:10.1111/j.1365-2729.2011.00458.x

Luckin, R., Clark, W., Garnett, F., Whitworth, A., Akass, J., & Cook, J. et al. (2010). Learner-Generated Contexts: A Framework to Support the Effective Use of Technology for Learning. In M. Lee, & C. McLoughlin (Eds.), *Web 2.0-Based E-Learning: Applying Social Informatics for Tertiary Teaching* (pp. 70–84). Hershey, PA: IGI Global. doi:10.4018/978-1-60566-294-7.ch004

Pachler, N., Bachmair, B., & Cook, J. (2010). *Mobile learning: Structures, agency, practices*. London: Springer. doi:10.1007/978-1-4419-0585-7

Parsons, D. (Ed.). (2013). *Innovations in Mobile Educational Technologies and Applications*. Hershey, PA: IGI Global.

Puentedura, R. (2006). *Transformation, Technology, and Education*. Retrieved 18 February, 2013, from http://hippasus.com/resources/tte/puentedura_tte.pdf

Salmon, G., & Angood, R. (2013). Sleeping with the enemy. *British Journal of Educational Technology, 44*(6), 916–925. doi:10.1111/bjet.12097

Sharples, M. (2009). *Learning at large*. Paper presented at the MLearn 2009: The 8th World Conference on Mobile and Contextual Learning, University of Central Florida, Institute for Simulation and Training. Orlando, FL.

Sheely, S. (2008). *Latour meets the digital natives: What do we really know*. Paper presented at the Hello! Where are you in the landscape of educational technology? ASCILITE 2008. Retrieved from http://www.ascilite.org.au/conferences/melbourne08/procs/sheely.pdf

Sternberg, R. J., Kaufman, J. C., & Pretz, J. E. (2002). *The creativity conundrum: A propulsion model of kinds of creative contributions*. Philadelphia: Psychology Press.

Swantz, M. L. (2008). Participatory Action Research as Practice. In P. Reason, & H. Bradbury (Eds.), *The SAGE Handbook of Action Research: Participative Inquiry and Practice* (2nd ed., pp. 31–48). London: SAGE Publications. doi:10.4135/9781848607934.d8

Traxler, J. (2010). Will student devices deliver innovation, inclusion, and transformation? [RCET]. *Journal of the Research Center for Educational Technology, 6*(1), 3–15.

Traxler, J. (2011). Introduction. In J. Traxler & J. Wishart (Eds.), Making mobile learning work: case studies of practice (pp. 4-12). Bristol: ESCalate, University of Bristol, Graduate School of Education.

Unterfrauner, E., & Marschalek, I. (2010). Appropriation of an online mobile community by marginalised young people: experiences from an Austrian case study. In M. Montebello, V. Camilleri & A. Dingli (Eds.), *Proceedings of MLearn 2010: The 9th International Conference on Mobile Learning* (pp. 276-281). Valletta, Malta: University of Malta.

White, D. S., & Le Cornu, A. (2011). Visitors and residents: A new typology for inline engagement. *First Monday, 16*(9). doi:10.5210/fm.v16i9.3171

ADDITIONAL READING

Blaschke, L. M. (2012). Heutagogy and lifelong learning: A review of heutagogical practice and self-determined learning. *International Review of Research in Open and Distance Learning, 13*(1), 56–71.

Canning, N., & Callan, S. (2010). Heutagogy: spirals of reflection to empower learners in higher education. *Reflective Practice: International and Multidisciplinary Perspectives, 11*(1), 71–82. doi:10.1080/14623940903500069

Conole, G. (2013). *Open, Social and Participatory Media Designing for Learning in an Open World* (Vol. 4, pp. 47–63). Springer New York. doi:10.1007/978-1-4419-8517-0

Fisher, M., & Baird, D. E. (2006). Making mLearning Work: Utilizing mobile technologies for active exploration, collaboration, assessment, and reflection in higher education. *Journal of Educational Technology Systems, 35*(1), 3–30. doi:10.2190/4T10-RX04-113N-8858

FitzGerald, E. (2012). Creating user-generated content for location-based learning: an authoring framework. *Journal of Computer Assisted Learning, 28*(3). doi:10.1111/j.1365-2729.2012.00481.x

Hase, S., & Kenyon, C. (2001). From Andragogy to Heutagogy. *ultiBASE Articles,* (December), 1-10. Retrieved from http://www.psy.gla.ac.uk/~steve/pr/Heutagogy.html

Rushby, N. (2012). Editorial: An agenda for mobile learning. *British Journal of Educational Technology, 43*(3), 355–356. doi:10.1111/j.1467-8535.2012.01313.x

Traxler, J., & Wishart, J. (Eds.). (2011). Making mobile learning work: case studies of practice. Bristol: ESCalate, University of Bristol, Graduate School of Education.

Verjans, S. (2013). Can we engage learners through Web 2.0 and mobile devices? *Research in Learning Technology, 21*(3). doi: http://dx.doi.org/10.3402/rlt.v21i0.23309

Waycott, J., Sheard, J., Thompson, C., & Clerehan, R. (2013). Making students' work visible on the social web: A blessing or a curse? *Computers & Education, 68*(0), 86-95. doi: http://dx.doi.org/10.1016/j.compedu.2013.04.026

KEY TERMS AND DEFINITIONS

COP: Community Of Practice.
Google Plus: Google's social network.
Heutagogy: Student-directed learning.
MOA: Mobile Airplay Screen.
SAMR: Substitution, Augmentation, Modification, Redefinition. A technology adoption framework.
WiFi: Wireless Ethernet.

Chapter 2
Developing Faculty to Effectively Use Mobile Learning Technologies in Collegiate Classes:
A Guide for Department Chairs

Richard E. Newman
University of Arkansas, USA

Michael T. Miller
University of Arkansas, USA

Kenda S. Grover
University of Arkansas, USA

ABSTRACT

Mobile devices have become a common accessory for many college students, and with the habits and tendencies that have formed from frequent use, colleges have begun to incorporate mobile devices into the delivery of education. As mobile learning has grown as a teaching strategy, some faculty have found it difficult to adapt to open access to computing, and others have simply attempted to ignore the new reliance on technology. Department chairs are uniquely situated to bridge the world of technology and the contemporary campus, and through strategic and intentional faculty development, they have the potential to successfully bring mobile learning to higher education. Throughout the chapter, strategies outline how to use adult learning to build faculty development programs that encourage the effective use of m-learning as an instructional strategy.

INTRODUCTION

Colleges and universities are being called upon to adapt to the changing nature of student interests, characteristics, and behaviors. Such changes range from the structure of residence hall rooms and the food selections offered in cafeterias to the kinds of digital materials libraries acquire and how technology is utilized to facilitate learning. The bulk of these kind of changes can be accounted for in Sporn's (1999) theory of adaptation, where organizations, including colleges and universities,

DOI: 10.4018/978-1-4666-6284-1.ch002

either change or adapt their operations to meet user needs, or they become obsolete. This is particularly true in competitive organizations, such as colleges and universities that must compete for students, faculty, and other resources.

One significant way that colleges and universities have adapted to recent changes in student and faculty behavior and interest is through the inclusion and integration of technology. Technology has become a common element in traditional classroom presentations and teaching (such as PowerPoint presentations), how learning is distributed (such as online courses), how students register and manage their enrollment, and even how students access their grades, plot progress toward graduation, and run simulations about changing majors. Most recently, college leaders have begun to look more critically at how mobile technologies can be used to enhance or augment the collegiate experience.

Mobile technologies are those that make use of wireless technologies to access some sort of data. In the case of higher education, these data are typically class lectures, notes, readings, assignments, etc. that students connect with to either participate fully or partially in coursework. This type of education has been termed "m-learning" and is most effective when it is interactive among two or more individuals (E-Learning, 2013). M-learning tools include such devices as cell phones, Kindles, Nooks, e-readers, iPads and other digital readers, and MP3 players. Each of these devices has the element of portability, allowing users to physically move about a campus without being attached to a single location.

There are multiple challenges for integrating m-learning into the college campus, including the challenge of developing buy-in or consensus about using these technologies by college faculty. Few argue the centrality of faculty members as the primary tool for student learning, although generational issues have sparked debate about the intention, role, and appropriate use of technology. Some of this debate has arisen from those who see 'digital-immigrants' as resisting technology. Digital immigrants are those who were raised or received their academic training prior to the internet revolution, and the argument holds that because they are new, or newer, to technology, they resist its use out of stubbornness or an unwillingness to see value in technology-mediated learning. The immigrants' primary rallying cry has been traced to any number of possibly related variables, such as poor student performance, poor student achievement in comparison to global competitors, an over-involvement from parents, grade inflation in high school, and even a diminished work ethic among the Millennial generation.

There is another camp of college faculty, a group that is rising and emerging on college campuses, that embraces technology as real mechanism for student learning. These faculty members support traditional classes with Blackboard (or privately hosted) websites, capture their lectures and classroom discussion through audio and video for easy replay by students, and even web-cast their classroom presentations to enhance accessibility, a challenge to the notion that a class lecture must meet at particular day and time. Another element is the rise of online coursework, an experience that can bring together students from anywhere in the world in real-time environments to share experiences and perspectives and to work toward a degree.

For policy makers broadly and college administrators specifically, there is a tremendous need to bridge the gap between the two extremes of faculty member behaviors and attitudes toward m-learning. Although this is a broad conversation, technology is both an administrative and instructional tool that has become a formal part of the higher education landscape and will continue to embed itself more deeply in the student experience. The most common administrator to deal with technology is the department chair, an administrative position that has been attributed with making 80% of all administrative decisions on the college campus.

For nearly 20 years, an emerging role for the department chair has been integrating technology into the curriculum. Seagren, Wheeler, Creswell, Miller, VanHorn-Grassmeyer (1994) identified the activity of working with faculty members to use technology in teaching in the early stages of the internet revolution. Concurrently, the Seagren team also identified faculty development as one of the primary duties of department chairs. The result is that as m-learning becomes common place in the academy, department chairs and heads are the ones most responsible for finding ways to help faculty learn how to use mobile technologies effectively. Subsequently, the current chapter was developed to explore faculty development for the purpose of integrating m-learning among faculty members in higher education.

CHALLENGES OF USING MOBILE LEARNING

Mobile learning, as a new instructional strategy, joins a long list of potential delivery methods for possible use by faculty. Within the academic department, there are notable factors that must be given (addressed) to determine if m-learning strategies are appropriate. Most notably, the use of m-learning must be driven not by convenience, but by a determined need that this is the most appropriate and strategic way to deliver material or help students focus their thinking about some content or its application. Too often, technologies are adopted and used without critical examination of how they help students learn, and this becomes a particularly important challenge for the contemporary department chair. And within this discussion of determining use, there are three distinct problems for chairs to consider: personnel, strategies (how), and assessment.

Personnel: Who Should Use M-Learning?

Faculty normally engage in a variety of functions contiguous to the tasks of teaching, advising, conducting research, and providing service. Increasingly, these task assignments have become more narrowly focused, with faculty directing their efforts in specific and less broad ways, meaning that some faculty are teaching more and conducting less research, while others are research-only faculty. The result in this growing stratification of faculty is that department chairs must find strategic ways to use their faculty to effectively reach their students. This means that chairs must assess their faculty members and find those who can use m-technologies in a meaningful way.

There are no clear delineations about who can or will effectively use m-learning technologies, although some claims have been made that younger faculty members who have grown up with technology will be more adaptable in their teaching methods to use and experiment with technology as a teaching tool. Conversely, however, some of the best faculty members in any given department are those digital-immigrants who did not grow up with technology, but are focused on assessing student learning and determining which teaching strategies best effect learning.

As is typically the case for department chairs, the question becomes one of human resource management and determining by which criteria faculty should be selected or encouraged to use or incorporate m-technologies into their classroom. Such criteria might include: topical area of the subject matter (does the subject lend itself to interaction or abbreviated communication?), are there other technologies that compliment m-learning situations, is interaction among students in the course an important part of developing deep learning, can m-learning improve real-time and real-world applications of content material, and do the faculty have the pre-dispositions of creatively and effectively accessing m-learning technologies and refreshing their use and skills on a regular basis. There are also traditional methods of instructional method selection that chairs might consider and these are typically driven by determining course learning objectives, student characteristics, and resource availability (Alexander & Davis, 1977).

Department chairs subsequently have the dual challenge of selecting both courses in which m-learning needs to be embedded along with identifying faculty who can strategically and effectively use m-learning. Accomplishing this task is critical to both the overall offering of courses in a department, and it reflects the important skill of successful chairs in managing their departments' curriculum delivery.

Strategies: How Do You Use M-Learning?

As an emerging teaching tool, there is relatively limited information on the impact of m-technologies on long-term student learning. There are, however, many creative approaches to using technology as a supplement to traditional coursework, and they fall into four unique domains of instruction: information delivery, peer learning support, community building, and content reinforcement.

Information delivery has been a critical focus of conversations in attempting to create effective teaching strategies. Information rich or dense topics lend themselves, for example, to the use and reliance on intensive reading, memorization, and explanations through lecture/discussions. Other course content can be related to comprehension and application, thus calling on instructors to employ a different set of information delivery strategies. M-learning technologies are typically used to deliver short or abbreviated material, as most are restricted in their word processing capabilities, and in some courses, this type of information sharing can be effective. For example, in hard science courses, text messages or mobile apps that highlight key or central concepts or ideas that are a foundation to other parts of a lesson can be distributed. Q-Readers, for example, might be placed on class handouts, and students can use their hand-held devices to go to a particular website to learn more about this foundational concept.

Exercise physiology and blood distribution at rest and in varying stages of exercise intensity would serve as a very good example. Visuals exist that display percentages of total blood volume at various sites in the human body during a pre-exercise state. You can then see how these blood flow sites and percentages change as exercise intensity increases toward a $VO_{2\,max}$ level of exertion. Delivery of oxygenated blood to the active muscle tissues and thermal regulation become priority functions, and these priority functions are accommodated by the physiological principle of vasoconstriction/vasodilation. The reverse of this adaptive response can be observed when the individual subsequently engages in active recovery and an ultimate return to a pre-exercise or resting state.

Peer learning support can also be critical to an effective college course, as students must understand that they are not alone in their studies and can rely on others to help them learn and process information. This type of support is grounded in student development theory where student growth in both maturity and academic knowledge are pillars of the collegiate experience (Evans, Forney, Guido, Patton, & Renn, 2009). The sharing of class information through mobile devices can allow increased contact among students and replaces the former strategy of sharing phone numbers or email addresses through a photocopied, pass-around sheet of paper. Also, group text messages can begin to instill a sense of common communication among students, and can be less formal than official university email messages. M-technologies, however, can also allow a group of students to have a common experience even though they are geographically dispersed, meaning that students can be on vacation, at an event, doing field work, etc., and can all communicate with each other in real-time to build the shared experiences that are important to group learning.

Community building is an extension of peer learning support and is critical to student retention outside of individual classes. By supporting dispersed real-time communication and the sharing of group events, students can feel supported and nurtured outside of formal classes, possibly improving retention and graduation rates. In a very traditional sense, community has been built on campuses through student organizations, and m-technologies can augment this collective process that can arise among students on campus. Some have argued that virtual communications has resulted in a different type of community emerging among young people and students, and left un-mitigated, naturally occurring virtual communities may indeed arise and become powerful experiences for students. An example of this power has been cited frequently as cyber-bullying. But, if used intentionally by campuses, including faculty and administrators, peer networks where individuals are accountable to each other can become critical enablers of student success.

Perhaps the most important variable from an academic perspective is whether m-technologies can be used to assist student learning in the classroom. By using mobile devices in the classroom, faculty can assign students different tasks in information gathering, having students report out to the class what they have found. Mobile devices can also bring visiting scholars' voices and images to individuals in a classroom in a real-time setting, and experiments, locations, field work, and applications can all be readily accessed. Additionally, material can be reinforced through video sharing, non-verbal communication, and even through the creation of gaming and simulation apps. The key to reinforcement of learning content is that mobile devices are used intentionally and in creative ways that respond to the habits and tendencies of students who have used mobile devices during their formative developmental years.

Assessment: Does M-Learning Work?

A critical component in any instructional environment is determining whether or not students have mastered or met the appropriate learning objectives of the given class or set of classes. Whether it is the acquisition of knowledge or the learning to apply knowledge or skills to a particular setting, there must be some form of assessment and determination about whether the m-technologies have added value to the course experience.

One of the most convenient strategies for addressing the effectiveness of m-learning is to include questions within end of course evaluations about whether the use of m-technologies made any perceived difference to the student. Similarly, faculty who teach by using m-technologies should be in a position to reflect critically on whether or not the technologies made a difference. Another approach that department chairs could consider is comparing control group grade point averages or assessment examinations, comparing those who have had classes where m-technologies play prominent roles as compared to traditional live-classes that did not use such tools. A fourth consideration would be to monitor m-technology use by students; even though the technology and device are included as an instructional practice, there must be some determination as to whether or not the tool was used, how often, and to what extent. Virtual fingerprinting, the process of noting when students logged on or off technology or into websites, can be easily tracked using contemporary technology, and should be a consideration to explore the extent of m-technology use.

The assessment of student learning can also be aided by using mobile devices. An extreme case might be random pop-quizzes, administered via mobile apps to students in a course, given anytime, anywhere, requiring students to be up caught up and current in their readings or homework. Another example might be to use tablets or other devices to administer exams in the classroom, or to use video technology for brief oral examinations or to monitor student test taking.

Overall, there is a significant need to look beyond preferences and basic discussions of m-technology performance to identify if and how these technologies impact learning. This research can and should be guided by department chairs (with deep content knowledge-?) and a thorough understanding of their students, and based on these findings, chairs can develop and use m-learning more effectively in their curricular offerings and in their academic programs.

SUCCESSFUL FACULTY DEVELOPMENT

This section focuses on two hypotheses. The first is that faculty development is based on a psychological contract (Wheeler, YEAR), and through this mental adoption of a needed change, department leaders become coaches of change. The second is that faculty development is grounded in adult learning theory, and that department leaders who want to create change among faculty must understand and incorporate the fundamentals of adult learning theory. These hypotheses will be specifically discussed in relation to different mobile learning technologies.

1. **Launch a Conference to Promote Mobile Initiatives and Engage Faculty:** Institutions and agencies engaged in upgrading their mobile technology and other IT infrastructure have come to realize "they must make professional development a priority if they are to engage faculty and produce successful outcomes" (CoyneSmith, 2012). As a result, a five step plan was proposed to maximize mobile learning through the use of professional development processes.

   Step one in the above mentioned plan involved initiating an in-house conference to promote mobile initiatives. The intent of this action was to engage faculty members but, at the same time, educate them about the perceived values associated with new technology. For illustrative purposes, CoyneSmith cited Adelphi University's annual *Teaching with Technology Conference*. This professional development initiative utilized peer teaching by fellow faculty members versus soliciting outside sources of expertise on mobile learning. Thus, conference participants were provided with an opportunity to learn teaching practices on various technologies from peer faculty who were judged to be credible as well as accessible. Accessibility to knowledge becomes an important professional development consideration, especially when continued learning is being sought by the conference's participants.

2. **Begin With an Implementation Strategy That Ties Mobile Learning to Your Institution's Academic Plan or Vision:** The second way that was suggested to enhance mobile learning through professional development was to start with an implementation strategy that ties mobile learning to the institution's academic plan or vision. CoyneSmith was very emphatic about this point when he stated that "to get faculty engaged in applications of mobile technology, place an emphasis on professional and community development around wireless applications, while explaining how it furthers the greater academic goals of the university" (p. 1). Facilitating an institution's academic strategies will certainly

make professional development funding easier to procure and, ultimately, it will most likely benefit faculty in terms of enhancing their workplace environment. Engaging in professional development becomes less difficult if you honestly believe the results of your efforts will ultimately improve the culture of your occupational environment. Engagement, enthusiasm, and motivation to improve oneself are normally tied to visualizing some type of positive reward for one's efforts toward self-improvement.

3. **Enable Faculty "Ambassadors" for Technology Maximization:** Capitalize on your existing assets to build consensus. CoyneSmith suggested that you use faculty who are influential and supportive to upgrading the mobile learning culture on one's campus. These "ambassadors" or advocates can serve as front line agents for new technology practices and techniques. At MBA@UNC was cited as an example that incorporated this strategic component. A small group of key faculty members aided other faculty in adopting and applying Facebook as a viable communication tool to utilize with students and/or among faculty. In essence, this step "created a community around technology maximization" according to Douglas Shackelford, Associate Dean for the online MBA program at the University of North Carolina.

4. **Link Technology to Learning Effectiveness:** Learning effectiveness is a key link to step number four in CoyneSmith's five step plan to maximize mobile learning through the use of professional development. According to the author, "faculty members are unlikely to adopt a new learning technology, mobile or otherwise, if they don't see the relationship between its use and learning outcomes" (CoyneSmith, p. 2). A reasonable premise, but the key becomes how do you create such a link? One method used to establish a solid connection featured the creation of an instructional technology fellows program like the one at Macaulay Honors College. This program was designed to connect graduate students with individual professors to collaborate on course activities. This collaborative venture enabled graduate students and faculty members "to design course syllabi, create activities and assignments, and determine new ways to enhance course instruction through the application of technology" (p. 2).

How and/or why was the preceding task of significance or value in terms of professional development endeavors? One rationale lies in discipline specific expertise versus technology expertise. While many prominent faculty are acknowledged for their mastery of content knowledge, they may lack the same level of proficiency in terms of technology abilities. Therefore, the creation of a technology fellows program can "provide a level of support that integrates both technology and pedagogy on a peer-to-peer level. It's extremely effective" (CoyneSmith p. 2).

5. **Dedicate Time and Resources to the Mobile Technology Adoption Effort:** The fifth and final step for maximizing mobile learning through professional development entailed the elements of time and resources. A quality professional development effort that produces lasting results is going to require substantial investments in terms of training opportunities, support, and adequate funding. In fact, Bailey and Powell indicated "that minus effective staff development and constant support, technology integration will never be satisfactorily achieved" (Bailey & Powell, 1998, p. 47). In addition, even with extensive professional development and coaching, it can take an individual from three to five years to reach the mastery and impact stages of technology use (Mandinach

& Cline, 1992). Thus, long-term commitments to professional development are a vital part of effective technology implementation (Cunningham, 2013). One-shot trainings and technology workshops do not yield the intended outcomes or long-term results sought via mobile learning initiatives. In part, the traditional sit-and-get training sessions or one-time-only workshops fail to make participants comfortable with using technology or proficient at integrating technology into their instructional methodologies (Rodriquez, 2000). In addition, effective professional development efforts will incorporate key points from adult learning theory. "Adults require relevant, concrete experiences with adequate support, appropriate feedback, and long-term follow-up" (Speck, 1996). To this end, it becomes clear why there must be a substantial investment and/or commitment of time and resources to any mobile technology adoption effort. There is simply no quick, inexpensive fix that will ensure that technology is used effectively and efficiently to foster new opportunities for learning and to promote student achievement.

NEXT GENERATION FACULTY DEVELOPMENT

Much work in the field of faculty development has focused on the diagnostic elements of improving teaching and research. Activities such as video recording teaching lessons, peer observations of teaching, micro-teaching exercises, peer coaching, self-reflection journaling, etc. have been described and advocated as useful tools in improving teaching. Developmental activities have also been identified and used to assist faculty with scholarly activities, including attending grant writing workshops, research methods and statistics refresher courses, and hiring editors and grant writers. The general approach for faculty development, as suggested from these types of activities, is that programs and practices are developed and implemented when needed and identified, such as in response to a particular problem. With the rate of change in technology and the expansion of knowledge, faculty development must fundamentally change and become an aggressive, assertive, and relevant part of the academy.

Future faculty development programs that can accommodate the current, and more importantly the future, of m-learning must be based on two concepts: faculty development as an adult learning activity, and faculty development as a constant, progressive, continuous activity.

Adult learning theory is grounded in the concept that education has different functions, and this functionality or practicality is important to how and why adults engage in learning activities. Clinton and Rieber (2010) highlighted the use of self-directed learning in adulthood, noting that adults are more likely to engage in learning that is applicable or directed to their interests and use. Adult education is often grounded in an individual's identification of a particular problem or perceived need, and learning is either sought after or self-defined to meet some practical need. As Stebbins (2001) has noted, however, often with adults learning can be crafted and developed around interests such as hobbies or leisure pursuits.

The key for adult education theory in faculty development is that the developmental aspect of faculty members is in response to something that the faculty member, as an adult, identifies a need for. Broad-based, shot-gun approaches to faculty development are not effective, particularly when faculty members might feel threatened or apprehensive about something, such as technology in general and mobile technologies specifically. Examples of what might have worked in the past include monthly faculty development luncheons or once-per-semester sessions highlighting some developmental activity. Instead, every department chair should be meeting regularly with faculty members to talk about how performance can be improved through developmental activities, and faculty development should be seen as a team approach, constantly identifying areas for improved performance to help faculty reach their potential.

For m-learning, this means that department chairs have to get to know their faculty members on a personal level and must understand how each faculty member approaches teaching and learning, and what individual skill levels might be, in addition to understanding the kinds of content and competencies required of each course taught. Once this more intimate level of understanding is created, department chairs can, in a non-threatening manner, help build competence, confidence, and intentionality in using m-learning.

In addition to this relevance, faculty development must evolve to become real-time, need-based, continuous, and evolving. With the frequency of change in technology, faculty members must become more concerned about how they use these resources, and department chairs are in the unique situation to encourage this concern. As colleges and universities are reflections of the quality of instruction that they offer, helping faculty members offer the highest quality of instruction possible is of critical importance. The key for department chairs, especially in working with m-learning technologies, is to be intentional in how technologies are used, and how faculty members are encouraged to incorporate these technologies into their curricula. Faculty members are not necessarily to be managed, but they must be coached and encouraged and their quality must be mentored. Much the same as talent or sports agents, department chairs must work in the best interests of their faculty members, and they must encourage, support, and provide essential resources for their faculty.

In the world of emerging m-learning, department chairs must explore changing how they offer developmental activities to their faculty. They must devise a plan to keep faculty members abreast of current technologies, and one that will also chart how m-learning should augment disciplinary learning. Mobile device use has become common among much of the educated population, especially among college students and even adult learners, and academic departments must have a plan and strategy to effectively use these devices to support effective instruction.

CONCLUSION

Mobile devices have become commonplace for much of the population, and with their rise in use and dependence, educational institutions have begun to more aggressively use them in providing instruction. As tablets, phones, laptops, and a growing number of apps demonstrate, these types of devices can be a significant contributor to how people communicate. Educational institutions have begun to embrace mobile learning technologies, and they are just beginning to structure educational activities and programs that make better use of the technology that is available to them.

One of the most critical determinants of m-learning success is the department chair; the individual responsible for the majority of all academic decisions being made on campus (Roach, 1976). As such, department chairs must learn to structure mobile learning as an element in a larger plan of how college-level education is offered. For the most part, much of the college curriculum has evolved without much regard to intentionality of instructional delivery, but with new technologies and applications available annually or monthly, chairs must provide the leadership necessary to focus on effective instructional delivery. With the broad reliance on mobile devices, m-learning has become critical to future college instruction, and will continue to emerge as an increasingly commonplace instructional strategy.

Department chairs can respond to the need for building expertise in m-learning by using faculty development as a continuous, intentional process. This perception of faculty development is different from previous incarnations of developmental activities that have been more stagnant. Faculty development that is current, continuous, and tied to specific objectives can lead to greater instructional outcomes and higher levels of faculty satisfaction. To accomplish this, however, department chairs must be willing to engage faculty on a constant basis and spend more time learning about the content of courses, the barriers to technology integration, and the personal motivations of their faculty members.

Importantly, there is a need for collaboration between faculty members, department chairs, and other administrators in creating a process to consistently identify and integrate new technologies into the teaching and learning process. Passive approaches to modifying teaching best practices can no longer be considered acceptable, as new generations of students are arriving on campus with very different perspectives about how communication can and should occur. Acknowledging the differences in Millennial students is a strong initial indication that an institution is willing to change and embrace different and creative thinking about student learning.

The use of mobile devices will most certainly continue, especially as cloud computing makes memory capacity and speed issues easier to deal with by the end user. And as speed and memory problems are erased from conversations about mobile technology, these technologies will become even more common place and a larger part of the collective population's toolbox. As institutions respond, the most basic level of administrator who can make a significant difference is the department chair. This figure must be intentional and creative in finding unique and meaningful ways to structure mobile learning into a student's curriculum, and this most often will be successfully accomplished through partnering with his/her faculty members. This partnership must be constructive, meaningful, supportive, and above all, centered on attempting to provide the best possible education for a new generation of college students.

REFERENCES

Alexander, L. T., & Davis, R. H. (1977). *Choosing instructional techniques*. East Lansing, MI: Michigan State University.

Bailey, G. D., & Powell, D. (1998). Technology staff development and support programs: Applying Abraham Maslow's hierarchy of need. *Leading and Learning with Technology, 26*(3), 47-51, 64.

Berge, Z. L., & Muilenburg, L. (Eds.). (2013). *Handbook of mobile learning*. New York, NY: Routledge.

Cahn, P. S., Benjamin, E. J., & Shanahan, C. W. (2013). Uncrunching time: Medical schools use of social media for faculty development. *Medical Education Online, 18*, 20995. doi:10.3402/meo.v18i0.20995 PMID:23810170

Clinton, G., & Rieber, L. R. (2010). The Studio experience at the University of Georgia: An example of constructionist learning for adults. *Educational Technology Research and Development, 58*, 755–780. doi:10.1007/s11423-010-9165-2

Collins, L. J., & Liang, X. (2013). Task relevance in the design of online professional development for teachers of ELLS: A Q methodology study. *Professional Development in Education, 39*(3), 441–443. doi:10.1080/19415257.2012.712752

Coyne-Smith, T. (2012, October 4). *5 Ways to Maximize Mobile Learning through Professional Development*. Retrieved from http://www.workforceanywhere.com/2012/10/04/5-ways-to-maximize-mobile-learning

Cunningham, J. (2013). Between technology and teacher effectiveness: Professional development teaching and learning. Retrieved from http://www.teachlearning.com/print.aspx?articleid=41214

E-Learning. (2013). *Introduction to mobile learning*. Retrieved from learning-india.com/E-learning-Articles/

Evans, N. J., Forney, D. S., Guido, F. M., Patton, L. D., & Renn, K. A. (2009). *Student development in college, theory research, and practice* (2nd ed.). San Francisco, CA: Jossey-Bass.

Han, J. H., & Finkelstein, A. (2013). Understanding the effects of professors' pedagogical development with clicker assessment and feedback technologies and the impact of students' engagement learning in higher education. *Computers & Education*, 65, 64–76. doi:10.1016/j.compedu.2013.02.002

He, W., & Abdous, M. (2013). An online knowledge-centered framework for faculty support and service innovation. *VINE: The Journal of Information & Knowledge Management Systems*, 43(1), 96–110. doi:10.1108/03055721311302160

Kerpen, D. (2011). *Likeable social media: How to delight your customers, create an irresistible brand, and be generally amazing on Facebook*. New York, NY: McGraw-Hill.

Mandinach, E., & Cline, H. (1992, April). *The impact of technological curriculum innovation on teaching and learning activities*. Paper presented at the Annual Conference of the American Educational Research Association. San Francisco, CA.

O'Hara, S., Pritchard, R., Huang, C., & Pella, S. (2013). Learning to integrate new technologies into teaching and learning through a design-based model of professional development. *Journal of Technology and Teacher Education*, 21(2), 203–223.

Roach, J. H. L. (1976). The academic department chairperson: roles and responsibilities. *The Educational Record*, 57(1), 13–23.

Seagren, A. T., Wheeler, D. W., Creswell, J. W., Miller, M. T., & VanHorn-Grassmeyer, K. (1994). *Academic leadership in community colleges*. Lincoln, NE: University of Nebraska.

Sporn, B. (1999). *Adaptive university structures*. Philadelphia, PA: Kingsley Publishers.

Stebbins, R. A. (2001, May/June). Serious leisure. *Society*, 53–57. doi:10.1007/s12115-001-1023-8

Udell, C. (2012). *Learning everywhere: How mobile content strategies are transforming training*. Nashville, TN: RockBench Publishing.

ADDITIONAL READING

Bhatti, M. T. (2012). Dimensions of good university teaching: Faculty and department chairs' perspectives. *Design and Technology Education*, 17(1), 44–53.

Bothma, C. H., & Cant, M. C. (2011). Adopting learning technologies: From belief to practice. *Educational Studies*, 37(4), 375–389. doi:10.1080/03055698.2010.511697

Bozeman, B., Fay, D., & Gaughan, M. (2013). Power to do....what? Department heads decision autonomy and strategic priorities. *Research in Higher Education*, 54(3), 303–328. doi:10.1007/s11162-012-9270-7

Campbell, J. P., & Bozeman, W. C. (2008). The value of student ratings: Perceptions of students, teachers, and administrators. *Community College Journal of Research and Practice*, 32(1), 13–24. doi:10.1080/10668920600864137

Evans, M. A., & Johri, A. (2008). Facilitating guided participation through mobile technologies: Designing creative learning environments for self and others. *Journal of Computing in Higher Education*, 20(2), 92–105. doi:10.1007/s12528-008-9004-1

Flood, T., & Black, T. (2011). Mobile technology and the unsettled ocean of student services. *College and University*, 86(3), 51–56.

Franklin, K. K., & Hart, J. K. (2006). Influence of web-based distance education on the academic department chair role. *Journal of Educational Technology & Society*, 9(1), 213–228.

Henning, T. B. (2012). Writing professor as adult learner: An autoethnography of online professional development. *Journal of Asynchronous Learning Networks, 16*(2), 9–26.

Jackson, L. D. (2009). Revisiting adult learning theory through the lens of an adult learner. *Adult Learning, 20*(3-4), 20–22.

Levinson-Rose, J., & Menges, R. J. (1981). Improving college teaching: A critical review of research. *Review of Educational Research, 51*(3), 403–434. doi:10.3102/00346543051003403

Lucas, K. (2011). Oral self critique: Raising student consciousness of communication (in) competence. *Communication Teacher, 25*(1), 12–15. doi:10.1080/17404622.2010.513993

Luna, G., & Cullen, D. (2011). Podcasting as complement to graduate teaching: Does it accommodate adult learning theories? *International Journal of Teaching and Learning in Higher Education, 23*(1), 40–47.

McDonald, I. (2001). The teaching community: Recreating university teaching. *Teaching in Higher Education, 6*(2), 153–167. doi:10.1080/13562510120045168

Moye, M. J., Henkin, A. B., & Floyd, D. J. (2006). Faculty-department chair relationships: Examining the nexus of empowerment and interpersonal trust in community colleges in the context of change. *International Journal of Educational Reform, 15*(2), 266–288.

Rossing, J. P. (2012). Mobile technology and liberal education. *Liberal Education, 98*(1), 68–72.

Rossing, J. P., Miller, W. M., Cecil, A. K., & Stamper, S. E. (2012). iLearning: The future of higher education? Student perceptions on learning with mobile tablets. *Journal of the Scholarship of Teaching and Learning, 12*(2), 1–26.

Ting, Y. L. (2013). Using mobile technologies to create interwoven learning interactions: An intuitive design and its evaluation. *Computers & Education, 60*(1), 1–13. doi:10.1016/j.compedu.2012.07.004

Woodard, C. A. (2007). Using adult learning theory for new-hire training. *Journal of Adult Education, 36*(1), 44–47.

Zerihun, Z., Beishuizen, J., & Van Os, W. (2011). Conceptions and practices in teaching and learning: Implications for the evaluation of teaching quality. *Quality in Higher Education, 17*(2), 151–161. doi:10.1080/13538322.2011.582793

KEY TERMS AND DEFINITIONS

Adult Education: For the purpose of this discussion, adult education references the unique learning style and characteristics of those who have reached a level of maturity to be referred to as an adult. Chronological age may be one criterion for referring to adults, but definitions may not entirely be limited to a specific age.

Department Chairs: Also referred to as department heads or academic directors, these individuals typically are faculty members who have been placed in a leadership role for a given academic unit. Units vary widely, with some including only a single degree program area, and others including multiple, loosely related programs.

Faculty Development: A process of helping college teachers improve their performance in certain or selected areas. In particular, the emphasis is on diagnosis and enhancement, noting that often individuals are not fully capable of self-identification and need external assistance to identify correcting or improvement measures.

M-Technologies: Mobile technology devices include tools such as cell phones, tablet computers, electronic readers, and might even include laptop or portable computers. The emphasis is on the ability for an individual to move freely while using the technology. Related are implications of m-technologies to learning, resulting in the concept of m-learning.

Chapter 3
A Case Study of Developing Suitable Mobile Learning Technology for a Distance Learning Masters Programme

Tracey Dodman
University of Leicester, UK

Terese Bird
University of Leicester, UK

David Hopkins
University of Leicester, UK

ABSTRACT

In 2012, following some development work, the Department of Criminology launched a new distance-learning course: the MSc Security, Conflict, and International Development (SCID). The target profile for students looking to enroll in this course were living or working in and around conflict regions; they may be forces personnel or professional staff stationed in areas of conflict or recent conflict. Therefore, reliable Internet connection (broadband or cellular) is often rare or intermittent. The course was designed to give learners a rich learning experience in such a way that their learning could remain largely uninterrupted when they experienced loss of Internet connection. Learners in this course were sent an Apple iPad as part of their course fees and given instructions to download a Course App comprising multimedia-rich learning resources. The programme enabled students to study and learn whilst on the move and provided an opportunity for study where otherwise it would have been very difficult, if not impossible for some. The authors believe they have widened participation and enhanced learning capacity through the innovative programme design. This programme is explored in this chapter.

DOI: 10.4018/978-1-4666-6284-1.ch003

INTRODUCTION

In October 2013 the University of Leicester was honoured to be shortlisted to the eLearning Awards in 2013 for 'best use of mobile learning' (University of Leicester, 2013a). Mobile learning is recognised as being a "relatively new phenomenon and the theoretical basis is currently under development" (Kearney, Schuck, Burden and Aubusson, 2012, n. p.) and that we need to approach the "whole process [of mobile learning] as a platform approach" (Quinn, 2013, p.161) and not just a different delivery mechanism. Despite the current trend toward mobile computing and 'always-on' learning (Wheeler, 2013), persistent Internet connectivity by a learner cannot be guaranteed, regardless of where the learner lives. The lessons learnt from developing and delivering this MSc course may be applied anywhere. Furthermore, while developing a course which may rely heavily on mobile learning, it is important to recognise that the pedagogic perspectives of the learning resources and provision of any required devices have potential to derail the workflow and timetable for development and take the team in an unforeseen direction. This risk can be mitigated by employing sound pedagogic principles in course design, as was done in the MSc Security, Conflict, and International Development.

As will be outlined in this chapter, our group of students for this case study was likely to be without Internet access for large periods of time. Hancock (2010) notes some potential problems when producing distance e-learning courses, such as parts of the developing world not having the infrastructure required for Internet access, and the fact that certain groups of students such as those in the armed forces on active service, prisoners, those in secure hospitals [in her case she was specifically referring to prisoners] simply do not have Internet access at all, or have intermittent access. This should be a consideration when designing courses. There are ways of identifying resources for student use; Hancock suggests "essential, desirable or optional" (p. 9), (we identified them as "required" and "useful") and efforts should be made to ensure ease of access to "essential" or "required" resources. Hancock rightly points out that "Internet access is taken for granted by many but, when constructing distance e-learning courses, we must not forget those for whom Internet access is spasmodic, limited or prohibited. If we do, we risk excluding large sections of the student body" (Hancock, 2010, p. 10).

There are, of course, cultural, educational and personal reasons that account for preferences in type of delivery. There are also pedagogic suggestions and claims regarding teaching delivery: "effective learning design should", as Wedgwood (2013, p. 96) notes, "always keep the ultimate goal for any learning uppermost and ensure that data can be collected to determine if the learners are gaining the required capability." Quinn (2013) continues this theme by saying that, when considering the provision of mobile learning, "your resources will include capabilities around devices, mobile-specific tools and infrastructure, and designers and developers" (p. 161) and that the skills required to keep up to date with the "still-dynamic field" will need to be kept fresh and fluid. Herrington, Mantei, Herrington, Olney and Ferry (2008) observe that there are few examples in literature, at the time the programme was being devised, where mobile devices may be used as cognitive tools to "solve complex problems and to engage students in authentic and meaningful tasks" (p. 419) beyond that offered by a simple replacement of the paper texts.

This chapter will look at the rationale behind the decisions made when developing the programme, the learning materials, and the iPad App. Investigations into the availability of appropriate technologies played a central role in the direction the programme and method of study took. We will outline the background and context for the provision and production of this new programme prior to discussing the rationale behind the decisions made. Results from student evaluations will be presented and considered before we consider solutions to problems faced and make recommendations for future development and research.

BACKGROUND

When distance learning was first offered by the department the Internet was often an under-utilised resource or tool: many students did not use computers on a regular basis, even for basic word processing purposes. Although Library provision had always been part of the course fees, at that time, this meant ordering books that would be posted to the student, with the student being responsible for the return postage. This was difficult for students, especially those based overseas, in terms of both cost and time. Whilst students were encouraged to access academic resources and source other material, essentially, students could pass the programme using only the module material and the texts they were sent from the department, as it was recognised at the time that it was very difficult for working people to be able to obtain any additional materials and resources.

As provision and use of computers and the Internet became more widespread, the electronic provision from the University Library greatly increased, with more and more electronic journal provision available each year and a growing number of e-books available. We have one undergraduate distance learning programme that is delivered online, via the Virtual Learning Environment (VLE), with downloads available for those who do not have good online provision. (Note that this chapter uses the UK term Virtual Learning Environment, or VLE, to refer a platform providing administrative and other learning support; in other countries, the term Learning Management System is used.) The main reason this programme moved to online delivery well before our other modules is that prior to this the course was delivered via CD ROM, so it was never just a module delivered via a traditional 'correspondence course' postal approach. The postgraduate programmes continue to be delivered via paper-based modules, although these can also be accessed online via the course VLE (Blackboard), but simply in PDF format. Photocopied readings are no longer provided; these looked very tired and rather old-fashioned and were dispensed with some years ago. We no longer provide large lever-arch files with each module, but a perfect bound product. Textbooks are still sent to students.

The postgraduate programmes consist of six modules plus a dissertation. The courses are distance learning and part time, so the full programme takes two years. In terms of the timetable, each module takes approximately 12 weeks and the dissertation five to six months. Each module contains nine units of written resource. During the units there are some reflective exercises and at the end of each unit there are some personal study questions (which are not submitted to the Department) and some suggested readings. Some of these readings will relate to a chapter from a course textbook they have been sent and others will either relate to a chapter of a book available in the Library which we have had scanned and made available via the Blackboard site (ensuring that we comply with UK Copyright provisions) or will be journal articles that can be electronically accessed via the University Library.

From student feedback and surveys we found that some of our students do not mind whether they receive paper or online materials; others prefer online and still others paper. There are clear pros and cons to each mode of delivery. Many of our students move around a reasonable amount for their work and therefore appreciate the portable nature of online delivery, but some students suffer from a lack of Internet access. As many of our students are of the more mature variety, some say they prefer paper as this is what they are 'used to' and like to make notes on the module material and we can appreciate this as this is often the way that we might feel that we prefer to study. However, whilst we may feel that we would prefer this in an ideal world, this is not always practicable.

RATIONALE AND LEARNING NEED

The courses that are offered are successful – they have reasonable levels of recruitment, the Security and Risk Management (SRM) programmes recruit very well, and provide education and academic achievement on subjects that are necessary, but seemingly under-provided for world-wide. The SRM programmes, for example, are not 'traditional' academic programmes; this is a relatively new area of academic study and the Department was one of the first providers of both undergraduate and postgraduate academic qualifications in this area. There has been a growing desire, and now, need, over the last decade for the professionalization of those working within the security industry in general, and one way of establishing this is via academic qualification. The Security Institute (UK based professional body), for example, recognises our programmes for their varying levels of membership. The Worshipful Company of Security Professionals was given a Royal charter by the Privy Council in March 2010 and runs the Register of Chartered Security Professionals in conjunction with the Security Institute. There are two routes to application, one being the 'standard path' requiring a bachelors or masters degree in a security-related discipline.

Following the success of offering such programmes by distance learning for over 20 years and in particular, the MSc SRM, the Department recognised the need for a further academic programme; one to meet the needs of students working in conflict and post-conflict countries. Several of our students on the MSc SRM programme were working in such environments, and we had received several enquiries from people working in this environment. Whilst the MSc SRM covers general principles, it was felt a tailored programme could be developed to meet the needs of this particular group of students working within the security arena, but in post-conflict environments.

The market was envisaged as being made up of students working for the United Nations, government bodies, Non Governmental Organisations (NGOs) and aid agencies – those already working – or hoping to work – in international development. Representatives from organisations that are particularly interested include:

- The United Nations (Political Affairs Officers; Programme Managers; Judicial Affairs Officers; Corrections Officers; Police Advisors; Policy and Planning Officers);
- Institutions such as the Organisation for Security and Co-operation in Europe (OSCE);
- European Union (EU);
- Council of Europe (CoE);
- Economic Community of West African States (ECOWAS);
- North Atlantic Treaty Organization (NATO);
- Non-governmental Organisations (NGOs) such as the Geneva Centre for the Democratic Control of Armed Forces (DCAF), Saferworld, International Alert, The Asia Foundation, Amnesty International; and Donor agencies and government bodies such as the UK's Department for International Development (DFID);
- The Open Society Institute (OSI) and the Soros Foundation Network.

Many students will be mid-career professionals who are looking to add an academic dimension to their professional profile. Many students may have an undergraduate qualification, although some will not, but it is increasingly recognised in certain organisations that a postgraduate qualification is required to reach a certain level with the profession – promotion may not be possible without this postgraduate qualification. Aside from the recognised qualification, the subject area alone makes the programme a very attractive option for those working within this area.

The programme was designed to develop skills, knowledge and understanding of conflict prevention and recovery with a particular emphasis upon: responding to the challenges of countries emerging from conflict; security sector reform; how to develop the rule of law; the importance of human rights in delivering justice and security; and broader issues relating to international security and the risks posed by countries emerging from, and vulnerable to, conflict. Given this, the department set about designing and developing an innovative and exciting postgraduate degree programme that focused on how to meet the strategic security and justice challenges of countries emerging from conflict, and the MSc in Security, Conflict and International Development was launched in March 2012. The module developer (also the main course tutor) has extensive knowledge and expertise of both working in, and researching, this subject area. The challenge was how to deliver the programme to the students that we would likely attract, given their particular needs.

The distance learning format makes it possible for students to study with us (or any other institution) from anywhere in the world and we knew from the subject area that we would be attracting students from a variety of locations worldwide. Many of our typical students on this programme will move around frequently (often at short notice) and will often be based for periods of time without Internet access. As noted in a recent report by Nie, Bird, Beck, Hayes and Conole (2013: 2), students on this type of programme face a number of challenges:

- **Access:** It is unlikely there will be a reliable and regular Internet connection in these post-conflict regions.
- **Travel:** Students travel considerably as part of their work.
- **Time:** Students are very busy and time-poor.
- **Resources:** It is unlikely there will be facilities such as a local Library in these post-conflict regions where students can find resources for their studies.

These challenges can have a great effect on whether keen applicants actually become students in the first place, and whether, once on a programme, students remain on it. These challenges can turn into barriers and this can mean that some students withdraw as they just find it too difficult to maintain the required level of study. The nature of distance learning means that the learning should ideally be designed to help working students achieve academic success. Quinn (2013) states that "if we're talking about looking at a full spectrum of solutions, we need to start from a bigger perspective than a course. We need to identify what the need is, and what the opportunity is" (p. 164), we therefore need to break down as many barriers as possible in order to ensure that we can widen participation and help committed students achieve their educational goals. Also identified, by Anderson and Dron (2010), is the intersection between the various approaches to distance education (cognitivist, behaviourist, and constructivist) "whether the learner is at the centre or part of a learning community or learning network, learning effectiveness can be greatly enhanced by applying ... an understanding of how people can learn more effectively" (p. 92). It was therefore important to consider how we might create a holistic learning experience, based on sound pedagogic principles and achievable learning outcomes, using technology creatively and effectively, with varying learning material formats and built-in collaborative activities, to address the needs of our students and enable them to achieve even beyond their own expectations.

In terms of *Access* – the unreliable nature or complete absence of the Internet in certain areas (and particularly broadband) could mean that online programmes may be difficult to access and if they are accessed, may be either incredibly time-consuming (if broadband is not available) or simply impossible to be able to access the programme for the requisite amount of time (some students in the armed forces or working in refugee camps, for example, may only be allowed limited Internet access a day or week and understandably, studying may not always be top of their list of things to do when contacting family and friends will also be counted during this time). This may suggest that a paper programme would be more suitable for this challenge / barrier. As mentioned though, these types of students are likely to travel regularly, often at very short notice. This can mean that large paper modules and textbooks are not part of the luggage allowance, or even a consideration when deploying or changing location at short notice.

Time is an issue for any student who has to combine studying with work (and/or family/caring responsibilities). Whilst not wanting to start an argument by suggesting that our students have the busiest working lives of all distance learning students, it is a fact that most of our students do not have a traditional working week and work in excess of the usual 37-40 hours of full time work, often exceeding the usual limits set in place by the European Commission Working Conditions - Working Time Directive (European Commission, 2013). It can be very difficult to maintain the recommended 10-15 hours of studying per week (in order to achieve the notional 150 study hours for each 20 credit module). Of course, whilst a certain number of study hours should be undertaken, due to the flexible nature of distance learning it is up to the student how this is achieved.

Whatever the mode of delivery, study will have to be undertaken. What is important therefore, is to be able to maximise the time available. This could be by spending less time searching for readings, by having them instantly available, or by maximising opportunities by reading or viewing a learning resource while on a break. Here, the benefits of online resources can be seen. Conversely, time is wasted when trying to connect where broadband service is poor or slow and trying to download a reading can take a great deal of time. In these circumstances, a paper based module could be of benefit (although not everything can be reproduced on paper).

Campus-based students should have access to all the required resources via their University Library and Learning Development unit (or equivalent unit that assists students with study skills resources and issues). UK Universities have reciprocal agreements for student access so that students can access other University libraries (University of Leicester, 2013b). Distance learning students may therefore access other libraries, often in countries outside of the UK. However, due to the nature of the work that many of the SCID students do, they are often unlikely to be based near to a University Library. This can put them in a detrimental position. The University of Leicester Library (like many others) has excellent electronic facilities, meaning that students can access a wide range of journals and e-books (although they will of course need Internet access in order to do so). Where possible, the University will purchase e-books alongside paper textbooks, although some publishers still will not provide access to e-books. In these cases, the librarians can copy one chapter of a book (adhering to UK Copyright legislation) and email this to a student (again, requiring Internet access). This is very useful, but students may want to read more than one chapter of a book. Leicester's Learning Development unit provides downloadable study guides and offers sessions with learning advisors by phone, email, and Skype for students who are unable to attend in person but, as with many students, this extremely useful resource is not accessed as much as educators might want, as highlighted by Minocha and Others (2009, p 116), where they discuss the relative benefits and issues surrounding the use of Skypecasts for tutorial work, especially in situations where reliable connectivity is an issue.

Therefore, neither our existing modes of delivery of paper-based modules for postgraduates nor current models of Internet/online delivery for undergraduates were considered ideal for this group of students. Unless distance learning students are motivated through well-designed learning activities that are linked to learning objectives that help learners understand how the activity itself can aid the realisation of personal goals, aspirations, or interests (Hartnett, George and Dron, 2011) they are unlikely to remain studying if they face such challenges/barriers. Indeed, even highly motivated students may become demotivated as a result of such challenges/barriers, resulting in a very disappointing learning experience. This led us to consider how we could provide quality educational resources that delivered for such a group of students. We decided on an approach that would allow us to provide a variety of up-to-date resources, whilst also giving students access to course materials when Internet access was unavailable. The main mode of delivery was to be the VLE, but with the provision of an Apple Ipad and specially designed course App.

COURSE DESIGN AND DEVELOPMENT

The University provides support for the design of new programmes. Our first port of call was the University's Beyond Distance Research Alliance, now renamed the Institute of Learning Innovation (ILI). This research group developed and teaches a course design workshop entitled Carpe Diem. Carpe Diem brings together course teams, subject librarians, and learning technologists to create an effective e-learning course design, encouraging more learner-centred approaches as opposed to didactic, teacher-centred approaches (Armellini and Jones, 2008). Course teams are encouraged and helped to use the VLE as more than just a repository for PowerPoint slides and the course handbook, and rather to enable collaboration, cooperation, and knowledge-building discussion between student and student, as well as between student and tutor. The Carpe Diem workshop was researched and developed with special focus on distance learning providers, an area of significant importance at the University of Leicester.

The Course Developer and Course Convenor attended the Carpe Diem workshop and discussed the nature of the course design. This would be a new programme; with no prior course aspects to have to deal with, there was a clear opportunity to follow principles of good course design explored in Carpe Diem. Rather than remain with the traditional nine unit-per-module model (as described earlier) used elsewhere in the department's Distance Learning programmes, designed initially to help students manage their time through the module (nine weeks for the units and then two-three weeks for preparing for the assignment), it was agreed that each module would have fewer units but contain more resources. In order to retain some consistency and uniformity for the students, it was agreed to have six units per modules, each containing three learning resources, and each learning resource containing fluid educational resources, depending on the subject and the most apposite way of meeting the learning outcomes for each module. The Course Developer is experienced in the subject area with expert knowledge of what should be contained in each module and was initially contracted on a part time basis to produce the modules. Five modules were produced by the course developer; the other, a research methods module, is common to all of the postgraduate programmes and developed separately but in the same format. The programme approval paperwork had been approved and this formed our framework for the development of programme content (Armellini and Jones, 2008).

It is clear that such a programme could not be developed and written without expertise in the area and we were very pleased to obtain the services of the Course Developer. This put us in a risky position in that should something untoward happen to the Course Developer during the development and writing of the modules, the department would have been in a difficult position in terms of finding a suitable replacement to complete the design and production in time. Luckily for all concerned, this was not an issue. We retained the Course Developer who is now a full time member of staff at the department and tutor on the programme.

All of the Department's MSc programmes require a total of 180 credits to be earned for graduation, and consist of six 20 credit modules plus a 60 credit dissertation. Each unit contains a welcome podcast (and transcript) from the Course Tutor and a bibliography listing further suggested reading, including weblinks where possible. Each learning resource is made up of a written document outlining the main themes, theories and concepts to be considered and additional resources. In this respect it is similar to the traditional programmes, as some amount of written narrative is felt to be very important to introduce and discuss the topics, relevant concepts and theoretical perspectives. Within these written sections, web links are live (requiring WiFi) together with a list of further activities and resources (videos, audio files and texts). Where possible, e-books are provided to students (via Amazon vouchers) for them to download and they will directed to read certain chapters at specific points of their learning journey and pathway through the modules. (Paper textbooks are sent when e-books are unavailable.) Where copyright permits, these additional resources are embedded in the course App enabling the student anytime access. The student is offered two types of resource – 'required', that should be reviewed as a necessary component of the programme and 'useful', which they are encouraged to review if they have time and/or specific interest in that area. It is important to ensure that sufficient content and resources are available for intrinsically motivated students who have the time and interest in order that they may have the necessary resources and guidance to meet their needs. Where copyright permission is unavailable, the App links the student to the relevant Internet site to enable them to access the material when possible, in an area with WiFi. We aim to make all the required resources available 24/7 so that students can always access their required readings, although this is not always possible. Approximately 80% of the required course materials can be accessed offline. We are very pleased with this as, as with all academic programmes at this level, students are not given absolutely everything that they need to read/listen to/watch in order to pass their assignments and programme. We have a collaborative approach (Armellini and Jones, 2008) and method to learning on the programme, making use of "e-tivities" (Salmon, 2013), discussion boards and wikis to drive discussion. Students are actively encouraged to undertake wider reading/listening/watching so they can engage in moderated e-tivities and discussions to broaden their knowledge base from which to then be in a good position to be able to address their assignments.

Course information is put on the App, consisting of the student course handbook and the Department's referencing guide. The App provides students with a number of additional study resources to help facilitate their learning. These sections contain study skills audio-visual presentations. Many of these are available 24/7, but a few of these require WiFi (students are notified, in the App, where an Internet connection is required to avoid disappointment or difficulties in access).

One aspect of effective online learning covered in Carpe Diem is the design and implementation of e-tivities. An e-tivity is an online activity, facilitated by the VLE, in which learners interact with each other and with the course tutor, who may be referred to as the e-moderator. The e-tivity begins with a 'spark' - a piece of information or a challenge, possibly in multimedia format. The spark is followed by short instructions inviting learners to respond to the spark in some way, through writing on the discussion board, adding to an online wiki, or even leaving a spoken recording on a 'voice board.' Learners are further invited to respond to each other's comments, to build on them and to construct knowledge and continue to develop ideas (Salmon, 2013). E-tivities therefore encourage distance learner motivation, engagement, and interest, and foster critical and other academic skills. The University's Course Design and Development Unit provided assistance to put multimedia and text material together via the University VLE and the Carpe Diem facilitators were always available for advice and support.

The University adopted VLE provision in 2001 with the decision to use Blackboard. The Department of Criminology was one of the first departments to take this on board and start to use it for the delivery of campus and distance learning programmes (although, particularly in the early years, this was used in an administrative and repository format in the main). We recognised a need to provide resources to students electronically so that they could access more resources than they currently did, such as scanned book chapters, as well as highlighting useful web resources to students. We also appreciated the electronic submission facility to enable a more efficient workflow for online assignment submissions (we used the Blackboard 'dropbox' facility in the first instance, prior to moving to Turnitin): reducing our paper handling and storage needs. Online submissions would also save students time as they would not have to complete their assignments earlier than the submission date in order to allow for the uncertainty of time needed for postage, which was especially pertinent for overseas students. We recognised that online submission may cause problems for students who did not have reliable or regular access to the Internet, but in the years of increasing computer usage and Internet and broadband provision, we felt it important that students need to have access to the Internet as part of the requirement for acceptance on to the programme of study, even if only once every three months to submit their assignment. We considered that most students would have more access than that, so that we could start to make more use of Internet resources available to students. We are not aware of instances where a student who would otherwise have joined the programme, did not, due to complete lack of Internet access, but this may have happened.

Our experience in offering distance learning programmes to students studying in unconventional situations led us to consider how we could begin to utilise new technologies to provide students with the opportunity to develop their professional careers in an area of growing strategic importance. It was decided to provide all those registering on the programme with an iPad and access to a bespoke course App (developed in association with a local company), enabling those on the move or with sporadic Internet connection to access course materials, even while offline. It also meant that the course designers could make use of a greater range of study materials – audio and video as well as text-based documents, which have been the traditional mode of learning on most distance learning courses.

We chose an iPad because at the time of course development (early 2011) it was the only tablet computer widely available with a suitably developed international network of support should the device need repair or replacement. Additionally, it was agreed that the intuitive interface would minimise the need for IT support, which can be challenging to deliver to students located across the globe and especially in countries emerging from conflict.

The Department worked closely with the App developer to create a design that would match the intuitiveness of the iPad. We needed the general point of flow for the programme to be clear, but in a non-linear manner. We did not want to have to continually inform the student what s/he should be moving on to next. Given the nature of the roles of many of the students and different amount of time and access that students might have, we wanted to have a number of resources for the student varying in amount of time required for study. We also wanted a variety of resource and information formats. It is clear, for example, that not all students respond to the written word in the same way, but this does not mean that they are not capable of appreciating, analysing and synthesising large amounts of complex information. By providing learning material in audio and video formats in addition to text, and by engaging students in e-tivities in which they build on their prior knowledge and construct new knowledge together with colleagues, we felt we were creating "self-directed learning opportunities… more likely to result in learning-related success" as expressed by Zhang and Bonk (2008, n.p.). Below are some figures of pages within the App.

The University of Leicester already had considerable experience and expertise with e-learning using VLEs and research into these and other technologies. The University's Institute of Learning Innovation (ILI) had recently completed a nationally-funded curriculum delivery project DUCKLING, in which distance-learning Masters students from the School of Education and School

Figure 1. Opening page in Course App

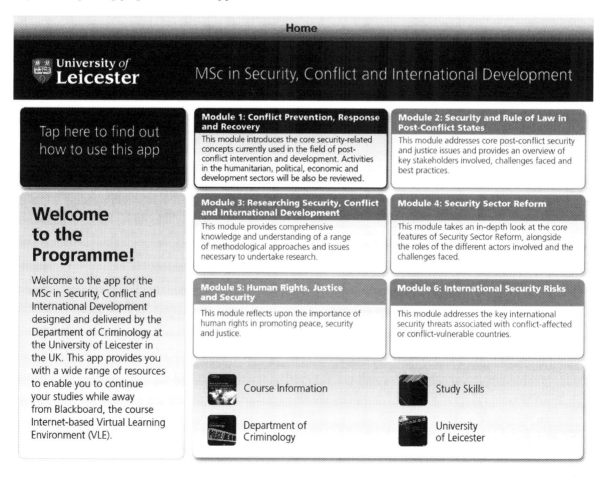

Figure 2. Demonstration of 'Module 1' section

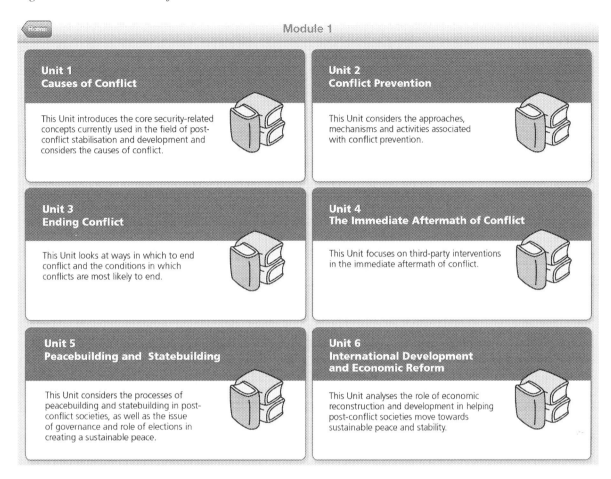

of Psychology received simple e-readers preloaded with course learning material. The students, most of whom were working full-time and had to fit study into free time, found the e-readers very useful in enabling study while on the move, fitting study into small periods through the day, and for holding learning materials in one compact device (Nie, 2010). Another nationally-funded project, OTTER, explored the creation, open licensing, and public release of open educational resources (OERs), examining issues of copyright of learning materials (Witthaus and Williamson, 2010). Findings from both of these projects laid groundwork for our new course requiring an App and iPad. At the time, the University had no experience of delivering study materials by means of an App in a commercial app store, and it was not able to assist us in designing and developing an App. We contacted a local App development company and discussed how the material could be put into an App to allow students maximum coverage and ease of access. UK Copyright legislation has a large part to play in determining what could be made available as 24/7 resources (available all the time) and what would require WiFi in order to be accessed. We had to work closely with the University's Copyright department to ensure that all resources were checked. This process takes time and is an area that must be planned for and timetabled into the design process of any programme developed in this manner. The resources had to be checked and for those that did not have a Creative Com-

Figure 3. Module 1, Unit 1 Resources (text, audio, video for offline learning)

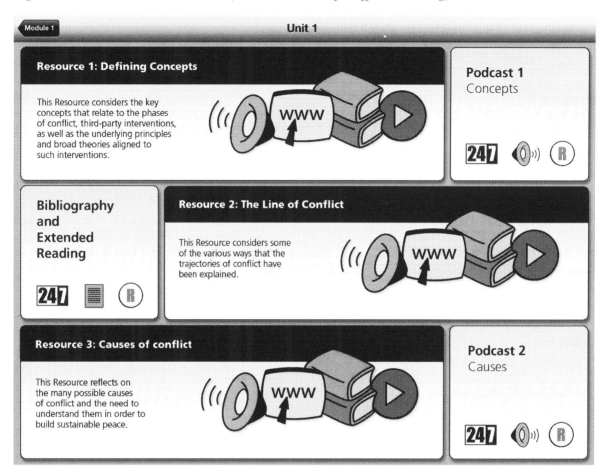

mons (CC) license, a request was made to be able to use the resource in the way we wanted. When a response was not forthcoming, reminder/chaser emails were sent. Sometimes the response would be affirmative, sometimes negative and sometimes we still received no response. After several chase communications, we had to abandon the use of those particular resources for 24/7 access. This of course had an impact on what we could offer as 24/7 course material and when we wanted an item to be 'required' reading/listening, we really wanted to have 24/7 access. Therefore, as part of the process, certain items had to change and replacements had to be found.

The App developers listened to our remit and understood our requirements. They worked with us to develop a user-friendly course App. We consulted on this and all spent some time ensuring all resources could be accessed and our views were fed back into the process and design. As the Course Convenor had no experience of using an iPad up to that point, it was a useful way of trialing the whole process to see how someone new to the product would be able to understand how to use the both the iPad and the App. Obviously, production time will vary, but a clear timetable must be in place and adhered to. Our production is outlined in the following workflow chart.

There was a matter of a contract with the App Developers to construct an agreement over work and payment as this project was without precedent. In University programme development,

A Case Study of Developing Suitable Mobile Learning Technology

Figure 4. Example of a learning resource

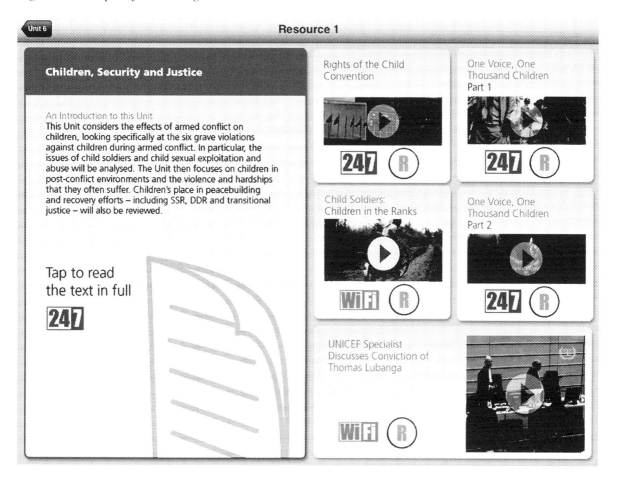

there is little money available for programme development and what is spent is often on time for the academic experts to develop/write the programme. Additionally, this was the first time that an App was going to be developed for one of our University programmes, so there was no precedent set. As such, it was agreed that payment would be via a commission paid per student on the programme. At the time, the University was paying Agents a commission per student enrolment where applicable so this was not so very different. The University has now moved away from using Agents and paying commission to the extent it once did, but given the lack of internal App-programming expertise and support, it was the only way this development could have taken place. We felt that the commission per student agreement a good one as, whilst we felt the course could be very popular, this was not a given, and high up-front development costs would have put an end to the programme before it had begun. The App Developers were also happy with this approach. It could lead to other contracts for them from other courses/departments, and the better the App, the more word of mouth, more students on the programme, more commission for them.

In addition to the course App the programme materials are fully available on the University's VLE, where students can view course materials, submit assignments, interact and engage with staff and other students and access the University's e-Library facilities. Additionally, some resources

Figure 5. Workflow chart for design and production of material

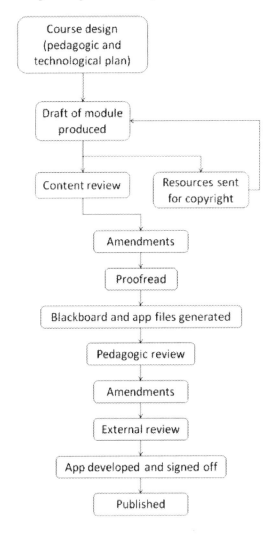

that cannot be viewed via an iPad (e.g. some flash videos) are also available via the VLE. Students are encouraged to use a range of communication methods including Twitter, wikis and blogs to share information, exchange ideas and develop networks. The next version of the course App will have greater communication functionality built in to enable this to happen more easily, incorporating chat areas and links to Twitter and RSS feeds, although this will require some online access. This will help to provide fuller portability and the increased communication and collaboration facilities will help to encourage learning to take place.

WHAT THE STUDENTS SAY

Student views and opinions are very important to the department and we continually monitor the student performance and their feedback on both our teaching and their learning. Their experiences of using the technologies we have implemented and made available to them have a huge impact on their involvement and engagement with the programme and the learning materials: therefore these views are very important to not only the success of the programme but also the ability for the students to progress and graduate. Alongside Departmental research and evaluation, the course

App was part of a wider piece of funded research evaluating student learning and mobile devices (Nie et al., 2013). We therefore have a wealth of data to present and discuss in the chapter.

Interestingly, research (University of Leicester, 2013c) found that 50% of student respondents used the course App on a daily basis and a further 42% used it at least two times a week which is remarkably high for a distance learning programme where students are in full-time employment (particularly so considering the types of employment roles these students hold). Over half of respondents said they used it in public places such as cafés, airports, etc. and 58% used it while on the move – on planes and trains, etc, making good use of what Traxler (2011) refers to as "dead time" (p. 8).

It is clear from our evaluations that not only do students prefer to access their materials via the iPad/course App interface, they are also more motivated to learn and access a greater range of materials. This model of distance learning has proven so effective that this is one of the main reasons why the Department has decided to adopt this model for the rest of its distance learning programmes.

The issue of portability came through strongly in much of the feedback from students:

I travel quite a lot for work making the use of iPad ideal.

For me, the course app is suitable based on the nature of my job which demands me to always be on the move. Print could be very bulky for me to move.

The course App allows you to access the information on the move without the paper clutter.

Often my Internet [connection] is of a poor standard so the App makes it easier to study.

When asked whether the iPad and course App had changed the way that students studied, responses included:

Firstly I am more motivated, as it is structured and organised. I am getting through more than I would if I was solely given a recommended reading list.

It has enabled me to read on the move or when working away from home.

The iPad has enabled me to broaden my research horizon as I am able to compare ideas and confirm issues faster as a result of the online capability of the iPad. Access to materials like [the] eLibrary has also brought the classroom closer to me.

I love the fact it is mobile, as I am constantly on the move. Travelling with books would be unrealistic.

It is more interactive than other conventional means of studying. You can use audio visual options plus get to online links which can help maintaining focus while studying.

When asked to summarise their experience with the iPad and course App, student responses included:

It is a dynamic learning tool, which has done an excellent job in filling the gap for the working student who is unable to be on campus, by making the material available everywhere you go.

A good way of bringing your study with you on the go.

Excellent as it allows for flexible study as you can access all the materials without having to carry lots of books and means you can study anytime anywhere.

It is clear from this evaluation that not only do students prefer to access their materials via the iPad/course App interface, they are also more motivated to study and access a greater range of materials. This is highly encouraging and is being reflected in a lower rate of failure compared with other distance learning programmes offered by the Department.

Tracking the first cohort's module evaluation responses throughout their programme shows that more found the provision of an iPad 'very useful' to their studies as the programme progressed. This could be due to a change in their work/access circumstances, but it could suggest that the students get used to the iPad and working on the device and find it more useful as time goes on as they can do more with it. This also applies to whether students found the App well set out and easy to use, with 100% of students agreeing by the time they were half way through their studies, compared with 80% after Module 1; possibly because they have become more accustomed to the App now. This finding is useful for developers and staff when starting new programmes to ensure that sufficient explanation and time is given at the beginning of a programme for students to get used to the App (or other electronic resource) and how to use it fully and effectively.

One of the obvious considerations, without wanting to be considered ageist (we do naturally seem to consider that younger students may prefer electronic content, but this is not a universal view, as highlighted in the research by Margaryan, Littlejohn and Vojt (2011) into the preconceived notions of 'digital natives') was whether more mature adults would find the delivery difficult, as these students may be much more used to traditional methods of reading and study. We have received some comments on evaluations such as:

I do however have some reservations about making effective use of the e-books, but that could just be a habit thing.

I found the format and the small screen of the iPad hard to adjust to.

I would prefer all my materials available in normal note format.

Preference is for all material to be available in easily printable form. Electronic was very challenging.

Interestingly, findings from the Places (University of Leicester, 2013c) survey showed that overall the App was the most favoured way for reading course materials. Students were asked to rank their preference for reading their course materials via printed material, the App and Blackboard. The responses showed that printed materials ranked equal first with the App, but in second place, the App scored much higher than printed materials, so overall, the App scored much more highly over first and second choice combined than any of the other options. Blackboard came last in order of first and second choice preference combined, but this could be due to access issues with this group of students. Printed material seemed to split the respondents more clearly, as can be seen from the table below:

Table1. Student response when asked how they would prefer to access their learning materials

Preferred Method of Accessing Learning Materials	1st Choice	2nd Choice	3rd Choice
Print	50%	8.3%	41.7%
App	50%	33.3%	16.7%
Blackboard	0%	50%	50%

In terms of preference, one student who had already completed a masters at this institution stated:

Having recently completed a ... MA with Leicester, I find that having access to the course materials via the I-app [sic] is much better than receiving piles and piles of binder materials. The App also contains a diverse range of materials (i.e. video, audio and reports), which I have found to be genuinely interesting and conducive to working through the material.

Other students also gave favourable responses to the App-approach:

Keep on with the App use. It is particularly useful for many of us who work full time and travel frequently.

Combining study with a fulltime job requires time management, and the use of the app allows me the flexibility to study when other methods are not readily accessible.

The iPad was great for travel and to keep in touch.

From my perspective, the app format, the portability (I have lived in 3 different countries during the course so far!) and the diversity of study materials it offers is great.

When asked to provide percentages for time spent studying via Blackboard and the App, some were strongly in favour of Blackboard, others the App, and some fairly equal. However, on average, students (n=39) spent just over a third of their time on Blackboard (37%) and just under two-thirds of their time on the App (63%). For one student who had spent all of his time on the App, his explanation was as follows:

...as being deployed was extremely reliant on the app to explain and breakdown everything as without Internet.

Some of the other comments are as follows:

As in the previous modules, and due to work related constraints and frequent travelling, Course App was used in some 70% of overall study time. The Course App is hugely helpful in allowing me to study even when away from home computer.

Blackboard and course app were pretty evenly split based upon the times at which I was able to sit down and focus on the module.

We encountered students (just two so far) who, due to geographical locations, could not download the App. One student was based in Sudan where, due to governmental impositions, he found it is not possible to access the Apple iTunes Store, nor use the Amazon vouchers to download the required textbooks. This issue was thankfully resolved for this student, as part of his work also meant he travelled to other countries where he could then access and download the materials. Geographical location is a serious consideration if planning to use/design a course using these types of resources. For students who did not have the opportunity to access the resources for download through travelling to different countries (one student in Nigeria encountered these issues) we resolved this by sending a paper copy of the textbook he was missing.

Many of the comments regarding the App and iPad refer to the portable aspect of it, as so many of these students travel. What is not clear is just how useful students would find it who are based in more permanent locations, and this is an area for future research. Many would presumably find it useful - who wouldn't, but the question is, what effect does this have on their learning?

One other aspect of this delivery method that is very useful to all students, not just distance learners, is the convenience of having a large amount of study materials in one place and on one device. There are disagreements over whether we, as education providers, should be giving students all the 'required' resources, for example, some might argue that part of the nature of studying is sourcing your own readings and material. If we really want students to read or watch or listen to something, perhaps we should make this easily available to avoid reasons and excuses for them not being able to access it.

The Places study (University of Leicester, 2013c) asked students if the iPad and Course App had changed the way they studied, and if so, to explain in what way. The responses from the nine students (out of a total of 12) who felt it had changed the way they studied are set out below:

Firstly I am more motivated, as it is structured and organised. I am getting through more than I would if I was solely given a recommended reading list.

It has enabled me to read the material without carrying a bundle of books and is very good for studying at work during ... free time.

Having access to the information wherever I go has allowed for better time management particularly as a distance learning student and under full time employment.

I have the ability to study on the move or when working away from home.

The iPad has enabled me to broaden my research horizon has [sic] I am able to compare ideas and confirm issues faster as a result of the online capability of the of the ipad. Access to materials like eLibrary has also brought the classroom closer to me.

I love the fact it is mobile, as I am constantly on the move. Travelling with books would be unrealistic.

It is more interactive than other conventional means of studying. You can use audio visual options plus get to online links which can help maintaining focus while studying. Plus this is like mobile education as you don't need to go to a physical space, e.g. Study room or Library, to study.

I see the iPad as a supplement to my studies rather than something that is changing the way I study.

More use of multimedia in studying. Use of other methods such as mind map and Goodreader type apps. Ability to tailor to your preferred study method. Everything in one place (i.e. no piles of paper).

As can be seen, many of the comments refer to portability and ease of access, which is fine so far as it goes and it is good to know that students appreciate this, but some do go further to consider ways in which focus can be maintained, how the use of Apps can help with studying, comparison of ideas, and broaden horizons. These start to get to issues about how learning could be enhanced. This is one of the key areas of interest: how do we know whether learning has been increased or enhanced through the use of such mobile technologies? This is not something we are necessarily able to answer in terms of this case study, as it is a newly designed programme, never delivered in any other way, so no direct comparisons are available. However, when compared with our other distance learning programmes, more SCID students score at the higher end of the marking range with merit and distinction level marks and slightly fewer SCID students fail assignments at first attempt (Bird, 2013).

SOLUTIONS AND RECOMMENDATIONS

The University is keen to maintain and enhance its solid reputation in widening participation. We are proud of the fact that the University of Leicester is the 'most socially inclusive of Britain's top-20 leading Universities' (University of Leicester, 2013d) and we strive to ensure that mature students are able to fulfil their potential and gain an academic qualification that they otherwise would not be in a realistic position to achieve. The University has made distance learning one of its priority areas. Simpson (2003) notes that widening participation has brought with it challenges for retention as these student groups are harder to retain and that distance learning has traditionally had low retention rates. We believe that as a result of the increased communication through moderated discussion and resources and activities such as e-tivities, together with the ease of study in terms of accessing the course materials, the retention rates on this programme are higher than for our other distance learning programmes (95% compared with 89% over the same time period).

The Department faced considerable challenges when it first investigated the possibilities of providing an iPad and specially designed course App to all students. The challenges were overcome, but some took considerable time, effort and persistence on the part of the Department not to give up its vision.

The University of Leicester is a top-20 ranked UK University (The Guardian, 2013; The Complete University Guide, 2013) and ranked 161 in the world (Times Higher Education, 2013), was founded in 1921 and was granted its Royal Charter in 1957. It is the only UK University to have won a Times Higher Education Award for seven consecutive years (University of Leicester, 2013e). Whilst it has forged ahead in many respects, getting an institutional framework agreement for a project such as the iPad provision and App was quite an undertaking. The two main areas for consideration were legal and IT-related. There were questions over the purchase of the iPad: who would own them, what would happen if something went wrong with one, or if it was broken, or if a student withdrew from the programme, or if a student already owned a device, or had an Android device? These questions are quite basic, but proved to be quite a challenge and time-consuming to address. As no precedent was set for such an undertaking, these challenges had to be worked through thoroughly. We quickly recognised that the iPads would have to be owned by the student and that they would have to register it and load up their course App and associated Apps. In addition, there would be little point in having iPads returned to us at the end of the programme as the iPads would be used and probably outdated by that point and it might be difficult to get one returned from a student who withdrew or who the University withdrew. In the initial stages we could have set up the iPads and pre-loaded the App, but considering up-scaling in the hope that the course would recruit well, this could be problematic in terms of staff time.

Apple's reputation for good customer service was one of the main reasons we chose to use Apple iPads. We knew that the University's IT Services would not be able to support any fault issues as these sort of devices were unsupported, and therefore we wanted to go with a device and provider that would offer good service should something go wrong. We did not want to provide a device as part of our course designed to make things easier for students that actually made things harder. We decided that there could be no reduction in course fees should a student decide they did not want an iPad (as the iPad would be provided as part of the course materials) and similarly, the App is designed for an iPad as this is what is provided to the student. There is no suggestion at this stage that we will have an App designed for an Android device.

We are building in more interactivity to the App for its next iteration. Students use the App so much that many state they would prefer to do everything on it, rather than have to submit their written assignments via Blackboard and complete their e-tivities via the App, rather than having to do this via Blackboard. Students would like discussion boards to be available via the App also. Some of this is possible, although it is doubtful that we will be able to link directly through to Blackboard via the App, but we can include other forums for live chat, etc. on the App. The suggestion that students would like more ability to connect with other students is a useful finding as with our other programmes and experience, we find it quite difficult to encourage students to consistently use the discussion boards on Blackboard to keep in touch and discuss academic issues. Evaluation of this initiative is recommended.

When considering a venture or development such as this, it is vital to ensure plenty of time for planning and design. Our workflow highlights the various stages we go through and this can take several months per module to complete in full. There is a need to prepare and plan well in advance, but, technological advancements are moving forward at a pace, so there is a fine balance here in terms of preparedness and planning and exploiting the most up-to-date features. This is a team effort and best use should be made of subject experts, educational experts and learning technologists, both in terms of the design stage and ongoing support. The research conducted into Carpe Diem workshops shows that more collaborative activities can be devised and put into place with ongoing technical support (Armellini and Jones, 2008). Academics can be put off by the technological challenge and advice and support are vital if developments are to take place.

We found this to be a steep learning curve for us at the time, but now that a precedent has been set, it is considerably more straightforward. Committed staff require the confidence to drive the issue with University management to ensure that learning can be enabled using examples of good practice and best fit for both the programme and the type of student.

CONCLUSION

We strongly believe that the provision of an iPad and course App has helped to attract many more students on to this programme and this is great news for widening participation and really responds to the objectives of distance learning. The existing distance learning models were not a good fit for the learning environment of the target audience. The main challenge our existing students face is having the time to study, given the fact that they move around a lot and do not have very good access to the Internet. Students on the SCID programme however, find the iPad very useful as they can study while on the move. Many find studying easier during their breaks at work also, due to the bite-sized nature of some of the resources. Many students prefer a variety of learning methods and this programme allows that. Many of these students simply would not be able to study effectively if they did not have access to the required resources on one small device. But this is not just an issue about access (although that is an important factor). Students have told us they are more motivated, and, as we know for distance learning students, high levels of motivation are a necessary factor in the completion of the programme. The SCID students are also more likely to use discussion facilities when they do have access to the Internet and this helps to scaffold and cement their learning.

The programme commenced in March 2012 and the first cohort of students is just completing their dissertations. Whilst difficult to determine with any degree of certainty, results suggest that students on this programme are responding very well to this mode of delivery and we have considerably lower attrition rates on this programme than we do on our other distance learning programmes (5% and 11% respectively, over the March 2012 - December 2013 timeframe). Preliminary evidence suggests that students on this programme have also tended to score higher in their formative assignments than distance learning students on our other programmes. Since the programme was launched student recruitment is 100% above target and we are confident that the innovative and flexible learning environment is a key part of this success.

The Department of Criminology wanted to provide distance education to a group of students working and living in often very difficult circumstances. They are time and resource poor, often with little or no Internet access. The traditional method of paper modules and textbooks, in an ever-increasing mobile world, is losing pace. It would be difficult – in terms of keeping the material up to date, in terms of getting the material to the students on several occasions throughout their studies, and in terms of the students accessing the additional resources they would need. The other method of providing online only programmes via the VLE is not suitable due to the online access issues. We therefore considered a method of providing up-to-date, innovative materials, making best use of the latest resources available whilst ensuring learner-centred approaches to maximise knowledge attainment, active engagement and deep learning. We considered that an App, at that time, was the only way that we could provide this.

REFERENCES

Anderson, T., & Dron, J. (2010). Three generations of distance education pedagogy. *International Review of Research in Open and Distance Learning*, *12*(3), 80–97. Retrieved from http://www.irrodl.org/index.php/irrodl/article/view/890

Armellini, A., & Jones, S. (2008). Carpe Diem: seizing each day to foster change in e-learning design. *Reflecting Education*, *4*(1), 17–29.

Bird, T. (2013). *Impact of University of Leicester Criminology iPad and Course App in distance learning*. Available at http://www.youtube.com/watch?v=iYspVOGs2zs

European Commission. (2013). *Working Conditions - Employment, Social Affairs and Inclusion - European Commission*. Retrieved from http://ec.europa.eu/social/main.jsp?catId=706&langId=en&intPageId=205

Guardian. (2013). *University Guide 2014: University League Table*. Retrieved from http://www.theguardian.com/education/table/2013/jun/03/university-league-table-2014

Hancock, V. (2010) Essential, desirable or optional? Making distance e-learning courses available to those without internet access. *European Journal of Open, Distance and E-Learning*, *11*. http://www.eurodl.org/materials/contrib/2010/Val_Hancock.pdf

Hartnett, M., St. George, A., & Dron, J. (2011). Examining motivation in online distance learning environments: Complex, multifaceted and situation-dependent. *International Review of Research in Open and Distance Learning*, *12*(6), 20–38. Retrieved from http://www.irrodl.org/index.php/irrodl/article/view/1030

Herrington, J., Mantei, J., Herrington, A., Olney, I., & Ferry, B. (2008). New technologies, new pedagogies: Mobile technologies and new ways of teaching and learning. In *Hello! Where are you in the landscape of educational technology? Proceedings ascilite Melbourne 2008*. Retrieved from http://www.ascilite.org.au/conferences/melbourne08/procs/herrington-j.pdf

iPad App - MSc in Security, Conflict and International Development from the University of Leicester and KuKu Apps. (n.d.). Retrieved from https://itunes.apple.com/gb/app/scid-course/id503579966

Kearney, M., Schuck, S., Burden, K., & Aubusson, P. (2012). Viewing mobile learning from a pedagogical perspective. *Research In Learning Technology*, *20*. doi:10.3402/rlt.v20i0.14406

Margaryan, A., Littlejohn, A., & Vojt, G. (2011). Are digital natives a myth or reality? University students' use of digital technologies. *Computers and Education*, *56* (2), 429-440.

Minocha, S., et al. (2009). A study on the effective use of social software by further and higher education in the UK to support student learning and engagement: final report. *JISC*.

Nie, M., Bird, T., Beck, A., Hayes, N., & Conole, G. (2013). *Adding Mobility to Distance Learning. Places Case Study*. Retrieved from: http://www.le.ac.uk/places-mlearn

Quinn, C. (2013). Mobile Learning. In The Really Useful eLearning Instruction Manual: Your toolkit for putting elearning into practice. Chichester, UK: Wiley and Sons.

Rowntree, D. (1992). *Exploring open and distance learning*. London: Kogan Page.

Salmon, G. (2013). *E-tivities: The key to active online learning* (2nd ed.). London: Routledge.

Simpson, O. (2003). *Student retention in Online, Open and Distance Learning*. London, UK: Kogan Page. doi:10.4324/9780203416563

The Complete University Guide. (2013). *Top UK University League Tables and Rankings 2014*. Retrieved from: http://www.thecompleteuniversityguide.co.uk/league-tables/rankings

Times Higher Education. (2013). *World University Rankings 2013-2014 - Times Higher Education*. Retrieved from http://www.timeshighereducation.co.uk/world-university-rankings/2013-14/world-ranking

Traxler, J. (2010). Students and mobile devices. *Research in Learning Technology*, *18*(2). doi:10.3402/rlt.v18i2.10759

Traxler, J. (2011). Introduction. In J. Traxler & J. Wishart (Eds.), *Making mobile learning work: Case studies of practice* (pp. 4-12). Bristol, UK: ESCalate. Retrieved from http://www.leeds.ac.uk/educol/documents/201799.pdf

University of Leicester. (2013a). *Armed Conflict Learning shortlisted for national e-learning award*. Retrieved from http://www2.le.ac.uk/colleges/socsci/college%20news/armed-conflict-learning-shortlisted-for-national-e-learning-award

University of Leicester. (2013b). *Using Other Libraries — University of Leicester*. Retrieved from http://www2.le.ac.uk/library/services/other-libraries/using-other-libraries

University of Leicester. (2013c). *Places: Adding Mobility to Distance Learning*. Retrieved from: http://www2.le.ac.uk/departments/beyond-distance-research-alliance/projects/places

University of Leicester. (2013d). *Our Achievements — University of Leicester*. Retrieved from http://www2.le.ac.uk/about/facts

University of Leicester. (2013e). *Times Higher Education Awards - University of Leicester*. Retrieved from http://www2.le.ac.uk/about/the-awards

Wedgwood, J. (2013). Blended Learning. In The Really Useful eLearning Instruction Manual: Your toolkit for putting elearning into practice. Chichester, UK: Wiley & Sons.

Wheeler, S. (2013). *'Always on' learning.* Retrieved from http://steve-wheeler.blogspot.co.uk/2013/10/always-on-learning.html

Witthaus, G., & Williamson, H. (2010). *OTTER Project Final Report.* Retrieved from http://www.jisc.ac.uk/media/documents/programmes/oer/otterfinalreport27april2010_v2 1.pdf

Zhang, K., & Bonk, C. J. (2008). Addressing diverse learner preferences and intelligences with emerging technologies: Matching models to online opportunities. *Canadian Journal of Learning and Technology, 34*(2). Retrieved from http://www.cjlt.ca/index.php/cjlt/article/view/496/227

ADDITIONAL READING

Batchelor, J., Herselman, M., Traxler, J., and Fraser, W. (2012). *Emerging Technologies, Innovative Teachers and Moral Cohesion,* 1–9.

Beetham, H., & Sharpe, R. (2013). *Rethinking Pedagogy for a Digital Age* (2nd ed.). London, UK: Routledge.

Center_for_Security_Studies. (2013). *Mobile Learning in Security and Defense Organizations.* ISN Website. Retrieved September 02, 2013, from http://www.isn.ethz.ch/Communities-and-Partners/ISN-CSS-Events/Detail/?lng=en&id=168413

Conole, G. (2011). The interconnectedness of design and e-pedagogy. In *The interconnectedness of design and e-pedagogy.* Sydney. Retrieved from http://www.slideshare.net/grainne/conole-sydney

Conole, G. (2013). *Designing for learning in an Open World.* New York, NY: Springer. doi:10.1007/978-1-4419-8517-0

Conole, G., & Dyke, M. (2004). What are the affordances of information and communication technologies? *ALT-J Research in Learning Technology, 12*(2), 113–124. doi:10.1080/0968776042000216183

Conole, G., & Fill, K. (2005). A learning design toolkit to create pedagogically effective learning activities. *Journal of Interactive Media in Education.* Retrieved from http://jime.open.ac.uk/article/2005-8/275

Conole, G., & Wills, S. (2013). Representing learning designs – making design explicit and shareable. *Educational Media International, 50*(1), 24–38. doi:10.1080/09523987.2013.777184

Edfutures. (2013). *BYOD - EdFutures. Edfutures Wiki.* Retrieved January 15, 2013, from http://edfutures.net/index.php?title=BYOD

Hawkridge, D., Armellini, A., Nikoi, S., Rowlett, T., & Witthaus, G. (2010). Curriculum, intellectual property rights and open educational resources in British universities—and beyond. *Journal of Computing in Higher Education, 22*(3), 162–176. doi:10.1007/s12528-010-9036-1

JISC. (2011). *Mobile Learning infokit / Home.* Retrieved August 22, 2012, from https://mobilelearninginfokit.pbworks.com/w/page/41122430/Home

JiscLegal. (2012). *Mobile Learning and the Law: Are you remotely interested?* Inverness.

Koole, M. L. (2009). A Model for Framing Mobile Learning. In M. Ally (Ed.), *Mobile Learning: Transforming the Delivery of Education and Training* (pp. 25–50). Edmonton.

Kukulska-Hulme, A. (2010). Mobile learning as a catalyst for change. *Open Learning The Journal of Open and Distance Learning*, 25(3), 181–185. Retrieved from http://oro.open.ac.uk/23773/1/Open_Learning_editorial_(Accepted_Manuscript).doc

Kukulska-Hulme, A., Pettit, J., Bradley, L., Carvalho, A. a., Herrington, A., Kennedy, D. M., & Walker, A. (2011). Mature Students Using Mobile Devices in Life and Learning. *International Journal of Mobile and Blended Learning*, 3(1), 18–52. doi:10.4018/jmbl.2011010102

Mac Callum, K., & Jeffrey, L. (2013). *The influence of students' ICT skills and their adoption of mobile learning*. Australasian Journal of Educational Technology.

Nie, M. (2010). A case study of integrating e-book readers into two Masters' distance learning programmes in Occupational Psychology. Leicester, UK. Retrieved from http://www2.le.ac.uk/departments/beyond-distance-research-alliance/projects/duckling/E-book reader for OP.pdf [Accessed: 13 Dec 2013]

Nie, Ming, Armellini, A., Witthaus, G., and Barklamb, K. (2011). How do e-book readers enhance learning opportunities for distance work-based learners? *Research in Learning Technology*, 19(1). doi: doi:10.3402/rlt.v19i1.17104

Nie, M., Witthaus, G., Armellini, A., Salmon, G., & Mukherjee, J. (2010). *JISC Final Report*. Leicester, UK. Retrieved from http://jweblv01.jisc.ulcc.ac.uk/media/documents/programmes/curriculumdelivery/DUCKLING_Final_Report.pdf

Ozdalga, E., Ozdalga, A., & Ahuja, N. (2012). The smartphone in medicine: a review of current and potential use among physicians and students. *Journal of Medical Internet Research*, 14(5), e128. doi:10.2196/jmir.1994 PMID:23017375

Quinn, C. (2013). Mobile Learning. In: Hubbard, R. eds. (2013). The Really Useful eLearning Instruction Manual: Your toolkit for putting elearning into practice. Chichester: Wiley & Sons, pp. 147-174.

Rogelberg, D. (2013). *Mobile Education - Lessons from 35 Education Experts on Improving Learning with Mobile Technology*. [e-book] Studio B Productions Inc. Available through: http://www.slideshare.net/DavidRogelberg/mobile-education-27782655 [Accessed: 14 Dec 2013]

Sharples, M. (2009). Methods for evaluating mobile learning. In G. N. Vavoula, N. Pachler, and A. Kukulska-Hulme (Eds.), *Methods* (Vol. 16, pp. 17–39). Peter Lang Publishing Group. Retrieved from http://www.peterlang.com/index.cfm?event=cmp.ccc.seitenstruktur.detailseiten&seitentyp=produkt&pk=50553&concordeid=11832

Sharples, M., Taylor, J., & Vavoula, G. (2007). A Theory of Learning for the Mobile Age (pre-print). In R. Andrews, & C. Haythornthwaite (Eds.), *The Sage Handbook of Elearning Research* (pp. 221–247). London.

Traxler, J. (2009). Current State of Mobile Learning. (M. Ally, Ed.) *Mobile Learning Transforming the Delivery of Education and Training*, 5(2), 9–24. Retrieved from http://www.aupress.ca/books/120155/ebook/01_Mohamed_Ally_2009-Article1.pdf

Traxler, J. (2010). Students and mobile devices. *Research In Learning Technology*, 18(2). doi:10.3402/rlt.v18i2.10759

Traxler, J. (2010). Will Student Devices Deliver Innovation, Inclusion, and Transformation? *Journal of the Research Center for Educational Technology*, 6(1), 3–15. Retrieved from http://rcetj.org/index.php/rcetj/article/view/56

Traxler, J., & Campus, P. (2009). 0288 Students and mobile devices : choosing which dream. In D. B. Responsibility (Ed.), *ALT-C 2009* (pp. 70–81).

Walker, R. Voce, J., and Ahmed, J. (2012). *TEL_survey_2012_final_ex_apps.pdf*. Oxford, UK. Retrieved from http://www.ucisa.ac.uk/~/media/groups/ssg/surveys/TEL_survey_2012_final_ex_app

Walker, Ros. (2013, June 9). "I don't think I would be where I am right now". Pupil perspectives on using mobile devices for learning. *Research in Learning Technology*. doi:10.3402/rlt.v21i0.22116

Wedgwood, J. (2013). Blended Learning. In: Hubbard, R. eds. (2013). The Really Useful eLearning Instruction Manual: Your toolkit for putting elearning into practice. Chichester: Wiley & Sons, pp. 91-106.

KEY TERMS AND DEFINITIONS

App: A software application developed for use on the Apple iPad.

Distance Learning: A form of education, often at HE level, where students study remotely and do not attend campus based lectures/classes.

iPad: A handheld tablet computing device produced by Apple Inc.

Learner Preferences: Approaches that individuals naturally prefer (often related to Honey and Mumford's learning styles).

Learning Technologies: A broad range of information and communication technologies that are used to support learning.

Mobile Learning: Learning that takes place via a mobile device such as an iPad, tablet or mobile phone.

Programme Development: Quality framework encompassing programme approval, specifications, content and assessment.

VLE: A virtual learning environment is an online educational system, typically containing course information, learning materials, discussion boards, and assignment features.

Chapter 4
Mobile Learning:
Trends, Issues, and Challenges in Teaching and Learning

Chien Yu
Mississippi State University, USA

Sang Joon Lee
Mississippi State University, USA

Carlos Ewing
Mississippi State University, USA

ABSTRACT

The purpose of this chapter is to provide the readers with an overview of the association between mobile learning technologies and the nature of teaching and learning. In addition to the benefits of using mobile learning, the current educational and strategic uses of the mobile technology are discussed. Based on a review of scholarly publications, the chapter delineates the current trends and issues pertinent to the development of mobile learning or e-learning at large. By outlining some fundamental issues and considerations, the chapter further presents some challenges and impacts of mobile learning in teaching and training as well. Additional examples drawn from literature are included to explore the use of mobile learning in education and the strategies of effective mobile learning applications.

INTRODUCTION

The rapid development of wireless communication and mobile technologies has not only enabled people to conveniently access the information anytime and anywhere, but also extended online learning modes further from e-learning to m-learning (Jeng, Wu, Huang, Tan, & Yang, 2010). M-learning (Mobile learning) refers to the use of mobile or wireless devices for the purpose of learning while on the move (Park, 2011). Typical examples of the devices used for mobile learning include cell phones, smart phones, palmtops, personal digital assistants (PDAs), handheld computers, tablet PCs, laptops, personal media players (Kukulska-Hulme & Traxler, 2005), even digital cameras and USB keys (Low & O'Connel, 2006).

DOI: 10.4018/978-1-4666-6284-1.ch004

Mobile learning, however, is not just about the use of portable devices. It is also about learning across contexts (Walker, 2006) with the emphasis on facilitating and extending the reach of the teaching and learning, such as the knowledge construction, the information collection and exchange, the collaborative learning (Hine, Rentoul, & Specht, 2004), independent learning (Bull & Reid, 2004) and lifelong learning (Attewell & Savill-Smith, 2004). Winters (2006) addresses the nature of mobile learning as "mediated learning through mobile technology" (p. 9). Lan and Sie (2010) view mobile learning as a type of learning model that allows learners using mobile technologies and the Internet to obtain learning materials anywhere and anytime. Laurillard and Pachler (2007) define mobile learning as the digital support of adaptive, investigative, communicative, collaborative, and productive learning activities in remote locations. Yi, Liao, Huang, and Hwang (2009) describe that mobile learning is an array of ways that people learn or stay connected with their learning environments including their classmates, instructors, and instructional resources while going mobile. Brown (2005) indicates mobile learning as "an extension of e-learning" (p. 299). Peters (2007) views mobile learning as a useful component of the flexible learning model.

Seppala and Alamaki (2003) claim that, given that 98% of university students possessed cell phones, the instruction via mobile devices would play an important role in education. They indicate the core characteristic of mobile learning enables learners to be in the right place at the right time, that is, to be where they are able to experience the authentic joy of learning. Ozdamli and Cavus (2011) view the core characteristic of mobile learning are ubiquitous, portable size of mobile tools, blended, private, interactive, collaborative, and instant information, because the common use of telephones and messaging for facilitating friendships and socialization (Taylor & Harper, 2002) has established a role for the mobile telephone as a means of collaborative learning.

With recent innovations in program applications and social software using Web 2.0 technologies (e.g., blogs, wikis, Twitter, and YouTube) or social networking sites (e.g., Facebook), mobile technologies and devices have been more dynamic and pervasive and also promised more educational potential (Park, 2011). For example, advances in handheld devices have facilitated the use of multimedia in mobile applications, which allows mobile learners to have access to a wide variety of richly diversified learning resources (Huang, Chen, & Chen, 2009). BenMoussa (2003) identifies several benefits of using mobile applications, which generally permit users to control or filter the flow of information and communication using individualized or personalized devices. Even without the intervention of a teacher or instructor, mobile devices and applications can still be deployed as learning tools to facilitate learning activities.

Although mobile learning has increasingly attracted the interest of educators, other researchers (Uzunboylu, Cavus & Ercag, 2009) also warn only few studies have investigated educational outcomes of mobile learning. Chen, Chang, and Wang (2008) state that mobile devices for learning are limited by screen size, computational power, battery capacity, input interface and network bandwidth; therefore, how to adapt information for delivery to mobile devices has become a critical issue in mobile learning environment (Jeng et al., 2010). In addition to the integration of suitable software and novel mobile technologies, many educators and researchers (McConatha, Praul & Lynch, 2008; Motiwalla, 2007; Patten, Arnedillo-Sánchez & Tangney, 2006; Thornton & Houser, 2002) also point out the importance of pedagogical implications for mobile learning. As a result, how to combine appropriate pedagogical strategies for enhanced learning applications has become another critical important issue in mobile learning environment (Jeng et al., 2010).

Without a doubt, a deeper insight into theory-based research is required to better understand how to adopt mobile learning elements and characteristics. Ozdamli and Cavus (2011) suggest the elements of mobile learning need to be well organized, and the interactions between the various elements need to be efficiently combined so that the mobile learning can be successful and the implementation can be efficient as well. The combination of collaborative, contextual, and constructivist principles should be derived from pedagogical learning process (Jeng et al, 2010). As a result, instructional designers and teachers not only need a solid theoretical foundation for mobile learning in the context of distance education, but also need more guidance about how to effectively utilize and integrate emerging mobile technologies into their teaching (Park, 2011).

The purpose of this chapter is to provide the readers with an overview of the association between mobile learning technologies and the nature of teaching and learning. In addition to the benefits of using mobile learning, the current educational and strategic uses of the mobile technology will be discussed. Based on a review of scholarly publications, the chapter delineates the current trends and issues pertinent to the development of mobile learning, or e-learning at large. By outlining some fundamental issues and considerations, the chapter further presents some challenges and impacts of mobile learning in teaching and training as well. Additional examples drawn from literature are included to explore the use of mobile devices in education and the strategies of effective mobile learning applications.

REVIEWING THE DEFINITIONS OF MOBILE LEARNING

Since the early studies of mobile learning, there has been a wide debate and interpretation on its exact definition (Alnuaim, Caleb-Solly, & Perry, 2012). As a result, the definition of mobile learning remains still unclear and uncertain (Rossing, Miller, Cecil, & Stamper, 2012). When the use of mobile devices in learning is generally referred to as mobile learning (m-learning), many other keywords such as *ubiquitous learning, handheld learning, hypermedia-assisted learning,* and *e-learning* have also been evolving towards the concepts and functions of mobile technologies (Rossing, Miller, Cecil, & Stamper, 2012).

In reviewing various prevalent definitions of mobile learning in literature, some researchers characterize mobile learning as an extension of e-learning. For example, Kadirire (2009) defines m-learning as a form of e-learning, which can take place anytime, anywhere with the help of a mobile communication device. Brown (2005) identifies mobile learning as "an extension of e-learning" (p. 299). Quinn (2000) defines mobile learning as "the intersection of mobile computing and e-learning (electronic learning): accessible resources wherever you are, strong search capabilities, rich interaction, powerful support for effective learning, and performance-based assessment" (p. 8). However, some researchers indicate that mobile learning is not a reduced version of e-learning. For example, Vavoula, Lefrere, O'Malley, and Sharples (2004) define it as "Any sort of learning that happens when the learner is not at a fixed, predetermined location, or learning that happens when the learner takes advantage of learning opportunities offered by mobile technologies" (p. 174).

On the other hand, some authors place emphasis on the mobile devices and the mobility of the user. For example, Traxler (2005) offers a definition as "any educational provision where the sole or dominant technologies are handheld or palmtop devices" (p. 263) that specifically links educational provision to a handheld device. Orr (2010) suggests to incorporate "mobile recording, imaging, or communication devices" as part of mobile learning. Wang, Wiesemes, and Gibbons (2012) simply defines it as, "learning through mobile devices" (p. 570). According to Yousef (2007), "Mobile learning is defined as the provision of education and training on mobile devices:

Personal Digital Assistants (PDAs), smart phones and mobile phones." (p. 117). Geddes (2004) states mobile learning as the acquisition of any knowledge and skill through using mobile technology, anywhere, anytime that results in an alteration in behavior. As a result, the learners and devices seem to be fundamentally linked together with mobile learning (Wright & Parchoma, 2011), and that has also become one of prevalent definitions of mobile learning in literature.

However, Woodill (2011) points out there is a shift in the perception of mobile learning by stating, "Ten years ago, mobile learning was about displaying e-learning on a small screen." (as cited in Alnuaim et al, 2012, p. 163), but now it allows people to learn in an "anywhere, anytime" manner and to access information when needed. This significant characteristic of ubiquity makes learners learn the right thing at the right time at the right place (Peng, Su, Chou, & Tsai, 2009). Laouris and Eteokleous (2005) indicate, "not only should we not constrain our definition of mobile learning to learning through mobiles, but we must shift focus from device to human" (p. 6). Sharples, Taylor, and Vavoula (2005) agree that "it is the learner that is mobile, rather than the technology" (p. 4), and the most essential difference between mobile learning and other types of learning activities is "learners are continually on the move" (Sharples et al., 2005, p. 1).

There are many different mobile learning perspectives in the related literature. Each definition focuses on the different features, but, it seems that three elements –*mobility, mobile devices* and *learning* have become the key concepts of mobile learning. As El-Hussein and Cronje (2010) state, mobile learning can be better defined as "any type of learning that takes place in learning environments and spaces that take account of the mobility of technology, mobility of learners, and mobility of learning" (p. 20).

BENEFITS AND POTENTIAL OF MOBILE LEARNING

Unlike a desktop computer that needs a fixed location and source of power, mobile devices have numerous unique characteristics, including: portability, connectivity, convenience, expediency, immediacy, accessibility, individuality and interactivity (Song, 2011). Because of the characteristics and opportunities, there are many advantages of using mobile technology, such as freedom to study with flexibility, low cost, timely application (Alzara & Zulkifli, 2007), improvement of experiential, authentic and reliable learning situations, enhanced availability of guidance, ease of use, support in learning situations (Seppala, Sariola, & Kynaslahti, 2002), fast production of digital learning materials and copyright issues, and flexibility of learning (Sharples, Corlett, & Westmancott, 2002). In addition, Alnuaim et al. (2012) also add that personalization is one of mobile learning's strengths. As Park (2011) emphasizes portability as the strongest advantage of learning with mobile devices, Pea and Maldonado (2006) agree portability as the most distinctive feature that distinguishes mobile devices from other emerging technologies and makes other technological attributes possible such as individuality and interactivity. Crescente and Lee (2011) describe the primary goal of mobile learning as "to provide the learner the ability to assimilate learning anywhere and at any time" (p. 112).

OVERVIEW FOR MOBILE LEARNING RESEARCH

In order to better understand the current status of mobile learning research, this section reviews and discusses some research areas that have been studied in educational uses of the mobile technologies and instructional practices of mobile learning.

Mobile Learning and the Effectiveness

According to a study of a meta-analysis and review of trends for mobile learning studies (Wu et al., 2012), evaluating the effects of mobile learning is the most common frequently-cited research purpose (58%). From their literature review among the 164 published articles from 2003 to 2010, a majority of the research studies show positive effectiveness of mobile learning. For instance, Baya'a and Daher (2009) found that students in Israel responded positively in terms of using mobile phones for learning mathematics. Al-Fahad (2009) found that mobile learning could improve retention among B.A. (Bachelor of Arts) and M.D. (Medicine) students. Evans (2008) examined the effectiveness of podcasting which can be played on a computer or a portable media player such as iPod and tablet, and students indicated podcasts to be preferable to their textbooks as a learning aid. Pfeiffer, Gemballa, Jarodzka, Scheiter, and Gerjets (2009) examined students' learning via mobile devices in a situated learning scenario, and revealed that students performed better after than before the mobile learning experience, and the mobile devices could be well implemented in a situated learning scenario.

Apart from the positive effectiveness, some research studies report neutral or negative findings regarding the effectiveness of mobile learning. Ketamo's study (2003) showed that mobile technologies can generally bring some added value to network-based learning, but they cannot replace conventional computers. Doolittle and Mariano (2008) investigated the effects of individual differences in working memory capacity (WMC) and found that students in a stationary instructional environment performed better, while interaction effects indicated that low-WMC students performed most poorly in a mobile instructional environment.

Mobile Learning and Learning Systems

As the second most-frequently-cited research purpose (32%), Wu et al (2012) found that the number of publications studied mobile learning system designs have been increased over time, and that could be possibly related to rapid technology development (e.g., new smart phones and wireless data networks) combined with the willingness of researchers to trial new technologies in developing mobile learning systems. Numerous studies have been done in order to customize a mobile learning environment to a particular learner's context. For example, Shen, Wang, and Pan (2008) developed a mobile learning system that can deliver real-time classroom lectures and provide various communication channels including text messaging and instant polls to increase interactivity in blended classrooms. Kuo, Huang, Liu, and Chang (2008) presented an implementation of a system using mobile devices for creation of authentic examples. In order to improve students' knowledge, De-Marcos et al. (2010) designed an application for mobile phones and found it improved student achievement, especially those who were younger learners with a relatively low impact on current teaching activities and methodologies.

Mobile Learning and Perceptions of Teachers and Students

Mobile technology and devices have increasingly influenced the popularity of mobile learning; therefore, a significant amount of literature studies deal with how educators and students perceived the use of mobile technologies for instruction.

- **Teachers:** Educators are expected to integrate technology in the classroom, therefore, Henderson and Chapman (2012) examined the perceptions of business educators for using mobile phones in the classroom. They found 46% of the respondents had used a mobile device for educational purposes, and also the associate professors tended to be slightly more accepting of mobile phone use in the classroom than middle school, high school, and community college educators. When Ifenthaler and Schweinbenz (2013) investigated the teachers' perspectives and acceptance of Tablet-PCs (TPCs) in classroom instruction, they found only a minority of respondents believed in improving learning and instruction through the use of TPCs and most participants were not quite clear how TPCs could be used as an innovative tool to facilitate learning and instruction. Aubusson, Schuck, and Burden (2009) discussed the role of mobile learning in teachers' professional learning, and reported that mobile learning has been embraced by teachers relatively low partially because limited perceptions of mobile devices that teachers possessed and mobile learning was not yet a part of mainstream professional learning. Serin (2012) studied the mobile learning perceptions and levels of the prospective teachers; the findings indicated that prospective teachers' mobile learning perception levels were in general low. Overall, teachers' perception or acceptance towards mobile technologies may have had considerable reservations, or teachers have been hesitant to embrace them with their pedagogical practices (Fuegen, 2012).
- **Students:** On the other hand, in the studies of student perceptions on the integration of emerging technology into classroom instruction, students generally reported positive experiences (Rossing et al., 2012). In a study of exploring student perceptions of learning and engagement by using a mobile device – iPads in the classroom, Rossing et al. found that the students perceived the novelty of the iPads contributed positively to their learning – the "fun" experience resulted in better student learning and engagement. Also, students predominantly agreed that iPads helped them "participate in the course activity in ways that enhanced" learning. In addition, students reported that the immediate access to information enhanced in-class discussion, and iPads were suited for collaborative learning because the devices allowed for easy viewing and sharing of online resources. Gupta and Manjrekar (2012) indicated that the students perceived that mobile learning could be highly useful in improving the quality in higher education. In a study by Kinash, Brand, and Mathew (2012), 51% of students were neutral when they were asked whether they perceived iPads could improve their learning; but there was the highest frequency of students (42%) who agreed using iPads motivated them to learn. Similarly, Sung and Mayer (2013) reported that effective instructional methods could improve learning outcomes across different media when they investigated online multimedia learning with mobile devices and desktop computers, but using hand-held instructional devices may increase students' willingness to continue to engage in learning.
- **Cross-Cultural Studies:** In order to explore the effect of national differences and investigate importance of cultural factors on the use of mobile technology, many studies have reviewed the cross-cultural perspectives, and outcomes have been various depending on the different cultures and countries. For example, Yang (2012) studied the attitudes and self-efficacy of using

mobile learning devices for college students in Taiwan, and showed that most students agreed their motivation for English learning was enhanced and most of the students had positive attitudes towards mobile learning. Lu's study (2008) reported students in Taiwan generally held positive attitudes towards learning vocabulary via mobile phones. When Al-Fahad (2009) explored students' attitudes and perceptions towards the effectiveness of mobile learning in Saudi Arabia, he found more than 50% of students strongly supported mobile learning as an effective method for learning. Suki and Suki (2011) examined students' acceptance of mobile technology usage for learning in Malaysia and found that the students had yet to accept that the concept of mobility in learning, but they were willing to explore more ideas of using mobile technology for learning, especially in a studio-based setting. Another Malaysian study by Hussin, Manap, Amir, and Krish (2012) focused on basic skills, psychological and budget readiness of students toward to mobile learning and found students were highly familiar with computing skills and they welcomed the integration of mobile learning in education. Alzaza and Yaakub (2011) found the students in Malaysia have adequate knowledge and awareness to use mobile technology in their education environment.

Mobile Learning, E-Learning, and Distance Education

So, what role does mobile learning play in distance education? Fuegen (2012) emphasized the potential for mobile devices to both effect and affect learning in distance education environments would be large. Yousef (2007) stated, "Facilitating mobile learning can improve the entire distance education [experience] by enhancing ways of communication among distance learners, tutors, and supporting staff" (p. 114). According to Yousef, mobile learning can bring many benefits to the distance learning experience:

- The provision of course content to off-campus students.
- The provision of feedback to off-campus students.
- The provision of student support services to off-campus students.
- Links to the WWW and other resources.
- Student-to-student interactivity.
- Student to tutor and institution interactivity (p. 117).

Fuegen indicated, "Mobile technologies, with their ability to create diverse learning contexts with increased dialogue and communication, have great potential to overcome the transactional distance divide that is inherently a part of distance education" (p. 50). As student and faculty expectations for mobile-integrated education grow, distance education program and institutions will need to keep up with demand too.

As a scale of devices decreases sizes from desktop to laptops, tablets and mobile phones, learning experience for learners has also been changed along with most digital technologies. Although by nature the mobile learning is "a form of existing d-learning (distance learning) and e-learning" (Georgiev, Georgieva, & Smrikarov, 2004, p. IV.28-1), some researchers (Woodill, 2013; Georgiev et al., 2004) sought to pinpoint the relationships and differences among mobile learning, e-learning and distance learning. As e-Learning offers new methods for distance education, mobile learning also offers new opportunities for e-learning. Therefore, Georgiev et al. viewed the mobile learning as part of e-learning and thus also part of distance learning (as shown in Figure 1).

Figure 1. The place of mobile learning as part of e-learning and distance learning.
(Source: Georgiev, Georgieva, & Smrikarov, 2004, p. IV.28-1)

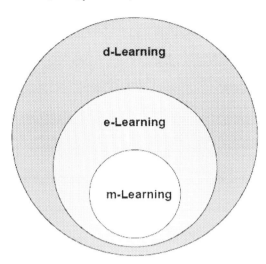

On the other hand, Woodill (2013) focused on the key differences between e-learning and mobile learning, including: the presence or absence of mobility (not the device that a learner uses), and different technologies (e.g., GPS, accelerometers and other onboard electronic sensors, multi-touch capabilities and gesture recognition, and dynamic maps). He further stated, "With e-learning in a fixed location, the learner is usually not situated or immersed in the environment he or she is learning about. Mobile allows a person to be in context, in the learner's immediate environment. This makes learning more authentic and relevant, and leads to inquiry-based learning drawing from questions generated from the situation" (p. 37).

Mobile Learning and Learning Theories

Bransford, Brown, and Cocking (1999) indicated, "a fundamental tenet of modern learning theory is that different kinds of learning goals require different approaches to instruction; new goals for education require changes in opportunities to learn" (p. 131). Lahiri and Moseley (2012) viewed that these new learning opportunities should take place in learning environments that are student-centered, knowledge-centered, assessment-centered, and community centered; and the new technologies such as mobile technologies need also to be consistent with the principles of new theories of learning.

Mobile learning has been a high multidisciplinary study field (Keskin & Metcalf, 2011). The learning theories together with mobile learning devices can help create a learning environment that allows participants to "use their knowledge and skills – by thinking critically, applying knowledge to new situations, analyzing information, comprehending new ideas, communicating, collaborating, solving problems, making decisions" (Honey, Mandinach, & McMillan, 2003, p. 9). According to Naismith, Lonsdale, Vavoula, and Sharples (2004), mobile learning can be divided into six types of learning. They are: behaviorist, constructivist, situated, collaborative, informal/lifelong, and support coordination. Thomas (2007; as cited in Hussin et al., 2012) viewed mobile learning could be adapted to behaviorism, constructivism, informal or situated learning, and collaborative learning by instructors. Although each learning theory has a different focus, Keskin and Metcalf (2011) stressed that mobile devices are well suited for different applications of various learning theories, such as behaviorist learning, cognitivist learning, constructive learning, situated learning, problem-based learning, context awareness learning, socio-cultural theory, collaborative learning, conversational learning, lifelong learning, informal learning, activity theory, connectivism, navigationism, and location-based learning.

Mobile Learning and Conceptual Frameworks/Models

According to Park (2011), the most serious issue faced by mobile learning is the lack of a solid theoretical framework that can guide effective instructional design and evaluate the quality of programs that reply significantly on mobile technologies. As a result, many researchers have attempted to develop models and conceptual frameworks to explain and analyze mobile learning, and various models for understanding mobile learning systems have also been created and adapted to measure performance, user acceptance, or understand the user's context. For example, Koole (2009) developed a framework for the rational analysis of mobile education (FRAME) model which presents three aspects of mobile learning: the device, the learner, and the social environment. Danaher, Gururajan, and Hafeez-Baig (2009) proposed a framework based on three key principles: engagement, presence and flexibility. Parsons, Ryu, and Cranshaw (2007) proposed a complex conceptual framework for m-learning with four perspectives: generic mobile environment issues, learning contexts, learning experiences and learning objectives. Vavoula and Sharples (2008) proposed a three-level framework for evaluating m-learning, comprising a micro-level concerned with usability, a meso level focusing on the learning experience and a macro level dealing with integration within existing organizational contexts. Al-Hmouz, Shen, Yan, and Al-Hmouz (2010) proposed a framework for learner personalization that takes into account different contexts. The four major statuses that they proposed included: situation status; learner status; knowledge and shared properties status, and educational activity status. Kearney, Schuck, Burden, and Aubusson (2012) proposed a pedagogical framework for m-learning from a socio-cultural perspective, including personalization, authenticity and collaboration as the three distinctive features. Park's (2011) pedagogical framework of mobile learning generated the following four types in the context of distance education, including:

1. High transactional distance and socialized mobile learning activity.
2. High transactional distance and individualized mobile learning activity.
3. Low transactional distance and socialized mobile learning activity.
4. Low transactional distance and individualized mobile learning activity.

Naismith et al. (2004) emphasized a conceptual framework for the design of mobile learning should ensure the achievement of learner-centered, highly situated, personal and collaborative mobile learning.

Although mobile learning has been popular in the field of educational technology, some researchers (Sharples et al., 2005 & 2007) express there is under-theorization about the nature, process, and outcome of mobile learning. As Sharples et al. (2005) indicated, "There is a need to re-conceptualize learning for the mobile age, to recognize the essential role of mobility and communication in the process of learning, and also indicate the importance of context in establishing meaning, and the transformative effect of digital networks in supporting virtual communities that transcend barriers of age and culture" (p. 1). They thus proposed a theory based on conversation for the design of mobile technology for learning and further offered an initial framework for mobile learning, and the following steps have been postulated into a theory of mobile learning:

1. To distinguish what is special about mobile learning compared to other types of learning activity.
2. To embrace the considerable learning that occurs outside classrooms and lecture halls as people initiate and structure their activities to enable educational processes and outcomes.
3. Based on contemporary accounts of practices that enable successful learning (e.g., learner centered; knowledge centered; assessment centered; community centered).
4. Take account of the ubiquitous use of personal and shared technology.

They also suggested that a theory of mobile learning have to be tested against the following criteria:

- Is it significantly different from current theories of classroom, workplace or lifelong learning?
- Does it account for the mobility of learners?
- Does it cover both formal and informal learning?
- Does it theorize learning as a constructive and social process?
- Does it analyze learning as a personal and situated activity mediated by technology? (p. 4)

Mobile Learning and the Technical Features

In the early studies, the designs of mobile devices mainly focused on the technical features of portability and accessibility, essentially accompanied by the limitations of tiny displays and limited input during the learning process (Ting, 2012). Now, more researchers indicate the use of mobile devices in learning should go beyond the technical functionalities, and stress the contextual use of mobile devices (Kjeldskov & Graham, 2003; Kukulska-Hulme, 2007; Ting, 2012). Some researchers (Jones & Issroff, 2007; Kukulska-Hulme, 2009) advocated the advanced features of mobile technologies need to include the situated and authentic access and interaction across different contexts of use.

A number of researchers have studied various methods to overcome the limitations of the mobile device and content adaption. For example, from the technical perspective, Morita (2003) suggested that learning contents should be designed to be studied only using arrow keys, so typing can be eliminated. Jones, Buchanan and Thimbleby (2003) recommended to adopt vertical scrolling rather than horizontal one. From the pedagogy-oriented means for the effective use of mobile devices for review and practice, Thorton and Houser (2002) suggested e-mailing students short mini-lessons in discrete chunks that could be easily read on the small screen. If taking an individual learner's cognitive capability point of view, Chen, Hsieh, and Kinshuk (2008) indicated that the learning content with pictorial annotation is more helpful in a mobile language learning environment for those learners with lower verbal and higher visual ability.

TRENDS IN MOBILE LEARNING

The following section reviews the trends for increasing learning with mobile technologies and devices.

Changing Dynamics of Learning

The number of students who own mobile devices has been tremendously grown. According to the EDUCASE report *ECAR Study of Undergraduate Students and Information Technology, 2012* (Dahlstrom, 2012), almost 9 out of 10 students own a laptop and more than 62% of students now have their own smartphone in the United States, although the percentage of students who own desktops and regular cell phones has decreased. Along with the increasing number of ownership of mobile devices, the use of mobile devices for teaching and learning has been growing and it is expected to enhance student learning experiences, regardless of online, blended, informal, social, or situated learning environments.

- **Online Learning:** Compared to traditional classroom settings, online learning has the advantage of flexibility and convenience allowing students to learn anywhere anytime when they have access to a computer and an internet connection. In 2012, the number of students taking at least online course was 6.7 million and 32% of students have taken at least one online course (Allen & Seaman, 2013). While sharing the advantages of online learning, online learners can use mobile and wireless technologies to extend the availability of online learning on various mobile devices such as laptops, PDAs, mobile phones, tablet computers, and digital media players (Evans, 2008).
- **Blended Learning:** With recent development of mobile and wireless technologies, mobile learning has the potential to change the way students interact with one another as well as to change the way learning materials are distributed. The most common use of mobile technologies in education is to enhance current online learning environments by providing alternative ways of accessing course materials on mobile devices. This trend results in an increase of blended or hybrid learning (Alexander, 2004). Students prefer blended learning environments and the hybrid learning has become the norm (Dahlstrom, 2012). Many students believe they learn most when instructors provide both online and face-to-face options (Dahlstrom, 2012). Even in the traditional classroom, many instructors provide streamed and recorded lectures for those who cannot attend lectures physically. Some students may decide to come to classrooms while others may choose to listen to or watch lectures on computers or other mobile devices. With the increased flexibility, student attendance is likely to decrease (Turney, Robinson, Lee, & Soutar, 2009).
- **Informal and Social Learning:** Mobile technologies can support social constructivist approaches to learning. Bryant (2006) also supported mobile technologies as tools to 'expand discussion beyond the classroom and provide new ways for students to collaborate and communicate within their class or around the world" (p. 61).

Recent days, students spent a lot of time on their mobile devices in social networking or social media sites. With the increased use of social media and networking sites such as: YouTube, Facebook, Twitter, LinkedIn, Google+, Pinterest, and Instagram, learners can not only connect to other people for online chat, text messaging, photo sharing, podcast or video streaming, but also form a collaborative learning community with those whom share the same interests. Social network provides various advantages for the educational context through personalization, collaboration, information sharing, cultivating common interests, language development and learning, active participation, and knowledge creation (Lahiri & Moseley, 2012). As social networks and media are everywhere, the social software has become inevitable for teaching and learning.

- **Situated Learning:** "Knowledge is information in context and knowledge creation is location-dependent and situation-dependent" (Ally, 2005, p. 5). Mobile learning devices can allow learners to learn wherever they are located and in their personal context so that the learning can be meaningful too (Sharples, 2000). With GPS-enabled wireless devices, mobile learning is context-aware so that it can locate individual students in the real world and provide context-specific support as well as guidance (Hwang, Yang, Tsai, & Yang, 2009). GPS-enabled mobile devices can provide personalized information based on learners' contexts and locations, which enables educational practitioners to create more contextualized learning activities (Alnuaim et al., 2012).

In addition, mobile technologies have the potential to deliver situated digital experiences to enhance student learning in authentic environments (Hull, Reid, & Geelhoed, 2002). Presenting digital objects to assist student interaction with and understanding of the authentic environments, the situated digital experiences can augment student's learning experiences. Chu, Hwang, and Tsai (2010) implemented the repertory grid method originated from Kelly's Personal construct theory in a natural science course at an elementary school. Based on the enhanced repertory grid approach, *Mobile Knowledge Constructor*, a Mindtool for context-aware ubiquitous learning, was developed to assist students in the authentic environment. Equipped with a mobile device to interact with plants and communicate with a computer server, students in a garden at the elementary school were asked to observe and classify plants. The learning system was able to detect individual students' locations and provide personalized guidance based on the students' locations and activities. By integrating real-world learning environments and the digital resources, students were involved in real situations dealing with problems with access to information and resources on mobile devices (Chu et al., 2010). Mobile technologies made it possible to bridge the gap between learning in and outside classroom (Johnson, Levine, Smith, & Haywood, 2010).

- **Tablet Learning (T-Learning):** The use of tablet learning (t-learning) has been noticeably popular in the recent couple of years (Little, 2013). Like m-learning has different parameters to e-learning, t-learning has its own parameters different from both m-learning and e-learning. Little provided some technological characteristics of tablets (e.g., screen size; personal issue) to distinguish the uniqueness of t-learning from m-learning and/or e-learning. As mobile devices, Little (2013) views tablets are more acceptable to learners in a group learning context because they do not ring like mobile phones; learners can thus have less distractions (e.g., calls or text messages) while using tablets. In addition, tablet screens are designed to make learners easily share their displays with others, so that would help collaborative learning take place.
- **Ubiquitous Learning (U-Learning):** When mobile learning offers the opportunity to move beyond the formal classroom and allow more freedom for learning anywhere, anytime (Stanton & Ophoff, 2013), there is also a growing interest in context-aware ubiquitous learning over the past few years. As a variant of m-learning, u-learning currently uses various advanced forms of mobile technologies such as GPS, sensor devices, radio-frequency identification (RFID) and Near Field Communication (NFC) technology to transmit information such as files, hyperlinks, and contacts from one device to another via physical proximity (Kambourakis, 2013).

- **E-Learning:** As Little (2012) indicated, "e-learning is well suited to formal learning, while mobile learning is ideal for electronic performance support, lifelong learning, just-in-time and close to the point of need learning. This implies those developing mobile learning materials need to construct them differently from the traditional methods of e-learning" (p. 403). Triantafillou, Georgiadou, and Economides (2008) stated the introduction of mobile devices into the learning process can complement e-learning, and mobile learning can intersect mobile computing with e-learning. Due to the characteristic of the "just enough, just in time, just for me" model of flexible learning, learners can often take advantage of unexpected free time as they frequently have their devices with them (Evans, 2008; Vavoula & Sharples, 2008). Without constraints of time or place, the learner can easily review information about courses, take exams, download notes, and share information.

Changing E-Learning Platforms

The availability and popularity of mobile portable wireless devices has brought changes in the e-learning platforms. With the advent of the Internet, many educational institutions have adopted their e-learning systems such as Blackboard, Moodle, and Angel to deliver course content to students (Goh, 2010). Since they started as a Web-based e-learning system, they are still limited in delivering learning materials to mobile devices and making all features available on the small screen. In addition, the learning management system (LMS) is fallen behind in integrating social networking sites and Web 2.0 tools and providing personalized learning environments (Ingerman & Yang, 2010).

The popular LMSs or course management systems (CMSs) have begun slowly allowing access to make learning content available to those who want to access online courses via mobile devices. In the preface of *Multiplatform E-Learning Systems and Technologies*, Goh (2010) defined *multiplatform e-learning systems* as "learning systems that generate support and provide appropriate learning content concurrently to a proliferation of mobile devices" (p. xx). Multiplatform e-learning systems are inclusive and comprehensive in that they provide access through multiple devices including laptops, PDAs, mobile phones, tablet computers, and digital media players. The affordances of information and communication technologies are expected to bring about ubiquitous learning, which enables anyone to learn anytime anywhere (Tan, Lin, Chu, & Liu, 2012).

Providing Adaptive (Personalized) Learning System and Assessment

While early perspectives of M-Learning focused on technology, new mobile learning perspective is the learner-centered focusing on individualism (Keskin & Metcalf, 2011). Recent developments in mobile and wireless technologies can facilitate personalized and contextualized learning and support (De Jong, Fuertes, Schmeits, Specht, & Koper, 2010). Thus, a number of studies have been conducted to examine adaptive learning systems and assessment applications for mobile learning. Kinshuk, Chang, Graf, and Yang (2010) introduced a personalized learning environment which adapts to learners' characteristics such as learning styles, performance, and preferences and to the contexts of their surroundings. The context-aware techniques can present learners with context-bound learning activities in their preferred ways. El-Bishouty and his colleagues (2010) developed a model of personalized collaborative ubiquitous learning environment which can detect a learner's surrounding objects and enable peer helpers to provide support in learning tasks or activities. Triantafillou et al. (2008) evaluated the use of computerized adaptive test on mobile devices, and reported positive comments from the users. Nedungadi and

Raman (2012) discussed a web-based Adaptive Learning and Assessment System (ALAS) that was designed for personalized assessment and learning on mobile devices. Shanmugapriya and Tamilarasi (2012) developed a mobile adaptive test for an Android-based m-learning environment to enhance the teaching-learning process with great emphasis on learner's knowledge acquirement via various assessment methods. Segall, Doolen, and Porter (2005) compared a PDA-based quiz and standard paper-and-pencil applications, and indicated the PDA-based quiz was more efficient because students could complete it in less time. Although no differences in efficiency and satisfaction were found between these two quiz types, they concluded that PDAs were an attractive test administration option for schools.

Implementing Augmented Reality (AR)

Augmented reality (AR) has been identified as one of key promising technologies in teaching and learning and drawn many interests from educational researchers and practitioners. Combined with both a camera and a wireless internet connection, AR and the related devices provide the user with information about their surroundings (places, events, or activities).

With a high fidelity of real world environments, AR places virtual objects or information to real world contexts to augment students' learning experiences. AR has students "act like professionals in the field as opposed to students in a classroom" (Wasko, 2013, p. 17). It can make learning immersive and authentic, by providing interactive, situated, and collaborative problem solving activities, which encourages students' engagement and understanding (Dunleavy, Dede, & Mitchell, 2009; Wasko, 2013). In the early days of AR, teachers and students used a separate display device mounted to a laptop computer (Wasko, 2013). Coupled with advancement in GPS, video, and handheld computers, AR has become available to teachers and students (Johnson et al., 2010). The recent development and availability of mobile devices and technologies has made it possible to create a mobile AR and use it in educational settings (Liestøl, 2011).

Using a handheld computer and GPS technology, Dunleavy et al. (2009) designed a scenario-based AR simulation, *Alien Contact!*, to teach math, language arts, and scientific literacy skills to middle and high school students. The students work in a team of four members, each of whom plays a role of chemist, cryptologist, computer hacker, and FBI agent and collets different clues or evidences to discover the purpose of the visit to Earth. While collaborating with the teammates, students navigate the AR space and have richer interaction with virtual characters and objects. They found that students were highly motivated and engaged in the AR simulations. In the forensic medicine department, Albrecht, Behrends, Von Jan, and Folta-Schoofs (2013) compared the impact of a mobile AR blended learning environment on medical students to textbook materials. They found that students in the mobile augmented group were emotionally involved in the learning process and performed better than the textbook group. With the advent of wearable technology, AR is expected to become more common experiences in the near future (Wasko, 2013).

Adopting Cloud Computing

Cloud computing is quickly being adopted as a popular tool for mobile learning (Kambourakis, 2013). Cloud computing is "a model for enabling ubiquitous, convenient, on-demand network access to a shared pool of configurable computing resources" (Mell & Grance, 2011, p. 2). It is a scalable computer infrastructure that hosts applications and provides software, services, and data resources to end-users over the Internet (Despotović-Zrakić, Simić, Labus, Milić, & Jovanić, 2013). Compared to traditional hosting, cloud computing can be more efficient and cost effective by providing on-demand resources and flexible IT capacities (Bora & Ahmed, 2013). Microsoft, Google, Amazon, and other big IT companies have showed their interests in cloud computing and expanded their cloud resources and services for their customers. They include networks, servers, infrastructures, platforms, storage, applications and services. Using the Internet, people can access their personal files from any computer and use applications and software without installing them on their individual computers (Bora & Ahmed, 2013).

As mobile and wireless technologies have expanded, cloud computing has been growing rapidly and utilized in many areas including the field of education, in particular e-learning. In e-learning environments, cloud computing can provide a ubiquitous learning environment in a reliable and efficient way (Despotović-Zrakić et al., 2013). In the National Institute of Standards and Technology (NIST) report, Mell and Grance (2011) identify three cloud computing service models including Software as a Service (SaaS), Platform as a Service (PaaS), and Infrastructure as a Service (IaaS). Butoi, Tomai, and Mocean (2013) add a Learning as a Service (LaaS) as a cloud-enabled learning tools. The LaaS includes cloud e-learning and m-learning systems. Because of its ability to increase the scalability, flexibility and availability of e-learning systems, cloud computing has emerged as a future e-learning infrastructure (Masud & Huang, 2012). Using cloud computing, teachers and students can have direct access to academic resources, research applications and educational services and tools on their personal mobile devices (Bora & Ahmed, 2013).

In addition, cloud computing has transformed the way people work together. Collaboration has long been identified as a fundamental skill in problem solving and learning (Baskin, Barker, & Woods, 2005; Fisher, Thompson, & Silverberg, 2004/2005; Williams, Morgan, & Cameron, 2011). Lave and Wenger (1991) state that learning requires collaboration by participating in the practice of a community. While supporting each other in a collaborative learning environment, students can discuss and explore multiple perspectives and negotiate meanings to achieve shared goals (Land & Hannafin, 2000). Particularly for adult learners, the ability to effectively work in groups is critical in their real lives. Cloud computing can enhance collaborative works by providing cloud-based platforms, services, and software of applications for sharing, communication and collaboration.

LIMITATIONS, ISSUES, AND CHALLENGES IN MOBILE LEARNING

While mobile technologies have great potential for learning, mobile technology and devices, however, have some limitations, issues and challenges as well. According to Elias (2011), a solid theoretical foundation in mobile learning addresses equitable use, flexible use, simple and intuitive interfaces, perceptible information, tolerance for error, low physical and technical effort, community of learners and support, and instructional climate (as cited in Fuegen, 2012). As literature (Cheon, Lee, Crooks, & Song, 2012) indicate there is little experience of how to deliver learning through mobile technology, many researchers also point out some common issues in mobile learning, such as usability, communication and interactivity (Ali, Ouda, & Capretz, 2012); cost, compatibility, equity of access, security, privacy and ethical concerns (Cobcroft, Towers, Smith, & Bruns, 2006; Traxler & Bridges, 2004). The following section reviews some of these issues and challenges related to mobile learning.

Design Issues and Principles

In addition to putting efforts to develop models and conceptual frameworks, current research around mobile learning design has been quite varied. For instance, Stanton and Ophoff (2013) suggested that mobile learning designs need to consider what needs to be delivered, how it will be done and the structure of such a delivery. Hemabala and Suresh (2012) identified three modules to mobile learning: 1) the content module (e.g. authoring tools such as development, management, distribution, collaboration, delivery); 2) the learning module (e.g., where learning takes place), and 3) the evaluation module (e.g., knowledge sharing and management). When designing a mobile course, Killilea (2012) proposed five best practices to the design and use of mobile learning. They are: 1) clear objectives to the course; 2) feedback; 3) content; 4) active learning techniques, and 5) realistic timeframes for lessons. Yau and Joy (2010) proposed an m-learning model consisting of five dimensions of mobile learning preferences. They are: location, level of distractions, time of day, level of motivation, and available time. Ryokai (2012) presented four design principles for mobile learning: 1) connect; 2) contextualize access, 3) capture, and 4) multimodal. These design principles refer to the importance of creating a connection between what takes place in the classroom and what is delivered through the mobile device; and the importance of creating a personal connection to the material for the learner by ensuring it is relevant and meaningful to the learner.

Technical and Usability Issues

There are a number of technical and usability issues that are associated with mobile learning. Usability focuses on making systems easy to learn and easy to use (Zhang & Adipat, 2005). Kukulska-Hulme (2007) summarized some of usability concerns, such as: a) physical attributes of mobile devices, such as small screen size, inadequate memory, and short battery life; b) content and software application limitations, such as a lack of built-in functions, the difficulty of adding applications, and differences between applications and circumstances of use; c) network speed and reliability; and d) physical environment issues,

such as problems with using the device outdoors and concerns about personal security. Crescente and Lee (2011) also described some usability challenges in mobile learning. For example, how to keep a mobile device charged for longer periods of use; limit activities such as reading because of small screen size; costs of connectivity; environmental factors such as sunshine and rain on the practicality of learning outdoors, and unexpected noise and interruptions on the quality of learning in public areas and when traveling.

In addition, Kant (2012) provided a comprehensive list of technical challenges, especially in the social and educational aspects, such as: accessibility and cost barriers for end users; how to assess learning outside the classroom; how to support learning across many contexts; content's security (or) pirating issues; frequent changes in device models/technologies/functionality; developing an appropriate theory of learning for the mobile age; conceptual differences between e- and m-learning; design of technology to support a lifetime of learning; tracking of results and proper use of this information; no restriction on learning timetable; personal and private information and content; no demographic boundary; disruption of students' personal and academic lives, and access to and use of the technology in developing countries.

Security and Privacy Issues

Kambourakis (2013) indicated that most mobile learning studies have focused on course development, deployment and delivery, but not paid enough attention to the security and privacy issues. In a study of frameworks and middleware for facilitating mobile and ubiquitous learning development, Martin et al. (2011) also concluded that privacy and security would be needed for the future development when building systems that guarantee user's rights. Lahiri and Moseley (2012) reported safety and privacy of young children would be the issues that arise against using mobile devices in K-12 educational settings. Kambourakis further identified several primary challenges in m-leaning, including: a) security and privacy of data and systems; b) ensuring actors' (user) privacy; c) mobile device related issues; such as safeguarding of data stored on mobile devices and prevention of offensive or illegal behavior; d) content filtering; e) protection of data in the cloud; f) security and privacy in multi-university consortiums; g) protection of copyright and Intellectual Property Rights (IPR), and f) u-learning. One example of the issue would be to reveal data about individuals that they might not know was accessible because some mobile devices are location-aware and can disclose the participant's movements (Sharples et al., 2005). Due to the constant interaction that the learner has with their environment information such as location, history of movement in space, and history interaction with other smart objects, security and privacy policies are required to offer advanced context-aware information control (Kambourakis, 2013).

Ethical and Legal Issues

Some of the major ethical issues associated with mobile learning include informed consent, anonymity and confidentiality, participant risk, payment to participants and cultural differences (Anderson & Kanuka, 2003; Hewson, Yule, Laurent, & Vogel, 2003; Traxler & Bridges, 2004). Sharples et al. (2005) complemented systems such as *myLifeBits* not only have the potential to be powerful tools helping those with failing memories by recording everyday life as sounds and pictures, but also allow parents or teachers to monitor every intimate detail of learning, so that play and leisure can be an extension of school activity by being checked and assessed as continuous records of achievement. However, Sharples et al. also warned this "as a deeply disturbing vision of childhood without privacy" (p. 5). Traxler and Bridges (2004) also concerned about the issue of ethics and emphasized that any ongoing online activity, including mobile learning, has an ethical dimension and this needs to be identified and explored as mobile learning evolves.

Broadband Connections and Infrastructure Issues

There are many several operating systems, video formats, hardware limitations, and internet connections all of which make it difficult to develop standards for mobile learning. Without any standards that are universally accepted and practiced, the capacities of mobile device will never be reached (Crescente & Lee, 2011).

Mobile learning is impossible without broadband connections. Some of well-established broadband technologies, such as DSL (Digital Subscriber Line), Cable Internet, Wireless Internet Service Providers, Satellite Internet, are still not yet prevalent in the rural area because of cost concern (Kant, 2012). Although WiMax (Worldwide Interoperability for Microwave Access) has been anticipated as the most dominant broadband technology in rural areas in the near future (Kant, 2012), the cost of implementing the infrastructure could be very costly (Kant, 2012). As a result, mobile learning designers not only have to understand what facilities and devices would be available to their learners, but also need to cooperate with technical consultants who can help with minimal technical specifications to make mobile learning more effective (Crescente & Lee, 2011).

Other Cost Concerns

In addition to the broadband connections, it is important to examine the other costs of mobile learning. Initially, organizations will have to invest a large sum of financial resources into mobile learning; these resources will be used to cover the cost of training, infrastructure, devices, content development, and testing (Kant, 2012). The time need for converting existing content into mobile learning content should be closely evaluated and tested for effectiveness (Crescente & Lee, 2011).

According to Crescente and Lee (2011), the cost for information technology (IT) would be a significant issue, because organizations would have to deal with device hardware issue failure, loss of access, security issues, lack of knowledge, and the need to access the vendor's support documents. The limitations of LMSs would be another cost issue. Due to their limitation, some organizations have to purchase a separate learning platform to support mobile learning (Crescente & Lee, 2011). To offset these costs, some organizations obtain sponsorship from device manufacturers, and this allows organizations the ability to provide devices to large groups of users (Kant, 2012). With the high cost of mobile devices, instructional designers need to ensure that the mobile devices they choose will be able to meet the learning needs of the users over an extended period of time (Crescente & Lee, 2011).

CONCLUSION

Without a doubt, mobile learning has emerged as a potential educational environment and a tool for the teaching and learning process. However, merely having the learning materials delivered through mobile technology does not make learning effective. Williams (2009) considers the major element of a successful mobile learning to be the instructional design. Literature (Armstrong, 2011; Rossing et al., 2012) indicated instructional design and comfort with technology are significant factors, and students have attributed negative qualities to instructional technology due to ineffective implementation in classrooms and learning activities. Little (2012) also agreed, "The real difference between effective and ineffective learning materials is the instructional design (ID). Well-designed learning presents content, guides the student in practice provides for independent practice by the learner and assesses how well the learning is doing." (p. 406). Therefore, to utilize the immense potential of mobile devices and technology for enhancing learning, it is essential to have well-defined principles of mobile learning pedagogy. As Lahiri and Moseley (2012) conclude, "Without pedagogical principles and supporting research evidence, mobile devices cannot be fully utilized as educational tools to enhance learning. Implementing mobile devices in the teaching-learning process without careful considerations of how to use mobile technology as a tool might lead to frustration, inequity, shallow learning, and distraction from the main purpose of enhancing learning and making students' competent professionals" (p. 11). Shifting from e-learning to mobile learning implies that instructional designers need to adopt new ways of facilitating learning, not in one way, but using multiple pedagogical strategies, to help people learn whenever they need and wherever they are.

REFERENCES

Al-Fahad, F. N. (2009). Students' attitudes and perceptions towards the effectiveness of mobile learning in King Saud University, Saudi Arabia. *The Turkish Online Journal of Educational Technology*, *8*(2), 111–119.

Al-Hmouz, A., Shen, J., Yan, J., & Al-Hmouz, R. (2010). Enhanced learner model for adaptive mobile learning. In *Proceedings of the 12th International Conference on Information Integration and Web-based Applications & Services - iiWAS 2010*, (pp. 783 – 786). iiWAS.

Albrecht, U. V., Behrends, M., Von Jan, U., & Folta-Schoofs, K. (2013). Effects of mobile augmented reality learning compared to textbook learning on medical students: Randomized controlled pilot study. *Journal of Medical Internet Research*, *15*(8). doi:10.2196/jmir.2497 PMID:23963306

Alexander, B. (2004). Going nomadic: Moblile learning in higher education. *EDUCAUSE Review*, *39*(5), 28.

Ali, A., Ouda, A., & Capretz, L. F. (2012). A conceptual framework for measuring the quality aspects of mobile learning. *Bulletin of the IEEE Technical Committee on Learning Technology*, *14*(4), 31–34.

Allen, I. E., & Seaman, J. (2013). *Changing course: Then years of tracking online education in the United States*. Babson Survey Research Group and Quahog Research Group, LLC.

Ally, M. (2005). Using learning theories to design instruction for mobile learning devices. In J. Attewell & C. Savill-Smith (Eds.), Mobile learning anytime everywhere. A book of papers from MLEARN 2004 (pp. 5–8). Retrieved from http://stu.westga.edu/~bthibau1/MEDT%208484-%20Baylen/mLearn04_papers.pdf#page=14

Alnuaim, A., Caleb-Solly, P., & Perry, C. (2012). A mobile location-based situated learning framework for supporting critical thinking: A requirements analysis study. In *Proceedings of IADIS International Conference on Cognition and Exploratory Learning in Digital Age*, (pp. 163-170). IADIS.

Alzaza, N. S., & Yaakub, A. R. (2011). Students' awareness and requirements of mobile learning services in the higher education environment. *American Journal of Economics and Business Administration*, *3*(1), 95–100. doi:10.3844/ajebasp.2011.95.100

Alzaza, N. S., & Zulkifli, A. N. (2007). Mobile Based Library Loan Service (MBLLS). In *Proceeding of the Rural ICT Development Conference*. Retrieved from http://citeseerx.ist.psu.edu/viewdoc/download?doi=10.1.1.97.7749&rep=rep1&type=pdf

Anderson, T., & Kanuka, H. (2003). *E-research: Methods, strategies and issues*. Boston, MA: Allyn and Bacon.

Armstrong, D. A. (2011). Students' perceptions of online learning and instructional tools: A qualitative study of undergraduate students use of online tools. *Turkish Online Journal of Educational Technology*, *10*(3), 222–226.

Attewell, J., & Savill-Smith, C. (2004). *Learning with mobile devices: research and development – a book of papers*. London: Learning and Skills Development Agency.

Aubusson, P., Schuck, S., & Burden, K. (2009). Mobile learning for teacher professional learning: Benefits, obstacles and issues. *ALT-J Research in Learning Technology*, *17*(3), 233–247. doi:10.1080/09687760903247641

Baskin, C., Barker, M., & Woods, P. (2005). When group work leaves the classroom does group skills development also go out the window? *British Journal of Educational Technology*, *36*(1), 19–31. doi:10.1111/j.1467-8535.2005.00435.x

Baya'a, N., & Daher, W. (2009). Learning mathematics in an authentic mobile environment: The perceptions of students. *International Journal of Interactive Mobile Technologies*, *3*, 6–14.

BenMoussa, C. (2003). *Workers on the move: New opportunities through mobile commerce*. Paper presented at the meeting of the Stockholm Mobility Roundtable. Stockholm, Sweden.

Bora, U. J., & Ahmed, M. (2013). E-learning using cloud computing. *International Journal of Science and Modern Engineering*, *1*(2), 9–13.

Bransford, J., Brown, A., & Cocking, R. (Eds.). (1999). *How people learn: Brain, mind, experience, and school*. Washington, DC: National Academy Press.

Brown, T. H. (2005). Towards a model for m-learning in Africa. *International Journal on E-Learning*, *4*(3), 299–315.

Bryant, T. (2006). Social software in academia. *EDUCAUSE Quarterly*, *2*, 61–64.

Bull, S., & Reid, E. (2004). Individualized revision material for use on a handheld computer. In J. Attewell, & C. Savill-Smith (Eds.), *Learning with Mobile Devices Research and Development* (pp. 35–42). London: Learning with Mobile Devices, Learning and Skills Development Agency.

Butoi, A., Tomai, N., & Mocean, L. (2013). Cloud-based mobile learning. *Informatica Economica*, *17*(2), 27–40. doi:10.12948/issn14531305/17.2.2013.03

Chen, G. D., Chang, C. K., & Wang, C. Y. (2008). Ubiquitous learning website: Scaffold learners by mobile devices with information-aware techniques. *Computers & Education*, *50*, 77–90. doi:10.1016/j.compedu.2006.03.004

Chen, N.S., & Hsieh, S.W., & Kinshuk. (2008). Effects of short-term memory and content representation type on mobile language learning. *Language Learning & Technology*, *12*, 93–113.

Cheon, J., Lee, S., Crooks, S. M., & Song, J. (2012). An investigation of mobile learning readiness in higher education based on the theory of planned behavior. *Computers & Education*, *59*(3), 1054–1064. doi:10.1016/j.compedu.2012.04.015

Chu, H. C., Hwang, G. J., & Tsai, C. C. (2010). A knowledge engineering approach to developing mindtools for context-aware ubiquitous learning. *Computers & Education*, *54*(1), 289–297. doi:10.1016/j.compedu.2009.08.023

Cobcroft, R., Towers, S., Smith, J., & Bruns, A. (2006). Mobile learning in review: Opportunities and challenges for learners, teachers, and institutions. In *Proceedings of OLT 2006 Conference*. Queensland University of Technology.

Crescente, M. L., & Lee, D. (2011). Critical issues of m-learning: Design models, adoption processes, and future trends. *Journal of the Chinese Institute of Industrial Engineers*, *28*(2), 111–123. doi:10.1080/10170669.2010.548856

Dahlstrom, E. (2012). *ECAR Study of Undergraduate Students and Information Technology, 2012 (Research Report)*. Louisville, CO: EDUCAUSE Center for Applied Research.

Danaher, P., Gururajan, R., & Hafeez-Baig, A. (2009). Transforming the practice of mobile learning: promoting pedagogical innovation through educational principles and strategies that work. In H. Ryu, & D. Parsons (Eds.), *Innovative mobile learning: Techniques and technologies* (pp. 21–46). Hershey, PA: IGI Global.

De Jong, T., Fuertes, A., Schmeits, T., Specht, M., & Koper, R. (2010). A contextualised multi-platform framework to support blended learning scenarios in learning networks. In T. T. Goh (Ed.), *Multiplatform E-Learning Systems and Technologies* (pp. 1–19). Hershey, PA: Information Sceince Reference.

De-Marcos, L., Hilera, J. R., Barchino, R., Jiménez, L., Martínez, J. J., & Gutiérrez, J. A. (2010). An experiment for improving students' performance in secondary and tertiary education by means of m-learning auto-assessment. *Computers & Education*, *55*(3), 1069–1079. doi:10.1016/j.compedu.2010.05.003

Despotović-Zrakić, M., Simić, K., Labus, A., Milić, A., & Jovanić, B. (2013). Scaffolding environment for e-learning through cloud computing. *Journal of Educational Technology & Society*, *16*(3), 301–314.

Doolittle, P., & Mariano, G. (2008). Working memory capacity and mobile multimedia learning environments: individual differences in learning while mobile. *Journal of Educational Multimedia and Hypermedia*, *17*(4), 511–530.

Dunleavy, M., Dede, C., & Mitchell, R. (2009). Affordances and limitations of immersive participatory augmented reality simulations for teaching and learning. *Journal of Science Education and Technology, 18*(1), 7–22. doi:10.1007/s10956-008-9119-1

El-Bishouty, M. M., Ogata, H., Rahman, S., & Yano, Y. (2010). Social Knowledge Awareness Map for Computer Supported Ubiquitous Learning Environment. *Journal of Educational Technology & Society, 13*(4), 27–37.

El-Hussein, M. O. M., & Cronje, J. C. (2010). Defining mobile learning in the higher education landscape. *Journal of Educational Technology & Society, 13*(3), 12–21.

Elias, T. (2011). Universal instructional design principles for mobile learning. *International Review of Research in Open and Distance Learning, 12*(2), 143–156.

Evans, C. (2008). The effectiveness of m-learning in the form of podcast revision lectures in higher education. *Computers & Education, 50*, 491–498. doi:10.1016/j.compedu.2007.09.016

Fisher, M., Thompson, G. S., & Silverberg, D. A. (2004/2005). Effective group dynamics in e-learning: Case study. *Journal of Educational Technology Systems, 33*(3), 205–222. doi:10.2190/YTJ7-PLQB-VNDV-71UU

Fuegen, S. (2012). The impact of mobile technologies on distance education. *TechTrends, 56*(6), 49–53. doi:10.1007/s11528-012-0614-0

Geddes, S. (2004). Mobile learning in the 21st century: Benefit for learners. *The Knowledge Tree: an e-Journal of Learning Innovation*.

Georgiev, T., Georgieva, E., & Smrikarov, A. (2004). M-learning: A new stage of e-learning. Retrieved from http://www.pttmedia.com/newmedia_knowhow/KnowHow_Design/Instructional%20Design/iMobile/mlearning.pdf

Goh, T. T. (2010). *Multiplatform e-learning systems and technologies: Mobile devices for ubiquitous ICT-based education.* Hershey, PA: Information Science Reference.

Gupta, M., & Manjrekar, P. (2012). Using mobile learning to enhance quality in higher education. *SIES Journal of Management, 8*(1), 23–30.

Hemabala, J., & Suresh, E. (2012). The frame work design of mobile learning management system. *International Journal of Computer and Information Technology, 1*(2), 179–184.

Henderson, R. G., & Chapman, B. F. (2012). Business educators' perceptions concerning mobile learning (M-Learning). *Delta Pi Epsilon Journal, 54*(1), 16–26.

Hewson, C., Yule, P., Laurent, D., & Vogel, C. (2003). *Internet research methods.* London: Sage Publications.

Hine, N., Rentoul, R., & Specht, M. (2004). Collaboration and roles in remote field trips. In J. Attewell, & C. Savill-Smith (Eds.), *Learning with Mobile Devices Research and Development* (pp. 69–72). London: Learning and Skills Development Agency.

Honey, M., Mandinach, E., & McMillan, K. C. (2003). *A retrospective on twenty years of education technology policy.* Education Development Center, Center for Children and Technology, U.S. Department of Education, Office of Educational Technologies.

Huang, C. J., Chen, H. X., & Chen, C. H. (2009). Developing argumentation processing agents for computer-supported collaborative learning. *Expert Systems with Applications, 36*, 2615–2624. doi:10.1016/j.eswa.2008.01.036

Hull, R., Reid, J., & Geelhoed, E. (2002). Creating experiences with wearable computing. *IEEE Pervasive Computing, 1*(4), 56–61. doi:10.1109/MPRV.2002.1158279

Hussin, S., Manap, M. R., Amir, Z., & Krish, P. (2012). Mobile learning readiness among Malaysian students at higher learning institutes. *Asian Social Science*, *8*(12), 276–283. doi:10.5539/ass.v8n12p276

Hwang, G.-J., Yang, T.-C., Tsai, C.-C., & Yang, S. J. H. (2009). A context-aware ubiquitous learning environment for conducting complex science experiments. *Computers & Education*, *53*(2), 402-413. http://dx.doi.org/10.1016/j.compedu.2009.02.016

Ifenthaler, D., & Schweinbenz, V. (2013). The acceptance of tablet-PCs in classroom instruction: The teachers' perspectives. *Computers in Human Behavior*, *29*, 525–534. doi:10.1016/j.chb.2012.11.004

Ingerman, B. L., & Yang, C. (2010). Top-10 IT issues, 2010. *EDUCAUSE Review*, *45*(3), 46–60.

Jeng, Y. L., Wu, T. T., Huang, Y. M., Tan, Q., & Yang, S. J. H. (2010). The add-on impact of mobile applications in learning strategies: A review study. *Journal of Educational Technology & Society*, *13*(3), 3–11.

Johnson, L. F., Levine, A., Smith, R. S., & Haywood, K. (2010). Key emerging technologies for elementary and secondary education. *Education Digest*, *76*(1), 36–40.

Jones, A., & Issroff, K. (2007). Motivation and mobile devices: Exploring the role of appropriation and coping strategies. *ALT-J. Research in Learning Technology*, *15*, 247–258. doi:10.1080/09687760701673675

Jones, M., Buchanan, G., & Thimbleby, H. (2003). Improving web search on small screen devices. *Interacting with Computers*, *15*, 479–495. doi:10.1016/S0953-5438(03)00036-5

Kadirire, J. (2009). Mobile Learning DeMystified. In R. Guy (Ed.), *The Evolution of Mobile Teaching and Learning*. California, USA: Informing Science Press.

Kambourakis, G. (2013). Security and privacy in m-learning and beyond: Challenges and state-of-the-art. *International Journal of U- and E-Service. Science and Technology*, *6*(3), 67–84.

Kant, K. (2012). The future of higher education: M-learning. *Indian Streams Research Journal*, *2*(11), 1–6.

Kearney, M., Schuck, S., Burden, K., & Aubusson, P. (2012). Viewing mobile learning from a pedagogical perspective. *Research in Learning Technology*, *20*, 1–17. doi:10.3402/rlt.v20i0.14406

Keskin, N. O., & Metcalf, D. (2011). The current perspectives, theories, and practices of mobile learning. *The Turkish Online Journal of Educational Technology*, *10*(2), 202–208.

Ketamo, H. (2003). xTask-an adaptable learning environment. *Journal of Computer Assisted Learning*, *19*, 360–370. doi:10.1046/j.0266-4909.2003.00037.x

Killilea, J. (2012). Leveraging mobile devices for asynchronous learning: Best practices. Retrieved from http://www.scs.org/upload/documents/conferences/autumnsim/2012/presentations/etms/4_Final_Submission.pdf

Kinash, S., Brand, J., & Mathew, T. (2012). Challenging mobile learning discourse through research: Student perceptions of Blackboard mobile learn and iPads. *Australasian Journal of Educational Technology*, *28*(4), 639–655.

Kinshuk, Chang, M., Graf, S., & Yang, G. (2010). Adaptivity and personalization in mobile learning. *Technology, Instruction. Cognition and Learning*, *8*, 163–174.

Kjeldskov, J., & Graham, C. (2003). A review of mobile HCI research methods. Proceedings of Mobile HCI 2003, Springer-Verlag. *Lecture Notes in Computer Science*, *2795*, 317–335. doi:10.1007/978-3-540-45233-1_23

Koole, M. L. (2009). A model for framing mobile learning. In M. Ally (Ed.), *Empowering learners and educators with mobile learning* (pp. 25–47). Athabasca, Canada: Athabasca University Press.

Kukulask-Hulme, A. (2007). Mobile usability in educational context: What have we learnt? *International Review of Research in Open and Distance Learning, 8*(2), 1–16.

Kukulska-Hulme, A. (2009). Will mobile learning change language learning? *ReCALL, 21*, 157–165. doi:10.1017/S0958344009000202

Kukulska-Hulme, A., & Traxler, J. (2005). *Mobile learning: A handbook for educators and trainers*. London: Routledge.

Kuo, Y. H., Huang, Y. M., Liu, T. C., & Chang, M. (2008). Collaborative creation of authentic examples with location for u-learning. *Proc. e-Learning, 2*, 16–20.

Lahiri, M., & Moseley, J. L. (2012). Is mobile learning the future of 21st century education? Educational considerations from various perspectives. *Educational Technology*, (July-August): 3–13.

Lan, Y. F., & Sie, Y. S. (2010). Using RSS to support mobile learning based on media richness theory. *Computers & Education, 55*(2), 723–732. doi:10.1016/j.compedu.2010.03.005

Land, S. M., & Hannafin, M. J. (2000). Student-centered learning environments. In D. H. Jonassen, & S. M. Land (Eds.), *Theoretical foundations of learning environments* (pp. 1–23). Mahwah, NJ: Erlbaum.

Laouris, Y., & Eteokleous, N. (2005). *We need an educationally relevant definition of mobile learning*. Paper presented at mLearn 2005. Cape Town, South Africa.

Laurillard, D., & Pachler, N. (2007). Pedagogical forms of mobile learning: Framing research questions. In N. Pachler (Ed.), *Mobile learning: towards a research agenda* (pp. 33–54). London: WLE Centre, IOE.

Lave, J., & Wenger, E. (1991). *Situated learning: Legitimate peripheral participation*. New York: Cambridge University Press. doi:10.1017/CBO9780511815355

Liestøl, G. (2011). *Learning through situated simulations: Exploring mobile augmented reality* (ECAR Research Bulletin 1). Boulder, CO: EDUCAUSE Center for Applied Research. Retrieved from http://www.educause.edu/ecar

Little, B. (2012). Effective and efficient mobile learning: issues and tips for developers. *Industrial and Commercial Training, 44*(7), 402–407. doi:10.1108/00197851211267983

Little, B. (2013). Issues in mobile learning technology. *Human Resource Management International Digest, 21*(3), 26–29. doi:10.1108/09670731311318361

Low, L., & O'Connell. (2006). Learner-centric design of digital mobile learning. *Proceedings of the OLT Conference*. Retrieved from: http://s3.amazonaws.com/academia.edu.documents/30832501/learner-centric-design-of-digital-mlearning-low-oconnell-2007.pdf?AWSAccessKeyId=AKIAIR6FSIMDFXPEERSA&Expires=1380491751&Signature=SX3KiZEbsd6eOrAc2Rp5TmWjmZ8%3D&response-content-disposition=inline

Lu, M. (2008). Effectiveness of vocabulary learning via mobile phone. *Journal of Computer Assisted Learning, 24*, 515–525. doi:10.1111/j.1365-2729.2008.00289.x

Martin, S., Diaz, G., Plaza, I., Larrocha, E. R., Castro, M., & Peire, J. (2011). State of the art of frameworks and middleware for facilitating mobile and ubiquitous learning development. *Journal of Systems and Software, 84*(11), 1883–1891. doi:10.1016/j.jss.2011.06.042

Masud, A. H., & Huang, X. (2012). An e-learning system architecture based on cloud computing. *World Academy of Science. Engineering and Technology, 62*, 74–78.

McConatha, D., Praul, M., & Lynch, M. J. (2008). Mobile learning in higher education: An empirical assessment of a new educational tool. *The Turkish Online Journal of Educational Technology, 7*(3), 15–21.

Mell, P., & Grance, T. (2011). The NIST definition of cloud computing. *Communications of the ACM, 53*(6), 50.

Morita, M. (2003). The Mobile-Based Learning (MBL) in Japan. In *Proceedings of the First Conference on Creating, Connecting and Collaborating through Computing*. Retrieved from http://origin-www.computer.org/csdl/proceedings/c5/2003/1975/00/19750128.pdf

Motiwalla, L. F. (2007). Mobile learning: A framework and evaluation. *Computers & Education, 49*(3), 581–596. doi:10.1016/j.compedu.2005.10.011

Naismith, L., Lonsdale, P., Vavoula, G., & Sharples, M. (2004). Literature review in mobile technologies and learning. Retrieved from http://telearn.archives-ouvertes.fr/docs/00/19/01/43/PDF/Naismith_2004.pdf

Nedungadi, P., & Raman, R. (2012). A new approach to personalization: Integrating e-learning and m-learning. *Educational Technology Research and Development, 60*, 659–678. doi:10.1007/s11423-012-9250-9

Orr, G. (2010). A review of literature in mobile learning: Affordances and constraints. In *Proceedings of the 6th IEEE International Conference on Wireless, Mobile, and Ubiquitous Technologies in Education*, (pp. 107–11). Kaohsiung, Taiwan: IEEE Computer Society Press.

Ozdamli, F., & Cavus, N. (2011). Basic elements and characteristics of mobile learning. *Social and Behavioral Sciences, 28*, 937–942.

Park, Y. (2011). A pedagogical framework for mobile learning: Categorizing educational applications of mobile technologies into four types. *International Review of Research in Open and Distance Learning, 12*(2).

Parsons, D., Ryu, H., & Cranshaw, M. (2007). A design requirements framework for mobile learning environments. *Journal of Computers, 2*(4), 1–8. doi:10.4304/jcp.2.4.1-8

Patten, B., Arnedillo-Sánchez, I., & Tangney, B. (2006). Designing collaborative, constructionist and contextual applications for handheld devices. *Computers & Education, 46*(3), 294–308. doi:10.1016/j.compedu.2005.11.011

Pea, R., & Maldonado, H. (2006). WILD for learning: Interacting through new computing devices anytime, anywhere. In R. K. Sawyer (Ed.), *The Cambridge handbook of the learning sciences* (pp. 427–441). Cambridge, UK: Cambridge University Press.

Peng, H., Su, Y., Chou, C., & Tsai, C. (2009). Ubiquitous knowledge construction: Mobile learning redefined and a conceptual framework. *Innovations in Education and Teaching International, 46*(2), 171–183. doi:10.1080/14703290902843828

Peters, K. (2007). M-learning: Positioning educators for a mobile, connected future. *International Journal of Research in Open and Distance Learning, 8*(2), 1–17.

Pfeiffer, V. D. I., Gemballa, S., Jarodzka, H., Scheiter, K., & Gerjets, P. (2009). Situated learning in the mobile age: Mobile devices on a field trip to the sea. *ALT-J. Research in Learning Technology, 17*(3), 187–199. doi:10.1080/09687760903247666

Quinn, C. (2000). M-learning: Mobile, wireless, in-your-pocket learning. *Linezine: Learning in the new economy*. Retrieved from http://www.linezine.com/2.1/features/cqmmwiyp.htm

Rossing, J. P., Miller, W. M., Cecil, A. K., & Stamper, S. E. (2012). iLearning: The future of higher education? Student perceptions on learning with mobile tablets. *Journal of the Scholarship of Teaching and Learning, 12*(2), 1–26.

Ryokai, K. (2012). Mobile learning with the engineering pathway digital library. *International Journal of Engineering Education, 28*(5), 1119–1126.

Segall, N., Doolen, T., & Porter, D. (2005). A usability comparison of PDA-based quizzes and paper-and-pencil quizzes. *Computers & Education, 45*, 417–432. doi:10.1016/j.compedu.2004.05.004

Seppala, P., & Alamaki, H. (2003). Mobile learning in teacher training. *Journal of Computer Assisted Learning, 19*, 330–335. doi:10.1046/j.0266-4909.2003.00034.x

Seppala, P., Sariola, J., & Kynaslahti, H. (2002). Mobile learning in personnel training of university teachers. In *Proceeding of the IEEE International Workshop on Wireless and Mobile Technologies in Education* (pp. 136-139). IEEE.

Serin, O. (2012). Mobile learning perceptions of the prospective teachers. *The Turkish Online Journal of Educational Technology, 11*(3).

Shanmugapriya, M., & Tamilarasi, A. (2012). Developing a mobile adaptive test (MAT) in an m-learning environment for Android based 3G mobile devices. *International Journal on Computer Science and Engineering, 4*(2), 153–161.

Sharples, M. (2000). The design of personal mobile technologies for lifelong learning. *Computers & Education, 34*, 177–193. doi:10.1016/S0360-1315(99)00044-5

Sharples, M., Corlett, D., & Westmancott, O. (2002). The design and implementation of a mobile learning resource. *Personal and Ubiquitous Computing, 6*(3), 220–234. doi:10.1007/s007790200021

Sharples, M., Taylor, J., & Vavoula, G. (2005). *Towards a theory of mobile learning*. Paper presented at mLearn 2005. Cape Town, South Africa.

Sharples, M., Taylor, J., & Vavoula, G. (2007). A theory of learning for the mobile age. In R. Andrews, & C. Haythornthwaite (Eds.), *The Sage Handbook of E-learning Research* (pp. 221–247). London: Sage.

Shen, R., Wang, M., & Pan, X. (2008). Increasing interactivity in blended classrooms through a cutting-edge mobile learning system. *British Journal of Educational Technology, 39*(6), 1073–1086. doi:10.1111/j.1467-8535.2007.00778.x

Song, Y. (2011). Investigating undergraduate student mobile device use in context. A. Kitchenham (Ed.), Models for interdisciplinary mobile learning: Delivering information to students (pp. 120–136). Hershey, PA: IGI Global for publication.

Stanton, G., & Ophoff, J. (2013). Towards a method for mobile learning design. *Issues in Informing Science and Information Technology*, *10*, 501–523.

Suki, N. M., & Suki, N. M. (2011). Using mobile device for learning: From students' perspective. *US-China Education Review*, 44-53.

Sung, E., & Mayer, R. E. (2013). Online multimedia learning with mobile devices and desktop computers: An experimental test of Clark's methods-not-media hypothesis. *Computers in Human Behavior*, *29*, 639–647. doi:10.1016/j.chb.2012.10.022

Tan, T.-H., Lin, M.-S., Chu, Y.-L., & Liu, T.-Y. (2012). Educational affordances of a ubiquitous learning environment in a natural science course. *Journal of Educational Technology & Society*, *15*(2), 206–219.

Taylor, A. S., & Harper, R. (2002). *Age-old practices in the 'New World': A study of gift-giving between teenage mobile phone users*. Paper presented to the Conference on Human Factors in Computing Systems. Minneapolis, MN.

Thorton, P., & Houser, C. (2002). M-learning in transit. In P. Lewis (Ed.), *The changing face of CALL* (pp. 229–243). Lisse, The Netherlands: Swets and Zeitlinger.

Ting, Y. (2012). The pitfalls of mobile devices in learning: A different view and implications for pedagogical design. *Journal of Educational Computing Research*, *46*(2), 119–134. doi:10.2190/EC.46.2.a

Traxler, J. (2005). *Defining mobile learning*. IADIS International Conference Mobile Learning 2005. Retrieved from http://www.marcosbarros.com.br/ead/file.php/10/200506C018.pdf

Traxler, J., & Bridges, N. (2004). Mobile learning: The ethical and legal challenges. Retrieved from http://www.mobilearn.org/download/events/mlearn_2004/presentations/Traxler.pdf

Triantafillou, E., & Georgiadou, E., & Economides. (2008). The design and evaluation of a computerized adaptive test on mobile devices. *Computers & Education*, *50*, 1319–1330. doi:10.1016/j.compedu.2006.12.005

Turney, C. S. M., Robinson, D., Lee, M., & Soutar, A. (2009). Using technology to direct learning in higher education: The way forward? *Active Learning in Higher Education*, *10*(1), 71–83. doi:10.1177/1469787408100196

Uzunboylu, H., Cavus, N., & Ercag, E. (2009). Using mobile learning to increase environmental awareness. *Computers & Education*, *52*, 381–389. doi:10.1016/j.compedu.2008.09.008

Vavoula, G. N., Lefrere, P., O'Malley, C., & Sharples, M. (2004). *Producing guidelines for learning, teaching and tutoring in a mobile environment*. Paper presented at the 2nd IEEE International Workshop on Wireless and Mobile Technologies in Education (WMTE). Taoyuan, Taiwan.

Vavoula, G. N., & Sharples, M. (2008). Challenges in evaluating mobile informal learning. In *Proceedings of the m-Learn 2008 conference* (pp. 296–303). Wolverhampton.

Walker, K. (2006). Introduction: Mapping the landscape of mobile learning. In M. Sharples (Ed.), *Big issues in mobile learning: Report of a workshop by the kaleidoscope network of excellence mobile learning initiative*. University of Nottingham.

Wang, R., Wiesemes, R., & Gibbons, C. (2012). Developing digital fluency through ubiquitous mobile devices: Findings from a small-scale study. *Computers & Education, 58*(1), 570–578. doi:10.1016/j.compedu.2011.04.013

Wasko, C. (2013). What Teachers Need to Know About Augmented Reality Enhanced Learning Environments. *TechTrends: Linking Research & Practice to Improve Learning, 57*(4), 17–21. doi:10.1007/s11528-013-0672-y

Williams, K. C., Morgan, K., & Cameron, B. A. (2011). How do students define their roles and responsibilities in online learning group projects? *Distance Education, 32*(1), 49–62. doi:10.1080/01587919.2011.565498

Williams, P. W. (2009). Assessing mobile learning effectiveness and acceptance. Retrieved from http://www.scribd.com/doc/95393980/Assessing-Mobile-Learning-Effectiveness-and-Acceptance

Winters, N. (2006). What is mobile learning? In M. Sharples (Ed.), *Big issues in mobile learning: Report of a workshop by the kaleidoscope network of excellence mobile learning initiative*. University of Nottingham.

Woodill, G. (2011). *The mobile learning edge: Tools and technologies for developing your teams*. New York: McGraw-Hill Professional.

Woodill, G. (2013). E-learning vs. m-learning: Same or different? *Chief Learning Officer, 12*(3), 37.

Wright, S., & Parchoma, G. (2011). Technologies for learning? An actor-network theory critique of 'affordances' in research on mobile learning. *Research in learning. Technology (Elmsford, N.Y.), 19*(3), 247–258.

Wu, W. H., Wu, Y. C., Chen, C. Y., Kao, H. Y., Lin, C. H., & Huang, S. H. (2012). Review of trends from mobile learning studies: A meta-analysis. *Computers & Education, 59*, 817–827. doi:10.1016/j.compedu.2012.03.016

Yang, S. (2012). Exploring college students' attitudes and self-efficacy of mobile learning. *The Turkish Online Journal of Educational Technology, 11*(4), 148–154.

Yau, J. Y-K, & Joy, M.S. (2010). Proposal of a mobile learning preferences model. *International Journal of Interactive Mobile Technologies, 4*(4). Retrieved from: http://eprints.dcs.warwick.ac.uk/638/1/yau_joy_ijim_4.pdf

Yi, C. C., Liao, W. P., Huang, C. F., & Hwang, I. H. (2009). Acceptance of mobile learning: a respecification and validation of information system success. Proceedings of World Academy of Science, Engineering and Technology, 41.

Yousef, M. I. (2007). Effectiveness of mobile learning in distance education. *Turkish Online Journal of Distance Education, 8*(4), 114–124.

Zhang, D., & Adipat, B. (2005). Challenges, methodologies, and issues in the usability testing of mobile applications. *International Journal of Human-Computer Interaction, 18*, 293–308. doi:10.1207/s15327590ijhc1803_3

KEY TERMS AND DEFINITIONS

Adaptive Learning: An educational method that enables individualized or personalized learning based on learners' needs, preferences, learning styles, performances, abilities, and contexts.

Augmented Reality: A virtual reality mediated by the use of technology that places digital objects to the real world context to assist people's interaction with and understanding of the context.

Broadband: A wide bandwidth enabling high speed data transmission.

Cloud Computing: A computing model for providing ubiquitous access to data, software applications, platforms, infrastructures, and services over the Internet. It is flexible and scalable in that it shares pools of computing resources to address on-demand network access.

E-Learning Platform: A framework or a learning environment that supports and enhances teaching and learning through information and communication technologies by integrating and providing tools, resources and services.

Mobile Learning: Learning mediated and facilitated by the use of wireless communication and mobile technologies.

Ubiquitous Learning: Anytime, anywhere learning that is made possible by advanced technologies.

Usability: The quality of a user's experience with products or systems. It focuses on making products and systems easy to learn and easy to use to increase their effectiveness, efficiency, and the overall satisfaction of the user.

Chapter 5
Teacher Development, Support, and Training with Mobile Technologies

Nance S. Wilson
State University of New York at Cortland, USA

Vassiliki (Vicky) I. Zygouris-Coe
University of Central Florida, USA

Victoria M. Cardullo
Auburn University, USA

ABSTRACT

Preparing teachers to integrate iPads into the classroom requires designing professional development that supports teacher knowledge development as well as the development of a teacher as metacognitive. In this chapter, the authors describe training and support that builds teachers' development of a Metacognitive Technological Pedagogical Framework (M-TPACK) for integrating iPads. The professional development emphasizes the metacognitive teacher with positive dispositions towards technology integration as a key factor in ensuring that teachers implement knowledge of content, technology, pedagogy, and students. Finally, this chapter presents authentic and relevant examples for teacher development with mobile technologies.

INTRODUCTION

Technological advancements have changed the way we communicate, learn, create, share, and publish information, and have even changed the way we live in the 21st century. Some predict that the number of mobile devices will exceed the entire planet's population at the end of 2013 (Cisco, 2012). The mobile learning (m-learning) transformation as well as the functionality and cost of mobile devices has made learning and education possible in diverse settings. Mobile devices have been changing the lives and learning of millions of people around the world in ways we could not have imagined a couple of decades ago. For example, a young woman in Bangladesh now

DOI: 10.4018/978-1-4666-6284-1.ch005

has access to countless English language lessons and quizzes where before her only access to an education would be at a brick and mortar school to which she was forbidden to attend. Mobile technologies, once marketed primarily for entertainment for communication purposes, have actually come to play a significant role in economies and cultures (United Nations Educational, Scientific and Cultural Organization [UNESCO], 2013). In addition to changing cultures and economies, mobile phones and tablet computers are used by educators around the world to access information, enrich students' education, and facilitate learning in various creative ways.

Mobile learning (m-learning) involves the use of mobile technologies, either alone or in combination with other information and communication technologies (ICT), to enable learning anytime and anywhere. Learning can manifest in different ways: people can use mobile devices to access educational resources, connect with others, or create content, both inside and outside classrooms. More and more schools are adopting m-learning devices because of portability, affordability, and flexibility factors. Cell phones, smartphones, iPods, Personal Digital Assistants (PDAs), tablets, and e-readers (i.e., iPad, Kindle, Nook) are increasingly becoming the teaching and learning tools of choice for today's K-20 educators. Mobile devices have the following common characteristics: they are digital, easily portable, are ubiquitous, usually owned and controlled by an individual rather than institution(s), can access the Internet, have multimedia capabilities, and can facilitate a number of tasks, particularly those related to communication.

Because m-learning technologies are more affordable and more easily managed than computers, m-learning requires reconceptualizing traditional models of technology use and implementation, as m-learning requires students to have uninterrupted, ubiquitous, and greater access to technology. Mobile learning technologies have tremendous potential for learning in innovative, creative, metacognitive, and rigorous ways. For example, the implementation of ConnectEd, a strategic initiative to connect 99% of American students to the internet within five years (Munoz & Sperling, 2013) will put more internet enabled devices such as iPads into the hands of more students. The ever-increasing availability of m-learning technologies in educational settings calls for policy makers to rethink m-learning's purpose in K-20 learning and requires a pedagogical framework for effective use of m-learning for teaching and learning purposes.

iPads are multifunction devices that can be used for everything from reading e-textbooks, document creation, video viewing, and creation to web surfing. iPads came to the market in 2010 with a promise to bring instant access to books, media, and affordable educational applications. The iPad allows for the user to move easily from reading an e-book to searching the Internet. Research on the use of mobile applications for academic purposes have demonstrated that effective and consistent use of particular applications will improve academic achievement (Perkins, Hamm, Pamplin, Morris, & McKelvain, 2011; Heinrich, n.d.; McClanahan, 2012). This research along with the promise of less expensive and updated e-books, hands-on personalized experiences, and the adaptive capabilities such as speech recognition and text to speech (D'Orio, 2011) have brought iPads into K-20 classrooms.

There is more to harnessing the power of the iPad than simply putting it in the hands of teachers and students. In a classroom where the teacher and students use iPads for academic purposes, the teacher needs to determine how they can best utilize the device to improve student achievement regarding curricular goals. This requires that the teacher develop knowledge of the device as well as the applications, and/or e-books that can support teaching and learning.

In this chapter, we will discuss the importance of teacher professional development and support with m-learning technologies and we will also offer suggestions for implementing iPads in the K-20 classroom. Our suggestions stem from lessons learned from research with elementary (Cardullo, Zygouris-Coe, Wilson, Craneen, & Stafford, 2012; Sheppard, 2011; Wilson, Zygouris-Coe, & Cardullo, In Press) and secondary level students and teachers (Cardullo, 2013; Perkins et al., 2011). We approach the training and support of the teacher from the standpoint of a Metacognitive Technological Pedagogical Content Knowledge (M-TPACK) (Wilson, Zygouris-Coe, Cardullo, & Fong, 2013). From this research we have learned that introducing the iPad into classrooms requires strategic and relevant professional development for teachers that focuses on both developing their knowledge about ways to use iPads to support teaching and learning as well as the development of metacognition in teachers. In this chapter, we describe why this type of professional development is called for and also provide specific examples for supporting teachers as they implement iPad use in their classrooms for academic learning purposes.

A FRAMEWORK FOR PROFESSIONAL DEVELOPMENT

The professional development framework for implementing iPads is built upon the Metacognitive Technological Pedagogical Content Knowledge (M-TPACK) framework (Wilson et al., 2013). The framework stems from two areas of work for effective teaching and learning: (a) Technological Pedagogical Content Knowledge (TPACK) (Mishra & Koehler, 2006) and (b) teacher dispositions towards technology in the classroom.

Technological Pedagogical Content Knowledge (TPACK)

TPACK (Mishra & Koehler, 2006) stems from the work on Pedagogical Content Knowledge by Shulman (1987). The premise of this work is that teachers have areas of overlapping and interacting knowledge that play key roles in teachers' success in the classroom. Mishra and Koehler (2006) bring Shulman's work into the era of technology with a strong focus on the flexible and intentional integration of technology knowledge in discipline specific teaching (Harris, Mishra, & Koehler, 2009). The TPACK framework emphasizes the connections between teachers' knowledge of content, pedagogy, and technology. In this model, teachers integrate content, pedagogical, and technical knowledge to create and utilize new knowledge throughout the instructional process. The complexity of teaching with technology affects how a teacher understands and approaches content as well as pedagogy thus forcing an examination of the interaction of all three factors of the framework. At the heart of TPACK, is the knowledge that teachers possess and the ways that they implement that knowledge. When implementing knowledge to integrate technology, teachers are faced with solving problems having large amounts of information without one correct solution (Voss & Post, 1988). These ill structured problems that are encountered by teachers result in beliefs playing a major role in teaching (Nespor, 1987). Beliefs are a part of the construct known as dispositions.

Teacher Dispositions about Technology

Merriam-Webster defines disposition (n.d.) as "a tendency to act or think in a particular way" (http://www.merriam-webster.com/dictionary/disposition10/2/13). Eberly, Rand, and O'Conner (2007) define disposition by how teachers respond in specific ways under specific conditions. All teachers have dispositions that affect how they plan, enact, and reflect upon instruction. Wasicsko (2004) states that teacher behaviors are based on her dispositions. In other words, dispositions refer to teacher attitudes, perceptions or beliefs, and personal characteristics that become the foundation for teacher behavior(s) (Damon, 2005). Key teacher dispositions include: (a) interactions with students; (b) professional ethics and practices; (c) effective communication; (d) planning and teaching for student learning; and, (e) sensitivity to diversity and equity. Since a teacher's dispositions are demonstrated by her verbal and non-verbal behaviors as she plans, teaches, and interacts with students, families, and other stakeholders, it is important to consider the role these affective teacher qualities play in effective instruction of students (National Council for Accreditation of Teacher Education, 2010). Thus, in classrooms aiming to integrate technology, a teacher's disposition(s) towards technology are important as according to Serdyuko and Ferguson (2011) "significantly affect how teachers will transfer knowledge into their classroom and how they will model the desired behaviors and attitudes" to their students (as cited in Serdyuko & Hill, 2007, p. 107). When designing professional development aimed at integrating iPads in the classroom, it is imperative that the experiences provided affect three categories of teachers' disposition toward technology: self, teaching, and text.

Disposition of self is known as self-efficacy. A teacher's self-efficacy is defined as her beliefs about capabilities to effect student learning. Bandura (1997) described self-efficacy as the beliefs of one's capabilities that influence everything from choice of behavior, to amount of effort, to emotional response to success. Ertmer and Ottenbreit-Leftwich (2010) explain the connection between self-efficacy and technology by stating "although knowledge of technology is necessary, it is not enough if teachers do not also feel confident using that knowledge to facilitate student learning" (p. 261). In support of the need to develop teachers self-efficacy for technology, Albion (2001) found that the amount of time spent using computers was directly related to self-efficacy. For instance, a teacher who is not adept or interested in using a computer for tasks such as tracking grades, emailing, or writing letters is less likely to envision ways to engage students with technology. Similarly, a science teacher who sees technology as something for writing papers may not be likely to engage with technology for laboratory simulations because she does not see a connection to this aspect of her content area. Based on this research, a teacher's self-efficacy regarding the use of iPads in the classroom is related to her integration of the technology. Therefore, in developing professional development for integrating iPads in the classroom, it is key that the training fosters the development of teacher self-efficacy.

A teacher's beliefs towards teaching are also a key factor in her disposition toward integrating iPads into the classroom. iPads, like much of the technology resources available in schools, offer a variety of ways to access content, process ideas, and have students demonstrate what they know (Wahl & Duffield, 2005). The technology lends itself to a student-centered teaching approach. Honey and Moeller (1990) found that teachers with a strong student-centered approach to teaching were more likely to integrate these types of technologies than teachers with more traditional approaches. Becker and Ravitz (2001) confirmed this when they found that constructivist beliefs foster computer use. Judson (2006) and Totter, Stutz, and Grote (2006) also confirmed the effect of student-centered beliefs on teacher technology integration. For instance, a teacher who conceives learning as teacher-centered may not be willing to use technology to individualize instruction or to create less structured tasks that allow students to engage in independent research. Teachers need support and training that foster a constructivist approach to teaching as they learn about integrating iPads into their classroom.

The discussion of teachers' dispositions regarding the integration of technology would not be complete without considering a teacher's beliefs about the nature of texts. A teacher who sees text as static or only print-based will not be disposed to teach students skills and strategies for reading and using interactive and multimodal text or for gaining knowledge from alternative forms of text.

For instance, iPads have the capacity to integrate video, audio recording, and text all within one e-book (Hurd, 2012). These changes in the way communication occurs in the classroom raise questions about how the teacher will implement literacy instruction (Bezemer & Kress, 2008; Jewitt, 2013; Leander & Frank, 2006; Unsworth, 2008). The changing nature of text in iPads highlights the importance of designing professional development for teachers that addresses their conception of text as they integrate iPads in the classroom.

The Role of the Metacognitive Teacher in M-Learning

Understanding a teacher's beliefs toward herself, teaching and text in the iPad classroom is incomplete without considering the manner in which the teacher will demonstrate these beliefs in the classroom. Since teaching and learning situations often bring about ill-defined problems involving a variety of competing forces (Lampert, 2001), teachers need to consider how they might need to adapt their teaching before, during, and after instruction. The adaptive teacher is metacognitive. She is informed by her knowledge and her beliefs and is flexible throughout the instructional process. For instance, when planning for instruction, teachers must anticipate the possible diverse learning paths of students, interruptions to classroom learning, and stumbling blocks that may arise within the execution of the lesson. For example, Vogt and Rogalla (2009) stated that during teaching a metacognitive educator "notices lack of understanding, diminishing of concentration, and the onset of disruptions and acts accordingly, adjusting the course of the planned lesson during implementation" (p. 1052). After teaching, the educator allows time for instructional adaptations. The metacognitive teacher responds immediately to unanticipated situations by making conscious and deliberate decisions utilizing her knowledge and dispositions (Duffy et al., 2009; Lin, Schwartz & Hatano, 2005). When Lin (2001) tried to implement a new technological artifact into her teaching she was forced to adopt new teaching routines from the presentation of material to how she had students working on math problems. As she evaluated her situation, she transitioned from her normal teaching approach to a more hands-on approach, thus becoming a more adaptive teacher. In this case, "metacognition served as a mechanism for problem finding, for setting adaptive goals, for identity building, and for value clarification" (Lin, Schwartz & Hatano, 2005, p. 249). The adaptations occurred during periods of reflection that followed teaching. A metacognitive teacher is disposed to responding to unanticipated and complex situations in an adaptive manner.

Being a metacognitive teacher is often defined as teacher disposition because it is influenced by the teacher's self-efficacy, beliefs about teaching and views of text, as well as the teacher's ability to reflect on an ongoing basis, monitor, and evaluate her instruction and students' learning. A teacher's disposition towards being metacognitive depends upon her beliefs regarding the need to adapt instruction throughout the instructional process. A teacher who believes that they have competency with technology and content while understanding their students' learning needs, and a variety of pedagogical approaches that will help them meet their goals, will be more likely to reflect, adjust, and adapt their teaching as needed. A teacher who is disposed to a learner-centered approach to teaching will be more likely to change course based on the students' needs. Finally, the teacher's view of text affects the ways in which the teacher adapts her curriculum to meet student needs and instructional goals. These separate dispositions partially determine how teachers respond to a teaching situation, and whether or not they make instructional adjustments and modifications to support students' learning needs. Thus the effective teacher in an e-reader classroom is a metacognitive teacher. This view is supported by research that demonstrated that the effective teacher adapts her instruction based on her knowledge of students, pedagogy, content, and context (Duffy, 2005; Duffy et al., 2010; Lin, 2001; Little et al., 2007; Zohar, 2006).

A classroom that integrates technology requires the metacognitive teacher to use her knowledge of students, technology, and content and pedagogy, to adapt her teaching to the specific needs of the class before, during, and after teaching. For instance, when planning to teach students about the presidential election, the teacher must first examine the learning goals, the content, the students' needs, tools (e.g. books, resources), and strategies prior to instruction. She will need to think about how she might organize the materials to assure that the lesson is differentiated and meets all students' needs. An app that can assist teachers in doing this is *Flipbook*. *Flipbook* allows the teacher to put numerous articles and materials into a digital magazine that students can flip through on their iPad. By creating her own magazine the teacher can use her knowledge of students' learning styles, comprehension, and background knowledge of the topic to prepare a combination of articles that is "just right" for her students.

If the teacher wants students to create a graphic organizer about the candidates, she has to choose another application using her knowledge of students' prior experiences with applications, such as *Glogster*, *Wordle*, or *Mindmeister*, as well as general experience with different kinds of graphic organizers. When guiding students to create the graphic organizer on the properties of matter, a teacher can use an application such as *Mindmeister* (Figure 1). The teacher will need to respond to students' content questions, web application questions, and possible issues when using both applications. After teaching this lesson, the teacher will need to review her choices to determine how they helped students to the curricular goals, how she used the iPad to meet instructional, pedagogical, content, technological, and learning goals, and how she managed student learning to determine if any changes in her instruction are necessary.

Metacognitive Technological Pedagogical Content Knowledge (M-TPACK)

The Metacognitive Technological Pedagogical Content Knowledge (M-TPACK) framework (Wilson, Zygouris-Coe, Cardullo, & Fong, 2013) is a valuable vehicle for understanding, building, and sustaining teacher integration of technology in the classroom. M-TPACK views teacher knowledge as the cornerstones of effective teaching and learning. It places teachers' metacognitive decision-making skills and dispositions at the front and center of the framework. The engine of knowledge moves the car; but it is the power steering of the metacognitive teacher that moves in the direction that builds student achievement. The framework includes four types of knowledge that are needed for moving student achievement in the iPad classroom: content, pedagogical, technological, and student knowledge (see Figure 2).

Content knowledge refers to the teacher's subject matter knowledge and pedagogical content knowledge. Subject matter knowledge is related directly to the intellectual ideas, facts, and information of a particular content. Pedagogical content knowledge (Shulman, 1987) is the interaction between the teaching process and content knowledge. This refers to content-specific techniques a teacher knows and uses for teaching content. The metacognitive teacher disposed toward technological integration in her teaching and in student learning will also be supported by her knowledge of content to evaluate and analyze websites and applications for appropriateness for teaching the content and assure that instruction facilitates student content knowledge.

Pedagogical knowledge refers to general classroom procedures as well as teaching methods and processes. The metacognitive teacher who uses iPads in her classroom for academic purposes establishes specific classroom procedures around the use of iPads including sharing information,

Figure 1. Image of Mindmeister

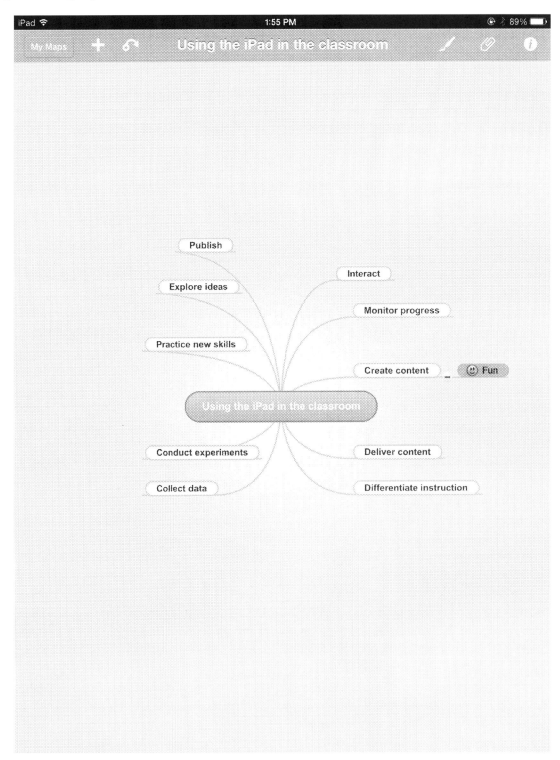

Figure 2. Pedagogical framework for e-readers in the classroom (Wilson, Zygouris-Coe, Cardullo, & Fong, 2013)

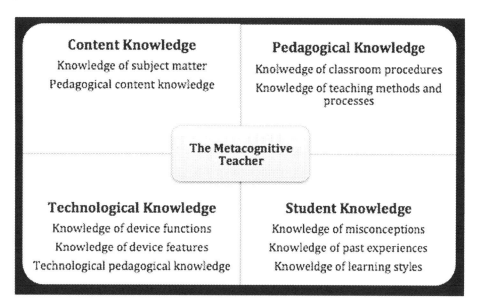

Note. This figure illustrates a pedagogical framework for using of e-readers in any classroom. The figure highlights the importance of explicit teacher instruction for the development of student metacognition that is particularly important to 21st century learning.

developing, retrieving and returning of assignments, as well as the sharing of the teacher's iPad with the class for modeling content and procedures. The teacher develops differentiated lessons using various texts and applications. She monitors student progress and evaluates both the effectiveness of the e-reader and the teaching methods and procedures.

The teacher's knowledge of her students includes knowledge of students' misconceptions and past experiences as well as their learning styles and learning needs. The teacher uses iPads to develop students' knowledge of technology, content, and learning needs and to develop appropriate curricular supports. The metacognitive teacher's knowledge of students equips her with flexibility in her application and implementation of iPads. The teacher's disposition towards technology and adaptability in teaching will affect the classroom environment and create a sense that all students can learn.

Lastly, the teacher's technological knowledge, her knowledge of the device's structure, functions and features, as well as her knowledge of how the device can be used to enhance student thinking and learning of the content, are important factors for effective use of iPads in any classroom. The teacher needs to understand the functions of the device and of each application. In using the iPad, the teacher needs to know how to choose relevant applications and download them, choose shortcuts for navigating from one application to another, ways to share website URLs with students, how to share her screen with students, how to use selected applications and device features for learning, etc.

At the center of the framework is the metacognitive teacher. The metacognitive teacher responds to the demands of a classroom integrating iPads by flexibly applying her knowledge of students, content, pedagogy, and technology within the content of her dispositions towards technology integration. The adaptations take place before, during, and after teaching. The metacognitive teacher has strong self-efficacy regarding her teaching with technology. She is confident in her knowledge of the technology, content, pedagogy, and students. The metacognitive teacher views teaching as student-centered by focusing her teaching on building students' understanding of content using technology. She also views learning as a multimodal undertaking. The teacher at the center of the framework uses different types of knowledge to make metacognitive decisions before, during, and after instruction. The framework highlights the role and importance of a metacognitive teacher; however only professional development and support that is geared at addressing teachers' dispositions will promote metacognitive teachers.

TEACHER TRAINING AND SUPPORT FOR iPAD INTEGRATION IN THE CLASSROOM

Professional development is the vehicle through which teacher educators train and support teachers to make changes in their practice. The goal of professional development is to improve student learning. In a study of twenty-five international school systems, Barber and Mourshed (2007) examined the factors that resulted in improved student outcomes including how school systems develop teachers' ability to teach well. They found that good professional development is concrete or relevant and classroom-based. When implementing iPads, individuals who have "reviewed the app, run trials of the app in the classroom with students, evidence of the impact on teaching and learning, and can convey this experience to others in a framework for replication" (Mahaley, 2013, p. 1). Other meta-studies of professional development initiatives have identified mentoring and coaching (Day, Sammons, Kington, Gu, & Stobart, 2006; Hobson et al., 2006, 2007; Vogt & Rogalla, 2009) which allows for two or more colleagues to work together to develop knowledge of the device and applications to support implementation. This type of professional development is sustained and has demonstrated effectiveness in developing teacher's abilities to improve student achievement (Cordingley, Bell, Thomason & Firth, 2005; Guskey & Yoon, 2009).

In designing professional development to ensure improved student learning and successful implementation of the iPad, teachers need training and support that follows what we know about successful professional development initiatives. Effective professional development must be concrete and classroom-based, involve mentoring and/or coaching, and be sustained overtime.

In the past, initiatives focused on preparing teachers for using technology in the classroom have been defined not by instructional content, but by the technology (Harris, 2008). The approaches that dominate past technology integration have been focused on software, sample resources, technology additions to current practices, technology-focused courses, and acquisition of hardware and software (Harris, Mishra, & Koehler, 2009). These initiatives lead to integration efforts constrained not by what students need to learn, but by the affordances of the technology. Classrooms, however, need technology integration that recognizes the realities of the content, students, and school (American Association of Colleges of Teacher Education, 2008). In order to prepare teachers to integrate technology in a manner that honors each discipline, students, technology, and pedagogy, we must also ensure that teachers approach teaching with self-regulation and awareness (Wilson et al., 2013).

The training and support to develop a pedagogical framework that ubiquitously and authentically integrates iPads into the classroom requires a teacher who is sensitive to the demands of implementing iPads in the classroom and willing to make changes to her pedagogical moves throughout the instructional process; in other words, it requires a teacher who is metacognitive. According to Duffy et al. (2010) ". . . teachers can learn to be metacognitive, and that both cognitive and dispositional aspects of professional development can be designed to intentionally encourage teachers to become metacognitive professionals" (p. 10). The need to design professional development for integrating iPads that builds metacognitive teachers is highlighted by the results garnered from a recent study on using the iPad for educational learning (Cardullo, 2013). Cardullo (2013) found that additional reading, cognitive, and technological demands were placed on the readers, as they read nonfiction text using the iPad. The new skills and strategies required by the device highlighted the need for the teacher who is:

1. Aware of students' levels of content and technological knowledge,
2. Cognizant of the pedagogical moves necessary for classroom management and application of the skills and strategies related to the content as well as the iPad,
3. The conscious application of "instructional techniques that support student thinking and learning along with an understanding of key instructional strategies" (Wilson et al., 2013, p. 13) is required.

Findings from this study (Cardullo, 2013), illustrated the changing role of the teacher and the need for a metacognitive teacher. Thus designing professional development that supports the M-PACK framework (Wilson et al., 2013).

Facilitating Teacher Metacognition

Professional development that builds the metacognitive teacher focuses on an educative model (Duffy, Miller, Parsons, & Meloth, 2009). In this model, the professional development is sustained and embedded in the classroom as teachers use what they are learning to construct knowledge that will improve practice. This model prepares teachers to address the ill-defined problems that are brought about by integrating iPads into teaching and learning. The professional development needs to first provide opportunities for teachers to build self-efficacy, constructivist views of teaching, and multi-modal views of text. The second step is to engage the teacher in mentoring and support activities over time that help teachers to integrate and reflect on iPads in the classroom, discuss challenges and problem solve and build reflective practice.

Promoting Positive Teacher Dispositions toward iPad Integration in the Classroom

The development of a metacognitive teacher should begin with building teachers' confidence with technology (Bauer & Kenton, 2005) and their confidence that their instructional goals will be addressed with technology (Wozney, Venkatesh, & Abrami, 2006). Below is a list of suggested activities developed by our own research and other studies included in this chapter aimed at building teachers' self-efficacy toward technology integration.

1. Support from the school administrator to learn, experiment, and collaborate with others about iPads and how to use them in the classroom (Somekh, 2008).
2. Demonstrations by instructional coaches, other teachers at the school, or professional development providers of how iPads can support student learning (Kanaya, Light, & Culp, 2005).
3. Time to acclimate, practice, and build knowledge of the iPads (Somekh, 2008).
4. Time to apply applications to content prior to introducing the devices and/or applications to students (Hennessey, Ruthven, & Brindley, 2005).
5. Time to reflect, discuss, and problem-solve about implementation, instructional, pedagogical, technological, or student learning challenges (Hennessey et al., 2005).

6. Collaborations with outside experts, peers, technology specialists, and curriculum coaches (Ertmer, Ottenbreit-Leftwich, & York, 2006).

Establishing positive experiences for teachers with iPads is key for building their beliefs in the technology and confidence to apply it as an instructional tool (Mueller, Wood, Willoughby, Ross, & Specht, 2008). For instance, when demonstrating the versitility of the application *DataAnalysis* (Figure 3) for the iPad, science teachers will be able to see how the iPad can provide students with practice understanding and creating data charts as well as the relationship between the data in an experiment. The nature of the application to relate specifically to the content will provide a frame for teachers to view the iPad as a positive component of their classroom instruction. Additionally, the use of this application can assist teachers in building their understanding of text as multi-modal. By viewing the data entered into the application in a variety of ways, and by manipulating the data the text is presented multi-modally.

This initial step involved providing teachers with time to learn how to use iPads. Teachers also need time to acclimate, practice, and build iPad knowledge. Once being introduced to the iPad teachers need to apply what they have learned for professional uses prior to planning classroom integration. They need time to build and change their beliefs about teaching and learning to develop a more student-centered perception of teaching and learning. A series of longitudinal studies found that being given time and support for integrating technology into the classroom led to changes in teachers' beliefs towards teaching and learning (Hennessey et al., 2005; Levin & Wadmany, 2005; Sandholtz, Ringstaff, & Dwyer, 1997). For instance, the application *Noteability* allows teachers to work with documents in a variety of formats and then save the documents to a shared folder through a cloud service such as *Dropbox* or *Google Drive*. Teachers can use *Noteability* to take notes during faculty meetings and then share these notes with colleagues. Teachers can also integrate flowcharts, images, or videos into their notes. Given adequate time to explore and use this application is particularly useful in building teachers' concept of text as multi-modal because they can create a document reflecting their own experiences that also includes a variety of texts. Thus, giving them the opportunity to practice skills that they will use with their students. Additionally, it will give them a chance to see any problems that arise which can then be addressed prior to working with students. This provides the teacher with the ability to understand the technological processes and develop adaptive teaching strategies to help differentiate learning for indiviudal students' needs. The teacher will also see how using the application can provide opportunities for more student-centered activities.

Also related to building positive dispositions and adaptive teaching through general practice with iPads, teachers need time to apply content-specific applications prior to requiring students to do so. These experiences should provide teachers with opportunities that support a student-centered approach to teaching. For instance, before having students use *Timeline Builder* (Figure 4), teachers should practice using the application to create their own timelines and then demonstrate for the entire class (or small groups of students) how the application works and its multimodal capabilities. Scaffolding both teacher and student experiences in these ways builds positive experiences with the device and provides teachers and students with multiple experiences that develop skills and adaptive learning and teaching strategies.

Providing Teacher Support for iPad Use in the Classroom

Once teachers have been provided with ample time to build academic experiences with the e-reader and its application, they will need support from peers and instructional coaches (curriculum and/

Figure 3. Image of scientific data

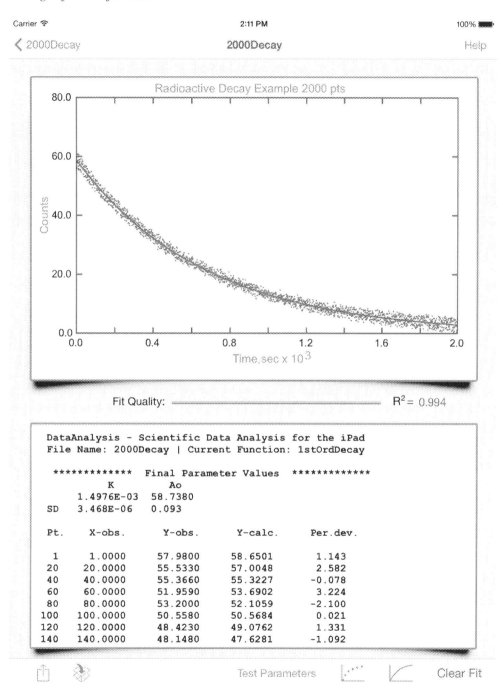

or technology) to successfully implement iPads to assure she acts as a metacognitive teacher. This support takes place most effectively with Professional Learning Communities (PLC) (Dufour, 2004) and co-teaching opportunities. PLCs that focus on technology integration in the classroom can be used to promote technology efforts and help teachers focus on improving student achievement,

Figure 4. Timeline builder

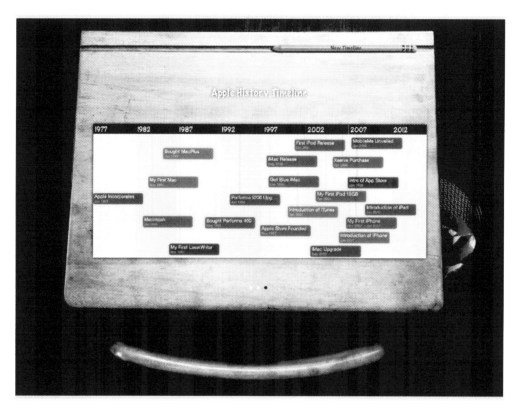

learning, and teacher collaboration. In addition, a PLC focused on the integration of iPads in the classroom, supports teachers possessing similar dispositions regarding teaching and learning.

Participation in a PLC focused on using iPads supports the teacher's disposition as a metacognitive teacher because it will allow her to discuss with colleagues the adaptations that are needed to ensure that all students are learning. The culture of collaboration created by the PLC provides a sounding board for developing best practices and solving problems. Finally, the fact that PLCs must focus on results will keep teachers grounded in developing effective ways to implement technology versus focusing on the potential problems that these technologies may pose. To be an effective metacognitive teacher, one has to envision the final objectives of technology integration (m-learning and iPads in the classroom). PLCs can be used as a means of school-based professional development to support this integration of technology.

The second factor in supporting the development of metacognitive teachers in their implementation of iPads is to create opportunities for co-teaching. Co-teaching is when two or more professionals deliver substantive instruction within a single classroom (Friend & Cook, 2003). Although co-teaching is most often associated with special education teachers and classroom teachers, we believe that co-teaching can serve as an effective model for supporting teachers when integrating iPads in the classroom. Co-teaching involves co-planning and active instruction by both teachers in the classroom. To support a teacher who is integrating iPads into the classroom, a professional development provider, a PLC teammate, or technology coordinator should co-plan a lesson with the classroom teacher. When co-planning the teachers work to assure both teachers are knowledgeable about the technology, the planned technology use, and determine the instructional techniques and/or co-teaching model that will support instruction, thus enhancing the learning of both teachers. When teaching the lesson it is important that the teachers stick to the co-teaching model decided upon during planning and to communicate using unobtrusive signals if adaptive strategies such as increased lesson time need to be implemented (Murawski & Dieker, 2004).

For example, when introducing *Subtext*, an iPad application that allows groups to read and annotate the same text simultaneously, to seventh graders the first author worked with the classroom teacher on several goals including: first, choose an appropriate text, second reviewing students' knowledge of close reading skills, and finally to practice using the application. When first introducing the application, the teacher and co-teacher showed the students their practice text with conversation, then modeled the first paragraph for the students, and continued to actively participate in the discussion of the text with the students throughout the reading process. While students were working both teachers walked around the room assisting students with questions on the technology, application, and close reading. This use of co-teaching supported the development of the metacognitive teacher because the classroom teacher had the opportunity to see adaptations in real time and had support when recognizing that adaptations need to be made.

Developing Teachers' Knowledge about Using iPads in the Classroom

The M-TPACK framework sets the stage for professional development that focuses on both developing the metacognitive teacher and building the knowledge cornerstones required to integrate technology. In the previous section, exemplars were provided that demonstrate techniques used to facilitate teacher metacognition by promoting positive dispositions toward iPad integration and providing teacher support for using iPads in the classroom. In implementing these practices, teachers develop strong self-efficacy towards their ability to integrate technology, envision teaching as student-centered, and see how the multi-modal aspects of the technology applies to their teaching. In developing these capacities, teachers will be more likely to transfer that knowledge to their classrooms (Hughes, 2005; Snoeyink & Ertmer, 2001/2002).

Many of the instructional strategies presented above also develop teachers' knowledge of technology and pedagogy. The following section presents techniques for supporting and training teachers in developing their knowledge cornerstones, i.e., content, pedagogy, technology, and students. In working to develop these support mechanisms, it is imperative to provide teachers with concrete applications, mentoring and/or coaching, as well as time to learn, apply, and integrate their knowledge into the classroom.

Training and Support That Develops Teacher Content Knowledge

Content knowledge consists of the teacher's knowledge of subject matter. With teachers who are implementing iPads in their classroom, it is important to demonstrate how certain applications can build their content knowledge. For instance, social studies teachers can explore the *Guttenberg Project* application, *History Maps of the World* (Figure 5), or *Today in History*. They can evaluate how these applications could support their curriculum and use them to build upon their own knowledge.

Training and Support That Develops Teacher Pedagogical Knowledge

Pedagogical knowledge refers to the teachers' knowledge of instructional techniques that support teaching and learning. In implementing iPads

Figure 5. History: Maps of the World

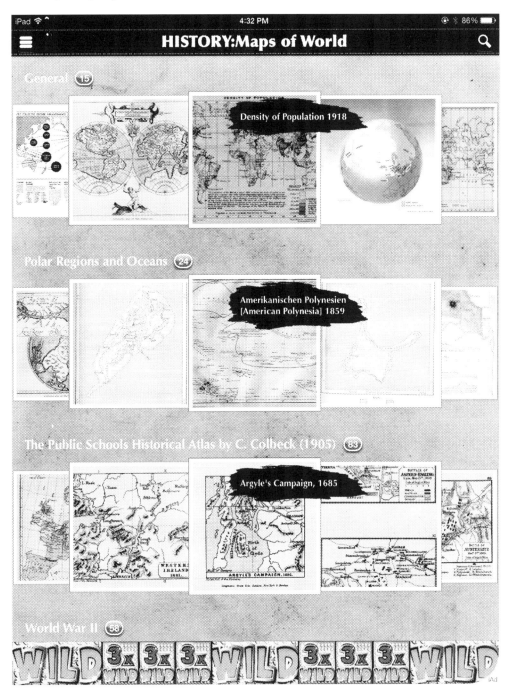

in the classroom, there are a multitude of issues to address when building teachers' pedagogical knowledge. These include, but are not limited to, techniques for sharing screens (Box 1), managing *Cloud* applications, and assessing student work on the iPad. For the purpose of this chapter, we are going to focus on training and supporting teachers to utilize the *Cloud*. The *Cloud* provides teachers

Box 1. Ways that teachers can share their iPad screen with students

> Sharing your screen with a projector:
> - VGA Adapter.
> - Document Camera.
> - AppleTV.
> - Reflector.
> - AirServer.
>
> Sharing your screen or presentations directly with students:
> - Haiku Deck.
> - Educreations.
> - Showme.
> - Nearpod.

and students opportunities to share documents and folders across devices without using email. Many of these tools work across platforms and devices. In working with a teacher to utilize *Google Drive*, we first helped the teacher set up the account. Then we worked with her to create folders, and then we shared folders with each other, and then shared documents within the folders. When introducing *Google Drive* to the students we co-planned and co-taught the lesson. First, helping students to create folders and share the folders. Then, we created a document using the class computer and shared it with the students. The students opened the document, saved it with their name and placed it in the shared folder with the teacher. The teacher was then able to assess students' knowledge regarding the use of *Google Drive*. Throughout this process we developed the teacher's pedagogical knowledge about managing student work while utilizing iPads. The pedagogical techniques for managing student work and actions around turning in and returning work added to the teacher's pedagogical knowledge about iPads. The co-teaching provided the coaching support while the availability of the support throughout the year helped to build pedagogical knowledge overtime.

Training and Support That Develops Teacher Technological Knowledge

Technological knowledge includes teachers' knowledge of the technology, how to use the technology, and how the technology can be integrated in the learning process. The support and training needed to build technology knowledge requires providing a variety of experiences using the technology in authentic contexts. These experiences involve demonstrations of how to move from one application to another, how to close an application, how to use a particular application, and how to take a screen shot with the device. This training occurs formally and informally. For instance, in demonstrating the capabilities of *Notability* (Figure 6) the technology coach may help a teacher find an appropriate website, bookmark it, then return to the home screen to open *Notability*, then add the website to a *Notability* document. To conserve battery life, the teacher needs to learn how to close programs by double clicking the "home" button and then "pushing" the open applications up. The teacher will also want to learn how to organize her applications. This can occur through a formal demonstration of holding down an application until it "shakes" then moving it on top of another application to create a "folder" of similar applications. All of these examples, as well as those discussed previously, are examples of ways to develop teachers' knowledge of iPad technology in ways that support technological knowledge.

Training and Support That Promotes Teacher Knowledge of Students

Knowledge of students includes knowledge of students' characteristics, academic needs, abili-

Figure 6. Notability

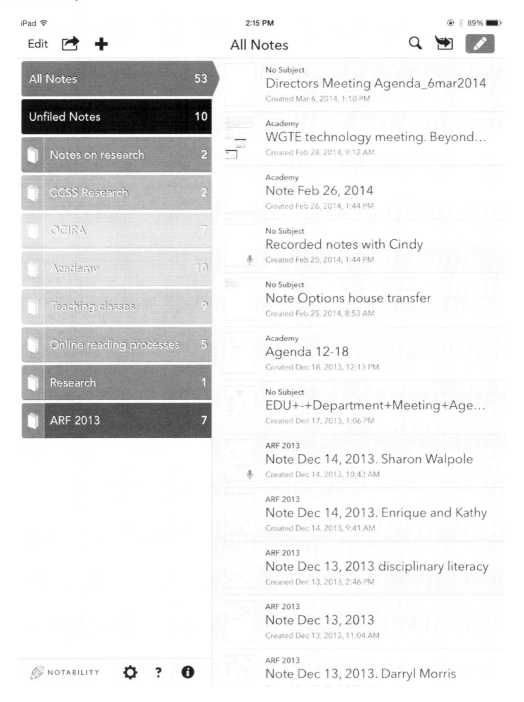

ties, content knowledge, prior experiences with iPads, and interests. Professional development that supports teachers' knowledge of students should focus on understanding the content expectations of the previous grades; the teacher will need to familiarize herself with the applications and techniques for which students have used the devices. If the iPads are new to the school, teachers need to find out what if any experience the students have had with the devices. This can be accomplished through informal class discussions, surveys, and observation. Next, the teacher needs to learn about her students' interests and learning styles. An interest survey that asks students about books, sports games, television shows, movies, etc. that they enjoy will inform the teacher of the students' personal interests. Another survey that could be helpful to teachers in planning instruction would be a survey on students' metacognitive skills (such as monitoring, strategy application, decision making processes) and/or knowledge of the iPad. Surveys of metacognitive skills such as the Metacognitive Awareness of Reading Strategies Inventory (Mokhtari & Reichard, 2002), can inform the teacher of a student's knowledge of ways to solve problems in reading. The teacher created student surveys for use on the iPad, which asked questions such how to switch between applications, what they need to do to open a new tab in Safari, how to put the device to sleep, etc. This survey, will inform the teacher about what students know about the iPad. Surveying students about their iPad knowledge, interests, and learning about content knowledge will provide teachers with some of the knowledge necessary to effectively implement iPads into the classroom.

CONCLUSION

Mobile learning will continue to revolutionize living and learning in our world. Mobile technologies have the potential to impact teaching and learning in ways that other technologies cannot. Mobile learning technologies can offer teachers a flexible, relevant, personalized, metacognitive, and innovative way to teach and support students' learning. As schools move toward mobile learning, it is important to support teachers through professional development on technological, pedagogical, and instructional issues. The M-TPACK (Wilson et al., 2013) m-learning framework provides a foundation for teacher training and professional development, and for student success. Effective instructional and learning decisions cannot be made solely by knowing how to use a device; teachers need to learn how to use m-learning technologies in instructionally, pedagogically, and technologically sound ways. A teacher who is willing to learn more about m-learning technologies and how to creatively and innovatively use them to facilitate student learning in the 21st century, is a teacher who is metacognitive and a lifelong learner. The m-learning revolution has resulted in more m-learning devices in our schools. Teacher professional development and support with m-learning technologies that is founded in the M-TPACK (Wilson et al., 2013) framework, will promote teacher knowledge and effective instructional decisions with m-learning uses for teaching and learning in the classroom. The question still remains: How will teachers learn to use m-learning in effective and ubiquitous ways to support and extend student learning? Further research in effective professional development initiatives for m-learning classroom integration is needed.

REFERENCES

Albion, P. (2001). Some factors in the development of self-efficacy beliefs for computer use among teacher education students. *Journal of Technology and Teacher Education*, 9(3), 321–347.

American Association of Colleges of Teacher Education (Ed.). (2008). *Handbook of technological pedagogical content knowledge (TPCK) for educators*. New York, NY: Routledge.

Bandura, A. (1997). *Self-efficacy: The exercise of control*. New York, NY: W.H. Freeman and Company.

Barber, M., & Mourshed, M. (2007). *How the world's best-performing school systems come out on top*. London, UK: McKinsey & Company.

Bauer, J., & Kenton, J. (2005). Toward technology integration in schools: Why it is not happening. *Journal of Technology and Teacher Education, 13*, 519–546.

Becker, H. J., & Ravitz, J. L. (2001). *Proceedings from the American Educational Research Association (AERA): Computer use by teachers: Are Cuban's predictions correct?* Retrieved from http://www.crito.uci.edu/tlc/findings/conferences-pdf/aera_2001.pdf

Bezemer, J., & Kress, G. (2008). Writing in multimodal texts: A social semiotic account of designs for learning. (Special Issue on Writing and New Media). *Written Communication, 25*(2), 166–195. doi:10.1177/0741088307313177

Cardullo, V. (2013). *Eighth-grade students reading nonfiction literature on the iPad: An exploratory case study*. (Unpublished doctoral dissertation). University of Central Florida, Orlando, FL.

Cardullo, V., Zygouris-Coe, V., Wilson, N. S., Craneen, P., & Stafford, T. (2012). Exploring think-alouds and text coding for comprehension of digital-based text. *American Reading Forum Online Yearbook, 32*. Retrieved from http://www.americanreadingforum.org/yearbook/12_yearbook/volume12.htm

Cisco (2012). *Cisco visual networking index: Global mobile data traffic forecast update, 2011-2016*. Retrieved from http://www.cisco.com/en/US/solutions/collateral/ns341/ns525/ns537/ns705/ns827/white_paper_c11-520862.html

Coiro, J., & Dobler, E. (2007). Exploring the online reading comprehension strategies used by sixth grade skilled readers to search for and locate information on the internet. *Reading Research Quarterly, 42*, 214–257. doi:10.1598/RRQ.42.2.2

Cordingley, P., Bell, M., Thomason, S., & Firth, A. (2005). The impact of collaborative continuing professional development (CPD) on classroom teaching and learning. Review: How do collaborative and sustained CPD and sustained but not collaborative CPD affect teaching and learning? In *Research Evidence in Education Library*. London, UK: EPPI-Centre, Social Science Research Unit, Institute of Education, University of London. Retrieved from www.eppi.ioe.ac.uk

D'Orio, W. (2011). iPads in Class. *Scholastic Administrator Magazine*. Retrieved from http://www.scholastic.com/browse/article.jsp?id=3755865

Damon, W. (2005). Personality test: The dispositional dispute in teacher preparation today, and what to do about it. *Fwd: Thomas Fordham Foundation, 2*(3), 1–5.

Day, C., Sammons, P., Kington, A., Gu, Q., & Stobart, G. (2006). Methodological synergy in a national project: The VITAE story. *Evaluation and Research in Education, 19*(2), 102–125. doi:10.2167/eri422.0

Dispositon. (n.d.). In *Merriam-Webster online dictionary*. Retrieved from http://www.merriam-webster.com/dictionary/disposition

Duffy, G. G. (2005). Developing metacognitive teachers: Visioning and the expert's changing role in teacher education and professional development. In S. E. Israel, C. C. Block, K. L. Bauserman, & K. Kinnucan-Welsh (Eds.), *Metacognition in literacy learning: Theory, assessment, instruction, and professional development* (pp. 299–314). Mahwah, NJ: Lawrence Erlbaum.

Duffy, G. G., Miller, S. D., Parsons, S. A., & Meloth, M. (2009). Teachers as metacognitive professionals. In D. J. Hacker, J. Dunlosky, & A. C. Graesser (Eds.), *Handbook of metacognition in education* (pp. 240–256). New York, NY: Routledge.

Dufour, R. (2004). What is a professional learning community? *Educational Leadership*, *61*(8), 6–11.

Eberly, J., Rand, M., & O'Conner, T. (2007). Analyzing teachers' dispositions towards diversity: Using adult development theory. *Multicultural Education*, *14*(4), 31–36.

Ertmer, P. A., & Ottenbreit-Leftwich, A. (2010). Teacher technology change: How knowledge, confidence, beliefs, and culture intersect. *Journal of Research on Technology in Education*, *42*(3), 255–284. doi:10.1080/15391523.2010.10782551

Ertmer, P. A., Ottenbreit-Leftwich, A., & York, C. (2006). Exemplary technology-using teachers: Perceptions of factors influencing success. *Journal of Computing in Teacher Education*, *23*(2), 55–61.

Friend, M., & Cook, L. (2003). *Interactions: Collaboration skills for school professionals. (4th editon)*. Boston, MA: Allyn and Bacon.

Guskey, T. R., & Yoon, K. S. (2009). What works in professional development? *Phi Delta Kappan*, *90*(7), 495–500.

Harris, J., Mishra, P., & Koehler, M. (2009). Teachers' technological pedagogical content knowledge and learning activity types: Curriculum-based technology integration reframed. *Journal of Research on Technology in Education*, *41*(4), 393–416. doi:10.1080/15391523.2009.10782536

Heinrich, P. (n.d.). *The iPad as a tool for education: A study of the introduction of iPads at Longfield Academy, Kent*. Naace and 9ine Consulting.

Hennessy, S., Ruthven, K., & Brindley, S. (2005). Teacher perspectives on integrating ICT into subject teaching: Commitment, constraints, caution, and change. *Journal of Curriculum Studies*, *37*, 155–192. doi:10.1080/0022027032000276961

Hobson, A., Malderez, A., Tracey, L., Giannakaki, M. S., Pell, R. G., & Kerr, K. ... Roper, T. (2006). Becoming a teacher: Student teachers' experiences of initial teacher training in England (Research Report 744). Nottingham, UK: DfES Publications.

Hobson, A. J., Malderez, A., Tracey, L., Homer, M., Mitchell, N., & Biddulph, M. ... Tomlinson, P. D. (2007). Newly qualified teachers' experiences of their first year of teaching: Findings from Phase III of the Becoming a Teacher project. Nottingham, UK: Department for Children, Schools and Families (9781847750204).

Honey, M., & Moeller, B. (1990). *Teachers' beliefs and technology integration: Different values, different understandings* (Technical Report 6). Center For Technology in Education.

Hughes, J. (2005). The role of teacher knowledge and learning experiences in forming technology-integrated pedagogy. *Journal of Technology and Teacher Education*, *13*, 277–302.

Hurd, B. (2012). *The Shoah: 101 keys to understanding the Holocaust*. Little Falls, MN: Zoomable Media.

Jewitt, C. (2013). Multimodality and digital technologies in the classroom. In I. de Saint-Georges, & J. J. Weber (Eds.), *Multilingualism and multimodality: Current challenges for educational studies* (pp. 141–152). Rotterdam, The Netherlands: Sense Publishers. doi:10.1007/978-94-6209-266-2_8

Judson, E. (2006). How teachers integrate technology and their beliefs about learning: Is there a connection? *Journal of Technology and Teacher Education*, *14*(3), 581–597.

Kanaya, T., Light, D., & Culp, K. M. (2005). Factors influencing outcomes from a technology-focused professional development program. *Journal of Research on Technology in Education, 37,* 313–329. doi:10.1080/15391523.2005.10782439

Lampert, M. (2001). *Teaching problems and the problems in teaching.* New Haven, CT: Yale University Press.

Leander, K., & Frank, A. (2006). The aesthetic production and distribution of image/subjects among online youth. *E-learning, 3*(2), 185–206. doi:10.2304/elea.2006.3.2.185

Levin, T., & Wadmany, R. (2005). Changes in educational beliefs and classroom practices of teachers and students in rich technology-based classrooms. *Technology, Pedagogy and Education, 14,* 281–307. doi:10.1080/14759390500200208

Lin, X., Schwartz, D. L., & Hatano, G. (2005). Toward teachers' adaptive metacognition. *Educational Psychologist, 40*(4), 245–255. doi:10.1207/s15326985ep4004_6

Lin, X. D. (2001). Reflective adaptation of a technology artifact: A case study of classroom change. *Cognition and Instruction, 19,* 395–440. doi:10.1207/S1532690XCI1904_1

Little, J. W. (Chair), Lampert, M., Graziani, F., Borko, H., Clark, K. K., & Wong, N. (2007, April). *Conceptualizing and investigating the practice of facilitation in content-oriented teacher professional development.* Paper presented at the 2007 Annual Meeting of the American Educational Research Association. Chicago, IL.

Mahaley, D. (2013, August 11). *iPad educator professional development - The three r's.* Retrieved from Emerging Ed Tech: http://www.emergingedtech.com/2013/08/ipad-educator-professional-development-the-three-rs/

McClanahan, B. (2012). A breakthrough for Josh: How use of an iPad facilitated reading improvement. *TechTrends, 56*(3), 20–28. doi:10.1007/s11528-012-0572-6

Mishra, P., & Koehler, M. (2006). Technological Pedagogical Content Knowledge: A framework for teacher knowledge. *Teachers College Record, 108*(6), 1017–1054. doi:10.1111/j.1467-9620.2006.00684.x

Mokhtari, K., & Reichard, C. (2002). Assessing students' metacognitive awareness of reading strategies. *Journal of Educational Psychology, 94*(2), 249–259. doi:10.1037/0022-0663.94.2.249

Mueller, J., Wood, E., Willoughby, T., Ross, C., & Specht, J. (2008). Identifying discriminating variables between teachers who fully integrate computers and teachers with limited integration. *Computers & Education, 51,* 1523–1537. doi:10.1016/j.compedu.2008.02.003

Munoz, C., & Sperling, G. (2013). *Bringing America's students into the digital age.* White House Blog. Retrieved October 1st, 2013, from http://www.whitehouse.gov/blog/2013/06/06/bringing-america-s-students-digital-age

Murawski, W. M., & Dieker, L. A. (2004). Tips and strategies for co-teaching at the secondary level. *Teaching Exceptional Children, 35*(5), 52–58.

National Council for Accreditation of Teacher Education. (2010). *Glossary, Professional Dispositions.* Retrieved from http://www.ncate.org/Standards/UnitStandards/Glossary/tabid/477/Default.aspx#P

Nespor, J. (1987). The role of beliefs in the practice of teaching. *Journal of Curriculum Studies, 19*(4), 317–328. doi:10.1080/0022027870190403

Perkins, S., Hamm, S., Pamplin, K., Morris, J., & McKelvain, R. (2011). Exploring learning with the iPad: ACU connected and the future of digital texts. In M. Koehler & P. Mishra (Eds.), *Proceedings of Society for Information Technology & Teacher Education International Conference 2011* (pp. 1640-1642). Chesapeake, VA: AACE.

Sandholtz, J. H., Ringstaff, C., & Dwyer, D. C. (1997). *Teaching with technology: Creating student-centered classrooms*. New York, NY: Teachers College Press.

Serdyuko, P., & Hill, R. (2007). Cultivating quality educators through innovative and comprehensive teacher preparation programs. *Journal of Research in Innovative Teaching, 4*(1), 106-119.106-107.

Serdyukov, P., & Ferguson, B. F. (2011). Teacher dispositions: What kind of candidates do we have in a teacher preparation program, and how can we make them better? *Journal of Research in Innovative Teaching, 4*(1), 106–119.

Sheppard, D. (2011). Reading with iPads – The difference makes a difference. *Education Today, 3*, 12–15.

Snoeyink, R., & Ertmer, P. A. (2001/2002). Thrust into technology: How veteran teachers respond. *Journal of Educational Technology Systems, 30*(1), 85–111. doi:10.2190/YDL7-XH09-RLJ6-MTP1

Somekh, B. (2008). Factors affecting teachers' pedagogical adoption of ICT. In J. Voogt, & G. Knezek (Eds.), *International handbook of information technology in primary and secondary education* (pp. 449–460). New York, NY: Springer. doi:10.1007/978-0-387-73315-9_27

Totter, A., Stutz, D., & Grote, G. (2006). ICT and schools: Identification of factors influencing the use of new media in vocational training schools. *The Electronic Journal of e-Learning, 4*(1), 95-102. Retrieved from www.ejel.org

UNESCO. (2013). *The future of mobile learning: Implications for policy makers and planners*. Retrieved from http://unesdoc.unesco.org/images/0021/002196/219637E.pdf

Unsworth, L. (Ed.). (2008). *New literacies and the English curriculum*. London, UK: Continuum.

Vogt, F., & Rogalla, M. (2009). Developing adaptive teaching competency through coaching. *Teaching and Teacher Education, 25*, 1051–1060. doi:10.1016/j.tate.2009.04.002

Voss, J. F., & Post, T. A. (1988). On the solving of ill-structured problems. In M. T. H. Chi, R. Glaser, & M. J. Farr (Eds.), *The nature of expertise* (pp. 261–285). Hillsdale, NJ: Lawrence Erlbaum.

Wahl, L., & Duffield, J. (2005). *Using flexible technology to meet the needs of diverse learners: What teachers can do*. Retrieved from http://www.wested.org/online_pubs/kn-05-01.pdf

Wasicsko, M. (2004). The 20-minute hiring assessment. *School Administrator, 61*(9), 40–42.

Wilson, N. S., Zygouris-Coe, V., & Cardullo, V. (2013). Trying to make sense of e-readers. *Journal of Reading Education*.

Wilson, N. S., Zygouris-Coe, V., Cardullo, V., & Fong, J. (2013). Pedagogical frameworks of mobile learning technologies in education. For publication. In S. Keengwe (Ed.), *Pedagogical applications and social effects of mobile technology integration* (pp. 1–24). doi:10.4018/978-1-4666-2985-1.ch001

Wozney, L., Venkatesh, V., & Abrami, P. C. (2006). Implementing computer technologies: Teachers' perceptions and practices. *Journal of Technology and Teacher Education, 14*(1), 173–207.

Zohar, A. (2006). The nature and development of teachers' metastrategic knowledge in the context of teaching higher order thinking. *Journal of the Learning Sciences, 15*(3), 331–377. doi:10.1207/s15327809jls1503_2

ADDITIONAL READING

Apple. (n.d.). *iPad in education*. Retrieved from http://www.apple.com/education/ipad/teaching-with-ipad/

Auburn. (2013, February 21). *Professional development of Auburn's iPad kindergarten teachers*. Retrieved from http://multiplepathways.wordpress.com/2012/02/21/professional-development-for-auburns-ipad-kindergarten-teachers/

Avvitt, J. T. (2011). An investigation of the relationship between self-efficacy beliefs about technology integration and technological pedagogical content knowledge (TPACK) among preservice teachers. *Journal of Digital Learning in Teacher Education, 27*(4), 134–143. doi:10.1080/21532974.2011.10784670

Baylor, A. (2002). Expanding preservice teachers' metacognitive awareness of instructional planning through pedagogical agents. *ETR&D, 50*(2), 5–22. doi:10.1007/BF02504991

Bebell, D., & O'Dqyer, L. (2010). Educational outcomes and research from 1:1 computing settings. *The Journal of Technology, Learning, and Assessment*, 5-15.

Borko, H., Whitcomb, J., & Liston, D. (2009). Wicked problems and other thoughts on issues of technology and teacher learning. *Journal of Teacher Education, 60*(1), 3–7. doi:10.1177/0022487108328488

Burns, M. (2010). How to help teachers use technology in the classroom: The 5J approach. *eLearn Magazine: Education and Technology in Perspective*. Retrieved from http://elearnmag.acm.org/featured.cfm?aid=1865476

Classroommaid. (2013, June 9). *MERLOT supports mobile learning*. Retrieved from classroom-aid: http://classroom-aid.com/2013/06/09/merlot-supports-mobile-learning/

Educational Technology and Mobile Learning. (2013, November). *The best 15 iPad apps for teacher professional development*. Retrieved from http://www.educatorstechnology.com/2013/11/the-best-15-ipad-apps-for-teacher.html

Edutopia. (2012, September). *Mobile devices for learning: What you need to know*. Retrieved from http://edutech4teachers.edublogs.org/files/2012/09/Edutopia-Mobile-Learning-Guide-color-o6f2ux.pdf

Edutopia Staff. (n.d.). *Mobile learning: Resource roundup*. Retrieved from http://www.edutopia.org/mobile-learning-resources

Evans, T., Guy, R., Honan, E., Kippel, L. M., Muspratt, S., & Paraide, P. ... Tawaiyole, P. (2006). PNG Curriculum Reform Implementation Project: Impact Study 6: Final report. Melbourne, Australia: Australian Government.

Ferriman, J. (2013, October 6). *Benefits of mobile devices in the classroom*. Retrieved from http://www.learndash.com/benefits-of-mobile-devices-in-the-classroom/

Fletcher, J. (2011, November 8). *Teacher training should start before iPad deployment*. Retrieved from http://thejournal.com/articles/2011/11/08/teacher-training-should-start-before-ipad-deployment.aspx

Hammerness, K., Darling-Hammond, L., Bransford, J., Berliner, D., Cochran-Smith, M., McDonald, M., & Zeichner, K. (2007). How teachers learn and develop. In L. Darling-Hammond, & J. Bransford (Eds.), *Preparing teachers for a changing world: What teachers should learn and be able to do* (pp. 358–389). Hoboken, NJ: Jossey-Bass.

Hartman, D. K., Morsink, P. M., & Zheng, J. (2011). From print to pixels: The evolution of cognitive conceptions of reading comprehension. In E. A. Baker (Ed.), *Multiple perspectives on new literacies research and instruction* (pp. 1–45). New York, NY: Guilford.

Heo, M. (2009). Digital storytelling: An empirical study of the impact of digital storytelling on pre-service teachers' self-efficacy and dispositions towards educational technology. *Journal of Educational Multimedia and Hypermedia*, *18*(4), 405–428.

Hoekstra, A., & Korthagen, F. (2011). Teacher learning in a context of educational change: Informal learning versus systematically supported learning. *Journal of Teacher Education*, *62*(1), 76–92. doi:10.1177/0022487110382917

Jennings, P. A., & Greenberg, M. T. (2009). The prosocial classroom: Teacher social and emotional competence in relation to student and classroom outcomes. *Review of Educational Research*, *79*(1), 491–525. doi:10.3102/0034654308325693

Kramarski, B., & Feldman, Y. (2000). Internet in the classroom: Effects on reading comprehension, motivation, and metacognitive awareness. *Educational Media International*, *37*, 149–155. doi:10.1080/09523980050184709

Larson, L. C. (2010). Digital readers: The next chapter in e-book reading and response. *The Reading Teacher*, *64*(1), 15–22. doi:10.1598/RT.64.1.2

Levin, T., & Wadmany, R. (2006). Teachers' beliefs and practices in technology-based classrooms: A developmental view. *Journal of Research on Technology in Education*, *39*(2), 157–181. doi:10.1080/15391523.2006.10782478

Mahaley, D. (2013, August 11). *iPad educator professional development -- The three R's*. Retrieved from http://www.emergingedtech.com/2013/08/ipad-educator-professional-development-the-three-rs/

Murray, O. T., & Olcese, N. R. (2011). Teaching and learning with iPads, ready or not? *TechTrends*, *55*(6), 42–48. doi:10.1007/s11528-011-0540-6

Ottenbreit-Leftwich, A., Glazewski, K., Newby, T., & Erter, P. (2010). Teacher value beliefs associated with using technology: Addressing professional and student needs. *Computers & Education*, 1321–1335. doi:10.1016/j.compedu.2010.06.002

Robson, R. (2003). *Mobile learning and handheld devices in the classroom.* Retrieved from http://www.eduworks.com/Documents/Publications/Mobile_Learning_Handheld_Classroom.pdf

Rosen, Y. (2011). Teacher-led technology-rich environment: Educational effects. In S. Barton et al. (Eds.), *Proceedings of global learn Asia Pacific 2011* (pp. 1878–1885). Chesapeak, VA: AACE.

Sahin, I., Akturk, A., & Schmidt, D. (2009). Relationship of preservice teachers' technological pedagogical content knowledge with their vocational self-efficacy beliefs. In C. D. Maddux (Ed.), *Research highlights in technology and teacher education 2009* (pp. 293–301). Chesapeake, VA: AACE.

SwiftLaunch. (2013). *Why teachers struggle with using and effectively integrating iPads in the classroom for education.* Retrieved from http://www.swiftlaunch.com/Blog/Why-teachers-struggle-with-using-and-effectively-integrating-iPads-in-the-classroom-for-education

TeachThought Staff. (2013, November 17). *Better teacher professional development: Pairing teachers.* Retrieved from http://www.teachthought.com/teaching/better-teacher-professional-development-pairing-teachers/

Titova, S. (2012). *Mobile learning in language classroom today.* Retrieved from http://www.slideshare.net/AnnaMlearn/mobile-learning-in-language-classroom

Tondeur, J., van Braak, J., Sang, G., Boogt, J., & Fisser, P. O.-L. (2011). Preparing pre-service teachers to integrate technology in education: A synthesis of qualitative evidence. *Computers & Education,* 1–11.

UNESCO. (2012). *Mobile learning for teachers in North America: Exploring the potential of mobile technologies to support teachers and improve practice.* Retrieved from http://unesdoc.unesco.org/images/0021/002160/216084E.pdf

UNESCO. (2013). *Policy guidelines for mobile learning.* Retrieved from http://unesdoc.unesco.org/images/0021/002196/219641E.pdf

Woodill, G. (2011, October 10). *Mobile devices in the classroom: Is this really mobile learning?* Retrieved from http://floatlearning.com/2011/10/mobile-devices-in-the-classroom-is-this-really-mobile-learning/

Wright, P. I., Neugent, L., & McGraw, T. (2011). *Beyond textbooks.* Common Wealth, Virginia: Virginia Department of Education.

Wylie, J. (n.d.). *Mobile learning technologies for 21st century classrooms.* Retrieved from http://www.scholastic.com/browse/article.jsp?id=3754742

Zimmerman, S. (2013, April 18). *Tips for initial teacher iPad training/professional development.* Retrieved from http://schoolipads.wordpress.com/2013/04/18/tips-for-initial-teacher-ipad-training-professional-development/

KEY TERMS AND DEFINITIONS

Application (App): A specialized program downloaded onto mobile devices.

Dispositions: Teacher attitudes, perceptions, and beliefs that effect their verbal and nonverbal behaviors when planning, teaching, and engaging with stakeholders.

iPads: Multifunction devices that can be used for everything from reading e-books, document creation, video viewing, and creation to web surfing.

Knowledge of Content: A teacher's subject matter knowledge and pedagogical content knowledge. Subject matter knowledge is related directly to the intellectual ideas, facts, and information of a particular content.

Knowledge of Pedagogy: A teacher's general classroom procedures and teaching methods and processes.

Knowledge of Students: A teacher's knowledge of her students includes knowledge of students' misconceptions and past experiences as well as their learning styles and learning needs.

Knowledge of Technology: A teacher's knowledge of the device's structure, functions, and features, as well as her knowledge of how the device can be used to enhance student thinking and learning of the content.

Metacognitive Teacher: A teacher who responds immediately to unanticipated situations by making conscious and deliberate decisions utilizing her knowledge and dispositions (Duffy et al., 2010; Lin & Schwartz, 2005).

Metacognitive Technological Pedagogical Content Knowledge (M-TPACK): A pedagogical framework that identifies the metacognitive teacher as central to the integration of technology in the classroom.

Mobile Learning (M-Learning): Involves the use of mobile technology, either alone or in combination with other information and communication technology (ICT), to enable learning anytime and anywhere.

Professional Development: The vehicle through which teacher educators train and support teachers to make changes in their practice that improves student learning.

Self-Efficacy: A teacher's beliefs about capabilities to effect student learning.

Technological Pedagogical Content Knowledge (TPACK): Teachers integrate content, pedagogical, and technical knowledge to create and utilize new knowledge throughout the instructional process (Mishra & Koehler, 2006).

Chapter 6
Using Mobile Technology for Student Teaching Observations of Special Education Candidates

Josh Harrower
California State University – Monterey Bay, USA

Cathi Draper Rodríguez
California State University – Monterey Bay, USA

ABSTRACT

Student teacher supervision has been an important part of teacher preparation almost since the inception of teacher education programs. The goal of this type of supervision is to strengthen the skills of the pre-service teacher. Providing this type of observation can be difficult for teacher preparation programs and university faculty. Many factors, including large numbers of students in teacher education programs and student placements in remote schools, contribute to this. In order to make the most effective use of faculty and pre-service teacher time, other options for providing this support need to be explored. The rapidly developing field of mobile technology (e.g., iPads, iPhones, Smart Phones) can be used to facilitate student teaching observations. This chapter discusses how teacher preparation programs can implement candidate field supervision using video conferencing via mobile technology to increase the ability to conduct observations in schools and in a more efficient manner. It also explores the security of video conferencing applications and the issues related to using video conferencing in special education classrooms, where student confidentiality is heightened.

INTRODUCTION

The No Child Left Behind (NCLB) Act and current reauthorization of the Individuals with Disabilities Education Act (IDEA) require that all teachers, including special educators, be highly qualified with an appropriate credential. Nationwide, shortages of highly qualified special education teachers have been reported in 98% of all school districts, with the greatest demand reported in the poorest schools (Brownell et al., 2005). While over 95% of California's teachers are highly qualified, nearly 10% of the State's special education teachers are not (U.S. Department of Education, 2008). With

DOI: 10.4018/978-1-4666-6284-1.ch006

a special education population in 2008-2009 of 678,105 students (California Department of Education [CDE], 2010), this gap represents a significant inequality for California's students with disabilities. In order to fill this gap, over 3000 special education teachers are needed to teach students with disabilities in California (CDE, 2010). These shortages are even more pronounced in the Central Coast Region of California, where many programs are located in remote and rural settings and are thus not easily accessible. Shortages of special education personnel are nowhere more severe than in rural schools (Ludlow, Conner & Schechter, 2005).

Additionally, under-prepared special education teachers (defined as those teaching on waivers, short term permits, provisional internship permits, and intern credentials) are more likely to be teaching in schools serving low income, minority, low-achieving, and English Language Learner students (Shields et al., 2003). In Monterey, Santa Cruz and San Benito Counties, the percentage of under-credentialed special education teachers of students with low incidence disabilities in 2008-2009 was 17.9%, 18.8%, and 33.3%, respectively (CDE, 2009). Traditional teacher preparation programs cannot meet this critical need. In California, enrolment in special education teacher preparation programs during 2007-08 was 11,040 students, yet only 3,592 special education credentials were issued during that time (CCTC, 2009).

With the development and increased accessibility of online instruction, much of the access issue with regards to candidate preparation in content and methods can now be readily addressed by preparation programs. Distance learning has been found effective in serving people across a broad geographical expanse (Jung et al., 2006) in addressing increased numbers of students (Spooner et al., 1998), and providing increased access to students with disabilities when universal design is used (Burgstahler, 2002). However, the clinical experience, or practicum, still requires direct supervision by program faculty of the candidate in field placement settings. Recent reform efforts in teacher preparation have focused on realigning program design around the clinical teaching experience, with coursework supporting supervised practical application in the field (National Council for Accreditation of Teacher Education, 2010). Similar to residency requirements in medical training programs, these reform efforts in teacher preparation place the emphasis of training on the supervised practical experiences of the teacher in training. While preparation programs can identify specific school sites for these practical training experiences for student teachers in general education, potential barriers to this model of prescribed placement exist for special education programs.

Given the shortages in the field combined with the fifth year post-baccalaureate model of teacher preparation in California, many teacher candidates in special education pursue their credential while employed in some capacity (e.g., Paraprofessionals, Behavior Technicians, etc.) in special education settings. Thus, university programs can be limited in their abilities to place candidates in close proximity to campus. Further, research has identified placement in rural settings during the teacher preparation program as a critical feature in addressing the even greater shortage issues seen in such settings (Barley & Brigham, 2008). Yet the time and mileage costs involved in providing direct, on-site supervision of teacher candidates in remote areas can pose workload and budgetary challenges for preparation programs in special education. As a result, teacher preparation programs in special education may want to consider technological solutions for providing ongoing direct supervision of teacher candidates who complete field placement requirements in remote school settings.

Therefore, this chapter will review preliminary studies that demonstrate the rationale for incorporating mobile learning into candidate field supervision. The authors will discuss the existing evidence regarding traditional student teacher observations along with limitations to conducting on-site supervision, such as cost, observer effects on candidate behavior, travel time, etc. Recommendations on how to effectively incorporate mobile technology into candidate field supervision will be presented. Finally, an overview of potential security issues of available software and the various requirements of education organizations (e.g., Council for Exceptional Children, National Association of School Psychologist) will be discussed.

OBSERVATIONS OF TEACHER CANDIDATES

A cornerstone of most teacher education programs is the field based experience, which requires the pre-service teacher to perform the tasks associated with being a teacher. This is typically completed at the end of the training program. Pre-service teachers usually complete this field-based experience with both a university and classroom-based supervisor. The President's Commission on Excellence in Special Education (2002) recommended field-based experiences with continual guidance, feedback, and induction into the teaching profession. Ongoing, individualized support and assistance of new teachers has been shown to increase teacher retention (Tushnet et al., 2002; Shields et al., 2003).

Impact of Pre-Service Teacher Observations

Many believe that the field experience is the most important part of the teacher preparation program (Guyton & McIntyre, 1990; Hollins & Guzman, 2005; Wilson, Floden, & Ferrini-Mundy, 2001). Rust (1999) stated that teachers who undergo meaningful field based experiences make the transition into their own classrooms much easier. They tend to evolve from student teacher to teaching professional with fewer difficulties.

Research suggests that there is a positive relationship between the student teaching experience and the ensuing achievement of the K-12 students once they become teachers (Boyd, Grossman, Lankford, Loeb, & Wyckoff, 2009; Ronfeldt, 2012). Boyd et al., measured the impact of specific teacher education program components on the teachers' value-added to their students. The researchers found university oversight of student teaching experiences was positively related to the teachers' impact on their own students' learning.

Their findings suggested very specific requirements in the field experience produced higher student achievement. The requirements included university involvement in field placement and a minimum of 5 visits by the university supervisor. Teachers who had these experiences during their preservice training produced higher levels of student achievement gains during the first year as the teacher of record than teachers who did not have these requirements during their preservice training. Because of these benefits, teacher education faculty are pressed to identify more ways to provide this level of support to their students.

Challenges of Providing Field Supervision

Despite the clear need to provide ongoing supervision of teacher candidates in the field, conducting on-site field supervision has long been known to be a significant expense for teacher preparation programs (Garret & Dudt, 1998), particularly for those serving candidates in rural settings. Travelling to remote school locations to provide direct, in-person supervision of teacher candidates can be difficult. Time spent in transit can lead to inequitable workload arrangements among supervisors, and mileage reimbursement can have significant impacts on increasingly limited teacher education budgets. These two issues can quickly become a barrier to conducting a sufficient level of supervision for candidates.

Another downfall of field based observations is that the presence of the university supervisor alone may alter the instructional setting. Research suggests that the presence of an unknown individual changes the behaviors of all in a classroom (Ardley, 2009; Diaz & Cartnal, 1999; Strauss, 1993). Diaz and Cartnal found that a visitor in the classroom may interrupt the daily routine. This can be particularly problematic in a special education classroom where some students do not handle changes in routine well. Ardley argued that it may not be best for the university supervisor to be a physical presence in the classroom as this may create an artificial viewing of the student teachers ability.

Given recent technological advances, supervision does not have to mean face-to-face, on-site, observations in the candidate's classroom. Instead, a supervisor remotely observing a teacher candidate utilizing video conferencing software can also provide the necessary supervision of, and feedback on, candidate teaching activities. With the possibility of video conferencing occurring without disrupting the day to day classroom functions, this type of observation as an additive to face-to-face observations would greatly benefit student teaching in general and special education classrooms.

UTILIZING VIDEO CONFERENCING FOR FIELD SUPERVISION

Video conferencing observations of candidates in field settings appear to offer a comparable alternative to on-site observations in clinical teaching experiences (Hamel, 2012). Using video observations has been shown to be an effective and reliable method for observing student teachers (Anderson & Petch-Hogan, 2001; Ardley, 2009; Conole & Culver, 2009; Hannon, 2009). Additionally, the benefits of web-based distance education such as fewer teachers, reaching more students, and low cost have been documented and recommended by representatives of California's institutes of higher education special education teacher preparation programs (Project Pipeline, 2003). Effective models for providing field supervision in special education at a distance have also been developed (Jung, Galyon-Keramidas, Collins & Ludlow, 2006).

Bolton (2010) conducted a study to determine the impact of teleconfering on student teacher performance. Through a survey of both the student teacher and the field-based supervisor, Bolton identified several areas, which this type of observation was useful in the student teacher training. The student teachers felt there was increased utility of university supervisor feedback because their were fewer student interruptions. Both the field based teacher and student teachers indicated that the video conferencing observations were able to take place with minimal interruption as compared to on-site visits. The participants in this study felt that the video conferencing allowed for greater collaboration between the university faculty, the school personnel and the student teacher. Finally, the student teachers felt that they were able to get more timely feedback from their university supervisor using teleconferencing as fax machines were used to provide the student teacher timely feedback.

All researchers believed that the use of video conferencing can be used to supplement face-to-face observations. This additional way to observe student teachers can allow for more frequent visits while overcoming some of the barriers of face-to-face observations, including cost, time involved and student distractions. While the field and research has moved toward this type of observation, it is vital for teacher preparation programs to understand what restrictions professional organizations may have on this type of supervision.

PROFESSIONAL ORGANIZATIONS REGULATIONS

Many professional organizations (e.g., National Council for Accreditation of Teacher Education, Council for Exceptional Children, National Association of School Psychologist) have a mission to oversee the preparation of educators (e.g., general education teachers, special education teachers, school psychologist, speech pathologists). The organizations often have standards, which dictate the need for teacher candidates to be observed during their university training.

In order to fully understand what these organizations require in terms of video conferencing for supervision, their websites were explored. In cases, where no information regarding policy or procedures about this type of observation was evident an email was sent to inquire about the organizations policy regarding video conferencing. All but one organization replied to the email requesting more information. Only one organization asked, American Psychological Association (APA), has guidelines related to the use of video conferencing for observations. While this is certainly not a scientific study, it clearly demonstrates that the rapid growth of technology is not matched by the educational organizations.

Due to the lack of guidance from accrediting agencies, teacher preparation program faculty need to explore legislation related to students right. In the case of special education students, this legislation is the Individuals with Disabilities Education Act (2004). IDEA (2004) requires that schools take actions to ensure the confidentiality of students receiving special education services. This includes maintaining any personally identifiable data, information, and records. While completing video supervision, university faculty must use mobile applications that can ensure this confidentiality.

While IDEA does not have specifics about how to protect the confidentiality, a comparable law, Health Insurance Portability & Accountability Act (HIPAA) of 1996, has confidentiality provisions for the health information of patients. HIPAA has detailed privacy standards for relaying information in electronic, paper and oral forms. The authors believe that mobile applications that meet HIPAA standards will meet confidentiality requirements set forth by IDEA (2004). More information regarding the HIPAA standards can be found at: http://www.cms.gov/Regulations-and-Guidance/HIPAA-Administrative-Simplification/.

MOBILE APPLICATIONS AVAILABLE FOR VIDEO CONFERENCING

Mobile technologies have been ubiquitous. Because of this many faculty and student teachers already possess the technologies needed to complete video observations of student teaching. There are many mobile applications available for video conferencing. A quick search in the Google Play Store (app purchasing device for Androids) revealed hundreds of applications with video conferencing capabilities. University faculty need to be aware of these and determine which of them meet their needs for use in the field. Due to the professional use of these applications only business minded or professional applications were reviewed. That is, no dating or social media applications were included. The information provided in Table 1 is the best available information at the time. These technologies are always changing and educators need to double check these information prior to use.

CASE STUDY IMPLEMENTATION OF VIDEO SUPERVISION

In 2011, CSU, Monterey Bay was awarded a Personnel Development Grant from the Office of Special Education Programs, U.S. Department of Education (H325K100428) to support individuals in pursuing a credential in low incidence disabilities by providing innovative technological supports and enhanced on-site and university faculty mentorship. Among a variety of other technological and mentorship supports, Project STREAM (Supporting teachers with Technology, Resources, Education And Mentorship) provides teacher candidates with additional observations

Table 1. Mobile technologies for video conferencing

App name	Platforms	Cost	Security Features Mentioned
Facetime	Apple devices only	Free	Calls encrypted and compatible with HIPAA standards when using proper encryption
Google Hangout	All but must have Google Plus Account	Free	Not clear; but Google Helpout a paid service is encrypted
OoVoo	PC, Mac, Android and iPhone	Free with added features for payment	Does not provide encryption.
Skype	Android; iPhone	Free	Calls encrypted
VidyoMobile	Apple and Android	Has cost structure dependent on many variables	Calls encrypted and compatible with HIPAA standards when using proper encryption
VSee	Apple and Windows devices	Free with added features for payment	Calls encrypted and compatible with HIPAA standards when using proper encryption

by University Faculty conducted remotely via video conferencing software programs available on various mobile technologies (Laptops, iPads, iPhones, etc.). Following the success of utilizing video conferencing to conduct remote observation of candidates in the Project STREAM program, these practices were adopted for use with all candidates pursuing a special education credential in both high incidence and low incidence disabilities, leading to the California Preliminary Education Specialist Mild to Moderate Credential or Preliminary Education Specialist Moderate to Severe Credential, respectively. As a result, remote video conferencing observations are conducted along with continued on-site observations by University Faculty, and allow for a cost-effective, efficient method for providing ongoing university supervision to teacher candidates. It is important to note that the candidates participating in the CSUMB special education credential programs satisfy their field experience requirements in three distinct ways.

First, the program supports traditional student teachers. These candidates are placed into an appropriate school setting/program in order to satisfy their field experience requirements. Second, the program supports candidates who are working full-time as the teacher of record under a California Intern Credential in special education. These candidates are able to utilize their employment position (i.e., classroom) as their field placement setting. The third group of candidates are those who are employed in an appropriate special education setting/program in a capacity other than that of the teacher of record. Examples of these types of employment positions include paraprofessionals and instructional aides. These candidates submit information on their employment setting and position for program approval for use as the field placement setting for program field experience requirements. Thus, when initiating this supervision delivery method, the program developed a variety of policies, procedures and documents to support the use of this practice across all candidates.

Authorization Procedures

For candidates in the program, a number of guidelines for securing site authorization to conduct remote supervision were developed and provided upon admission to the program. A video conferencing site authorization procedure was developed, consisting of two options for verifying/obtaining authorization to conduct the remote observations (see Appendix A). The first option was for the school or district site administrator (e.g., building principal, district special education director, etc.)

to verify their approval for the University Faculty to conduct remote observations of the teacher candidate in their field placement site. Furthermore, this site authorization includes verification by the administrator that remote observation protocols were in place at the school/district site, and that parent/guardian consent or assent for these protocols had been obtained. This School/District Compliance Form (see Appendix B) was provided to the appropriate site administrator, along with the contact information for the Program Director so that any questions or concerns could be addressed. The second option, if the site administrator could not verify appropriate remote supervision protocols, was a parent/guardian consent process. In this option the teacher candidate would deliver a Parent/Guardian Consent Form (see Appendix C) to a parent or guardian for each student who would appear in the live video feed during the remote observation. When parents/guardians did not provide consent for their child to participate in the remote observation, the teacher candidate, their cooperating teacher and the site administrator made arrangements for these students to participate in an alternate activity. These two forms, along with the description of the procedures for following these two options, were provided to all teacher candidates in their Program Handbooks, as well as in the course syllabi for all field experience courses. Furthermore, they were presented and reviewed with all teacher candidates during the orientation meeting for their initial semester field experience course.

Accounting for Technological Limitations in the Field

While the vast majority of field experience sites possess the technological capabilities to support remote supervision, based on reports in the literature on technological difficulties inherent with remote supervision (O'Connor, Good & Greene, 2006), the program developed a petition procedure for any candidates participating in settings lacking the adequate technology. The petition process allows program personnel to identify the nature of the technological limitation (Wi-fi capabilities, computer availability, video camera functions, district access to video conferencing software programs, etc.) at the site, and to make decisions regarding future use/approval of the site for the program field experience requirements. Typically, the petition process allows program personnel the opportunity to follow up with site administration in order to clarify and/or problem-solve the reported limitation. This follow up has resulted in the following examples of district efforts to enhance the availability of technology to candidates placed or employed at their sites: 1) lifting of district-wide restrictions on teacher access to video conferencing software on district computers, 2) temporary or permanent provision of external video camera devices, and 3) authorization for the candidate to utilize video conferencing software on their personal tablet or mobile device. The extent to which districts provide authorization and/or accommodations to program candidates regarding their ability to participate in video conferencing impacts program decisions around student teacher placement and program approval of employment settings for meeting the field experience requirements.

Supporting University Faculty in Conducting Remote Observations

Additionally, the program has provided procedures and support in the use of video conferencing for each of the University Faculty involved in providing field supervision of candidates. First, written procedures on the use of video conferencing supervision were developed and included in the Field Supervisor Handbook (see Appendix D for relevant excerpt) distributed to all supervising faculty. Copies of all forms and procedures disseminated to candidates, site administrators and parents/guardians were also provided to faculty providing remote field supervision, and all materials are reviewed with supervising faculty in meetings held during each semester's faculty planning week and revisited during ongoing program meetings.

Lastly, program faculty who are more experienced with the use of video conferencing software for conducting remote field supervision have provided opportunities for those less familiar to sit in on and observe how remote observations are conducted. Additionally, after obtaining school/district assurance of compliance and parent/guardian consent to do so, supervising faculty have conducted group video conference observations of candidates conducted in a conference room with the video feed projected on a screen for university faculty training. This allowed supervising faculty to discuss a common experience with remote supervision as a part of their professional development in this area.

Planning for the Remote Observation

When preparing to conduct a remote observation there are a number of considerations to be addressed. In addition to the typical preparation involved in conducting an on-site observation, such as 1) scheduling a date/time, 2) prompting the candidate to provide lesson plans and other relevant materials, 3) allocating a period of time following the observation to provide immediate feedback, etc. preparing for a video conferencing observation brings its own set of preparations to be arranged. Depending on the video conferencing software program to be used, there may be particular set up requirements before the program can be utilized. These might include downloading the program to the device or computer to be used, testing the video/audio feed, exchanging contact information (e.g., cell phone number, software program contact identification, etc.), and determining where to physically position the device/camera to display the activity to be observed. To address these set up considerations, we have maintained an initial on-site visit by the University Faculty to the candidate's field placement site. This initial visit serves a number of additional useful purposes, such as meeting the Cooperating Teacher, Site Administrator, Students, etc. However in terms of preparing for the remote observations, this initial visit allows the supervising faculty to review the computer/device to be used for appropriate video conferencing software, audio/video functioning, as well as to assist the candidate in determining appropriate classroom activities to conduct, and thus where/how to position the computer/device/camera, for the remote observation.

Conducting the Remote Observation

Just as with preparing for the remote observation, conducting the observation remotely differs in many ways from conducting an observation on-site. For example, while an in-person visit to the classroom can pose as a distraction to students, the appearance of another person on a computer or other device can become an even greater distraction to students. However, most video conferencing programs have options for removing the video feed on one end of the conference (i.e. on the computer/device in the classroom), either by opening other programs to "cover" the video picture or by minimizing the frame of the video feed. Additionally, most video conferencing programs possess a mute option to block distracting noises (e.g., phone calls, campus construction, etc.) coming from the university supervisor's end of the conference. Also, even with the best performing technology (e.g., software programs, computers/devices, internet bandwidths, etc.) video conferencing is limited in the extent to which a supervisor can visually observe all potential relevant features in the classroom setting. Thus, in addition to benefiting from an initial on-site visit to get a "lay of the land" perspective, university faculty request specific materials be submitted to them prior to conducting the remote observation. Many teacher preparation programs now use online student course management systems, which allow for any number or type of electronic documents to be uploaded for supervisor review. Candidates in our program maintain an electronic portfolio in this type of a system, where supervisors review items submitted, including lesson plans, journal reflections, summaries of assigned experiences in the field (e.g. attending an IEP meeting), and provide written feedback on assignments and observations (on-site and remote). Thus, in advance of a remote observation, programs can instruct candidates to submit relevant materials to be used during that lesson, making it accessible to the university faculty as they conduct their observation.

CONCLUSION

Providing direct supervision of teacher candidates in practical field settings is a crucial feature of effective teacher preparation programs. Yet, with less than optimal budget scenarios, increasing faculty workloads and the need to provide field experience in rural and often remote settings, the costs and time involved in providing on-site supervision can serve as a burden to faculty and preparation programs alike. However, with recent technological advances, teacher preparation programs are now able to make use of distance learning approaches in the provision of field supervision of credential candidates remotely. Video conferencing programs available on mobile or portable devices (e.g. cell phones, tablets, laptops, etc.) can provide an efficient medium for conducting field supervision. Ensuring that secure software programs are used, and that appropriate authorization and consent protocols are followed, are just a few of the important considerations facing teacher preparation programs taking advantage of these technologies to supervise the field experiences of teacher candidates.

ACKNOWLEDGMENT

The contents of this chapter were developed under grant from the U.S. Department of Education (H325K100428). However, those contents do not necessarily represent the policy of the U.S. Department of Education, and you should not assume endorsement by the Federal Government.

REFERENCES

Barley, Z. A., & Brigham, N. (2008). Preparing teachers to teach in rural schools (Issues & Answers Report, REL 2008–No. 045). Washington, DC: U.S. Department of Education, Institute of Education Sciences, National Center for Education Evaluation and Regional Assistance, Regional Educational Laboratory Central. Retrieved from. Retrieved from http://ies.ed.gov/ncee/edlabs

Boyd, D. J., Grossman, P. L., Lankford, H., Loeb, S., & Wyckoff, J. (2009). Teacher preparation and student achievement. *Educational Evaluation and Policy Analysis*, *31*(4), 416–440. doi:10.3102/0162373709353129

Brownell, M. T., Sindelar, P. T., Bishop, A. G., Langley, L. K., Seo, S., Rosenburg, M. S., & Bishop, L. (2005). *Growing and Improving the Special Education Teacher Workforce*. University of Florida.

Burgstahler, S. (2002). *Bridging the Digital Divide in Postsecondary Education: Technology access for youth with disabilities*. Minneapolis, MN: University of Minnesota.

California Commission on Teacher Credentialing. (2009). *Teacher Supply in California: A Report to the Legislature, Annual Report 2007-2008*. Sacramento, CA: Author.

California Department of Education. (2009). Educational Demographics Office – DataQuest. Sacramento, CA: Author.

California Department of Education. (2010). Educational Demographics Office – DataQuest. Sacramento, CA: Author.

Garret, J. L., & Dudt, K. (1998). Using video conferencing to supervise student teachers. *Technology and Teacher Education Annual*, 1084-1088.

Guyton, E., & McIntyre, D. J. (1990). Student teaching and school experience. In W. R. Houston (Ed.), *Handbook of research on teacher education 7* (pp. 514–534). Thousand Oaks, CA: Corwin Press.

Hamel, C. (2012). Supervision of pre-service teacher: Using internet collaborative tools to support their return to their region of origin. *Canadian Journal of Education*, *31*(2), 141–154.

Hollins, E. R., & Torres Guzman, M. (2005). Research on preparing teachers for diverse population. In M. Cochran-Smith, & K. Zeichner (Eds.), *Studying teaching education: The report of the AERA Panel on Research and Teacher Education* (pp. 477–544). Mahwah, NJ: Lawrence Erlbaum.

Jung, L. A., Galyon-Keramidas, C., Collins, B., & Ludlow, B. (2006). Distance Education Strategies to Support Practica in Rural Settings. *Rural Special Education Quarterly*, *25*(2), 18–24.

Ludlow, B. L., Conner, D., & Schechter, J. (2005). Low Incidence Disabilities and Personnel Preparation for Rural Areas: Current Status and Future Trends. *Rural Special Education Quarterly*, *24*(3), 15–24.

National Council for Accreditation of Teacher Education. (2010). Transforming teacher education through clinical practice: A national strategy to prepare effective teachers. Washington, DC: Author.

O'Connor, K. A., Good, A. J., & Greene, H. C. (2006). Lead by example: The impact of teleobservation on social studies methods courses. *Social Studies Research and Practice*, *1*(2), 165–178.

President's Commission on Excellence in Special Education. (2002). A New Era: Revitalizing special education for children and their families. Washington, DC: Department of Education, Office of Special Education and Rehabilitative Services.

Project Pipeline. (2003). *Seeking Out Special Educators: An in-depth look at California's special education teacher shortage*. Sacramento, CA: Project Pipeline.

Ronfeldt, M. (2012). Where should student teachers learn to teach? Effects of field placement school characteristics on teacher retention and effectiveness. *Educational Evaluation and Policy Analysis*, *34*(1), 3–26. doi:10.3102/0162373711420865

Rust, F. O'C. (1999). Professional conversations: New teachers explore teaching through conversation, story, and narrative. *Teaching and Teacher Education*, *15*(4), 367–380. doi:10.1016/S0742-051X(98)00049-3

Shields, P., Esch, C., Humphrey, D., Wechsler, M., Chang-Ross, C., & Gallagher, H. et al. (2003). *The Status of the Teaching Profession*. Santa Cruz, CA: The Center for the Future of Teaching and Learning.

Spooner, F., Spooner, M., Algozzine, B., & Jordan, L. (1998). Distance Education and Special Education: Promises, practices, and potential pitfalls. *Teacher Education and Special Education*, *22*(2), 97–109. doi:10.1177/088840649902200203

Tushnet, N. et al. (2002). *Independent Evaluation of the Beginning Teacher Support and Assessment (BTSA) System*. San Francisco, CA: WestEd.

U.S. Department of Education. (2008). *Personnel in Full Time Equivalency of Assignment Employed To Provide Special Education Programs. Data Analysis Systems (DANS)*. Washington, DC: Office of Special Education Programs.

Wilson, S. M., Floden, R. E., & Ferrini-Mundy, J. (2001). *Teacher preparation research: Current knowledge, gaps, and recommendations.* Seattle, WA: University of Washington.

KEY TERMS AND DEFINITIONS

Field Supervision: Observations by faculty of teacher candidates participating in classroom settings as a requirement of the preparation program.

Mobile Device: Portable electronic computing device, such as a smart phone, tablet or laptop computer.

Video Conferencing: Software program allowing two parties to access visual and audio feeds displayed via a camera and speakers on an electronic computing device.

APPENDIX A

Sample Written Guidelines on the Use of Video Conferencing

Supervision Permission Forms

The use of video conferencing software in your field placement requires that you secure permission to include children in the video stream. Therefore, you must secure parental permission and document for the Special Education Program the existence of the signed permission forms.

Two forms are provided to meet this requirement. Each is used in a different situation. Please read the descriptions below and select the option and form that fits your situation. If you have any questions, contact the appropriate program coordinator.

Option 1

You may use the form, *School/District Compliance Form* if your school has secured permission for the students in your class to be viewed remotely by a Faculty Supervisor during video conferencing supervision activities. These forms must be kept on file at the school. The form simply requires your administrator's signature as documentation that the school holds the forms. You *do not* need to submit the individual student forms in this case.

Option 2

If the school does not have signed permission forms on file for the students in your class, then you must collect the permissions yourself. Use the form entitled *Student Permission Form*. You must get a signature from a parent or guardian for each child in the classroom who may appear on camera during the video conferencing supervision. If you are unable to get such permission from one or more parents, under no circumstances can those children appear during the video conferencing supervision.

Once you have collected the forms (under either Option 1 or Option 2) they must be submitted to the SPED, where they will be kept on file. If you have questions about the permission process, please contact your Faculty Supervisor.

APPENDIX B

Box 1. Sample school/district compliance form

Special Education Candidates must verify consent of parents/legal guardians of all children and from any adults who appear on camera during a video conferencing supervision meeting before such meetings can occur.

I hereby affirm that I have followed the privacy conventions and permission requirements of my program and/or school district. I certify that I have secured and am holding on file signed copies of all necessary permission forms from all responsible individuals, or otherwise confirmed their consent.

_____ _____
Administrator's Name   Date

_____
School Name/Address

****

_____ _____
Candidate Name   Date

_____ _____
Teacher's Name/Room Number   Date

Please submit this form with an original signature to the Special Education Program Office

---

APPENDIX C

Box 2. Sample parent/guardian consent form

     Your child is in a classroom being taught by a Special Education Credential student enrolled at University. One basis for provision of quality instruction to our credential students is the use of observation. These observations provide opportunities for educational training, monitoring and planning for future sessions. Some of our observations will be done in person, while others will be done through live video. This live video observation activity involves an observation by a University Faculty Supervisor, observing remotely via video conferencing software, of a lesson taught in your child's class.

     Although both the teacher and various students would be within view during the video conference observation, the primary focus is on the teacher's instruction, not on the students in the class. Video conferences *will not* be recorded. No student's name will appear on any submitted materials. All materials will be kept confidential. Please complete and return the attached Video Conferencing Supervision Permission Form to document your permission for these activities.

I am the parent/legal guardian of the child named above. I have received and read your letter regarding the teacher candidate video conferencing observation, and agree to the following:

_____I DO give permission to include my child's image during the video conferencing observation as he or she participates in a class conducted at_____(Name of School) by_____(Teacher-Candidate Name). I understand that no student images will be recorded or otherwise permanently captured.

_____I DO NOT give permission to you to include my child's image during the video conferencing observation as he or she participates in a class conducted at_____(Name of School) by_____(Teacher-Candidate Name)

Signature of Parent/Guardian: _____Date: _____

APPENDIX D

Excerpt on Video Conference Supervision from the CSUMB Special Education Program Field Supervisor Handbook

Observations are conducted via a mixture of on-site visits and remote observations via video conferencing technology. Students are expected to make arrangements with their supervisors to participate in on-site and remote video conference observations.

1. Typical on-site visits include an observation and a private post-observation conference (post-observation conferences may be done by phone after the initial personal meeting).
    a. Normally, observations should cover a full lesson and a minimum of 15 minutes should be spent in the post-observation conference.
    b. The post-observation conference should occur as soon after the observation as possible and can be used as a pre-observation conference for the next observation.
2. Typical remote supervision includes the arrangement of video conferencing utilizing the supervisor's preferred software program (e.g., Skype, Google Hangout, etc). Therefore, the candidate must make proper arrangements with their site administration to ensure access to and approval for this activity. Please see Appendix A for the Video Conferencing Procedures and Authorization Forms. Remind your candidates to read over the two options carefully, select the appropriate form (District Authorization or Parent/Guardian Consent), obtain the relevant signatures and submit to you by the end of the second week of the semester.
    a. Normally, the video conferencing observations should cover a short 20-30 minute lesson, either with a large/small group or individual one-on-one instruction. The first 5 minutes of the observation should be set aside for ensuring that the technology is working properly, and the final 5-10 minutes should be reserved for a post-conference.
    b. In the event that a candidate has thoroughly pursued all available options to properly arrange for video supervision and not been granted authorization by the site administration and/or has not been provided with proper technology to conduct the video conference, the candidate may appeal to their Program Coordinator requesting that the video conference requirement be replaced with an on-site observation. The Program Coordinator will then make a determination as to the outcome of the appeal.

Chapter 7
Mobile Technology in Higher Education:
Patterns of Replication and Transferability

Meghan Morris Deyoe
University at Albany (SUNY), USA

Dianna L. Newman
University at Albany (SUNY), USA

Jessica M. Lamendola
University at Albany (SUNY), USA

ABSTRACT

Innovative instructional strategies and approaches are in high demand in STEM higher education. Currently, interest lies in the integration of mobile technology within these settings to provide learning opportunities that are flexible and feasible enough to increase student understanding using critical inquiry. Although the positive impact of the use of mobile technology in many pilot settings is known, there are still numerous questions left unanswered in relation to the effectiveness of the use of mobile technology as it is replicated from developer across enthusiastic replicator use to required use. This chapter examines the replication and transferability patterns related to the use of a mobile technology device within and across multiple instructors, settings, context, and content areas. Key variables explored relate to student and instructor prior use and experience with the mobile technology, pedagogical goals, and similarly, content and context to original use.

INTRODUCTION

With the continuous development and expansion of mobile technologies comes the need for more planned integration into education. This is especially true in the areas of science, technology, engineering, and math (STEM), the domains which spawned much of technology's early development and use. This growth has left the field with a plethora of resources, tools, pilot curricula, and eager instructors, but very little confirmation of evidence-based use and outcomes.

DOI: 10.4018/978-1-4666-6284-1.ch007

What we do know, however, is that in the STEM domain, incorporating technology into teaching and learning is fundamental if we are to represent and meet twenty-first century needs of students (DeHaan, 2005). Surprisingly, greater inclusion in higher education, the site of much of STEM's digital development, is especially needed. Inclusive, purposeful technology use within advanced and applied STEM settings is essential if today's students are to learn to navigate through complex problems that will prepare them for the future; today's students are tomorrow's professionals and they must have the ability to use flexible digital resources to solve problems efficiently and effectively if they are to move the society to new levels of economic greatness (Newman, Clure, Morris Deyoe, & Connor, 2013; Newman, Morris Deyoe, Lamendola, & Clure, 2014). To achieve the professions and society's goals, future workers need not only to be able to problem-solve and navigate through technology, they also must be able to combine their communication skills, their professional knowledge, and their work styles.

To meet these twenty-first century needs, both within the classroom and in future employment, more digitally supported devices, especially mobile devices, are being designed, developed, and piloted. The first generation impact of these tools is known; pilot studies show that mobile technology and its use enhances and promotes knowledge, both short-term and long-term, when coupled with active experimentation grounded in authentic settings (Hwang & Chang, 2011; National Council for Accreditation, 2008; Sultan, Woods, & Koo, 2011; Wong, Chin, Tan, & Liu, 2010). Most of the results of these studies, however, are limited in that they are based solely on use by developers or enthusiastic replicators. What we do not know is what happens to implementation, outcomes, and long-term adaptation of tools when the use of these devices becomes ubiquitous. Many questions still remain; for example: Are planned processes still used? What adaptations are crucial? How much prior user training is needed for the "typical" instructor? And, what developmental stages of instruction are supported?

A key area open for debate is the state of replicated use. Wiggins and McTighe's (2005) research on and investigation of transferring new educational resources into practice suggests that to reap the benefits of using mobile technology as a means of enhancing learning, instructors must know not only how to use the new technology, but also how to integrate the tool into meaningful learning experiences. Research suggests, however, that in cases where technology and course materials are implemented solely on perception of content and industry needs, generally by the person who developed and designed the material, student learning outcomes and perceptions, are positive at first use, but tend to decline when materials are adopted by a non-developer instructor (Cordray, Harris, & Klein, 2009; Newman et al., 2013; Teclehaimanot, Mentzer, & Hickman, 2011). These studies suggest that something appears to be lost when technology, especially mobile technology, goes "ubiquitous." Very little research has tracked this "loss" and determined when, where, and how much of it occurs.

This chapter attempts to begin a discussion of that loss and how to counteract it when using mobile technology in authentic education approaches. The chapter documents the patterns of replicability and transferability of a multiyear project which focused on replication and transferability of authentic use of a mobile hand-held technology across multiple contexts, pedagogies and practicums, tracking changes as the device moved from development to mass integration in undergraduate STEM courses. The chapter attempts to develop a pattern of use and subsequent outcomes detailing: 1) issues related to replicability across content, context, sites, and instructors, and 2) unexpected transferability to external, unplanned use. The role of prior use and experience for both instructors and students, as well as the embedded goals of pedagogy in authentic education will be addressed within the discussions of replicability and transferability.

OVERVIEW OF LITERATURE

In higher education STEM training, innovative, modified, and refined methods of adapting instruction and resources are increasingly being sought (Mastascusa, Snyder, & Hoyt, 2011). Faculty are looking for ways to strengthen student learning and understanding, as well as methods of creating more engaging, feasible, and flexible ways to provide students with learning opportunities. Embedded within this search is the common primary goal of increasing understanding through critical inquiry and problem-solving in a way that will promote twenty-first century career needs (Mastascusa et al., 2011). This drive to improve students' learning occurs at all levels, but it is especially important at the college level as we strive to meet the increasing demands of the workforce for the next generation. Consequently, new and old instructional methods, grounded in evidenced-based constructivist, guided inquiry, and discovery learning theory, are being implemented, reinvented, or reinstated. An increasing number of campuses, classes, and instructors are now integrating, or considering implementing, peer instruction, collaborative learning, student-based learning, application-based learning, service learning, problem-based learning, and instructor-guided inquiry into their student learning patterns (Swanson, 2013).

In support of this increased emphasis on effective instructional techniques, a new focus is evolving that is based on developing and implementing resources and instructional tools which support learning; this new focus also emphasizes tools that make use of the increasingly sophisticated and easily available technology advancements (e.g., iPads, iPods, Senseo Response Systems, SMART Boards, etc.). As a result, inexpensive, readily available multimedia and digital devices now are playing a major role in supporting and providing application and constructivist-based learning opportunities (Akhras & Self, 2000; Cheng, 2006; Newman & Gullie, 2009). Within STEM classrooms, the use of technology as a tool and support for instruction is now perceived as a requirement when teaching students the skills and knowledge needed within those professions. In STEM higher education settings faculty-researchers are developing and implementing new technological tools for their own classroom; many instructors are expected to and are planning on replicating, adopting, or adapting these new technologies and instructional methods for their own use in different domains and settings. While development is ongoing, replication is the new "name of the game."

This replication, however, has resulted in a transfer problem. Most new technologies are designed and implemented by the "developer(s)" of the products. These instructors have limited problems adapting the materials to different classes because they developed the tool to meet their instructional needs. Research touting the effectiveness of many of these methods is based on efforts and uses of the developers, not ubiquitous use. Unfortunately, new instructors who want to adopt these tools are often without the necessary resources, knowledge, or skills used by the original developer to implement with fidelity; consequently, replication users frequently find no immediate effect and abandon the attempt, reverting to less successful methods. Very little research is available on the replicability and transfer patterns of new STEM innovations and what we can expect to have happen when we move materials from their original setting to new sites and uses.

Literature indicates that accurate replication and transfer of instructional techniques is a major problem that may be affected by several factors including familiarity with the content, familiarity using the tool, and the amount of instructor practice

(O'Donnell, 2008; Rogers, 2003). Many of these factors reflect both formal and informal models of instructor-based professional development (Guskey, 2000) as well as the need for a common design that authenticates the diversity of use (Wiggins & McTighe, 2005). For instance, while prior research has shown that reflective practice and cross-site comparison is vital in changing classroom practices (Desimone, 2009; Guskey, 2002), we know that factors related to how, when, and where professional development is offered can promote change. This includes variations in sustained and embedded site-based training, the use of professional learning communities and peer-based communication, the availability of follow-up and support opportunities for users, and continuous evaluation of outcomes (Garet, Porter, Desimone, Birman, & Yoon, 2001; Guskey, 2000; Hawley & Valli, 1991; Keengwe, Kidd, & Kyei-Blankson, 2009). In addition, we know that some factors appear to greatly enhance the transferability and replication of new technologies in educational settings. Several researchers have noted that ongoing, intensive examination of and reflection on new technologies affects educational improvements (Garet, 2001; Guskey, 2000; Hawley & Valli, 1991; Johnson & Daugherty, 2008). Keengwe and colleagues (2009, when reviewing a series of research studies that investigated the adoption and use of technology at higher education sites (e.g., Frank, Zhao, & Borman, 2004; Schrum, Skeele, & Grant, 2002; Spotts, 1999)), found that both reflection and formative assessment were "critical to the adoption process" (p.24).

Expected Adaptation: Fidelity of Use

A major issue in the use of resources and tools developed by others is a distinction between adoption and adaptation, that is, fidelity of intended use. According to Rogers (2003), true adoption of an innovation or technology is supposed to be an exact replication of the technology or innovation's use as conducted in its developed setting and as documented in early research. In most settings, however, this does not happen. Instead, new users adapt, or modify, the tool, its use, and its expected outcomes to meet their own needs. As a result, debates and inquiries about fidelity of implementation are common and critics as well as funders now call for research that focuses on the changes that ensue as adoption, replication, and adaptation occur across individuals and settings. As an example of this debate, O'Donnell (2008), when discussing fidelity of implementation, found that it reflected two components: efficacy and effectiveness. Efficacy refers to evidence that an innovation, program, or intervention achieved the desired outcome "under the most favorable conditions" (O'Donnell, 2008, p.41) and represents implementation as documented by the developer. Typically, this reflects the critical elements which are still tightly controlled or monitored, ensuring that confounding factors within the design are maximized as necessary to make the innovation work. Effectiveness, on the other hand, is related to movement away from the developer to new users or new settings, and represents how well the innovation or program or intervention works when it is replicated, transferred, or adapted to naturalistic settings, non-controlled settings, where the influence of mediating and moderating factors is inevitable (O'Donnell, 2008). O'Donnell notes that because variations in fidelity will occur in natural settings, these may be variations in both process and student outcomes, thus impacting the perception of the innovation's widespread replicability and transferability. Borrergo, Cutler, Prince, Henderson, and Froyd (2013) note the importance of understanding and documenting both types of fidelity when integrating instructional methods within STEM education; they note the need for evidence-based studies within both developer and non-developer domains.

Some authors, however, note a disconnect between the two types of studies, prioritizing one or the other (e.g., Desimone, 2009; O'Donnell, 2008). They note that efficacy studies address specific relevance and usefulness, while effectiveness studies more accurately address the outcomes of replication, transfer, and adaptation. A review of literature indicates there is a need for both. Studies conducted on the effectiveness of technology-based instruction are typically conducted on a "solo pilot" level (i.e., only one location, one subject, and one instructor are studied). It is the results of meta-analyses of these "solo" studies that have been used to show that the use of technology in education does have positive affective (i.e., interest and motivation) and cognitive (i.e., knowledge retention) outcomes for students (Blok, Oostdam, Otter, and Overmaat, 2002; Cheung & Slavin, 2012; Lee, Waxman, Wu, Michko, & Lin, 2013; Soe, Koki, & Chang, 2000; Tamim, Bernard, Borokhovski, Abrami, & Schmid, 2011; Waxman, Lin, & Michko, 2003). As more specific examples, Newman, Rienhard, & Clure (2007) and Newman, Clure, Morris Deyoe, & Connor (2013) found that at one higher education site, the integration of multimedia-based tools as well as local technology in STEM education met both individual and group needs and supported a transfer of knowledge and skills to real life experiences, use of differentiated data sets, and outcomes to simulated professional problems. A study in a single school district on the use of instructional technology within ELA classrooms coupled with self-reflection led to increases in student attendance, student ELA test scores, and higher motivation to read (Newman, Coyle, & McKenna, 2013). Similarly, a study on the use of instructional technology and professional development within science classrooms, again in only one school district, led to documented increases in student attendance and science test scores, as well as reduced math anxiety for teachers (Newman, Gullie, & Hunter, 2012).

Although these studies have shown efficacy of the new tools, they provide only limited evidence of replication, transfer, and adaptation. If present, it is only at localized sites, with little or limited documentation describing the process of transferability and areas of common effectiveness across the sites. Further evidence is necessary on the actual process of implementation from developer to replicator (adopter), including what that replication looks like (e.g., fidelity); how differences occur across individuals, content areas, and contexts (e.g., adaptation); and how these differences impact outcomes. This knowledge is particularly needed in STEM higher education. The following study provides an in-depth investigation into the replication and transferability of a mobile technology within and across instructors, content, contexts, and institutions. Patterns of losses, gains, and potential confounding variables also are identified.

BACKGROUND OF THE STUDY

Data collected from a six-year project studying the use of a handheld mobile technology device were analyzed to investigate potential patterns of use reflecting fidelity of implementation including efficacy and effectiveness of outcomes. Settings included multiple instructors, content areas, and institutions. As shown in Figure 1, the proposed implementation pattern took on a "bulls-eye" pattern beginning with the developer at the center and each level of implementation following a different setting of replication or transfer. The *Developer* of the technology represented the original designer and developer of the tool and the curriculum. Two levels of use are portrayed by this instructor, the first, *Developer Piloting*, is the original use of the tool and its supporting curriculum, conducted by the author/developer; this use reflects stand-alone implementation needed for piloting and refinement. The second level, *Developer Integration*, reflects full use of the entire sequence of modules throughout a semester. This level includes refinement and adaptation to different classroom and student needs. The next major instructor breakout represents *Content Replication* instructors (two levels); participants represent faculty who teach

Figure 1.

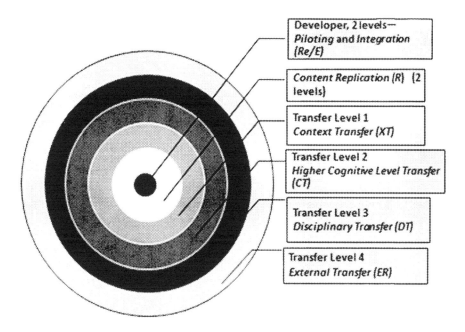

the same course as the developer, at the same institution, but who were not part of the design, development, piloting and structured refinement of the tools. First level use by these *Content Replication* faculty involves direct transfer of the tool and curriculum; it is intended that replication will occur with maximum fidelity. Second level use by *Content Replication* faculty allowed these instructors to refine their use and adapt the curriculum to their specific style of teaching; there is fidelity within content and curriculum, but pedagogical styles and some expected student outcomes are allowed to differ. The role of *Transfer Instructors* has four levels. The first level of *Transfer Instruction* represents *Context Transfer*; the resources are utilized in a similar content, but offered for a different purpose or audience (in this case a course on the same content for nonmajors, for instance, a course on electric circuits for majors other than electrical engineering). The second level of *Transfer Instruction, Higher Cognitive Level Transfer,* represents movement of the tool to an advanced course on the same content. Expected goals and use of the tool may be different, supportive or exploratory, and not reflect those of early learning. The third level of *Transfer Instruction, Disciplinary Transfer,* moves the use outside the original design's disciplinary domain to a topic-specific use where content overlaps, such as the specific use of a math formula in an applied content class. The fourth level of *Transfer Instruction, External Transfer,* supports original content, but the tool is utilized at different institutions. The use in this setting may reflect differences in content, context, and instructional goals and support. All of these levels of use, from developer to offsite uncontrolled use, were expected to have issues of replication, transferability and adaptation that might affect fidelity of the process of use, as well as fidelity of outcomes. The analyses presented in this chapter seek to determine the adequacy of the proposed pattern and issues related to fidelity as implementation shifted away from the developer, the specific context, and the specific site.

The Tool and Its Use

The tool discussed in this study was part of a larger project[1], and revolved around an innovative, handheld device developed and implemented for use in an engineering electric circuits course at a private college. The function of the tool was to simulate large laboratory equipment typically used in science and engineering classrooms (e.g., oscilloscope, function generator, etc.). The technology, the Mobile Studio Learning Platform™, consisted of an electronic input/output board, downloadable Mobile Studio Software™ for laptops, and a materials kit (e.g., batteries, wire, pliers, wire strippers, resistors, capacitors, and inductors). Over the course of a six year, 17 term, implementation project, the technology was used by 10 different instructors across five content domains (Electric Circuits, Electronic Instrumentation, Introduction to Electronics, Physics II, and Elements of Electrical Engineering) at multiple sites.

Eight instructors (including the developer) utilized the technology at the initial site of development; and two instructors implemented it at external schools of higher education. A brief summary of the levels of use and key contextual variables related to replication, transferability, and adaptation may be found in Table 1. The developer taught four semesters of the key content course Electric Circuits; in this setting, students represented primarily those majoring in electrical engineering. These classes reflected *Levels One and Two of Developer* use. Three subsequent semesters of this course were taught by a non-developer, or *Content Replication* instructor. This use reflects levels one and two uses of *Content Replication* instructors. The next levels of adoption, transfer occurred in different courses at the developing site. Use in Electronic Instrumentation represented the first level of *Transfer, Context*, to an engineering course comprised of students who did not have a background in electronics. Use in Introduction to Electronics represented the second level *Transfer, Cognitive,* a higher level course within the same content area—electrical engineering. The third level of *Transfer, Disciplinary*, was to a Physics course with use of the module moved to support other disciplines. The final and fourth level of *Transfer, External*, was to courses taught at external sites, but in content similar to that of the developer's original course.

Data Collection

The effectiveness of the technology on student learning and perceptions was examined when the technology was utilized by the *Developer, Content Replication* instructors within the same content area, *Transfer* instructors across contexts and disciplines, and *External Transfer* instructors. As can be seen in Table 2, the majority of students providing documentation for this chapter represent undergraduate electrical or computer systems engineering majors, with less reported evidence from students enrolled in the *Context Transfer* course and the *Discipline Transfer* course. Students in the *Discipline Transfer* courses were predominantly dual mechanical, aeronautical, chemical, and/or biomedical engineering majors.

Several data collection methods were involved. Pre-surveys (n=960), administered within the first two weeks of each course, assessed the status of replication and transferability (e.g., course, academic status and major), as well as potential confounding learner variables such as attitudes toward learning the context. Students' perceptions on the particular course in which they were enrolled, the format and setting of the tool and resources used, the benefits of its use and self-reported learning outcomes were assessed in matched post-course surveys, administered during the class in the last week of the course. Post-course interviews of students and instructors (n=90), administered in-person and via telephone at the end of the course, validated pre- and post-surveys and assessed overall perceptions of students' experiences with the technology used directly within the course, outside the course, and perceived long-term

Table 1. Technology implementation level and rank of instructor familiarity

Level of Implementation	Rank of St. Background Knowledge*	Course/Student Majors	Rank of Instructor Familiarity	Instructor Familiarity
Developer • Piloting. • Integration.	1	Electric Circuits/ Electronic Engineering Majors	1	Developed technology/Lead on project
Replication • Content Replication.	1		2	Some familiarity, sat in on classes where technology was used
Context Transfer • Replicate Instructor and Replacement project lead.	2	Electronic Instrumentation/ Non-electronic Engineering Majors	3	Replacement lead on project
Higher Cognitive Level Transfer I • Replicate Instructor (TAs).	1	Introduction to Electronics/ Electronic Engineering Majors	4	TAs served as instructors when technology was used, TAs had prior experience using the technology in instruction
Higher Cognitive Level Transfer II • Replicate Instructor (TAs).	1		7	TAs served as instructors when technology was used, TAs did not have experience using the technology in instruction
Disciplinary Transfer I • Replicate Instructor.	3	Physics II/Required course for a variety of majors, non-engineering and engineering	8	Instructor had no prior experience with the I/O board
Disciplinary Transfer II • Replicate Instructor.	3		6	Instructor(s) had prior experience, trained TAs in how to use the technology
External Transfer	1	Electrical Engineering/ Electronic Majors	5	A part of the project since its development

*Background knowledge refers to knowledge and experience with the content and concepts related to the Mobile Studio Learning Platform™(i.e., circuits, electrical engineering, etc.)

Key: 1=most familiarity or background knowledge. Highest # in each column equals the lowest amount of familiarity/background knowledge.

Table 2. Data sample

Phase	Year Three			
	Pre-Survey	Post-Survey	Interviews	Observations
Developer Integration/ Refinement	73	70	5	14
Content Replication	65	65	4	7
Higher Cognitive Level Transfer	67	67	1	2
Context Transfer	42	42	1	3
Disciplinary Transfer	84	84	3	5
External Transfer	24	9	0	0

outcomes. Observations (n=104) in all courses also confirmed survey and interview responses. A representative sample of the data is used for the purposes of this chapter; see Table 2 for more information on the instruments and sample.

IMPLEMENTATION

Examination of the overall data set identified several key patterns of use related to replicability and transferability of the data. In general, the expected pattern was verified with the device appearing to be transferrable and relevant to many users, contexts, and instructional needs. The device was successfully implemented in a variety of settings, where both experiential and didactic pedagogical goals were represented. In addition, support for both autonomous and collaborative learning was documented, as well as diverse instructional goals including scaffolded learning, demonstration, and guided inquiry. With the exception of the class depicting *Disciplinary Transfer*, almost all students found the mobile learning platforms to reflect course content and noted that it supported hands-on experience for learning (see Appendix Tables 3 & 6 for more information on use). Within this general finding, however, several different patterns of use were derived from the data for subsets of users. These patterns, along with confounding variables are discussed below.

The Role of Instructor Familiarity

A predominant factor involved in the pattern of implementation and replication was level of instructor familiarity with the mobile technology itself (i.e., how to use Mobile Studio Learning Platform™, familiarity and experience in using it in a class before, etc.). Analyses of the data indicated that instructor knowledge of the tool, practices in using it, and instructional goals were related to the patterns of perceptions of utility and relevance. As noted above, overall, the majority of the students had positive perceptions of the technology, but a decreasing pattern of the positive perception was noted by key instructional variables. When the faculty member had greater connections to the technology and its designed use, students had higher positive perceptions than students of instructors who were not as familiar with the technology and its prescribed use. As instructor levels of familiarity shifted from the initial use, where the familiarity was highest (i.e., *Developer*), to levels where the instructor was most removed from both the development and the original context (i.e., *Transfer Instructors*), perceptions of effectiveness decreased. Further examination indicated that familiarity with content, context, and development did form a series of concentric rings resembling the proposed bulls-eye (see Figure 2) where the *Developer* is the center of the bulls-eye with adjacent rings denoting higher levels of use and greater levels of disparity on adoption and replication with only minor variations. This pattern varied from the expected fidelity pattern.

As can be seen in Figure 2 and documented in Table 3 (see Appendix), students had more positive perceptions of use, the role of the instructor, and supplementary materials in *Developer* and *Content Replication* courses, with more disparity from the target found for *Higher Cognitive Level Transfer* and *Context Transfer* courses. That is, those students taught by the instructors with less familiarity with the technology and its intended use yielded the lowest ratings. More specifically, students in classes taught by more experienced instructors perceived the hands-on practice of the Mobile Studio Learning Platform™: 1) to better reflect real life situations grounded in the course content, and 2) that supporting resources were positive aspects of its use and were relevant to the course they were taking (see Appendix Table 3). Lower perceptions of these variables were presented by the *Disciplinary Transfer* classes where instructor knowledge in the major concepts crossed disciplinary use. In this setting, students'

Figure 2. Bulls-eye pattern with instructor familiarity variable

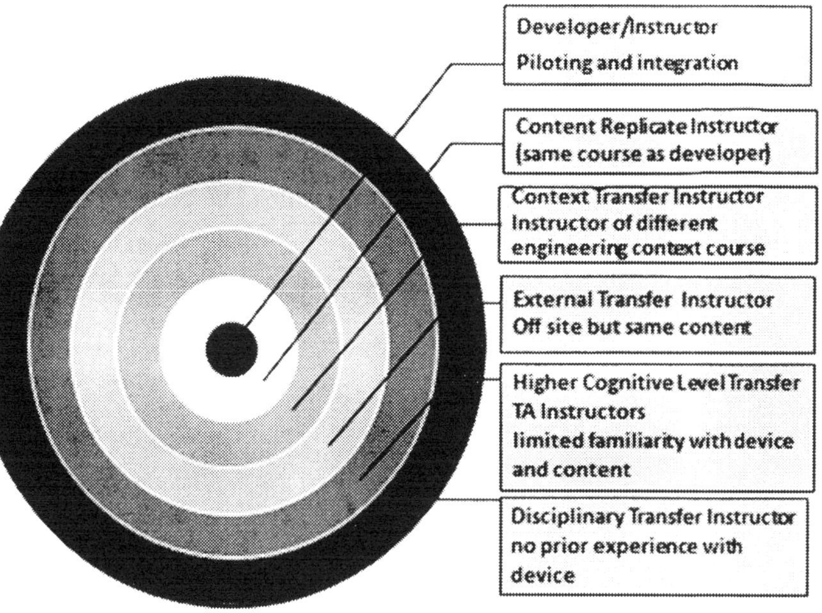

- Developer/Instructor Piloting and integration
- Content Replicate Instructor (same course as developer)
- Context Transfer Instructor Instructor of different engineering context course
- External Transfer Instructor Off site but same content
- Higher Cognitive Level Transfer TA Instructors limited familiarity with device and content
- Disciplinary Transfer Instructor no prior experience with device

perceptions of the device were less than in the courses where the instructors had familiarity with content. The settings where adaptation was managed by teaching assistants with lesser familiarity of both the device and the content served as the outer ring of the bulls-eye.

The Role of Students' Prior Experience

Data indicated student background knowledge embedded within the phase of implementation also changed the pattern of perceptions toward contextual knowledge acquisition. On average, responses to context knowledge generation ranged from a high percentage of agreement to a low percentage (see Figure 3), and again followed the expected replication pattern based on similarity to original purpose, content and context: that is, *Developer Integration, External Transfer, Context Transfer, Replication, Higher-Level Cognitive Transfer,* and *Disciplinary Transfer*. It is noteworthy, however, that for this variable—student prior experience—sites with *External Transfer* moved from the outer ring to one of closer proximity to the *Developer* (see Figure 4). In this setting, it appears the external users were transferring the tool to settings that reflected the same content and context as the *Developer*, as were *Context Transfer* settings in which students were learning similar content but for different uses; they also rated higher than did other adaptions. An unexpected deviation from the proposed pattern, but one that could be explained by instructor familiarity that occurred in transfer courses where the adaptation was managed by teaching assistants who were unfamiliar with the device. In these courses, where replicating and transfer should have mirrored courses with parallel content, it was found that student perceptions were markedly lower.

More specifically, as shown in Figure 5a, the majority of students in all phases of implementation within the same discipline (i.e., engineering) agreed that the use of the tool in active experimentation and hands-on activities enhanced their cognition of theories and concepts related to their course. It would appear that instructor familiarity moderates this value of active experimentation;

Figure 3. Support for context knowledge generation

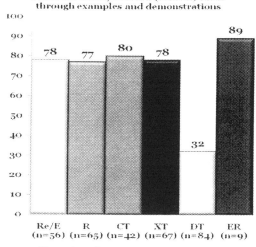
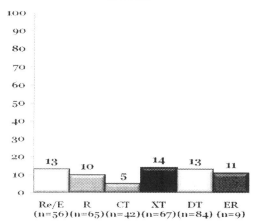
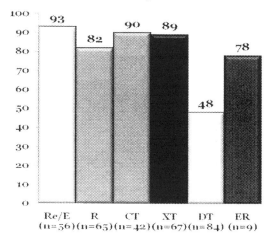
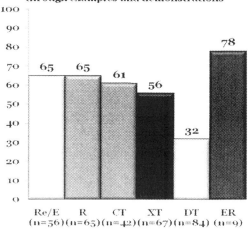

only one-third of students in the *Disciplinary Transfer* course reported the device as helpful in practicing concepts compared to over 70% of users by the *Developer*, *Content Replication* instructors and *External Transfer* instructors.

Examination of Figure 5b, the need to have someone model concepts instead of using hands-on exploration, indicated less than one-half of the students perceived a need for active demonstration provided by someone else for learning. This was most notable among those students where the instructor and the content were most removed from the original use (e.g., *Disciplinary Transfer*). These students may have placed less need to understand the content and context as they did not see instructors relating relevance. Overall, however, over half of each group no longer perceived a need for external support, but were satisfied with their own authentic hands-on experience (as shown in Figure 5a).

As further noted in Figure 6, for variables related to content generation (i.e., developing interest,

Mobile Technology in Higher Education

Figure 4. Bulls-eye pattern with student prior experience variable

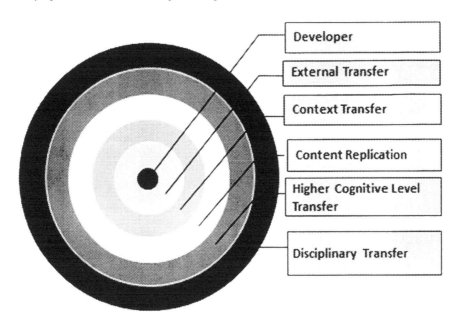

Figure 5.

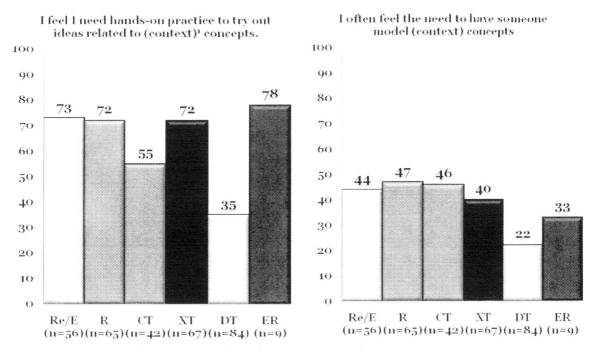

Re/E=Developer Integration/Refinement phase; R=Replication phase ; CT= Cognitive Transfer phase;
XT= Context Transfer phase ; DT= Disciplinary Transfer phase; ER= External Transfer phase
Figures 5a & 5b (respectively): Support for Knowledge Generation

Figure 6. Student perceptions on I/O Board benefits for learning outcomes

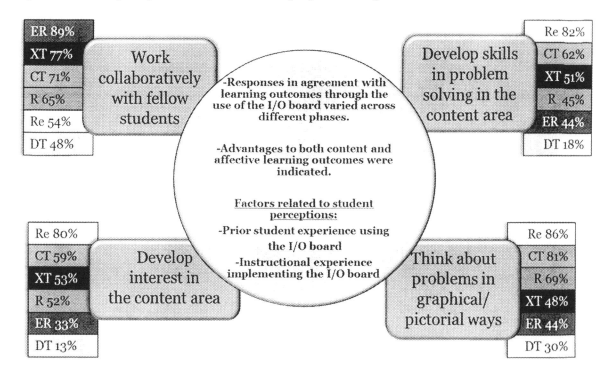

Re/E=Developer Integration/Refinement phase ; R=Replication phase ; CT= Cognitive Transfer phase; XT= Context Transfer phase ; DT= Disciplinary Transfer phase ; ER= External Transfer phase

developing problem-solving skills, and thinking about problems in a graphical way) the more the use correlated with the developers original idea in terms of content, context, and outcomes, the more learning outcomes were reported. A different pattern of concentric rings was noted (see Figure 7), however, when student skills in collaboration were assessed. In those settings where greater leaps in transfer were made (i.e., different sites, content or context) students relied more on collaboration with their peers.

Overall, both student and instructor familiarity emerged as factors related to use of the mobile technology and its effectiveness within the course(s). While the general format of a concentric ring of a bulls-eye was followed, the placement of some of these rings varied for some outcomes by user variables.

THE ROLE OF CONFOUNDING VARIABLES

Lack of Formal Training in Tool Integration

Formal training and professional development related to the use of the Mobile Studio Learning Platform™ and assistance in how to implement it within instruction did not occur for this device at the higher education level. Although all of the instructors were believed to be familiar with the content and the traditional tools the technology simulates (i.e., oscilloscope and function generator), methods of learning about the tool and its potential uses varied greatly. For example, the *Content Replication* instructor learned to use the technology through individual practice sup-

Figure 7. Bulls-eye pattern with collaboration variable

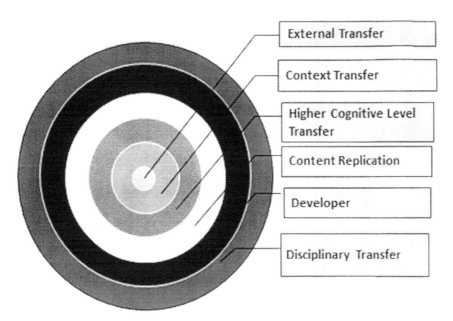

ported by in-class observations of the developer; this resulted in direct knowledge of the tool and its expected usage. Similarly, the instructor of the *Context Transfer* course also noted using autonomous hands-on experimentation to facilitate transfer of the tool within his own course.

For replication and transfer instructors who did not have these experiences, more adaption, transfer, and adoption problems were noted. Some instructors who did not have direct support turned that segment of their course over to other "more competent" instructors or delayed, decreased, or omitted use. Observations also indicated that, at times, this use was not integrated into the standard curriculum, but was perceived as an "add on" experiential opportunity. As noted earlier, experience levels of the teaching assistants also were important. The assistants in the first *Higher Cognitive Level Transfer* class had prior experience using the technology in one of the replication classes and one was part of the development process and worked directly on its design and refinement with the developer. These assistants were able to help with or provide the necessary transfer experience and support the instructor. Those teaching assistants, however, who taught the second *Higher Cognitive Level Transfer* class, did not have prior experience in using the device, nor did they receive any training in how to use it. As can be seen in Tables 3-6 in the Appendix, perceptions of the process and outcomes were lower in this setting. On the other hand, scores for the *External Transfer* instructor were higher; this instructor had received informal feedback and took part in several discussions about use with peer content providers. Although no formal training was provided, these developer/instructor conversations reflected informal best uses and advice on support were provided that guided implementation and adaptation.

Instructional Approaches and Instructional Goals

The device successfully supported multiple teaching styles that exemplified differing pedagogical approaches and varied levels of support. The *Developer* initially focused on autonomous learning with some opportunity for partner-work supported by scaffolded, guided inquiry approach to learning. In using this approach, the instructor demonstrated and modeled concepts that students then practiced individually through active experimentation until they mastered the concepts. Students in this setting received multiple instructor demonstrations using the tool during the class or "lecture" portion of the course, as well as time set aside for immediate individual use. In addition, the *Developer's* students were the only group where more than half of the students reported using the tool for homework and to practice outside the classroom (56% of students reported using the board independently for homework; 22% reported using it with a partner to complete homework). These students evidenced greater long-term retention.

Although the *Content Replication* instructor utilized a similar approach to instruction, there was more emphasis on partner-work when using the mobile device over individual use.[2] In addition, demonstrations during the "lecture" period were reported much less frequently (13%) at the replication level; these students had more hands-on trial and error authentication. In this setting, though retention was not as great as the previous setting, perceived knowledge of possible affective outcomes increased pre to post.

Because in the *Higher Cognitive Level Transfer* classes nearly all the students had prior experience with the Mobile Studio Learning Platform™ and the content, use of the device was restricted to lab time only. Although demonstration was provided to the class by a teaching assistant familiar with the tool, the majority of students learned through a cooperative peer learning approach. In addition, approximately two-thirds of these students reported using the device independently while in class. In this setting, two major course objectives were supported through the use—students had gains in knowledge as well as increased opportunity to learn team building skills.

Similar goals were met in the learning environment in the *Context Transfer* class. This setting utilized collaborative student inquiry and self-regulated learning conducted in teams of two and four working at their own pace. Observations noted that depending on students' division of tasks, some students also worked autonomously with the Mobile Studio Learning Platform™. Learning outcomes appeared to vary by role of the student.

The *External Transfer* instructor primarily implemented a collaborative learning setting; however, autonomous learning also was reported (see Appendix Table 6). The majority of students (78%) in the *External Transfer* course reported using the Mobile Studio Learning Platform™ with a partner in lab and independently during class. The *External Transfer* instructor also utilized demonstration techniques in both lab and lecture. For instance, approximately one-third of these students indicated they used the Mobile Studio Learning Platform™ and 56% of students reported using the Mobile Studio during class time. These students reported greater gains in content and relevance of materials.

In the *Disciplinary Transfer* courses, considerably fewer students reported positive use of the Mobile Studio Learning Platform™ in any capacity and observers noted major differences in instructional goals as well as practice. In the first *Disciplinary Transfer* course, nearly 25% of students reported use through instructor demonstration, whereas only 8% reported use through instructor demonstration for the second *Disciplinary Transfer* course. Observations indicated that in an attempt to move beyond demonstration, strong support was needed for the instructor and for the student. In the first *Disciplinary Transfer* course, the initial instructional approach began by using a guided inquiry approach; however, as the semester went on, feedback and informal assessments led the instructor to reduce use to more of a direct instruction approach to ensure student understanding. In the second *Disciplinary Transfer* course, the instructional approach was based on constructivist, guided inquiry with direct scaffolding via lab handouts.

Figure 8. Implementation of mobile studio approach

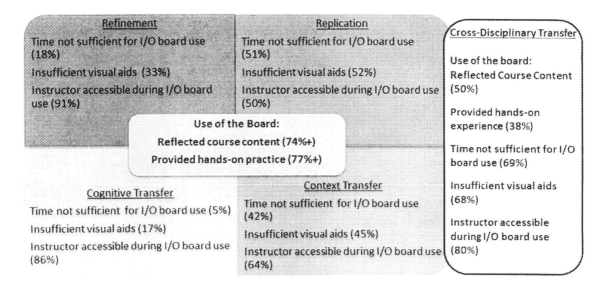

CONCLUSION AND IMPLICATIONS

This six year, 17-term development and replication project found that use of a mobile technology was successful in assisting and supporting higher education STEM learning. Overall, use of the mobile technology supported multiple instructional styles and students' knowledge generation when replicated and transferred across multiple settings. Use and experience, however, was related to the instructors' pedagogical goals and approach in the classroom but these in turn appear to be related to instructor familiarity. For example, instructor accessibility and time allotted for use of the device and supporting materials appears to be concomitantly dependent upon the instructor's targeted use in the classroom and how that use was perceived to support learning (i.e., teacher-directed vs. student-directed learning, constructivist learning vs. direct instruction), as well as, instructor familiarity with the technology. Instructors who were more familiar with the device, and whose course goals more closely matched the original concept tended to move toward more students-centered, hands-on approach to use. The further the use was removed from the original concept, the more instructors tended to use the device as a "drop in" aid to curriculum and instruction. As the instructor gained in familiarity with the tool and saw potential for practice and exploration, however, use did increase. This use might not have, and frequently did not, replicate the original development goals, but was viewed as partially successful by students.

Data patterns indicate the implementation level, instructor familiarity, and student background knowledge (i.e., knowledge in content related to electrical engineering) influenced participants' perceptions of mobile technology-related learning outcomes. Differences in familiarity with the tool, as well as instructional style, led to the variations in student responses towards a need for supporting visual aids, and more time allotted for use.

Although pedagogical goals may be based on students' level of familiarity with the mobile device and the advanced standing of the course (i.e., more emphasis was placed on student-centered constructivist learning), instructor familiarity and congruence with original *Developer* goals played major roles.

Use in courses taught by the *Developer* and in the first *Higher Cognitive Level Transfer* course yielded the most positive perceptions of the benefits of using the mobile technology by both student and instructor on the device's ability to assist in specific learning outcomes (i.e., thinking about problems graphically, pictorially and developing content-related problem solving skills). These outcomes are directly related to student ability to demonstrate knowledge in specified domains that can later be transferred.

Use of the mobile technology also was perceived beneficial in promoting more general learning outcomes related to long-term learning and professional needs. Two-thirds or more of students perceived the device to promote collaboration if they were students enrolled in courses where the device was used to support hands-on practice in cooperative group work (i.e., *External Transfer, Content Replication, Higher Cognitive Level Transfer,* and *Context Transfer*).

Increases in affect necessary to promote learning also were supported differentially. In settings where both the instructor and the student had more familiarity with content and context, greater gains in the important variables were noted. For example, more than half of the students in the developer's classes, first *Higher Cognitive Level Transfer* course, and the second *Content Replication* course perceived the device to benefit affective learning. Students in *Disciplinary Transfer* demonstrated less change.

These findings and the resultant patterns have implications for both developers of technology and for higher education faculty adopters. Researchers need to expand the design and development activities as well as supporting materials to ensure transfer to those who are novices in the use of the tool. This includes more discussion and instruction on how to use these tools in different course configurations, as well as different phases of support systems. Designers need to build into their development, the documentation of exemplary practices and acceptable transformation of use in ways that will still result in fidelity of outcomes. This means that design and development is not complete when the tool has been proven to work in the local pilot setting. Instead, if proven successful in this setting, designers need to promote and document use in alternate settings and assist in creating replicable, transferable, and adaptive uses.

Instructors in higher education settings also need to be more aware of the time, resources, and convergence of goals on their intended adoption. If new technological devices are to be introduced into a higher education classroom, instructors should look for those that have documented suggestions for use, plan on at least two repetitions, and allocate time for adaption, not just adoption and replication.

The role of technology in higher education settings is here to stay, either as a content to be learned or as a support to learning and instruction. While it can be used well, it also can be used poorly. More development and documentation of successful patterns of use is needed to assist in creating "good use".

REFERENCES

Akhras, F. N., & Self, A. J. (2000). System intelligence in constructivist learning. *International Journal of Artificial Intelligence in Education, 11*(4), 344–376.

Blok, H., Oostdam, R., Otter, M. E., & Overmaat, M. (2002). Computer-assisted instruction in support of beginning reading instruction: A review. *Review of Educational Research, 72*(1), 101–130. doi:10.3102/00346543072001101

Borrergo, M., Cutler, S., Prince, M., Henderson, C., & Froyd, J. E. (2013). Fidelity of implementation of research-based instructional strategies (RBIS) in engineering science courses. *Journal of Engineering Education, 102*(3), 394–425. doi:10.1002/jee.20020

Cheng, Y. C. (2006). New paradigm of learning and teaching in a networked environment: Implications for ICT literacy. In L. T. Wee Han, & R. Subramaniam (Eds.), *Handbook of research on literacy in technology at the K-12 level*. Hershey, PA: IDEA Group, Inc. doi:10.4018/978-1-59140-494-1.ch001

Cheung, A. C., & Slavin, R. E. (2012). How features of educational technology applications affect student reading outcomes: A meta-analysis. *Educational Research Review, 7*(3), 198–215. doi:10.1016/j.edurev.2012.05.002

Cordray, D., Harris, T., & Klein, S. (2009). A research synthesis of the effectiveness, replicability, and generality of the VaNTH challenge-based instructional modules in bioengineering. *Journal of Engineering Education, 98*(4), 335–348. doi:10.1002/j.2168-9830.2009.tb01031.x

Dehaan, R. L. (2005). The impending revolution in undergraduate science education. *Journal of Science Education and Technology, 14*(2), 253–269. doi:10.1007/s10956-005-4425-3

Desimone, L. M. (2009). Improving impact studies of teachers' professional development: Toward better conceptualization and measures. *Educational Researcher, 38*(3), 181–199. doi:10.3102/0013189X08331140

Frank, K. A., Zhao, Y., & Borman, K. (2004). Social capital and the diffusion of innovations within organizations: Application to the implementation of computer technology in schools. *Sociology of Education, 77*(2), 148–171. doi:10.1177/003804070407700203

Garet, M. S., Porter, A. C., Desimone, L., Birman, B. F., & Yoon, K. S. (2001). What makes professional development effective? Results from a national sample of teachers. *American Educational Research Journal, 38*(4), 915–945. doi:10.3102/00028312038004915

Guskey, T. (2000). *Evaluating Professional Development*. Thousand Oaks, CA: Corwin Press.

Guskey, T. R. (2002). Professional development and teacher change. *Teachers and Teaching: Theory and Practice, 8*(3/4), 381-391.

Hawley, W., & Valli, L. (1991). The essentials of effective professional development. In L. Darling-Hammond, & G. Sykes (Eds.), *Teaching as the Learning Profession: Handbook of Policy and Practice*. San Francisco, CA: Jossey Bass Publishers.

Hwang, G., & Chang, H. (2011). A formative assessment-based mobile learning approach to improving the learning attitudes and achievements of students. *Computers & Education, 56*(4), 1023–1031. doi:10.1016/j.compedu.2010.12.002

Johnson, S. D., & Daugherty, J. (2008). Quality and characteristics of recent research in technology education. *Journal of Technology Education, 20*(1), 16–31.

Keengwe, J., Kidd, T., & Kyei-Blankson, L. (2009). Faculty and technology: Impact for faculty training and technology leadership. *Journal of Science Education and Technology, 18*(1), 23–28. doi:10.1007/s10956-008-9126-2

Lee, Y. H., Waxman, H., Wu, J. Y., Michko, G., & Lin, G. (2013). Revisit the effect of teaching and learning with technology. *Journal of Educational Technology & Society, 16*(1), 133–146.

Mastascusa, E. J., Snyder, W. J., & Hoyt, B. S. (2011). *Effective instruction for STEM disciplines: From learning theory to college.* San Francisco, CA: John Wiley & Sons, Inc.

National Council for the Accreditation of Teacher Education. (2008). *Professional Standards for the Accreditation of Schools, Colleges, and Departments of Education.* Washington, DC: NCATE.

Newman, D., Clure, G., Morris Deyoe, M., & Connor, K. (2013). Using technology in a studio approach to learning: Results of a five year study of an innovative mobile teaching tool. In J. Keengwe (Ed.), *Pedagogical applications and social effects of mobile technology integration* (pp. 114–132). Hershey, PA: IGI Global. doi:10.4018/978-1-4666-2985-1.ch007

Newman, D., Coyle, V., & McKenna, L. (2013). Changing the face of ELA classrooms: A case study of TPACK in professional development. In J. Keengwe (Ed.), *Research perspectives and best practices in educational technology integration.* Hershey, PA: IGI Global.

Newman, D., & Gullie, K. (2009). *Using constructivist methods in technology-supported learning: Evidence of student impact.* Paper presented at the Annual Meeting of the American Educational Research Association. San Diego, CA.

Newman, D., Gullie, K., & Hunter, K. (2012). *Syracuse city school district urban natural science initiative.* Paper presented at the Math Science Partnership Regional Conference. New Orleans, LA.

Newman, D., Morris Deyoe, M., Connor, K., & Lamendola, J. (2014). Flipping STEM learning: Impact on students' process of learning and faculty instructional activities. In J. Keengwe, & G. Onchwari (Eds.), *Promoting active learning through a flipped classroom model.* Hershey, PA: IGI Global. doi:10.4018/978-1-4666-4987-3.ch006

Newman, D., Reinhard, D. E., & Clure, G. (2007). *Using constructivist methods in technology supported learning: Evidence of student impact.* Paper presented at the American Educational Research Association. Chicago, IL.

O'Donnell, C. L. (2008). Defining, conceptualizing, and measuring fidelity of implementation and its relationship to outcomes in K–12 curriculum intervention research. *Review of Educational Research, 78,* 33–84. doi:10.3102/0034654307313793

Rogers, E. M. (2003). *Diffusion of innovations* (5th ed.). New York, NY: Free Press.

Schrum, L., Skeele, R., & Grant, M. (2002). One college of education's effort to infuse technology: A systemic approach to revisioning teaching and learning. *Journal of Research on Technology in Education, 35*(2), 256–271. doi:10.1080/15391523.2002.10782385

Soe, K., Koki, S., & Chang, J. M. (2000). *Effect of Computer-Assisted Instruction (CAI) on reading achievement: A meta-analysis.* Honolulu, HI: Pacific Resources for Education and Learning.

Spotts, T. H. (1999). Discriminating factors in faculty use of instructional technology in higher education. *Journal of Educational Technology & Society, 2*(4), 92–99.

Sultan, W. H., Woods, P. C., & Koo, A. (2011). A constructivist approach for digital learning: Malaysian schools case study. *Journal of Educational Technology & Society, 14*(4), 149–163.

Swanson, J. A. (2013). *Emerging adults: Analysis of learning patterns in collegiate classrooms.* (Unpublished doctoral dissertation). University at Albany, State University of New York, Albany, NY.

Tamim, R. M., Bernard, R. M., Borokhovski, E., Abrami, P. C., & Schmid, R. F. (2011). What forty years of research says about the impact of technology on learning a second-order meta-analysis and validation study. *Review of Educational Research, 81*(1), 4–28. doi:10.3102/0034654310393361

Teclehaimanot, B., Mentzer, G., & Hickman, T. (2011). A mixed methods comparison of teacher education faculty perceptions of the integration of technology into their courses and students feedback on technology proficiency. *Journal of Technology and Teacher Education, 19*(1), 5–21.

Waxman, H., Lin, M., & Michko, G. (2003). *A meta-analysis of the effectiveness of teaching and learning with technology on student outcomes.* Naperville, IL: Learning Point Associates.

Wiggins, G., & McTighe, J. (n.d.). *Understanding by design®* (2nd ed.). Alexandria, VA: Association for Supervision and Curriculum Development.

Wong, L., Chin, C., Tan, C., & Liu, M. (2010). Students' personal and social meaning making in a Chinese idiom mobile learning environment. *Journal of Educational Technology & Society, 13*(4), 15–26.

ADDITIONAL READING

Bybee, R. W. (2010). Advancing STEM education: A 2020 vision. *Technology and Engineering Teacher, 70*(1), 30–35.

Collins, A., & Hlaverson, R. (2009). *Rethinking education in the age of technology.* New York, NY: Teachers College Press.

D'Angelo, J. M., & Wooley, S. A. (2007). Technology in the classroom: Friend or foe? *Education, 127*(4), 462–471.

Fisher, M., & Baird, D. E. (2006). Making mlearning work: Utilizing mobile technology for active exploration, collaboration, assessment, and reflection in higher education. *Journal of Educational Technology Systems, 35*(1), 3–30. doi:10.2190/4T10-RX04-113N-8858

Franklin, T., Sun, Y., Yinger, N., Anderson, J., & Geist, E. (2013). The changing roles of faculty and students when mobile devices enter the higher education classroom. In J. Keengwe (Ed.), *Pedagogical applications and social effects of mobile technology integration* (pp. 238–257). Hershey, PA: IGI Global. doi:10.4018/978-1-4666-2985-1.ch014

Gappa, J., Ausin, A., & Trice, A. (2007). *Rethinking faculty work: Higher education's strategic imperative*. San Francisco, CA: Jossey-Bass.

Gupta, B., & Koo, Y. (2010). Applications of mobile elearning in higher education: An empirical study. *International Journal of Information and Communication Technology Education*, *6*(3), 75–87. doi:10.4018/jicte.2010070107

Henderson, C., Beach, A., & Finkelstein, N. (2011). Facilitating change in undergraduate STEM instructional practices: An analytic review of the literature. *Journal of Research in Science Teaching*, *48*(8), 952–984. doi:10.1002/tea.20439

Katehi, L., Pearson, G., & Feder, M. (Eds.). (2009). *Engineering in K-12 education: Understanding the status and improving the prospects*. Washington, DC: National Academies Press.

Keefe, B. (2010). *The perception of STEM: Analysis, issues, and future directions. Survey*. Entertainment and Media Communication Institute.

Kim, S. H., Mims, C., & Holmes, K. P. (2006). An introduction to current trends and benefits of mobile wireless technology use in higher education. *AACE Journal*, *14*(1), 77–100.

Labov, J. B., Singer, S. R., George, M. D., Schweingruber, H. A., & Hilton, M. L. (2009). Effective practices in undergraduate STEM education. Part 1: Examining the evidence. *CBE Life Sciences Education*, *8*(3), 157–161. doi:10.1187/cbe.09-06-0038 PMID:19723807

Looi, C. K., Seow, P., Zhang, B., So, H. J., Chen, W., & Wong, L. H. (2009). Leveraging mobile technology for sustainable seamless learning: A research agenda. *British Journal of Educational Technology*, *41*(2), 154–169. doi:10.1111/j.1467-8535.2008.00912.x

Metcalf, D. S., & DeMarco, J. M. (2006). mLearning: Mobile learning and performance in the palm of your hand. Amherst, MA: HRD Press, Inc.

Moore, K., Fairweather, J., Amey, M., Ortiz, A., Mabokela, R., & Ruterbusch, M. (2000). *Best practices for reform in undergraduate education in science, math, engineering, & technology: A knowledge framework*. East Lansing, MI: Center for the Study of Advanced Learning Systems, Michigan State University.

Naismith, L., Sharples, M., Vavoula, G., & Lonsdale, P. (2004). Literature review in mobile technologies and learning.

National Research Council (NRC). (2010). *Exploring the intersection of science education and 21st century skills: A workshop summary*. Washington, DC: National Academies Press.

Pursell, D. P. (2009). Adapting to student learning styles: Engaging students with cell phone technology in organic chemistry instruction. *Journal of Chemical Education*, *86*(10), 1219–1222. doi:10.1021/ed086p1219

Roschelle, J. (2003). Keynote paper: Unlocking the learning value of wireless mobile devices. *Journal of Computer Assisted Learning*, *19*, 260–272. doi:10.1046/j.0266-4909.2003.00028.x

Samson, P. J. (2010). Deliberate engagement of laptops in large lecture classes to improve attentiveness and engagement. *Computers & Education*, *1*(2), 1–19.

Sanders, M. (2009). Integrative STEM education primer. *Technology Teacher*, *68*(4), 20–26.

Shih, J. L., Chuang, C. W., & Hwang, G. J. (2010). An inquiry-based mobile learning approach to enhancing social science learning effectiveness. *Journal of Educational Technology & Society*, *13*(4), 50–62.

Trigwell, K., & Prosser, M. (1996). Congruence between intention and strategy in university science teachers' approaches to teaching. *Higher Education*, *32*(1), 77–87. doi:10.1007/BF00139219

Volkmann, M. J., & Zgagacz, M. (2004). Learning to teach physics through inquiry. The lived experiences of a graduate teaching assistant. *Journal of Research in Science Teaching, 41*(6), 584–602. doi:10.1002/tea.20017

Walcyk, J. J., & Ramsey, L. L. (2003). Use of learner-centered instruction in college science and mathematics classrooms. *Journal of Research in Science Teaching, 40*(6), 566–584. doi:10.1002/tea.10098

Wangler, T. G., & Ziliak, E. M. (2013). Increasing student engagement and extending the walls of the classroom with emerging technologies. In J. Keengwe (Ed.), Research Perspectives and Best Practices in Educational Technology Integration (44-60). Hershey, PA: IGI Global.

Wiggins, G., & McTighe, J. (1998). *Understanding by design*. Alexandria, VA: Association for Supervision and Curriculum Development.

Wiggins, G., & McTighe, J. (2013). *Essential questions: Opening doors to student understanding*. Alexandria, VA: Association for Supervision and Curriculum Development.

Wiggins, G., & McTighe, J. (2013). *Schooling by design: Mission, action, and achievement*. Alexandria, VA: Association for Supervision and Curriculum Development.

KEY TERMS AND DEFINITIONS

Authentic Education: Education experiences grounded in real world, problem-based activities designed to encourage multiple perspectives and cross-disciplinary knowledge application and transfer.

Constructivism: Learning theory that states an individual's learning is contextual and is based on their building of knowledge through their experiences.

Effectiveness: How well an innovation can be used across multiple sites and settings.

Efficacy: How well an innovation produces desired results.

Mobile Devices: Any technological device that has portability and mobility that allows for internet connectivity.

Mobile Studio Learning Platform™: A hardware platform designed for use with a laptop and appropriate software to simulate hardware used in electronics laboratories.

Replication: The reproduction of the use of a tool or innovation in another setting, by the same or another individual.

SMART Board: an interactive whiteboard that allows for the use of multimedia tools (e.g., videos, images, websites) into instruction.

Understanding by Design®: A framework designed by Wiggins and McTighe (1998) to improve student achievement in learning that includes the interrelation of learning goals, assessments, and learning activities.

ENDNOTES

[1] Partial support for this project was provided by the Engineering Research Centers Program of the National Science Foundation Grant under NSF Cooperative Agreement EEC-0812056 and the NSF Division of Undergraduate Education under DUE-0717832.

[2] The second year of replication, external factors (e.g., delays in manufacturing) caused students to only have access to the Mobile Studio Learning Platform™ during lab and "open shop" time set aside for them to work on assignments.

APPENDIX

Table 3. Student perceptions of Mobile Studio I/O Board use in the classroom*

Statement	% Agree**											
	D Pilot/ Integ. Sp 08 (n=76)	D Integ. F08-Sp09 (n=138)	D I/Re F09 (n=56)	R Sp10 (n=65)	R/Re F10-Sp11 (n=115)	CT I Sp10 (n=42)	CT II F10-Sp11 (n=66)	XT Sp10 (n=67)	XT F10-Sp11 (n=109)	DT I F09 (n=84)	DT II Sp12 (n=66)	ER F09 (n=9)
Role of Instructor (including the Teaching Assistants)												
The instructor was accessible during I/O board use/exercises.	83	89	91	50	77	86	39	64	75	80	74	67
The time allotted for I/O board use was adequate.	59	70	82	49	63	95	74	58	65	72	51	56
Format and Setting during I/O Board Use												
The use of the I/O boards reflected course content.	90	87	93	74	81	88	68	84	87	50	46	100
The I/O boards provided opportunities for students to practice content.	90	91	93	77	81	86	71	84	87	38	49	89
The use of the I/O boards reflected real practice.	80	79	82	60	58	64	56	65	74	27	42	--
Supplementary Instructional Materials												
The visual aids (e.g. diagrams) used with I/O boards were clear and helpful.	45	66	67	48	58	87	45	55	64	32	46	89

* Numbers represent percentages of participants who responded "Strongly Agree" or "Agree" on a 6-point Likert-type scale.
***D=Developer, D Integ=Integration, D Re= Developer Refinement, Re/E=Refinement/Expansion phase, R=Replication phase, CTI=Cognitive Transfer phase with experienced TA instructors, CT II=cognitive transfer with inexperienced TA instructors, XT=Context Transfer phase, DT I=Disciplinary Transfer phase with inexperienced instructor, DT II= Disciplinary transfer with experienced instructors, ER=External Transfer

*Table 4. Support for context knowledge generation**

Learning Engineering Statements	% Agree**											
	D Pilot/ Integ. Sp 08 (n=76)	D Integ. F08 Sp09 (n=138)	D I/Re** F09 (n=56)	R** Sp10 (n=65)	R/Re F10 Sp11 (n=115)	CT I Sp10 (n=42)	CT II F10-Sp11 (n=66)	XT Sp10 (n=67)	XT F10 Sp11 (n=109)	DT I*** F09 (n=84)	DT II*** Sp12 (n=66)	ER F09 (n=9)
Using hands-on manipulatives will enhance my understanding of engineering concepts.	83	86	93	82	83	90	83	89	85	48%	61	78%
I have the ability to learn engineering ideas through examples and demonstrations.	77	82	78	77	78	80	74	78	85	32%	73	89%
Sometimes I need hands-on practice to try out ideas related to engineering concepts.	68	71	73	72	70	55	68	72	67	35%	49	56%
I have the ability to communicate engineering ideas with classmates through examples and demos.	64	66	65	65	60	61	59	56	71	32%	29	78%
Using hands-on manipulatives to learn engineering concepts would make me nervous.	9	13	13	10	10	5	15	14	17	13%	8	11%

* D=Developer, D Integ=Integration, D Re= Developer Refinement, Re/E=Refinement/Expansion phase, R=Replication phase, CTI=Cognitive Transfer phase with experienced TA instructors, CT II=cognitive transfer with inexperienced TA instructors, XT=Context Transfer phase, DT I=Disciplinary Transfer phase with inexperienced instructor, DT II= Disciplinary transfer with experienced instructors, ER=External Transfer
**Percentages represent those participants who responded, "Strongly Agree" or "Agree" on a 6-point Likert-type scale.
***The word "engineering" in each item was replaced with "physics" for items for the disciplinary transfer course.

Table 5. Student perceptions of learning outcomes*

Perception Toward Mobile Studio Learning Platform™ Benefits	% Agree**											
	D Pilot/ Integ. Sp 08 (n=76)	D Integ. F08 Sp09 (n=138)	D I/Re F09 (n=56)	R Sp10 (n=65)	R/Re F10-Sp11 (n=115)	CT I Sp10 (n=42)	CT II F10-Sp11 (n=66)	XT Sp10 (n=67)	XT F10-Sp11 (n=109)	DT I F09 (n=84)	DT II Sp12 (n=66)	ER F09 (n=9)
Specific content learning												
Think about problems in graphical/pictorial/practical ways.	75	78	86	69	65	81	64	49	64	30	36	44
Develop skills in problem solving in the content area.	70	69	82	45	54	62	49	51	54	18	23	44
General learning												
Develop different ways of solving problems.	65	66	71	42	50	55	45	35	46	17	27	44
Work collaboratively with fellow students.	53	56	54	65	76	71	67	77	67	48	42	89
Affective learning												
Develop interest in the content area.	75	74	80	52	55	59	47	53	49	13	18	33
Become motivated to learn course content.	63	63	68	37	50	55	30	31	39	8	12	33

*Percentages represent those participants who responded, "Strongly Agree" or "Agree" on a 6-point Likert-type scale. The word "engineering" in each item was replaced with "physics" for the disciplinary transfer course.

**D=Developer, D Integ=Integration, D Re= Developer Refinement, Re/E=Refinement/Expansion phase, R=Replication phase, CTI=Cognitive Transfer phase with experienced TA instructors, CT II=cognitive transfer with inexperienced TA instructors, XT=Context Transfer phase, DT I=Disciplinary Transfer phase with inexperienced instructor, DT II= Disciplinary transfer with experienced instructors, ER=External Transfer

Table 6.* % of student self-reported approaches to Mobile Studio Learning Platform™ use

Statements	% of Students***						
	D Pilot thru Refinement (n=270)	Replication (n=180)	Transfer to Higher level (n=108)	Transfer Outside Original Context (n=176)	DT I (n=84)	DT II (n=66)	ER (n=9)
Prior I/O Board Experience							
Yes	22	36	94	16	--**	11	--**
No	78	64	6	85	--**	89	--**
Instructor Used I/O boards to Demonstrate Material/Concepts							
In Class	43	13	12	64	15	3	11
In Lab	91	70	45	33	24	8	56
Students Used I/O Boards Independently							
In Class	43	13	12	64	35	8	56
In Lab	90	55	65	62	37	38	33
Homework	56	16	8	22	4	3	0
Students Used I/O Boards with 1 Peer							
In Class	24	25	17	92	27	5	44
In Lab	51	93	88	95	28	32	78
Homework	21	18	8	17	2	3	0
Students Used I/O Boards with 2 or More Peers							
In Class	9	13	5	51	35	11	33
In Lab	19	19	26	54	43	46	33
Homework	10	7	4	9	2	1	0

*Numbers represent mean percentages of participants who answered both pre and post-surveys who responded "often"/"most of the time."

**Item not on survey

***D=Developer, D Integ=Integration, D Re= Developer Refinement, Re/E=Refinement/Expansion phase, R=Replication phase, CTI=Cognitive Transfer phase with experienced TA instructors, CT II=cognitive transfer with inexperienced TA instructors, XT=Context Transfer phase, DT I=Disciplinary Transfer phase with inexperienced instructor, DT II= Disciplinary transfer with experienced instructors, ER=External Transfer

Chapter 8
Improving the Work Integrated Learning Experience through Mobile Technologies

Chris Dann
The University of the Sunshine Coast, Australia

Tony Richardson
The University of the Sunshine Coast, Australia

ABSTRACT

The inclusion of technological solutions in higher education has led to a vast array of options for educators. An educational problem has driven each solution and the associated research into defining the effectiveness of those solutions. This chapter describes some of the problems faced by a teacher education program, triggered by the use of Work Integrated Learning (WIL), to connect theory taught in universities to the realities of a teacher's life. The underlying beliefs of the authors are that there needs to be critical discourse about the teaching and learning models used to engage students in the art of workplace learning, that this critical discourse needs to be based on facilitating a teaching and learning environment that is highly effective, and that the nexus is that the student's Work Integrated Learning (WIL) experience will not be counterproductive. This chapter highlights a concrete example of how one university implemented these beliefs in a structured and proactive manner.

INTRODUCTION

A Paradox: 19th Century Working Views Defining 21st Century Practicum

For over 200 years the nature of work and education has been inexorability linked. The public school system was initially designed to train factory workers and teach farm children the basic skills needed for industrialization; reading, writing, arithmetic, and most importantly the significance of conforming to externally mandated rules and regulations. Consequently, it is difficult not to disassociate our current models of education with the advancement that society continues to undergo. This outcome was the direct result of the skills required for the successful implementation of the Industrial Revolution. These models, which centred on the creation of an industry

DOI: 10.4018/978-1-4666-6284-1.ch008

model, facilitated by willing workers; educated for the linear development of production via the assembly line, has been deeply engrained in our education systems and work places.

This has become an issue for students undertaking (W.I.L.). One of the major impediments to this application has been the continued use of the 'Master-Apprentice' philosophy. This philosophy has been based around the notion of the passing of information from the expert to the learner; an expert who is all knowing and all powerful. They (the expert) are the fountain of all knowledge and the giver of all skills pertaining to their area of work. In essence they speak the leaner listens, they act and the learner acts, they think and the learner thinks. Under this regime it is very difficult for the learner to deviate from their chosen path, a path moulded and manipulated by the expert. In this model the learner is not permitted to question or more importantly to think for themselves. They are not permitted to express an opinion nor have a point of view that differs from the expert. There is no deviation from the way in which the skill and content is passed onto the learner. In order to 'succeed' the learner; so that they too can become a master, has to effectively regurgitate all of what they have been shown by the expert, with very little margin for error.

Whilst this approach may have been successful in supplying willing and competent workers for the assembly lines of the Industrial Revolution the continued use of such a model in the 21st century is complete anathema. What has transpired, with respect to the continued use of this model, has culminated in disconnectedness; which is the result of a dysfunctional relationship between a rapidly changing 21st century work environment and the antiquated 19th century models still in use. This belief is not new amongst influential academics, such as, Sir Ken Robinson, who in 2009 expressed the view that our present system was designed for 19th century industrialism and unfortunately, that system is now dangerously overheating. From Robinson's (2009) perspective it is now necessary to re-think education as a whole because he argues that an industrialized model, founded on the notion that one-size-fits-all, is drastically inadequate for the 21st century. Robinson (2009) contends that the industrial model, once the main stay of education, needs to reflect a more organic environment. In this way, Robinson (2009) believes, that individuals are allowed to grow within the context of their differing environments. Hence, the need to conform and the associated rigidity required to function effectively in the 19th century is not easily juxtaposed to the requirement of organic growth in the 21st century. Therefore, the skills required for the 21st century are diametrically opposed to those of the 19th century. Consequently, the 21st century work environment that has changed significantly when compared to its 19th century predecessor. This change is most evident with respect to the master – apprentice relationship, which was the main stay of the 19th century industrial model.

Previously, the expectation was that the apprentice would be required to, as Patrick (2013) suggests, cooperate with the master. However, in today's environment Patrick (2013) argues, that the situation has changed markedly whereby, the apprentice and the master are now engaged in collaboration, as opposed to cooperation. Collaboration is now an important part of this new type of relationship. Collaboration is built between the master and the apprentice and as such, it has a significant impact on the old master –apprentice model, which has operated in the work place for over 200 years. The introduction of this new approach, to work place relationships, moves away from the notion of recognizing only the professional experience and expertise of the master.

This perspective establishes a relationship that is not one bound by the constraints exemplified through the master-apprentice model. Instead, it encourages a more symbiotic connection reflected via the focus on a mentor - learner relationship, as opposed to a master –apprentice application. In this way what is created between the mentor and the leaner, is a community of practice, defined by a relationship built on trust and respect facilitated by transparency. By undertaking this approach, each member in that community can contribute equally to the success of the organization. Hence, the skills required for the 21st century focus less on the dogged, regimented adherence to conformity and wrote learning, as exemplified in the 19th century, to an emphasis on the "development of critical thinking, analytical reasoning, problem solving skills, creativity and research techniques that together support the ability of lifelong learning" (Institute of Chartered Accounts of Australia & CPA Australia, 2009, p.3, as cited in Leong & Kavanagh, 2013).

Therefore, the challenge confronting us today is to address this situation so that our work places and consequently, the Work Integrated Learning experiences for our students, align with the requirements of the 21st century; as opposed to those of the antiquated 19th century. This chapter proposes that there needs to be a change from the master-apprentice model to one that focuses on collaborative and cooperation relationships. It is argued that undertaking a focus on relationships helps to build communities of practice. Within this community there is no expert, just individuals who want to share and learn from each other in an open, honest and transparent way.

ACADEMIC ISSUE

The Significance of Real-Time Feedback in Filling a 'Gap-of-Knowledge'

The challenge for academics is how to know what their students are doing on placement and where they need increased support? These two areas reflect the significance of feedback, and in particular the need for that feedback to be clear and concise. For feedback to fall into this domain it needs to be ongoing, because ongoing feedback can provide the student with responses, which are more structured, as opposed to fragmented. Structured feedback relates to the way, and manner, in which the feedback is delivered to the student. Within the context of structured feedback the student, through real-time responses to their actions, obtain a much clearer picture of their performance on a daily basis. This approach would prove to be more beneficial to the student; as opposed to a fragmented approach because the information comes to them in broken uncoordinated snips. If students are able to obtain ongoing feedback, during their placement on a daily basis, then that assistance can culminate in enhanced outcomes. As a result of this ongoing feedback, a strong possibility exists that it could be beneficial in helping the student with their teaching and learning outcomes.

This ongoing feedback represents a formative assessment approach, as the student receives feedback on their performance not at the culmination of their practicum but rather has they perform in real-time. Assessment is essential for the teaching and learning process, without it there would be great difficulty in attempting to qualify a student's exit level, based on their performance. However, the use of formative assessment, as opposed to summative assessment, focuses on a systematic and continuous process where evidence is constantly being gleaned from the environment. The use of this type of feedback can provide a much more detailed outline of the student's performance. This more detailed outline of the student's performance is achieved by the feedback being capable of identifying the gaps that may exist between the student's current levels of application, with a task, compared to the desired learning outcome associated with that task (Sadler, 1989). Information obtained in this way represents *real-time* feedback. Real-time feedback focuses on capturing data on a student's performance, based against agreed standards, and the observer marking or commenting on that performance as it unfolds. In this way real-time feedback assists in helping to address the 'gap-of-knowledge' and, as result, provides enhanced feedback because it attempts to highlight to the student their conceptions, misconceptions, skills and knowledge base in a moment-by-moment basis.

Hattie and Clinton (2001) argue that when engaged in conducting assessment it is important that three key areas are addressed; credibility, dependability and fairness. Within the context of this application feedback would fall under the umbrella of assessment. This would be the situation because the feedback provided, for the student, is in response to their performance. It is their performance that is being assessed and therefore, commented on. Hence, having the capacity to deliver real-time feedback assists a student with any gap-of-knowledge associated with their performance.

However, it is important that both the analysis and interpretation of that feedback is very accurate. If the analysis and interpretation of the feedback is erroneous then the evidence, by which the assessment is undertaken, cannot be credible and as a result dependable. This could ultimately lead to errors in instructional steps, for the student, which could culminate in an inability to effectively close their gap-of-knowledge. When using formative assessment it is critical to ensure that the evidence, by which the assessment is undertaken, remains as accurate as possible because it is pivotal to the effectiveness of the assessment process. Failure to do so would have dire consequences. Therefore, the effectiveness of formative assessment is based on the action taken, from the evidence elicited from the data, which will close a student's gap-of-knowledge (Black, Harrison, Lee & Wiliam, 2003; Sadler, 1989; Wiliam &Thompson, 2007). By utilizing this approach a much more effective process could be implemented to assist in ameliorating concerns about current W.I.L. assessment practices.

A number of researchers (Hodges, Smith & Jones, 2004; Coll & Zegwaard, 2006) have documented concerns associated with the current assessment process surrounding W.I.L. The main focus of this concern relates to these assessment practices being rushed and frequently, not under the best conditions (Hodges, Smith & Jones, 2004; Coll & Zegwaard, 2006). Added to this, Wellington, Thomas, Powell and Clarke's (2002) research found many tertiary institutions still utilize traditional summative assessment tools, such as exams, to assess a student's W.I.L. performance. By aligning their assessment tools in this way tertiary institutions, according to Hodges et al (2004) and Col and Zegwaard (2006), have created a problematic situation. The issue at hand stems directly from the feedback because it is summative in nature and has a penchant to focus on the 'negative' outcomes highlighted by the student. Pepper's (1996) research suggests that industry tends to focus on delivering feedback that is restricted to negative comments about the experiences of students. Further to this, McNamara (2008) suggests, that this negative feedback could impact on students through the 'creation' of more gaps-of-knowledge.

The purpose of the W.I.L. experience is for the student to apply the knowledge that they acquired through their university discipline and then experience the application of that knowledge in the work place. Kolb (1984) argues that the transformation that occurs, due to this process, is described in terms of professional development (P.D). This term, within the context of W.I.L., reflects the professional development of the student not in a 'PD' application but rather linking their university experience with that of the work place. In this way the student is acquiring industry skills within the framework of the profession in which they are entering. Consequently, their skills are being developed within the context of their chosen profession as they learn more about what it is they will be expected to undertake. The effectiveness of this professional development is dependent upon the opportunities, which are provided to the student, at the work site. In conjunction with this, the learning process that the student undertakes is also dependent upon their capacity to observe, apply and reflect on their actions. Hence, feedback can also be given, via a reflective process, whereby the student reviews their actions against those observed or expected. In this way students acquire critical professional knowledge to prescribed tasks that they have performed. However, McNamara (2008) and Cates (2005), highlight that feedback back from supervisors is often difficult to obtain and concentrates on analysis as opposed to outcomes. It is essential that students are in a position to maximize their learning and therefore, whilst reflective individual practice can be useful the knowledge gained from supervisor feedback could be counterproductive. Consequently, there needs to be a balance of information to ensure that what the student is receiving does not have a negative impact on their W.I.L. experience whilst also ensuring that they can effectively learn from their mistakes. To try and obtain a balance there needs to be a movement away from the master-apprentice model; as the issue here relates to the manner in which feedback is given, by the master, under the current model.

The problem with this would be reflected in the continued or increasing 'gap-of-knowledge' that the student maybe experiencing due to their mentor's unstructured feedback. This situation would no doubt impact, in a counterproductive way, on the student's W.I.L. experience. As a result, with respect to their higher education accreditation, there would also be commensurate gap/s-of-knowledge about the student's performance by their visiting *workplace academic supervisor*. This development would occur because there would be a lack of understanding, by the academic, about what students have undertaken during their placement and, more importantly, how they could have been effectively supported. The student, due to the nature of their relationship with their supervisor; a master-apprentice approach, could find themselves struggling with diminishing their gaps-of-knowledge; as the feedback provided by their master maybe fragmented. Coupled with this the academic responsible for the student's W.I.L. experience would receive feedback which is dysfunctional, and due to the nature of this feedback, would not be in a position to diminish their 'gap-of–knowledge'. This gap-of-knowledge would relate to that student's performance during and after their W.I.L. experience. Hence, the whole W.I.L. experience could be quite negative for the workplace academic supervisor, the student and their master because none of them really know the full story; the journey that the student is taking along the way, as opposed to, simply focusing on their destination. In order to address this situation there needs to be greater collaboration between workplaces and the higher education sector. It is essential for the student's W.I.L. experience to be productive.

To facilitate this positive experience it is important to ensure that the feedback provided by the workplace is structured and delivered so that it assists in diminishing the gaps-of-knowledge of the master, the student and their workplace academic supervisor. One way of ensuring that this does happen is to obtain feedback in real-time. Whereby, the focus is on capturing data on a student's performance, based against agreed standards, and the observer marking or commenting on that performance as it unfolds. Real-time feedback assists in helping to address the challenge of gap/s-of-knowledge. It achieves this by providing enhanced feedback because it highlights to the student their conceptions, misconceptions, skills and knowledge base in a moment-by-moment basis; and most significantly credible, dependable and fair feedback which is outcomes based. However, one important element is to facilitate a high level of collaboration and cooperation between all interested parties.

COLLABORATION AND COOPERATION

Schools and Higher Education

While W.I.L. can be seen in a number of work related situations one of the key areas of its application relates to the school. There is enough research that reflects the significance of education and its links with a country's economic growth. Added to this research, there is also enough evidence to link teacher quality with student outcomes. Consequently, if the quality of the teacher can have an impact on the outcomes of students, then the nexus to this is, that better student outcomes would equate to a better system of education. This in turn would suggest a better level of economic growth for the country. Based on this association the quality of a country's education system would be linked to the quality of their teachers. One of the seminal applications for the process of teacher education focuses on teacher preparation. This process is inextricably linked with W.I.L. through the practicum that each potential teacher must undertake as a part of their teacher training. Consequently, as Zeichner (1990) claims, because the practicum is essential for teacher preparation it defines the quality of teacher education. Within the framework of this association the student applies the theory that they have acquired, at university, within the learning environment. Clearly, a student's ability to not just simply know the knowledge but more importantly, apply that knowledge, within the work place, would be of paramount importance. Therefore, W.I.L. undertaken within the context of teacher preparation has a significant role to play in the quality of teaches, and as a result, the economic growth of a nation. Yet, research by Haigh, Ell and Mackisack (2013), identifies issues with current W.I.L practices and that this has culminated, in international concerns over the problematic nature of those issues.

Haigh et al. (2013) argue that whilst the practicum is recognized as a seminal application for teacher preparation programmes there are international concerns about its capacity to adequately address the magnitude of that importance. This is reflected by, Haigh et al (2013), who highlight concerns over the capacity of the programs to recognize teacher candidates that can make a positive difference, to student outcomes, and also, the use of systems, which have the ability to recognize those teacher candidates during their practicum. This situation directs attention, as Tynjälä (2012) argues, to explore new ways of developing different kinds of professional expertise, new forms of collaboration and most importantly, new ways of learning. Clearly, one such focus would need to reflect a much greater association between the work place and higher education sector. This would be reflected within the framework of education via enhanced collaboration and cooperation between schools, the higher education sector teachers and their pre-service teacher.

Jorgenson and Howard (2005) suggest that assessment methods associated with W.I.L. programs should reflect the integration of theory and practice. It is here that the issues associated with W.I.L. assessment methods are more apparent with the focus on addressing both the needs of the workplace and the higher education institution. The challenge is to have cogent links between the traditional subject's disciplines, of higher education, matched against the variability of the workplace. The central issue is the discipline specific content of higher education, which relates to the theory application of the W.I.L. experience, juxtaposed to the needs of the workplace. This is because the workplace, where the W.I.L. experience is undertaken, is a more complex environment comprised of numerous variables and, as such, there is difficulty in developing assessment to match all areas. This has culminated in, as Costly and Armsby (2007) suggest, a need to meet the requirements of both the workplace and the university. Consequently, there is a movement away from individual assessment to the development of generic skills agreed to by the university and the workplace. By undertaking this approach, Bates (2004) argues, that there is a tendency to focus on generic skills, which tend to be linked with the workplace, and, as a result, this can be quite problematic.

For W.I.L. to be successful there needs to be established links between the workplace and higher education. The continued tension between meeting the needs of the discipline controlled higher education and the multi-faceted roles of the workplace will no doubt continue to fuel this ongoing debate. It is evident, as Patrick, Peach, Pocknee, Webb, Fletcher and Pretto (2009) highlight, that there needs to be consideration given to resources along with the commitment of the employer to the W.I.L. experience. Patrick et al. (2009) further argue, that the "development and implementation of effective assessment methods were key issues in higher education" (p.42). Without the development of a close relationship, between higher education and the workplace, there is little chance there being a truly worthwhile W.I.L. experience. One of the key developments that need to take place, with respect to this collaboration, relates to the way in which students are assessed. The relationship that exists between the school and higher education focuses very much on ensuring that the student is capable of meeting the requirements of the course work. The higher education institution has clearly defined criteria, by which they expect students to be graded against and allocated an outcome. Similarly, the workplace, via its association with the standards set by the various governing bodies; for example accreditation associated with Teaching, Engineering and Nursing, has outcomes that it too would like the student to attain. Yet, within the context of the W.I.L. experience the most important person, with respect to quality of the applicant, is clearly the student. Their effectiveness as an educator, engineer or nurse is of the upmost significance. To assist in ensuring that this transpires one of the key elements of the collaboration between the workplace and higher education is the need to move away from summative to formative assessment. However, within the context of this paper the notion of formative assessment relates to assessing the student within a 'real-time' framework. By undertaking this approach the authors believe that there will be more effective student learning and a better development of program design.

ASSESSING STUDENTS IN 'REAL-TIME'

Sheldon and Thornthwaite (2005) express the view that contemporary businesses expect their employees to hit the ground running. The expectation is that they come to the workplace capable of undertaking the task/s expected of them to fulfil the requirements of their employment. Consequently, if the graduate has the capacity to meet the needs of their employer they are in a better position to obtain employment over those who are also graduates but less skilled (Sheldon & Thornthwaite, 2005). Therefore, given the significance of this situation the importance of the W.I.L. application plays a seminal role in ensuring that graduates are work place ready. One of the key aspects of this role relates to the preparation of students for employment. Cranmer (2006) outlines that one of the features of W.I.L. is its ability to link the discipline focus of the university with the generic skill development required for the workplace. However, Wellington, Thomas, Powell and Clarke (2002) found that universities continue to assess students through traditional assessment tools like exams. Unfortunately, this situation can be problematic, as it does not focus on the plethora of learning experiences located within the workplace (Coll & Zegwaard, 2006; Foley, 2004). Hence, the assessment tools used within the context of the workplace and the university are complex and therefore, not easily developed. However, what this section argues is that no matter what assessment tool is used its emphasis needs to be formative as opposed to summative. The following will outline the case for this course of action.

Assessment, within the context of providing a response to an individual so as to add value to their knowledge, is most effective when it is delivered through high level feedback. Unfortunately, Pepper (1996) highlights, that feedback delivered within the context of the workplace and articulated for the purpose of providing knowledge to add-value can often be negative, and as a result, culminate in decreasing the performance of those who receive it (Ilgen & Davis, 2000). Further to this McNamara (2008) states that supervisor feedback tends to be analytical in nature and often difficult to obtain. Therefore, for feedback to be effective it needs to be delivered by supervisors or mentors who are well versed in unpacking an individual's performance in a clear, concise and positive way. Added to this, supervisors or mentors need to feel a sense of self-confidence when it comes to a capacity to evaluate and assess the performance of others (Eisenberg, Heycox & Hughes, 1996). Consequently, for assessment to be effective it needs to reflect feedback that is of a high calibre. This can be achieved by ensuring that those charged with delivering feedback are well versed in the skills associated with ensuing that their feedback is filling 'a gap-of-knowledge'. For feedback to be of a high calibre it is the view of this paper that it needs to be both formative and summative and obtained in 'real-time'.

For summative assessment to be effective, Jones, Jackson, Coiacetto, Budge, Coote, Steele, Gall & Kennedy (2009) argue, it is important that students are made aware of learning goals and that they understand those learning goals. Hence, summative assessment focuses on attaining an outcome at the end of the task. In this way the student has the learning goals outlined to them and then based on those learning goals they are then evaluated on their ability to meet those learning goals. On the other hand, formative assessment is a systematic process whereby data is collected about a student's performance about their learning goals (outcomes). The concept of real-time, with respect to feedback, has an impact on how assessment is viewed. Real-time relates to the capacity of technology to be in a position to structure feedback against agreed learning goals on a daily basis. Hence real-time, when explored through an assessment application, is a combination of both a summative and formative approach. The formative application is continually re-defining a student's progress towards their learning goals, as they are viewed and enacted upon by agreed standards. This formative approach supports the summative application at it gives direction and focus to the student's learning goals. Therefore, real-time is about working 'towards learning goals' that are assessed, via agreed standards, on a regular basis. This formative assessment process attempts to have a strong impact on the student's 'gap-of-knowledge'.

The role of the supervisor or mentor is to assist the student in closing their 'gap of knowledge'. When students enter the workplace they have varying levels of knowledge and experience that is associated with that workplace. It is the supervisor or mentor's role to obtain evidence about the student's performance. This advice centres on supplying feedback on, as Heritage, Kim, Vendlinski and Herman (2008) outline, evidence that focuses on areas of interest related to the student; conceptions, misconceptions, skills and knowledge. Based on responses to these areas the supervisor or mentor will be in a position, continue Heritage et al. (2008), to close the student's gap of knowledge by identifying the student's emerging understanding or associated skills so that they can hopefully build on, and then modify, their growth. Heritage et al. (2008) suggest that based on this approach the analysis and interpretation of evidence plays a pivotal role in the effectiveness of the feedback supplied. Given that the effectiveness of the feedback is based on the capacity of the supervisor or mentor to unpack the evidence provided by the student's formative assessment then, real-time has the capacity to deliver the most effective feedback. This is evident because real-time provides evidence on the student's demonstrated performance at that time.

As previously mentioned, real-time represents a combination of both summative and formative assessment applications. If the emphasis were only on delivering feedback at the completion of the work place experience then the student's gap-of-knowledge would only be impacted upon at the end of their placement. A situation like this would prove to be counterproductive. Feedback delivered in this format would be counterproductive as the purpose of the W.I.L. experience is to ensure that the student is ready to be a part of the workforce from day one. Suppling feedback to the student on a regular basis would be more beneficial as it would be able to fill gaps-of-knowledge within the assessment period, as opposed to the end of the assessment period. In this way the student would be receiving continuous feedback as they undertake the task. This would then give them an enhanced access to regular feedback thereby, placing them in an improved position to reflect and review their performance. The challenge, with respect to any workplace, is to address the myriad of micro skills that a student will confront each day. Whilst there are agreed standards, which reflect the student's capacity demonstrate learning goals, there are also a plethora of micro skills associated with each individual workplace. One of the key elements of formative assessment is that it is designed to obtain evidence to close the student's gap-of-knowledge (William & Thompson, 2007). However, formative assessment based on the real-time paradigm, undertakes this task with a view to closing a student's gap-of-knowledge through their knowledge-in-practice; as their task is being performed. Consequently, the emphasis is not on exploring what the student learnt but rather how the student learnt it and displays it. This approach emphasises a reflective practice that centres on unpacking the negotiated steps that the student is undertaking as the action is delivered.

Real time is about offering the learner the experience of 'viewing' their knowledge and upon reflection, understanding the difference between the learning goal and the viewed experiences. This highlights the behaviours and skills that the student may have accomplished, and also those elements of behaviour or skills, that they have yet to demonstrate. One of the key elements is the functional understanding of knowledge-in-practice. This concept needs to reside with the supervisor as well as the student to gain full benefit of the W.I.L. experience. Boud and Walker (1998) caution the use of reflective practice because if it is not undertaken correctly the possibility exists that it could have a negative impact on the learning experience of students. Boud and Walker (1998) suggest that when reflective practices are used that they do not always lead to learning. It is the view of the authors that this failure to lead to learning is a direct result of an inability to provide effective reflective practice through real time feedback.

KNOWLEDGE-IN-PRACTICE

A Reflective Process
Understanding What You Learnt

What you do is important but more importantly is to understand why you did it? Hence, 'knowledge-in-practice' is about supplying students with information about what they did as they were doing it. The emphasis is on creating a situation whereby, the student is able to reflect on their performance after they had undertaken a task. In this way the student is able to review aspects of their performance based on their actions, linked against the agreed standards that are aligned with the stated learning goals. The student is able to reflect on their performance with a view to being in a position to address both their strengths and weaknesses. Consequently, 'knowledge-in-practice' is about ensuring that the student obtains feedback on their performance as it happens. In this way the supervisor or mentor is providing the student with information, feedback, which is highly effective because it deals with what transpired during the delivery of the presentation; as it actually transpired.

Students need to acquire acknowledge about their practice, how it was that they undertook the task which in turn would allow them to extrapolate this information to why they undertook a specific course of action? By focusing on what the student did, as it happened, allows them to then be in a position to accurately reflect on their practice by providing knowledge of that practice, in real-time. Hence, 'knowledge-in-practice' allows the supervisor or mentor to provide the student with details about their actions, in real-time. As an adjunct to that, the student is then in a position to reflect on their practice based on knowledge of their own practice/s as it unfolded. In this way the student is in a position to view their actions, and reflect on those actions, through effective feedback. This would take place because the student is in a position to review their performance based not just on what they did but also why they did it.

CASE STUDY

Timeline of Development

Technology placements in higher education have taken many forms. iRIS® video streaming, PDF forms for teacher to complete, student generated portfolios of work are all current and common forms of technological use in W.I.L. placement in the UK, US and Australia. The Australian Teaching and Learning Council have funded numerous projects investigating technological uses in W.I.L. These include the

- Enhancing access, participation and progression in WIL (2013).
- The assessment of the impact of WIL on Student readiness (2011).
- Using a Distributed leadership approach to WIL (2011).
- Facilitating WIL skill through e-portfolios (2009) Building leadership capacity of field work coordinators.
- WIL and national framework for best practice (2007).

Only one of the projects mention has explicit ties between assessment and the W.I.L. This project was initiated in 2010 and looked at the use of professional standards and the relationship they had to the assessment of the W.I.L. experience. There is still a project that looks at the dynamic interplay that assessment plays in the W.I.L. and how this assessment can be enhanced using current electronic means. Further search of the O.L.T. project database, using the term 'assessment', highlights projects in all faculties of higher education. Within these projects there are studies that focused on the use of technology to 'improve students' learning and assessment reliability'; 2010 the development of a competencies assessment tool for use across Australia nursing. Much of the tool kit developed from this was paper based and electronically delivered. Even in 2010, a tool for assessment was developed as a paper-based representation of skills and knowledge, presented and recorded on a template for ongoing reproduction by users; electronically limited. Further analysis of the overall funding shows increasingly little funding being placed in the exploration of electronic assessment processes. Current technological advancements are being explored and activated in industries and private enterprise and are yet to appear in the W.I.L. assessment space.

Case Study Use of Technology

Technology has been used primarily as an administrative support for communication and delivery of information to schools. At the case study university this took the form of delivering documentation to support a teacher and the school, in their role as manager of the student; while the student was on placement, as well as support of the summative assessment process. The system was a commercial system called SONIA and allowed the placement administrative staff to upload documents and make these available to schools. The system also allowed students to log in and see the details of their school and supervising teacher. Documents could be downloaded from the site and then printed for completion at the school.

This system became the conduit of communication, once the initial commitments from the school were made verbally, and via email, clarified how many students a school could take and details relating to that student's placement at that school. The university would then send out a hard copy of the policies and procedures to the school coordinator and the university's job was considered complete, in terms of administering the placement.

Ongoing communication between the school and the university was facilitated by 'academic liaisons officers' who were sometimes lecturers from the teacher education programs and sometimes ex-teachers to university tutors employed to visit the students in the schools. These academic liaison officers did not have a formal role in the assessment of the students. Their role was to ensure open communication between the school, the teacher and the students. If a student was found to be experiencing difficulties, and was at risk of failing the placement, it was the academic liaison officer's role to refer the situation to the placement office. From there, the liaison office would then assign a senior member of the placement office to take the case and support the student and the school. The academic liaison officer was to record their visit on the SONIA system and deliver all email correspondence to the placement officer who had taken on the case.

The software used in the trial, at the case study university, attempted to make use of current technological process such as smart phones, with their video capability, touch screen swap interface and cloud based storage. The trail reported by Dann and Toohey (2013) also sought to place these technologies in the workplace and measure the pedagogical impact on such an immersion. The sections below give a brief description of the stages the author and his team went through from 2008- 2013.

DEVELOPING THE SYSTEM

The problem of inconsistency, reliability and equity arose in the placement office through the collation of teacher, academic and student complaints and comments. These were all anecdotally recorded as part of the administrative role of the placement coordinator at the university. To correct these issues invitations were sent out to teachers, students, principals and academics involved in placement assessment to attend focus groups and collaboratively work through the issues.

Over a 12-month period, the group meet regularly and developed an approach to the assessment that involved a refocus on the formative phase of the assessment so that an open, transparent process driven by explicit understanding of the required competencies was developed. This process required delivery of the explicit competencies to each of the stakeholders in the assessment process. It required each teacher to complete regular, formative assessments of a student's performance of the designated explicit competencies. It charged the student with the responsibility of viewing the feedback and acting on it. Added to this, it also provided the university with a way of seeing how a student was going and to understand how the teacher was supporting the student in achieving their required competencies.

This process brought up the problem of teacher workload. Lecturers, tutors, school teachers and individuals working in a workplace have a primary objective and the team needed to work out how a teacher could complete the assessment feedback with limited impact on their primary classroom roles. Part of the answer came with the advent of smart phone technology and the "App" wave that smart phones triggered.

The functionality and requirements of the system were developed with the App environment in mind and this introduced the opportunity to engage the video collection function of smart phones and mobile devices. The system would be capable of collecting video evidence of performance to support teacher feedback and support the planning for improvement.

A 12-month period of technical development occurred before delivery of the research capable system. This development required the contracting of three external companies and realisation of the requirements of the group within the capability of the technology.

Ethical Approvals

As the system approached its completion ethical approval was sought for use in schools. The use of a mobile phone in a classroom was considered a risk due to its ability to capture video and images. The need to protect the children in the room was the largest hurdle to overcome. This reduced the trial to one school with full permissions from the school, the teachers, the student teacher and the families of the students in the classroom. As part of addressing this system the following measures were put in place.

1. Images could only be uploaded when the phone was in a school wireless environment.
2. Images were to be stored on a locked server in Australia.

A parallel trial was conducted that did not use the mobile device. This trial used a web interface only and the image capture was taken out of this system. This system allowed a teacher to go online and complete the feedback on each competency and had the capacity for students to view their feedback and plan for improvements.

Implementing a Trial

The first trial found that the phones (iPhones) had to access a site via the wireless system of the school and this system had firewalls that stopped access to the systems server. That was the end of that trial until the technicians in the education system approved the access to the research server. A second attempt was then conducted in the same school and found that the schools wireless environment was weak in many areas of the school.

Once these technical issues were addressed a third trial was conducted and reported by Dann et al (2013) and surveys, interviews and analytic data were collected over a four week period of use.

Incidental Learning from the Trials

There were a number of incidental learning outcomes from the trials. They include:

1. The wireless networks in workplaces need to be capable of covering the entire site.
2. Teachers wanted mobility and did not want a system that required training outside of the classroom.
3. Teachers prudently used the video capability.
4. The iPhone typing screen was too small for most teachers and they proffered a keyboard to type.
5. Students were initially uncomfortable with being videoed but this changed during the four week trial.
6. Certain interface and work flow changes were needed for the system.

The full data from the trials has previously been reported in Dann and Allen (2013) and shows a number of important points from the three data collection techniques. Data was collected via interview, surveys from pre and post use and finally analytical data collected by the system during the trial period. Interview data was coded and themed and indicated that students did become more comfortable with the videoing and wanted to develop the system so that they could have planned and unplanned video observations. Students also found that they could now 'see' the engagement in the classroom and were making connections between their actions and the terms so often used in the formal University course work. Terms such as engagement, transitions, teacher tone, and concepts such as rapport were becoming realities for the student. Teachers that used the system reported that this was the 'way to go' but felt that they had 'too many' competencies to grade over the term of the placement (four weeks). This was an issue for the placement and course leaders rather than the system itself but still very useful information. Survey data was limited by the trial numbers and not statistically relevant and this is one of the limitations of the study to date. Further studies require broad scale testing and data collection.

The analytic data showed that students were accessing their video after 9.30pm on the day of it being taken and they were accessing the feedback at the same time. It also showed that teachers were able to use the system in the classroom. Most use was done in the mornings during the teacher of subjects such as maths and English and data upload into the system was almost exclusively done before 12 noon. The length of video taken was on average 2.17 sec with one teacher trying to video a whole lesson and crashing the server.

Commercialisation

The awareness of the commercial applications of the system became apparent during demonstration to education faculty and other faculty academics. Presentation to academics outside of the case study university also triggered the possibility of commercial application of a simple assessment system that required limited training and a simple mobile interface. The lead researcher initiated a commercialisation and IP process but unfortunately, from that point, the development of the system ceased, as funding ran out, and the focus shifted to writing up the findings of the trials and dealing with the commercial aspects of the system.

One of the challengers, faced with the development of the system, related to the size and age of the case university. As a young regional university it lacked, at the time, the necessary infrastructure that a much larger established city university had at its disposal. Consequently, the process from initial formal contact with the university's research office, through to the signing of the licence agreement, had a number of challengers that need to be navigated. However, with continued support, and ongoing assistance from the university, a product is now being commercialised at the University's Innovation Centre. One other factor was the disclosure of the concept.

Researchers are bound to seek ethical clearance, conduct their research and then present this publically for peer review. The initial stage of development of this system was followed up by a presentation to a national conference. The presentation showed the system, its functionality and the research method used. In commercial terms the IP system could no longer be defended in a number of countries around the world and the IP needed to be registered in Australia, within 12 months of the disclosure if any IP was to be claimed. The decision to present should have been given much more consideration with respect to the commercial implication of presenting functionality, screen layout and the processes used in the system.

Blue Sky Dreaming

Feedback will be aggregated to form an avatar capable of interacting with the user and showing the user their progress towards a professional standard. This means that a user will be able to select a standard or a number of related competencies related to a standard. Consequently, the basic avatar developed by the student will then manifest itself showing how the student looks when demonstrated that standard.

Research in to the aggregation of video captured against each competency would be required and the research would then be driving the development of technology in the educational assessment space as technology research drove space exploration and medical research. This drive will have subtle differences in each training environment. Nursing environments, along with other training environments have specific requirements regarding patient care, negligence and operational procedures. The workspace can be complex and the use of mobile technology many need to be abandoned in favour of wearable technology capable of capturing de-identified images and verbal feedback for later reference.

CONCLUSION

We live in a world of advanced technology solutions were simple solutions can be overlooked. This chapter has identified a paradox between the 19th century models we are trying to apply to a 21st century workplace environment. This does not refer to the technology per say, but rather to the learning and societal environment in which we are operating. The case study university has developed a possible solution to address a small part of a complex problem and does not presume to have 'the' solution but rather a step forward. During the evolution of the research a number of concepts have become clear; the need for real-time feedback, the importance of feeding information to students so they can bridge their gap-of-knowledge. In order to achieve this there needs to be increased levels of collaboration and cooperation between the university and the school site/s.

If the collaboration and cooperation can be conducted to bring a solution that produces real-time feedback to the students and the university, as well as allow students to identify and plan improvements to their personal gap-of-knowledge, then a possibility exist that knowledge in practice levels of our next generation teachers will be improved.

REFERENCES

Bates, M. (2004). From knowledge to action and back again: Building a bridge. *Asia-Pacific Journal of Cooperative Education*, 5(1), 7–14.

Black, P., Harrison, C., Lee, C., & Wiliam, D. (2003). *Assessment for learning: Putting it into practice*. New York, NY: Open University Press.

Boud, D., & Walker, D. (1998). Promoting reflection in professional courses: The challenge of context. *Studies in Higher Education*. Retrieved 7/12/13 from http://www.tandfonline.com/doi/abs/10.1080/03075079812331380384#.UvYlJGKSyuM

Cates, C. (2005). *Building a bridge between university and employment: Work-Integrated learning*. Brisbane, Australia: Research Publications and Resources Section.

Coll, R. K., & Zegwaard, K. E. (2006). Perceptions of desirable graduate competencies for science and technology new graduates. *Research in Science & Technological Education*, 24(1), 29–58. doi:10.1080/02635140500485340

Costly, C., & Armsby, P. (2007). Work-based learning assessed as a field or a mode of study. *Assessment & Evaluation in Higher Education*, 32(1), 21–33. doi:10.1080/02602930600848267

Cranmer, S. (2006). Enhancing graduate employability: Best intentions and mixed outcomes. *Studies in Higher Education*, 31(2), 169–184. doi:10.1080/03075070600572041

Dann, C. E., & Allen, B. (2013). Using mobile video technologies to enhance the assessment and learning of preservice teachers in Work Integrated Learning (WIL). In *Proceedings of the Society for Information Technology & Teacher Education International Conference AACE*. New Orleans, LA: AACE.

Eisenberg, M., Heycox, K., & Hughes, L. (1996). Fear of the personal: Assessing students in practicum. *Australian Social Work*, *49*(4), 33–40. doi:10.1080/03124079608411186

Foley, G. (2004). Introduction: The state of adult education and learning. In G. Foley (Ed.), *Dimensions of Adult Learning: Adult education and training in a global era* (pp. 3–19). Crows Nest, Australia: Allen & Unwin.

Haigh, M., & Ell, F. (2013). And Mackisack, V. *Judging Teacher candidates' readiness to teach. Teaching and Teacher Education*, *34*, 1–11. doi:10.1016/j.tate.2013.03.002

Hattie, J., & Clinton, J. (2001). The assessment of teachers. *Teaching Education*, *12*, 279–300. doi:10.1080/10476210120096551

Heritage, M., Kim, J., Vendlinski, T. P., & Herman, J. L. (2008). From Evidence to Action: A Seamless Process in Formative Assessment? (CRESST Report 741). National Centre for Research on Evaluation, Standards and Student Testing (CRESST). University o California.

Hodges, D., Smith, B. W., & Jones, P. D. (2004). The assessment of cooperative education. In R. K. Cool, & C. Eames (Eds.), *International handbook for cooperative education: An international perspective of the theory, research and practice of work-integrated learning* (pp. 49–64). Boston, MA: World Association for Cooperative Education.

Ilgen, D. R., & Davis, C. A. (2000). Bearing Bad news: Reactions to negative performance feedback. *Applied Psychology: An International Review, 49* (3), 550 – 565.

Jones, M., Jackson, J.T., Coiacetto, E., Budge, T., Cote, M., Steele, W., Gall, S., & Kennedy, M. (2009). *Generating academic standards in planning practice education: Final report to the Australian Learning and Teaching Council*. Retrieved from https://www.google.com.au/?gfe_rd=ctrl&ei=0x_2UuTZG6qN8Qey94G4Dw&gws_rd=cr#q=generating+academic+standards+in+planning+practice+education%3A+Final+report+to+the+australian+learning+nd+teaching+council

Jorgensen, D., & Howard, P. (2005). *Assessment practice for orientation education. (J. Goldson, Trans.).* Rockhampton, Australia: Central Queensland University.

Kolb, D. A., (1984). Experiential learning: Experience as the source of learning and development. Englewood Cliffs, NJ: Prentice Hall.

Leong, R., & Kavanagh, M. (2013). A work-integrated learning (WIL) framework to develop graduate skills and attributes in an Australian university's accounting program. *Asia-Pacific Journal of Cooperative Education*, *14*(1), 1–14.

McNamara, J. (2008, December). *The challenge of assessing student employability skills in legal internships.* Paper presented at the WACE Asia Pacific Conference. Sydney, Australia.

Patrick, C. J., Peach, D., & Pocknee, C. (2009). The WIL (Work Integrated Learning) report: A national scoping study. Strawberry Hills, Australia: Australian Learning and Teaching Council in association with the Australian Collaborative Education Network.

Patrick, C. J., Peach, D., Pocknee, C., Webb, F., Fletcher, M., & Pretto, G. (2009). *The WIL report: A national scoping study.* Brisbane, Australia: Academic Press.

Patrick, R. (2013). *"Don't rock the boat": Conflicting mentor and pre-service teacher narratives of professional experience.* The Australian Association for Research in Education.

Pepper, N. (1996). Supervision: A positive learning experience or an anxiety provoking exercise? *Australian Social Work, 49*(3), 55–64. doi:10.1080/03124079608415690

Robinson, K. (2009). *Transform Education? Yes, We Must.* Retrieved from http://www.huffingtonpost.com/sir-ken-robinson/transform-education-yes-w_b_157014.html

Robinson, K. (2009). *The elements: How finding your passion changes everything.* London, UK: Penguin.

Sadler, D. R. (1989). Formative assessment and the design of instructional systems. *Instructional Science, 18,* 119–144. doi:10.1007/BF00117714

Sheldon, P., & Thornthwaite, L. (2005). Employability skills and vocational education and training policy in Australia: An analysis of employer association agendas. *Asia-Pacific Journal Resources, 43*(3), 404–425. doi:10.1177/1038411105059100

Tynjälä, P. (2012). Toward a 3-P Model of Workplace Learning: a Literature Review. *Vocations and Learning, 6,* 11 – 36.

Wellington, P., Powell, T. I., & Clarke, B. (2002). *Authentic assessment applied to engineering business undergraduate consulting teams.* Melbourne, Australia: Department of Mechanical Engineering Monash University.

Wiliam, D., & Thompson, M. (2007). Integrating assessment with learning: What will it take to make it work? In C. A. Dwyer (Ed.), *The future of assessment: Shaping teaching and learning.* Mahwah, NJ: Lawrence Erlbaum Associates.

Zeichner, K. (1990). Changing directions in the practicum: looking ahead in the 1990s. *Journal of Education for Teaching, 16*(2), 105–132. doi:10.1080/0260747900160201

KEY TERMS AND DEFINITIONS

Analytics: All data automatically generated by the computer system and its application.

Competencies: Specific behaviours when combined with other behaviours create a demonstration of a professional standard.

Gap-of-Knowledge: Relates to information that an individual may require to understand or perform a task.

Knowledge-in-Practice: Data collected in real-time for use by student to observe their performance at that moment.

Master-Apprentice: The term used to describe the relationship that exists within the context of the Industrial Model.

Professional Standards: Are the professional requirements that universities must adhere to as to gain accreditation for their courses.

Real-Time: Events that are occurring as they unfold during the collection of data.

W.I.L.: Work Integrated Learning.

Chapter 9
Opportunities and Challenges of Mobile Technologies in Higher Education Pedagogy in Africa:
A Case Study

Frederick Kang'ethe Iraki
United States International University, Kenya

ABSTRACT

Since the late 1990s, Kenya has undergone a real technological revolution, especially in the domain of mobile telephony and Internet connectivity. From a negligible number of handsets in the hands of the political elites, today almost every adult Kenyan has a mobile phone, or access to one. This is thanks to reduced costs following expansion and diversification of the market niche. Despite this remarkable progress, research has shown that cell phones are used mainly for financial transactions, social communication, and entertainment, but hardly for learning purposes. This means that despite the impressive number of smartphone owners in the university, for example, the devices are not used for enhancing student learning or teaching. In Kenya, more than 60% of the population employs mobile banking, thus underscoring the immense potential that the cell phones have for education. This chapter explores the benefits and challenges in employing mobile telephony to improve the quality of teaching and learning.

Mobile phones are the future of the Internet –Google Vice-President (2007)

INTRODUCTION

Cell phones have revolutionized communication and businesses in Africa in the last 15 years or so. In Kenya, for instance, mobile telephony has significantly impacted small-scale businesses whose owners could hardly afford banking fees. Indeed, about 60% of Kenyans employ mobile phones to access banking and financial services[1]. Among the most successful money transfer services include M-Pesa, M-Shwari and M-Banking. Further, due to the dramatic reduction of prices, mobile phones have simply become ubiquitous. On average, a basic cell phone costs USD 24 in Kenya. Cell phones are now increasingly improving rural health in

DOI: 10.4018/978-1-4666-6284-1.ch009

some countries, notably India and Nigeria (Egbunike 2013). In Kenya, mobile applications are beginning to improve farming, especially livestock management, hence, improving incomes. In the same vein, mobile phones are used in the slums of Kibera in Nairobi to make medical prescriptions, thus enhancing health at an affordable cost to the financially challenged populations[2]. Nevertheless, there is hardly any evidence of using cell phones to enhance academic achievement in Kenya. In a recent survey in Kenyan public universities, it was noted that faculty and students hardly use Web 2.0 technologies for learning (Murungi & Gitonga 2013). These technologies include wikis, blogs, social networking, folksonomies, podcasting, Wikipedia, YouTube, Facebook, MySpace, Flickr[3]. Researches are ongoing on the efficacy of cell phones to improve language learning (Susan 2008, Fangyi 2011). Given the ubiquity and capabilities of cell phones, it would be of interest to examine whether students can engage more with the learning materials, fellow students and their lecturers (Maria & Muyinda 2013). Cell phones, especially smart phones, provide learning opportunities such as SMS, videos and applications. In the current study, university students enrolled in a French literature course were encouraged to employ SMS messages to comment on posted thematic questions and also their reading materials, mainly French novels. The purpose was to establish whether cell phones could improve students' performance in French literature.

LITERATURE REVIEW

In 2013, an E-learning conference was held in Nairobi, Kenya, and among the highlights was M-learning. Nonetheless, the M-learning sessions went little more than stating that mobile phones had great potential for improving learning. There was no evidence of usage of cell phones for learning and yet these communication tools are ubiquitous due to increased affordability and popularity, especially among teenagers and university students. It is estimated that 75% of teenagers intend to use cell phones for the rest of their lives (CTIA and Harris Interactive survey cited in Montgomery 2010)[4]. This implies that most of these young people will be having a cell phone at hand for the better part of their lives. The World Bank has been collaborating with mEducation Alliance (previously known as m4Ed4Dev[5]) to explore the potential of mobile education in enhancing progress in the developing countries in view of the ubiquity of mobile phones. The Alliance seeks to establish how mobile phones can improve education and spur development in the developing world. To be sure, there are groups of youths in Ghana, Morocco, Uganda and Maharashtra creating mobile phone networks to enhance e-learning[6]. In an iHub debate entitled *How can mobile devices enhance learning in classrooms*, the experts were unequivocal about how mobile phones can be used to enhance assessment, access learning content and build networks for learning, especially in the developing world[7]. The E-learning Africa conference in 2011 noted that there were more than 500 million cell phone subscribers in Africa, up from 246 million in 2008[8]. Clearly, there are more cell phones in Africa than in the US. Cell phones, especially SMS have promoted distance learning in areas remote of access, devoid of electricity or Internet, notably in Mozambique. Indeed, Gerald Henzinger in a paper entitled "New Technologies in Restricted Environment", salutes the significant contribution of cell phones in Mozambique in promoting access to content for many students, interaction with faculty about the subject matter and on administrative issues. The inexpensive technology of SMS can be employed to promote education and contribute to the development of a country (Attewell, 2005). By facilitating access to education, cell phones are promoting equity and equality. In fact, students from impoverished rural homes can enjoy the same quantity and quality of education as anyone else. Further, the conviviality of mobile technologies makes learning fun (Vinod Ganjoo, cf. endnote 5). Vinod noted "These new technologies have provided flexible and cheap learning channels for many students in classrooms and outside classrooms." Children learning mathematics in South Africa through mobile phones described the experience as "cheap, efficient and very exciting" according to Riitta Vänskä (cf. endnote 5.)

T.M. Sakunthala Yatgammana Ekanayake notes that education via mobile phones is all the more exciting since they provide a raft of possibilities since they are "spontaneous, personal, informal, contextual, portable, ubiquitous, pervasive and avail functions such as talk, text, still camera, video, radio, and the internet (Kukulska-Hulme et. al. 2005)." Furthermore, it is suggested that mobile education should mainly target the teenagers "because the front-end research showed that teenagers had a higher than average interest in every mobile phone activity that was evaluated."[9]. Ombaka (2013) observes that mobile technologies can be instrumental in developing human capital in Kenya but this dimension has not been explored at all. Dominic Mentor and Nabeel Ahmad (2010) observe that mobile telephony has helped bridge the digital divide between the developed and developing nations. Indeed, the cell phones have become ubiquitous in Asia and Africa where they are used mainly to "communicate and connect with friends and family, schedule appointments and reminders, and play games."[10] However, the use of mobile phones for educational purposes is only beginning, even in the developed world. In view of the immeasurable potential of mobile phones in transforming lives in Africa through education, there is need to embark on research to test the extent to which cell phones can be used to improve access to knowledge and academic achievement. The current study sought to test the efficacy of SMS in enhancing achievement in a French literature course at the United States International University (USIU) in Kenya.

THE CURRENT STUDY

In view of the rapid proliferation of mobile phones in Kenya, especially among university students, the study sought to understand to what extent these devices could be used to enhance student learning and achievement. Previous research had established that university students at USIU were using their mobile phones almost exclusively for communication and not as learning tools (Iraki, 2011). Nonetheless, it was noted that since no effort had been made by faculty to introduce the cell phones as learning tools, little wonder students could not conceptualize the phones as such. The current study set out to explain to students how their cell phones could help them achieve better results in learning French literature.

In another class in spring 2013, the researcher had encouraged students to use their cell phones to visit specific language learning sites or dictionaries but no systematic survey was conducted to establish the effects of the initiative on their academic achievement in French. As a result, in fall 2013 a more targeted approach was adopted in a French literature course to ascertain whether the use of cell phones could impact academic achievement. If cell phones could be employed productively to enhance academic achievement at university level it could herald changes in pedagogy in this direction. Considering the large presence of cell phones among students, their use as friendly learning devices could have significant positive impact on academic performance, among other positives.

Central Research Questions

The research aimed at ascertaining the following:

1. Can cell phones enhance student achievement and how?
2. What are the constraints in using cell phones for learning?

3. What do students think about using their cell phones for class learning?

METHODOLOGY

The study was designed to establish how cell phones could impact student achievement in French literature, a course conducted mainly in French. The course, FRN 3001, code-named Literature in France, was organized in terms of lectures, discussions and student presentations. The course was conducted in French as per the requirements. The students were required to read a French literary book and summarize it in form of a PowerPoint presentation. For each theme or literary movement discussed in class, the lecturer prepared one question and required the students to either call or send him an SMS (short message) before end of week. For instance, " What lesson can we draw from reading Montesquieu's *De l'Esprit des Lois*" or "What's the moral of Jean de la Fontaine's fable, *la cigale et la fourmi*? Further, the students were required to call or send SMS concerning the books they were reading. For instance, a student could call or text a question to the lecturer such as "I don't quite understand why Jean-Paul Sartre's book is called *les mains sales*. Please help." Students were required to send at least three SMS and a call per week. All in all, the lecturer posted 10 questions over the 13-week course, the 13th and 14 weeks were dedicated to review and examinations respectively. At the end of the course, the students were requested to describe their experience of using cell phones as part of schoolwork.

DATA COLLECTION AND ANALYSIS

The data consisted mainly of SMS messages that the students sent to the lecturer regarding the questions posted and their literary books. The calls came a cropper since only one male student called the lecturer who was also male. This was due to inhibitions, cultural or linguistic, that made it very difficult to get the students to call their lecturer in a language that they had not mastered well. Other constraints will be discussed shortly. Other data came from students' comments about their experience using cell phones to learn French literature.

Brief Profile of the Sample

The FRN 3001 class was made up of ten regular Kenyan students studying French as a minor at the United States International University (USIU). Two of the students were male and the rest female; their ages ranged from 21-23 years and none of them had lived in a French-speaking country. The students' level of French could be gauged as B1[11], which is lower Intermediate.

FINDINGS AND DISCUSSION

Previous studies established that Kenyans liked making calls as opposed to sending text messages (Iraki, 2011). Nevertheless, the students under study were extremely reluctant to call their lecturer but instead preferred sending text messages. Firstly, the students explained: "it was just odd" to call the lecturer on their mobile phones since *stricto sensu* he was not "their friend". This is hardly surprising in Kenya where the lecturer-student distance is normally greater than say in the US. For instance, students are usually very formal when dealing with faculty and since cell phones are considered "very private", students found it rather uncomfortable to call their lecturer. Secondly, calling meant using French in real time in the conversation as compared to texting, which could be done offline. Calling, therefore, had a much higher cognitive cost and the students just avoided it, despite the high dividends promised in form of "class participation" marks. The lecturer discussed the issue with the students and modified the requirements; they were to just focus on sending the required SMS.

In terms of SMS sent, the initial messages were extremely short in content and students made considerable effort to employ abridged forms of French SMS.[12] In addition, the messages were slow in coming and the students had to be reminded that it was a course requirement. After three weeks, the messages picked momentum, both in terms of discussion points and queries about their literary books. The messages also became longer and longer. Students were encouraged also to use dictionaries and spell-checkers before sending the SMS. This had the effect of increasing the volume and frequency of SMS.

The lecturer responded to all SMS instantly in an effort to maintain the "flow" of ideas. Messages popped in at all times, including late hours and very early mornings. Even during weekends and public holidays, the students kept sending in their messages and queries.

Overall, the performance in the final examination was very good – 8 A's and 2 B's - and this could be explained by a number of factors. Firstly, despite the initial hesitations the students sent in a great deal of messages and queries that helped them understand the French literature course better. The students said they were "intimidated" at the beginning. Secondly, by texting more and using dictionaries and spell-checkers, students became significantly better at writing French. One student remarked "it made me use my French dictionary more often." Thirdly, students came to appreciate the fact that even when away from the university, their cell phones were unwieldy learning devices that they could employ at all times to improve their academic performance. Indeed, in their final remarks about the experience, the students expressed surprise and satisfaction that their own cell phones had helped them learn so much about French literature. Such a realization is significant in the context of self-directed learning since forthwith the students had identified a formidable learning tool. Fourthly, the students came to realize that their cell phones were more reliable than the university's internet connectivity; this meant that their learning could continue uninterrupted wherever they were as long they had Wi-Fi in restaurants and bars. This had a liberating effect on the students as they felt they could manage and direct their learning. They felt that they could access knowledge from their lecturer anytime anywhere. Finally, the students said that the experience was new, exciting and fun as it made them use French almost everyday.

From the faculty perspective, the experience was an eye-opener in many respects. Firstly, I had in spring 2013 encouraged the same class of students to use their cell phones to access language learning sites and dictionaries since the Internet on university computers was invariably down or dead slow. However, I had not tried to gauge how such an initiative could impact student learning. Therefore, the fall 2013 experiment, though modest, had promising results. Secondly, the current study attempted to focus on only two uses of cell phones, i.e. calling and texting, even though there are many more tools such as websites and clouds for more interactivity (Ferriter 2010, Dunn 2011, Ormiston 2013): www.polleverywhere.com, Evernote, School Town, wiffiti.com, Dropbox, Youtube, Study Boost, Tweetcall, Scavenger Hunt (SCVNGR), just to mention a few. In future, it might be interesting to test these tools to ascertain their importance and relevance in enhancing student achievement in higher education. Thirdly, the student inhibitions came as a rude surprise as I had not factored in the culture in Kenyan universities where the distance between faculty and student is relatively great. This implies that the cultural dimension matters considerably in deciding how to use cell phones as learning cum communication tools. Fourthly, it was extremely important to maintain the "immediacy" of SMS messages by responding immediately to maintain the flow. This was quite challenging since the messages arrived at times at odd times and moments. Finally, the feeling of being "locked-in" with the students was as fulfilling as it was challenging. I felt my students were learning at all times, and this was a great feeling. The downside was that I had to respond immediately in fear of breaking the conversation.

One would have expected the students to raise the constraint of cost in regard to sending SMS, which is about USD 0.02 per SMS. However, the target group remarked that the cost was insignificant and they did not even think about it. To wit, the students had even "discovered" how to send free SMS from their respective airtime companies. Another barrier one would have expected was ethical in nature.

The lecturer made it abundantly clear that the cell phone communications would be guided by a clear set of rules or net ethics (netiquette). These included mutual respect, decent and polite language, timeliness and confidentiality. Furthermore, the messages were exclusively for learning purposes within the target group and therefore could not be shared with outsiders. Abridged versions of the French language were allowed to create an air of naturalness in the exchanges. The issue of confidentiality and "privacy" of cell communication may have contributed to the initial "shyness" among the target group. In a different report regarding eHealth, the question of medical confidentiality with respect to patient information continues to raise eyebrows in Kenya (Gathura 2014). The report by the Kenya Medical Research Institute (KEMRI) called for more vigilance, especially in relation to HIV subjects while noting that "the use of mobile phones or other electronic media is on the rise in the medical field." The use of passwords could help avoid breaches of privacy, even within a learning context. Nevertheless, the target audience did not raise the issue of confidentiality.

IMPLICATIONS OF THE FINDINGS

The study, thanks to qualitative data, had made a case for using cell phones to enhance student interaction with the lecturer and the learning resources. No doubt, the use of SMS and eventually phone calls increase access and frequency of discussion with lecturers and fellow students. This alone can impact positively on academic achievement. Further, the study confirmed that the use of cell phones for learning could lead to autonomy on the part of students thus promoting long life learning or self-directed learning. The interactions with faculty at all times and in all places was key in promoting not only deep and transformative learning but also self-paced learning; faculty could develop problem-solving skills via their questions and also each of the students could progress at their own pace. Slower students could communicate their obstacles and get help whereas those with special talents can also outpace the rest and create their own momentum with the faculty. There is no gainsaying the importance of dealing with the cultural barriers that may mitigate the results of such an undertaking.

Cultural specificities such as distance, contact vs. non-contact cultures, writing vs. oral cultures, individual vs. collective considerations are key to the success of an initiative touching on a device considered by many as "private and personal". In view of the above opportunities and constraints, faculty should be encouraged to embrace the emerging mobile technologies to enhance student performance in various subjects. It goes without saying that more research need be conducted to further investigate the import of cell phones in enhancing student achievement in other courses. In Kenya, almost every university student has a cell phone; hence the potential for using the gadget to promote learning is immeasurable. Furthermore, the major mobile telephony companies in

Kenya could partner with schools and universities within the Private Public Partnership framework to provide affordable rates for using cellphones to promote learning.

CONCLUSION

The study sought out to ascertain whether cell phones could impact student achievement at university level by focusing on the French literature course for Minor students in fall 2013. It also sought to identify the constraints in employing the cell phones for learning and the students' perceptions of using cell phones to learn French literature. The modest findings point to the positive effect of using cell phones in teaching and learning. The intensity and frequency of lecturer-student interactions via SMS had a lot to do with the improvement in the final grade. Further, students reported that they found the experience enriching and fulfilling despite the initial cultural bottlenecks. In addition, the study established that the cultural parameter is key to the success of using cell phones for teaching and learning and should be integrated in the pedagogy. Issues regarding the cultural perceptions of teachers/lecturer relationship were very important. Furthermore, ethical issues such as netiquette and confidentiality of information shared are of paramount importance. No information about the students should be revealed to outsiders.

In view of the immense potential, a partnership between mobile phone companies in Kenya and the public sector (government, schools and universities) could further reduce the cost of using cell phones for learning. There is need, therefore, to explore to what extent the private sector can chip in within its Corporate Social Responsibility docket to promote mobile learning. Finally, the study recommended further investigation to test the import of other tools available in cell phones with respect to promoting student achievement in higher education. These include phone calls, blogs, wikis and innovative mobile applications: www.polleverywhere.com, Evernote, School Town, wiffiti.com, Dropbox, Youtube, Study Boost, Tweetcall, Scavenger Hunt (SCVNGR).

REFERENCES

Attewell, J. (2005). *Mobile technologies and learning: a technology update and m-learning project summary*. London: Learning and Skills Development Agency.

Dunn, J. (2011). *How should Students Use Cell Phones In School?*. Retrieved from http://www.edudemic.com/phones-in-classroom/

Egbunike, N. A. (2011). New Media and Health Communication: Communication Strategies in Malaria Control in Nigeria. In D. Ndirangu Wachanga (Ed.), Cultural Identity and New Communication Technologies (pp. 197-213). Hershey, PA: IGI Global.

Ferriter, W.M. (2010). *Digitally Speaking/Cell phones as Teaching Tools*. Retrieved from http://www.ascd.org/publications/educational-leadership/oct10/vol68

Gathura, G. (2014, January 27). eHealth poses risks, says Kemri. The Standard.

Iraki, F. K. (2011). The Cultural, Economic and Political Implications of New Media: A Case Study on Mobile Telephony among University Students in Kenya. In D. Ndirangu Wachanga (Ed.), Cultural Identity and New Communication Technologies, (pp. 90-110). Hershey, PA: IGI Global.

Kukulska-Hulme, A., Sharples, M., Milrad, M., Arnedillo-Sánchez, I., & Vavoula, G. (2005). Innovation in Mobile Learning: a European Perspective. *International Journal of Mobile and Blended Learning*, *1*, 1.

Maria, M., & Muyinda, P. B. (2013). *A Ubiquitous Method for Sustainable Use of Mobile Learning in the Classroom*. Paper presented at the e-learning Innovations Conference & Expo. Nairobi, Kenya.

Mitra, S. (2011). *Can Mobile phones be used to Improve The Quality of Learning*. Retrieved from https://www.google.com/search?q=n+Mobile+Phones+Be+Used+To+Improve+The+Quality+Of+Learning++In+Open+Schooling%3F&ie=utf-8&oe=utf-8&aq=t&rls=org.mozilla:en-US:official&client=firefox-

Murungi, C. G., & Gitonga, R. K. (2013). *Are lecturers and Students in Our Public Universities Interacting with Technology in the Blended/Hybrid Classes?*. Paper presented at the e-learning Innovations Conference & Expo. Nairobi, Kenya.

Ormiston, M. (2013). *How to Use Cell Phones as Learning Tools*. Retrieved from http://www.teachhub.com/how-use-cell-phones-learning-tools

Saran, M. (2008). Use of Mobile Phones in Language Learning: Developing Effective Instructional Materials. In *Proceedings of Fifth IEEE International Conference on Wireless, Mobile, and Ubiquitous Technology in Education (wmute 2008)*, (pp. 39-43). IEEE.

Spindler, G. (1963). *Education and Culture: Anthropological Approaches*. New York, NY: Holt, Rinehart and Wilson.

Wycliff, O. (2013). *Developing Human Capital Through e-learning and Mobile Technologies*. Paper presented at the e-learning Innovations Conference & Expo. Nairobi, Kenya.

Xia, F. (2011). *Research on the Use of Mobile Devices in Distance EFL Learning*. Retrieved from http://link.springer.com/chapter/10.1007%2F978-3-642-23321-0_16#page-1

KEY TERMS AND DEFINITIONS

Convivial: Friendly and make one feel comfortable and welcome.

Culture: Sum total of a people's values and norms that define their way of thinking and acting.

Deep Learning: Learning that involves understanding and application of ideas to solve problems. It is opposed to surface learning where rote learning is the norm.

European Common Reference Framework for Languages (ECRFL): Norms for evaluating European languages: A1 & A2 (basic level); B1 &B2 (Intermediate) and C1 & C2 (Advanced level).

Innovation: New ideas and processes.

Learning: Gain knowledge or experience of something.

Mobile Technologies: Texting, SMS, online applications available on mobile phones.

Netiquette: Polite manners while communicating via the Internet.

Pedagogy: Methods and principles of teaching.

Self-Directed Learning: Lifelong learning after formal directed education.

SMS: Short Message Service.

Ubiquitous: Available everywhere.

ENDNOTES

[1] Kenya Bankers Association Survey, 2014.
[2] With over 800,000 poor people, Kibera is easily the biggest slum in Africa.
[3] http://www.unimelb.edu.au/copyright/information/guides/wikisblogsweb2blue.pdf
[4] http://thinkingmachine.pbworks.com/w/page/22187713/Think%20Mobile%20Phones%20for%20Learning

5. Mobile for Education for Development. http://web.worldbank.org/WBSITE/EXTERNAL/TOPICS/EXTEDUCATION/0,,contentMDK:22267518~pagePK:148956~piPK:216618~theSitePK:282386,00.html
6. http://www.theguardian.com/global-development/2012/may/30/mobile-phone-developing-world-elearning
7. http://www.wise-qatar.org/content/how-can-mobile-devices-enhance-learning-classrooms.
8. http://www.elearning-africa.com/eLA_Newsportal/more-africans-learning-by-mobile-phone/
9. http://www.schoolnet.lk/research/mobile_phones_for_teaching_learning_science/
10. http://www.educause.edu/ero/article/teaching-americas-first-course-mobile-phone-learning
11. See Common European Framework for Languages.
12. The students had had a visiting lecturer who introduced them to French abbreviations for SMS.

Chapter 10
Promoting Strategic Reading Using the iBooks Author Application

Natalia Auer
University of Leicester, UK

ABSTRACT

Students are increasingly bringing their own mobile devices into the classroom. However, they do not take advantage of the various features that technology offers for supporting learning. The focus of the chapter is on digital reading in learning and particularly in foreign language learning with tablets. The author reviews the literature on digital reading and discusses briefly the use of reading strategies to promote reading comprehension. This is followed by a discussion of how the application iBooks Author was used in a research project in September 2012 in an Adult Education Centre in Denmark. The aim of the project was to determine to what extent students employ reading strategies when using tablets and which functions in the tablets support reading comprehension. Using a theoretical framework for learning strategies, the author discusses the design of digital material embedding reading strategies. The chapter concludes with practical suggestions for teachers and educational designers for promoting strategic reading using the iBooks Author application.

INTRODUCTION

With the arrival of technology in the classroom, more and more textbooks and reading materials are published in a digital format. There is much debate on whether the print format is more effective for learning than the digital media (Baron 2013, Szalavitz 2012, Wolf 2010*)*. Wolf (2010) suggests that the way we read is influenced by the medium. She claims that digital reading may hinder deeper reading processes such as analyzing and reflecting (Wolf 2010). Mangen, Bente, & Brønnick (2013) argue that reading texts on a computer screen is detrimental for reading comprehension. Their study used pdf files as digital material, thus, it did not take advantage of all the possibilities of the medium, such as inserting a table of contents where you can click to navigate to specific chapters or sections, or embedding a video or an audio.

DOI: 10.4018/978-1-4666-6284-1.ch010

Moreover, students need to learn how to read digital texts because as, Strømsø and Bråten (2008) put it:

Digital texts are key information resources in today's society, and we must learn to use them in order to participate in it. We cannot drop digital texts. (Strømsø and Bråten, 2008, p.202, my own translation from the Danish.)

That is to say, students need to learn how to use information from digital texts if we want to prepare them for today's society. Therefore, the debate should focus not so much on what media are best for learning, print or digital, but on what our students need to learn. There is a need to prepare students for "the changing demands of new electronic literacies in a globally competitive world" (Leu, 2000, p.748). In addition, UNESCO notifies us that:

To live, learn, and work successfully in an increasingly complex, information-rich and knowledge-based society, students and teachers must utilize technology effectively. (ICT Competency Standards for Teachers, UNESCO, 2008, p.1)

Furthermore, mobile devices are nowadays learning tools. Research shows that learning takes place everywhere and that young students use these devices for informal learning (Levinsen & Sørensen, 2008). Since students increasingly read digital texts for their courses, we need to support their reading process in the digital media. Their success in learning depends on their ability to understand and use the information in these texts.

According to Perfetti, Landi, & Oakhill (2005), reading comprehension "occurs as the reader builds a mental representation of a text message" (p.228).

Research evidence indicates that there is a positive relationship between the use of metacognitive awareness of reading strategies and foreign reading ability (Sheorey & Mokhtari, 2001). Raising students' awareness of the various cognitive and metacognitive strategies that they can use for reading will enable them to choose the appropriate strategies for better comprehension. These strategies are also crucial in comprehending e-material (Verezub & Wang, 2008).

In order to help students to be aware of their reading skills teachers can help them to model reading strategies. For example, think-aloud is an approach that relies on the teacher's help to model, for students, metacognitive strategies such as activating background knowledge, inferring the meaning and monitoring. In the think-aloud approach, the teacher verbalizes what she is thinking while she is reading, as it is important to visualize that reading is an active process in which we actively construct meaning from the text based on our existing knowledge. We need to give students more tools for text comprehension and encourage them to be active in the process of reading, that is to say, students should use reading strategies as they read such as asking questions about the content, identifying the main ideas or testing the logic and credibility of a text. Technology can also help the learner by modelling such reading strategies as the teacher does in the think-aloud approach. That is to say, technology can take the role of the teacher as mediator.

Being aware of one's thought process is important in face-to-face teaching but perhaps even more so in e-learning where the e-learning design leaves students with a higher degree of autonomy. In e-learning, it is essential for students to self-evaluate and monitor their knowledge. For example, Virtual Learning Environments (VLEs) are fairly well established in education and increasingly teachers are creating much digital material for uploading to the VLE. The development of students' autonomy in using digital material is essential. For students to develop digital competency, teachers must explain and support the use of' strategies that can help them to reflect on and self-evaluate their reading.

READING DIGITAL TEXTS AND READING COMPREHENSION

Research on reading has shown that the use of reading strategies enhances reading comprehension, but most of this research has been conducted with print texts. The research on the use of reading strategies with digital texts has been conducted mainly with pdf files and with students reading from stationary computers. Missing from the research on reading processes are studies that investigate the use of foreign language (FL)[1] reading strategies in reading from tablets, such as the iPad. Research on reading digital material with pdf files showed that the group reading digital material (in pdf format) scored less on comprehension measures than the group reading print (Mangen et al., 2013). Mangen et al. (2013) argue that issues of navigation within the document, among other things, might be the cause for the lower scores in reading comprehension. In their experiment, the pdf format they used did not take advantage of the digital medium. For example, it did not include an outline, or other reading strategies. It is different to read a pdf format where you do not have a table of contents or features that support comprehension. Research using the potential of digital materials is still needed.

Gegner, Mackay, & Mayer (2009) have shown that in computer-based environments embedding reading strategies such as activating background knowledge enhances students' reading comprehension. Azevedo (2005) provides a useful approach of teaching learning strategies in computer environments by modelling metacognitive strategies while learning with hypermedia. Bundsgaard (2009) points out that reading on the Web is a challenge for students and he provides an approach to searching for information and reading it on the Web. His approach stresses the importance of using reading strategies when the students surf the Web with a purpose.

To address the issues mentioned by Mangen et al (2013), there is a need to develop digital reading material grounded in research-based theories of reading comprehension. Further, research is needed to identify successful reading strategies for reading digital texts and to determine how they can be best embedded in the digital media.

My own study addresses this gap by investigating students' use of reading strategies when using tablets. This study draws from two research fields: metacognition applied to reading and foreign language and technology. There is an increasing use of digital material such as websites, podcasts, and e-books for foreign language learning, but there is a need to evaluate digital content drawing on foreign language acquisition research (Chapelle, 2009). Research in the field of metacognition provides a model for self-regulated learning, which in the context of mobile learning is one of the components for success (Sharples, 2002). Moreover, self-management is paramount for self-directed language learners in virtual learning environments because in them students will find for themselves the most advantageous conditions for their learning (Hauck, 2005).

Metacognition and Metacognitive Strategies in FL

Flavell and/or his colleague Brown[2] introduced the concept of metacognition in the 1970s. It refers to awareness of one's thinking processes (Flavell, 1979). The notion has been applied to different fields such as reading, writing, language acquisition, memory, attention, social interactions, self-instruction and education. In foreign language learning studies, Flavell's model has been widely used as the framework to explore learners' metacognitive knowledge of language learning (Wenden 1998; Goh 1998).

In foreign language learning, metacognitive strategies are actions used to control the processes involved in language learning (Oxford, 1990). Research has shown that the use of metacognitive strategies enhances both listening comprehension (Vandergrift 2004, Goh 2000) and reading comprehension (Boulware-Gooden et al. 2007, Macaro 2009) at different education levels. Research on reading (Arnbak, 2003) has shown that a good understanding of a text[3] requires that learners use metacognitive strategies such as: activating background knowledge, identifying and planning the task, monitoring and self-evaluating their own progress.

Nevertheless, research has shown that foreign language learners do not use metacognitive strategies as often as other strategies such as cognitive strategies (Oxford, 1990). Besides, the repertoire of metacognitive strategies that are used is limited; language learners use planning but they use very little self-monitoring and self-evaluation (Oxford, 1990). Therefore, learners should know more about metacognitive strategies, which can be learned through instruction (Chamot, Barnhardt, El-Dinary, & Robbins, 1999; Nunan, 1997).

Interactive comprehension instruction is research-based reading instruction where the teacher models these metacognitive strategies while reading a text and thinking aloud at the same time (Lapp, Fisher, & Grant, 2008). Based on a constructivist approach to learning, the teacher uses scaffolding in reading and assists the students by modelling the strategies. Since learning now takes place more and more outside the classroom through mobile devices (Levinsen & Sørensen, 2008) learning how to use metacognitive strategies in FL reading should be mediated by interaction with technology. That is to say, technology should take the role of the teacher as mediator.

Researchers have categorized learning strategies in different ways (O'Malley & Chamot, 1990, Oxford, 1990, Wenden & Rubin 1987) but most agree on the detailed definitions of metacognitive strategies, i.e. that these include: planning, monitoring, and evaluating. These strategies are also crucial in comprehending e-material (Verezub & Wang, 2008). Few studies have examined in which way technology (Chun & Plass 1997; Gegner et al., 2009, Mayer & Moreno 2003) should be developed for improving reading in L1[4] and in L2[5].

The findings in this developing field can be used to facilitate the process of L2 reading comprehension. With the integration of technology both in the classroom and outside the classroom, there is a need to find which types of software supports best the process of L2 reading comprehension. For example, technology can assist using metacognitive strategies such as activating background knowledge since it is otherwise more difficult to get background information when reading outside the classroom (Mayer, 1997).

Metacognitive strategies in foreign language learning have been predominantly studied with conventionally produced texts. Therefore, the question of how students use strategies through technology to understand a foreign language seems relatively unexplored. My study focuses on metacognitive awareness and foreign language reading comprehension processes in a mobile environment based on the Strategic Self-Regulation (S^2R) Model of language learning (Oxford, 2011).

Defining Language Learning Strategies: The S^2R Model

The S^2R model of language learning (Oxford, 2011) is based on social constructivist theory, which assumes that knowledge is constructed through a dialogue between the more competent person and the learner. This theoretical framework can better explain the learning process in the digital media since one important characteristic of these media is the possibility of interaction and collaboration. The S^2R model assumes that L2 strategies can be learnt through "mediation from others". In this way, the teacher assists the learner by modelling L2 learning strategies. The model supports a view that in informal learning this mediation is facilitated with books, media or technology.

In the S²R model, Oxford (2011) defines self-regulated L2 learning strategies as "deliberate, goal-directed attempts to manage and control efforts to learn the L2" (p.12). As mentioned before, researchers have categorized L2 learning strategies in different ways. In a review, Hsiao and Oxford (2002) compared classification theories of language learning strategies. From all the models, the model chosen for my study, Oxford's 6-factor strategy taxonomy, is the most consistent with learners' strategy use (Hsiao and Oxford, 2002). Therefore, I have chosen this model and not other well-known theoretical models such as Macaro's (2006), O'Malley and Chamot's (1990) and Wenden's (1998). Moreover, Oxford (2011) includes in her model other dimensions relevant for L2 learning than the cognitive, namely the affective and the sociocultural-interactive (SI) dimension. In her model, cognitive strategies support learners in constructing and applying L2 knowledge. Affective strategies help learners to cope with their feelings and attitudes in order to keep motivated. Sociocultural interactive strategies assist the learner with communication, sociocultural contexts, and identity. These strategies are controlled by metastrategies such as planning, monitoring and evaluating. Therefore, her model includes three types of metastrategies: Metacognitive strategies, meta-affective strategies and meta-SI strategies. Figure 1 shows metastrategies and strategies in the S²R Model.

As mentioned above the S²R considers three dimensions for L2 learning. In my study, I focus on the cognitive dimension. This learning dimension is supported by two types of strategies: cognitive

Figure 1. Metastrategies and strategies in the S²R Model. (Source: Oxford (2011, p. 17). Reprinted with permission.)

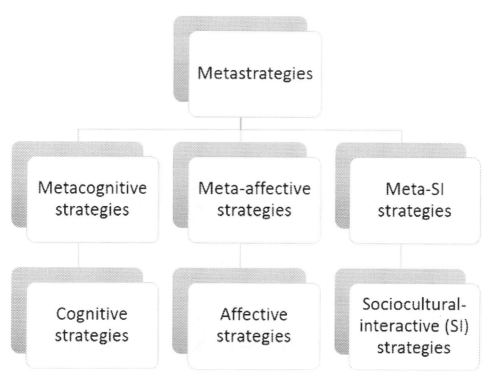

and metacognitive strategies. Metacognitive strategies control cognitive processes in L2 learning. Oxford (2011, p.45) includes the following:

- Paying attention to cognition.
- Planning for cognition.
- Obtaining and using resources for cognition.
- Organizing for cognition.
- Implementing plans for cognition.
- Orchestrating cognitive strategy use.
- Monitoring cognition.
- Evaluating cognition.

Cognitive strategies assist the learner in constructing and applying L2 knowledge. The S^2R Model comprises 6 cognitive strategies (Oxford, 2011, p.46):

- Using the senses to understand and remember.
- Activating knowledge.
- Reasoning.
- Conceptualizing with details.
- Conceptualizing broadly.
- Going beyond the immediate data.

Research has shown the importance of using metacognitive strategies in formal instruction (Oxford 1990) and in distance foreign language learning (White, 1995). Research also shows that metacognitive awareness of reading strategies is related to foreign language reading ability (Sheorey and Mokhtari, 2001). Increasing students' awareness of these strategies can help them choose appropriate strategies for understanding FL texts.

Tablets for Modelling Metacognitive Reading Strategies

The primary purpose of my study with iPads was to investigate students' use of FL reading strategies through this technology. To investigate this phenomenon I studied two cases: 1) Case study 1 Vestegnen HF & VUC and 2) Case study 2 Ørestad High School. In this chapter, I will describe case study 1.

Vestegnen HF & VUC (VUCV) is an adult education centre in Albertslund, Denmark. VUCV is a self-governing institution that offers full-time 2-year programmes and single subject courses leading to the Higher Preparatory Examination (general adult education at high school level). Additionally, VUCV offers courses in special education for dyslexic people and in Danish as a second language. About 2700 students attend courses at VUCV every year. They are men and women of all ages and backgrounds. Most of the teaching takes place between 8.00 am and 10.30 pm Monday-Friday in classes of between 25 to 30 participants. A small part of the teaching is made up of flexible offerings, wholly or partly as e-learning, individually adjusted to the participants' other work and family life.

The school offers language courses in the morning, afternoon and evening. In most courses, print books and Fronter, the virtual learning environment of the school, are used.

The study lasted 10 months, from September 2012 to March 2013. 7 Spanish students from VUCV were willing to participate in the study. They had already completed one year of learning Spanish (200 hours). VUCV delivers Spanish courses that attract 30-40 face-to-face students and about 70 e-learning students a year.

Students were asked to go to the centre to borrow iPads for 4-6 weeks. iPad 2 was the model of tablet chosen for the study. Then they met me and I introduced them to the technology. I showed them how the hardware and the application iBooks functioned. For example, I told them how they could look up the definition of words using a built-in Spanish dictionary (see Figure 2), highlight any word or passage of text within a book, create a

Promoting Strategic Reading Using the iBooks Author Application

Figure 2. Reading tools: Highlight function and dictionary

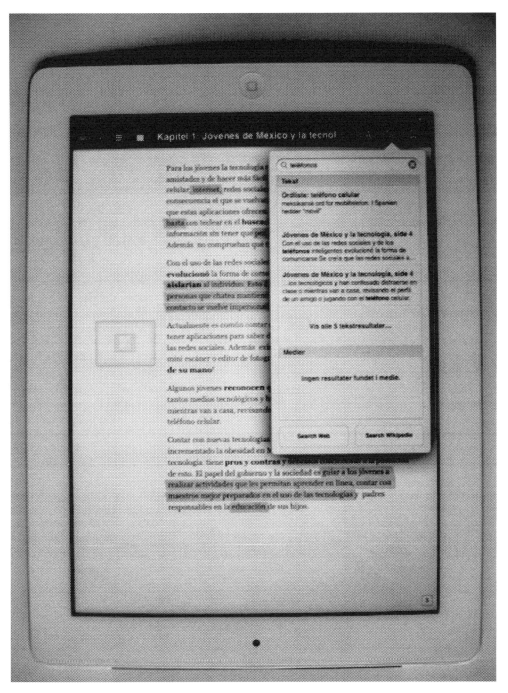

note and review their highlights and notes by tapping the table of contents button. These features support important reading strategies: highlighting the text is a strategy that helps the students focus as they read and helps them identify the main ideas in the text; note-taking helps the students to reflect on what they have read by asking questions about the text or checking comprehension as well as organizing learning material.

Then I showed them how to download e-books and e-material for iBooks. I told them that they could download to the tablets any other application and material they wanted. Finally, I showed them the iBook I had created for the study in the iBooks Author application (see Figure 3).

The aim of the guided hands-on session was to give participants the opportunity to get acquainted with the functions of the tablet so they would be able to proceed to reading the Spanish material. Table 1 shows the steps I followed to prepare the e-book with the iBooks app and to get students acquainted with the functions of the iPads and the iBooks app.

Embedding Reading Strategies in the Digital Text Using the iBooks Author Application

iBooks Author (see Figure 4) is an Apple product. The app is free and can be downloaded in the Mac App Store. It is an app for creating interactive books, originally created for producing textbooks but it is possible to produce any kind of text. It is simple to add text, graphics, movies by dragging and dropping a Microsoft Word document for example to the Book pane (see Figure 4). In addition, the widgets feature (see Figure 4) allows you to add among other things, photo galleries, animations and 3D objects for interaction.

The iBook can be viewed on the iPad. When I saw the presentation of iBooks Author in 2012, I thought that it was a very powerful tool, but that the exercises proposed did not take full advantages of the application for learning purposes. The type of exercises they proposed were based on behaviourist theories, for example quizzes and flash cards.

iBooks author is an application for writing books for students to read. Since reading is a constructive process, the different features of the application can be used to model metacognitive thought to make reading more effective. I used the feature "Shapes" (see Figure 4) for embedding reading strategies.

As shown in Figure 3, not only reading strategies are presented (guided practice) but also why

Figure 3. Spanish iBook created with iBooks Author application for the study

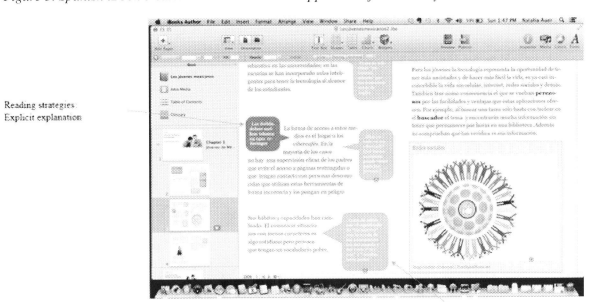

Promoting Strategic Reading Using the iBooks Author Application

Table 1. Guidance on the use of tablets for reading

Step	Description
A. Creating the iBook with iBooks Author application	I created an iBook with 3 Spanish texts and embedded reading strategies in a version that could be read in an iPad and shared with a link.
B. Guidance: 1. Introduction to the tablet 2. Setting up the iPad 3. Presentation of App Store and iBooks application 4. Introduction to the Spanish iBook with embedded strategies and features supporting FL reading	I introduced the technology, showing the students how the hardware and the software functioned. I introduced to the App Store those students unfamiliar with Apple devices, and showed them how to download the iBooks application. The iBook with embedded reading strategies was presented as well as the features in the app that supported FL reading.
C. Delivery	The tablets were delivered to students

Figure 4. iBooks Author

the presented strategy should be used (explicit explanation). The three Spanish texts were written in Word document by a Mexican e-learning researcher and two of her students. The theme is about youth in Mexico and each text is approximately 500 words. I imported the Spanish texts to the iBooks Author application and I used the feature "Shapes" to model reading strategies.

Then, I exported the book in iBooks format to be read on the students' iPads. Finally, the iBook file was uploaded to a Dropbox Public folder and the URL copied and I sent by mail the link to the iBook with the Spanish texts. Figure 5 shows the steps for making the Spanish texts available on the students' iPads.

Figure 5. The process of designing an iBook with the iBooks Author app for promoting the use of reading strategies

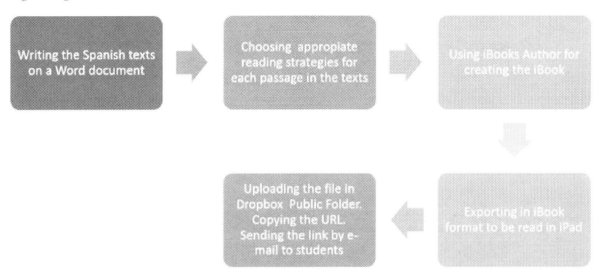

RESULTS OF INTERVIEWS OF STUDENTS

To identify my students' reading strategies I carried out semi-structured interviews with them after they had had an iPad on loan for 4-6-weeks.

Students' Use of Reading Strategies

My study showed that the students made use of some metacognitive and cognitive strategies as defined by Oxford (2011) when reading a foreign language on the iPads (see Table 2). Some students felt that the speech bubbles with reading strategies increased their awareness of the strategies. As one student commented:

Maybe the embedded strategies helped me to be conscious of how I read.

Another student commented that the e-book was very clear contrary to the scanned pdf files he had encountered before:

… so when you get such old copies [scanned pdf files] so you cannot, or if you have to read them online, you cannot see the text properly and … here [the e-book] has a better layout. You can go back and forth, you can zoom, you can click on the words and then you find [the word] you do not need to have a dictionary next to you.

This result is interesting since some research on reading digital texts has been conducted with pdf files (Mangen et al., 2013). Mangen et al. (2013) argued that comprehension performance of the group who read in print was higher than the group reading digital material (PDF format) due to issues of navigation within the document. Nevertheless, the PDF format did not take advantage of the digital media by giving an outline, or embedding strategies. It is different reading a pdf format where you do not have a table of contents or features to support comprehension. Therefore, more research using the potential of digital materials is needed.

My study shows that the different features and the embedded strategies in the iBook developed for this study optimized the reading experience.

Evaluating knowledge proved to be an effective strategy for reading comprehension, one student compared what she knew before reading the text

Table 2. Students' use of metacognitive and cognitive strategies when reading an iBook on an iPad

Metacognitive Strategies	Student Quotes
Paying attention to cognition	"… it is only one page [of the text] I have to concentrate on now, so I can look through the notes so that I can better remember those words I do not know what they mean"
Implementing plans for cognition	"So I used a lot [the note function], at least in the beginning, to create a note of these words … how it should be translated"
Monitoring	"Thus there were some times where I looked up [a word/sentence] in Google Translate where I thought 'it makes no sense at all'"
Evaluating	"things you think you know turn out not to be correct, I could not imagine that it [technology in Mexico] was so used as it appears to be "
Cognitive Strategies	**Student Quotes**
Using the senses to understand and remember	"I do not read aloud, I read 'in between'. No one can hear me, but I use my lips it helps me to make sure whether I have understood the text or not"
Conceptualizing broadly	"When a text contains a picture, it gives then an overview, so I when I read (the text), it becomes easier for me"
Activating knowledge	"I use my own knowledge about technology, so it was easy"
Going beyond the immediate data, inferring	"But mostly, I can understand the meaning (of a word) from the sentence…"

and afterwards and realized the gap: *…things you think you know turn out not to be correct, I could not imagine that it [technology in Mexico] was so used as it appears to be.*

Functions in the Tablets That Support Reading Comprehension

Some students valued the note function for reviewing learning material. This helped them to study the new words learnt through reading, as one student commented:

I found that out that if you go here [table of contents], it's pretty smart (…) you can get a full list of the words you have looked up, (…) as a kind of reviewing.

Students also identified advantages using the built-in search feature of the iBooks mobile application. They could search any word or phrase in the Internet, one student stated:

…you do not necessarily need a dictionary to have by your side, you can tap the word, and then you can go on the internet and then find out how you say the word.

Students did not realize that they could also use the built-in search feature for finding a word or phrase anywhere in the iBook but in the interview the researcher showed it and it was valued. One student stated:

So it is a good feature to review, perhaps, when you read to learn something and say, 'I'm sure I learned it', but you cannot remember…

It is important to show students the functions that are available and that can help their reading. For example, in my study many students were unaware of the possibility of looking for specific text within the iBook with the search function. I had showed them the feature but not all the possibilities. The search function gives three options: search on Wikipedia, search on the web or search throughout the book. The last one is very useful if you are looking for specific text within the book. Two students did not find it easy to use an Apple product. They were PC users and had some difficulties in the beginning. Eventually, they obtained advice from a peer who is familiar with iOs, the iPad's operating system.

Most of my students wished that iPads had the possibility of having more than one window open. When they found information on the Internet, it was difficult to remember when they went back to the text:

I like to be able to see things. That is to say, ... when I looked up on Google, I could be in doubt what it was the context, and then I had to return to see what it said before or after [the word] that could help to understand it, do not.

This is an issue since it is important when reading to be able to relate fast to the context. Though they had problems, students had a positive experience reading texts in a foreign language with an iPad. In summary, the tablet, the embedded strategies and the different features of the mobile application iBooks reader helped students to use a wide range of reading strategies for reading comprehension.

RECOMMENDATIONS

My recommendations on how best to use iPads to support FL reading comprehension are drawn from my small study:

- Show students applications and functions in iPads that support FL reading comprehension.
- Embed reading strategies in the digital material that support cognitive and metacognitive processing by using an application for creating e-books.
- Engage students in cognitive and metacognitive processes through using the embedded reading strategies and explain why they should do so.

FUTURE RESEARCH DIRECTIONS

Research on students' reading of digital material has focused on comparing reading on screen versus paper and on stationary computers, not laptops, tablets or mobile phones. I know of no studies that have measured the effect of the use of reading strategies on FL reading comprehension when reading digital texts with tablets. Due to time limitations in my own study, the use of video and audio as reading strategies were not used. These tools can provide opportunities for investigating the effects of video and audio in reading comprehension. It would be fruitful to research the effect of using these tools for enhancing reading comprehension within a multimodal learning perspective (Mayer, 2001).

My study presents students' use of FL reading strategies using iPads, but future research could focus more on these reading strategies, which play such an important role in FL reading comprehension. The effect of awareness of FL reading strategies on reading performance could also be investigated.

Research is also needed into how a research-based reading intervention might be implemented with tablets. In my research, the iBook that was created contained various reading strategies, thus modelling reading processes required for good comprehension. Students used a wide range of reading strategies, taking advantage of the digital media. Nevertheless, there is not enough research evidence to guide teachers and material developers in the process of using the full potentials of the iBooks Author app or other similar applications to create learning materials for the purpose of promoting the use of reading strategies.

CONCLUSION

The case study I presented in this chapter was aimed at investigating students' use of reading strategies when reading digital texts in a foreign language with tablets and to determine which functions in the tablet support reading comprehension and enable awareness of reading strategies. While the value of reading strategies in print texts is recognized, embedding reading strategies in digital texts is especially beneficial with mobile devices. Thus, students can take advantage of the various features that technology offers for supporting learning. Since much learning takes place also outside the classroom, we need to help students by providing activities that engage them in cognitive and metacognitive processes.

Although my study was based on a small sample of participants, the findings suggest that students use a wide range of cognitive and metacognitive reading strategies reading with tablets, thus engaging in higher-level processes. These findings contribute to the current literature in various ways. First, we have to be cautious about generalizing findings from different digital texts because each digital text contains different features to support comprehension. For example, a PDF format does not take full advantage of the digital media. As mentioned before, it is different to read a pdf format where you do not have a table of contents or features to support comprehension than reading and iBook with embedded reading strategies. We need to distinguish in digital reading research the kind of digital material used in the studies to be able to draw valid conclusions for practice. Second, the various types of digital texts require the use of different strategies from the reader. Finally, it is important to teach our students a wide repertoire of reading strategies so they can navigate and create meaning from the texts they read. However, additional research is needed to examine the potential of digital materials and other mobile technology applications to help learners model effective reading strategies.

REFERENCES

Arnbak, E. (Ed.). (2003). *Faglig læsning*. Copenhagen, Denmark: Gyldendal.

Azevedo, R. (2005). Using hypermedia as a metacognitive tool for enhancing student learning? The role of self-regulated learning. *Educational Psychologist*, *40*(4), 199–209. doi:10.1207/s15326985ep4004_2

Baron, N. (2013). Redefining Reading: The Impact of Digital Communication Media. *PMLA*, *128*(1), 193–200. doi:10.1632/pmla.2013.128.1.193

Boulware-Gooden, R., Carreker, S., Thornhill, A., & Joshi, R. M. (2007). Instruction of metacognitive strategies enhances reading comprehension and vocabulary achievement of third-grade students. *The Reading Teacher*, *61*(1), 70–77. doi:10.1598/RT.61.1.7

Bundsgaard, J. (2009). Skærmlæsning. In A. Mangen (Ed.), *Lesing på skjerm* (pp. 35–41). Stavanger, Norway: Lesesenteret, Universitetet i Stavanger.

Chamot, A. U., Barnhardt, S., El-Dinary, P. B., & Robbins, J. (1999). *The learning strategies handbook*. White Plains, USA: Addison Wesley Longman.

Chapelle, C. A. (2009). The relationship between second language acquisition theory and computer-assisted language learning. *Modern Language Journal*, *93*, 741–753. doi:10.1111/j.1540-4781.2009.00970.x

Chun, D. M., & Plass, J. L. (1997). Research on text comprehension in multimedia environments. *Language Learning & Technology*, *1*(1), 60–81.

Flavell, J. H. (1979). Metacognition and cognitive monitoring: A new area of cognitive-developmental inquiry. *The American Psychologist*, *34*, 906–911. doi:10.1037/0003-066X.34.10.906

Gegner, J. A., Mackay, D. H. J., & Mayer, R. E. (2009). Computer-supported aids to making sense of scientific articles: Cognitive, motivational, and attitudinal effects. *Educational Technology Research and Development, 57*(1), 79–97. doi:10.1007/s11423-008-9088-3

Goh, C. M. (1998). Strategic processing and metacognition in second language listening. *RELC Journal, 29*(2), 173–175.

Goh, C. M. (2000). A cognitive perspective on language learners' listening comprehension problems. *System, 28*(1), 55–75. doi:10.1016/S0346-251X(99)00060-3

Hauck, M. (2005). Metacognitive knowledge, metacognitive strategies, and CALL. In J. L. Egbert, & G. Petrie (Eds.), *CALL research perspectives. ESL and applied linguistics professional series* (pp. 65–86). New Jersey, USA: Lawrence Erlbaum.

Hsiao, T., & Oxford, R. L. (2002). Comparing theories of language learning strategies: A confirmatory factor analysis. *Modern Language Journal, 86*(3), 368–383. doi:10.1111/1540-4781.00155

Lapp, D., Fisher, D., & Grant, M. (2008). "You can read this text-I'll show you how": Interactive comprehension instruction. *Journal of Adolescent & Adult Literacy, 51*(5), 372–383. doi:10.1598/JAAL.51.5.1

Leu, D. J. (2000). Literacy and Technology: Deictic Consequences for Literacy Education in an Information Age. In M. L. Kamil, P. Mosenthal, P. D. Pearson, & R. Barr (Eds.), *Handbook of Reading Research* (Vol. III, pp. 743–771). Mahwah, US: Lawrence Erlbaum Associates Publishers.

Levinsen, K., & Sørensen, B. H. (2008). *It, faglig læring og pædagogisk videnledelse: Rapport vedr. projekt it læring 2006-2007*. København, Danmark: Danmarks Pædagogiske Universitetsforlag.

Macaro, E. (2006). Strategies for language learning and for language use: Revising the theoretical framework. *Modern Language Journal, 90*(3), 320–337. doi:10.1111/j.1540-4781.2006.00425.x

Macaro, E., & Mutton, T. (2009). Developing reading achievement in primary learners of french: Inferencing strategies versus exposure to 'graded readers'. *Language Learning Journal, 37*(2), 165–182. doi:10.1080/09571730902928045

Mangen, A., Bente, R., & Brønnick, K. (2013). Reading linear texts on paper versus computer screen: Effects on reading comprehension. *International Journal of Educational Research, 58*, 61–68. doi:10.1016/j.ijer.2012.12.002

Mayer, R. E. (1997). Multimedia learning: Are we asking the right questions? *Educational Psychologist, 32*(1), 1–19. doi:10.1207/s15326985ep3201_1

Mayer, R. E. (2001). *Multimedia learning*. New York, USA: Cambridge University Press. doi:10.1017/CBO9781139164603

Mayer, R. E., & Moreno, R. (2003). Nine ways to reduce cognitive load in multimedia learning. *Educational Psychologist, 38*(1), 43–52. doi:10.1207/S15326985EP3801_6

Nunan, D. (1997). Does learner strategy training make a difference? *Lenguas Modernas, 24*, 123–142.

O'Malley, J. M., & Chamot, A. U. (1990). *Learning strategies in second language acquisition*. Cambridge, UK: Cambridge University Press. doi:10.1017/CBO9781139524490

Oxford, R. L. (1990). *Language learning strategies: What every teacher should know*. Rowley, USA: Newbury House.

Oxford, R. L. (2011). *Teaching and researching language learning strategies*. Harlow, UK: Pearson Education.

Perfetti, C., Landi, N., & Oakhill, J. (2005). The acquisition of reading comprehension skill. In M. Snowling, & C. Hulme (Eds.), *The science of reading* (pp. 227–247). Malden, USA: Blackwell. doi:10.1002/9780470757642.ch13

Sharples, M. (2002). Disruptive devices: Mobile technology for conversational learning. *International Journal of Continuing Engineering Education and Lifelong Learning*, *12*(5/6), 504–520. doi:10.1504/IJCEELL.2002.002148

Shaughnessy, M. F., Vennemann, M. V. E., & Kleyn-Kennedy, C. (Eds.). (2008). *Meta-cognition: A recent review of research, theory, and perspectives*. New York, USA: Nova Science Publishers, Inc.

Sheorey, R., & Mokhtari, K. (2001). Differences in the metacognitive awareness of reading strategies among native and non-native readers. *System*, *29*(4), 431–449. doi:10.1016/S0346-251X(01)00039-2

Strømsø, H. I., & Bråten, I. (2008). Forståelse af digitale tekster - nye udfordringer. In I. Bråten (Ed.), Læseforståelse (pp. 201-224). Århus, Danmark: Klim.

Szalavitz, M. (2012, March 14). Do E-books make it harder to remember what you just read? *Time*. Retrieved from http://healthland.time.com/2012/03/14/do-e-books-impair-memory/

United Nations Educational, Scientific and Cultural Organization (UNESCO). (2008). ICT competency standards for teachers: Policy framework (No. CI-2007/WS/21). UNESCO's Communication and Information Sector.

Vandergrift, L. (2004). Listening to learn or learning to listen. *Annual Review of Applied Linguistics*, *24*, 3–25. doi:10.1017/S0267190504000017

Verezub, E., & Wang, H. (2008). The role of metacognitive reading strategies instructions and various types of links in comprehending hypertexts. In Hello! Where are you in the landscape of educational technology? Proceedings Ascilite Melbourne 2008. Retrieved from http://www.ascilite.org.au/conferences/melbourne08/procs/verezub.pdf

Wenden, A., & Rubin, J. (Eds.). (1987). *Learner strategies in language learning*. Englewood Cliffs, NJ: Prentice Hall International.

Wenden, A. L. (1998). Metacognitive knowledge and language learning. *Applied Linguistics*, *19*(4), 515–537. doi:10.1093/applin/19.4.515

White, C. (1995). Autonomy and strategy use in distance foreign language learning: Research findings. *System*, *23*(2), 207–221. doi:10.1016/0346-251X(95)00009-9

Wolf, M. (2010). *Our "deep reading" brain: Its digital evolution poses questions*. Retrieved on June 22, 2013, from http://www.nieman.harvard.edu/reports/article/102396/Our-Deep-Reading-Brain-Its-Digital-Evolution--Poses-Questions.aspx

KEY TERMS AND DEFINITIONS

Cognitive Strategies: Actions and procedures learners use in order to consolidate and elaborate their knowledge.

Digital Reading: Reading texts in digital environments such as the Web, computers, e-book reading and mobile devices.

Hypermedia: Computer-based environment which includes audio, video, animation, graphics and/or text which is designed and structured for learning.

iBook: An electronic book designed for Apple's iPad.

iBooks App: An e-book reader and e-bookstore. It has reading features for enhancing reading: annotations, highlighting, and bookmarks. You can import ePub and PDF formatted books to read in iBooks.

iBooks Author: iBooks Author is an Apple product. The app is free and can be downloaded in the Mac App Store. It is an app for creating interactive books, originally created for producing textbooks but it is possible to produce any kind of text. For more information visit: http://www.apple.com/ibooks-author/.

Learning Strategies: Conscious actions selected by students in order to learn.

Metacognition: The ability of thinking about your own thinking.

Metacognitive Strategies: Intentional actions by which learners plan, monitor and evaluate their learning.

Reading Comprehension: The extraction of meaning through interaction with a written text.

Strategic Reading: Understanding the meaning of the text by readers through the effective and appropriate use a wide variety of strategies.

Strategic Self-Regulation Model of Language Learning (S^2R): S^2R (Oxford, 2011) proposes a theoretical framework for language learning strategy from three different perspectives of learning theory: psychological, social-cognitive, and sociocultural.

ENDNOTES

[1] The terms foreign language (FL) and second language (SL or L2) are used interchangeably in the literature when referring to a language that is not the mother tongue.

[2] In an interview conducted by Shaugnessy (2008), Flavell has stated that he is not sure whether it was him or his colleague Brown that coined the term "metacognition".

[3] I use Hallyday's (1987) definition of text: "Any passage, spoken or written, of whatever length, that does form a unified whole" (p.1).

[4] L1 is the first language or mother tongue.

[5] L2 the second language is any language learnt after the first language.

Chapter 11
Using Mobile Technologies to Co-Construct TPACK in Teacher Education

Cornelis de Groot
University of Rhode Island, USA

Jay Fogleman
University of Rhode Island, USA

Diane Kern
University of Rhode Island, USA

ABSTRACT

How student teachers might benefit from using their mobile technologies during teaching experiences is a timely question for teacher educators. This chapter describes efforts to use the TPACK framework (Mishra & Koehler, 2006) to investigate how students use iPad computers during their student teaching and design appropriate supports. A design-based approach (Sandoval & Bell, 2004) was used over two years with two cohorts of student teachers (N=60). Descriptions of the use of the TPACK framework in this endeavor and findings from surveys and field notes about how and to what degree mobile technology can facilitate activities and interactions in planning, teaching, reflecting, and sharing are included. The case is made for co-learning and co-constructing by student teachers and teacher educators of the various TPACK domains of teacher knowledge in the context of mobile technology. Implications for developing supportive learning environments for 21st century student teachers are also discussed.

INTRODUCTION

During the past two decades, digital tools have transformed most knowledge-related professions as well as many jobs that do not, at first glance, seem data-dependent. Throughout higher education, as predicted, students have adopted mobile devices rapidly and are beginning to view these tools, including laptops, smartphones, and tablet computers, as critical for effective learning (Alexander, 2004; Chen & Denoyelles, 2013). Since their students increasingly rely on personal

DOI: 10.4018/978-1-4666-6284-1.ch011

technologies, colleges and universities are moving quickly to incorporate technology as part of the learning environment (Dahlstrom, 2012). The question is how specific university programs, such as teacher education, will integrate these tools to prepare their graduates to begin careers in teaching more effectively.

The transformative potential of personal technologies is especially apparent in pre-professional programs such as education and medicine. These programs often require novices to complete internships that call for rapid application of knowledge that they have been accumulating over an extended sequence of coursework. Medical schools are trying to discern what the affordances of personal digital devices might be in these settings (George, Dumenco, Doyle, & Dollase, 2013; Shurtz, Halling, & McKay, 2011). In teacher education programs, several studies have tried to gauge the role that mobile devices might play in pedagogical coursework as well as in clinical teaching experiences (Amador-Lankster & Naffziger, 2013; Geist, 2011; Maher, 2013; Newhouse, 2006; Swenson, 2011).

In this chapter, we seek to add to this discussion by describing our efforts to integrate mobile devices, including iPad tablet computers, into learning environments for English, mathematics, and science secondary student teachers. We begin by describing our approach based on the recognition that the knowledge necessary for teaching is complex and that student teachers learn by engaging in the professional work of teaching. We then describe our efforts to provide student teachers with iPads to use during their student teaching experience as well as our efforts to integrate iPads into our classroom observations and seminar activities. We will share observations and survey data on how student teachers used iPads during student teaching, and discuss how these data inform subsequent efforts to help student teachers enhance their experiences through the use of mobile technology. We are interested in what features of mobile technology can be incorporated into the teaching experiences and coursework that can help student teachers bridge the gap between personal uses and using these and other technologies effectively with their students in their respective learning environments.

BACKGROUND

Teaching is a challenging profession. Shulman (1986) explained that teachers must address a multitude of student needs almost simultaneously, and to do this they must bring to bear several different types of knowledge. Furthermore, they must be able to anticipate the effects of their actions ahead of time and make quick adjustments in the act of teaching (Dolk, 1997). This requires teachers to have strong capacity for reflecting on action and in action. We are interested in establishing skilled planning as well as reflecting on action and moving this toward reflecting in action. Labaree (2004), explained that there are four main reasons why "teaching is an enormously difficult job that looks easy":

1. Aim of teaching is to change the behavior of the client. Thus, the success of teaching depends on the willingness of the client to cooperate.
2. Client is brought into the relationship under compulsion. A major job for the teacher is to manage the emotions that are inherent to this relationship.
3. Teachers must carry out their practice (of convincing the client to cooperate) in conditions of structural isolation.
4. Teachers must live with chronic uncertainty about the effectiveness of their efforts to teach.

We are interested in how digital tools can support dealing with these challenges inherent to teaching.

Some of the knowledge teachers have and need to acquire is unique to their professional role. Shulman noted that in addition to very specialized curricular knowledge, teachers must also develop pedagogical content knowledge (PCK), which is generally an understanding of how the curriculum is perceived and processed by a range of students, and how to address and refine these understandings through instruction. PCK, therefore, is knowledge of how to support student learning of the curriculum. In 2006, Mishra & Koehler augmented Shulman's taxonomy of knowledge for teaching to address the added demands of integrating technology into instruction. Technological pedagogical content knowledge (TPACK) is an amalgamation of Shulman's PCK with the knowledge teachers need to incorporate technology into their professional practices.

The TPACK framework (Mishra & Koehler, 2006; Koehler, Mishra, Yahya, 2007) represented the relationship between a teacher's knowledge for teaching and his or her knowledge of technology as a Venn diagram consisting of three knowledge domains. This is model is shown in Figure 1.

In addition to the central concept of TPACK, which is the knowledge teachers need to help their students use technology for learning, this model also illuminates six other compound knowledge types that constitute knowledge for teaching, which are also described by Mishra & Koehler (2006).

Our observations of classroom practice, as well as our own experiences, support the central

Figure 1. TPACK Framework (Reproduced by permission of the publisher, © 2012 by tpack.org)

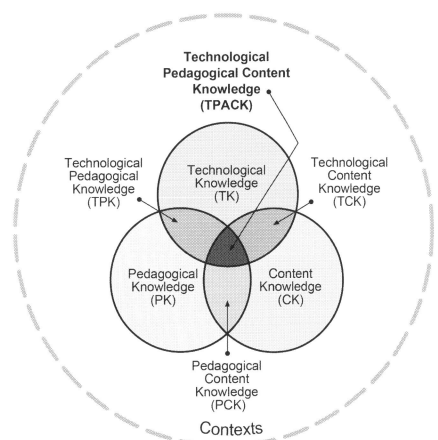

ideas within the TPACK framework, i.e. that in order for teachers to use technology effectively with students robust knowledge of students, the curriculum, and technological tools is required. In addition to TPACK, we focus on how the other technological domains of teachers' knowledge for teaching (i.e. TPK and TCK) provide opportunities to think about how best to incorporate mobile technologies into student teaching.

The TPACK framework also presents a challenge to teacher educators working with student teachers just before and during student teaching. Concerns have been raised regarding the limitations of TPACK as a tool for designing student teaching learning experiences (Graham, 2011; Archambault & Barnett, 2010). As instructors, we consider our student teachers' experiences with K-12 students, as well as the preceding planning and subsequent reflecting, as the central elements in building their knowledge of learners and learning environments. Furthermore, we expect that these deliberate experiences will either address or elevate student teachers' concerns about their practice. This apparent space between the TPACK framework and the experiences we have designed for our student teachers has led us to posit a model for how we are building toward TPACK, TCK, and TPK in our courses. This model is shown in Figure 2.

Our model represents a constructivist description of TPACK. This perspective is based on the idea that people build new understandings by augmenting, revising, and reorganizing their prior knowledge in light of new experiences and ideas (Brandsford, Pellegrino, & Donovan, 2003). Externally, a student teacher's knowledge of teaching can be understood in terms of the familiar TPACK framework; internally, each student teacher's knowledge takes the form of schema, some consisting of combinations of concepts that are pedagogical, technological, and content related. These schemas, resulting from the student teachers' diverse experiences and reflecting on these experiences, are idiosyncratic and complex. Initially, a student teacher's knowledge of teaching is grounded in the personal gestalt, represented by the dotted loop in our model. Each student teacher's experiences are bounded by his or her individual context.

The development of schema is supported by designing and providing tailored experiences that allow for just enough disruption and skill development accompanied by systematic reflection on these experiences. According to Korthagen and Kessels (1999), this leads to personal theories about teaching they label as phronesis, or theory with a lower case t. Korthagen and Kessels argue that teachers then continue to develop their schema into theories with an upper case T (episteme), also supported by systematic reflection processes. Working with student teachers, we are particularly interested in how to support the development of their schema related to teaching. Korthagen and Kessels also claim that the development from gestalt formation, to schematization and theory formation, supported by reflection processes, must lead to what they term as level reductions in order for the developed notions to become actionable in the moment of teaching (Dolk, 1997). In our model, we want to represent this development, and we view TPACK, TPK, and TCK to exist at the Theory (episteme) development phase for teachers. We want to convey that initially, in the process of teacher education, there is not likely a 1-1 mapping with the TPACK framework for our students and that teacher educators should be careful not to impose it too strictly on the learning of beginning teachers. We posit that we should aim first at experiences that lead to schematization. As such we have been interested in how digital tools and devices can support this work.

Figure 2. A Constructivist Model of TPACK

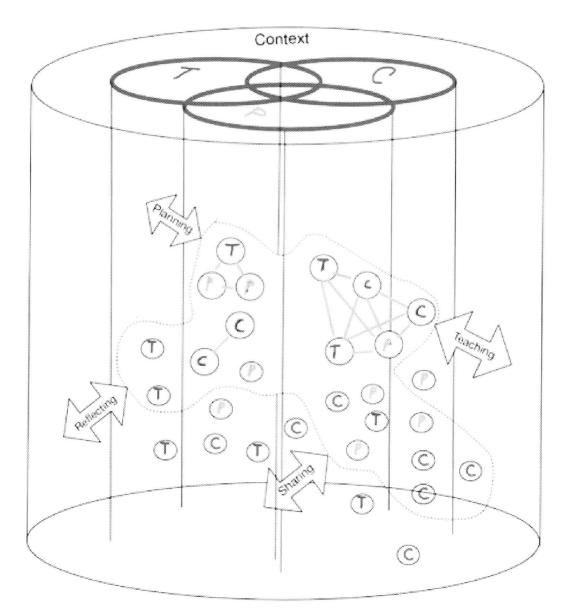

USING MOBILE TECHNOLOGIES TO CO-CONSTRUCT TPACK IN TEACHER EDUCATION

Our work with student teachers has goals that are naturally in tension with each other. On the one hand, as teacher educators, we seek to influence the learning of student teachers; on the other hand, we seek to provide a path to autonomous, self-monitored, and self-regulated learning and decision-making. Furthermore, we are not the only ones who have goals in mind for student teachers. Influences of practicum supervisors, cooperating teachers and their colleagues, peers, students, friends, and family also play a role. Student teachers interact with these influences through activities and experiences that include planning, teaching, reflecting, and sharing. We identify the total of these influences and interactions as the learning environment for the student teacher. In our model we have represented these domains of interaction as arrows into and from the gestalt. It should be understood that each student teacher, in turn, is an active agent in such a socially constructed complex set of influences in which teacher identity is formed; student teachers also exert their own influences on the learning environment.

The challenge of helping student teachers develop their knowledge for teaching is compounded by several factors related to the cultural context of traditional teacher education. The first factor is the tenuous expertise of the faculty and field instructors involved in the process. While it is not uncommon for teacher educators to have extensive classroom experience, this experience is likely situated in the past with technology that predates current innovations. As some of their TPACK may be generalizable across this divide, the staggering pace of innovation has potentially made their specific repertoire of technological tools obsolete. A second factor is the nature of digital innovation. Mobile technologies are entering classrooms on the coattails of Web 2.0-based applications and the emergence of the potential of these devices is still becoming apparent. Currently, new technological disruptions appear before current technologies are understood and implemented effectively. These pressures challenge us as teacher educators to develop effective student teaching learning environments while we must continually learn about teaching with emerging innovations.

In our early exploration of student teachers' use of mobile technologies for teaching, we have been interested in how these mobile technologies influence the student teachers' learning experiences. Additionally, we were interested in how interactions with others, including supervisory experiences and sharing experiences during seminar were influenced by these technologies. Within this context, we sought to link personal uses of mobile technology with professional uses. We are hoping our student teachers' comfort with personal technology will result in their use of their mobile devices in their teaching activities, and also very interested in whether their use of the devices for planning, teaching, reflecting, and sharing have any influence on their confidence using technology with their students as well as their choices to use the devices with their students.

Our research questions for this work are:

1. How do student teachers use iPads to build their knowledge for teaching?
2. What influences affect student teachers' use of iPads for building their knowledge for teaching?
3. What benefits and drawbacks of iPads did student teachers perceive during their student teaching?
4. How do student teachers and faculty members participate and contribute in learning environments designed to support the use of mobile technology for teaching?

We will report our approach and our findings in the next section, followed by a discussion of these findings. We will close with our conclusions and recommendations.

METHOD

We strive to help student teachers learn to use familiar mobile technology tools to improve their early teaching and to provide an environment in which they can explore the roles these technologies might play with their students in classrooms. We have used an iterative, design-based approach in our work. A design-based approach is often used to develop theory alongside innovations aimed at improving a system (Sandoval & Bell, 2004; Cobb, Confrey, Lehrer, & Schauble, 2003). An essential characteristic of a design-based approach is an effort to understand aspects of how an innovation and its purpose are understood by participants as well as how these understandings inform the theoretical basis of the innovation itself. In our case, our students are increasingly comfortable with using mobile devices in their everyday lives. They learn to use new "apps" as these are warranted, and rely on maintaining an almost constant connection to the Internet. The emergence of digital technologies as classroom tools leads us as teacher educators to ask how best to help our student teachers build on their technological acumen to better prepare to teach. The iterative nature of our work is represented in Table 1.

Our work has focused on using tablet computers and appropriate scaffolds to help our student teachers plan, teach, reflect and share in ways that enrich student teaching. We investigated how student teachers in secondary science, mathematics, and English language arts education developed spontaneous and deliberate uses of tablet computers underpinned by how they developed and managed their personal notes (Fogleman, de Groot, Kern, Byrd, 2013; Fogleman, de Groot, Kern, Byrd, 2014). Furthermore, we investigated the ways student teachers used these tools in relationship to their personal uses of mobile technology as well as in relationship to the perceived technological efficacy they reported about their cooperating teachers (de Groot, Fogleman, & Kern, 2013, Fogleman, de Groot, Kern, 2013; Kern, Fogleman, de Groot 2013). In this chapter, we extend this work by focusing on how student teachers use iPads to build their knowledge for teaching and how these results have contributed to the design of our student teaching learning environments. We consider our study of student teachers' use of iPads an opportunity to reinforce an atmosphere of co-learning similar to how teachers generally

Table 1. Iterative design of study of student teachers' use of iPads

Study Duration:	Spring 2011- 2012	Spring 2012- 2013
Research Focus	Student Teachers' (STs) use of iPads during student teaching for professional and personal use to build knowledge for teaching Perceptions of STs use of iPads by cooperating teachers (CTs)	STs use of iPads during student teaching for professional and personal use to build knowledge for teaching Role of classroom technology and CTs on iPad use
Research Questions	1. How do STs in secondary science, mathematics, and English Language Arts use iPads to plan, teach, and reflect during their student teaching practice? 2. Does having access to iPads for personal use influence STs' use of the iPads for professional purposes? 3. What other factors influence STs use of iPads during student teaching? 4. What barriers do STs experience while trying to use iPads during their student teaching?	1. How do student teachers use iPads to build their knowledge for teaching? 2. How do classroom conditions affect student teachers' use of iPads for teaching? 3. How do student teachers and faculty members participate and contribute in learning environments designed to support the use of mobile technology for teaching?
Intervention	STs in ELA, Math, and Science borrow iPads and video adapter for semester. Digital storytelling project Notability-based observations	STs in ELA, Math, and Science borrow iPads and video adapter for semester. Subject-specific shared resource notebooks. Notability-based observations w/ reflections "Hold hands and stick together" shared notebook
Data Collected	iPad use survey CT Survey Student Reflections on Teaching (Math) Digital Storytelling Samples (Science)	iPad Use Survey Student Reflections on Teaching (Math)

rely on peers for learning day-to-day (Jackson & Bruegmann, 2009; Kubitskey, Fishman, & Marx, 2003).

Procedure

Three years ago, our school of education began the process of integrating iPads into our curriculum by purchasing iPads so that faculty members could begin to familiarize themselves with possible uses of the devices in our teacher education coursework. In 2011, when the iPad 2 was released, our school used a technology grant to purchase two class sets of thirty iPads along with iPad carts to be used in classes on an as needed basis. In spring of 2012, the faculty members working with student teachers at the secondary level in English language arts, mathematics, and science were allowed to use one of the iPad carts continuously to begin this study. At the beginning of the semester, 30 iPad 2s were distributed to each of our student teachers as they began student teaching.

We managed the lending of the iPads to allow our student teachers to customize their iPad with their own apps. Before distribution, each iPad was restored to its factory settings and distributed with a charger and a video adapter to allow each student teacher to project his or her iPad in their classroom. Each student had to initialize the iPad by establishing a free iTunes account with Apple. This allowed each student teacher to download apps of their choosing. They were encouraged to use the iPads for both professional and personal uses. During the first iteration in 2012, we did not distribute screen covers with the iPads, and we had five iPads that were damaged. During the second iteration in the spring in 2013, we distributed the iPads with Apple "smart" covers and none of them were damaged over the duration of the semester.

In this next section, we describe aspects of the learning environment, including the participants. The measures we used to understand how and if our student teachers were using their iPads, as well as some of the strategies used to support them.

Participants

Participants included secondary level student teachers during their student teaching semester in the spring of the last year of their teacher education program. The participants were both graduate and undergraduate students, with the majority being undergraduate students. The study included approximately thirty secondary English language arts, mathematics, and science education student teachers during spring 2012 and thirty during the spring 2013 student teaching semesters. These participants are summarized in Table 2. In the spring of 2012, we also conducted a user group for field supervisors to discuss their shared experiences using iPads in a supervisory setting. In addition to the student teacher participants, we also considered ourselves participants and learners over the course of our study. As we were afforded prior opportunities to explore iPads beginning the study, we were aware of powerful ways the iPads might enhance our work as teacher educators. We found it valuable and important that we extended this exploratory stance into our work with student teachers to learn alongside them and from them. In this context, we regard ourselves as participants and will represent our voices and learning as part of the data in this chapter. We will reflect on this role further in the discussion section.

Data Collection

The main source of data for this study is a survey that we used to gauge student teachers' use of their iPads during their student teaching. In addition to demographic information, the survey asked about how often they used their iPads for planning, teaching, and reflecting. In addition, we also asked them about how they used Evernote to study and develop materials related to their teaching. In 2012, numerous student teachers said that their classrooms did not support effective use of the iPads, so we added questions in 2013 about how classrooms and cooperating

Table 2. Student teacher participants 2012-2013

		Year		Total
		2012	2013	2012-2013
		n	n	N
Undergraduate or Graduate?	Undergraduate	14	18	32
	Graduate	8	5	13
Own a smartphone?	Yes	9	21	30
	No	13	2	15
Used Evernote this semester?	Yes	13	19	32
	No	9	4	13
Content Area?	English	6	7	13
	Mathematics	8	10	18
	Science	8	6	14

teachers supported the student teachers' use of their iPads. Student teachers were asked to share a variety of instructional plans, reflections, and survey responses during their student teaching seminars in both years. We will describe results from each of these data sources. The survey items are summarized in Table 3.

We categorized the survey questions pertaining to student teachers' planning, teaching, reflecting, and Evernote use according to the definitions of the various knowledge elements included in the TPACK framework (Mishra & Koehler, 2006). We categorized each item based on the TPACK definitions and some guiding questions derived from those definitions. These working definitions of each knowledge type, the questions we used to categorize each type of activity, and the categorized activities are shown in Table 4.

RESULTS

We were interested in what impact mobile technology, coupled with deliberate scaffolds for supporting using these technologies for teaching, might have for student teachers on their learning to teach, their planning, instruction, and reflection. We investigated student teachers' personal and professional uses of these tools as well as circumstances that promote these uses in detail. In this chapter, we share selected results from the student survey and discuss a small number of cases based on the learning environment in each of our seminar courses.

1. How Did Students Use Their iPads to Build Their Knowledge for Teaching? TK, TCK, TPK, TPACK?

Our intention was to foster a learning environment for student teachers that provided them with conditions in which they could use iPads for authentic teaching tasks. After categorizing these tasks in terms of the types of knowledge for teaching they required, we examined their reported iPad use for these tasks. There was very little difference in the task breakdown for years 2012 and 2013. The overall distribution of activity is shown in Figure 3.

Figure 3 suggests that the student teachers used their iPads to build their knowledge for teaching in a variety of ways on average once per week per activity. (2.00 = "less than once per week", 3.00 =

Table 3. Survey scale items

Survey Scale	Item
Planning	1. Researching lesson options
	2. Researching academic concepts
	3. Professional reading
	4. Exploring instructional apps or websites
	5. Eliciting/sharing ideas with colleagues or cooperating teacher
	6. Eliciting/sharing ideas with student teachers
	7. Mapping a unit
	8. Creating a weekly (or unit) planning grid
	9. Writing lesson plans
	10. Developing student materials, e.g. worksheets and handouts
	11. Developing presentations
	12. Developing tests and/or quizzes
Teaching	1. Presenting material
	2. Annotating presentation material "live" in front of students
	3. Showing videos
	4. Showing simulations
	5. Having students interact with iPad individually at their desks
	6. Help with lesson pacing
	7. Formative assessment
	8. Summative assessment
	9. Grading/recording grades
Reflecting	1. Making post-lesson notes in lesson plans between periods
	2. Making post-lesson notes in lesson plans between periods
	3. Post-lesson journaling
	4. Writing post-observation reflection
	5. Sharing ideas with colleagues or fellow student teachers

"one or two times per week") Since the composite variables for each type of knowledge are averages of several contributing activity types, the strength of the graph is to show that students used their iPads to build knowledge of each type, using the iPads slightly more for their own learning (TCK) than for other purposes. Looking at this same data separated by discipline is shown in Figure 4. In this graph, student teachers in all disciplines relied on their iPads to build all types of technological knowledge for teaching, slightly more for building their TCK, i.e. reviewing academic concepts in preparation for teaching. Student teachers in each discipline were least likely to use their iPads in activities that addressed their TPACK.

The experiences that student teachers had in building their technological knowledge correlated with their iPad use in general. How student teachers chose to use their iPads, or the number of experiences that they had to build their knowledge for teaching using their iPads, was strongly interrelated and significantly related to how much they

Table 4. Survey items measuring iPad use by type of knowledge for teaching

Framework Element	Definition (Mishra & Koehler, 2006)	Planning	Teaching	Reflection
TK	Understanding how to use various technological tools, including operating systems and productivity applications.	Researching lessons Mapping a unit Developing planning grid Writing a lesson plan Developing instructional materials Developing presentations Developing tests and quizzes. Using Evernote to research lesson ideas Using Evernote to capture web pages Using Evernote to write lesson plans Using Evernote to take notes	Emailing Presenting Showing videos	Journaling Using Evernote to journal
TPK	Understanding of how technologies are used in teaching and learning, and how these technologies might change teaching and learning	Sharing ideas with colleagues Sharing ideas with peers Using Evernote to sequence lessons	Annotating presentations live in front of students Showing simulations Help with lesson pacing Formative assessment Summative assessment Grading	Between lesson notes End of day notes Post observation reflections Sharing in seminar
TCK	Understanding of how technology contributes to understanding	Professional reading Research concepts Using Evernote to record concept research		
TPACK	Understanding of technologies and pedagogical approaches that take into account students prior knowledge and help them learn	Exploring instructional apps	Having students interact with iPad in front of class Having students use iPad individually at their desk	Using Evernote to capture student work samples

used their iPads for non-instructional purposes. The correlations between their technological knowledge for teaching and iPad use are summarized in Table 5.

2. What Factors Influence Student Teachers' Use of iPads for Building Their Knowledge for Teaching?

How student teachers' were able to use their iPads to engage in knowledge-building experiences was influenced by several factors. Feedback from the first iteration of this study indicated that some student teachers did not have access to technology in their classrooms, such as wireless Internet access and projectors, which was necessary for using their iPads for teaching. In addition, since lack of wireless access would limit their access to documents stored "in the cloud" by several iPad apps, including Evernote and Dropbox, their iPads were no longer reliable for accessing or creating planning or reflecting on artifacts.

We were also interested in whether cooperating teachers might have an effect on their student teachers' use of their iPads. Based on this feedback, we modified our post-use survey in 2013 to include

Figure 3. Student teachers' use of iPads for building their knowledge for teaching (TK)

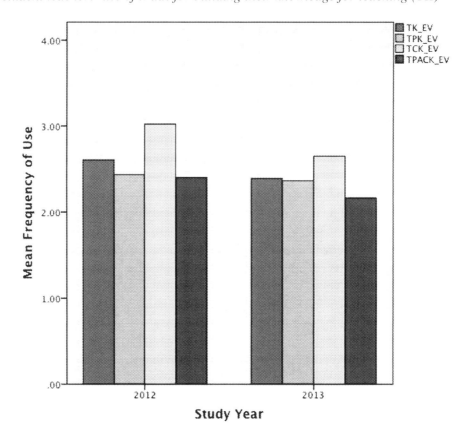

questions about the technology available in their classrooms, as well as the student teachers' perceptions of their cooperating teachers' attitudes toward using technology in the classroom.

Three composite variables were created to help us understand the effects that these conditions had on student teachers' iPad use. ClassroomTech is a measure of the degree that technology is available in the classroom. It was computed by taking the mean of a series of yes/no questions about whether specific technology (e.g. projector, wireless Internet, printer, online grade book, etc.) was available in a student teachers' classroom. The mean of the survey items asking about the presence of wireless Internet and a classroom projector was labeled as ClassroomIPadFriendly. The survey also asked student teachers to assess their cooperating teachers' level of technology use, from 1 = "tech enthusiast / early adopter" to 6 = "tech reluctant." This item was recoded afterwards as a 0 to 1 scale, with 1 = "tech enthusiast / early adopter" and 0 = "tech reluctant."

Because of the low sample size, bivariate correlations were used to look for relationships between opportunities for building different types of knowledge for teaching, TK, TPK, TCK, TPACK and these learning environment factors. This table is shown in Table 6.

The 2013 survey provided evidence about factors that influence student teachers' use of their iPads. In addition to their non-instructional iPad use, the degree that classrooms were equipped technologically had significant effects. The student teachers' ability to build their TPK and TPACK were significantly correlated to the degree that classrooms supported using their iPads for teach-

Figure 4. Student teachers' use of iPads for building knowledge for teaching by discipline

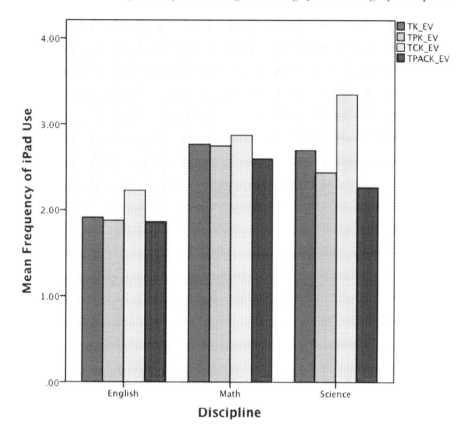

ing. The degree to which cooperating teachers were comfortable with technology significantly influenced student teachers' use of their iPads to build their own content understandings (TCK) as well as the degree that classrooms were equipped technologically.

3. What Benefits and Drawbacks of iPads Did Student Teachers Perceive During Their Student Teaching?

In 2013, we posed three open-ended questions for additional insight into our student teachers'

Table 5. Correlations between technological knowledge for teaching and non-teaching uses of iPads

Subscale	TK	TPK	TCK	TPACK	Non-teaching iPad use
Student teachers (n = 45)					
TK	-	.913**	.731**	.765**	.500**
TPK		-	.676**	.865**	.476**
TCK			-	.518**	.541**
TPACK				-	.405**
Non-teaching iPad use					-

**p < .01

Table 6. Correlations between technological knowledge for teaching and classroom factors

Subscale	TK	TPK	TCK	TPACK	Classroom Tech	Classroom iPad Friendly	CT Tech
Student teachers (n = 23)							
TK	-	.930**	.698**	.804**	.510*	.466	.370
TPK		-	.707**	.887**	.533*	.540*	.255
TCK			-	.571**	.587*	.475	.511*
TPACK				-	.578*	.542*	.105
Classroom Tech					-	.681**	.568*
Classroom iPad Friendly						-	.405
CT Tech							-

*p < .05 **p < .01

experiences. We wanted to know what disadvantages they found in using iPads, what lesson enhancements they could identify during student teaching, and whether the iPad helped them be more effective as a student teacher. We posed these questions as follows:

- What disadvantages or drawbacks do you see for using iPads for student teaching? (N=19)
- What were you able to do during student teaching using your iPad that would have been more difficult or impossible without it? (N=20)
- Do you believe that an iPad helped you be more effective as a student teacher? Why or why not? (N=23)

Disadvantages of Using iPads

Several student teachers identified difficulties with using their iPads. Seven student teachers identified difficulties in operation, problems connecting to the Internet and other technological barriers. These students teachers also reported that the iPad was, at times, a distraction for their students and cited challenges in managing a device that is relatively expensive, fragile and easy to steal. The remaining student teachers identified several challenges, such as reliability of operation, having no iPads available for their students, and the lack of compatibility of various technology components. A few students saw their own competence with the device as a challenge. Last, occasionally student teachers found it a barrier that they could not keep the device beyond the student teaching semester and weren't willing to make an investment of time in something they could not continue to use in the future. In contrast, avid users in the group were sad to have to give it up at the end of student teaching. Seven out of twenty-three student teachers did not answer this question.

Enhancements to the Student Teaching Experience

Twelve student teachers identified ways that the iPad enhanced their experiences. They identified the following: being able to find on-line resources (videos, websites, apps) in a variety of places and on the spot to address student interest or questions; being able to use the idiosyncratic capabilities of iPad apps for teaching (seating charts, taking attendance, keeping track of student behavior, using electronic whiteboards such as Educreations, and using interactive apps); being able to project and display student work and student thinking for class discussion; being able to do tasks that a laptop does not allow, such as hand-writing notes during supervisory visits; and uses for planning (looking up notes and information, resources) especially in places where a laptop is too bulky or intrusive a device.

There were eight students who did not identify any ways that the iPad enhanced their student teaching experience. A typical response was as follows, " I don't think there is anything that I wouldn't be able to do without the iPad in the classroom. I was fortunate to be placed in two classrooms with a fair amount of technology available." This suggests that the reasons for lack of enhancement were not necessarily related to poor technological infrastructure.

Effectiveness as a Student Teacher

Eleven student teachers did find that using the iPad contributed to their effectiveness. They identified several aspects of iPads that were helpful to them. They stated that it provided access to a great variety of resources all in one device and that this access allowed for on-the-spot actions and responses with their students. They remarked that it allowed them to engage their students more intensely, both inside and outside the classroom, and that they were able to use it for professional tasks. They saw a personal benefit for maintaining a better organization in their work and that they were able to do tasks more efficiently and quickly. A typical response was, "I loved using the iPad and its apps! The students loved the change and were eager to use it themselves. I'm sad to give it back!"

Ten student teachers did not feel that the iPad helped them be more effective as a student teacher. Results fell into three groups. One group indicated they did not have sufficient opportunity to use the device in a productive manner. A typical response was, " I don't think it necessarily helped me be a more effective teacher considering I hardly used it. The classrooms I taught in didn't have accessibility for iPad use and certainly did not have enough technological devices for each student." It seemed that this group does see the device as having potential for increasing their effectiveness but was not able to overcome these barriers. A second group was more prone to use their own devices (laptops, smartphones), sometimes because the iPad did not seem to offer any unique capabilities. A typical response was, "I also have an iPhone and MacBook. Everything that can be done on the iPad could be done on either of those." The third group of students had set themselves on a path in the pre-student teaching semester for using technology that was available in their student teaching sites, which did not include iPads. A typical response was, "I don't believe that it made me a more effective student teacher. Most of my lessons had been outlined before receiving the iPad, so I planned to use the technology already available in the classroom."

4. How Do Student Teachers and Faculty Members Participate in and Contribute to Learning Environments Designed to Support the Use of Mobile Technology for Teaching?

We will address this question by discussing our findings from our seminars in four areas of activity and interaction that we focus on throughout our teacher education program: planning, teaching, reflecting, and sharing. The bi-directional arrows in our theoretical model represent the four areas of activity and their interactions (see Figure 2).

Sharing

Our student teachers and we took a co-learning, collaborative approach to explore ways to do our work with the support of mobile technologies. During student teaching, we have a 3-hour seminar once a week. We routinely began each seminar with opening the floor for anything student teachers wanted to share with the whole group regarding their student teaching experiences of the past week. About every three weeks we would more specifically ask how they were using their iPads to address their concerns during student teaching and also to share ways we were using these tools.

These discussions often let student teachers share novel iPad uses. One student teacher explained she was concerned about having her back to a particular class for any length of time. She decided to use the iPad as a mobile whiteboard that she could draw and write on while facing the students. This solved a significant classroom management dilemma for her and she was able to establish better control of the class and to encourage participation of her students.

Another student teacher explained he wanted to be more available to his students after class, but many could not meet with him in person in school for a variety of reasons. He established a Twitter account for his class to which his students could send a question they had at any time. He then used Educreations to fashion a response to the student and sent the URL for this response back to the student, who could view this online at his or her convenience. Since this worked nicely on either the iPad or his smartphone, he was able to respond under many circumstances.

A third student teacher was interested in creating more student engagement and classroom discourse in her classes. She decided to use PollEverywhere to pose interesting questions and problems to which students individually text their response with their cell-phones. She reported that the students became much more focused on each others' thinking and less so on her thinking as the ultimate judge of correctness. She found it changed her role in the classroom.

A last example is from a student teacher who wanted to improve her questioning techniques. She found an app called Stick Pick. This app allows the teacher to enter all the names of a class and assign a questioning level according to Bloom's revised taxonomy. Then when the app randomly picks a given student, question stems for that particular level of the taxonomy show up on the iPad screen. While initially she was a little distracted, eventually, with practice, she found that this really helped her ask better questions and effectively use wait time.

To facilitate sharing among student teachers and teacher educators, several apps and scaffolds were needed to extend the capacity of the iPads. We began by modeling how Evernote and Dropbox could be used on the iPads for planning and sharing. During the first year, we were able to provide most student teachers and each of us with a premium license for Evernote. We then provided class time to install Evernote and DropBox. Student teachers worked in pairs to complete an Evernote quest, which was a self-guided activity to help student teachers learn to use Evernote. This led to the idea to create a shared notebook in Evernote called "Hold Hands and Stick Together" to which all secondary science, mathematics, and English language arts student teachers and teacher educators were invited. Contributions to this notebook included uses for Evernote, apps of interest or websites one found helpful in learning to teach or to do the work of teaching. Sharing continued through the Evernote notebook and also in person regularly during a segment of class time for the rest of the semester.

Planning

During the pre-student teaching semester, student teachers were required to design a unit plan in their respective disciplines. In the past paradigm, we had each student teacher submit such a plan in a word-processed format, where plans consisted of a sequence of lesson plans. Using the capabilities of the iPad, we have come to rethink planning activities. For example, student teachers can use photo or scanning apps to capture handwritten (brainstorming) records and many other resources. In the past, we were not able to provide many tools for organizing and creating unit plans or other plans for that matter. (Figure 5)

We thought to use shared Evernote notebooks to provide planning templates and other tools. We provided options for a variety of planning approaches and encouraged student teachers to modify and customize these templates for their needs. The mobility of the iPad allowed student teachers to do on-the-spot work. We found that initially a good number of the student teachers were more comfortable using established word processors and other software external to Evernote. These students were able to drag these files into a note to keep a shared record. This ameliorated the limitations of the word processing capabilities in Evernote for some, but limited the immediate visibility of the work.

We strive to place student teachers in pairs in a school as much as we can. In these instances, we see that student teachers are prone to plan together, especially in cases where they have the opportunity to co-teach. We have noticed that in such pairs the iPad is a strong partner in their planning and teaching. This works particularly well with apps that have good potential for collaboration. During supervision of these pairs, we also stimulated student teachers to be involved with observing each other and to co-reflect. Again the

Figure 5. Example of Evernote notebook of shared resources for student teaching

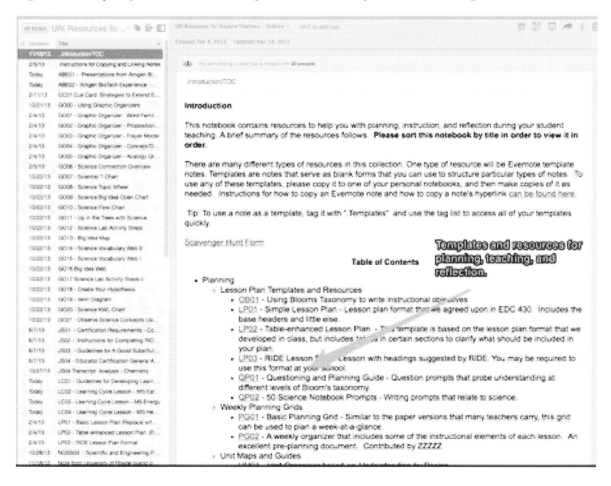

iPad's sound, photo, and video recording capabilities enhanced this experience. For example, one pair, in mathematics, used the video recording capability of iPads to look back and reflect on co-taught lessons and revised their original plan and co-teaching strategies to share with their supervisor.

Teaching

A major task in the student teaching seminar course is to conduct a case study to use student assessment data to inform instruction. We discovered that the use of the iPad's photo capability eased the burden of scanning sets of student work and allowed the student teacher to get corrected work back to their students right away. Several student teachers used Evernote and DropBox to organize, store, and share lesson plans. A lesson on Shakespeare's *The Merchant of Venice* with high school seniors involved the PollEverywhere app on the student teacher's iPad connected to a projector. The students were asked to use their personal devices to write a Tweet as a character in the play after events in Act III. Student teachers started to think how they could employ the iPad as an assessment tool during their teaching. Two mathematics student teachers asked groups of their students to solve problems on an electronic whiteboard and record their think aloud while they wrote their work on the iPad. These recordings were used for the whole class to review and critique and used for subsequent assessment by the student teachers as well. They learned to adapt instruction based on the rich information from these recordings. These are a few examples of how the iPad helped with the tangible productivity of learning to teach. Several other examples are given in the section on reflecting below.

Reflecting

Because of our interest in developing the reflective capacity of student teachers during our role as university supervisors, we realized that the Notability app for the iPad might be useful during a student teacher observation. Notability, which is able to record sound and sync with handwritten or typed notes and photos, allows one to go instantly to particular episodes in an observation that the observer or the student teacher want to discuss further. This tool seemed unobtrusive and thus viable as an observation and reflection medium. For example, during a given observation the student teacher asked one question after another without waiting for any student responses. When confronted with this practice after the lesson, the student teacher could not remember the occurrence. The university supervisor was able to go to that moment in time instantly by tapping on notes in Notability and together with the student teacher listened to the audio of this episode, jogging the student teacher's memory and helping her to reflect in that moment. This experience had a positive impact on her teaching behavior in subsequent observations. Not only were we able to share notes and recordings with the student teachers immediately following the lesson to support reflecting-on-action, we were also able to send notes and recordings to them for further reflection, using a shared Dropbox folder. (see Figure 6 and Figure 7)

FUTURE RESEARCH DIRECTIONS

Developing a Student Teaching Learning Environment Supported by Mobile Technology

By focusing on how student teachers used their iPads, we learned about how they built their technological knowledge for teaching. The TPACK framework extends Shulman's (1986) efforts to classify the complex knowledge teachers develop as they build their expertise. Researchers and teacher educators have struggled to operationalize TPACK into a guide for integrating technology

Using Mobile Technologies to Co-Construct TPACK in Teacher Education

into learning experiences of preservice teachers (Angeli, 2005; Archambault & Barnett, 2010; Graham, 2011). As our student teachers described how they chose to integrate their iPads into their teaching, it became clear that how they were able to build technological knowledge of each type depended on their familiarity with their iPad (TK) as well the degree that their instructional use of the iPad (TPK, TPACK) was supported by their classroom context. Bullock (2004) noted that importance of the cooperating teacher (CT) as modeler and encourager, but we found that our student teachers' use of their iPads was not tightly linked to their CT's attitudes towards technology, except in the case of TCK, which can be understood as their use of their devices for their own just-in-time learning.

Mobile technology, in our view and experience, can enable teacher educators and other actors in the learning environment to address several areas of pertinent need and concern of and for student teachers. We feel that it is crucial that these needs and concerns are shared in this environment. Thus we were prone to create an environment in which co-learning and co-constructing of meaning is a central tenet. In other words we made every effort to heed the congruence principle (Koster & Korthagen, 1997). We have attempted to represent this stance in our conceptual model (see Figure 2).

In such an environment, we share the student teacher's need for autonomy, while we also desire to maintain influence. In order to support the student teacher on this path to autonomy we created a variety of scaffolds for using mobile technology so that we were able to increase the likelihood that they were able to generate a cache of useful teacher knowledge that could be enacted on-the-spot. At the same time, we respected that

Figure 6. Example of observation notes taken using Notability

Figure 7. Example of a post-observation dialog using a shared note in Evernote

Taxonomy of Reflection	Description
Remembering: What did I want, do, feel, and think? What did the student(s) want, do, feel, and think?	How much help is too much help? I felt like I gave a lot of help to most of my students during the test. Some did better but some still didn't get it. I think that the test was pretty difficult because we got the questions from a common core program. They were not used to the type of questions they saw on it. When students would raise their hands to ask a question I would go to them and respond with a leading question. This would help them to realize it on their own. Even when giving students the greatest advantage (using a calculator, omitting questions, open notes etc.) and some still fail or get less than a 75. Should I consider not giving these advantages anymore? Do I need to start critiquing my teaching style or the way I teach that specific topic? I feel like I'm the one that had failed them when they do not do well on a test. I have spoken with my CT about taking this sort of thing so personally. S_____ with the way I teach so its up to them to put that extra effort in to study. I am starting to see that maturity is a really big part of why students either care or don't. I see so many students who are completely capable of doing the work but just don't because of pure laziness. Are you sure about that? Do you equate disengaged with lazy? Seems a little bit like an "easy" explanation...maybe. I'm very excited to start teaching at the high school now because I feel like I may start getting some of that effort back (at least in _____)
Understanding: What was important about it? For me? For the student(s)? For both of us?	What is important about this is I need to know where to draw the line with allowing my students extra help on tests or quizzes. S_____ under more pressure than others when taking tests so they choke. This has definitely happened to me before so having that foldable handy during the test would always come in handy, but would always take advantage of it. What I am now seeing is students not taking advantage of such an easy thing. It just is beyond me because I never would have passed up the opportunity to be able to use something like that on my tests. How can some do so terrible on a tests where the answers are practically right in front of you? Granted (let me clarify) not ALL or even a lot of students failed, but I just don't think ANY should have. So maybe your expectations (realistic or not) drive how you experience the results of your students. It seems unacceptable to you that even with all these aids there are students who do not do very well. How is that possible? Yes?
Applying: Where can I use this again?	I'm really curious to see where I can use this when I go to the high school. Will it be too much by letting them use a foldable? What if they have a question on the test? Can I still give them the sort of leading questions I gave the middle schoolers? I know that I want to be sure my students are prepared to take the test before I give it out. I like a sort of pre-assessment to help myself be sure if they will do well. Yes, how will you know that students are ready for the test? Or do you give the test when you had it planned, ready or not? How ill you know that your students are able to take advantage of the tools you give them?
Analyzing: Do I see any patterns in what I did?	Eventually I just got really tired of helping students try to improve their grade. I put so much effort into helping them get it up so they can pass the class or test or quiz but they only rely on that. They don't bother putting the effort into studying. That is what really got to me I think. I just was working so hard to help them understand and not getting anything in return from some of them was frustrating. Clear! So did you notice this at the time of the test or was this apparent as you taught the unit? If so, what did you do to make the students work hard instead of you?
Evaluating: What was effective and what was not effective?	What is not effective is trying to get them to put extra effort into learning the curriculum. If they don't want to do it then they aren't going to. What was effective was giving incentives (points) to certain students who came to a review session that I held before the class. The 4 students who showed up got 10 extra points on their tests. (I felt like this was too many points but my CT insisted so I agreed.) This may seem effective, but in essence these are bribes and not learning incentives. Do you think these students would do okay on the same test a week later?
Creating: What could I do next?	I will be bringing my new findings into the high school with me this next quarter. I'll definitely give a pre-assessment to see where each student is at. This can help figure out if the students need 1, 2 maybe 3 days to keep seeing it. Bravo! I will need to draw a limit though on how many days because some students may get bored. So, you need to differentiate and not try to keep everyone do the same dance in the same place. This made me think of another issue with this though! What if you wanted to make a limit on how long you spent on something? Well, I really believe that you need to tend to the students' needs. I will move on once the majority of the class understands the topic. This can lead to more problems though of boredom from those who are ahead. But what if 2 or 3 students in the class are really struggling? When do you move on? This type of situation is something I feel like I'm currently wanting to really develop a plan/understand how to handle. Excellent. Look into differentiating your instruction. What have you learned about this in the past that may be useful? What resources can you find, in the classroom? On the internet? In the Curriculum Materials Library?

Excerpts from student teacher's reflection with followup prompts from supervisor

some student teachers did not feel room for mobile technology in their learning environment due to the added investment needed.

For those student teachers that did explore the use of mobile technology, we feel that the enhancements this provided them easily outweighed the needed investment. We have realized we should not overestimate the readiness of our student teachers. We also realized that we did not spend enough time learning about student teachers' gestalts in relationship to mobile technology and we may have been asking them to develop schema for which the T, C, and P elements were not well organized or ready. As such, we need to begin this work in the pre-student teaching semester and even earlier so that, when they enter student teaching, there is less burden in realizing the potential of mobile technology. More than 90% of the student teachers regarded themselves tech savvy, but it appears that roughly 60% could realize this technological skill into practice during student teaching.

We have been working on helping student teachers with systematic reflection and providing fast and useful feedback to them. We have been able to enhance this aspect of our work through the use of mobile technology. Student teachers have indicated a high appreciation for this. This issue of relative immediacy appears to resonate with the way in which many of our students communicate in their personal lives. They tend to be able to act on these conversations and interactions effectively.

In the end, most student teachers collected a wealth of information, documents, resources, artifacts, and memories that had found a singular portable place where these elements lived together and allowed for sense making. It is understandable from this perspective that many of them were sad to have to return the iPads. By providing student teachers with strategies early on to preserve their notes, plans, reflections and other artifacts, they were all able to sync their records to their computer for future use. This ability to accumulate a corpus of teaching materials that can be accessed anytime and persist across platforms is consistent with early ideas about how teachers might use technology to construct, situate and distribute their knowledge (Borko & Putnam, 2000).

ENHANCING OUR OWN TPACK

Koster and Korthagen (1997) introduced the congruence principle for teacher educators. This principle states that the pedagogical actions of a teacher educator must correspond with the pedagogical actions that he/she wants to promote in student teachers and experienced teachers; therefore, teacher educators must be able to bring to bear their specialized knowledge in a similar fashion as they strive their student teachers to do. To us this means that we must also engage and immerse ourselves in similar learning environments as our students. This principle does not just pertain to our instructional practices but very much guides us in our own learning. Furthermore, we view ourselves as co-learners learning from and with our student teachers (Friere, 1998). We value experiences with innovations and ideas on a collegial level. For the most part, student teachers choose to be in our program. This is a distinct advantage compared to compulsory schooling at the K-12 level (Labaree, 2004). In fact, we likely learn more from them than they learn from us as we have very limited opportunity to implement mobile technology devices and tools in K-12 practice. While we do not lack ideas and theoretical schema (episteme), we do lack practical experiences on the ground (phronesis) in this area. In the realm of TPACK, we very much rely on our student teachers to develop our own constructs through their eyes.

The effect of this stance is that we invite participation in more open experiences in which we explore the possibilities alongside our students. It is in this environment where our institutional practice meets the K-12 school practice. It is the place where we are all forging a bridge between our experiences through reflections, such as this chapter writing has allowed us, as we gradually integrate the TPACK framework into our gestalts as teacher educators.

There were three main sources that provided this learning for us. First, there were the seminars during which student teachers regularly shared their experiences and innovations, some of which we have highlighted in this chapter. Second, we learned about student teachers use of iPads through surveys, which included the opportunity in three questions for the student teachers to explain their experiences. Third, we regularly exchanged experiences and ideas with a field supervisor user group. Since all three of us supervise student teachers and since our offices are adjacent, we had many informal opportunities to have impromptu reflexive conversations. For example, in one conversation we discussed how we are avid users of e-mail and how our students are avid users of texting. We discussed the different socially constructed expectations for e-mail and texting, such as the expectation of an immediate response to a text message, very much as in a face-to-face conversation, and that such an expectation does not really seem to exist in e-mail communication. This made us think more deeply about electronic media that address the need for immediacy well and what might be useful implications of immediacy in an educational setting.

We considered our reliance on and comfort with e-mail as a possible mismatch in communication. We do value this immediacy in providing feedback to our students on their work. We have found Evernote to be a good tool for this purpose. As we provide feedback to work posted in a shared notebook, our students can see our feedback in progress as we sync it and, vice versa, we are much closer witnesses to their work in progress. This is an advantage that we have not had before. It gives us opportunities for influence in the moments of creation. This offers a new perspective for us on how technological tools can bring depth to our work that is empowering to our student teachers and us simultaneously, socially reciprocal, and pedagogically congruent.

CONCLUSION

Mobile technology has become a ubiquitous companion for students in higher education, but the role that mobile learning might play in their learning and maturation as creative professionals is still largely unexplored territory. We believe that in order to help our students use their devices effectively for learning, knowing, reflecting, and creating, we must integrate supports for using these tools into student teachers' academic and professional experiences. Recent efforts to characterize teachers' technological knowledge are useful in helping teacher educators and student teachers shape productive learning environments.

Our design-based approach allowed us to explore facets of our learning environment that have emerged over the course this study. The theme of *immediacy* has emerged from this work: responding on-the-spot to students, student teachers' affinity for text messaging and social media versus e-mail, the use of shared planning notebooks and witnessing work in progress, the capability of field supervisors to prompt student teachers with audio clips of their teaching provides new windows on their practice, opportunities for informal feedback on the go, and access to resources or mentors. The iPads and our student teachers' smartphones also *eroded classroom isolation*, a second theme that emerged from this study. Twenty-first century student teachers are now able to communicate with faculty and peers real-time throughout their day. We continue to explore how these themes might be used to enhance our students' learning experiences.

REFERENCES

Alexander, B. (2004). Going nomadic: Mobile learning in higher education. *Educause Review*, *39*(5). Retrieved from https://www.educause.edu/pub/er/erm04/erm0451.asp

Amador-Lankster, C., & Naffziger, L. (2013). Power of using iPads during clinical practice with teacher candidates. In R. McBride & M. Searson (Eds.), *Proceedings of Society for Information Technology & Teacher Education International Conference 2013* (pp. 2534-2539). Chesapeake, VA: AACE. Retrieved January 19, 2014 from http://www.editlib.org/p/48484

Angeli, C. (2005). Transforming a teacher education method course through technology: Effects on preservice teachers' technology competency. *Computers & Education*, *45*(4), 383–398. doi:10.1016/j.compedu.2004.06.002

Archambault, L. M., & Barnett, J. H. (2010). Revisiting technological pedagogical content knowledge: Exploring the TPACK framework. *Computers & Education*, *55*, 1656–1662. doi:10.1016/j.compedu.2010.07.009

Borko, H., & Putnam, R. (2000). What do new views of knowledge and thinking have to say about research on teacher learning. *Educational Researcher*, *29*, 4–15. doi:10.3102/0013189X029001004

Brandsford, J. D., Pellegrino, J. W., & Donovan, S. (Eds.). (1999). *How people learn: Bridging research and practice*. Washington, D.C.: National Academy Press.

Bullock, D. (2004). Moving from theory to practice: An examination of the factors that preservice teachers encounter as the attempt to gain experience teaching with technology during field placement experiences. *Journal of Technology and Teacher Education*, *12*(2), 211–237.

Chen, B., & Denoyelles, A. (2013). Exploring students' mobile learning practices in higher education. Boulder, CO: Educause Center for Applied Research. Retrieved from http://www.educause.edu/ero/article/exploring-students-mobile-learning-practices-higher-education

Cobb, P., Confrey, J., Lehrer, R., & Schauble, L. (2003). Design experiments in educational research. *Educational Researcher*, *32*(1), 9–13. doi:10.3102/0013189X032001009

Common Core Standards. (n.d.). Retrieved from https://itunes.apple.com/us/app/common-core-standards/id439424555?mt=8

Dahlstrom, E. (2012). *ECAR study of undergraduate students and information technology*. Boulder, CO: Educause Center for Applied Research.

de Groot, C., Fogleman, J., & Kern, D. (2013, November). *STEM student teachers' uses of iPads: Planning, teaching and managing, and reflecting*. Paper presented at the Annual meeting of the School Science and Mathematics Association. San Antonio, TX.

Dolk, M. L. A. M. (1997). *Onmiddellijk onderwijsgedrag; over denken en handelen van leraren in onmiddellijke onderwijssituaties* [Immediate teaching behavior: About thinking and acting of teachers in immediate classroom situations]. Utrecht, The Netherlands: IVLOS, Utrecht University.

Dropbox. (n.d.). Retrieved from http://www.dropbox.com

Educreations. (n.d.). Retrieved from http://www.educreations.com

Evernote. (n.d.). Retrieved from https://evernote.com

Fogleman, J., de Groot, C., Kern, D., & Byrd, D. (2013). *Infusing tablet computers into the student teaching triad: Student teachers' use of iPads for planning, teaching, and reflection*. Paper presented at the annual meeting of the Association of Teacher Educators. Atlanta, GA.

Fogleman, J., de Groot, C., Kern, D., & Byrd, D. (2014). *Using Evernote to support preservice teachers' personal knowledge management*. Paper presented at the annual meeting of the Association of Teacher Educators. St. Louis, MO.

Freire, P. (1998). *Pedagogy of the oppressed*. New York: Continuum.

Geist, E. (2011). The game changer: Using iPads in college teacher education classes. *College Student Journal*, *45*(4), 758–768.

George, P., Dumenco, L., Doyle, R., & Dollase, R. (2013). Incorporating iPads into a preclinical curriculum: A pilot study. *Medical Teacher. Informa Healthcare*, *35*(3), 226–230.

Graham, C. R. (2011). Theoretical considerations for understanding technological pedagogical content knowledge (TPACK). *Computers & Education*, *57*(3), 1953–1960. doi:10.1016/j.compedu.2011.04.010

Jackson, C. (Kirabo), & Bruegmann, E. (2009). Teaching students and teaching each other: The importance of peer learning for teachers. *American Economic Journal: Applied Economics*, *1*(4), 85–108.

Kern, D., Fogleman, J., & de Groot, C. (2013). *Hold hands and stick together: Using iPad technology to enhance teachers' planning, instruction and reflection*. Paper presented at the annual meeting of the Association of Literacy Educators and Researchers. Dallas, TX.

Koehler, M. (2013). *TPACK*. Retrieved from http://www.matt-koehler.com/tpack/using-the-tpack-image/

Koehler, M. J., Mishra, P., & Yahya, K. (2007). Tracing the development of teacher knowledge in a design seminar: Integrating content, pedagogy and technology. *Computers & Education, 49*(3), 740–762. doi:10.1016/j.compedu.2005.11.012

Korthagen, F. A. J., & Kessels, J. P. A. M. (1999). Linking theory and practice: Changing the pedagogy of teacher education. *Educational Researcher, 28*(4), 4–17. doi:10.3102/0013189X028004004

Koster, B., & Korthagen, F. A. J. (1997). Opleiden in een snel veranderende samenleving: enkele aspecten van de professionalisering van lerarenopleiders. [Educating in a fast changing society: Several aspects of the professionalization of teacher educators.]. *PML-Nieuwsbrief, 2*, 2–4.

Kubitskey, M. E., Fishman, B. J., & Marx, R. W. (2003). *The relationship between professional development and student learning: Exploring the link through design research*. Paper presented at the annual meeting of the American Education Research Association. New Orleans, LA.

Labaree, D. F. (2004). The trouble with Ed schools. New Haven, CT: Yale University Press.

Maher, D. (2013). *Pre-service primary teachers' use of iPads to support teaching: Implications for teacher education*. Retrieved from http://ersc.nmmu.ac.za/articles/Vol2No1_Maher_pp48-63_April_2013.pdf

Mishra, P., & Koehler, M. (2006). Technological pedagogical content knowledge: A framework for teacher knowledge. *Teachers College Record, 108*(6), 1017–1054. doi:10.1111/j.1467-9620.2006.00684.x

Newhouse, C. (2006). *Mobile education devices for pre-service teachers*. Australian Council for Computers in Education. Retrieved from http://acce.edu.au/sites/acce.edu.au/files/archived_papers/conf_P_288_newhouse_mobiles_fin.doc

Notability. (n.d.). Retrieved from http://www.gingerlabs.com

PollEverywhere. (n.d.). Retrieved from http://www.polleverywhere.com

Sandoval, W. A., & Bell, P. (2004). Design-based research methods for studying learning in context: Introduction. *Educational Psychologist, 39*(4), 199–201. doi:10.1207/s15326985ep3904_1

Shulman, L. S. (1986). Those who understand: Knowledge growth in teaching. *Educational Researcher, 12*(2), 4–14. doi:10.3102/0013189X015002004

Shurtz, S., Halling, T. D., & McKay, B. (2011). Assessing user preference to circulate iPads in an academic medical library. *Journal of Electronic Resources in Medical Libraries, 8*(4), 311–324. doi:10.1080/15424065.2011.626342

Stick Pick. (n.d.). Retrieved from https://itunes.apple.com/us/app/stick-pick/id436682059?mt=8

Swenson, P. W. (2011). iPad - The third hand. *National Social Science Technology Journal, 1*(3). Retrieved from http://www.nssa.us/tech_journal/volume_1-3/vol1-3_article_9.htm

Twitter. (n.d.). Retrieved from https://www.twitter.com

KEY TERMS AND DEFINITIONS

Congruence Principle: The pedagogical actions of a teacher educator must correspond with the pedagogical actions that he/she wants to promote in student teachers and experienced teachers; therefore, teacher educators must be able to bring to bear their specialized knowledge in a similar fashion as they strive their student teachers to do (Koster & Korthagen, 1997).

Episteme: General *conceptions*, applicable to a wide variety of situations; this knowledge is based on research and can be characterized as "objective" theory, with a big T (Korthagen & Kessels, 1999).

Gestalt: The personal conglomerates of needs, concerns, values, meanings, preferences, feelings and behavioral tendencies, united into one inseparable whole (Korthagen & Kessels, 1999).

Level Reduction: Through practical experiences and reflection upon these, the theory level can become self-evident to the teacher, and the knowledge can be used in a less conscious, "intuitive" way. It is as if the whole schema or theory has been reduced to one Gestalt (Korthagen & Kessels, 1999).

Phronesis: Knowledge that is situation-specific and related to the context in which they meet a problem or develop a need or concern, knowledge that brings their already existing, and subjective *perception* of personally relevant classroom situations one step further. We could also call it "theory with a small t" (Korthagen & Kessels, 1999).

TPACK: Technological Pedagogical Content Knowledge (TPACK) is a framework that identifies the knowledge teachers need to teach effectively with technology. The TPACK framework extends Shulman's idea of Pedagogical Content Knowledge (Koehler, www.tpack.org).

Chapter 12
Reconceptualizing Learning Designs in Higher Education:
Using Mobile Devices to Engage Students in Authentic Tasks

Nathaniel Ostashewski
Curtin University, Australia

Sonia Dickinson-Delaporte
Curtin University, Australia

Romana Martin
Curtin University, Australia

ABSTRACT

This goal of this chapter is to provide a design and development roadmap for the adaptation of traditional classroom activities into engaging iPad-based digital learning activities. Reporting on an ongoing longitudinal case study, the chapter provides an overview of rationale and design considerations of the authentic iPad learning design implementation project, and the outcomes and improvements made over time. The iPad activities described provide further details of the approach taken and adaptations made. Since implementing iPad activities into this higher education environment several terms ago, the lecturer reports significantly higher levels of student engagement. Additionally, students report that the classroom activities in the post-graduate marketing course are authentic, transferrable, and are more engaging due the use of the iPad-based activities.

INTRODUCTION

With an increasingly connected global economy, university education continues to be challenged to provide students with opportunities to develop workplace skills. University administration and teaching staff are often concerned about the implications of the global economy, as more and more opportunities exist for students to select which institution they study at based on the types learning experiences they seek and the range of workplace skills they hope to graduate with. Uni-

DOI: 10.4018/978-1-4666-6284-1.ch012

versity lecturers are now, even more that in the past, expected to develop and implement a wide range of activities that prepare students for their working life and, at the same time, move away from the traditional lecture style of educational delivery towards more contemporary learning methods. In this educational environment, opportunities to implement classroom technologies that can engage students in authentic tasks, which are transferable to a digital workplace, are becoming more important. This chapter provides a design and development roadmap for the adaptation of traditional classroom activities to create engaging iPad-based digital activities which is informed by one lecturer's successes over the past three years.

Education trends in higher education over the past few years have increasingly pointed towards increased student collaboration using digital tools and resources. For instance, The New Media Consortium's (NMC) yearly Horizon Report, a well-respected report on key emerging technologies in education, has identified digital collaboration tasks and mobile computing as up-and-coming trends. The 2012 Horizon report (Johnson, Adams, & Cummins, 2012) identified mobile apps as one of the fastest growing mobile technologies in higher education. Always-on mobile devices, the availability of Wi-Fi and 3G networks, and the affordances of current mobile devices have made mobile software applications both powerful and very productive. The Horizon 2013 report makes note that tablet computing, with iPads and similar devices, has particular implications for higher education according (Johnson, Adams Becker, Cummins, Estrada, Freeman, & Ludgate, 2013). Specifically, the report outlines tablet-based learning activities as having carved out a niche in higher education. Higher education institutions have embraced tablet technologies and are developing software, best practice guidelines, and support systems for lecturers and students who want to utilize them in learning activities. The impact of educational technologies can be significant when incorporated meaningfully into classrooms, and the implementation described here in this chapter, is one example of successful iPad tablet computing in higher education.

The advantages afforded by iPads are numerous, and include high levels of mobility with immediate access to the WWW, appealing characteristics such as touch screens, access to apps, games and a wide range of media (Johnson, Adams, & Cummins, 2012; McCombs, S., & Liu, Y., 2011). iPads provide opportunities for greater engagement of students in learning activities that foster creativity and build skills in the use of digital media (Martin, Ostashewski, & Dickinson-Delaporte, 2013). Based on a survey of 36 universities in 2010-2011, Murphy (2011) proposed a six-point typology of the capabilities of these post-PC devices (PPDs) that includes iPads. Murphy's six-point typology includes utilizing PPDs in the contexts of course materials, enrolment and administration, content generation, research and material yielding, collaboration and engagement, and productivity enhancement. The use of iPads however, is still relatively new in higher education so that learning engagement and collaboration opportunities in the classroom have not yet been fully uncovered. In many higher education settings, tablet implementation issues surrounding the cost of equipment, management of devices, need for supportive classroom requirements, and institutional policies, present a range of barriers to their adoption (Colorado, 2012). In some cases, the willingness of lecturers to adopt iPads in their discipline area can be minimal, as in the case of a law school pilot documented by Jaworowski (2011). Regardless, when technologies become more accepted by staff and students in everyday life, their use for education seems to be inevitable. iPads, with their wide range of capabilities including the recording and display of multimedia, are ideally suited for complex learning tasks such as digital collaboration and artifact creation.

This chapter presents a detailed roadmap, informed by the adaptation of traditional classroom activities, for the creation of a series of mobile iPad activities supported by active learning methodologies. The activities described in this chapter include: group-based online research, digital collage creation, large group presentations, and audiovisual TV commercial creation. Key from the lecturer's perspective was the intent to develop engaging learning activities that support critical thinking and collaboration. The key takeout from this chapter is one process for the translation of traditional classroom activities into collaborative iPad activities. Other takeouts include implementation challenges and solutions, as well as several classroom activities that may be transferred to other learning contexts. Finally, some thoughts about the supports required for university lecturers embarking on the integration of tablet or iPad activities are provided based on the experiences of the research team.

iPAD TABLET BACKGROUND

Since the release of the Apple iPad tablet in April of 2010, there has been considerable interest in how this device can be used in educational settings. This interest stems from the popularity of this iDevice (Reid & Ostashewski, 2011) and its ease of use as a mobile media device. From the initial release of the iPad, global sales have increased yearly from 19 million sold by March 2011, to 67 million in April 2012, and over 170 million near the end of 2013 (Costello, 2013). According to the NPD Group (2013), a commercial reseller sales tracking company, tablet sales in the United States made up over 22 percent of personal computing device sales, with the Apple iPad tablet accounting for 59 percent of all tablet sales. While other tablet devices are coming onto the market – the iPad has an overwhelming share of the tablet market.

There are numerous reasons for selecting the iPad as the mobile educational technology for this project. From a physical perspective, iPads offer several advantages over smaller mobile devices. Larger screens, built-in speakers and high-resolution imaging, provide the requirements needed for collaborative and small group activities (Bonsignore, Quinn, Druin, & Bederson, 2013; Elbert, Code, & Irvine, 2013a; 2013b; Ostashewski, Reid, & Ostashewski, 2011). Other advantages of iPads for use in learning activities relate to the iPad's design characteristics which allow for immediate, mobile, and flexible usage. The touch screen makes iPads an interactive and engaging tool while artifacts created on iPad Apps are sharable and often revisable. Other technologies provide many of these same characteristics; however, the combination of these characteristics - particularly audio and visual recording, web access, and inexpensive software applications - make the iPad an excellent mobile educational device. The implementations described in this chapter provide further evidence to support the use of iPads for teaching and learning, as the study involves a successful example of how these devices can be effectively used in collaborative, authentic learning activities for postgraduate learners.

TEACHING CONTEXT

The School of Marketing (SOM) is one of seven teaching areas within the Curtin Business School (CBS), which is one of the most comprehensive business schools in Australia. CBS has considerable experience in providing high-quality and transformative education across Australia and the Asian region. This commitment to high-quality and transformative education is a university-wide strategy that unites the Curtin community, with the aim being to evolve a contemporary and future proof student experience. The School of Marketing offers postgraduate level courses, designed to provide students with advanced professional knowledge that is in-touch with industry. The courses are industry-focused, with an emphasis on topics that are relevant to the marketing profession. They also provide regular interaction with practitioners through guest speakers and industry-based projects.

Global Marketing Communications is a graduate course in the Master of Marketing program which has been designed to provide an overview of the current developments and management of marketing communication programs. The focus of the course is on how businesses plan, develop and implement marketing communication programs to support various sales and marketing initiatives nationally, regionally and globally. The course investigates various alternatives and challenges of marketing communications across borders, across cultures and across communication systems. The unit has two deliveries per year, with a total of approximately 40 students in each delivery. As well, there is a significant ratio of students enrolled in this postgraduate course, approximately 50%, who are international.

iPADS IN TEACHING AND LEARNING

Over the past decade, mobile device ownership has increased rapidly, with most university students owning or having access to more than one mobile device (Jones, Ramanau, Cross, & Healing, 2010; Kennedy et al., 2009). Studies have also documented a steady increase in students' ownership of mobile technologies and students' IT literacy, particularly in younger students or school leavers (e.g. Salaway, Caruso, & Nelson, 2007; Salaway, Caruso, & Nelson, 2008; Smith & Caruso, 2010; Smith, Salaway, & Caruso, 2009). For instance, Apple iPads have had a high and rapid adoption rate in the mobile device market and have become mainstreamed in a very short timeframe (Alyahya & Gall, 2012; Meeker, 2012). Furthermore, iPads have been adopted in both K12 schools and higher education, with a number of universities now providing students with iPads pre-loaded with electronic resources, e-textbooks and Apps (Cross, 2010; Murphy, 2011; Georgieva, 2012).

Despite the advantages of iPads for learning being acknowledged by many educators and administrators, the finer points of making effective use of iPads in learning and teaching are often addressed on the fly. In many situations, iPads are being used in class for individual tasks such as searching the web and accessing email, but little forward planning is made to integrate the use of iPads into the learning designs or adapting the learning designs to ensure the iPads add value. A pilot study by Dogan (2012) found that although students used iPads in class for notetaking, Twitter and accessing the web, they were keen to see their lecturers integrating iPads more into teaching. Some examples of effective use of iPads in higher education include using iPads for:

- Providing content and e-textbooks (Brand & Kinash, 2010; Cross, 2010);
- Conducting assessment activities (Jalali, Trottier, Tremblay, & Hincke, 2011);
- Communicating with students, producing video lectures and marking assignments (Manuguerra & Petocz, 2011);
- Teaching practicums (Sachs & Bull, 2012);

Nevertheless, the full scope for using iPads to foster engagement in learning is as yet untapped and the sharing of strategies on how to integrate iPads in to learning designs could overcome this deficit. In the case of university lecturers, who are often unfamiliar with educational design, integrating new technologies can be both frustrating and very time consuming. Therefore, projects such as the one described in this chapter contribute to the dissemination of strategies that can be used in university settings, where collaboration using digital tools and resources is a learning priority.

ENGAGEMENT AND AUTHENTIC TASKS

When planning implementations of active learning and student engagement in authentic tasks within the university setting, it is critically important to be clear about the proposed course learning goals and assessments. While K-12 education may allow for more breadth in terms of learning tasks and time spent on them, university courses are often very resource dense and time efficient. This is particularly true in business schools, where learning tasks are often governed by external certification board requirements for licensing and accreditation. While business schools are charged with providing industry-related skills and tasks to prepare their students for the workplace, there may still be a digital divide present. This means that some lecturers may not have the skill-base required. Some of the challenges lecturers have voiced in the past to members of this research team were: "How can I become expert at using all these mobile devices" or "How can I possibly provide active learning and authentic engagement tasks and get through all of the course material that the university requires of me?" One solution is to ensure that only one device is introduced (e.g. the iPad) and that the active learning and authentic tasks originate from existing learning activities in these courses. In this way, learning goals and assessments remain the same, but the activities are reconceptualized and moved to a digital world providing enriched, rather than alternative activities.

For the purposes of this study, student engagement, mobile learning, and authentic learning descriptions were clearly articulated as part of the process. There are a number of definitions of student engagement in learning. However, the research team found the following description by Coates most relevant, whereby student engagement is defined as: "active and collaborative learning, participation in challenging academic activities, formative communication with academic staff, involvement in enriching educational experiences and feeling legitimated and supported by university learning communities" (2007, p. 122).

Similarly, the term "mobile learning" encompasses a wide range of interpretations. However, research indicates that there is a range of opportunities for the design of engaging mobile-learning activities for the classroom. Some of these are:

- Learner-centered constructivist learning activities and learning designs (Herrington, Herrington, Mantei, Olney & Ferry, 2009; Oliver, Harper, Hedberg, Wills & Agostinho, 2002)
- Active learning (Kukulska-Hulme & Traxler, 2007; Pfeiffer, Gemballa, Jarodzka, Scheiter & Gerjets, 2009),
- Authentic learning (Herrington, et al., 2009), and
- Situated learning designs (Olney, Herrington & Verenikina, 2009).

Furthermore, the literature reports that mobile learning can impact positively on students' *engagement* in learning in the areas of:

- Participation in activities and communication (Cochrane & Bateman, 2010; Dyson, Litchfield, Raban & Tyler, 2009; Shen & Shen, 2008),
- Mastery of content and theoretical concepts (Dyson et al., 2009); and,
- Mobile learning can support engagement in experiential and active learning (Olney et al., 2009; Wang et al., 2009).

Engaging mobile activities, where students get opportunities for hands-on participation and collaboration, were the focus of the iPad implementation in this project. The key purpose of the mobility aspect related to the types of tasks embedded in the activities that could make use of the iPad attributes. For this reason, mobile WWW access, mobile photography and videography, and small group collaboration (Ostashewski, Reid, & Ostashewski, 2011), were what the lecturer and research team used as guideposts for reconceptualizing existing learning activities.

Finally, authentic learning tasks, an institutional goal of the university context of this study, were already established and well described in the literature (Herrington & Herrington, 2006). Herrington, Reeves, & Oliver (2009) state that in order for authentic learning to occur, lecturers need to provide learners with an opportunity to be engaged in an inventive and realistic task in the form of a complex collaborative activity. Furthermore, (Rule, 2006) describes authentic learning as being characterized by the presence of the following themes:

1. Real-world problems that engage learners in the work of professionals;
2. Inquiry activities that practice thinking skills and metacognition;
3. Discourse among a community of learners; and
4. Student empowerment through choice. (p. 1)

In summary, this research team conceptualised authentic learning tasks in higher education as learner-centred, collaborative, complex, and industry-related activities. Implementing these learning tasks using iPads in ways that engaged students and are fun to participate in therefore met the challenge of the university setting.

ACTIVITY DESIGN PROCESS

The initial work on this iPad activity project began with a series of discussions about technology in the classroom. The lecturer had been working on another project with the primary researcher, supporting the development of online learning in a course. The discussions led to a conversation about the use of iPads and their potential use in a post-graduate course that the lecturer was teaching. The lecturer, who had recently purchased an iPad and had begun utilizing it at home, asked if there were any types of classroom-based iPad activities that might engage students. The lecturer wanted to increase student access to online resources in small groups in the classroom, as well as provide some activities that would develop students' digital literacy in the discipline area. The first discussions led to the development of a series of classroom activities that have now become an integral part of this lecturer's teaching strategies. After initial meetings, the lecturer procured a set of 8 iPads to begin working with in the classroom. A second educational technology researcher, who was familiar with mobile devices and implementations, was also brought on board to provide activity design support. This initiated a team consisting of the lecturer and two supporting academics with learning design expertise, to form the design and research team for this project.

The development of iPad activities, based on existing paper and pencil-based activities followed. While many lecturers are familiar with delivering classroom activities, the adaptation of activities to utilize another technology or tool can be difficult. In this regard, the educational technology researchers, fluent in many communication and media technologies, were key to driving the initial steps of the adaptation process. With an ever-expanding technology toolset, the selection of hardware, software, and classroom processes needed for an effective classroom implementation is increasingly complex. In addition, university lecturers often lack the learning design background necessary to develop activities that can take full advantage of what technologies can offer. In this case, the lecturer was a subject matter expert in the field of business marketing who had recently taken over the course and activities developed by previous lecturers. The lecturer had made significant changes to many of the learning activities in the course based on her industry experience, but finding iPad Apps and developing iPad activities for students presented a completely new set of challenges. Discussions between the lecturer and the two researchers/learning designers focused on finding out what types of activities could be adapted to take advantage of the iPads.

One of the first learning activities selected for the iPad adaptation was a collage creation activity – where small groups of students were tasked with presenting a target audience for a given brand in a visual format. The team explored familiar free iPad Apps, such as Drawing Pad, and developed a learning design and classroom sequence for the lecturer to implement the activity. After installing the required Apps on the iPads, the team introduced this first activity to the class. The presence of the whole team in the classroom on this initial trial was critical for the lecturer, who was not fully adept at using many of the iPad-specific hardware and software functions needed for the task. This was because the lecturer was still a relatively new iPad user, but also because login access to the campus networks, patchy Wi-Fi access, and students using their own iPads, presented some initial stumbling points for the activity. By the end of the first trial activity, students were interested in engaging with the iPads more, and many of the iPad issues had been resolved.

As the team met following the first trial activity, the lecturer's enthusiasm and feedback from students provided further encouragement to continue to refine the activity. The next semester's student cohort participated in the same activity, but some revisions included sharing of the collages with each other via a classroom Dropbox, and more time for presentation of the collages at the class level in addition to the small group discussions students had while creating the collages. Subsequent implementations of the lecturer's iPad activities have evolved into a scaffolded series of activities increasing in both conceptual complexity and the level of digital literacy and iPad skills required. The scaffolding from basic to challenging tasks with increased levels of collaboration and complexity encouraged student engagement throughout the semester. The creative educational design thinking on the part of the lecturer, points to one of the truly desirable outcomes of the project – whereby the lecturer becomes authentically engaged in the scholarship of teaching and learning and through having initial educational design support gains the confidence to independently create engaging student learning activities augmented by learning technologies. Indeed, the iPad activity project also placed the lecturer's course and teaching in the spotlight as an example of a successful technology-enriched implementation modeling the learning transformation aimed for by the university. Further developments have seen this course moved into a newly refurbished collaborative classroom environment where small groups work at mobile collaborative workstations allowing more streamlined sharing of iPad artifacts. The success of this lecturers scaffolded set of collaborative learning designs using iPads, and the fact that students also report the activities as being fun and exciting, is an example of where utilizing technology has provided a significant benefit. That the learning activities relate directly to industry tasks also meets the requirement of being authentic and highly relevant for students taking this course.

ACTIVITY DEVELOPMENT PROCESS

The creation of new iPad activities and several adaptations of traditional paper-and-pencil activities into iPad activities resulted in the research team's development of an iPad activity design model. The model is transferrable for use with any type of tablet device; however, the Apps, collaboration tasks and processes would likely need to be revised accordingly. Further research utilizing other types of tablet devices and exploring their capabilities for delivering the same kinds of tasks is an area of research planned for the near future. It was not practical for this project to utilize more than one type of tablet device, as the lecturer was only able to secure 8 iPads for a class of approximately 30. The process of creating classroom activities using iPad technology-enhanced tasks is presented in Figure 1: The iPad Activity Design Process. The model presented in Figure 1 describes a process that can be used to develop completely new activities, but also captures the cycle of existing classroom activity translation into iPad-based activities. The five steps in this model are further described below and, in addition to a roadmap series of these five steps, further considerations relating to developing authentic activities, as well as practice-based comments that can aid in development are provided in the following descriptions.

Step 1: Identify Learning Outcomes of the Authentic Activity

Step 1 of the process begins with identifying the learning outcomes of the classroom activity, and in the case of an iPad activity, this also included the development of an output or artifact of the activity. Overall, the iPad provides opportunities for students to become engaged in undertaking something that results in a product or output.

Step 1 Tasks

- Identify learning outcomes.
- Identify outputs (artifacts, assessments etc.).
- Review traditional approaches to the tasks and note areas where resources are used.

Step 1 Considerations

1. Choose authentic activities that students would be undertaking if employed in the workplace.
2. Adapting may be easier than creating, so a careful review of traditional resources such as textbook activities may be worthwhile,

Figure 1. iPad activity design process

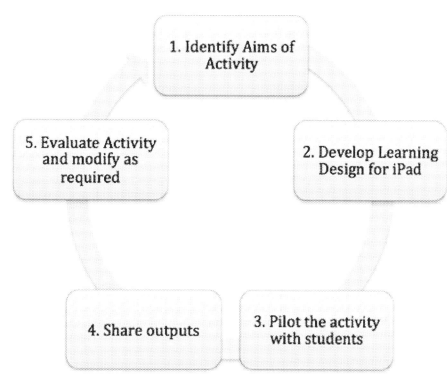

with the view to infusing the activity with iPad technology. Can the artifact be improved by having it presented in an audio/visual format?

Step 2: Adapt/Develop Learning Design for the iPad

Step 2 of the process involves developing the activity flow. This also includes identifying Apps, which will support the intended activity or outputs, and testing them on the iPad. Once a suitable App has been found, the development of the sequence of tasks students will need to follow can be completed. Testing and revision and further testing of this sequence, which may mean finding new Apps prepares the lecturer for Step 3.

Step 2 Tasks

- Develop a sequence of tasks to be undertaken by learners.
- Identify tasks which could be supported by iPads (e.g. researching, graphics creation, e-book creation) matched to alternative options for students without iPads (e.g. drawing on paper, creating graphics in Photoshop; creating PDFs).
- Source, install and test apps that could be used to support tasks.
- Test and revise activity design until streamlined.

Step 2 Considerations

1. Access support from learning designers or other iPad users where possible.
2. Determine relevance of iPad, and what it adds to the activity – evaluate whether adding the iPad is worth the effort (e.g. what does it enable that was not possible before).
3. Prepare a non-iPad alternative should some students not have access to an iPad or experience technical difficulties.
4. Develop tasks and sequence on the iPad and consider trying more than one option.
5. Be prepared to find and install apps and test by trying a range of Apps, if available.
6. Revise activity design/task sequence and document the steps for later reference.

Step 3: In Class: Pilot the Activity with Students

Step 3 is the implementation of the learning activity in the classroom setting. As mentioned previously, and often reported in education technology literature, there may be a need for technical support for the lecturer at the initial trial of the activity. In this step 3, the lecturer demonstrates the activity for students and, as with any other classroom activity, then goes on to support the students while they engage in the iPad activity.

One key finding from this study was that demonstrating on an iPad to a classroom can be a challenge, as students need to see the physical touch movements made on the iPad during the demonstration while the iPad is connected to a projector. This can be done by using a document camera projected to a screen.

Step 3 Tasks

- Describe outputs to students and show examples if available (image, video, interview, booklet).
- Explain the learning outcomes and purpose of the learning activity.
- Demonstrate Apps and the required processes. Provide information about non-iPad alternatives, if required.
- Provide guidance and support for students as they work on the learning activity.
- Note areas of difficulty and support needs.

Step 3 Considerations

Pilot the Activity with Students:

1. Explain the authenticity of activity and relevance to workplace settings.
2. Demonstration of the app, especially if not used in previous activities.
3. Provide continual support for students during the activity.
4. Noting difficulties provides a helpful reference for revising and updating the activities for the next cohort.

Step 4: Share Outputs

Step 4 of the iPad activity design process focuses on sharing of the outputs or artifacts created during the classroom activity. Some of the activities result in an artifact being developed by the students and shared to the whole class in a presentation. Many outputs of the iPad activities, such as collages or digital pages or booklets can be further shared online or even uploaded to student or class portfolios. The flexibility and revise-ability of the iPad-generated outputs provides for further future discussions and learning opportunities as well.

Step 4 Tasks

- Students present and discuss outputs in class (project to main screen).
- Students share artifacts online and discuss via discussion forum or blog.
- Students upload artifacts to an e-portfolio (an optional assessment strategy).

Step 4 Considerations

1. Plan to share and critique outputs among students.
2. How can students present artifacts and engage in related discussions at the classroom or large group level? How can they discuss these online?
3. Digital artifacts might be shared via email or a cloud-based repository such as Dropbox. Consider these options before the class so the output can be captured there and then.

Step 5: Evaluate Activity and Modify as Required

The final Step 5 of the process is the lecturer review of the effectiveness of the learning design. Until activities have been tested with students and in various settings they can only be designs. However, after putting activities into practice in the classroom revisions of a learning design are often needed. Putting classroom sets of iPads, and managing the constraints of classroom environments often brings to light new challenges that need to be resolved. As such step 5 is a post-activity evaluation and revisiting of the learning outcomes, particularly reviewing the whole process for teaching including the intended learning outcomes.

Step 5 Tasks

- Gather student feedback.
- Review artifact quality and authenticity.
- Review processes for iPad users and alternative approaches.
- Review any technical or other challenges (e.g. facilities, apps, capturing and storing artifacts).

Step 5 Considerations

1. Did the activity encourage engagement?
2. Did the activity allow for collaboration and sharing of ideas between students?
3. Did activity enhance students' digital literacy and digital media skills?
4. Was the focus on the activity rather than the iPad – the technology should ideally become transparent with the focus being on student learning and the task at hand.
5. What were the challenges – technological and other? Some examples are:

a. Instructor familiarity with the iPads and Apps? Familiarity is required but need not be an expert.
b. Lecturer should be able to troubleshoot Apps, but may need initial support with iPads. Was sufficient support available?
c. Managing artifacts. Lecturer needs a process in place for students to send artifacts for archiving or assessment – consider an email account or Dropbox created for this purpose.
d. Consider login issues, critical for Wi-Fi access (iPad Management); Consider Wi-Fi access in lesson venues.
e. Other equipment requirements. For example, there is a need for a document camera in order to be able to demonstrate the App use to students – in order to allow students to see the touch-screen finger movements.
f. Consider when iPads will be charged and how (iPad carts and charging stations are helpful).
g. Consider how Apps will be updated or reset: how, by whom, where.

iPAD ACTIVITY EXAMPLES

In each case, the iPad activities created by the design team took advantage of an affordance provided by the device. The series of five iPad activities described in the section that follows represents the result of several iterations of design, implementation, and evaluation of each activity. This series also demonstrates some of the iPad skill development and conceptual scaffolding showing increasingly complex learning activities from the first to the fifth activity. These learning activities have been used by the lecturer in a business marketing course, but can be adapted for use in a wide range of university classroom settings.

The activities are intended for small groups of 2 to 4 students in a classroom setting where the attendance pattern is a single three hour interactive seminar style class. Below a brief description of each activity is provided as well as the App used, description of the student task, the original classroom activity that it was based upon, and a description of how the activity was enhanced by using the iPad.

Example 1: Developing a Cognitive Map

In this activity students in small groups were tasked with developing a concept or cognitive map relating to a topic in the course. The topic used in this marketing course was to develop a visual map/depiction of a person's knowledge and memories regarding a market brand.

1. **iPad App:** Mindjet Maps for iPad, by Mindjet LLC.
2. **Student task:** Think about a consumer's knowledge and memories related to a brand and develop a visual cognitive map. **Example:** Rolex brand, see Figure 2: Cognitive map produced using Mindjet App.
3. **Original Activity:** Do the same mapping exercise using pens and large sheets of paper.
4. **iPad Enhancement:** The Mindjet App allows for users to use touch movements and the virtual keyboard to add nodes to the map, The App allows for: rearrangement of nodes easily as creation of the map develops, images to be imported from a camera roll, and supports individual visual designs. A Mindjet map can be saved and revised at a later date be shared with others or submitted as an assessment. Figure 2 shows an example of a Mindjet map created by students on an iPad.

Figure 2. Cognitive Map produced using Mindjet App

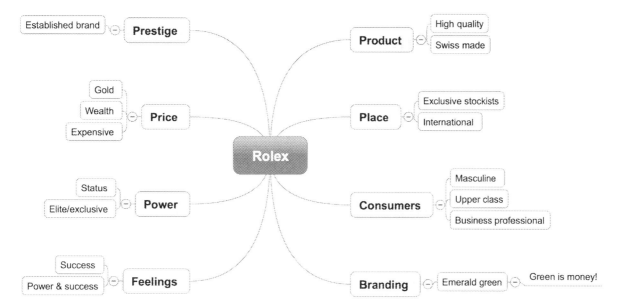

Example 2: Creating a Digital Collage

1. **iPad App:** Drawing Pad for iPad, by Darren Murtha Design & Safari for iPad by Apple.
2. **Student Task:** Create a digital collage, where students use multiple profiling elements (geographic, demographic, psychographic and behavioral elements) to holistically create a visual snapshot of a target audience for a product or service. In marketing terms this is a target market visual profile.
3. **Original Activity:** Students would use scissors and glue to cut and paste images from magazines to create a paper collage.
4. **iPad Enhancement:** The Drawing Pad App allows for users to: access text and images from various sources on the iPad (camera roll, Internet, or via screen capture), manipulate images and layers as the collage is developed, share and email their collage to others (or the lecturer for assessment), immediate display of the collage (supports a presentation to the whole class which is facilitated using a cable connecting the iPad to a projector or a collaborative workstation computer with large display screen).

Example 3: Design a Movie Advertisement

1. **iPad App:** iMovie, by Apple.
2. **Student Task:** Students are asked to develop a mock audio-visual TVC advertisement (a movie trailer) that uses one of a number of three advertising appeal types: e.g. Fear, scarcity, humor, or rational marketing appeals.
3. **Original Activity:** Students were given ten coloured print advertisements, and in small groups, they had to identify the type of appeal that was depicted.

4. **iPad Enhancement:** App allows for users to develop, video-record, edit, and present a TVC in a short period of time.

Example 4: Critiquing Activity

1. **iPad App:** iPad camera, Safari web browser by Apple.
2. **Student Task:** Marketing Communication Integration analysis - Review of marketing communication by a brand across multiple channels, and assessment of the level of integration. Students were asked to aggregate outcomes of the research using artifacts collected in the iPad such as photos of the physical spaces (signage), YouTube artifacts, Pinterest, Twitter, Facebook.
3. **Original Activity:** Students were asked to think of a brand that had strong communication integration and discuss communication touch-points that provided evidenced of integration. They did not provide examples or artifacts. Discussion only.
4. **iPad Enhancement:** The students' preferred App (e.g. Facebook) was used to capture, record, edit, revise and share the digital artifacts from all of the sources explored in their research, and then this collection of aggregated artifacts was shared with the class or teacher as an assessment.

Example 5: Final Assessment Case Study

1. **iPad App:** Mindjet, Drawing Pad, Safari, iMovie.
2. **Student Task:** Students apply all of the previous 4 activities described above to a particular brand as one of the final course activities. This activity was to be completed as a small group activity during one 3 hour class.
3. **Original Activity:** None.
4. **iPad Enhancement:** The Apps applied in this activity allow students to work as a team, to collaborate and develop a final case study project and a set of digital artifacts. The resulting artifacts can be stored or shared as required and provide a resource base for future cohorts.

CONCLUSION

The implementation of the iPad activities described in this chapter, can only be described as successful if they have met the learning outcomes intended in the course. From the lecturer's perspective, the classroom activities that were adapted to utilize an iPad, allowed students to meet and exceed beyond the required learning goals. The iPad-based activities provided an enhanced learning experience and a more engaging series of classroom activities, according to the lecturer's previous experiences in teaching the course. The lecturer further reported that in all of the cohorts students continued to be engaged in the learning activities often beyond the course. Students' enthusiasm and feedback provided additional encouragement for the lecturer to continue to refine the activities for successive rounds of the course. In summary, one conclusion is that *well-designed iPad-based activities can effectively support student achievement of learning outcomes.*

The second conclusion that *well-designed iPad activities can support active, authentic, and technology-enhanced learning* can be drawn from the numerous examples of feedback the lecturer and research team received from students. Anecdotal feedback from students to the instructor included many positive statements. Themes in the feedback provided by students regarding the value of the iPad activities included the following:

- **Supporting Active Learning:** The interactive nature of the activities allowed stu-

Reconceptualizing Learning Designs in Higher Education

dents to participate and actively do something rather than just listening or working individually with traditional media.
- **Supported Collaboration:** The activities provided consistent opportunities for group collaboration in groups of between 2 and 4 students. The activities also supported full class collaboration with opportunities for all students to review and discuss others' work.
- **Extended Communication Theory:** Students reported that the activities helped them to understand communication theory due to the applied nature of the tasks.
- **Authentic Learning:** According to students the activities were real – the activities brought real-life situations into the classroom. This is a key intended outcome of the instructor who had planned the learning tasks to reflect industry practices. This demonstrates that when the instructor maintains industry connectedness and brings it into the classroom, the authentic nature of the activity is valued by students.
- **Supported Creativity:** Students indicated that the use of the iPad provided a sense of creativity in the classroom that is often missing in Postgraduate classes. This may be due to the novelty and fun nature of the activity, especially in comparison with traditional paper and pencil activities in other courses.
- **Transfer of Digital Skills:** Students saw opportunities to transfer knowledge and processes used on the iPad into other classes and disciplines of study. Students reported that they planned to use the Apps and tools to complete assessments/activities in other courses of their study.
- **Constructionism Evidenced:** The group activities allowed for student negotiation and joint creation as groups moved to produce the artifacts

A third conclusion that emerges in this implementation research is that *iPad activities adapted from paper-and-pencil activities can enhance student engagement with complex collaborations*. The Instructor noted that while the activities were collaborative in nature even prior to the iPads being incorporated, the iPad-based activities were further amplified in the "Collaborative Learning Space", the newly refurbished learning spaces with collaborative workstations. Additionally, classroom observations by the research team made it obvious that the iPads offered a range of affordances that were difficult to replicate even in standard computer laboratories. Examples of these kinds of affordances were that students working in groups could pass the iPad around, take photos or video with the iPad, record audio segments and embed all of the media in their work on the fly. They could display and present their work to the entire class with the minimum of effort. And there was also the "fun factor". Students appeared to enjoy the activity and whether this was due to the novelty of the activity, the learning design, or the iPad tasks the research team believes that bringing fun into the learning environment will assist in student engagement in learning.

This goal of this chapter was to provide readers with a design and development roadmap for the development of engaging classroom activities using iPad technology. The activities described and development process shared provide readers with such a roadmap, as well as bringing to light several other advantages of iPads for classroom activities. The design and research team feel that in this higher education case, many of the activities could be adopted for use, even when attendance patterns are not in three-hour blocks of time. Additionally, the digital nature of iPad artifacts provided an opportunity for sharing artifacts and discussions between on-campus and online students, an increasing trend seen in some universities. Finally, it is hoped that the design and implementation model will provide encouragement for teaching academics to enhance their classrooms with more engaging and fun collaborative tasks for learning.

REFERENCES

Alyahya, S., & Gall, J. E. (2012). iPads in Education: A Qualitative Study of Students' Attitudes and Experiences. In *Proceedings of World Conference on Educational Multimedia, Hypermedia and Telecommunications* (Vol. 1, pp. 1266-1271). Academic Press.

Bonsignore, E., Quinn, A. J., Druin, A., & Bederson, B. (2013). Sharing Stories "in the Wild": A Mobile Storytelling Case Study Using StoryKit. *ACM Transactions on Computer-Human Interaction*, *20*(3), 18. doi:10.1145/2491500.2491506

Brand, J., & Kinash, S. (2010). Pad-agogy: A quasi-experimental and ethnographic pilot test of the iPad in a blended mobile learning environment. The *Proceedings of the 27th Annual Conference of the Australian Society for Computers in Learning in Tertiary Education* (ASCILITE). Sydney, Australia: ASCILITE.

Coates, H. (2007). A model of online and general campus-based student engagement. *Assessment & Evaluation in Higher Education*, *32*(2), 121–141. doi:10.1080/02602930600801878

Cochrane, T., & Bateman, R. (2010). Smartphones give you wings: Pedagogical affordances of mobile Web 2.0. *Australasian Journal of Educational Technology, 26* (1), 1-14.

Colorado, J. (2012). Teaching 21st Century Learners with Mobile Devices. In *Proceedings of World Conference on Educational Multimedia, Hypermedia and Telecommunications* (Vol. 1, pp. 2247-2252). Academic Press.

Costello, S. (2013). What are iPad Sales All Time? *About.com Website*. Retrieved from http://ipod.about.com/od/ipadmodelsandterms/f/ipad-sales-to-date.htm

Cross, K. (2010). *iPad replaces uni textbooks at University of Adelaide Science Faculty*. Retrieved from http://www.adelaidenow.com.au/news/ipad-replaces-uni-textbooks-at-university-ofadelaide-science-faculty/story-fn5jhv6y-1225918213032

Dogan, B. (2012). Integration of IPad in Higher Education: A Pilot Project. Global Time, 1, 27-30.

Dyson, L. E., Litchfield, A., Raban, R., & Tyler, J. (2009). Interactive classroom mLearning and the experiential transactions between students and lecturer. In R. J. Atkinson & C. McBeath (Eds.), *Same places, different spaces: Proceedings of ASCILITE Auckland 2009, 26th Annual ASCILITE International Conference* (pp. 233-242). Auckland, New Zealand: ASCILITE.

Elbert, J., Code, D. J., & Irvine, D. V. (2013b). iPads on Practicum: Perspective of a Student-Teacher. *The Arbutus Review*, *4*(1), 1–18.

Elbert, J., Code, J., & Irvine, V. (2013a). Integrating iPads: Perspectives and Possibilities in a High School ELA Context. In *Proceedings of World Conference on Educational Multimedia, Hypermedia and Telecommunications* (Vol. 1, pp. 1739-1742). Academic Press.

Georgieva, M. (2012). Learning in the Apps: Enabling A Student-Centered Approach to Learning with Mobile Technology. In *Proceedings of World Conference on Educational Multimedia, Hypermedia and Telecommunications* (Vol. 1, pp. 358-363). Academic Press.

NPD Group. (2013). *U.S. Commercial Channel Computing Device Sales Set to End 2013 with Double-Digit Growth, According to NPD*. Retrieved from https://www.npd.com/wps/portal/npd/us/news/press-releases/u-s-commercial-channel-computing-device-sales-set-to-end-2013-with-double-digit-growth-according-to-npd/

Herrington, J., Herrington, A., Mantei, J., Olney, I., & Ferry, B. (Eds.). (2009). *New technologies, new pedagogies: Mobile learning in higher education*. Wollongong: University of Wollongong.

Herrington, J., Reeves, T. C., & Oliver, R. (2009). *A guide to authentic e-learning*. Routledge.

Herrington, T., & Herrington, J. (2006). Authentic Learning Environments in Higher Education. Information Science Publishing.

Jalali, A., Trottier, D., Tremblay, M., & Hincke, M. (2011). Administering a gross anatomy exam using mobile technology. *e-Learn Magazine, 2*.

Jaworowski, S. (2011). Law professors and the iPad: A likely innovation? Global TIME, 1, 21-26.

Johnson, L., Adams, S., & Cummins, M. (2012). *The NMC Horizon Report: 2012 Higher Education Edition*. Austin, TX: The New Media Consortium.

Johnson, L., Adams Becker, S., Cummins, M., Estrada, V., Freeman, A., & Ludgate, H. (2013). *NMC Horizon Report: 2013 Higher Education Edition*. Austin, TX: The New Media Consortium.

Jones, C., Ramanau, R., Cross, S., & Healing, G. (2010). Net generation or digital natives: Is there a distinct new generation entering university? *Computers & Education, 54*(3), 722–732. doi:10.1016/j.compedu.2009.09.022

Kennedy, G. E., Dalgarno, B., Bennett, S., Gray, K., Waycott, J., Judd, T. S., et al. (2009). *Educating the Net Generation: A handbook of findings for practice and policy*. Retrieved from http://www.voced.edu.au/td/tnc_97.139

Kukulska-Hulme, A., & Traxler, J. (2007). Designed and user-generated activity in the mobile age. *Journal of Learning Design, 2*(1), 1–13. doi:10.5204/jld.v2i1.28

Manuguerra, M., & Petocz, P. (2011). Promoting student engagement by integrating new technology into tertiary education: The role of the iPad. *Asian Social Science, 7*(11), 61–65. doi:10.5539/ass.v7n11p61

Martin, R., Ostashewski, N., & Dickinson-Delaporte, S. (2013). Creating authentic iPad activities to increase student engagement: A learning design approach. In *Proceedings of World Conference on Educational Multimedia, Hypermedia and Telecommunications* (Vol. 1, pp. 249-253). Academic Press.

McCombs, S., & Liu, Y. (2011). *Channeling the channel: Can iPad meet the needs of today's M-Learner*. Paper presented at the Society for Information Technology & Teacher Education International Conference 2011. Nashville, TN. Retrieved from http://www.editlib.org/p/36322

Murphy, G. D. (2011). Post-PC devices: A summary of early iPad technology adoption in tertiary environments. *e-Journal of Business Education & Scholarship of Teaching, 5*(1), 18-32.

Oliver, R., Harper, B., Hedberg, J., Wills, S., & Agostinho, S. (2002). Formalising the description of learning designs. In A. Goody, J. Herrington, & M. Northcote (Eds.), *Quality Conversations: Research and Development in Higher Education* (Vol. 25, pp. 496–504). Jamison, Australia: HERDSA.

Olney, I., Herrington, J., & Verenikina, I. (2009). Digital story telling using iPods. In J. Herrington, A. Herrington, J. Mantei, I. Olney, & B. Ferry (Eds.), *New technologies, new pedagogies: Mobile learning in higher education* (pp. 36–44). Wollongong, Australia: University of Wollongong.

Ostashewski, N., Reid, D., & Ostashewski, M. (2011). The iPad as mobile teaching device: multimedia database access in a classroom context. In *Proceedings of Global TIME 2011* (pp. 49–53). AACE.

Pfeiffer, V. D. I., Gemballa, S., Jarodzka, H., Scheiter, K., & Gerjets, P. (2009). Situated learning in the mobile age: mobile devices on a field trip to the sea. ALT-J. *Research in Learning Technology*, *17*(3), 187–199. doi:10.1080/09687760903247666

Reid, D., & Ostashewski, N. (2011). iPads in the Classroom–New Technologies, Old Issues: Are they worth the effort? In *Proceedings of World Conference on Educational Multimedia, Hypermedia and Telecommunications* (Vol. 1, pp. 1689-1694). Academic Press.

Rule, A. C. (2006). The components of authentic learning. *Journal of Authentic Learning*, *3*(1), 1–10.

Sachs, L., & Bull, P. (2012). Case study: Using iPad2 for a graduate practicum course. In *Proceedings of Society for Information Technology & Teacher Education International Conference* (Vol. 1, pp. 3054-3059). Academic Press.

Salaway, G., Caruso, J. B., & Nelson, M. R. (2007). *The ECAR study of undergraduate students and information technology, 2007*. Boulder, CO: EDUCAUSE Center for Applied Research.

Salaway, G., Caruso, J. B., & Nelson, M. R. (2008). The ECAR study of undergraduate students and information technology, 2008 (Vol. Research Study, Vol. 8). Boulder, CO: EDUCAUSE Center for Applied Research.

Shen, L., & Shen, R. (2008). The pervasive learning platform of a Shanghai online college: A large-scale test-bed for hybrid learning. Lecture Notes in Computer Science, 5169, 178-189.

Smith, S., & Caruso, J. (2010). *The ECAR study of undergraduate students and information technology, 2010 Key Findings* (Vol. 6, pp. 1–13). Boulder, CO: EDUCAUSE Center for Applied Research.

Smith, S., Salaway, G., & Caruso, J. B. (2009). *The ECAR study of undergraduate students and information technology, 2009*. Boulder, CO: EDUCAUSE Center for Applied Research.

Wang, M., Shen, R., Novak, D., & Pan, X. (2009). The impact of mobile learning on students' learning behaviours and performance: Report from a large blended classroom. *British Journal of Educational Technology*, *40*(4), 673–695. doi:10.1111/j.1467-8535.2008.00846.x

KEY TERMS AND DEFINITIONS

Active Learning: Active learning involves students *doing* tasks with the materials or resources they are learning about, engaging with the materials in some manner as opposed to listening someone lecture about the topic.

Affordance: In education, an attribute of an object or environment that allows learners to perform an action.

Authentic Learning: Learners are provided with an opportunity to be engaged in an inventive and realistic task in the form of a complex collaborative activity.

Engagement: Active and collaborative learning, participation in challenging academic activities, formative communication with academic staff, involvement in enriching educational experiences and feeling legitimated and supported by university learning communities.

iPad Device: The Apple iPad is a tablet device that provides an interactive touch-screen, audio and image recording capability, WIFI access, a virtual keyboard, and speakers. The device has been on the market since April of 2010 and continues to get more powerful and offer high-resolution graphics, while at the same time providing access to over 1 million inexpensive software applications for users to utilize.

Learning Activities: Activities involved in the delivery of education or training.

Mobile Learning: Learning that utilizes any form of mobile personal computing device in the learning process.

Scaffolding: Provision of numerous levels of support for learners during the learning process, often related to supporting a variety of levels of previous experience.

Chapter 13
Framing Mobile Learning:
Investigating the Framework for the Rationale Analysis of Mobile Education

Kim A. Hosler
University of Denver, USA

ABSTRACT

The purpose of this chapter is to introduce faculty and instructors, and those interested in using mobile technologies to support teaching and learning, to the Framework for the Rationale Analysis of Mobile Education (FRAME; Koole, 2009). This chapter discusses how mobile or handheld devices can be used to promote inquiry-based learning and constructivist and authentic pedagogies. Additionally, the chapter discusses Koole's (2009) FRAME model as a scaffold for guiding "the development of learning materials, and the design of teaching and learning strategies for mobile education" (p. 25). Lastly, the FRAME model is used to guide the implementation of an inquiry-based instructional unit incorporating mobile or handheld devices.

INTRODUCTION

As we enter the second decade of the 21st century, technology tools supporting increased virtual social interactions and augmenting educational practices abound (El-Hussein & Cronje, 2010; Traxler, 2007; Haag, 2011). Today's undergraduate and graduate college students are more connected to each other and the World Wide Web than ever before. Smartphones, netbooks, e-readers, and tablet computing offer broadband and wireless (WiFi) "instant on" connections to the Internet and the expansive amount of resources it offers. According to Dahlstrom (2012), portable devices are the academic champions (in all their diverse brands and platforms), across campuses today, with students favoring small, portable devices. Johnson, Levine, Smith, and Stone (2010), found mobile devices have become an accepted, integrated, and ubiquitous part of our daily lives, allowing access to video and audio files, geo-locating, social networking, personal productivity, informational and academic resources, and just-in-time learning. More recently, Johnson, Becker, Cummins, Estrada, Freeman, and Ludgate (2013), proclaimed, "tablets are proving to be powerful tools for learning inside and outside of the classroom" (p. 4). As such, the immediacy,

DOI: 10.4018/978-1-4666-6284-1.ch013

convenience, and ubiquity of hand-held mobile devices readily support inquiry-based pedagogies and authentic, real-world questions.

Mobile learning (or m-learning) by its very name invokes the mobility of the learner with a portable handheld device, resulting in a corresponding mobility of learning (El-Hussein & Cronje, 2010). According to El-Hussein and Cronje (2010), "These observations emphasize the mobility of learning and the significance of the term 'mobile learning'" (p. 14). Because many definitions of mobile learning exist, El-Hussein and Cronje urged the consideration of the relationship of the words mobile and learning in any definition of mobile learning, but acknowledged the difficulty of ascribing one fixed definition to the term. They advocated for the concept of mobility to be an interdependent tripartite classification--the mobility of the technology, the mobility of the learner, and the mobility of learning "that augments the higher education landscape" (p. 17). According to Laouris and Eteokleous (2005), m-learning is not only defined as ever-changing mobile technology (i.e., faster processors, smaller devices, varying output characteristics), but it should also be explained with "… a socially and educationally responsible definition [that views] the learner as the one being mobile and not his/her devices! What needs to move with the learner is not the device, but his/her whole learning environment" (p. 6). This definition offers a more learner-centered, device independent focus when describing mobile learning, which underpins Traxler's (2007) explanation that mobile learning is personal, contextual, and situated. Sharples, Taylor, and Vavoula (2007), proposed a theory of learning directed towards a mobile society where learning is supported not only by mobile devices but also by the mobility of people and knowledge. Similar to Laouris and Eteokleous (2005), Sharples et al. (2007) claimed that the foundation for a theory of mobile learning needed to be grounded in the awareness that learners are always on the move.

We learn across space as we take ideas and learning resources gained in one location and apply or develop them in another. We learn across time, by revisiting knowledge that was gained earlier in a different context, and more broadly, through ideas and strategies gained in early years providing a framework for a lifetime of learning. We move from topic to topic, managing a range of personal learning projects, rather than following a single curriculum. We also move in and out of engagement with technology, for example as we enter and leave cell (mobile) phone coverage (p. 222).

These postulated theories, definitions, and explanations of mobile learning point towards the ubiquitous and personally managed, contextual, networked, and active-oriented nature of m-learning. Intrinsically then, mobile learning readily lends itself to a learner-centered, constructivist pedagogy underpinned by learner-centered theories and constructivist philosophy.

CONSTRUCTIVIST ENVIRONMENT

Constructivism entails humans making meaning and constructing knowledge from active participation and inquiry that is social in nature. Constructivism as a theory embodies knowledge as "emergent, developmental, nonobjective, viable, constructed explanations by humans engaged in meaning making in cultural and social communities of discourse" (Fosnot, 2005, p. ix). A social constructivist view takes into consideration not only what is going on inside the learner's mind, but how the meaning is shaped, validated and shared with others. According to van Merrienboer and de Bruin (2014), "Social constructivist theory discourages the use of traditional lectures, because of the minimal opportunities for communication and discussion with the teacher and fellow students" (p. 27) They posited *"the construction of meaning and knowledge through the interaction with others*" to be the most essential factor shaping learning (p. 27). Kim (2001), similarly noted that social constructivism is reality fashioned through human activity and that learning is a social process because reality is not discovered, but rather comes into existence through social invention.

Therefore, from a constructivist perspective, instructors can provision students through the creation of authentic tasks and inquiry-based approaches using mobile devices, which integrates their understanding of a problem or situation from multiple perspectives through reflection, interaction, and discourse. Instructors and faculty members seeking to capitalize on the affordances of mobile learning and its constructivist necessities, are hard pressed to be the sage on the stage, but instead function as the guide on the side (King, 1993), orchestrating context and content driven mobile activities that support inquiry-based learning in the natural or material world. As explained by the Institute for Inquiry (1996), "Inquiry is an approach to learning that involves a process of exploring the natural or material world, that leads to asking questions and making discoveries in the search for new understandings" (A description of inquiry section, para. 2).

EXPLICATING INQUIRY-BASED LEARNING

The Academy of Inquiry Based Learning (AIBL, n.d.), offered that inquiry-based learning (IBL) is a pedagogy, engaging "students in sense-making activities. Students are given tasks requiring them to solve problems, conjecture, experiment, explore, create, and communicate" (What is IBL section, para. 2). Lin and Tallman (2006), identified IBL as a learning process, stating, "It usually begins with posing a problem or question, followed by generating and pursuing strategies for investigating, collaborating, reflecting, and justifying the solutions of the problem or answers to the question, and communicating the conclusions" (p. 1).

According to Alberta Learning (2004), inquiry-based learning is a process,

... where students are involved in their learning, formulate questions, investigate widely and then build new understandings, meanings and knowledge. That knowledge is new to the students and may be used to answer a question, to develop a solution or to support a position or point of view. The knowledge is usually presented to others and may result in some sort of action. (p. 1)

Hmelo-Silver, Duncan, and Chinn (2007) claimed that inquiry-based learning situates the learning in complex tasks, noting that inquiry learning is "organized around relevant, authentic problems or questions" where students learn content as well as reasoning skills through investigations, collaborations, and activity (p. 100). The authors added that inquiry learning has its roots in scientific inquiry and "places a heavy emphasis on posting questions, gathering and analyzing data, and constructing evidenced-based arguments" (p.100).

Colburn, (2000) defined inquiry-based learning as an environment where "students are engaged in essentially open-ended, student centered, hands-on activities" (p. 42) targeting pursuits where students can answer questions via investigation. He focused on inquiry as a pedagogy (teaching technique). Prince and Felder (2006) who also affixed their definition of IBL in science and engineering wrote, "Inquiry learning begins when students are presented with questions to be answered, problems to be solved, or a set of observations to be explained" (p. 127). In a similar characterization, Savery (2006) described inquiry-based learning as

A student-centered, active learning approach focused on questioning, critical thinking, and problem solving. Inquiry-based learning activities begin with a question followed by investigating solutions, creating new knowledge as information

is gathered and understood, discussing discoveries and experiences and reflecting on new-found knowledge. (p. 16)

An inquiry-based learning environment can capitalize on students' probing, data collection and synthesis, evidenced-based argumentation and presentation. The active, context-rich, and authentic experience mobile learning affords supports such an environment. When implemented purposefully, mobile learning endeavors underwrite an instructor's ability to engage students in inquiry-based activities. Mobile learning by its very name implies the mobility of the learner with a portable handheld device, which in turn allows the learner to explore and investigate in a learner-centered, self-directed manner. According to Keys and Bryan (2001), "There is not one true definition of inquiry waiting to be discovered, but an understanding of inquiry is constructed by individual participants" (p. 633). This statement aligns with constructivist philosophy, which posits knowledge is not independent of the meaning a learner ascribes to an experience, but rather constructivist philosophy assumes "knowledge is constructed by learners as they attempt to make sense of their experiences" (Driscoll, 2005, p. 387). Consequently, inquiry-based learning aligns with constructivist philosophy as Lee, Greene, Odom, Schechter, and Slatta (2004) noted when they wrote that inquiry-guided learning refers "to a range of strategies used to promote learning through students' active and increasingly independent investigation of questions, problems and issues, often for which there is no single answer" (p. 5). Regardless of whether inquiry-based learning (IBL) is viewed as a pedagogy, instructional strategy, or a process, common characteristics among these definitions are the ideas of meaning making, constructing knowledge in union with others, exploring and investigating in authentic contexts inspired by a probing question or driving curiosity.

These authors and other researchers anchored the IBL concept in the sciences; however, it is wholly applicable across most disciplines and should not be reserved for science inquiry alone. Thus, students using mobile or hand-held devices are appropriately positioned for inquiry and problem-based approaches to learning because these methods can be located within student experiences (individually or collaboratively), within the students' physical environment in real-world situations, and across disciplines. Kukulska-Hulme and Traxler (2013) posited, "Mobile learning enables these conditions for authentic learning to be met, allowing learning tasks designed around content creation, data capture, location awareness and collaborative working in real-world settings" (p. 250). It does however, fall to the instructor to create a scaffolded, information-rich, and inquiry-inspired learning environment, one that exploits the anytime, anywhere, in-my-pocket availability mobile learning offers. To do this effectively, it becomes necessary to follow a conceptual model or framework that can inform mobile learning activities.

APPLYING A FRAMEWORK

By ascribing to a model or conceptual framework, instructors can approach the pedagogical task of creating mobile learning units from an organized foundation. Conceptual frameworks provide coherency and a way to present ideas and practices so that others may readily understand. When considering the adoption and implementation of a technology such as mobile learning, it is important to be purposeful and deliberate about why that technology should be considered, how its use will support inquiry-based activities, and the availability of that technology to students and instructors. By ascribing to a model or framework, instructors will be able to approach the pedagogical task of creating mobile learning activities from an ordered and systematic foundation. Frameworks are also models informing or supporting action, processes, parameters, or specific practice. Miles and Huberman (1994) described a conceptual framework as a visual or written product that

... explains, either graphically or in narrative form, the main things to be studied—the key factors, concepts, or variables—and the presumed relationships among them. Frameworks can be rudimentary or elaborate, theory-driven or commonsensical, descriptive or casual. (p. 18)

Theoretical and conceptual frameworks provide a way to examine and identify fundamental ideas and the relationships among those ideas. Concepts (abstractions/ideas) represent the rational or intellectual interpretation of an aspect of reality acquired from observations made about phenomena. When applied to instructional endeavors, frameworks or conceptual models offer instructors the basis from which to identify and refine the issues, ideas, and challenges involved in creating instruction suitable for mobile learning.

FRAMEWORK FOR THE RATIONALE ANALYSIS OF MOBILE EDUCATION (FRAME)

Koole's (2009) Framework for the Rationale Analysis of Mobile Education (FRAME) is a model for guiding the development of learning materials, mobile pedagogy, and learning strategies, and is readily applied to inquiry-based, authentic learning experiences. In a 2011 interview, Koole stated, "Basically the model is a heuristic; that is, it is a tool, like a lens, that allows someone to critically examine a given phenomenon" (Is the FRAME model still current section, para. 3).

FRAME presents mobile learning as a process model resulting from the "convergence of mobile technologies, human learning capacities, and social interaction" (Koole, 2009, p. 25).

The model specifically addressed information overload, knowledge navigation, and collaboration that guide and inform the creation of course content, as well as the design and development of teaching and learning strategies for mobile education. These are all critical considerations when implementing inquiry-based mobile learning activities. Koole's model considered not only the technology element of mobile learning, but also the social and personal aspects of learning, including constructivism and activity theory, key concepts behind inquiry-based methods. As she wrote, "The FRAME model describes a mode of learning in which learners may move within different physical and virtual locations and thereby participate and interact with other people, information, or systems – anywhere, anytime" (Koole, 2009, p. 26). (see Figure 1)

FRAME is depicted in a Venn diagram with three overlapping circles representing the characteristics of the device, (D) the learner, (L) and the social aspects of learning (S). As Koole (2009) noted, the intersection of the three circles represents "a convergence of all three aspects, define[ing] an ideal mobile learning situation" (p. 27). She believed that by examining all dimensions of the FRAME model in an m-learning context, "practitioners [could] use the model to design more effective mobile learning experiences" (p. 27).

Where the circles intersect and overlap are the attributes belonging to both aspects. The device aspect (D) represents "the physical, technical, and functional characteristics of a mobile device" (Koole, 2009, p. 28); whereas, the learner aspect (L) considers the emotions and motivations of the learner as well as how learners use prior knowledge, and encode, store, and transfer information. She posited that mobile learning could help learners activate episodic memory, memory grounded in actual events and authentic experiences. The social aspect (S) of the model concerns social interactions and cooperation, which she believed were governed by rules determined by a learner's culture. Device usability (DL) addresses character-

Framing Mobile Learning

Figure 1. The framework for the rational analysis of mobile education model © (Koole, 2009, p. 27). Used with permission. This work is licensed under a Creative Commons License (CC BY-NC-ND 2.5 CA)

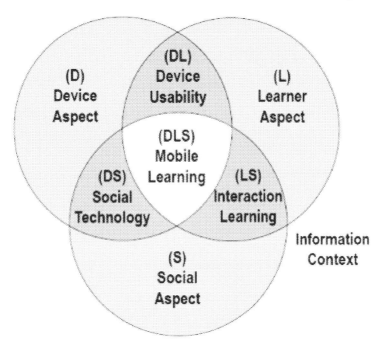

istics belonging to both the device and the learner, such as cognitive tasks related to manipulating and storing information, portability of the mobile device (weight, size), and aesthetics of the interface (how intuitive it is). The social technology intersection (DS) is where Koole considered the social aspect of mobile learning. She described this area as "the means of information exchange and collaboration between people with various goals and purposes" including factors such as co-authoring documents and coordinating tasks and activities (p. 34). Accordingly, she claimed her model placed more of an emphasis on constructivism where learning is a collaborative process, and meaning and understanding are gleaned from multiple perspectives.

The overlap of device usability (DL) and social technology (DS) describes the affordances of mobile technology; the area labeled interaction learning (LS) "contains instructional and learning theories with an emphasis on social constructivism" (Koole, 2009, p. 27). The center, where all three aspects converge, represents exemplar mobile learning situations. She indicated that her model, through the consideration of all aspects within a mobile learning situation (i.e., the technical, social, and personal), could assist practitioners in designing more effective mobile learning experiences and help them "better comprehend the complex nature of mobile learning" (Koole, 2009, p. 41). To better understand the FRAME model in a mobile, inquiry-grounded learning experience, each of the primary elements of the model need to be clarified in light of inquiry-based learning characteristics.

Examining Inquiry-Based Learning through FRAME

The device aspect of the FRAME model (D), refers to the physical properties of the hand-held or mobile device. It includes such things as how the user may manipulate the device, how the user can move with the device, the size and weight

243

of the device, input mechanisms such as a keyboard, touchscreen, or voice, as well as output mechanisms such visual or audio elements. The device aspect of the model bears consideration because "the hardware and software design of the devices ... have a significant impact on the physical and psychological comfort levels of the users" (Koole, 2009, p. 28), and it is the device that acts as the link or interface between the mobile learner and his or her inquiry-learning activities. Without a device that facilitates exploration in a convenient and highly portable manner, (i.e. its usability) structuring inquiry-guided mobile activities would become cumbersome and burdensome for the learner. Because finding and investigating data through questioning, observation, and experimentation are significant characteristics of inquiry-based learning, asking students to complete an exercise lugging around a five or six-pound laptop in the field invokes an unreasonable, if not amusing visual.

The learner aspect of the FRAME model (L), reflects the learner's cognitive abilities, memory, prior knowledge, and to some extent their motivations. Koole (2009) elaborated on this concept by stating that episodic memory (declarative, personalized memory of an event or episode) allows the learner to use ideas actively, which supports the transfer of the concept or idea to other contexts. Engaging the learner in mobile learning activities coupled with authentic and contextually rich experiences grounded in inquiry-based pedagogies, can support learner recall, information transfer, and "may stimulate the learner to develop skills to filter, choose, and recognize relevant information in different situations" (p. 30). By engaging with questions presented in a specific and authentic context, and supported by a mobile device, the learner has the opportunity to explore actively possible answers and solutions, thereby moving that experience and event into episodic memory in support of knowledge acquisition.

The social aspect of the FRAME model (S), describes "the processes of social interaction and cooperation" (Koole, 2009, p. 31), whether that interaction is physical, virtual or both. The precepts of social constructivism are evidenced in the social element of the model as learners figure out how to work together in a cooperative and collaborative manner during the exploration and problem solving that often accompany inquiry-based learning. Conversation, effective communication, and cultural understanding all influence the social aspect of the FRAME model as learners work together or individually through an inquiry-based activity and present the results of their findings. As Kuhlthau and Todd (2012) noted, "Inquiry learning is responsive to students' personal, social and cultural worlds, valuing differences and cultivating an inclusive community" (p. 9).

Where the device and learner (DL) aspects of the model intersect, (device usability) learner actions, tasks, memory and encoding of information meet the affordances of the mobile device, and how easily (or not) that device allows the learner to move between physical and virtual worlds. Characteristics such as the portability, physical robustness and physical comfort of the device, as well as its ease of use, will bear on the learner's ability to exploit it in physical and virtual environments. Considerations such as the device's capacity to permit adequate acquisition, storage, and retrieval of information are important when deliberating the use of the device in an anytime, anywhere manner. As Koole (2009) noted, "Highly portable devices must resist humidity, dust, and shock. Information access complements portability, and it enables information to travel with the user rather than the user moving to the information" (p. 33). The juncture of the device and learner aspects of the FRAME model support inquiry based learning by allowing students to effectively and efficiently mobilize their opportunities to learn with the device, thus experiencing realistic and authentic environments as they investigate, explore, and discover answers to problems and queries they have.

The intersection of the device aspect of the model with the social aspect (DS), Koole labeled the social technology intersection. The social technology intersection addresses how mobile devices support communication and collaboration among many individuals and across various systems. These intersecting elements address the social property of multiple learners working and learning together, while being connected where network connectivity is a given and available in an unobtrusive and ubiquitous manner. Connectivity speaks to Internet access, social media access and sharing, virtual data storage and retrieval, in addition to email and text message exchanges that often accompany learners working together using mobile devices. The learner in tandem with her mobile device, other learners, and network connectivity, can move fluidly in the learning environment and participate in community learning situations.

The element resulting from the learner intersecting with the social aspect (LS) Koole called interaction learning. She posited that interaction learning, "Represents a synthesis of learning and instructional theories, but relies very heavily upon the philosophy of social constructivism" (p. 36). Here the emphasis is on social interactions of the learner, with less emphasis on the device and more focus on "the needs of distance learners as individuals who are situated within unique cultures and environments. [Where] such settings impact a learner's ability to understand, negotiate, integrate, interpret, and use new ideas" (p. 36). At the learner and social aspect intersection (LS) (interaction learning), situated cognition, authentic experiences, learning communities, and other forms of student to student, student to content and student to instructor interactions occur. The interaction learning element of the model supports inquiry-based methods through consideration of social constructivism, and the importance of others working together in a contextually rich environment to arrive at shared meanings. Questioning and searching for answers in a collaborative manner are critical elements of inquiry, and effectively generating knowledge is one of several desired outcomes of this method.

The central intersection where Device, Learning, and Social (DLS) aspects of the model meet depicts the integration of all three aspects, and represents an effective mobile learning experience. By considering the device, its usability, the learner, (memory, prior knowledge, motivations) the social aspects (collaboration, conversation, social interactions, constructivism), and system connectivity, the Framework for the Rationale Analysis of Mobile Education offers a process model which can inform, structure, and provide appropriate parameters for implementing inquiry-based learning.

Inquiry-Based Mobilized Activity

With a sufficient understanding of inquiry-based learning, and the FRAME model for mobile learning, the next step is to look at how the model may be applied to an inquiry-based learning context or activity. What follows is an inquiry-based activity from a graduate level course addressing communication for change management. The course title, Communication for Change Management, supports learners in becoming effective change leaders within their organizations. This course engaged students through a focus on understanding critical change dynamics, including organizational structures and roles. Each student studied and applied communication competencies that may allow organizational members to direct change dynamics in effective ways. Concepts, models, and practices of coaching and facilitation for change are explored, as are methods of supporting leaders during times of change. The specific inquiry-based activity in this class represents a microcosmic look at using the FRAME model to consider and support a mobile inquiry-based assignment. Through the application of the FRAME model, it is possible to foresee how *mobilizing* the inquiry-based activity has the potential to enrich and augment the learner's experience.

A new or emerging model is only as good as its ability to inform, structure, and improve practice and or learning. In order to trial the Framework for the Rationale Analysis of Mobile Education (FRAME) (Koole, 2009), and its ability to inform, improve student inquiry abilities, and *mobilize* an inquiry-grounded activity, it is necessary to begin with an inquiry oriented pursuit that has the potential to go mobile. Owens, Hester, and Teale (2002) noted the availability of technology to support the process of inquiry-based learning offered IBL a "new element" (p. 620). They wrote:

At its most simplistic level, technology allows students to organize and edit their projects more easily. At a more complex level, technology allows students to communicate with experts around the world, to access information from a vast array of resources, and to create high-quality presentations that combine text, sound, and visual images. (p. 620)

The inquiry activity assigned was part of a fully online class called Communication for Change Management, a graduate level course within an Organizational and Professional Communication degree program. The assignment necessitated students interview an individual they deemed to be a change leader or change management role model. This individual could be someone from the private or government sector, someone in non-profit, education, or religion. Students had latitude in choosing the change leader they wanted to interview as well as the questions to ask. Owens, et al. (2002), believed that successful inquiry-based activities "emerge from topics that are of real interest to the students. These topics may be derived from themes studied as a class, but if so, it is imperative that students have a choice of topics about which they truly wonder and care" (p. 617). This interview assignment offered students an activity embedded as a central theme in the course, as well as a choice about whom to interview. To help scaffold students in this assignment, the instructor suggested they start with several interview questions such as:

- What kinds of organizational change have you experienced?
- What leadership role(s) have you taken in these instances?
- How did you help people become committed to the change(s)?
- Were there any models or frameworks you followed to support the change initiative?
- Tell me about a change effort in your organization that was successful and one that was not so successful. What did you learn from these experiences?

The purpose of this assignment was to help students better understand change leadership as it transpired in a situated, real-world context, while offering them the opportunity to discuss and question change strategies with an experienced other. Students' ability to seek out new perspectives and information through questioning is a central tenet of inquiry-based learning, whether inquiry is promoted by questions from the instructor or by a structured activity where the learner formulates his or her own questions. Additionally, effective inquiry is more than just asking questions. It involves synthesizing, reflecting upon, and organizing the data, along with the complex process of converting the acquired data into useful knowledge such as in a paper, presentation, or other form of de-briefing. The Educational Broadcasting Corporation (2004) noted, "Useful application of inquiry learning involves several factors: a context for questions,

Table 1. Applying the FRAME model (planning for the mobile learning environment)

Frame Aspect (element)	What to Consider	Application to the Activity
DEVICE (D)	• Do learners have a handheld device adequate / comfortable (to them) for the assignment? • Can the device record audio, take pictures? • Is there a note-taking app on the device? • Does the device permit the storage and retrieval of data?	Learners can use the mobile device for the interview as a way to record the live interview and/or capture their immediate ideas and thoughts about the interview before leaving the site.
LEARNER (L)	• Have you (instructor) designed the assignment around authentic activities, contexts, and audiences? • Does the activity build on the learner's prior knowledge? • Does the learning situation allow for the transfer of concepts and procedures to different contexts? • Does the assignment encourage learners to explore, discover, select information relevant to their own unique problems/interests? • Are learners familiar with using the handheld device? Do they know how to take photos, record audio or take notes on the device?	Learners have the opportunity to situate themselves in the interviewees actual work environment. Assignment is offered mid quarter, learners should have basic knowledge about organizational change. Interviewing is a skill that can be used in many situations /disciplines. Learners may add or change interviewing questions to meet their needs and that of the situation.
SOCIAL ASPECT (S)	• Are there any clarifying definitions, cultural behaviors (etiquette), or symbols that participants may require while interacting? • Is there sufficient, accurate and relevant communications established among participants in the mobile learning space?	The social aspect of the assignment occurs when learners are presenting/exchanging the results of their interviews in online discussion boards. No clarifications needed, other than clear presentation directions. Social interaction among participants while completing the assignment is not immediately relevant.
DEVICE USABILITY (DL) intersection	• What type of location and climate will the learner be in when using this device? • Will the learner's device permit access to information whenever and wherever needed (just-in-time learning)? • Are the assignment's content & required activities/tasks considerate of the device's usability? (e.g. screen size, keyboard, portability, personalization of the device)	The device will be used indoors presumably in a climate-controlled office. If used outside, students need to be cognizant of weather conditions (cold, rain, wind, dust etc.) Advise students they may want to use a WiFi enabled device. If in an environment where WiFi is not available, interview can still be completed. Any portable device with audio recording capability & data input ability will work for the interview.
SOCIAL TECHNOLOGY (DS) intersection	• Have you (instructor) selected appropriate collaboration software to meet the learning needs or social tasks? • Is wireless connectivity available for student collaboration? Is it secure and of adequate speed?	Collaboration takes place in the Learning Managements System's (LMS) online discussion forum during learners' exchange & sharing of interview experience & results. Students will be connected via the LMS for data sharing.

continued on following page

Table 1. Continued

Frame Aspect (element)	What to Consider	Application to the Activity
INTERACTION LEARNING (LS) intersection	• What are the learner's relationships with other learners, experts, & the systems they are using? • What are the learner's preferences for social interaction? • Have you (instructor) provided opportunities for mobile learning to develop communities of practice, apprentices, mentoring between learners and experts?	Learning community should already be established in first few weeks of class within the LMS, via discussion boards. Stipulate in assignment that effective use of the mobile device entails students be familiar with the apps and tools they will be using prior to interview. Collaboration and information exchange takes place in the LMS. Assignment provides for interaction between learner & knowledgeable (expert) other. Communities of practice established in the LMS via the shared experience of the assignment, the interview, & follow up paper.
DEVICE/ LEARNER & SOCIAL (DLS) intersection	• How may the mobile device change the interaction processes among the learners, their communities of practice & systems? • Does the assignment permit learners to use effectively the mobile device(s) to access other learners, systems, & devices; to recognize & evaluate information & processes to achieve their goals? • How can learners become more independent in navigating through data & filtering information? • When implementing a mobile learning activity, have you (instructor) considered how your role & that of the learner will change? Have you prepared students for that change?	The mobile interview assignment may affect learner actions during the interview. Learners may be more self-conscious, reticent when using a mobile recording device or mobile data input when face to face with a change leader. A mobile device allows students to capture & record their ideas, thoughts & events authentically & in real-time, thereby supporting recall & enabling more accurate synthesis of information later than mere note taking. Using the device to capture interview data supports acquisition of mobile navigation skills & data filtering skills as students organize data into a meaningful paper. For this assignment, use of a mobile device to capture & record data allows learners to be more autonomous, self-directed, & independent. Instructor does not specifically direct the actual assignment, but scaffolds the learner with interview question prompts while allowing the learner to conduct, process, & present the inquiry driven interview data.

Adapted from Koole, 2009 (pp. 45-47).

a framework for questions, a focus for questions, and different levels of questions. Well-designed inquiry learning produces knowledge formation that can be widely applied" (A context for inquiry section, para. 3).

The final presentation of the interview data required students to write a three to four page summary of the interview. In this paper, students described the change leader's style and the context within which the change leader operated. They also summarized three to four key learnings or insights gained from the interview, with a focus on change management and strategic communication for change. The interview summary paper allowed students to critically reflect on and document their experience and newfound knowledge in an organized manner. This reflection allowed them to more deeply process the experience, while synthesizing what they learned from the change leader. Furthermore, students shared and discussed their papers within online discussion forums following the paper submission. Lee et al., (2004) posited that students learn through the active investigation process itself and the presentation of results. The authors wrote, "This process involves the ability to formulate good questions, identify and collect appropriate evidence, present results systematically, analyze and interpret results, formulate conclusions and evaluate the worth and importance of those conclusions" (p. 9).

Applying FRAME

Once an activity has been identified as being inquiry-based, it falls to the instructor to see if mobilizing the learner with a hand-held device has the potential to better support active learning in the field within the circumstances of the inquiry. In this example, students were presented the opportunity to interview a change leader within the leader's operating environment, thereby gathering data real-time, in authentic and contextually vivid surroundings. While inquiry-based learning generally begins with an investigative type of question to be explored (grounded historically in the sciences), assigning students to interview expert others within a specific knowledge domain can also be considered authentic, inquiry-based learning.

A checklist accompanied Koole's (2009) model as support for the planning, development, and analysis of mobile learning environments, and the suitability of the activity to a mobile learner. By using the checklist, instructors can proactively ensure they are implementing a mobile learning assignment that students can successfully achieve. Table 1 illustrates the adaptation and application of Koole's checklist depicting various sub-items and the elements from her model as applied to the inquiry-based, change leader interview assignment.

Figure 2. Mobile learning and inquiry-based learning characteristics juxtaposed

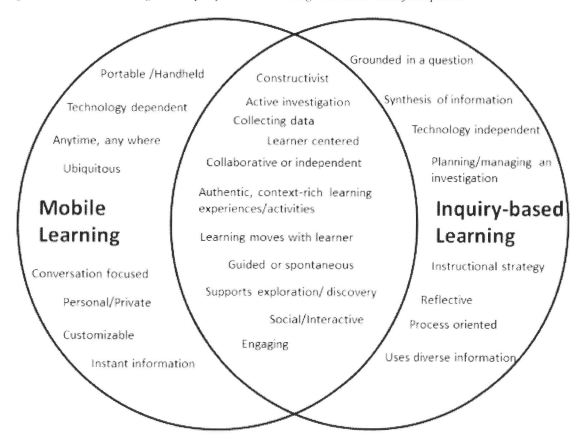

FINAL THOUGHTS

A model or process framework such as FRAME can offer a road map to the development of effective and efficient mobile learning with an inquiry-based predisposition. In the course of understanding and applying a structured model, instructors can more purposefully and thoroughly deploy mobile learning activities and assignments in their courses. Although initially grounded in scientific inquiry and offered as an opportunity "for students to improve their understanding of both science content and scientific practices" (Edelson, Gordin, & Pea, 1999, p. 391), inquiry-based learning when combined with mobile learning can be applied to other disciplines as this non-science, change management example illustrates. The juxtaposition of the descriptive aspects of FRAME and characteristics of mobile learning, with inquiry-based learning descriptors as depicted in Figure 2, helps ensure effective, engaging, and authentic learning.

Central to creating learner-centered, investigative, and authentic educational experiences are the tenets of inquiry-based learning joined with key characteristics and capabilities found in mobile learning. Ozdamli and Cavus (2011) found that it was critical for elements of mobile learning to be "organized correctly and the interactions between the various elements ... combined in an efficient and optimum way so that the mobile learning is successful and the implementation is efficient" (p. 937). When elements of both mobile learning and inquiry-based learning are combined and then informed by the application of a framework, the potential to design effective, constructivist, real world, and situated learning activities is strengthened. Learners can be invigorated by contextually rich endeavors that allow them to freely and independently capture and record events, data, and personal reflections in an anytime, anywhere, convenient manner. These digitally captured experiences are then available for later deliberation, synthesis and evaluation, presentation, and sharing by the learner; fundamental attributes of inquiry-based learning.

REFERENCES

Academy of Inquiry-based Learning. (n.d.). What is inquiry-based learning? *Retrieved from* http://www.inquirybasedlearning.org/?page=What_is_IBL

Alberta Learning. (2004). Focus on inquiry: A teacher's guide to implementing inquiry-based learning. Alberta, Canada: Alberta Learning. Retrieved from http://www.learning.gov.ab.ca/k_12/curriculum/bySubject/focusoninquiry.pdf

Colburn, A. (2000). An inquiry primer. *Science Scope, 6*(23), 42–44.

Dahlstrom, E. (2012). ECAR study of undergraduate students and information technology. Louisville, CO: EDUCAUSE Center for Applied Research. Retrieved from http://www.educause.edu/library/resources/ecar-study-undergraduate-students-and-information-technology-2012

Driscoll, M. P. (2005). *Psychology of learning for instruction*. New York, NY: Pearson Education.

Edelson, D. C., Gordin, D. N., & Pea, R. D. (1999). Addressing the challenges of inquiry-based learning through technology and curriculum design. *Journal of the Learning Sciences, 8*(3-4), 391–450. doi:10.1080/10508406.1999.9672075

Educational Broadcasting Corporation. (2004). Concept to classroom: What is inquiry-based learning. Retrieved from http://www.thirteen.org/edonline/concept2class/inquiry/index.html

El-Hussein, M. O., & Cronje, J. C. (2010). Defining mobile learning in the higher education landscape. *Journal of Educational Technology & Society, 13*(3), 12–21.

Exploratorium Institute for Inquiry. (1996). A description of inquiry. Retrieved from http://www.exploratorium.edu/ifi/resources/inquirydesc.html#inquiry

Fosnot, C. T. (2005). *Preface. In Constructivism: Theory, perspectives and practice* (pp. ix–xii). New York, NY: Teachers College Press.

Haag, J. (2011). From eLearning to mLearning: The effectiveness of mobile course delivery. *The Interservice/Industry Training, Simulation and Education Conference*. National Training Systems Association. Retrieved from http://www.ww.adlnet.org/wp-content/uploads/2011/12/e_to_mLearning_paper.pdf

Hmelo-Silver, C. E., Duncan, R. G., & Chinn, C. A. (2007). Scaffolding and achievement in problem-based and inquiry learning: A response to Kirschner, Sweller and Clark (2006). *Educational Psychologist*, *42*(2), 99–107. doi:10.1080/00461520701263368

Johnson, L., Adams Becker, S., Cummins, M., Estrada, V., Freeman, A., & Ludgate, H. (2013). *NMC Horizon Report: 2013 Higher Education Edition*. Austin, TX: The New Media Consortium.

Johnson, L., Levine, A., Smith, R., & Stone, S. (2010). *The 2010 horizon report*. Austin, TX: The New Media Consortium.

Keys, C. W., & Bryan, L. A. (2001). Co-constructing inquiry-based science with teachers: Essential research for lasting reform. *Journal of Research in Science Teaching*, *38*(6), 631–645. doi:10.1002/tea.1023

Kim, B. (2001). Social constructivism. In M. Orey (Ed.), Emerging perspectives on learning, teaching, and technology. Retrieved from http://epltt.coe.uga.edu/index.php?title=Social_Constructivism

King, A. (1993). From sage on the stage to guide on the side. *College Teaching*, *41*(1), 30–35. doi: 10.1080/87567555.1993.9926781

Koole, M. (2009). A model for framing mobile learning. In M. Ally (Ed.), Mobile learning: Transforming the delivery of education and training (pp. 25–47). Edmonton, AB: AU Press, Athabasca University. Retrieved from http://www.aupress.ca/index.php/books/120155

Koole, M. (2011, July 9). *Thoughts, writing & snippets. Mobile learning: Is the FRAME model still current?* [Web log comment]. Retrieved from http://kooleady.ca/thoughts/?p=619

Kuhlthau, C., & Todd, R. (2012). *Guided inquiry*. Retrieved from http://ebookbrowsee.net/guided-inquiry-by-carol-kuhlthau-and-ross-todd-doc-d347681374

Kukulska-Hulme, A., & Traxler, J. (2013). Design principles for mobile learning. In H. Beetham, & R. Sharp (Eds.), *Rethinking Pedagogy for a Digital Age: Designing for 21st Century Learning* (pp. 244–257). New York, NY: Taylor and Francis.

Laouris, Y., & Eteokleous, N. (2005). We need an educational relevant definition of mobile learning. Retrieved from http://www.mlearn.org.za/CD/papers/Laouris%20&%20Eteokleous.pdf

Lee, V. S., & Greene, D. B., Odom, J., Schechter, E., & Slatta, R. W. (2004). What is inquiry-guided learning?. In V. S. Lee (Ed.), Teaching and learning through inquiry (pp. 3-16). Sterling, VA: Stylus.

Lin, J., & Tallman, J. (2006). A theoretical framework for online inquiry-based learning. In C. Crawford et al. (Eds.), *Proceedings of Society for Information Technology & Teacher Education International Conference* (pp. 967-974). Chesapeake, VA: AACE. Retrieved from http://editlib.org/p/22178/

Miles, M. B., & Huberman, A. M. (1994). *Qualitative data analysis: An expanded sourcebook*. Thousand Oaks, CA: Sage Publications.

Owens, R., Hester, J. L., & Teale, W. H. (2002). Where do you want to go today? Inquiry-based learning and technology integration. *The Reading Teacher*, 55(7), 616–625.

Ozdamli, F., & Cavus, N. (2011). Basic elements of mobile learning. *Social and Behavioral Sciences Procedia*, 28, 937–942. doi:10.1016/j.sbspro.2011.11.173

Prince, M. J., & Felder, R. M. (2006). Inductive teaching and learning methods: Definitions, comparisons, and research bases. *Journal of Engineering Education*, 95(2), 123–138. doi:10.1002/j.2168-9830.2006.tb00884.x

Savery, J. R. (2006). Overview of problem-based learning: Definitions and distinctions. *Interdisciplinary Journal of Problem-based Learning*, 1(1), 9–20. doi:10.7771/1541-5015.1002

Sharples, M., Taylor, J., & Vavoula, G. (2007). A theory of learning for the mobile age. In R. Andrews, & C. Haythornthwaite (Eds.), *The Sage handbook of e-learning research* (pp. 221–247). London: Sage.

Traxler, J. (2007). Defining, discussing, and evaluating mobile learning: The moving finger writes and having writ..... *International Review of Research in Open and Distance Learning*, 8(2), 1–12.

Van Merrienboer, J. J. G., & de Bruin, A. B. H. (2014). Research paradigms and perspectives on learning. In M. Spector, D. Merrill, J. Elen, & M. Bishop (Eds.), *Handbook of research on educational communications and technology* (pp. 21–29). New York, NY: Springer. doi:10.1007/978-1-4614-3185-5_2

KEY TERMS AND DEFINITIONS

Authentic Learning: Generally, an activity or exercise conducted in a real-world setting or in the actual context of what is being investigated, explored, questioned or discovered. By learning within the actual context of a situation, the learner is confronted with ill-structured and complex problems and questions. Authentic learning promotes/supports realism in learning because of the genuineness of the situation in which the learner finds him or herself.

Conceptual Framework: A conceptual framework represents assumptions, beliefs, concepts (ideas) and theories used to underpin research. It presents key elements about what is to be studied, and the relationships among those elements. A conceptual framework is generally founded upon (or builds on) prior research and existing theories. It represents a schematic or model about what you are investigating compiled in a systematic manner to guide research and inquiry. The term is often used interchangeably with the word model.

Constructivism: Constructivism entails learners making meaning and constructing knowledge from active participation and inquiry that is social in nature. Learners create knowledge by and through their social interactions with others, because knowledge is not independent of the meaning a learner ascribes to an experience. A constructivist approach to teaching is less content oriented and more learner-centered.

Inquiry-Based Activity: An activity grounded in an initial question or series of questions that drives or promotes further active investigation. This initial question(s) can be student sponsored or come from the instructor. Inquiry-based activities or Inquiry-based assignments focus on the process of discovery, active exploration, relevant data gathering and synthesis and presentation of the data/answers found.

Learning Management System: Commonly referred to as a LMS, it is a web-based software application used for administration of student records (tracking, grading, attendance etc.), the delivery of content and instruction, communication. Learning management systems are commonly used in higher education contexts to support classroom and distance learning.

Mobile Learning: Mobile learning is broadly defined as the mobility of the learner in tandem with the handheld mobile device, a wireless Internet connection, and the learner's ability to move fluidly across time and place with access to content, information, other people and students, and discourse anytime, anywhere. In this definition, the exploratory, situated, and constructivist nature of mobile learning is implied, and it comprises a learner-centered focus.

Pedagogy: The artisanship of teaching, including instructional methods. The way one instructs or approaches instruction including instructional strategies and materials. The activities, methods, and work of the instructor.

Process Model: A process model represents a logical collection of actions, steps or procedures into a coherent framework or model. A process model offers a visual or narrative account of how something works, comes together, or proceeds, and how those actions, steps or procedures lead to specific results.

Venn Diagram: A Venn diagram visually (and circularly) represents the logical relationships among items or groups of items that have something in common. . When items within the Venn diagram overlap, the area they have in common is called a union. The union encompasses the items or groups of items each of the separate areas have in common.

Chapter 14
Integrating Mobile Technologies in Multicultural Multilingual Multimedia Projects

Melda N. Yildiz
Kean University, USA

Kristine Scharaldi
Independent Scholar, USA

ABSTRACT

This chapter explores the role of mobile technologies, such as Global Positioning System (GPS) and cell phones and tablet PC technologies, in higher education and professional development; offers creative strategies and possibilities for integrating GPS and mobile technologies into the curriculum with limited resources; outlines participants' projects and digital stories; and demonstrates examples that integrates Maps, Mathematics, and Media Education using cell phones, tablet PCs, and GPS devices in a gallery walk. The study explores a wide range of meanings participants associated with experiential project-based learning activities; the impact of mobile technologies in developing multicultural and multilingual curriculum that promotes inclusive and differentiated instruction; the ways in which participants integrated math, maps, and media into their learning; and how they gained alternative points of view on global education and renewed interest and commitment to community service and socially responsible teaching. This chapter will benefit teacher candidates and teacher educators who seek innovative and cost-effective strategies and tools in higher education.

INTRODUCTION

"Only when you say it in Russian I will do it," my kindergarten child said when we were living in Turkmenistan. My children attended an international school where they studied all subjects in English but also learned Turkmen, the official language of Turkmenistan, as well as an elective language, Russian. Our friends and neighbors spoke different languages and came from different countries- French, South Korea, China, Britain. Turkmenistan was truly a multilingual and multicultural experience for my family as well as for my scholarship. I ended up working

DOI: 10.4018/978-1-4666-6284-1.ch014

with faculty who were seeking innovative ways to integrate new technologies into their curriculum. I had the privilege working closely with over 20 higher education faculty as well as countless number of university and high school students who took courses, workshops or participated in my research projects.

Every day, my Turkmen language skills grew and knowing a few words in Turkmen opened so many doors. I was invited to speak at various occasions (e.g. seismology institute, women groups) and interviewed by Turkmen Television, Radio and Newspapers. For the first time, I prepared and presented all my talks in a multilingual format. For instance, if my slides are in English, I had a couple translators who translated my presentations to Turkmen and Russian. Sometimes. I had a chance to work with the translators ahead of time and prepared some of my slides in Russian or Turkmen to supplement my talks. Knowing Turkish was a big plus, because most of the Turkmen students I worked with went to Turkmen Turkish bilingual education schools. In short, my children and I had a true immersion into Turkmen culture and language throughout our stay. I was challenged to develop workshops, presentations, lessons and projects in a multilingual format as well as to integrate The Universal Design for Learning – UDL model in order to be more inclusive, innovative, multilingual and transdisciplinary for my Turkmen students.

Our experiences teaching new media and technologies (e.g. mobile phones, GPS) to K-16 students and providing professional development workshops to in-service teachers in multicultural and multilingual settings provided us ample examples to highlight in this paper.

The "m" in mLearning generally refers to mobile, in this chapter we will share our experiences with in-service and pre-service teachers and their experiences with *mlearning* in context of multicultural and multilingual education while creating their innovative transdisciplinary lesson plans and interactive multimedia projects. We integrated 7 state core curriculum and 2 common core standards in designing our K12 curriculum projects. We call our curriculum design 9M model. (e.g. Multilingualism is for World Languages standard.)

We used various mobile devices such as laptops, cell phones, GPS devices in our teacher education classes and professional development workshops. Each participant developed their mlearning model for developing their lesson plans and projects using mobile technologies. In-service and pre-service teachers are encouraged to work toward the development of an eclectic model using current educational research and frameworks. This chapter outlines some of the best practices, assessment tools, and curriculum models that promote transdisciplinary teaching models for P16 curriculum; argues the challenges and advantages of mobile learning technologies in teacher education and professional development; introduces the innovative use of mobile technologies (e.g. GPS, cell phones and apps) in developing multilingual and multicultural multimedia projects; demonstrates creative strategies and possibilities for engaging teacher candidates (undergraduates) and in-service teachers (professional development) in project-based globally connected activities integrating mobile technologies; and investigates the role of mobile technologies as a means to promote problem-based, project-based and inquiry-based curricula among in-service and pre-service teachers.

Mobile devices and technologies have been bringing new opportunities and challenges for teaching and learning and expanding the walls of our classrooms by promoting education in a formal or informal context anytime anywhere for anybody. From pre-school to graduate school, from English language learners to special education students, the use of mobile technologies are evident. With the advent of handheld devices such as GPS devices in our mobile phones, there will be an expanded access to alternative resources and global connections. Teaching and learning have potential to be a continuous life-long process; it is personalized, learner-centered, situated, collaborative, and ubiquitous. Suter, Alexander, and Kaplan (2005) summarized the notion of social interaction software "as a tool (for augmenting human social and collaborative abilities), as a medium (for facilitating social connection and information interchange), and as an ecology (for enabling a 'system of people, practices, values, and technologies in a particular local environment')." (p.48)

Education is no longer space bound, time bound, or restricted to one language. Anybody with a mobile device can access instruction anytime and anywhere in the world in a chosen language. Mlearning devices provide tools, resources and access to information such as pocket dictionary to check meaning, to practice pronunciation, to watch a video or to find a location using a built in GPS in many languages. Mostly, translations were done by the participants or the community of learners. For instance, in coursera.org, translations of the lectures are done by the participants, in TED.com, translation are completed by volunteers worldwide as part of the TED Open Translation Project. Another example, 7billionothers.org website not only provides a multilingual option to explore the website itself but also showcases the voices of the participants in their native languages with subtitles edited by the world community. On the internet, most content comes in multilingual content and the information can be switched into the language choice of the user. (e.g. Internet browsers such as Firefox, or tablet PCs, Macs or Ipads can be switched to work on another language). Formal education blends in with informal learning opportunities.

While focusing on teaching 21st century skills and eliminating participation gap (Jenkins et al., p. 59) among Turkmen youth who had limited access to internet and mobile technologies, Maps, Math and Media project was first developed in Turkmenistan integrating geography, numerical and media literacy skills in 2009. Cummins (2007) argues the importance of multilingual classrooms and sees the students who are learning English (L2) needs to be built on their native language (L1).

In this chapter, we hope to outline difficulties and unique characteristics of mobile technologies, discuss the power of social interaction software in developing 21st century skills into developing culturally and linguistically responsive curriculum and outline innovative interdisciplinary multilingual and multicultural multimedia projects using mobile devices in teacher education; offers creative strategies for developing projects for K-16 while integrating world languages, geography and 21st century skills; provides the results of participatory research projects among high school students, in-service and pre-service teachers; describes participants' reactions and experiences with new technologies and showcases the participants' multimedia projects.

According to UNESCO (2012), today there are over 5.9 billion mobile phone subscriptions worldwide and for every one person who accesses the internet from a computer two access it using a mobile device. Given the ubiquitous nature of mobile technologies, UNESCO, World Bank, USAID and many other organizations are optimistic about the potential use of mobile technologies for accessible, equitable, and individualized education around the world. These new wireless technologies and GPS built-in devices are transforming the way we teach and learn. As the traditional textbooks are being replaced by interactive ones, the need for multilingual and multicultural context and information literacy skills are becoming more important.

These mobile technologies are transforming the traditional classroom-based learning into teaching and learning into anytime and anywhere education. Therefore, this chapter investigates the use of mobile technologies in teacher education with particular reference to the use of GPS devices. Our results show that participants in each activity enjoyed interdisciplinary approach to lesson activities with the help of their mobile phones. We believe that using the M9 model as an lesson plan developing tool will contribute to the success of teachers and teacher candidates. These findings have implications for teacher candidates, K16 educators and students, parents, media specialists, and administrators who seek alternative strategies and tools in teaching and learning 21st Century Skills and interdisciplinary curriculum focusing on globally connected participatory projects.

BACKGROUND

Mobile technologies, such as iPads, empower educators and teacher candidates through the creation and exploration of flexible digital resources. Built-in tools, such as the camera, microphone, and speaker, allow users to record and listen to spoken voice and save images and video. Other native features, such as language keyboards and computerized text-to-speech, provide supports for users while reading and writing digital text as well as language tools and keyboards. These tools are integrated into various apps that allow for the production and sharing of digital products such as screencasts and interactive eBooks.

Screencasting applications, such as *ShowMe*, *ScreenChomp,* and *Educreations*, allow teachers and students to voice over annotated screens to create short movies. These apps have a simple iconic interface that make it accessible to users of various ages and abilities. Teachers are using these apps to create tutorials and customized instructional videos that are shared online for students and parents to view outside of school to support learning. Screencasting apps are also being utilized by students to demonstrate what they know and to work on fluency. These digital products become tools for assessment that can inform instruction as well as to provide evidence of learning. Screencasting applications offer open-ended opportunities for peer instruction, collaboration, and creative expression across content areas and grade levels.

Mobile devices offer users the ability to interact with text, allow customization of reading and writing experiences, and have access to digital materials from all over the world. When using eBook applications and web sites on the iPad, the text and font can be adjusted to be comfortable for the individual user, and there are options for hearing words read aloud while highlighting them one by one. In the *iBooks* and *Safari* apps the reader can tap on an unfamiliar word and have it spoken and defined on the screen. Thousands of eBooks are available to download for free, and there are opportunities to read books that are translated in numerous languages, such as those from the International Children's Digital Library Foundation *(ICDL)*. The *ICDL* app has a large collection of favorite books from over sixty countries and can be read in the native language and also translated into additional languages. The stories and illustrations in the books provide opportunities to explore other cultures as well as versions of familiar stories. Teachers and students are able to interact and annotate on screens on their mobile devices to further engage with the digital materials. In the *iBooks* app users can highlight text with various colors and add digital sticky notes on pages of the book they are reading to mark important passages, make connections, and ponder questions. The *Skitch* app is being used as a personal digital whiteboard to draw, label, and annotate over any type of screen content to save and share with others. For example, students are able to take a captured map image and use digital pen ink to draw over it to show intersecting lines, types of angles, and other geometric concepts. These versatile tools in the hands of learners and educators are offering alternative ways of representing curricular content and demonstrating ideas and concepts, and engaging in the construction and exploration of digital products.

Mobile digital storytelling and publishing applications allow teachers and students to develop and share their own digital products, such as multimedia eBooks. The *StoryKit* app is being used on the iPad, iPhone, and iPod Touch to capture images, insert photos, add voice recordings, and typed text on pages of an electronic book. Users of *StoryKit* are developing learning logs, how-to books, multimedia journals, and storybooks, and are creating individual elements as well as collaborative pieces. This mobile app, with its basic features and simple screen interface, is allowing students of all ages and abilities to contribute to a meaningful digital product. The finished projects are accessible online and are shared with family members near and far and can be sources of pride for students outside of school. *Book Creator* is another iPad application that is being embraced by educators to help develop and publish digital books that include pictures, music, narration, text and other elements. Whether it is a cookbook, scrapbook, group story, or poetry anthology, students are able to be "real" published authors and illustrators and share their unique contributions to an audience that can be local and global through these modern technologies.

From Khan Academy to MathTrain.tv, most mobile apps, computer software and games use the mastery learning approach to individualized learning providing badges, levels of each step with a star or certificates of accomplishment as well as allows user to interact with others showcasing their work and accomplishments in other social networking sites such as facebook. Additionally, Social Interaction Technologies and Collaboration Software have been changing the way we experience our world. GPS and SIS technologies are no longer for the corporation, government and media professionals. Software such as google earth, facebook, and skype are successfully adopted by many, although their use in education is still in its infancy. (Hendron, 2008, p. 238). From developing and showcasing digital portfolios (google sites) to posting online reflections and journals (wordpress), co-writing books (wikibooks), collecting data (GPS device) and co-creating interactive maps (communitywalk) to co-producing digital stories (voicethread), new mobile technologies is increasingly being used for educational and lifelong learning environments. GPS? SIS technologies provide new space for its participants to co-construct meaning using multilingual (Google Translator) and multimedia (slideshare) tools. The usage of social interaction software develops opportunities and supports "Open Learning" practices and processes, and promotes exchanges, connections, and collaboration among people who share common ideas and interests. Participants are bricoleur (Levi-Strauss, 1998) where they are the author as well as the cast, collector, and the director of their projects. In this participatory culture, content of the knowledge is co-constructed by the participants.

Research documents how Global Positioning System (GPS) and Social Interaction Software (SIS) can be used to support traditional literacy practices as well as facilitate the further development of multiple and critical literacies. According to Jenkins, Purushotma, Clinton, Weigel, and Robinson (2006), "The new literacies almost all involve social skills developed through collaboration and networking. These skills build on the foundation of traditional literacy, research skills, technical skills, and critical analysis skills taught in the classroom. (p. 4)" National Standards such as International Society for Technology in Education (ISTE) and International Reading Association (IRA) advocates the use a wide range of instructional tools, and curriculum materials to support instruction and promotes access for students to a new media and technologies in classrooms and libraries.

The Partnership for 21st Century Skills (2007) suggests that teaching and learning in the 21st century requires that students and teachers have:

subject specific knowledge, learning skills, use 21st century tools to foster learning, teach and learn in the 21st century context, connect learning to the real world, and use assessments that measure 21st century learning. Therefore, in our study, our twelve students and I got familiar with GPS and SIS technology to better prepare ourselves for the literacy demands we encounter as global citizens in the 21st century.

With the advent of new handheld devices such as GPS and social interaction software, there will be an expanded access to alternative resources and global connections. Teaching and learning have potential to be a continuous life-long process; it is personalized, learner-centered, situated, collaborative, and ubiquitous. Suter, Alexander, and Kaplan (2005) summarized the notion of social interaction software "as a tool (for augmenting human social and collaborative abilities), as a medium (for facilitating social connection and information interchange), and as an ecology (for enabling a 'system of people, practices, values, and technologies in a particular local environment')." (p.48)

Growing number of initiatives and projects directed for K16 education such as Oercommons. org[1] were shared during the workshop not only to seek out for teaching and learning content around the world but also to share and showcase our multilingual multimedia projects such as World Digital Library (http://www.oercommons.org/libraries/world-digital-library), attend online conferences and webinars (e.g. Global Education Conference -http://www.globaleducationconference.com/) and collaborate others using Web 2.0 features (e.g. classroom 2.0 - http://www.classroom20.com/).

Mejias (2006) wrote in response to his teaching and using social interaction software in his classrooms: "Social interaction software allows students to participate in distributed research communities that extend spatially beyond their classroom and school, beyond a particular class session or term, and technologically beyond the tools and resources that the school makes available to the students."

Despite all the concerns and challenges integrating social interaction technologies into the curriculum, there is a growing number of research and support by academics. For instance, Digital Youth Research [http://digitalyouth.ischool.berkeley.edu/] is a collaborative project that studies number of empirical and theoretical work on youth subcultures, new media, and popular culture. Wesch (2008a) argued the importance of welcoming social media into the classroom as powerful learning tools and wrote: "When students recognize their own importance in helping to shape the future of this increasingly global, interconnected society, the significance problem fades away." (p.7)

MAPS, MATH, MEDIA PROJECT

There is a huge impact GPS and SIS make in our teaching that has implications for global education, creativity and collaboration among our participants. In our projects, we explored wide range of meanings participants associated with Global Positioning System (GPS) and Social Interaction Software (SIS); impact of 21st century tools and activities such as gallery walk, geocaching and digital video in the curriculum; and ways in which participants integrated mobile technologies and SIS into their multilingual multimedia projects.

Teacher candidates argued challenges and advantages of mobile devices as classroom tools; developed skills in deconstructing existing curricula for improving student outcomes. Participants co-created Multilingual Digital Stories integrating mobile technologies and social interaction software (i.e, wikis, google earth) to foster connectivity among the students, faculty and community. Their projects focused on the role of multiliteracies (i.e. numerical, geographical and media literacy) through the lens of multiculturalism.

The purpose of this study was to meaningfully integrate geography, mathematics and social networking sites into "Maps, Math, and Media" workshops as a means of further developing their 21st century skills and to develop innovative interdisciplinary multilingual multimedia projects and teaching strategies and possibilities of integrating global literacies with limited resources and equipment in global education context. Our goal was to: a) To present the role of new technologies in order to argue the challenges and advantages of Global Positioning System (GPS) and Social Interaction Software (SIS) in K-16 curriculum across content area s (i.e. math, geography, cultural studies); b) To introduce maps and media across content areas in developing multiple literacies (i.e information, technology, geography, media literacy): c) To demonstrate creative strategies and possibilities for engaging K-16 students in meaningful integration of 21st century literacy activities while incorporating math, maps and media.

Today new generation use variety of mediums to communicate and form communities of interest outside "the classroom." There is an obvious disconnect between current educational practices and what the students are exposed to in their daily lives. Social Interaction Technologies and Collaboration Software have changed the way we experience our world. From showcasing digital portfolios (google sites) to posting online reflections and journals (wordpress); co-writing books (wikibooks) to co-producing digital stories (voicethread); co-creating interactive maps (mapsengine.google) to collecting data (GPS device) to solve community based issues, new technologies are increasingly being used for educational and lifelong learning environments as part of 21st century skill. The usage of social interaction software develops opportunities and supports "Open Learning" practices and processes, and promotes exchanges, connections, and collaboration among people who share common ideas and interests.

H5 TO NATURE PROJECT

In Fall 2008, I was assigned to teach a differentiated instruction course to teacher candidates in various subject fields. It gave me an opportunity to rethink and redesign the way I teach. I decided to model and showcase the differentiated instruction theories and approaches in the class and provide activities that students can engage in various disciplines and subject fields. I read and inspired by various GPS projects such as Hopeworks (http://www.hopeworks.org/) in Camden, NJ that energizes youth to become producer of knowledge using GPS devices. I wrote a mini grant to get a GPS data collecting device and developed an interdisciplinary Hi5 to Nature project involving my teacher candidates. We have developed, coordinated and conducted the Hi5 to Nature based on this differentiated instruction course.

For this project, we collaborated with our curriculum librarian at the university. She provided library instruction, research skills to my students and helped me prepare a gallery walk on integrating geography into every subject field. Teacher candidates received an information literacy support from the library and they collected activities and resources for their research over a couple of month period. For their project, teacher candidates deconstructed and assessed the national and local curriculum and standards; interviewed educators, expert in the fields, and documented their research in order to articulate their analysis, and dialog. Each week, they wrote a journal[2] on their findings, discoveries, and completed tasks. They responded to each other, shared resources on their social networking site that was created and managed by themselves. I was part of their social network as a guest.

For Girl Scout students, my teacher candidates and I developed an outdoor experiential learning activity that we called Hi5 (Hiking for Health, Happiness, Head, Hand and Heart) to Nature. While our teacher candidates were working on their unit and I was working on my Gallery Walk. I found out a local Junior Girl Scouts was looking for a hiking activity. I volunteered to developed an outdoor experiential learning activity that we called Hi5 (Hiking for Health, Happiness, Head, Hand and Heart) to Nature and I chose an unmarked trail called Buttermilk Falls in High Mountain Reserve in Wayne, NJ. Girl Scout leader told me this is their first hiking experience and most of them had never hiked before. Just like how I wanted to share my passion of geography across subject fields to my teacher candidates, I decided to develop Hi5 to Nature: Maps and Media project for the Girl Scouts. Hi5 stands for Hiking for Health, Happiness, Head, Hand and Heart.

Hi5 Nature involved Media Literacy, Technology, Environmental Science, Nature Ethics, Mathematics, and Community Service. The goal of the project was to showcase creative strategies and possibilities to my teacher candidates integrating mobile devices such as GPS device and provide a rich educational experience to Girl Scout students including science to environmental ethics. Before I took the scouts, I explored the neighboring hiking trails to organize a hiking experience that could take approximately 2 hours and hiked on this unmarked trail three times with my GPS device. After being lost twice, on my third trial I became familiar with the trail and also buried number of items (e.g. hand sanitizers, pens, coins) for our scavenger hunt, recorded the coordinates. I also explored the plants and rock formations and added what I saw to the list of items for the scouts to locate. Then, I started exploring the web for further information and printed information and scavenger hunt for the juniors. I wanted to make sure that they could explore the trail with purpose. My primary goal was to emphasize the ethics of hiking and to make sure this hiking experience was enjoyable, educational so that they would be encouraged to hike in future.

Fifteen junior scouts, two scout leaders and two parents participated in our first educational hiking project that included a GPS device and scavenger hunt (geocaching.com). Juniors were given a quick survey and a list of instructions[2] and items such a gloves and bags to collect garbage prior to their hiking experience. They were told to be kind and considerate to the lives of animals and plants, staying in the trail. They were told to just take pictures and leave only their foot prints. We each took turn exploring the GPS device and checked our coordinates and the map view of our location.

First, we passed through a creek. I had to point them out it was dried. We discussed how we need to be observant on how the creeks may dry and how the leaves in the Fall season may hide the trails. After that, Juniors started checking the items that they saw on the trail more carefully. They were excited about learning new things. For instance, we all learned different types of trees and compared their leaves. Most confusing ones were sycamore and maple tree leaves. At the end of the day, they learned different rock formations (i.e. shale, conglomerate rock) and different plants on our way to Buttermilk Fall.

Juniors exercised their body, used their hands to clean the trail while hiking, their head to explore rocks, plants and animal habitats, and their heart to be sensitive to the nature. Except one junior reported having a tick, our overall the hiking experience was memorable. They all were tired and happy at the end and even some clearly indicated they had fun and would love to hike again. Juniors not only enjoyed outdoor and learned about various plants, rock formations, they also cleaned up the garbage on the trail. They were happy to be part of this experiential learning opportunity. They certainly had a Hi5 to nature. As a final stage of our hiking experience, scouts were invited to add their pictures and stories on the community walk page.[3]

Research Participants

This research is based on the participatory action research (PAR) conducted while teaching transdisciplinary technology courses and professional development workshops related to mobile learning and investigated over 15 high school student and 40 teacher candidates in a state university in the United States and over 10 high school student and 10 K12 teachers in Turkmenistan.

The participants first de-constructed maps, learned basic map terminology, explored Gallery Walk by exploring maps and different projection of maps (e.g. upside down map, peters projection), later attended a geocaching activity using GPS device, and finally constructed their multilingual multimedia project of their choice. In some instances, due to availability of limited mobile technologies in Turkmenistan, participants worked on a group project. High school students borrowed the only available GPS device each day to collect data on bus routes in the city and eventually uploaded their waypoints and eventually made two maps one for bus routes in the city and later on historical cites for the tourist map in Turkmen, Russian and English. Each Turkmen participant knew English as well as Turkmen and Russian.

High school students during the 2011 and 2012 summer camp project created historical city map using communitywalk.com adding the pictures and video clips they took, links that they created using wikispaces based on research they conducted by interviewing, sorting facts and information for each historical site they visited during the camp. They shared their map on the internet and showcased their projects to their teachers, parents, as well as peers as a culminating activity at the end of the summer camp.

As an outcome of the educational technology courses, teacher candidates developed lesson plans integrating 9M model, presented their project in class and posted their lesson plan to their portfolio. Each candidate picked a topic or theme of their choice as long as they find the matching common core or state standard for the grade level they are planning to teach. After the introduction to Maps, Math, and Media modules, gallery walk, they were encouraged to develop lesson plans using The Universal Design for Learning – UDL (http://www.cast.org/udl/) model. Their UDL module lesson plans were designed using re-constructivist theory (Freire, 2002) focusing on global competencies and critical autonomy (Masterman, 1985/2001) and activism among K12 students who can research and co-construct meaningful multicultural multimedia projects that can be in the form of podcasts and digital stories among other products.

UNIVERSAL DESIGN FOR LEARNING

An important framework that is being used to support learners is Universal Design for Learning. The principles of Universal Design for Learning (UDL) have been compiled by David H. Rose, Ed.D., Co-Founder and Chief Education Officer at Center for Applied Special Technology (CAST), and Jenna Gravel, M.Ed., doctoral student at Harvard, and are based on research in the field of neuroscience. They have been studied and revised through the Center for Applied Special Technology (CAST) and have been put into practice in schools throughout the world. In using UDL principles to plan curriculum and activities, educators are taking into account the variability of all learners on the outset of a learning endeavor. This is a proactive approach to designing learning experiences and materials that are flexible and rich in ways to represent and engage with content, and options for the expression and assessment of student understanding.

According to the latest version of the UDL Guidelines put forth by the National Center on the Universal Design for Learning, the three main principles of Universal Design for Learning are to provide multiple means of representation, action and expression, and engagement (CAST, 2011). This framework addresses the need to consider the different networks that come into play, or the "what," "how," and "why" of learning (CAST, 2011). The UDL Guidelines go further to include specific recommendations for each principle. For multiple means of representation, it is important that educators offer options and alternatives for visual and auditory information, offer clarity and support for language, expressions and symbols, and options for comprehension in order to assist learners in processing new information (CAST, 2011). For multiple means of action and expression, curriculum should be designed so that there are options for learners in terms of physical action, choice of various tools and media to compose and communicate, and scaffolding of learner's skills and executive functions (CAST, 2011). And, in providing multiple means of engagement, it is essential that educators optimize student affect and motivation to engage student interest and persistence, such as being mindful of what is of relevant and meaningful to learners (CAST, 2011). These research-based recommendations, when applied to educational practice, help students of all abilities and backgrounds have opportunities to be appropriately challenged, accommodated and supported (110th Congress, 2007).

Research studies of the implementation of Universal Design for Learning have been conducted over many years and yield results that inform and shape the UDL Guidelines as they evolve, as well as point to effective practices in various learning situations. Of particular interest to our work are the studies of classrooms that share findings in relation to mobile technologies, multimedia, multicultural, and multilingual use, with a student-centered approach, such as inquiry- and project-based learning.

In a research project that spanned two years, the use of mobile technologies in primary-level Early French Immersion classes to support inclusive strategies for instruction was examined (Pellerin, 2013). IPods, iPads, and laptop computers were available for daily use by the teachers and students, and digital applications such as audio books and apps to record students' voices, augmented traditional materials such as leveled books. Key findings were that "the use of digital technologies contributed to the development of new and more inclusive instructional strategies" and that "the use of digital technologies provided multiple means of representation, action and expression, and engagement, based on the UDL Framework" (Pellerin, 2013). Pellerin (2013) indicated that

Integrating the use of digital devices such as iPods and iPads allowed the teachers to adopt new instructional strategies that included more individualized and guided practice, as well as a more student-centered approach. Students became more engaged in their learning and displayed greater autonomy during learning activities. As a result, teachers felt empowered to shift their instructional approach from a teacher-centered or transmission-oriented approach to a more student-centered approach. (Pellerin, 2013, p. 53)

Teachers participating in the study reported that the mobile technologies enabled them to design learning experiences that were more responsive to the needs and interests of their students, as well as provide alternative options for assessment, including recordings in audio and video formats, that served to document individual student learning in new ways and could inform further support through scaffolding and modifications of instruction (Pellerin, 2013). The findings outlined how the use of the mobile technologies supported the UDL principles in specific ways. For example, students had access to books in printed and audio formats and were given opportunities to choose what books to read or listen to based on individual interest and ability, were able to read or listen alone or with peers, and were encouraged to discuss the readings in groups. In having these options, the barriers to accessing the text were reduced for students who might have otherwise struggled, and teachers reported that by having the digital tools available students were more autonomous as they did not have to rely as often on adult assistance with the text (Pellerin, 2013). In terms of providing multiple means of action and expression, the mobile devices enabled students to use various modalities to share their thoughts and demonstrate what they know. By creating oral recordings using apps such as *Show Me*, students were able to speak their ideas and listen back to them. For some students, this removed the barriers of writing with pen and paper who might have struggled with fine motor skills or written composition. Instead, students were able to first record their ideas and then go back to listen and write them down. According to Pellerin (2013), "the use of alternative ways of expression was beneficial to all learners in the respective classrooms, because it provided opportunities to develop the wider range of expression associated with the communicative skills necessary for the 21st century." Additionally, findings in this research project suggest that the mobile tools did indeed offer multiple means of engagement that served to increase motivation and focus on the learning tasks (Pellerin, 2013).

It was noted that in the areas of fluency and skill practice, teachers observed higher levels of engagement with the use of the technological tools, particularly for students who were struggling, otherwise reluctant or who had attention disorders (Pellerin, 2013). For instance, in a Grade 4 classroom, students preferred working on reading fluency using the iPad rather than read aloud to others. The teacher reported "they liked the idea that they could listen to the recording of their voice and identify their own mistakes without fear of being ridiculed by others" (Pellerin, 2013). As a result of this research project, Pellerin concludes that instructional approaches that include principles of Universal Design for Learning and the use of mobile tools enhance learning through the opportunities to support all learners. (Pellerin, 2013).

Basham & Marino (2013) assert that in STEM education, the integration of the fields of Science, Technology, Engineering, and Mathematics, the Universal Design for Learning framework can improve learning experiences for diverse learners as well as increase the accessibility of learning materials in these curriculum areas. An emphasis on design, problem-solving, and reflection is inherent in this discipline as well as in developing educational experiences within various constraints. In creating learning activities that promote engagement, provide instructional supports, and advance higher-level thinking skills, UDL principles offer ways to accommodate individual variability and maximize learning opportunities for all students (Basham & Marino, 2013). Basham and Marino (2013) recommend that "teachers should employ a variety of evidence-based teaching practices such as ... guided inquiry, supporting multiple literacies, and instructional scaffolding, as well as incorporate technology tools (e.g., iPads, books, movies, software) to enhance students' content knowledge and metacognitive skills." Educators should also be considerate of the necessity of developing curriculum and materials through a design process that involves the continuous collection and analysis of data that informs redesign to improve instructional outcomes (Basham & Marino, 2013). The UDL framework outlines ways to plan for the presentation of, engagement in, and expression of learning content so that every student has the opportunity to become an expert learner. By offering flexible and varied materials, strategies, assessments and tools in the context of STEM as well as other content areas, educators provide diverse learners with supportive environments to develop skills and knowledge.

Preparing and Assisting Teachers in Implementing Effective Practices with Mobile Technologies

As mobile technologies are increasingly being provided as tools in classrooms and schools, it is becoming more important to prepare and train teachers to learn more about these technologies and the pedagogies that shape the use and effective integration in the design of modern learning experiences. The wave of mobile technologies is making its way into classrooms in many forms ranging from school and district-wide adoption of one type of device (such as iPads or Chromebooks), to smaller-scale implementation of devices available via movable carts or kits for classroom sharing or sign-out, as well as "bring your own device/technology" (also known as BYOD or BYOT) for which students and their families furnish the devices of either one type or one of their own choosing (such as a smartphone or tablet). No matter the specifics of the technology influx and its related infrastructure and technical issues, there is a growing need to rethink not only the role of the devices in the learning process but the larger questions of how teachers can design environments and reimagine how learning takes places in and out of the classroom. Most teachers are working with what they are given and required to do by administrators and mandates, and have limited control over issues of time, resources, and other factors that directly impact what can be done in the classroom.

In our work with pre- and in-service teachers we are well-aware that there are barriers and stumbling blocks to as well as constant change in the field of education and technology, but we have successfully utilized a number of strategies in helping teachers and teacher candidates in their professional learning about the integration of mobile tools. First, we have found that it is optimal that each teacher has his or her own device to use during the training so that the experience is as personal and hands-on as possible. Teachers have reported that they appreciate the time and opportunity to work at their own pace and on apps that they choose rather than be asked to spend the time watching a demonstration or sharing devices. We have also found it very helpful to share a list of apps that will be used in the workshop prior to the session so that the workshop time is spent more effectively. This also gives the participants the chance to have assistance before the workshop should they need help with logins, passwords or other technical issues. Another successful strategy is to have professional learning resources available during and after the workshop in both paper and digital formats. Sharing links, recommendations, and descriptions of applications allows the teachers to spend less time taking notes and more time interacting and engaging.

In preparing and presenting the workshop, it is most helpful to know as much as possible about the teacher audience such as the grade levels, subject areas, and levels of experience with the technology so that pertinent applications and examples can be provided. And, having teachers introduce themselves and telling the group about their goals for attending and their experiences in their respective teaching situations yields a collegial environment for learning in which people are more likely to share ideas with each other. It is of utmost importance to have a workshop facilitator that understands the demands of the teacher's position, experience with a variety of apps and tools, makes relevant connections between technology and curricular goals, and creates a comfortable learning environment for the teachers to explore and talk with each other. We have found that when the teachers become more fluent with the devices and apps, and are aware of the ways others are successfully integrating them, they are more willing to try new tools in their teaching situations.

USE OF MOBILE APPS

Handal, El-Khoury, Campbell, & Cavanagh (2013) make a case for the advantageousness of mobile learning in mathematics education and share a framework that categorizes mobile apps that can help teachers determine how to integrate the technologies into the curriculum. Within three clusters of tools they describe as investigative, productivity, and instructive, they specifically label apps in nine categories as "(1) emulation, (2) simulation, (3) guided discovery, (4) measurement, (5) drawing/graphing, (6) composing, (7) informative, (8) drill and practice, and (9) tutorial apps (Handal, El-Khoury, Campbell, & Cavanagh, 2013, p144)." The instructional role of the technology tools and the teacher depends on the types of tasks and activities the students are working on and the context of the learning situation planned by the teacher. For example, students who use apps that offer opportunities for guided discovery, tutorials, and simulations may explore concepts on their own with the teacher as facilitator. The ability to engage in problem-solving, authentic, open-ended, and interactive activities can empower students using mobile apps to direct their learning and build understanding. (Handal, El-Khoury, Campbell, & Cavanagh, 2013).

In our work, we have paid particular attention to mobile tools that offer flexibility and multi-modal options to support various tasks as we strive to meet the needs of all learners. The framework for use of mobile apps in mathematics outlined by Handal, El-Khoury, Campbell, & Cavanagh (2013) prove helpful in sharing strategies for teachers in learning about and choosing apps for implementation in their classrooms. Composing apps have been a big part of our teacher workshops due to their open-endedness and usefulness across curriculum areas and for instructional and assessment purposes. Specifically, we find apps for screencasting and digital storytelling to be extremely versatile and usable in most teaching and learning situations, whether is a one- or few- device classroom or a 1:1 model of implementation.

We have also found that often there are apps, whether in the same or different categories, that are effectively used in tandem to interactive with, capture, and demonstrate ideas and understanding. Often we will design activities that pair investigative apps and productivity apps so users can engage in exploration of a concept, create something related to it, and share a product all using the same device. Also, the built in features such as the camera, microphone, and speakers are being integrated into more and more apps to provide multi-modal mobile tools, recordings, and experiences.

One example of pairing apps in this way using iPads is the combination of an informative app (*Google Earth*) and a drawing app (*Skitch*) to support learning in the area of geometry. Teachers explored maps and views in *Google Earth* by zooming in and out, panning the screen, and searching for particular locations by name or address. Geometric concepts and terms that relate to angles, lines, shapes, etc. can be pointed out in authentic contexts. Vocabulary such as "intersecting" and "acute" and concepts such as perimeter and polygons can be illustrated with a map app in meaningful ways. Teachers were taught how to take a screen capture to save the map image on the screen so that it can be used in another application. We opened the *Skitch* app to show how a saved image can be annotated over in a variety of ways. Depending on the purpose of the activity, teachers and students can freehand draw on top of the image with different color pen ink, add arrows to point to areas of the image, type in text boxes that can move over the picture to label different items, and then save the screen as new image on the device for further use that might include emailing it to the teacher, posting it on a class webpage, and exporting it to another app for additional work (such as to add a voice recording).

We have also used two composing apps in tandem to create a collaborative body of work and/or to make use of the unique features of different apps in creating multimedia products. One example of this is the use of the app *PicCollage* to create a digital poster and then the app *Tellagami* to create a talking movie with the custom background and a personalized avatar. *PicCollage* is an easy-to-use app that allows the user to add selected images and inputted text to the screen and then have the ability to save, share, and export the finished collage. Teachers and students are designing digital collages that include photographs and text headings and captions for purposes ranging from building background knowledge of a time period prior to reading a novel by creating a collage of historical pictures, to building a visual dictionary of terms and images taken in the classroom environment or from the internet to support language learning and academic vocabulary. The finished collage can be saved in *Photos* and then imported into the *Tellagami* app as a background for users who then type or record their message to then be made into an animated movie that can be exported out of the app for sharing or additional work. Other examples include creating scenes in apps such as *Yakit* and *PuppetPals* and then importing them into apps like *iMovie* and *Videolicious* to produce longer movies. Another way apps are being combined is in the authoring of multimedia ebooks using apps such as *StoryKit* and *Book Creator* and adding elements created in other apps like *BuddyPoke* and *GarageBand*. The app-combination approach works particularly well for collaborative work and in situations where iPads are shared and rotated among students as they create and then can be exported.

INSTRUCTIONAL APPROACHES IN HIGHER EDUCATION AND PROFESSIONAL DEVELOPMENT

Pre- and in-service teachers were provided with various approaches for learning about and with mobile technologies. Each facilitator provided a combination of demonstration and hands-on practice as well as opportunities for discussion, sharing, and reflection in all scenarios. There were instances of whole-group technology use, small-group exploration and individual, self-directed examination of the devices and applications. Participants were provided with an iPad if they did not have access to their own personal devices. In many instances, teachers and teacher candidates used multiple devices during the sessions, including Smartphones, tablets, and laptops made by different manufacturers. The professional learning classes and workshops were focused on technology tools with emphasis on curriculum connections. Participants were provided with paper handouts as well as online resources for use during and after the training to help support a dynamic learning environment during which the facilitator(s) could walk around and offer support to the teacher-learners as desired.

In one scenario, a class of undergraduate teacher education students spent one class session examining how mobile technologies can support learning in Math and Science with a Universal Design for Learning approach. Participants were given the opportunity to rotate through four stations, each with a different technology focus, with the goal of discovering how these tools could be used to support content area learning and the creation of digital products. By structuring the learning environment into four learning stations--Multimedia Content Apps, Screencasting, Creating and Annotating with Apps, and Digital

Storytelling--the teacher candidates were able to work in small groups to make discoveries and engage with the devices, the two facilitators, and each other as desired. The undergraduates were instructed to complete a reflection piece, specifically addressing their own content-related topic they are working on as part of a larger, ongoing course project.

Professional learning workshops for in-service teachers consisted of either a one-day workshop held outside of their school buildings, typically in a university classroom or training facility, or a half-day workshop held in a conference room in the school building as part of an ongoing series of training days. Most of the participating teachers had self-selected the option to attend the workshop for the particular technology-related topic. Topics included "Using iPads for Projects Across the Curriculum," "Surprisingly Simple Movie-Making and Video Production Using the iPad," "Technology Tools, Applications and Resources To Support Math Education," and "Digital Storytelling and More!" The participating teachers were given the list of apps to download in advance so that the workshop time could be used more efficiently to focus on the applications. The learning environments were designed to promote active participation and dialogue among the teachers. In setting up the room in a U shape configuration, and by providing curated resources in both paper and online formats, the facilitator had more opportunities to address the needs and goals of each individual participant.

Inquiry Based Multilingual Multicultural Projects: Example

A fifth-grade teacher implemented a project with her students that utilized mobile technology and supported the principles of Universal Design for Learning. The classroom teacher in this case study, and her co-teacher who provides in-class support, attended workshops that focused on open-ended applications and tools available for the iPad. The teacher designed a project to support her students' learning of science, in particular, the classification of animals. In this project, students were given the assignment to work in pairs to research, create, and present what they learned to the class. The students were provided with an animal group, a list of characteristics to research, iPads and with several recommended apps already downloaded to use for the project, and other materials and resources to utilize. The teacher allotted class time for students to research their particular animal group, as well as time to create and produce both a digital and poster presentation. Students were given a rubric in advance that detailed the required components and the point value for completing the requirements. The project took several days to complete. It should be noted that there are students in this class that receive special services for various academic and other needs.

In this project, Universal Design for Learning guidelines were implemented and provided opportunities for all students to engage with the learning content and compose products using multiple media. The teacher left it up to the students to determine what resources to use to research ie. digital text, images, video, etc. (with the exception of requiring that at least one book be used as a source of information). Use of the iPads provided opportunities to utilize flexible digital resources and applications that incorporate speech and other auditory recordings. This project was designed so that different products could be made, and the results were varied and creative. Most students created talking videos that were shared in class and posted online. Two apps that were popular were *Tellagami* and *Yakit*. Using the app *Tellagami* students chose a custom background such as the habitat in which the animal lives and created an avatar on the screen that speaks the students' own voice or typed text telling about the animal group. Another app students used was *Yakit*, which allowed students to add a moving mouth to a picture of the animal that they imported to the screen and then record their voice to make it seem like the animal was animated. All of the students' movies were shared in class and online using a special YouTube channel.

After the project was completed, the participating teachers reflected on the process and offered valuable insights and feedback. The teachers shared that there was high student interest to work on the project and that every student participated; in their words, "everyone had a mission." They also indicated that there were no behavior problems in the classroom during the entire project. An aspect of the project that was unexpected was the time that it took to complete the work. One reason was that since there were some new apps on the iPads there were a few extra steps needed to configure them to have permission to use the camera and microphone. An notable comment from the teachers was that they noticed that many of the students did not prefer to have their own "normal" voice recorded in their projects, but instead either typed it to be read digitally or changed the pitch of their voice to make it sound quite different. This demonstrates the significance of providing flexible and multi-modal options for sharing their work.

STRUCTURE OF THE MAPS, MATH, AND MEDIA WORKSHOP

In the study, 9M stands for Maps, Math, Media, Multicultural, Multilingual, Multimedia:

- Maps is for integrating geographical literacy, GPS, GIS, google earth;
- Math is for integrating logic, critical thinking;
- Media is for integrating Music, Video, Art, Poetry, Literature, and Cartoons;
- Multicultural is for integrating Global literacy, addressing the needs of all the students;
- Multilingual is for addressing the language diversity of the classroom;
- Multimedia is for integrating Mobile Technologies into the curriculum designing lessons focused on co-constructing knowledge and developing producers of knowledge in the classroom vs. consumers.

Prior to each Maps, Math, & Media workshop, the presentation area has been decorated with maps with different projection, laptop computers with interactive maps, games, video and music clips, and Ipads with apps. Depending on the number of participants and the availability of laptops or Ipads, we provided various multimedia projects and slideshows around the room. In addition, participants were provided with books related to Art in Geography, Cartography, Environmental Ethics, GPS/ GIS in Education and even links to music in a Ipod touch such as "Follow the Drinking Gourd"- the lyrics of this song served as a map to freedom via the Underground Railroad.

Participants were given a questionnaire some in print and some online4 to determine their prior knowledge and also the post survey after completing the workshop. Girl scout groups and the youth groups in Turkmenistan completed the questionnaire in a paper format due to limited mobile devices. Vocabulary relating to this visual medium were presented and discussed. These terms include but are not limited to: latitude and longitude, Global Positioning System (GPS), Social Interaction Software (SIS), geocaching, Web 2.0, social networking, ning, and googleearth, KML file, waypoint. Formally presenting this information at the beginning of the session will facilitate participants' ability to explore and participate in the virtual activities that follow.

After the formal introduction to workshop that I presented in Ashabat Turkmenistan and New Jersey, USA and a three minute slideshow about USA to Turkmen participants and Turkmenistan to USA participants, all participants were invited to explore a Gallery Walk1 that was designed for exploring the role of and different types of maps, google earth and various interactive map tools and games. Gallery Walk for this project was a collection of artifacts (i.e. maps, pictures, posters, audio and video clips) designed to showcase the importance of geography across content areas. It also provided learning centers for each individual to interact and complete the tasks while interacting in group discussions and writing responses. There were different maps were available for participants to view and explore. The participants wrote their reactions and questions next to these maps. Teachers and teacher candidates were asked to discuss the significance and possibilities for incorporating these maps and technology across curriculum areas.

Maps, Math and Media Activities (Suggested Sample Activities)

Station 1-Giving Directions: Please give direction to get to X from our current location. There are more than one way to give directions. Are you comfortable giving directions? Do you draw maps, provide landmarks? Multiple ways to see and learn. We will provide books and material and bibliography on children's books.

Station 2-Printed Maps: Pleas explore different maps with various orientation and leave a note what you learned. What made you surprised? Why are there different representation?

Station 3-Community Walk: Explore maps on communitywalk.com created by high school students and view their historical site project linking their research, picture, video and the GPS coordinates on a their community walk map.

Station 4-Upside Down Map: Look at the video clip- http://www.odt.org/Pictures/map.mp4 or http://www.odt.org/Pictures/mapsmall.mov Please discuss what other ways we may be able to map the world. What about drawing maps side up? Why is it important to bring alternative maps into the classroom?

Station 5-GPS in the Classroom: Go though the attached slides and write how you may be able to include maps/ GIS/ geography in your classroom/ discipline.

Station 6-Layered Maps on GoogleEarth: Check Google earth and find Ataturk Dam and layered maps. You can see the changes between 1976 to today. Record your changes and share with the class. This activity is intended to show them how the ecology will change based on human intervention on the earth by comparing maps in two different era.

After the gallery walk activity, participants had hands on experience with using GPS devices as well as to use new technologies to develop interactive maps and social interaction modules online. First, participants engaged in Geocaching - high-tech treasure hunting game using GPS device. After geocaching, they continued to explore GPS and SIS software such as googleearth.com and communitywalk.com, collecting data using GPS device (Turkmen students collected data on the bus routes and historical sites in the city of Ashgabat while the student in New Jersey created historical map of their town in NJ) and created interactive maps and online projects of their own.

Our investigation was guided by these questions:

- What are the participants' personal experiences and reactions in GPS, SIS and geocaching and mapping and multimedia projects?
- What skills, methods, strategies, and tools do we need to provide to our students to improve 21st century skills and global competencies?
- How do we design and implement culturally and linguistically responsive curriculum that is community based, globally connected instruction models with limited resources and equipment? How to design differentiated and effective interdisciplin-

ary instruction (e.g integrating world languages, math, geography, and media literacy) using mobile technologies?
- What common problems and discoveries do the participants share during the process of co-creating projects such as developing maps and using GPS and SIS?
- What suggestions do participants make in order to improve teaching and learning?

Methodology includes analysis of background and digital media surveys, process papers, video narratives, questionnaires, electronic journals and reflection papers, responses to online activities and the process of producing documentaries, transcripts of interviews, and the content analysis of multimedia projects and presentations. The study used three theoretical framework; multicultural education, global competency and 21st Century Teaching Skills.

Lessons Learned from the Teacher Education Faculty and Teacher Candidates

Participants' voices and their reaction to curriculum and multilingual and multicultural multimedia projects support our goal of the study. During the Maps, Math, and Media workshops, the teachers argued the challenges and advantages of integrating new media into Turkmen curriculum; developed 21st Century skills in researching and creating digital resources and media messages using ning, voicethread and community walk; examined their national curriculum and GPS/SIS software in developing global understanding; experienced how a critical approach to the study of new media combines knowledge, reflection, and action to promote educational equity, and prepares new generation to be socially responsible members of a multicultural, global society. Some Turkmen teachers worked on several multilingual multimedia projects such as voicethread.com project with my students in the US, developed interactive maps (e.g. communitywalk.com) projects involving their communities on issues from education to business, and creating podcasts and video narratives reflects not only on their experiences but also international issues and perspectives through their online contact to global community. Their stories articulate the realities of conditions in their schools through their research, analysis, and dialog.

One Turkmen teacher participant said, "We are grateful for giving us the courage to think and deconstruct." Another wrote, "This project gave me chance to reflect on my own teaching. I think about integrating Maps, Math, Media in all my classes." Although at the beginning, most of the teachers argued that they do not have mobile technologies available in their schools, each workshop, they found the activities and the resources engaging and helpful in understanding the role and unique characteristics of mobile technologies.

The participants repeatedly claimed that they were intimidated by the social software but they eventually enjoyed being part of the world community while we used skype, voicethread and created blogs. As one said, "I don't believe what you see on television or read on the Internet. After recently producing a my own video [podcast]; I believe anything is visually possible with the help of fancy equipment." By actively involving participants in producing media (i.e facebook, communitywalk, toondoo, wikis, blogs and digital stories), they understood the conventions of the medium and gained alternative points of view on their environment and renewed interest and commitment to community service. As they became the producers of their own media projects, they developed 21st Century skills, and became informed consumers and citizen of the world.

FUTURE RESEARCH DIRECTIONS

As the theme of the book focuses on Mobile Pedagogies, this chapter intend to provide voices from the field who has used and been using mobile technologies in co producing and co-developing multilingual book, digital stories, podcasts and E-portfolios using various mobile devices. As we continue to teach and learn from our teacher candidates, we hope using the M9 model will inspire them to learn a language or two, see their ELL students who speak another language as an asset not a deficit, prepare them for globally connected world.

CONCLUSION

With the help of mobile technologies, we hope to explore how the use of SIS and mobile devices in teacher education combine knowledge, reflection, and action; promote global literacies and mutual understanding; and prepares new generation to be responsible members of a multicultural, global society. Teachers were more encouraged to use mobile technologies in the classroom. By actively involving teacher candidates and in-service teachers in producing multilingual multimedia using mobile technologies, they understood the conventions of the medium, developed innovative projects and gained alternative points of view on new technologies in education and renewed interest and commitment to multilingual and multicultural inquiry based projects. As they became the producers of their own multimedia using various mobile technologies, they developed multicultural and multilingual curricula in teaching math and science for every student in the classroom in every ability and language proficiency level.

REFERENCES

Basham, J. D., & Marino, M. T. (2013). Understanding STEM Education and Supporting Students Through Universal Design for Learning. *Teaching Exceptional Children*, *45*(4), 8–15.

Blau, A. (2004). The future of independent media. *Deeper News*, *10*(1). Retrieved February 3, 2008, from http://www.gbn.com/ArticleDisplayServlet.srv?aid=34045

boyd, d. (2008). Why youth (heart) social network sites: The role of networked publics in teenage social life. In D. Buckingham (Ed.), *Youth, Identity, and Digital Media* (pp. 119-142). Cambridge, MA: MIT Press.

Brundrett, M., & Silcock, P. (2002). Achieving competence, success and excellence in teaching. New York, NY: Routledge.

Bugeja, M. (2008, January-February). The Age of Distraction: The Professor or the Processor? *The Futurist*, *42*(1), 66.

Burkhardt, G., Monsour, M., Valdez, G., Gunn, C., Dawson, M., Lemke, C., et al. (2003). *21st century skills: Literacy in the digital age*. Retrieved January 29, 2008, from http://www.ncrel.org/engauge

CAST. (2011). *Universal Design for Learning Guidelines version 2.0*. Wakefield, MA: Author. Retrieved from http://www.udlcenter.org/aboutudl/udlguidelines

Christie, A. (2007). Using GPS and geocaching engages, empowers & enlightens middle school teachers and students. *Meridian: A Middle School Computer Technologies Journal*, *10*. Retrieved September 19, 2009, from http://ncsu.edu/meridian/win2007/gps/index.htm

Collison, C., & Parcell, G. (2001). *Learning to fly: Practical lessons from one of the world's leading knowledge companies.* Milford, CT: Capstone Pub.

Cummins, J. (2007). Rethinking monolingual instructional strategies in multilingual classrooms. *Canadian Journal of Applied Linguistics, 10*(2), 221–240.

Driscoll, M. (2002). "Blended Learning: Let's get beyond the hype." IBM Global Services. Retrieved from https://www-07.ibm.com/services/pdf/blended_learning.pdf

Dyck, B. (2007, October 11). *VoiceThread.* Retrieved December 31, 2008, from Education World Web site: http://www.education-world.com/a_tech/columnists/dyck/dyck019.shtml

Eco, U. (1996, November 12). *From Internet to Gutenberg.* Retrieved February 3, 2008 from, http://www.italianacademy.columbia.edu/pdfs/lectures/eco_internet_gutenberg.pdf

Franklin, T., & Van Harmelen, M. (2007). *Web 2.0 for content for learning and teaching in higher education.* Retrieved February 3, 2008, from http://www.jisc.ac.uk/media/documents/programmes/digital_repositories/web2-content-learning-and-teaching.pdf

Freire, P. (2002). *Pedagogy of the oppressed.* New York, NY: Continuum.

Gould, E. (2003). *The university in a corporate culture.* New Haven, CT: Yale University Press.

Handal, B., El-Khoury, J., Campbell, C., & Cavanagh, M. (2013). *A framework for categorising mobile applications in mathematics education.* Retrieved from http://researchonline.nd.edu.au/cgi/viewcontent.cgi?article=1072&context=edu_conference

Haythornthwaite, C. (2000). Online personal networks: Size, composition and media use among distance learners. *New Media & Society, 2*(2), 195–226. doi:10.1177/14614440022225779

Hendron, J. G. (2008). RSS for educators: blogs, newsfeeds, podcasts, and wikis in the classroom. Washington, DC: Academic Press.

H.R. 4137--110th Congress: Higher Education Opportunity Act. (2007). In www.GovTrack.us. Retrieved December 28, 2013, from http://www.govtrack.us/congress/bills/110/hr4137

International Society for Technology in Education. (2007). *National educational technology standards for students: The next generation.* Retrieved January 18, 2008, from http://cnets.iste.org/NETS_S_standards-1-6.pdf

Ito, M., Horst, H., Bittanti, M., boyd d., Herr-Stephenson, B., Lange, P.G., Pascoe, C.J., & Robinson, L. (2008). *Living and Learning with New Media: Summary of Findings from the Digital Youth Project.* Chicago: The MacArthur Foundation. Retrieved Dec 31, 2008, from http://www.macfound.org/atf/cf/%7BB0386CE3-8B29-4162-8098-E466FB856794%7D/DML_ETHNOG_WHITEPAPER.PDF

Jenkins, H. (2006, October 20). *Confronting the challenges of participatory culture: Media education for the 21st century (part one).* Retrieved March 20, 2008, from http://www.henryjenkins.org/2006/10/confronting_the_challenges_of.html

Jenkins, H., Purushotma, R., Clinton, K., Weigel, M., & Robinson, A. (2006). *Confronting the challenges of participatory culture: Media education for the 21st century.* Chicago, IL: The MacArthur Foundation. Retrieved from http://www.newmedialiteracies.org/wp-content/uploads/pdfs/NMLWhitePaper.pdf

Kahn, R., & Keller, D. (2007). Paulo Freire and Ivan Illich: Technology, politics and the reconstruction of education. *Policy Futures in Education, 5*(4), 431–448. doi:10.2304/pfie.2007.5.4.431

Lary, L. M. (2004). Hide and seek: GPS and geocaching in the classroom. *Learning and Leading with Technology, 31*(6), 14–18.

Lévi-Strauss, C. (1998). *The savage mind*. London: Weidenfeld & Nicolson.

Lieberman, G. A., & Hoody, L. L. (1998). *Closing the achievement gap: Using the environment as an integrating context for learning*. San Diego, CA: State Education and Environment Roundtable.

Masterman, L. (1985/2001). *Teaching the media*. New York, NY: Routledge. doi:10.4324/9780203359051

Matherson, L., Wright, V., Inman, C., & Wilson, E. (2008). Get up, get out with geocaching: Engaging technology for the social studies classroom. *Social Studies Research and Practice, 3*(3), 80-85. Retrieved from http://www.socstrp.org/issues/PDF/3.3.6.pdf

Mejias, U. (2006, June/July). Teaching social software with social software. *Journal of Online Education, 2*(5).

New London Group. (2000). A pedagogy of multiliteracies: Designing social futures. In B. Cope, & M. Kalantzis (Eds.), *Multiliteracies: Literacy learning and the design of social futures* (pp. 9–38). London: Routledge.

Noon, D. (2007, June 14). Democracy 2.0. *Borderland*. Retrieved from http://borderland.northernattitude.org/2007/06/14/democracy-20

Oblinger, D., & Oblinger, J. L. (2005). *Educating the net generation*. Boulder, CO: EDUCAUSE.

Oldenburg, R. (1999). *The great good place: Cafes, coffee Shops, bookstores, bars, hair salons and other hangouts at the heart of a community* (2nd ed.). New York, NY: Marlowe & Company.

Owen, M., Grant, L., Sayers, S., & Facer, K. (2006). Social software and learning. Futurelab. Retrieved from http://www.futurelab.org.uk/research/opening_education.htm

Partnership for 21st Century Skills. (2007, July 23). *Framework for 21st century learning*. Retrieved from http://www.21stcenturyskills.org/documents/frameworkflyer_072307.pdf

Pellerin, M. (2013). E-inclusion in Early French Immersion Classrooms: Using Technologies to Support Inclusive Practices That Meet the Needs of All Learners. *Canadian Journal of Education, 36*(1), 44-70.

Pew Internet and American Life Project. (2007, December 19). *Teens and social media*. Retrieved from http://www.pewinternet.org/pdfs/PIP_Teens_Social_Media_Final.pdf

Prensky, M. (2005). *Search vs. research. Or, the fear of The Wikipedia overcome by new understanding for a digital era*. Retrieved from http://www.marcprensky.com/writing/Prensky-Search_vs_Research-01.pdf

Rheingold, H. (2008, October) *Writing, Reading, and Social Media Literacy Writing, Reading, and Social Media Literacy*. Harvard Business Publishing: Retrieved from http://discussionleader.hbsp.com/now-new-next/2008/10/the-importance-of-social-media.html

Rice, M. L., & Wilson, E. K. (1999). How technology aids constructivism in the social studies classroom. *Social Studies, 90*, 28–34. doi:10.1080/00377999909602388

Richardson, W. (2006). *Blogs, wikis, podcasts and other powerful web tools for classrooms*. Thousand Oaks, CA: Corwin Press.

Schlatter, B. E., & Hurd, A. R. (2005). Geocaching: 21st century hide and seek. *Journal of Physical Education, Recreation & Dance, 76*(7), 28–32. doi:10.1080/07303084.2005.10609309

Shaunessy, E., & Page, C. (2006). Promoting inquiry in the gifted classroom through GPS and GIS technologies. *Gifted Child Today*, *29*(4), 42–53.

Soukup, C. (2006). Computer-mediated communication as a virtual third place: Building Oldenburg's great good places on the World Wide Web. *New Media & Society*, *8*, 421–440. doi:10.1177/1461444806061953

Srinivasan, R. (2006). Where information society and community voice intersect. *The Information Society*, *22*(5), 355–365. doi:10.1080/01972240600904324

Stimson, B. (2007, October). *An Educator's Manifesto! Arise! You have nothing to lose but your chains!* Classroom 2.0. Retrieved from http://www.classroom20.com/forum/topics/649749:Topic:56987

Suter, V., Alexander, B., & Kaplan, P. (2005). Social software and the future of conferences—Right now. *EDUCAUSE Review*, *40*(1).

Tucker, P. (2007, January-February). The overmediated world. *The Futurist*, *16*, 12–13.

UNESCO. (2012). Turning on mobile learning: Global themes. Paris, France: United Nations Educational, Scientific and Cultural Organization.

Unsworth, L.(2008). Multiliteracies, e-literature and English teaching. *Language and Education: International Journal*, *22* (1).

VirtualAbility. (2008). *Virtual Ability Our People*. Retrieved from Virtual Ability, Inc. Web site: http://virtualability.org/ourpeople.aspx

Wesch, M. (2008a). Anti-Teaching: Confronting the Crisis of Significance. *Education Canada*, *48*(2), 4–7.

Wesch, M. (2008b, October 21). *A Vision of Students Today (& What Teachers Must Do)*. Britannica Blog. Retrieved from http://www.britannica.com/blogs/2008/10/a-vision-of-students-today-what-teachers-must-do/

ADDITIONAL READING

Ally, M. (2009). Mobile Learning: Transforming the Delivery of Education and Training. Retrieved from http://www.aupress.ca/index.php/books/120155

Arthus-Bertrand, Y. (2009). *6 billion others: Portraits of humanity from around the world*. New York: Abrams. E- Book English version. Retrieved from http://www.7billionothers.org/content/electronic-book

Cavus, N., & Ibrahim, D. (2009). M-learning: An experiment in using SMS to support learning new English language words. *British Journal of Educational Technology*, *40*(1), 78–91. doi:10.1111/j.1467-8535.2007.00801.x

Learning and Skills Development Agency. (2005). Mobile learning anytime everywhere: A book of papers from MLEARN 2004 Edited by Jill Attewell and Carol Savill-Smith Retrieved September 30, 2012, from http://elearning.typepad.com/thelearnedman/mobile_learning/reports/mLearn04_papers.pdf

Learning and Skills Development Agency. (2005). A technology update and m-learning project summary (J. Attewell, Ed.). Retrieved from. http://www.m-learning.org/archive/docs/The%20m-learning%20project%20-%20technology%20update%20and%20project%20summary.pdf

UNESCO. (2012). *Mobile learning for teachers: Global themes*. Paris, France: United Nations Educational, Scientific and Cultural Organization.

United States Agency for International Development (USAID). (2011). Mobile phones, eBooks turning the page on education. Frontlines. September/October. Retrieved from.http://www.usaid.gov/press/frontlines/fl_sep11/FL_sep11_EDU_MOBILE.html

World Bank. (2011). The Use of Mobile phones in education in developing countries. Retrieved from.http://web.worldbank.org/WBSITE/EXTERNAL/TOPICS/EXTEDUCATION/0,,contentMDK:22267518~pagePK:148956~piPK:216618~theSitePK:282386,00.html

KEY TERMS AND DEFINITIONS

21st Century Skills: It is outlined by the Partnership for 21st Century Skills (http://www.p21.org/) as 21st century teaching and learning skills that are required by students and teachers in order to have subject specific knowledge, learning skills, use 21st century tools to foster learning, teaching in the 21st century context, connect learning to the real world, and use assessments that measure 21st century learning.

Acceptable Use Policies (AUP): AUP is a document with a set of rules developed by schools and school districts to prevent potential legal action, to inform parents of the use of new media and technologies in the school, and to provide guidelines for educators and students.

Avatar: An avatar is a representation of a person or character in graphical form in 2 or 3 dimensions. A user may create and use an avatar in their likeness while participating in digital spaces, such as online games, virtual worlds, or internet communities. There are applications that allow users to create customized avatars as characters that can speak using computerized or recorded speech.

Badges: Digital badges are typically icons that represent a skill or achievement that has been earned. Badges may be earned from various websites or awarded by others. People usually display their badges online in a digital community, blog, game, or other online space to share their skills and accomplishments for public recognition.

Banking Education: In the banking concept of education, education is an act of depositing, in which the students are the depositories and the teacher is the depositor.

Bricoleur/Bricolage: A term used in the construction or creation of a work from a diverse range of things which happen to be available or a work created by such a process. It is in essence building by trial and error and is often contrasted to *engineering*: theory-based construction. A person who engages in bricolage is called a *bricoleur* and usually invents his or her own strategies for using existing materials in a creative, resourceful, and original way.

Critical Autonomy: The process by which a member of the audience is able to read a media text in a way other than the preferred reading. Also used to describe the ability of media literacy students to deconstruct texts outside the classroom.

Culturally and Linguistically Responsive Curriculum: It is a pedagogical approach involving the learner characteristics, having high expectations for all the students, providing student-centered instruction, connecting with families and their experiences, and reshaping the education based on the needs of the students.

Distributed Learning: Distributed learning can occur anytime, anywhere, in multiple locations, using one or more technologies. Learners complete courses and programs at home or work by communicating with faculty and other students through various forms of computer-mediated communication and Web-based technologies. Learners participate in classroom activities at their own pace and at a self-selected time.

English Language Learner (ELL): ELL is an English language learner who is learning

English as foreign language (EFL) or a English as a second (ESL) language in addition to their native language.

Gallery Walk: Gallery Walk is based on Museum approach to teaching. *Gallery Walk* can be collection of artifacts (i.e. maps, pictures, posters, audio and video clips) designed to present the particular topic to the audience.

Geocaching: It is an outdoor hide and seek activity in which the participants use a Global Positioning System (GPS) to find "geocaches" located around the world.

Global Positioning System GPS: GPS is a satellite navigation system that provides the coordinates of a particular location as well as information on time, weather, altitude on the on earth surface. It is maintained by the US government with 25 satellites orbiting the earth. It is free and accessible anywhere in the world with a GPS device. It is used in military to agriculture, seismology to making maps.

Geographic Information System GIS: GIS may also stand for geographical information science or geospatial information studies. It is a system for managing, storing, manipulating, analyzing as well as presenting any types of geographical data.

Learning Communities: Learning communities are informal learning environments. Emphasis is on authentic and collective learning. Learning communities are formed by groups of people who work together on projects, support one another, and engage in socio-cultural experiences.

Open Learning: Open or flexible learning is a type of distance education where the focus is on learning rather than teaching.

Participatory Culture: Participatory culture as opposite to a consumer culture is a new term in which each person acts as a contributor or co-producer. With the advent of Web 2.0, Internet was no longer a static place, it turned into a dynamic environment each participants becomes part of the meaning making process.

Read/Write Web: This term refers to the new era of Internet, sometimes used to describe "Web 2.0." User will be able to contribute and publish content on the web in addition to passively read or search information.

Social Media Classroom: (SMS) is a free and open-source web service that integrates wikis, chat, blogs, tagging, media sharing, social bookmarking, RSS, and other read/write web tools. SMS provides teachers and learners with an integrated set of social media that each course can use for its own purposes and includes curricular material: syllabi, lesson plans, resource repositories, screencasts and videos.

Social Reconstructivist Theory: Social Reconstructivist Paradigm represents knowledge as socially constructed through language and interpersonal social processes. The role of education is to enhance students' learning through the interpersonal negotiation of meaning.

Third Place: The sociologist Ray Oldenburg coined the term *third place* or *great good places* to describe the public spaces used for informal social interaction outside of the home and workplace.

ENDNOTES

[1] http://mnyildiz.googlepages.com/eje -suggested steps for journaling

[2] http://buttermilkfalls.wikispaces.com – this wikispace includes our page on Community Walk map that has the trail information, handout for checklist and pictures

[3] Pre- and Post questionnaire - http://ku.us2.qualtrics.com/SE/?SID=SV_aaeNpYQL5XL11UF

Chapter 15
Web 2.0 Technology Use by Students in Higher Education:
A Case of Kenyan Universities

Rhoda K. Gitonga
Kenyatta University, Kenya

Catherine G. Murungi
Kenyatta University, Kenya

ABSTRACT

Web 2.0 technologies are technologies on the Internet such as blogs, wikis, and online forums that allow people to create, share, collaborate, and communicate their ideas. Blogs are known to enhance team cooperation and foster a learning community within the class. Wikis have been used to promote group work. Online discussion forums assist with problem-based learning. Facebook/Twitter have the potential to support social learning through community networking services such as wall pasting, chatting, content-sharing, and tagging. Despite the enormous potential and apparent cost effectiveness of new learning media for facilitating social-networked learning, problem-based learning, and promoting group work, its application by institutions of higher learning in developing African countries is low. The purpose of the study was to investigate the use of Web 2.0 technologies in teaching and learning in Kenyan universities. The researchers used surveys to collect data for this study. The findings reveal that the use of Web 2.0 technologies by students in Kenyan universities was quite low. Finally, other implications need to be explored in the context of the study, including the learners and the Web 2.0 technology resources available.

INTRODUCTION

The need for effective functioning in the knowledge society and coping with continuous change has led to the demand for higher levels of competencies (Kozma, 2005). There are new learning approaches such as resource-based, problem-based, project-based and competency-based learning that demand a high degree of information literacy. These new learning approaches demand a paradigm shift from dominant teaching methods involving pre-packaging information for the students, to

DOI: 10.4018/978-1-4666-6284-1.ch015

facilitating learning in authentic and information rich contexts. There are different ways in which teaching and learning can be made more efficient especially in program delivery through the use of ICT. Some of these ways include the use of Web 2.0 technologies such as blogs, wikis, video podcasts, social networks, and newsgroups, audio programs, video compact discs, use of electronic journals as well as use of online courses. Web 2.0 technologies are technologies that make easy knowledge sharing, interaction, collaboration and communication.

These technologies enable students collaborate and engage other students and lecturers in a common space where they have shared interests (Mazman & Usluel, 2009). Web 2.0 technology tools enable students to make links between internal thinking and external social interaction through the keyboard to improve the social and intellectual developments (Vygotsky, 1962). For example, wikis can enable group members edit each other's contributions. They provide an opportunity to work with other people and share knowledge. Web 2.0 technology tools offer rich learning support in line with social constructivism theories of learning (Vygotsky, 1978) which emphasize experiential learning, personalization, collaboration, information sharing, common interests, active participation, cooperative learning and group work support. (Newby, Lehman, Rushell & Stepich, 2010). Web 2.0 technologies therefore supports social networked learning and knowledge constructivism in which students use these tools to learn at their own pace as well as collaborate in problem-based learning.

Web 2.0 technologies have been used in students learning in various fields. Makoul etal., (2010) engaged in a project where medical students were using online forums to give them an opportunity to reflect, brief and respond to others about their experiences. He concluded that the online forums assisted with problem based learning. This was by providing a template that encouraged students to reflect and dialogue about challenging communication situations. Ramanau and Geng, (2009) on the other hand researched on the use of wikis to facilitate group work. Their work reflected on the experience of introducing Wiki technology into a "Japanese for Beginners" module at one of the universities in the UK and the evaluation of learner experiences that came thereafter.

Although most students were not sure how group work on the wiki fitted into their studies, they agreed that resources created by their peers in the wiki spaces were easier to understand than textbooks. McDermott, Eccleston and Brindley, (2010) discussed a project where students were encouraged to engage in using blogs to document their learning experiences. They found out that the experience of the students on reading and commenting on the blog was worthwhile due to the quality of information brought together on the student learning experience. From this experience, blogs were found to be useful in promoting reflective learning among students.

Despite the enormous potential and cost effectiveness of Web 2.0 technologies to support social networked learning and knowledge constructivism, it's application in institutions of higher learning in developing African countries is low (Ndume et al., 2008). Because of the functionalities provided by the social networking tools, higher education institutions need to ensure that effective usage of these tools is made by both students and lecturers (Kroop et al., 2010).

LITERATURE REVIEW

Learning with technology has evolved from software that supports students' individual learning based on mechanical drills to more advanced learning environments like the more developed cognitive tools and collaborative learning environments (Valtonen, 2011; Stahl et al., 2006; Jonassen, 1992). Technology in teaching has been known to use various formats ranging from traditional computer labs and presentation technologies to online learning and personal environments and social software. There have been several phases in the development of technology in Education. Koschmann (1996; 2001) and Lehtinen (2006) describe four phases of technology use in education.

The first phase was regarded as computer aided instruction or utopia of tireless and individual trainer, where learning goals were divided into smaller tasks that students could accomplish. Technology tools were able to provide instant feedback and control over the different tasks. The second phase was the utopia of intelligent tutor. This is where software was developed to emulate the thinking and problem solving of domain experts. The software was to provide students with personal tutors that followed the progress of learning and provided feedback and support. The third phase was the Utopia of the micro-worlds which was grounded in the constructivist theories of learning. Learning was seen as subjective construction of knowledge. Technology was used to provide students with environments for active inquiry and discovery. The computer provided the students with a safe environment for working and testing ideas. The fourth phase is regarded as Computer Supported Collaborative Learning (CSCL) Paradigm‖ (Koschmann, 1996; 2001) or utopia of collaborative learning‖ (Lehtinen, 2006). In this phase, the emphasis is on the collaborative and social factors of learning.

Technology is used in education to support students' collaborative knowledge building through collaborative work, sharing and explicating ideas and unique knowledge structures to provide a means of communication and inquiry and collaborative creations of knowledge. Lehtinen (2006) later described another phase, Utopias of multimedia and virtualization where evolution in technology is providing new technologies that are providing possibilities to effectively and interactively illustrate difficult content areas for students. Students can learn anytime and in any place through the developments in the Internet. This is where innovations from the Internet such as use of Web 2.0 technologies come in handy to promote social networked learning, problem solving based learning and collaborative learning.

The purpose of this study was to investigate the use of Web 2.0 technologies in learning by university students in Kenya. To establish this, the students were asked whether they knew about the identified Web 2.0 technologies and whether they were using them for learning purposes. The identified Web 2.0 technologies included blogs, wikis, Online discussion groups, Face-book/twitter, Online experts, Video podcasts, and use of Skype.

METHODOLOGY

Research Design

Descriptive survey can be used to describe the characteristics of a particular individual or group of variables (Kothari, 2007). It can also be used to determine how people feel about a particular issue by enabling them to describe their experiences (Mc Burney & White, 2004). In this study, it enabled students to describe their experiences in using Web 2.0 technologies.

Location of the Study

The study was carried out in the Nairobi metropolitan. According to the Ministry of Nairobi Metropolitan (2008), Nairobi metropolitan is that region that extends some 32,000 square kilometers from Nairobi city centre. This covers 15 No. local authority areas – City Council of Nairobi (684 km2); County Councils of Kiambu, Olkejuado, Masaku and Thika; Municipal Councils of Ruiru, Thika, Kiambu, Limuru, Mavoko, and Machakos; and Town Councils of Karuri, Kikuyu, Kajiado, and Kangundo. This region includes areas in which the institutions of the study are located. This region significantly depends on the city for employment and social facilities. This region has the highest number of both public and private universities.

Target Population

The target population comprised of all individuals and objects that the researcher could reasonably generalize findings to (Cooper & Schindler, 2006; Mugenda, 2008). The target population for this study was all the students, in all the public and private universities in Nairobi Metropolitan totaling to 66,081. There were some key characteristics of the population that were of interest in this study. Nairobi metropolitan area has experienced a decline in the cost per megabyte in KES of data transmitted. ICT services are closer to the people than any other region in Kenya (Kenya National Bureau of Statistics, 2010). This area has highest proportion of the population in Kenya using computers and the Internet. The region leads in the ownership of all basic households ICT equipment and Internet connectivity in the country. This implies that the population in this region is likely to be exposed to higher experiences in using Web 2.0 technologies and has a generally good ICT infrastructure.

Sampling Procedures and Sample Size

Purposive sampling was used to select the universities from which the sample was drawn. The main objective in this type of sampling was to pick cases that were typical of the population being studied. The researcher's judgment was used to select the respondents who best met the purposes of the study. Three public universities were selected because they were the only public universities with their main campuses within Nairobi metropolitan. The three private universities were selected because they were among the first established among all the private universities. Simple random sampling was then used to select the respondents namely the students from the target population.

The sample size was determined using Mugenda and Mugenda (1999), formulae. According to Mugenda and Mugenda (1999), the minimum sample size can be determined using the following formula: Where: $n=$ the minimum sample size if the target population is greater than 10,000 $Z=$ the standard normal deviate at the required confidence level. $p =$ the proportion in the target population estimated to have characteristics being measured. Use 0.5 if unknown. $q = 1-p$ $d=$ the margin of error. If the target population is less than 10,000 then the minimum sample size is obtained using the formula: Where: $ns=$ the minimum sample if the target sample size is less than 10,000 $n =$ the minimum sample size if the target population is greater than 10,000 $N =$ the estimate of the population size.

Using the Mugenda and Mugenda formulae, the relationship between sample size and total population was that as the population increases the sample size increases at a diminishing rate and remains relatively constant at slightly more than 380 cases. A sample size of 386 students was obtained. Once the required sample size was determined, proportional allocation was used to obtain the number of students that were included in the sample from each of the selected universities. To select individual respondents, the researcher visited the university students' common halls where the questionnaires were given to the individual students who had identifications. The respondents of interest in this case were the university students and hence, there was no need to identify the respondents through their departments or faculties.

Response Rate

Two hundred and thirty one (231) students' questionnaires were filled, and returned. This gave a response rate of 60%. This response rate was favorable according to Mugenda and Mugenda

(2003) in which they assert that a 50% response rate is adequate, 60% good and above 70% rated very well. Saunders, Lewis and Thornhill (2007) suggest that an average response rate of 30% to 40% is reasonable for deliver and collect survey method. Hager, Wilson, Pollack and Rooney (2003) recommend 50% while Sekaran (2003) recommends 30% as an adequate response rate for descriptive surveys. Based on these assertions, this implied that the response rate for this study was adequate.

RESEARCH RESULTS AND DISCUSSIONS

The purpose of this paper was to investigate the use of Web 2.0 technologies in learning by students in Kenyan Universities. To establish this, students were asked whether they were aware of the availability of Web 2.0 technologies for learning in their universities. Their responses were as shown in Table 1.

Table 1 shows that students were not aware of Web 2.0 technologies for learning such as online discussion groups (47.8%), Video podcasts (22.3%) and Skype (39.1%). This may be attributed to the fact that they were likely not to be using them as part of the learning tools in their programs. In a study conducted to determine undergraduate and high school students' attitudes towards the use of Web. 2.0 technologies in English, Yalcin (2011) reported that lack of awareness of Web 2.0 tools by both students and lecturers reduced their usefulness in teaching and learning. However, it was interesting to note the awareness of Web 2.0 technologies like Facebook (80.8%), Blogs (54.9%) and Wikis (53.1%) for learning. This could be attributed to the fact that Facebook is heavily relied on by students for social networking purposes. Waema (2000) and Rockman (2004) established that students may have picked skills for sending emails, chatting and communicating through social networks like in Facebook, but many had not learnt how to use Web 2.0 technologies in learning. The following section contains a report of students' perception of Web 2.0 technologies use in learning. Students were asked whether they used the Web 2.0 technologies in learning. Their responses were as shown on Table 2.

Table 2 shows that the percentages of students using Web 2.0 tools such as blogs (34.4%), wikis (41.6%), video podcasts (19.2%), and online discussion forums (34.2%) were very low. This probably was a result of ignorance, negative attitude, lack of appropriate skills on Internet use and/or technophobia. Some recent studies have found out that many students lack the required skills to use Web 2.0 tools efficiently (Bawden et al., 2007; Hudges, 2009, Al-Daihani, 2010). In a study to investigate whether the social software was really a "killer app" in the education of net generation students, Feuer (2011) pointed out that students reported a moderate amount of usage

Table 1. Awareness of Web 2.0 resources available for learning

Web 2.0 Resources	N	Yes	No
Online discussion groups	226	47.8	52.2
Blogs	224	54.9	45.1
Wikis	226	53.1	46.9
Face-book/twitter	224	80.8	19.2
Online experts	219	53.0	47.0
Video podcasts	224	22.3	77.7
Skype	225	39.1	60.9

Table 2. Web 2.0 technologies use in learning by students

Web 2.0 Technologies	N	Agree	Neutral	Disagree
Online discussion forums	228	34.2	15.8	50.0
Blogs	230	34.4	25.2	40.4
Wikis	226	41.6	19.0	39.4
Face book/Twitter	228	59.7	13.1	27.2
Online experts	225	36.5	15.9	47.6
Video podcasts	229	19.2	20.1	60.7
Skype	228	21.4	20.2	58.4

of Web 2.0 applications with the exception of social networking technologies whose adoption was common place. In a study to explore Internet access and use among undergraduate students in three Nigerian universities, Ani (2010) affirms a relatively poor level of use of online resources, electronic journals and online databases by students. Kenyan students like wise perceived a high difficulty level in using several Web 2.0 applications, such as video podcasts, wikis and online discussion forums, while they felt at ease in participating in online social communities such as Facebook. Yoo and Huang (2011) in their paper Comparison of Web 2.0 Technology Acceptance Level based on Cultural Differences, argued that though students already use a variety of Web 2.0 applications on a daily basis, they might not know how to use them efficiently for gaining new knowledge or developing new skills.

CONCLUSION

This research investigated the use of Web 2.0 technologies in learning by university students in Kenya. The data obtained indicates that the majority of students were aware of the availability of Facebook/ twitter, blogs and wikis for learning within their institutions but there was a relatively poor level of use of Web 2.0 resources, such as blogs, wikis and online discussion forums by students in Kenyan Universities. Considering the high rate of awareness of Facebook/twitter adoption of this Web 2.0 technology in learning is higher than the other technologies and this is not surprising. Web 2.0 technologies can support dialogue and collaborative learning in both campus-based courses and off-campus ones. Students can share documents simultaneously and everyone can edit together in real time. Collaborative benefits extend to faculty and staff as well. However, in view of the central role those Web 2.0 technologies are expected to play in the social networked learning and in knowledge construction, more work is needed to establish the extent to which these technologies support educational objectives. From Table 2, the use of Web 2.0 technologies for learning is still low in the Kenyan University setting as was observed by Ndume, et al., (2008).

RECOMMENDATIONS

Students' use of Web 2.0 technologies for academic purpose is greatly influenced by their lecturers use of this technology in the classroom. Training of lecturers and students on the use of these new technologies in teaching and learning would be essential if they are to confidently use them in teaching and learning. Introducing Web 2.0 tools into the curriculum would be the most effective way to teach students the use of a variety of Web 2.0 tools such as blogs, wikis and online discussion forums among others.

Students have changed over the years perhaps due to technology rich upbringing. They appear to have different needs, goals, and learning preferences than students in the past (Oblinger & Oblinger, 2005). The kind of students today are interested in self-directed learning opportunities, interactive environments, multiple forms of feedback, and assignment choices that use different resources to create personally meaningful learning experiences. They want assignments and class activities that have more hands-on, inquiry-based approaches to learning (Glenn, 2000). Hay (2000) argues that these students want more of hands-on, inquiry-based approaches to learning, and are less willing simply to absorb what is put before them. According to Carlson (2005), students demand independence and autonomy in applying their learning styles, which is impacting on a broad range of educational choices and behaviors, from "what kind of education they buy" *to* "what, where, and how they learn" hence the need to accommodate these students through the use of ICT such as use of Web 2.0 technologies in learning. Finally, other implications need to be explored, but in the context of the study, including the learners and the web 2.0 technology resources available.

REFERENCES

Al-Daihani, S. (2010). Exploring the use of social software by master of library and information science students. *Library Review*, *59*(2), 117–131. doi:10.1108/00242531011023871

Ani, E. O. (2010). Internet access and use: A study of undergraduate students in three Nigerian universities. The Electronic Library, 28 (4), 555 – 567.

Bawden, D., Robinson, L., Anderson, T., Bates, J., Rutkauskiene, U., & Vilar, P. (2007). Towards curriculum 2.0: library/information education for a Web 2.0 world. *Library and Information Research*, *31*(99), 14–25.

Carlson, S. (2005). The Net Generation goes to college. *The Chronicle of Higher Education, Section: Information Technology, 52*(7), A34. Retrieved October 30, 2010 from http://www.msmc.la.edu/include/learning_resources/todays_learner/The_Net_Generation.pdf

Cooper, D. R., & Schindler, P. S. (2006). *Business research methods* (9th ed.). McGraw- Hill Companies, Inc.

Feuer, G. (2011). Is social software really a "killer app" in the education of net generation students? Findings from a case study. *Library Hi Tech News*, *28*(7), 14–17. doi:10.1108/07419051111184043

Glenn, J. M. (2000). Teaching the Net Generation. *Business Education Forum*, *54*(3), 6–14.

Hager, M. A., Wilson, S., Pollak, T. H., & Rooney, P. M. (2003). Response Rates for Mail Surveys of Nonprofit Organisations: A Review and Empirical Test. *Nonprofit and Voluntary Sector Quarterly*, *32*(2), 252–267. doi:10.1177/0899764003032002005

Hay, L. E. (2000). Educating the Net Generation. *School Administrator*, *57*(54), 6–10.

Hudges, A. (2009). Higher education in a Web 2.0 world, General Publications. *JISC*. Retrieved August 7, 2012, from www.jisc.ac.uk/ publications/generalpublications/2009/heweb2.aspx

Jonassen, D. (1992). What are cognitive tools? In P. A. Kommers, D. H. Jonassen, & J. T. Mayers (Eds.), *Cognitive tools for learning* (pp. 1–6). Berlin, Germany: Springer-Verlag NATO Scientific Affairs Division. doi:10.1007/978-3-642-77222-1_1

Kenya National Bureau of Statistics (2010). *Kenya - National Information and Communication Technology Survey 2010*. KNE-KNBS-NICTS-2010-v01. Author.

Koschmann, T. (1996). Paradigm shifts and instructional technology: an introduction. In T. Koschmann (Ed.), *CSCL: Theory and Practice of an Emerging Paradigm* (pp. 1–23). Mahwah, NJ: Lawrence Erlbaum.

Koschmann, T. (2001). Revisiting the paradigms of instructional technology. In G. Kennedy, M. Keppell, C. McNaught & T. Petrovic (Eds.), *Meeting at the Crossroads, Proceedings of the 18th Annual Conference of the Australian Society for Computers in Learning in Tertiary Education* (pp. 15-22). Melbourne: Biomedical Multimedia Unit, The University of Melbourne.

Kothari, C. R. (2007). *Research methodology: Methods and techniques* (2nd ed.). India: New Age Publications.

Kozma, R. (2005). *ICT, education reform, and economic growth.* Chandler, AZ: Intel Corporation.

Kroop, S., Nussbaumer, A., & Fruhhman, K. (2010). *Motivating Collaborative Learning Activities by Using Existing Web 2.0 Tools.* Retrieved from http://mature-ip.eu/files/matel10/kroop.pdf

Lehtinen, E. (2006). Teknologian kehitys ja oppimisen utopiat. In S. Järvelä, P. Häkkinen, & E. Lehtinen (Eds.), Oppimisen teoria ja teknologian opetuskäyttö (pp. 264-278). Porvoo: WSOY.

Makoul, G., Zick, A. B., Aakhus, M., Neely, K. J., & Roemer, P. E. (2010). Using an online forum to encourage reflection about difficult conversations in medicine. *Patient Education and Counseling, 79*(1), 83–86. doi:10.1016/j.pec.2009.07.027 PMID:19717269

Mazman, S. G., & Usluel, Y. K. (2009). The usage of social networks in educational context. World Academy of Science, Engineering and Technology, 49(1).

Mc Burney, D. H., & White, T. L. (2004). Research methods (6th ed.). Thomson: Wadsworth Publishing.

McDermott, R., Brindley, G., & Eccleston, G. (2010). Developing tools to encourage reflection in first year students blogs. In *Proceedings of the 15th Annual Conference on Innovation and Technology in Computer Science Education, ITiCSE'10.* Ankara, Turkey: ITiCSE.

Ministry of Nairobi Metropolitan Development. (2008). *Nairobi Metro 2030 A World Class African Metropolis.* Government of the Republic of Kenya. Retrieved from http://www.tatucity.com/DynamicData/Downloads/NM_Vision_2030.pdf

Mugenda, A. G. (2008). *Social science research: Theory and principles.* Nairobi: Applied research and training services.

Mugenda, M. O., & Mugenda, G. A. (1999). *Research methods: Quantitative and qualitative approaches.* Nairobi, Kenya: ACTS press.

Mugenda, M. O., & Mugenda, G. A. (2003). *Research Methods Quantitative and Qualitative Approaches.* Nairobi, Kenya: ACTS press.

Ndume, V., Tilya, F. N., & Twaakyondo, H. (2008). Challenges of adaptive e-learning at higher learning institutions: a case study in Tanzania. *International Journal of Computing and ICT Research, 2*(1), 47–59.

Newby, T. J., Lehman, J., Russell, J., & Stepich, D. A. (2010). *Instructional Technology for Teaching and Learning: Designing Instruction, Integrating Computers, and Using Media* (4th ed.). Allyn & Bacon.

Oblinger, D. G., & Oblinger, J. L. (2005). Educating the Net Generation. In D. Oblinger & J. Oblinger (Eds), *Educating the Net generation* (pp. 2.1–2.20). Boulder, CO: EDUCAUSE. Retrieved August14, 2013 from http://net.educause.edu/ir/library/pdf/pub7101m.pdf

Ramanau, R., & Geng, F. (2009). Researching the use of Wiki's to facilitate group work. *Procedia Social and Behavioral Sciences*, *1*(1), 2620–2626. doi:10.1016/j.sbspro.2009.01.463

Rockman., I., F. (2004). *Integrating Information Literacy into the Higher Education Curriculum; Practiccal Models for Transformation*. John Wiley Publishers.

Saunders, M., Lewis, P., & Thornhill, A. (2007). *Research Methods for Business Students* (4th ed.). Harlow: FT Prentice Hall.

Sekaran, U. (2003). *Research method of business: A skill Building Approach* (4th ed.). New York, NY: John Willey & Sons, Inc.

Stahl, G., Koschmann, T., & Suthers, D. (2006). Computer supported collaborative learning: An historical perspective. In R. K. Sawyer (Ed.), *Cambridge handbook of the learning sciences* (pp. 409-426). Cambridge, UK: Cambridge University Press. Retrieved from http://www.cis.drexel.edu/faculty/gerry/cscl/CSCL_English.pdf

Valtonen, T. (2011). *An Insight into Collaborative Learning with ICT: Teachers' and Students' Perspectives. University of Eastern Finland*.

Vygotsky, L. S. (1962). *Thought and Language*. Cambridge, MA: MIT Press. doi:10.1037/11193-000

Vygotsky, L. S. (1978). *Mind and Society: The Development of Higher Mental Processes*. Cambridge, MA: Harvard University Press.

Waema, E. F. (2000). *The impact of introducing computers into library services: The case of the University of Dar es Salaam*. (MA dissertation). University of Dar es Salaam, Dar es Salaam, Tanzania.

Yalçan, F. (2011). An international dimension of the student's attitudes towards the use of English in Web 2.0 technology. *The Turkish Online Journal of Educational Technology*, *10*(3), 63–68.

Yoo, S. J., & Huang, W.-H. D. (2011). Comparison of Web 2.0 Technology Acceptance Level based on Cultural Differences. *Journal of Educational Technology & Society*, *14*(4), 241–252.

KEY TERMS AND DEFINITIONS

Blogs: Websites or part of a website allowing people to post comments. These websites maintain an ongoing chronicle of information. In this study, a blog was a part of a website where students and lecturers could post comments about topics learnt in class and allowed users to reflect, share opinions, and discuss various topics in the form of an online journal while readers commented on posts.

Podcasts: This is a multimedia digital file (either audio or video) made available on the Internet for downloading to a portable media player or a computer. For the purpose of this study, a podcast was a series of digital media files meant for teaching and learning (either audio or video) that were released episodically by the lecturers and often downloaded by students from the university website to their computers.

Problem Based Learning: This is where students learn about a subject through the experience of problem solving. In this work, students collaboratively come together in order to solve a particular problem.

Social Networked Learning: A social network is a social structure made up of individuals (or organizations) called "nodes", which are tied (connected) by one or more specific types of interdependency, such as friendship, kinship, common interest, financial exchange, dislike, sexual relationships, or relationships of beliefs, knowledge or prestige. For the purpose of this study, a social network referred to a social structure made up of individuals with a common interest that is sharing knowledge.

Student: According to Cambridge Advanced Learner's Dictionary, a student is a person who is learning at a college or university, or sometimes at a school. For the purpose of this study, a university student was a person enrolled in a degree program in one of Kenya's Public or private universities.

Technologies: These are collections of tools and resources used to support learning. In this case they include blogs, wikis, face-book/twitter, Skype, video podcast amongst others.

Web 2.0 Technologies: Web 2.0 has been referred to as technology (Franklin and Van Harmelen, 2007), as second generation web-based tools and services (Guntram, 2007), and as a community-driven online platform or an attitude rather than technology (Downes, 2005; Virkus, 2008). Some of the Web 2.0 applications and services are blogs, wikis, tagging and social bookmarking, multimedia sharing, podcasts, and social networking. For the purpose of this study Web 2.0 technologies referred to news groups, blogs, wikis, podcasts and social networking through face book and twitter.

Wiki: This is a website that allows the creation and editing of any number of interlinked web pages via a web browser using a simplified markup language or a text editor. In this study, a wiki referred to a website that was used collaboratively by multiple users especially students for personal note taking.

Related References

To continue our tradition of advancing research in the field of education, we have compiled a list of recommended IGI Global readings. These references will provide additional information and guidance to further enrich your knowledge and assist you with your own research and future publications.

Abrami, P. C., Savage, R. S., Deleveaux, G., Wade, A., Meyer, E., & LeBel, C. (2010). The learning toolkit: The design, development, testing and dissemination of evidence-based educational software. In P. Zemliansky, & D. Wilcox (Eds.), *Design and implementation of educational games: Theoretical and practical perspectives* (pp. 168–188). Hershey, PA: Information Science Reference. doi:10.4018/978-1-61520-781-7.ch012

Ackfeldt, A., & Malhotra, N. (2012). Do managerial strategies influence service behaviours? Insights from a qualitative study. In R. Eid (Ed.), *Successful customer relationship management programs and technologies: Issues and trends* (pp. 174–187). Hershey, PA: Business Science Reference. doi:10.4018/978-1-4666-0288-5.ch013

Adi, A., & Scotte, C. G. (2013). Barriers to emerging technology and social media integration in higher education: Three case studies. In M. Pătruţ, & B. Pătruţ (Eds.), *Social media in higher education: Teaching in web 2.0* (pp. 334–354). Hershey, PA: Information Science Reference. doi:10.4018/978-1-4666-2970-7.ch017

Aldana-Vargas, M. F., Gras-Martí, A., Montoya, J., & Osorio, L. A. (2013). Pedagogical counseling program development through an adapted community of inquiry framework. In Z. Akyol, & D. Garrison (Eds.), *Educational communities of inquiry: Theoretical framework, research and practice* (pp. 350–373). Hershey, PA: Information Science Reference.

Alegre, O. M., & Villar, L. M. (2011). Faculty professional learning: An examination of online development and assessment environments. In G. Vincenti, & J. Braman (Eds.), *Teaching through multi-user virtual environments: Applying dynamic elements to the modern classroom* (pp. 66–93). Hershey, PA: Information Science Reference. doi:10.4018/978-1-60960-783-8.ch119

Alegre, O. M., & Villar, L. M. (2012). Faculty professional learning: An examination of online development and assessment environments. In *Organizational learning and knowledge: Concepts, methodologies, tools and applications* (pp. 305–331). Hershey, PA: Business Science Reference.

Related References

Alegre-Rosa, O. M., & Villar-Angulo, L. M. (2010). Training of teachers in virtual scenario: An excellence model for quality assurance in formative programmes. In S. Mukerji, & P. Tripathi (Eds.), *Cases on transnational learning and technologically enabled environments* (pp. 190–213). Hershey, PA: Information Science Reference. doi:10.4018/978-1-61520-749-7.ch011

Andegherghis, S. (2012). Technology and traditional teaching. In I. Chen, & D. McPheeters (Eds.), *Cases on educational technology integration in urban schools* (pp. 74–79). Hershey, PA: Information Science Reference.

Anderson, K. H., & Muirhead, W. (2013). Blending storytelling with technology in the professional development of police officers. In H. Yang, & S. Wang (Eds.), *Cases on formal and informal e-learning environments: Opportunities and practices* (pp. 143–165). Hershey, PA: Information Science Reference.

Anderson, S., & Oyarzun, B. (2013). Multi-modal professional development for faculty. In J. Keengwe, & L. Kyei-Blankson (Eds.), *Virtual mentoring for teachers: Online professional development practices* (pp. 43–65). Hershey, PA: Information Science Reference.

Annetta, L. A., Holmes, S., & Cheng, M. (2012). Measuring student perceptions: Designing an evidenced centered activity model for a serious educational game development software. In R. Ferdig, & S. de Freitas (Eds.), *Interdisciplinary advancements in gaming, simulations and virtual environments: Emerging trends* (pp. 165–182). Hershey, PA: Information Science Publishing. doi:10.4018/978-1-4666-0029-4.ch011

Austin, R., & Anderson, J. (2006). Re-schooling and information communication technology: A case study of Ireland. In L. Tan Wee Hin, & R. Subramaniam (Eds.), *Handbook of research on literacy in technology at the K-12 level* (pp. 176–194). Hershey, PA: Information Science Reference. doi:10.4018/978-1-59140-494-1.ch010

Ayling, D., Owen, H., & Flagg, E. (2014). From basic participation to transformation: Immersive virtual professional development. In S. Leone (Ed.), *Synergic integration of formal and informal e-learning environments for adult lifelong learners* (pp. 47–74). Hershey, PA: Information Science Reference. doi:10.4018/978-1-4666-5780-9.ch025

Ayoola, K. A. (2010). An appraisal of a computer-based continuing professional development (CPD) Course for Nigerian English teachers and teacher-trainers. In R. Taiwo (Ed.), *Handbook of research on discourse behavior and digital communication: Language structures and social interaction* (pp. 642–650). Hershey, PA: Information Science Reference. doi:10.4018/978-1-61520-773-2.ch041

Baia, P. (2011). The trend of commitment: Pedagogical quality and adoption. In S. D'Agustino (Ed.), *Adaptation, resistance and access to instructional technologies: Assessing future trends in education* (pp. 273–315). Hershey, PA: Information Science Reference.

Banas, J. R., & Velez-Solic, A. (2013). Designing effective online instructor training and professional development. In J. Keengwe, & L. Kyei-Blankson (Eds.), *Virtual mentoring for teachers: Online professional development practices* (pp. 1–25). Hershey, PA: Information Science Reference.

Banks, W. P., & Van Sickle, T. (2011). Digital partnerships for professional development: Rethinking university–public school collaborations. In M. Bowdon, & R. Carpenter (Eds.), *Higher education, emerging technologies, and community partnerships: Concepts, models and practices* (pp. 153–163). Hershey, PA: Information Science Reference. doi:10.4018/978-1-60960-623-7.ch014

Barbour, M. K., Siko, J., Gross, E., & Waddell, K. (2013). Virtually unprepared: Examining the preparation of K-12 online teachers. In R. Hartshorne, T. Heafner, & T. Petty (Eds.), *Teacher education programs and online learning tools: Innovations in teacher preparation* (pp. 60–81). Hershey, PA: Information Science Reference. doi:10.4018/978-1-4666-4502-8.ch011

Bartlett, J. E. II, & Bartlett, M. E. (2009). Innovative strategies for preparing and developing career and technical education leaders. In V. Wang (Ed.), *Handbook of research on e-learning applications for career and technical education: Technologies for vocational training* (pp. 248–261). Hershey, PA: Information Science Reference. doi:10.4018/978-1-60566-739-3.ch020

Baylen, D. M., & Glacken, J. (2007). Promoting lifelong learning online: A case study of a professional development experience. In Y. Inoue (Ed.), *Online education for lifelong learning* (pp. 229–252). Hershey, PA: Information Science Publishing. doi:10.4018/978-1-59904-319-7.ch011

Beedle, J., & Wang, S. (2013). Roles of a technology leader. In S. Wang, & T. Hartsell (Eds.), *Technology integration and foundations for effective leadership* (pp. 228–241). Hershey, PA: Information Science Reference.

Begg, M., Dewhurst, D., & Ross, M. (2010). Game informed virtual patients: Catalysts for online learning communities and professional development of medical teachers. In J. Lindberg, & A. Olofsson (Eds.), *Online learning communities and teacher professional development: Methods for improved education delivery* (pp. 190–208). Hershey, PA: Information Science Reference. doi:10.4018/978-1-61520-869-2.ch020

Begg, M., Dewhurst, D., & Ross, M. (2010). Game informed virtual patients: Catalysts for online learning communities and professional development of medical teachers. In R. Luppicini, & A. Haghi (Eds.), *Cases on digital technologies in higher education: Issues and challenges* (pp. 304–322). Hershey, PA: Information Science Reference. doi:10.4018/978-1-61520-869-2.ch020

Benton, C. J., White, O. L., & Stratton, S. K. (2014). Collaboration not competition: International education expanding perspectives on learning and workforce articulation. In V. Wang (Ed.), *International education and the next-generation workforce: Competition in the global economy* (pp. 64–82). Hershey, PA: Information Science Reference.

Benus, M. J., Yarker, M. B., Hand, B. M., & Norton-Meier, L. A. (2013). Analysis of discourse practices in elementary science classrooms using argument-based inquiry during whole-class dialogue. In M. Khine, & I. Saleh (Eds.), *Approaches and strategies in next generation science learning* (pp. 224–245). Hershey, PA: Information Science Reference. doi:10.4018/978-1-4666-2809-0.ch012

Related References

Betts, K., Kramer, R., & Gaines, L. L. (2013). Online faculty and adjuncts: Strategies for meeting current and future demands of online education through online human touch training and support. In M. Raisinghani (Ed.), *Curriculum, learning, and teaching advancements in online education* (pp. 94–112). Hershey, PA: Information Science Reference. doi:10.4018/978-1-4666-2949-3.ch007

Biesinger, K. D., & Crippen, K. J. (2010). Designing and delivering technology integration to engage students. In J. Yamamoto, J. Leight, S. Winterton, & C. Penny (Eds.), *Technology leadership in teacher education: Integrated solutions and experiences* (pp. 298–313). Hershey, PA: Information Science Reference. doi:10.4018/978-1-61520-899-9.ch016

Bledsoe, C., & Pilgrim, J. (2013). Three instructional models to integrate technology and build 21st century literacy skills. In J. Whittingham, S. Huffman, W. Rickman, & C. Wiedmaier (Eds.), *Technological tools for the literacy classroom* (pp. 243–262). Hershey, PA: Information Science Reference.

Bloom, L., & Dole, S. (2014). Virtual school of the smokies. In S. Mukerji, & P. Tripathi (Eds.), *Handbook of research on transnational higher education* (pp. 674–689). Hershey, PA: Information Science Reference.

Bober, M. J. (2005). Ensuring quality in technology-focused professional development. In C. Howard, J. Boettcher, L. Justice, K. Schenk, P. Rogers, & G. Berg (Eds.), *Encyclopedia of distance learning* (pp. 845–852). Hershey, PA: Information Science Reference. doi:10.4018/978-1-59140-555-9.ch121

Bober, M. J. (2009). Ensuring quality in technology-focused professional development. In P. Rogers, G. Berg, J. Boettcher, C. Howard, L. Justice, & K. Schenk (Eds.), *Encyclopedia of distance learning* (2nd ed., pp. 924–931). Hershey, PA: Information Science Reference. doi:10.4018/978-1-60566-198-8.ch129

Boling, E. C., & Beatty, J. (2012). Overcoming the tensions and challenges of technology integration: How can we best support our teachers? In R. Ronau, C. Rakes, & M. Niess (Eds.), *Educational technology, teacher knowledge, and classroom impact: A research handbook on frameworks and approaches* (pp. 136–156). Hershey, PA: Information Science Publishing.

Bovard, B., Bussmann, S., Parra, J., & Gonzales, C. (2010). Transitioning to e-learning: Teaching the teachers. In I. Association (Ed.), *Web-based education: Concepts, methodologies, tools and applications* (pp. 259–276). Hershey, PA: Information Science Reference.

Bowskill, N. (2009). Informal learning projects and world wide voluntary co-mentoring. In P. Rogers, G. Berg, J. Boettcher, C. Howard, L. Justice, & K. Schenk (Eds.), *Encyclopedia of distance learning* (2nd ed., pp. 1169–1177). Hershey, PA: Information Science Reference. doi:10.4018/978-1-60566-198-8.ch167

Bowskill, N., & McConnell, D. (2010). Collaborative reflection in globally distributed inter-cultural course teams. In G. Berg (Ed.), *Cases on online tutoring, mentoring, and educational services: Practices and applications* (pp. 172–184). Hershey, PA: Information Science Reference.

Bradley, J. B., Rachal, J., & Harper, L. (2013). Online professional development for adults: Utilizing andragogical methods in research and practice. In V. Bryan, & V. Wang (Eds.), *Technology use and research approaches for community education and professional development* (pp. 171–193). Hershey, PA: Information Science Reference.

Braun, P. (2013). Clever health: A study on the adoption and impact of an ehealth initiative in rural Australia. In M. Cruz-Cunha, I. Miranda, & P. Gonçalves (Eds.), *Handbook of research on ICTs and management systems for improving efficiency in healthcare and social care* (pp. 69–87). Hershey, PA: Medical Information Science Reference. doi:10.4018/978-1-4666-3990-4.ch004

Breen, P. (2014). An intramuscular approach to teacher development in international collaborative higher education. In S. Mukerji, & P. Tripathi (Eds.), *Handbook of research on transnational higher education* (pp. 368–390). Hershey, PA: Information Science Reference. doi:10.4018/978-1-4666-5780-9.ch101

Brown, C. A., & Neal, R. E. (2013). Definition and history of online professional development. In J. Keengwe, & L. Kyei-Blankson (Eds.), *Virtual mentoring for teachers: Online professional development practices* (pp. 182–203). Hershey, PA: Information Science Reference.

Brown, C. W., & Peters, K. A. (2013). STEM academic enrichment and professional development programs for K-12 urban students and teachers. In R. Lansiquot (Ed.), *Cases on interdisciplinary research trends in science, technology, engineering, and mathematics: Studies on urban classrooms* (pp. 19–56). Hershey, PA: Information Science Reference. doi:10.4018/978-1-4666-4502-8.ch091

Burgess, M. (2013). Using second life to support student teachers' socio-reflective practice: A mixed-method analysis. In R. Lansiquot (Ed.), *Cases on interdisciplinary research trends in science, technology, engineering, and mathematics: Studies on urban classrooms* (pp. 107–127). Hershey, PA: Information Science Reference.

Burner, K. J. (2012). Web 2.0, the individual, and the organization: Privacy, confidentiality, and compliance. In V. Dennen, & J. Myers (Eds.), *Virtual professional development and informal learning via social networks* (pp. 25–38). Hershey, PA: Information Science Reference. doi:10.4018/978-1-4666-1815-2.ch002

Buzzetto-More, N. (2010). Applications of second life. In H. Song, & T. Kidd (Eds.), *Handbook of research on human performance and instructional technology* (pp. 149–162). Hershey, PA: Information Science Reference.

Bynog, M. (2013). Development of a technology plan. In S. Wang, & T. Hartsell (Eds.), *Technology integration and foundations for effective leadership* (pp. 88–101). Hershey, PA: Information Science Reference.

Calway, B. A., & Murphy, G. A. (2011). A work-integrated learning philosophy and the educational imperatives. In P. Keleher, A. Patil, & R. Harreveld (Eds.), *Work-integrated learning in engineering, built environment and technology: Diversity of practice in practice* (pp. 1–24). Hershey, PA: Information Science Reference. doi:10.4018/978-1-60960-547-6.ch001

Related References

Carlén, U., & Lindström, B. (2012). Informed design of educational activities in online learning communities. In A. Olofsson, & J. Lindberg (Eds.), *Informed design of educational technologies in higher education: Enhanced learning and teaching* (pp. 118–134). Hershey, PA: Information Science Reference.

Cassidy, A., Sipos, Y., & Nyrose, S. (2014). Supporting sustainability education and leadership: Strategies for students, faculty, and the planet. In S. Mukerji, & P. Tripathi (Eds.), *Handbook of research on transnational higher education* (pp. 207–231). Hershey, PA: Information Science Reference.

Cavanagh, T. B. (2011). Leveraging online university education to improve K-12 science education: The ScienceMaster case study. In M. Bowdon, & R. Carpenter (Eds.), *Higher education, emerging technologies, and community partnerships: Concepts, models and practices* (pp. 221–233). Hershey, PA: Information Science Reference. doi:10.4018/978-1-60960-623-7.ch020

Chapman, D. L. (2013). Overview of technology plans. In S. Wang, & T. Hartsell (Eds.), *Technology integration and foundations for effective leadership* (pp. 71–87). Hershey, PA: Information Science Reference.

Chapman, D. L., Bynog, M., & Yocom, H. (2013). Assessment, evaluation, and revision of a technology plan. In S. Wang, & T. Hartsell (Eds.), *Technology integration and foundations for effective leadership* (pp. 124–150). Hershey, PA: Information Science Reference.

Chylinski, R., & Hanewald, R. (2009). Creating supportive environments for CALL teacher autonomy. In R. de Cássia Veiga Marriott, & P. Lupion Torres (Eds.), *Handbook of research on e-learning methodologies for language acquisition* (pp. 387–408). Hershey, PA: Information Science Reference.

Chylinski, R., & Hanewald, R. (2011). Creating supportive environments for CALL teacher autonomy. In I. Association (Ed.), *Instructional design: Concepts, methodologies, tools and applications* (pp. 840–860). Hershey, PA: Information Science Reference. doi:10.4018/978-1-60960-503-2.ch403

Clouse, N. K., Williams, S. R., & Evans, R. D. (2011). Developing an online mentoring program for beginning teachers. In S. D'Agustino (Ed.), *Adaptation, resistance and access to instructional technologies: Assessing future trends in education* (pp. 410–428). Hershey, PA: Information Science Reference.

Colomo-Palacios, R., Tovar-Caro, E., García-Crespo, Á., & Gómez-Berbís, J. M. (2012). Identifying technical competences of IT professionals: The case of software engineers. In R. Colomo-Palacios (Ed.), *Professional advancements and management trends in the IT sector* (pp. 1–14). Hershey, PA: Information Science Publishing. doi:10.4018/978-1-4666-0924-2.ch001

Corbeil, M. E., & Corbeil, J. R. (2012). Creating ongoing online support communities through social networks to promote professional learning. In V. Dennen, & J. Myers (Eds.), *Virtual professional development and informal learning via social networks* (pp. 114–133). Hershey, PA: Information Science Reference. doi:10.4018/978-1-4666-1815-2.ch007

Corbitt, B., Holt, D., & Segrave, S. (2008). Strategic design for web-based teaching and learning: Making corporate technology systems work for the learning organization. In L. Tomei (Ed.), *Online and distance learning: Concepts, methodologies, tools, and applications* (pp. 897–904). Hershey, PA: Information Science Reference.

Corbitt, B., Holt, D. M., & Segrave, S. (2008). Strategic design for web-based teaching and learning: Making corporate technology system work for the learning organization. In L. Esnault (Ed.), *Web-based education and pedagogical technologies: Solutions for learning applications* (pp. 280–302). Hershey, PA: IGI Publishing.

Coutinho, C. P. (2010). Challenges for teacher education in the learning society: Case studies of promising practice. In H. Yang, & S. Yuen (Eds.), *Handbook of research on practices and outcomes in e-learning: Issues and trends* (pp. 385–401). Hershey, PA: Information Science Reference.

Cowie, B., Jones, A., & Harlow, A. (2011). Technological infrastructure and implementation environments: The case of laptops for New Zealand teachers. In S. D'Agustino (Ed.), *Adaptation, resistance and access to instructional technologies: Assessing future trends in education* (pp. 40–52). Hershey, PA: Information Science Reference.

Crichton, S. (2007). A great wall of difference: Musings on instructional design in contemporary China. In M. Keppell (Ed.), *Instructional design: Case studies in communities of practice* (pp. 91–105). Hershey, PA: Information Science Publishing. doi:10.4018/978-1-59904-322-7.ch005

Croasdaile, S. (2009). Inter-organizational e-collaboration in education. In N. Kock (Ed.), *E-collaboration: Concepts, methodologies, tools, and applications* (pp. 1157–1170). Hershey, PA: Information Science Reference. doi:10.4018/978-1-60566-652-5.ch086

Croasdaile, S. (2009). Inter-organizational e-collaboration in education. In J. Salmons, & L. Wilson (Eds.), *Handbook of research on electronic collaboration and organizational synergy* (pp. 16–29). Hershey, PA: Information Science Reference.

Csoma, K. (2010). EPICT: Transnational teacher development through blended learning. In S. Mukerji, & P. Tripathi (Eds.), *Cases on technological adaptability and transnational learning: Issues and challenges* (pp. 147–161). Hershey, PA: Information Science Reference. doi:10.4018/978-1-61520-779-4.ch008

Cunningham, C. A., & Harrison, K. (2011). The affordances of second life for education. In G. Vincenti, & J. Braman (Eds.), *Teaching through multi-user virtual environments: Applying dynamic elements to the modern classroom* (pp. 94–119). Hershey, PA: Information Science Reference.

Curwood, J. S. (2014). From collaboration to transformation: Practitioner research for school librarians and classroom teachers. In K. Kennedy, & L. Green (Eds.), *Collaborative models for librarian and teacher partnerships* (pp. 1–11). Hershey, PA: Information Science Reference.

Cuthell, J. P. (2010). Thinking things through: Collaborative online professional development. In J. Lindberg, & A. Olofsson (Eds.), *Online learning communities and teacher professional development: Methods for improved education delivery* (pp. 154–167). Hershey, PA: Information Science Reference.

D'Agustino, S., & King, K. P. (2011). Access and advancement: Teacher transformation and student empowerment through technology mentoring. In S. D'Agustino (Ed.), *Adaptation, resistance and access to instructional technologies: Assessing future trends in education* (pp. 362–380). Hershey, PA: Information Science Reference.

Related References

Dana, N. F., Krell, D., & Wolkenhauer, R. (2013). Taking action research in teacher education online: Exploring the possibilities. In R. Hartshorne, T. Heafner, & T. Petty (Eds.), *Teacher education programs and online learning tools: Innovations in teacher preparation* (pp. 357–374). Hershey, PA: Information Science Reference.

Dawson, K., Cavanaugh, C., & Ritzhaupt, A. D. (2013). ARTI: An online tool to support teacher action research for technology integration. In R. Hartshorne, T. Heafner, & T. Petty (Eds.), *Teacher education programs and online learning tools: Innovations in teacher preparation* (pp. 375–391). Hershey, PA: Information Science Reference.

De Simone, C., Marquis, T., & Groen, J. (2013). Optimizing conditions for learning and teaching in K-20 education. In V. Wang (Ed.), *Handbook of research on teaching and learning in K-20 education* (pp. 535–552). Hershey, PA: Information Science Reference. doi:10.4018/978-1-4666-4249-2.ch031

Dennen, V. P., & Jiang, W. (2012). Twitter-based knowledge sharing in professional networks: The organization perspective. In V. Dennen, & J. Myers (Eds.), *Virtual professional development and informal learning via social networks* (pp. 241–255). Hershey, PA: Information Science Reference. doi:10.4018/978-1-4666-1815-2.ch014

Dexter, S. (2002). eTIPS - Educational technology integration and implementation principles. In P. Rogers (Ed.), Designing instruction for technology-enhanced learning (pp. 56-70). Hershey, PA: Idea Group Publishing. doi: doi:10.4018/978-1-930708-28-0.ch003

Dickerson, J., Winslow, J., & Lee, C. Y. (2013). Teacher training and technology: Current uses and future trends. In V. Wang (Ed.), *Handbook of research on technologies for improving the 21st century workforce: Tools for lifelong learning* (pp. 243–256). Hershey, PA: Information Science Publishing.

DiMarco, J. (2006). Cases and interviews. In J. DiMarco (Ed.), *Web portfolio design and applications* (pp. 222–276). Hershey, PA: Idea Group Publishing. doi:10.4018/978-1-59140-854-3.ch012

Doherty, I. (2013). Achieving excellence in teaching: A case study in embedding professional development for teaching within a research-intensive university. In D. Salter (Ed.), *Cases on quality teaching practices in higher education* (pp. 280–290). Hershey, PA: Information Science Reference. doi:10.4018/978-1-4666-3661-3.ch017

Donnelly, R. (2009). Transformative potential of constructivist blended problem-based learning in higher education. In C. Payne (Ed.), *Information technology and constructivism in higher education: Progressive learning frameworks* (pp. 182–202). Hershey, PA: Information Science Reference. doi:10.4018/978-1-60566-654-9.ch012

Donnelly, R. (2010). The nature of complex blends: Transformative problem-based learning and technology in Irish higher education. In Y. Inoue (Ed.), *Cases on online and blended learning technologies in higher education: Concepts and practices* (pp. 1–22). Hershey, PA: Information Science Reference.

Donnelly, R., & O'Farrell, C. (2006). Constructivist e-learning for staff engaged in coninuous professional development. In J. O'Donoghue (Ed.), *Technology supported learning and teaching: A staff perspective* (pp. 160–175). Hershey, PA: Information Science Publishing. doi:10.4018/978-1-59140-962-5.ch010

Downing, K. F., & Holtz, J. K. (2008). Virtual school science. In K. Downing, & J. Holtz (Eds.), *Online science learning: Best practices and technologies* (pp. 30–48). Hershey, PA: Information Science Publishing. doi:10.4018/978-1-59904-986-1.ch003

Ehmann Powers, C., & Hewett, B. L. (2008). Building online training programs for virtual workplaces. In P. Zemliansky, & K. St.Amant (Eds.), *Handbook of research on virtual workplaces and the new nature of business practices* (pp. 257–271). Hershey, PA: Information Science Reference. doi:10.4018/978-1-59904-893-2.ch019

Ellis, J. B., West, T. D., Grimaldi, A., & Root, G. (2013). Ernst & Young leadership and professional development center: Accounting designed for leaders. In R. Carpenter (Ed.), *Cases on higher education spaces: Innovation, collaboration, and technology* (pp. 330–355). Hershey, PA: Information Science Reference.

Falco, J. (2008). Leading the art of the conference: Revolutionizing schooling through interactive videoconferencing. In D. Newman, J. Falco, S. Silverman, & P. Barbanell (Eds.), *Videoconferencing technology in K-12 instruction: Best practices and trends* (pp. 133–143). Hershey, PA: Information Science Reference.

Farmer, L. (2009). Fostering online communities of practice in career and technical education. In V. Wang (Ed.), *Handbook of research on e-learning applications for career and technical education: Technologies for vocational training* (pp. 192–203). Hershey, PA: Information Science Reference. doi:10.4018/978-1-60566-739-3.ch015

Farmer, L. (2010). Lights, camera, action! Via teacher librarian video conferencing. In S. Rummler, & K. Ng (Eds.), *Collaborative technologies and applications for interactive information design: Emerging trends in user experiences* (pp. 179–188). Hershey, PA: Information Science Reference.

Farmer, L. S. (2012). Curriculum development for online learners. In V. Wang, L. Farmer, J. Parker, & P. Golubski (Eds.), *Pedagogical and andragogical teaching and learning with information communication technologies* (pp. 88–104). Hershey, PA: Information Science Publishing.

Farmer, L. S. (2013). Assessment processes for online professional development. In J. Keengwe, & L. Kyei-Blankson (Eds.), *Virtual mentoring for teachers: Online professional development practices* (pp. 161–180). Hershey, PA: Information Science Reference.

Farmer, L. S. (2014). The roles of professional organizations in school library education. In V. Wang (Ed.), *International education and the next-generation workforce: Competition in the global economy* (pp. 170–193). Hershey, PA: Information Science Reference.

Fok, A. W., & Ip, H. H. (2009). An agent-based framework for personalized learning in continuous professional development. In M. Syed (Ed.), *Strategic applications of distance learning technologies* (pp. 96–110). Hershey, PA: Information Science Reference.

Fragaki, M., & Lionarakis, A. (2011). Education for liberation: A transformative polymorphic model for ICT integration in education. In G. Kurubacak, & T. Yuzer (Eds.), *Handbook of research on transformative online education and liberation: Models for social equality* (pp. 198–231). Hershey, PA: Information Science Reference.

Fuller, J. S., & Bachenheimer, B. A. (2013). Using an observation cycle for helping teachers integrate technology. In A. Ritzhaupt, & S. Kumar (Eds.), *Cases on educational technology implementation for facilitating learning* (pp. 69–84). Hershey, PA: Information Science Reference. doi:10.4018/978-1-4666-3676-7.ch004

Gairin-Sallán, J., & Rodriguez-Gómez, D. (2010). Teacher professional development through knowledge management in educational organisations. In J. Lindberg, & A. Olofsson (Eds.), *Online learning communities and teacher professional development: Methods for improved education delivery* (pp. 134–153). Hershey, PA: Information Science Reference.

Related References

Gairín-Sallán, J., & Rodríguez-Gómez, D. (2012). Teacher professional development through knowledge management in educational organisations. In *Organizational learning and knowledge: Concepts, methodologies, tools and applications* (pp. 1297–1315). Hershey, PA: Business Science Reference.

García, K., & Suzuki, R. (2008). The blended learning classroom: An online teacher training program. In M. Lytras, D. Gasevic, P. Ordóñez de Pablos, & W. Huang (Eds.), *Technology enhanced learning: Best practices* (pp. 57–80). Hershey, PA: IGI Publishing. doi:10.4018/978-1-59904-600-6.ch003

Gerbic, P., & Stacey, E. (2009). Conclusion. In E. Stacey, & P. Gerbic (Eds.), *Effective blended learning practices: Evidence-based perspectives in ICT-facilitated education* (pp. 298–311). Hershey, PA: Information Science Reference. doi:10.4018/978-1-60566-296-1.ch016

Gibbons, A. N. (2010). Reflections concerning technology: A case for the philosophy of technology in early childhood teacher education and professional development programs. In S. Blake, & S. Izumi-Taylor (Eds.), *Technology for early childhood education and socialization: Developmental applications and methodologies* (pp. 1–19). Hershey, PA: Information Science Reference.

Gonzales, C., Bussmann, S., Bovard, B., & Parra, J. (2007). Transitioning to e-learning: Teaching the teachers. In R. Sharma, & S. Mishra (Eds.), *Cases on global e-learning practices: Successes and pitfalls* (pp. 52–72). Hershey, PA: Information Science Publishing.

Gormley, P., Bruen, C., & Concannon, F. (2010). Sustainability through staff engagement: Applying a community of practice model to web 2.0 academic development programmes. In R. Donnelly, J. Harvey, & K. O'Rourke (Eds.), *Critical design and effective tools for e-learning in higher education: Theory into practice* (pp. 326–345). Hershey, PA: Information Science Reference. doi:10.4018/978-1-61520-879-1.ch020

Grandgenett, N., Ostler, E., Topp, N., & Goeman, R. (2012). Robotics and problem-based learning in STEM formal educational environments. In B. Barker, G. Nugent, N. Grandgenett, & V. Adamchuk (Eds.), *Robots in K-12 education: A new technology for learning* (pp. 94–119). Hershey, PA: Information Science Reference. doi:10.4018/978-1-4666-0182-6.ch005

Grant, M. R. (2010). Train the trainer: A competency-based model for teaching in virtual environments. In W. Ritke-Jones (Ed.), *Virtual environments for corporate education: Employee learning and solutions* (pp. 124–146). Hershey, PA: Business Science Reference. doi:10.4018/978-1-61520-619-3.ch008

Griffin, P., Care, E., Robertson, P., Crigan, J., Awwal, N., & Pavlovic, M. (2013). Assessment and learning partnerships in an online environment. In E. McKay (Ed.), *ePedagogy in online learning: New developments in web mediated human computer interaction* (pp. 39–54). Hershey, PA: Information Science Reference. doi:10.4018/978-1-4666-3649-1.ch003

Griswold, W. (2013). Transformative learning and educational technology integration in a post-totalitarian context: Professional development among school teachers in rural Siberia, Russia. In E. Jean Francois (Ed.), *Transcultural blended learning and teaching in postsecondary education* (pp. 128–144). Hershey, PA: Information Science Reference.

Gruich, M. R. (2013). Defining professional development for technology. In S. Wang, & T. Hartsell (Eds.), *Technology integration and foundations for effective leadership* (pp. 152–170). Hershey, PA: Information Science Reference.

Guidry, K. R., & Pasquini, L. (2013). Twitter chat as an informal learning tool: A case study using #sachat. In H. Yang, & S. Wang (Eds.), *Cases on formal and informal e-learning environments: Opportunities and practices* (pp. 356–377). Hershey, PA: Information Science Reference.

Gunn, C., & Blake, A. (2009). Blending technology into an academic practice qualification for university teachers. In E. Stacey, & P. Gerbic (Eds.), *Effective blended learning practices: Evidence-based perspectives in ICT-facilitated education* (pp. 259–279). Hershey, PA: Information Science Reference. doi:10.4018/978-1-60566-296-1.ch014

Hanewald, R. (2013). Professional development with and for emerging technologies: A case study with Asian languages and cultural studies teachers in Australia. In J. Keengwe (Ed.), *Pedagogical applications and social effects of mobile technology integration* (pp. 175–192). Hershey, PA: Information Science Reference. doi:10.4018/978-1-4666-2985-1.ch010

Hansen, C. C. (2012). ABCs and PCs: Effective professional development in early childhood education. In I. Chen, & D. McPheeters (Eds.), *Cases on educational technology integration in urban schools* (pp. 230–235). Hershey, PA: Information Science Reference.

Hao, S. (2012). Turn on your mobile devices: Potential and considerations of informal mobile learning. In V. Dennen, & J. Myers (Eds.), *Virtual professional development and informal learning via social networks* (pp. 39–58). Hershey, PA: Information Science Reference. doi:10.4018/978-1-4666-1815-2.ch003

Harteis, C. (2010). Contributions of e-collaborative knowledge construction to professional learning and expertise. In B. Ertl (Ed.), *E-collaborative knowledge construction: Learning from computer-supported and virtual environments* (pp. 91–108). Hershey, PA: Information Science Reference. doi:10.4018/978-1-61520-729-9.ch005

Hartsell, T., Herron, S. S., Fang, H., & Rathod, A. (2011). Improving teachers' self-confidence in learning technology skills and math education through professional development. In I. Association (Ed.), *Instructional design: Concepts, methodologies, tools and applications* (pp. 1487–1503). Hershey, PA: Information Science Reference. doi:10.4018/978-1-60960-503-2.ch609

Hartsell, T., Herron, S. S., Fang, H., & Rathod, A. (2012). Improving teachers' self-confidence in learning technology skills and math education through professional development. In L. Tomei (Ed.), *Advancing education with information communication technologies: Facilitating new trends* (pp. 150–164). Hershey, PA: Information Science Reference.

Related References

Hartsell, T., & Wang, S. (2013). Introduction to technology integration and leadership. In S. Wang, & T. Hartsell (Eds.), *Technology integration and foundations for effective leadership* (pp. 1–17). Hershey, PA: Information Science Reference.

Hauge, T. E., & Norenes, S. O. (2010). VideoPaper as a bridging tool in teacher professional development. In J. Lindberg, & A. Olofsson (Eds.), *Online learning communities and teacher professional development: Methods for improved education delivery* (pp. 209–228). Hershey, PA: Information Science Reference.

Haythornthwaite, C., & De Laat, M. (2012). Social network informed design for learning with educational technology. In A. Olofsson, & J. Lindberg (Eds.), *Informed design of educational technologies in higher education: Enhanced learning and teaching* (pp. 352–374). Hershey, PA: Information Science Reference.

Heinrichs, L., Fellander-Tsai, L., & Davies, D. (2013). Clinical virtual worlds: The wider implications for professional development in healthcare. In K. Bredl, & W. Bösche (Eds.), *Serious games and virtual worlds in education, professional development, and healthcare* (pp. 221–240). Hershey, PA: Information Science Reference. doi:10.4018/978-1-4666-3673-6.ch014

Helleve, I. (2010). Theoretical foundations of teachers' professional development. In J. Lindberg, & A. Olofsson (Eds.), *Online learning communities and teacher professional development: Methods for improved education delivery* (pp. 1–19). Hershey, PA: Information Science Reference.

Hemphill, L. S., & McCaw, D. S. (2009). Moodling professional development training that worked. In L. Tan Wee Hin, & R. Subramaniam (Eds.), *Handbook of research on new media literacy at the K-12 level: Issues and challenges* (pp. 808–822). Hershey, PA: Information Science Reference. doi:10.4018/978-1-60566-120-9.ch050

Hensley, M. K. (2010). Teaching new librarians how to teach: A model for building a peer learning program. In E. Pankl, D. Theiss-White, & M. Bushing (Eds.), *Recruitment, development, and retention of information professionals: Trends in human resources and knowledge management* (pp. 179–190). Hershey, PA: Business Science Reference. doi:10.4018/978-1-61520-601-8.ch010

Hernández-Gantes, V. M. (2011). Helping faculty design online courses in higher education. In V. Wang (Ed.), *Encyclopedia of information communication technologies and adult education integration* (pp. 779–794). Hershey, PA: Information Science Reference.

Herrington, J., & Oliver, R. (2006). Professional development for the online teacher: An authentic approach. In T. Herrington, & J. Herrington (Eds.), *Authentic learning environments in higher education* (pp. 283–295). Hershey, PA: Information Science Publishing.

Hicks, T. (2013). Adding the "digital layer": Examining one teacher's growth as a digital writer through an NWP summer institute and beyond. In K. Pytash, & R. Ferdig (Eds.), *Exploring technology for writing and writing instruction* (pp. 345–357). Hershey, PA: Information Science Reference. doi:10.4018/978-1-4666-4341-3.ch020

Hinson, J. M., & Bordelon Sellers, R. (2004). Professional development recommendations for online courses. In C. Cavanaugh (Ed.), *Development and management of virtual schools: Issues and trends* (pp. 135–157). Hershey, PA: Information Science Publishing.

Hirtle, J., & Smith, S. (2010). When virtual communities click: Transforming teacher practice, transforming teachers. In H. Yang, & S. Yuen (Eds.), *Handbook of research on practices and outcomes in e-learning: Issues and trends* (pp. 182–196). Hershey, PA: Information Science Reference.

Holland, I. E. (2007). Evolution of the Milwaukee public schools portal. In A. Tatnall (Ed.), *Encyclopedia of portal technologies and applications* (pp. 397–401). Hershey, PA: Information Science Reference. doi:10.4018/978-1-59140-989-2.ch067

Holt, J., Unruh, L., & Dougherty, A. M. (2011). Enhancing a rural school-university teacher education partnership through an e-mentoring program for beginning teachers. In M. Bowdon, & R. Carpenter (Eds.), *Higher education, emerging technologies, and community partnerships: Concepts, models and practices* (pp. 212–220). Hershey, PA: Information Science Reference. doi:10.4018/978-1-60960-623-7.ch019

Hood, D. W., & Huang, W. D. (2013). Professional development with graduate teaching assistants (TAs) teaching online. In J. Keengwe, & L. Kyei-Blankson (Eds.), *Virtual mentoring for teachers: Online professional development practices* (pp. 26–42). Hershey, PA: Information Science Reference.

Hu, X. C., & Meyen, E. L. (2013). A comparison of student and instructor preferences for design and pedagogy features in postsecondary online courses. In M. Raisinghani (Ed.), *Curriculum, learning, and teaching advancements in online education* (pp. 213–229). Hershey, PA: Information Science Reference. doi:10.4018/978-1-4666-2949-3.ch015

Hucks, D., & Ragan, M. (2013). Technology expanding horizons in teacher education: Transformative learning experiences. In J. Keengwe (Ed.), *Research perspectives and best practices in educational technology integration* (pp. 61–79). Hershey, PA: Information Science Reference.

Hui, D., & Russell, D. L. (2009). Understanding the effectiveness of collaborative activity in online professional development with innovative educators through intersubjectivity. In L. Tomei (Ed.), *Information communication technologies for enhanced education and learning: Advanced applications and developments* (pp. 283–302). Hershey, PA: Information Science Reference.

Hulme, M., & Hughes, J. (2006). Patchwork e-dialogues in the professional development of new teachers. In J. O'Donoghue (Ed.), *Technology supported learning and teaching: A staff perspective* (pp. 210–223). Hershey, PA: Information Science Publishing. doi:10.4018/978-1-59140-962-5.ch013

Hunt, L., & Sankey, M. (2013). Getting the context right for quality teaching and learning. In D. Salter (Ed.), *Cases on quality teaching practices in higher education* (pp. 261–279). Hershey, PA: Information Science Reference. doi:10.4018/978-1-4666-3661-3.ch016

Hur, J. W., Brush, T., & Bonk, C. (2012). An analysis of teacher knowledge and emotional sharing in a teacher blog community. In V. Dennen, & J. Myers (Eds.), *Virtual professional development and informal learning via social networks* (pp. 219–239). Hershey, PA: Information Science Reference. doi:10.4018/978-1-4666-1815-2.ch013

Hurst, A. (2012). Reflections on personal experiences of staff training and continuing professional development for academic staff in the development of high quality support for disabled students in higher education. In D. Moore, A. Gorra, M. Adams, J. Reaney, & H. Smith (Eds.), *Disabled students in education: Technology, transition, and inclusivity* (pp. 288–304). Hershey, PA: Information Science Reference.

Related References

Hyatt, K. J. (2011). Technology: A reflective tool for professional development. In L. Tomei (Ed.), *Online courses and ICT in education: Emerging practices and applications* (pp. 134–142). Hershey, PA: Information Science Reference.

Jackson, T. (2012). Ways to mentor methods' faculty integration of technologies in their courses. In D. Polly, C. Mims, & K. Persichitte (Eds.), *Developing technology-rich teacher education programs: Key issues* (pp. 519–534). Hershey, PA: Information Science Reference. doi:10.4018/978-1-4666-0014-0.ch033

Jamieson-Proctor, R., & Finger, G. (2009). Measuring and evaluating ICT use: Developing an instrument for measuring student ICT use. In L. Tan Wee Hin, & R. Subramaniam (Eds.), *Handbook of research on new media literacy at the K-12 level: Issues and challenges* (pp. 326–339). Hershey, PA: Information Science Reference. doi:10.4018/978-1-60566-120-9.ch021

Jarvis, D. H. (2012). Teaching mathematics teachers online: Strategies for navigating the intersection of andragogy, technology, and reform-based mathematics education. In A. Juan, M. Huertas, S. Trenholm, & C. Steegmann (Eds.), *Teaching mathematics online: Emergent technologies and methodologies* (pp. 187–199). Hershey, PA: Information Science Reference.

Jimoyiannis, A., Gravani, M., & Karagiorgi, Y. (2012). Teacher professional development through virtual campuses: Conceptions of a 'new' model. In H. Yang, & S. Yuen (Eds.), *Handbook of research on practices and outcomes in virtual worlds and environments* (pp. 327–347). Hershey, PA: Information Science Publishing.

Johnson, E. S., & Pitcock, J. (2008). Preparing online instructors: Beyond using the technology. In K. Orvis, & A. Lassiter (Eds.), *Computer-supported collaborative learning: Best practices and principles for instructors* (pp. 89–113). Hershey, PA: Information Science Publishing.

Johnson, K., & Tashiro, J. (2010). Interprofessional care and health care complexity: Factors shaping human resources effectiveness in health information management. In S. Kabene (Ed.), *Human resources in healthcare, health informatics and healthcare systems* (pp. 250–280). Hershey, PA: Medical Information Science Reference. doi:10.4018/978-1-61520-885-2.ch015

Johnson, K., & Tashiro, J. (2013). Interprofessional care and health care complexity: Factors shaping human resources effectiveness in health information management. In *User-driven healthcare: Concepts, methodologies, tools, and applications* (pp. 1273–1302). Hershey, PA: Medical Information Science Reference. doi:10.4018/978-1-4666-2770-3.ch064

Johnson, M. L. (2014). Moving from theory to practice: Integrating personal learning networks into a graduate-level student development theory course. In S. Leone (Ed.), *Synergic integration of formal and informal e-learning environments for adult lifelong learners* (pp. 165–177). Hershey, PA: Information Science Reference.

Johnson, V. (2009). Understanding dynamic change and creation of learning organizations. In P. Rogers, G. Berg, J. Boettcher, C. Howard, L. Justice, & K. Schenk (Eds.), *Encyclopedia of distance learning* (2nd ed., pp. 2187–2191). Hershey, PA: Information Science Reference. doi:10.4018/978-1-60566-198-8.ch323

Jones, M. G., & Harris, L. (2012). Using student choice to promote technology integration: The buffet model. In D. Polly, C. Mims, & K. Persichitte (Eds.), *Developing technology-rich teacher education programs: Key issues* (pp. 192–204). Hershey, PA: Information Science Reference. doi:10.4018/978-1-4666-0014-0.ch013

Joyes, G., Fisher, T., Firth, R., & Coyle, D. (2014). The nature of a successful online professional doctorate. In K. Sullivan, P. Czigler, & J. Sullivan Hellgren (Eds.), *Cases on professional distance education degree programs and practices: Successes, challenges, and issues* (pp. 296–330). Hershey, PA: Information Science Reference.

Kelly, D. (2009). Modeling best practices in web-based academic development. In R. Donnelly, & F. McSweeney (Eds.), *Applied e-learning and e-teaching in higher education* (pp. 35–55). Hershey, PA: Information Science Reference. doi:10.4018/978-1-60566-982-3.ch085

Kelly, D. K. (2010). Modeling best practices in web-based academic development. In A. Tatnall (Ed.), *Web technologies: Concepts, methodologies, tools, and applications* (pp. 1578–1595). Hershey, PA: Information Science Reference.

Kelly, R. (2014). Administration: Making a connection with the library's strongest advocate. In K. Kennedy, & L. Green (Eds.), *Collaborative models for librarian and teacher partnerships* (pp. 175–184). Hershey, PA: Information Science Reference.

Kennedy-Clark, S., & Thompson, K. (2013). A MUVEing success: Design strategies for professional development in the use of multi-user virtual environments and educational games in science education. In S. D'Agustino (Ed.), *Immersive environments, augmented realities, and virtual worlds: Assessing future trends in education* (pp. 16–41). Hershey, PA: Information Science Reference. doi:10.4018/978-1-4666-4502-8.ch036

Kent, A. M. (2013). Teacher leadership: Learning and leading. In J. Lewis, A. Green, & D. Surry (Eds.), *Technology as a tool for diversity leadership: Implementation and future implications* (pp. 230–242). Hershey, PA: Information Science Reference.

Keppell, M. J. (2007). Instructional designers on the borderline: Brokering across communities of practice. In M. Keppell (Ed.), *Instructional design: Case studies in communities of practice* (pp. 68–89). Hershey, PA: Information Science Publishing. doi:10.4018/978-1-59904-322-7.ch004

Kidd, T. T., & Keengwe, J. (2012). Technology integration and urban schools: Implications for instructional practices. In L. Tomei (Ed.), *Advancing education with information communication technologies: Facilitating new trends* (pp. 244–256). Hershey, PA: Information Science Reference.

King, K. P. (2008). The transformation model. In C. Van Slyke (Ed.), *Information communication technologies: Concepts, methodologies, tools, and applications* (pp. 1102–1108). Hershey, PA: Information Science Reference. doi:10.4018/978-1-59904-949-6.ch073

King, K. P. (2012). Impact of podcasts as professional learning: Teacher created, student created, and professional development podcasts. In S. Chhabra (Ed.), *ICTs for advancing rural communities and human development: Addressing the digital divide* (pp. 237–250). Hershey, PA: Information Science Reference. doi:10.4018/978-1-4666-0047-8.ch016

Related References

Kitchenham, A. (2011). Blending professional development for rural educators an exploratory study. In D. Parsons (Ed.), *Combining e-learning and m-learning: New applications of blended educational resources* (pp. 225–238). Hershey, PA: Information Science Reference. doi:10.4018/978-1-60960-481-3.ch014

Klieger, A., & Oster-Levinz, A. (2010). How online tasks promote teachers' expertise within the technological pedagogical content knowledge (TPACK). In T. Yuzer, & G. Kurubacak (Eds.), *Transformative learning and online education: Aesthetics, dimensions and concepts* (pp. 219–235). Hershey, PA: Information Science Reference. doi:10.4018/978-1-61520-985-9.ch015

Koh, S., Lee, S., Yen, D. C., & Havelka, D. (2005). Information technology professional career development: A progression of skills. In M. Hunter, & F. Tan (Eds.), *Advanced topics in global information management* (Vol. 4, pp. 142–157). Hershey, PA: Idea Group Publishing. doi:10.4018/978-1-59140-468-2.ch009

Kopcha, T., & Valentine, K. D. (2013). A framework for developing robust online professional development materials to support teacher practice under the common core. In D. Polly (Ed.), *Common core mathematics standards and implementing digital technologies* (pp. 319–331). Hershey, PA: Information Science Reference. doi:10.4018/978-1-4666-4086-3.ch021

Koumpis, A. (2010). Culture of services. In A. Koumpis (Ed.), *Service science for socio-economical and information systems advancement: Holistic methodologies* (pp. 312–347). Hershey, PA: Information Science Reference.

Kyei-Blankson, L., & Keengwe, J. (2013). Faculty-faculty interactions in online learning environments. In L. Tomei (Ed.), *Learning tools and teaching approaches through ICT advancements* (pp. 127–135). Hershey, PA: Information Science Reference.

Larson, L., & Vanmetre, S. (2010). Learning together with the interactive white board. In N. Lambropoulos, & M. Romero (Eds.), *Educational social software for context-aware learning: Collaborative methods and human interaction* (pp. 69–78). Hershey, PA: Information Science Reference.

Laurillard, D., & Masterman, E. (2010). TPD as online collaborative learning for innovation in teaching. In J. Lindberg, & A. Olofsson (Eds.), *Online learning communities and teacher professional development: Methods for improved education delivery* (pp. 230–246). Hershey, PA: Information Science Reference.

Lawrence, J., Burton, L., Summers, J., Noble, K., & Gibbings, P. D. (2013). An associate dean's community of practice: Rising to the leadership challenges of engaging distance students using blended models of learning and teaching. In J. Willems, B. Tynan, & R. James (Eds.), *Global challenges and perspectives in blended and distance learning* (pp. 212–222). Hershey, PA: Information Science Reference. doi:10.4018/978-1-4666-3978-2.ch017

Lee, D. M. (2004). Organizational entry and transition from academic study: Examining a critical step in the professional development of young IS workers. In M. Igbaria, & C. Shayo (Eds.), *Strategies for managing IS/IT personnel* (pp. 113–142). Hershey, PA: Idea Group Publishing.

Leh, A. S., & Grafton, L. (2009). Promoting new media literacy in a school district. In L. Tan Wee Hin, & R. Subramaniam (Eds.), *Handbook of research on new media literacy at the K-12 level: Issues and challenges* (pp. 607–619). Hershey, PA: Information Science Reference. doi:10.4018/978-1-60566-120-9.ch038

Lehew, A. J., & Polly, D. (2013). The use of digital resources to support elementary school teachers' implementation of the common core state standards. In D. Polly (Ed.), *Common core mathematics standards and implementing digital technologies* (pp. 332–338). Hershey, PA: Information Science Reference. doi:10.4018/978-1-4666-4086-3.ch022

Leng, J., & Sharrock, W. (2010). Collaborative practices in computer-aided academic research. In I. Portela, & M. Cruz-Cunha (Eds.), *Information communication technology law, protection and access rights: Global approaches and issues* (pp. 249–270). Hershey, PA: Information Science Reference. doi:10.4018/978-1-61520-975-0.ch016

Ley, K., & Gannon-Cook, R. (2010). Marketing a blended university program: An action research case study. In S. Mukerji, & P. Tripathi (Eds.), *Cases on technology enhanced learning through collaborative opportunities* (pp. 73–90). Hershey, PA: Information Science Reference. doi:10.4018/978-1-61520-751-0.ch005

Linton, J., & Stegall, D. (2013). Common core standards for mathematical practice and TPACK: An integrated approach to instruction. In D. Polly (Ed.), *Common core mathematics standards and implementing digital technologies* (pp. 234–249). Hershey, PA: Information Science Reference. doi:10.4018/978-1-4666-4086-3.ch016

Lithgow, C. M., Wolf, J. L., & Berge, Z. L. (2011). Virtual worlds: Corporate early adopters pave the way. In S. Hai-Jew (Ed.), *Virtual immersive and 3D learning spaces: Emerging technologies and trends* (pp. 25–43). Hershey, PA: Information Science Reference.

Lloyd, M., & Duncan-Howell, J. (2010). Changing the metaphor: The potential of online communities in teacher professional development. In J. Lindberg, & A. Olofsson (Eds.), *Online learning communities and teacher professional development: Methods for improved education delivery* (pp. 60–76). Hershey, PA: Information Science Reference.

Lockyer, L., Patterson, J., Rowland, G., & Hearne, D. (2007). ActiveHealth: Enhancing the community of physical and health educators through online technologies. In M. Keppell (Ed.), *Instructional design: Case studies in communities of practice* (pp. 331–348). Hershey, PA: Information Science Publishing. doi:10.4018/978-1-59904-322-7.ch017

Loose, C. (2013). Teachers as researchers and instructional leaders. In V. Wang (Ed.), *Handbook of research on teaching and learning in K-20 education* (pp. 710–725). Hershey, PA: Information Science Reference. doi:10.4018/978-1-4666-4249-2.ch041

Luetkehans, L. M., & Hunt, R. D. (2014). School librarians as significant other: Using online professional learning communities for the development of pre-service teachers. In K. Kennedy, & L. Green (Eds.), *Collaborative models for librarian and teacher partnerships* (pp. 56–66). Hershey, PA: Information Science Reference. doi:10.4018/978-1-4666-5780-9.ch078

Related References

Lyublinskaya, I., & Tournaki, N. (2012). The effects of teacher content authoring on TPACK and on student achievement in algebra: Research on instruction with the TI-Nspire™ handheld. In R. Ronau, C. Rakes, & M. Niess (Eds.), *Educational technology, teacher knowledge, and classroom impact: A research handbook on frameworks and approaches* (pp. 295–322). Hershey, PA: Information Science Publishing.

Mackey, J. (2009). Virtual learning and real communities: Online professional development for teachers. In E. Stacey, & P. Gerbic (Eds.), *Effective blended learning practices: Evidence-based perspectives in ICT-facilitated education* (pp. 163–181). Hershey, PA: Information Science Reference. doi:10.4018/978-1-60566-296-1.ch009

Mackey, J., & Mills, A. (2003). An examination of ICT planning maturity in schools: A stage theory perspective. In T. McGill (Ed.), *Current issues in IT education* (pp. 376–395). Hershey, PA: IRM Press.

Manathunga, C., & Donnelly, R. (2009). Opening online academic development programmes to international perspectives and dialogue. In R. Donnelly, & F. McSweeney (Eds.), *Applied e-learning and e-teaching in higher education* (pp. 85–109). Hershey, PA: Information Science Reference.

Marinho, R. (2010). Faculty development in instructional technology in the context of learning styles and institutional barriers. In S. Mukerji, & P. Tripathi (Eds.), *Cases on interactive technology environments and transnational collaboration: Concerns and perspectives* (pp. 1–38). Hershey, PA: Information Science Reference. doi:10.4018/978-1-61520-909-5.ch001

Mark, C. L. (2013). Evaluating and funding the professional development program. In S. Wang, & T. Hartsell (Eds.), *Technology integration and foundations for effective leadership* (pp. 206–226). Hershey, PA: Information Science Reference.

Marshall, J. C. (2013). Measuring and facilitating highly effective inquiry-based teaching and learning in science classrooms. In M. Khine, & I. Saleh (Eds.), *Approaches and strategies in next generation science learning* (pp. 290–306). Hershey, PA: Information Science Reference. doi:10.4018/978-1-4666-2809-0.ch015

Marshall, K. (2008). E-portfolios in teacher education. In G. Putnik, & M. Cruz-Cunha (Eds.), *Encyclopedia of networked and virtual organizations* (pp. 516–523). Hershey, PA: Information Science Reference. doi:10.4018/978-1-59904-885-7.ch068

Martin, M. (2008). Integrating videoconferencing into the classroom: A perspective from Northern Ireland. In D. Newman, J. Falco, S. Silverman, & P. Barbanell (Eds.), *Videoconferencing technology in K-12 instruction: Best practices and trends* (pp. 253–268). Hershey, PA: Information Science Reference.

Maurer, M. J. (2012). Telementoring and virtual professional development: A theoretical perspective from science on the roles of self-efficacy, teacher learning, and professional learning communities. In *Organizational learning and knowledge: Concepts, methodologies, tools and applications* (pp. 1158–1176). Hershey, PA: Business Science Reference.

McAnuff-Gumbs, M., & Verbeck, K. (2013). Toward a model of multi-level professional learning communities to guide the training and practice of literacy coaches. In H. Yang, & S. Wang (Eds.), *Cases on online learning communities and beyond: Investigations and applications* (pp. 361–402). Hershey, PA: Information Science Reference.

McCarthy, J. (2012). Connected: Online mentoring in Facebook for final year digital media students. In A. Okada, T. Connolly, & P. Scott (Eds.), *Collaborative learning 2.0: Open educational resources* (pp. 204–221). Hershey, PA: Information Science Reference. doi:10.4018/978-1-4666-0300-4.ch011

McConnell, D. (2005). Networked collaborative e-learning. In E. Li, & T. Du (Eds.), *Advances in electronic business* (Vol. 1, pp. 222–257). Hershey, PA: Idea Group Publishing.

McCormack, V. (2010). Utilizing VoiceThread to increase teacher candidates' reflection and global implications for usage. In J. Yamamoto, J. Kush, R. Lombard, & C. Hertzog (Eds.), *Technology implementation and teacher education: Reflective models* (pp. 108–123). Hershey, PA: Information Science Reference. doi:10.4018/978-1-61520-897-5.ch007

McGrath, E., Lowes, S., McKay, M., Sayres, J., & Lin, P. (2012). Robots underwater! Learning science, engineering and 21st century skills: The evolution of curricula, professional development and research in formal and informal contexts. In B. Barker, G. Nugent, N. Grandgenett, & V. Adamchuk (Eds.), *Robots in K-12 education: A new technology for learning* (pp. 141–167). Hershey, PA: Information Science Reference. doi:10.4018/978-1-4666-0182-6.ch007

McGuigan, A. (2012). Blogospheric learning in a continuing professional development context. In A. Okada, T. Connolly, & P. Scott (Eds.), *Collaborative learning 2.0: Open educational resources* (pp. 222–237). Hershey, PA: Information Science Reference. doi:10.4018/978-1-4666-0300-4.ch012

McIntosh, S. (2005). Expanding the classroom: Using online discussion forums in college and professional development courses. In K. St.Amant, & P. Zemliansky (Eds.), *Internet-based workplace communications: Industry and academic applications* (pp. 68–87). Hershey, PA: Information Science Publishing.

McNair, V., & Marshall, K. (2006). How eportfolios support development in early teacher education. In A. Jafari, & C. Kaufman (Eds.), *Handbook of research on eportfolios* (pp. 474–485). Hershey, PA: Idea Group Publishing. doi:10.4018/978-1-59140-890-1.ch042

McNair, V., & Marshall, K. (2008). How eportfolios support development in early teacher education. In L. Tomei (Ed.), *Online and distance learning: Concepts, methodologies, tools, and applications* (pp. 2130–2137). Hershey, PA: Information Science Reference.

McPherson, M., Baptista Nunes, M., Sandars, J., & Kell, C. (2008). Technology and continuing professional education: The reality beyond the hype. In T. Kidd, & I. Chen (Eds.), *Social information technology: Connecting society and cultural issues* (pp. 296–312). Hershey, PA: Information Science Reference. doi:10.4018/978-1-59904-774-4.ch019

Related References

Medina, A. L., Tobin, M. T., Pilonieta, P., Chiappone, L. L., & Blanton, W. E. (2012). Application of computer, digital, and telecommunications technologies to the clinical preparation of teachers. In D. Polly, C. Mims, & K. Persichitte (Eds.), *Developing technology-rich teacher education programs: Key issues* (pp. 480–498). Hershey, PA: Information Science Reference. doi:10.4018/978-1-4666-0014-0.ch031

Meletiou-Mavrotheris, M. (2012). Online communities of practice as vehicles for teacher professional development. In A. Juan, M. Huertas, S. Trenholm, & C. Steegmann (Eds.), *Teaching mathematics online: Emergent technologies and methodologies* (pp. 142–166). Hershey, PA: Information Science Reference.

Meltzer, S. T. (2013). The impact of new technologies on professional development. In V. Bryan, & V. Wang (Eds.), *Technology use and research approaches for community education and professional development* (pp. 40–52). Hershey, PA: Information Science Reference.

Milman, N. B., Hillarious, M., O'Neill, V., & Walker, B. (2013). Going 11 with laptop computers in an independent, co-educational middle and high school. In J. Keengwe (Ed.), *Pedagogical applications and social effects of mobile technology integration* (pp. 156–174). Hershey, PA: Information Science Reference. doi:10.4018/978-1-4666-2985-1.ch009

Moon, B. (2012). Teaching teachers: The biggest educational challenge in sub-Saharan Africa. In R. Hogan (Ed.), *Transnational distance learning and building new markets for universities* (pp. 198–209). Hershey, PA: Information Science Reference. doi:10.4018/978-1-4666-0206-9.ch012

Mørch, A. I., & Andersen, R. (2012). Mutual development: The software engineering context of end-user development. In A. Dwivedi, & S. Clarke (Eds.), *End-user computing, development, and software engineering: New challenges* (pp. 103–125). Hershey, PA: Information Science Reference. doi:10.4018/978-1-4666-0140-6.ch005

Morrow, D., & Bagnall, R. G. (2010). Hybridizing online learning with external interactivity. In F. Wang, J. Fong, & R. Kwan (Eds.), *Handbook of research on hybrid learning models: Advanced tools, technologies, and applications* (pp. 24–41). Hershey, PA: Information Science Reference.

Mountain, L. A. (2008). Videoconferencing: An alternative to traditional professional development in the K-12 setting. In D. Newman, J. Falco, S. Silverman, & P. Barbanell (Eds.), *Videoconferencing technology in K-12 instruction: Best practices and trends* (pp. 213–225). Hershey, PA: Information Science Reference.

Mouzakis, C., & Bourletidis, C. (2010). A blended learning course for teachers' ongoing professional development in Greece. In J. Yamamoto, J. Kush, R. Lombard, & C. Hertzog (Eds.), *Technology implementation and teacher education: Reflective models* (pp. 1–24). Hershey, PA: Information Science Reference. doi:10.4018/978-1-61520-897-5.ch001

Mouzakis, C., Tsaknakis, H., & Tziortzioti, C. (2012). Theoretical rationale for designing a blended learning teachers' professional development program. In P. Anastasiades (Ed.), *Blended learning environments for adults: Evaluations and frameworks* (pp. 274–289). Hershey, PA: Information Science Reference. doi:10.4018/978-1-4666-0939-6.ch014

Murphy, M. G., & Calway, P. B. (2011). Continuing professional development: Work and learning integration for professionals. In P. Keleher, A. Patil, & R. Harreveld (Eds.), *Work-integrated learning in engineering, built environment and technology: Diversity of practice in practice* (pp. 25–51). Hershey, PA: Information Science Reference. doi:10.4018/978-1-60960-547-6.ch002

Mustapha, W. Z. (2012). The art and science of designing and developing an online English language training module for adult learners. In N. Alias, & S. Hashim (Eds.), *Instructional technology research, design and development: Lessons from the field* (pp. 270–286). Hershey, PA: Information Science Reference.

Mutohar, A., & Hughes, J. E. (2013). Toward web 2.0 integration in indonesian education: Challenges and planning strategies. In N. Azab (Ed.), *Cases on web 2.0 in developing countries: Studies on implementation, application, and use* (pp. 198–221). Hershey, PA: Information Science Reference.

Newman, D. L., Clure, G., Deyoe, M. M., & Connor, K. A. (2013). Using technology in a studio approach to learning: Results of a five year study of an innovative mobile teaching tool. In J. Keengwe (Ed.), *Pedagogical applications and social effects of mobile technology integration* (pp. 114–132). Hershey, PA: Information Science Reference. doi:10.4018/978-1-4666-2985-1.ch007

Newman, D. L., Coyle, V. C., & McKenna, L. A. (2013). Changing the face of ELA classrooms: A case study of TPACK professional development. In J. Keengwe (Ed.), *Research perspectives and best practices in educational technology integration* (pp. 270–287). Hershey, PA: Information Science Reference.

Ng, A. W., & Ho, F. (2014). Dynamics of knowledge renewal for professional accountancy under globalization. In P. Ordóñez de Pablos, & R. Tennyson (Eds.), *Strategic approaches for human capital management and development in a turbulent economy* (pp. 264–278). Hershey, PA: Business Science Reference.

Ng, F. F. (2005). Knowledge management in higher education and professional development in the construction industry. In A. Kazi (Ed.), *Knowledge management in the construction industry: A socio-technical perspective* (pp. 150–165). Hershey, PA: Idea Group Publishing.

Ng, F. F. (2008). Knowledge management in higher education and professional development in the construction industry. In M. Jennex (Ed.), *Knowledge management: Concepts, methodologies, tools, and applications* (pp. 2355–2368). Hershey, PA: Information Science Reference.

Nguyen, V., & Szymanski, M. (2013). A state of the art cart: Visual arts and technology integration in teacher education. In J. Keengwe (Ed.), *Research perspectives and best practices in educational technology integration* (pp. 80–104). Hershey, PA: Information Science Reference. doi:10.4018/978-1-4666-4502-8.ch013

Niemitz, M., Slough, S., St. John, K., Leckie, R. M., Peart, L., & Klaus, A. (2010). Integrating K-12 hybrid online learning activities in teacher education programs: Reflections from the school of rock expedition. In J. Yamamoto, J. Kush, R. Lombard, & C. Hertzog (Eds.), *Technology implementation and teacher education: Reflective models* (pp. 25–43). Hershey, PA: Information Science Reference. doi:10.4018/978-1-61520-897-5.ch002

Related References

Norris, D. M. (2005). Driving systemic change with e-learning. In C. Howard, J. Boettcher, L. Justice, K. Schenk, P. Rogers, & G. Berg (Eds.), *Encyclopedia of distance learning* (pp. 687–695). Hershey, PA: Information Science Reference. doi:10.4018/978-1-59140-555-9.ch100

Northrup, P. T., & Harrison, W. T. Jr. (2011). Using learning objects for rapid deployment to mobile learning devices for the U.S. coast guard. In I. Association (Ed.), *Instructional design: Concepts, methodologies, tools and applications* (pp. 527–540). Hershey, PA: Information Science Reference. doi:10.4018/978-1-60960-503-2.ch303

Northrup, P. T., Rasmussen, K. L., & Dawson, D. B. (2004). Designing and reusing learning objects to streamline WBI development. In A. Armstrong (Ed.), *Instructional design in the real world: A view from the trenches* (pp. 184–200). Hershey, PA: Information Science Publishing. doi:10.4018/978-1-59140-150-6.ch011

Northrup, P. T., Rasmussen, K. L., & Dawson, D. B. (2008). Designing and reusing learning objects to streamline WBI development. In S. Clarke (Ed.), *End-user computing: Concepts, methodologies, tools, and applications* (pp. 1–1). Hershey, PA: Information Science Reference. doi:10.4018/978-1-59904-945-8.ch037

Oigara, J. N. (2013). Integrating technology in teacher education programs. In J. Keengwe (Ed.), *Research perspectives and best practices in educational technology integration* (pp. 28–43). Hershey, PA: Information Science Reference.

Orrill, C. H., & Polly, D. (2012). Technology integration in mathematics: A model for integrating technology through content development. In D. Polly, C. Mims, & K. Persichitte (Eds.), *Developing technology-rich teacher education programs: Key issues* (pp. 337–356). Hershey, PA: Information Science Reference. doi:10.4018/978-1-4666-0014-0.ch022

Ostashewski, N., & Reid, D. (2013). The networked learning framework: A model for networked professional learning utilizing social networking sites. In J. Keengwe, & L. Kyei-Blankson (Eds.), *Virtual mentoring for teachers: Online professional development practices* (pp. 66–83). Hershey, PA: Information Science Reference.

Ostashewski, N., & Reid, D. (2013). The iPad in the classroom: Three implementation cases highlighting pedagogical activities, integration issues, and teacher professional development strategies. In J. Keengwe (Ed.), *Pedagogical applications and social effects of mobile technology integration* (pp. 25–41). Hershey, PA: Information Science Reference. doi:10.4018/978-1-4666-2985-1.ch002

Pachler, N., Daly, C., & Turvey, A. (2010). Teacher professional development practices: The case of the haringey transformation teachers programme. In J. Lindberg, & A. Olofsson (Eds.), *Online learning communities and teacher professional development: Methods for improved education delivery* (pp. 77–95). Hershey, PA: Information Science Reference.

Parker, D. (2013). Implementing the professional development program. In S. Wang, & T. Hartsell (Eds.), *Technology integration and foundations for effective leadership* (pp. 190–205). Hershey, PA: Information Science Reference.

Payne, A. (2013). Designing a professional development program. In S. Wang, & T. Hartsell (Eds.), *Technology integration and foundations for effective leadership* (pp. 171–189). Hershey, PA: Information Science Reference.

Peacock, S., & Dunlop, G. M. (2006). Developing e-learning provision for healthcare professionals' continuing professional development. In J. O'Donoghue (Ed.), *Technology supported learning and teaching: A staff perspective* (pp. 106–124). Hershey, PA: Information Science Publishing. doi:10.4018/978-1-59140-962-5.ch007

Piecka, D. C., Ruberg, L., Ruckman, C., & Fullwood, D. (2012). NASATalk as a discovery learning space: Self-discovery learning opportunities. In S. Hai-Jew (Ed.), *Constructing self-discovery learning spaces online: Scaffolding and decision making technologies* (pp. 49–71). Hershey, PA: Information Science Reference.

Pilkington, R. (2010). Building practitioner skills in personalised elearning: Messages for professional development. In J. O'Donoghue (Ed.), *Technology-supported environments for personalized learning: Methods and case studies* (pp. 167–184). Hershey, PA: Information Science Reference.

Polly, D. (2011). Preparing teachers to integrate technology effectively: The case of higher-order thinking skills (HOTS). In S. D'Agustino (Ed.), *Adaptation, resistance and access to instructional technologies: Assessing future trends in education* (pp. 395–409). Hershey, PA: Information Science Reference.

Polly, D. (2013). Designing and teaching an online elementary mathematics methods course: Promises, barriers, and implications. In R. Hartshorne, T. Heafner, & T. Petty (Eds.), *Teacher education programs and online learning tools: Innovations in teacher preparation* (pp. 335–356). Hershey, PA: Information Science Reference.

Polly, D., Grant, M. M., & Gikas, J. (2011). Supporting technology integration in higher education: The role of professional development. In D. Surry, R. Gray Jr, & J. Stefurak (Eds.), *Technology integration in higher education: Social and organizational aspects* (pp. 58–71). Hershey, PA: Information Science Reference.

Polly, D., Mims, C., & McCombs, B. (2012). Designing district-wide technology-rich professional development. In I. Chen, & D. McPheeters (Eds.), *Cases on educational technology integration in urban schools* (pp. 236–243). Hershey, PA: Information Science Reference.

Powell, E. (2009). Facilitating reflective teaching: Video-stimulated reflective dialogues as a professional development process. In V. Wang (Ed.), *Handbook of research on e-learning applications for career and technical education: Technologies for vocational training* (pp. 100–111). Hershey, PA: Information Science Reference. doi:10.4018/978-1-60566-739-3.ch008

Prisk, J., & Lee, K. (2012). How to utilize an online community of practice (CoP) to enhance innovation in teaching and learning. In V. Wang (Ed.), *Encyclopedia of e-leadership, counseling and training* (pp. 532–544). Hershey, PA: Information Science Reference.

Prpic, J. K., & Moore, G. (2012). E-portfolios as a quantitative and qualitative means of demonstrating learning outcomes and competencies in engineering. In K. Yusof, N. Azli, A. Kosnin, S. Yusof, & Y. Yusof (Eds.), *Outcome-based science, technology, engineering, and mathematics education: Innovative practices* (pp. 124–154). Hershey, PA: Information Science Reference. doi:10.4018/978-1-4666-1809-1.ch007

Pullman, N., & Streff, K. (2009). Creating a security education, training, and awareness program. In M. Gupta, & R. Sharman (Eds.), *Handbook of research on social and organizational liabilities in information security* (pp. 325–345). Hershey, PA: Information Science Reference.

Related References

Quinton, S. (2007). Delivering online expertise, online. In M. Keppell (Ed.), *Instructional design: Case studies in communities of practice* (pp. 193–214). Hershey, PA: Information Science Publishing. doi:10.4018/978-1-59904-322-7.ch010

Reali, A. M., Tancredi, R. M., & Mizukami, M. D. (2012). Online mentoring as a tool for professional development and change of novice and experienced teachers: A Brazilian experience. In V. Dennen, & J. Myers (Eds.), *Virtual professional development and informal learning via social networks* (pp. 203–218). Hershey, PA: Information Science Reference. doi:10.4018/978-1-4666-1815-2.ch012

Redmon, R. J. Jr. (2009). E-mail reflection groups as collaborative action research. In J. Salmons, & L. Wilson (Eds.), *Handbook of research on electronic collaboration and organizational synergy* (pp. 349–361). Hershey, PA: Information Science Reference.

Rice, M. L., & Bain, C. (2013). Planning and implementation of a 21st century classroom project. In A. Benson, J. Moore, & S. Williams van Rooij (Eds.), *Cases on educational technology planning, design, and implementation: A project management perspective* (pp. 76–92). Hershey, PA: Information Science Reference. doi:10.4018/978-1-4666-4237-9.ch005

Richardson, S. L., Barnes, S. L., & Torain, D. S. (2012). Using technology to support algebra teaching and assessment: A teacher development case study. In I. Chen, & D. McPheeters (Eds.), *Cases on educational technology integration in urban schools* (pp. 224–229). Hershey, PA: Information Science Reference.

Rieber, L. P., Francom, G. M., & Jensen, L. J. (2011). Feeling like a first year teacher: Toward becoming a successful online instructor. In D. Surry, R. Gray Jr, & J. Stefurak (Eds.), *Technology integration in higher education: Social and organizational aspects* (pp. 42–57). Hershey, PA: Information Science Reference.

Ring, G., & Foti, S. (2006). Using eportfolios to facilitate professional development among pre-service teachers. In A. Jafari, & C. Kaufman (Eds.), *Handbook of research on eportfolios* (pp. 340–357). Hershey, PA: Idea Group Publishing. doi:10.4018/978-1-59140-890-1.ch031

Riverin, S. (2009). Blended learning and professional development in the K-12 sector. In E. Stacey, & P. Gerbic (Eds.), *Effective blended learning practices: Evidence-based perspectives in ICT-facilitated education* (pp. 182–202). Hershey, PA: Information Science Reference. doi:10.4018/978-1-60566-296-1.ch010

Robertshaw, M. B., Leary, H., Walker, A., Bloxham, K., & Recker, M. (2009). Reciprocal mentoring "in the wild": A retrospective, comparative case study of ICT teacher professional development. In E. Stacey, & P. Gerbic (Eds.), *Effective blended learning practices: evidence-based perspectives in ICT-facilitated education* (pp. 280–297). Hershey, PA: Information Science Reference. doi:10.4018/978-1-60566-296-1.ch015

Robertson, L., & Hardman, W. (2013). More than changing classrooms: Professors' transitions to synchronous e-teaching. In P. Ordóñez de Pablos, & R. Tennyson (Eds.), *Strategic role of tertiary education and technologies for sustainable competitive advantage* (pp. 156–175). Hershey, PA: Information Science Reference.

Rockland, R., Kimmel, H., Carpinelli, J., Hirsch, L. S., & Burr-Alexander, L. (2012). Medical robotics in K-12 education. In B. Barker, G. Nugent, N. Grandgenett, & V. Adamchuk (Eds.), *Robots in K-12 education: A new technology for learning* (pp. 120–140). Hershey, PA: Information Science Reference. doi:10.4018/978-1-4666-0182-6.ch006

Rockland, R., Kimmel, H., Carpinelli, J., Hirsch, L. S., & Burr-Alexander, L. (2014). Medical robotics in K-12 education. In Robotics: Concepts, methodologies, tools, and applications (pp. 1096-1115). Hershey, PA: Information Science Reference. doi: doi:10.4018/978-1-4666-4607-0.ch053

Rodesiler, L., & Tripp, L. (2012). It's all about personal connections: Pre-service English teachers' experiences engaging in networked learning. In V. Dennen, & J. Myers (Eds.), *Virtual professional development and informal learning via social networks* (pp. 185–202). Hershey, PA: Information Science Reference. doi:10.4018/978-1-4666-1815-2.ch011

Ronau, R. N., & Rakes, C. R. (2012). A comprehensive framework for teacher knowledge (CFTK): Complexity of individual aspects and their interactions. In R. Ronau, C. Rakes, & M. Niess (Eds.), *Educational technology, teacher knowledge, and classroom impact: A research handbook on frameworks and approaches* (pp. 59–102). Hershey, PA: Information Science Publishing.

Rosen, Y., & Rimor, R. (2013). Teaching and assessing problem solving in online collaborative environment. In R. Hartshorne, T. Heafner, & T. Petty (Eds.), *Teacher education programs and online learning tools: Innovations in teacher preparation* (pp. 82–97). Hershey, PA: Information Science Reference.

Ruberg, L., Calinger, M., & Howard, B. C. (2010). Evaluating educational technologies: Historical milestones. In L. Tomei (Ed.), *ICTs for modern educational and instructional advancement: New approaches to teaching* (pp. 285–297). Hershey, PA: Information Science Reference.

Russell, D. L. (2007). The mediated action of educational reform: An inquiry into collaboative online professional development. In R. Sharma, & S. Mishra (Eds.), *Cases on global e-learning practices: Successes and pitfalls* (pp. 108–122). Hershey, PA: Information Science Publishing.

Sáenz, J., Aramburu, N., & Rivera, O. (2010). Exploring the links between structural capital, knowledge sharing, innovation capability and business competitiveness: An empirical study. In D. Harorimana (Ed.), *Cultural implications of knowledge sharing, management and transfer: Identifying competitive advantage* (pp. 321–354). Hershey, PA: Information Science Reference.

Sales, G. C. (2009). Preparing teachers to teach online. In P. Rogers, G. Berg, J. Boettcher, C. Howard, L. Justice, & K. Schenk (Eds.), *Encyclopedia of distance learning* (2nd ed., pp. 1665–1672). Hershey, PA: Information Science Reference. doi:10.4018/978-1-60566-198-8.ch244

Sales, G. C. (2011). Preparing teachers to teach online. In I. Association (Ed.), *Instructional design: Concepts, methodologies, tools and applications* (pp. 8–17). Hershey, PA: Information Science Reference. doi:10.4018/978-1-60960-503-2.ch102

Related References

Sampson, D. G., & Kallonis, P. (2012). 3D virtual classroom simulations for supporting school teachers' continuing professional development. In J. Jia (Ed.), *Educational stages and interactive learning: From kindergarten to workplace training* (pp. 427–450). Hershey, PA: Information Science Reference. doi:10.4018/978-1-4666-0137-6.ch023

Sari, E., & Lim, C. P. (2012). Online learning community: building the professional capacity of Indonesian teachers. In J. Jia (Ed.), *Educational stages and interactive learning: From kindergarten to workplace training* (pp. 451–467). Hershey, PA: Information Science Reference. doi:10.4018/978-1-4666-0137-6.ch024

Scheckler, R. (2010). Case studies from the inquiry learning forum: Stories reaching beyond the edges. In J. Lindberg, & A. Olofsson (Eds.), *Online learning communities and teacher professional development: Methods for improved education delivery* (pp. 42–59). Hershey, PA: Information Science Reference.

Schifter, C. (2008). "Making teachers better": A brief history of professional development for teachers. In C. Schifter (Ed.), *Infusing technology into the classroom: Continuous practice improvement* (pp. 41–57). Hershey, PA: Information Science Publishing. doi:10.4018/978-1-59904-765-2.ch003

Schifter, C. (2008). Effecting change in the classroom through professional development. In C. Schifter (Ed.), *Infusing technology into the classroom: Continuous practice improvement* (pp. 259–274). Hershey, PA: Information Science Publishing. doi:10.4018/978-1-59904-765-2.ch014

Schifter, C. (2008). Continuous practice improvement. In C. Schifter (Ed.), *Infusing technology into the classroom: Continuous practice improvement* (pp. 58–86). Hershey, PA: Information Science Publishing. doi:10.4018/978-1-59904-765-2.ch004

Schifter, C. (2008). Finger painting to digital painting: First grade. In C. Schifter (Ed.), *Infusing technology into the classroom: Continuous practice improvement* (pp. 109–126). Hershey, PA: Information Science Publishing. doi:10.4018/978-1-59904-765-2.ch006

Schrader, P., Strudler, N., Asay, L., Graves, T., Pennell, S. L., & Stewart, S. (2012). The pathway to Nevada's future: A case of statewide technology integration and professional development. In I. Chen, & D. McPheeters (Eds.), *Cases on educational technology integration in urban schools* (pp. 204–223). Hershey, PA: Information Science Reference.

Scott, D. E., & Scott, S. (2010). Innovations in the use of technology and teacher professional development. In J. Lindberg, & A. Olofsson (Eds.), *Online learning communities and teacher professional development: Methods for improved education delivery* (pp. 169–189). Hershey, PA: Information Science Reference.

Scott, D. E., & Scott, S. (2012). Multi-faceted professional development models designed to enhance teaching and learning within universities. In A. Olofsson, & J. Lindberg (Eds.), *Informed design of educational technologies in higher education: Enhanced learning and teaching* (pp. 412–435). Hershey, PA: Information Science Reference.

Scott, S. (2010). The theory and practice divide in relation to teacher professional development. In J. Lindberg, & A. Olofsson (Eds.), *Online learning communities and teacher professional development: Methods for improved education delivery* (pp. 20–40). Hershey, PA: Information Science Reference.

Semich, G. W., & Gibbons, B. (2011). The professional development school: A building block for training public school faculty on new technologies. In L. Tomei (Ed.), *Online courses and ICT in education: Emerging practices and applications* (pp. 99–108). Hershey, PA: Information Science Reference.

Shambaugh, N. (2013). A professional development school technology integration and research plan. In A. Ritzhaupt, & S. Kumar (Eds.), *Cases on educational technology implementation for facilitating learning* (pp. 45–68). Hershey, PA: Information Science Reference. doi:10.4018/978-1-4666-3676-7.ch003

Sherman, G., & Byers, A. (2011). Electronic portfolios in the professional development of educators. In S. D'Agustino (Ed.), *Adaptation, resistance and access to instructional technologies: Assessing future trends in education* (pp. 429–444). Hershey, PA: Information Science Reference.

Simelane, S. (2010). Professional development programme in the use of educational technology to implement technology-enhanced courses successfully. In S. Mukerji, & P. Tripathi (Eds.), *Cases on technology enhanced learning through collaborative opportunities* (pp. 91–110). Hershey, PA: Information Science Reference. doi:10.4018/978-1-61520-751-0.ch006

Skibba, K. (2013). Adult learning influence on faculty learning cycle: Individual and shared reflections while learning to teach online lead to pedagogical transformations. In J. Keengwe, & L. Kyei-Blankson (Eds.), *Virtual mentoring for teachers: Online professional development practices* (pp. 263–291). Hershey, PA: Information Science Reference.

Skinner, L. B., Witte, M. M., & Witte, J. E. (2010). Challenges and opportunities in career and technical education. In V. Wang (Ed.), *Definitive readings in the history, philosophy, theories and practice of career and technical education* (pp. 197–215). Hershey, PA: Information Science Reference. doi:10.4018/978-1-61520-747-3.ch012

Slabon, W. A., & Richards, R. L. (2012). Story-based professional development: Using a conflict management wiki. In V. Dennen, & J. Myers (Eds.), *Virtual professional development and informal learning via social networks* (pp. 256–275). Hershey, PA: Information Science Reference. doi:10.4018/978-1-4666-1815-2.ch015

Spaulding, D. T. (2008). Virtual field trips: Advantages and disadvantages for educators and recommendation for professional development. In D. Newman, J. Falco, S. Silverman, & P. Barbanell (Eds.), *Videoconferencing technology in K-12 instruction: Best practices and trends* (pp. 191–199). Hershey, PA: Information Science Reference. doi:10.4018/978-1-59904-955-7.ch060

Speaker, R. B., Levitt, G., & Grubaugh, S. (2013). Professional development in a virtual world. In J. Keengwe, & L. Kyei-Blankson (Eds.), *Virtual mentoring for teachers: Online professional development practices* (pp. 122–148). Hershey, PA: Information Science Reference.

Related References

Stacey, E., & Gerbic, P. (2009). Introduction to blended learning practices. In E. Stacey, & P. Gerbic (Eds.), *Effective blended learning practices: Evidence-based perspectives in ICT-facilitated education* (pp. 1–19). Hershey, PA: Information Science Reference. doi:10.4018/978-1-60566-296-1.ch001

Stanfill, D. (2012). Standards-based educational technology professional development. In V. Wang (Ed.), *Encyclopedia of e-leadership, counseling and training* (pp. 819–834). Hershey, PA: Information Science Reference.

Steel, C., & Andrews, T. (2012). Re-imagining teaching for technology-enriched learning spaces: An academic development model. In M. Keppell, K. Souter, & M. Riddle (Eds.), *Physical and virtual learning spaces in higher education: Concepts for the modern learning environment* (pp. 242–265). Hershey, PA: Information Science Reference.

Stewart, C., Horarik, S., & Wolodko, K. (2013). Maximising technology usage in research synthesis of higher education professional development research. In J. Willems, B. Tynan, & R. James (Eds.), *Global challenges and perspectives in blended and distance learning* (pp. 1–16). Hershey, PA: Information Science Reference. doi:10.4018/978-1-4666-3978-2.ch001

Stieha, V., & Raider-Roth, M. (2012). Disrupting relationships: A catalyst for growth. In J. Faulkner (Ed.), *Disrupting pedagogies in the knowledge society: Countering conservative norms with creative approaches* (pp. 16–31). Hershey, PA: Information Science Reference.

Stockero, S. L. (2010). Serving rural teachers using synchronous online professional development. In J. Yamamoto, J. Leight, S. Winterton, & C. Penny (Eds.), *Technology leadership in teacher education: Integrated solutions and experiences* (pp. 111–124). Hershey, PA: Information Science Reference. doi:10.4018/978-1-61520-899-9.ch007

Stylianou-Georgiou, A., Vrasidas, C., Christodoulou, N., Zembylas, M., & Landone, E. (2006). Technologies challenging literacy: Hypertext, community building, reflection, and critical literacy. In L. Tan Wee Hin, & R. Subramaniam (Eds.), *Handbook of research on literacy in technology at the K-12 level* (pp. 21–33). Hershey, PA: Information Science Reference. doi:10.4018/978-1-59140-494-1.ch002

Szecsy, E. M. (2011). Building knowledge without borders: Using ICT to develop a binational education research community. In G. Kurubacak, & T. Yuzer (Eds.), *Handbook of research on transformative online education and liberation: Models for social equality* (pp. 67–85). Hershey, PA: Information Science Reference.

Tawfik, A. A., Reiseck, C., & Richter, R. (2013). Project management methods for the implementation of an online faculty development course. In A. Benson, J. Moore, & S. Williams van Rooij (Eds.), *Cases on educational technology planning, design, and implementation: A project management perspective* (pp. 153–167). Hershey, PA: Information Science Reference. doi:10.4018/978-1-4666-4237-9.ch009

Taylor, D. B., Hartshorne, R., Eneman, S., Wilkins, P., & Polly, D. (2012). Lessons learned from the implementation of a technology-focused professional learning community. In D. Polly, C. Mims, & K. Persichitte (Eds.), *Developing technology-rich teacher education programs: Key issues* (pp. 535–550). Hershey, PA: Information Science Reference. doi:10.4018/978-1-4666-0014-0.ch034

Tedford, D. (2010). Perspectives on the influences of social capital upon internet usage of rural Guatemalan teachers. In S. Mukerji, & P. Tripathi (Eds.), *Cases on technological adaptability and transnational learning: Issues and challenges* (pp. 218–243). Hershey, PA: Information Science Reference. doi:10.4018/978-1-61520-779-4.ch012

Terantino, J. M. (2012). An activity theoretical approach to examining virtual professional development and informal learning via social networks. In V. Dennen, & J. Myers (Eds.), *Virtual professional development and informal learning via social networks* (pp. 60–74). Hershey, PA: Information Science Reference. doi:10.4018/978-1-4666-1815-2.ch004

Thompson, T. L., & Kanuka, H. (2009). Establishing communities of practice for effective and sustainable professional development for blended learning. In E. Stacey, & P. Gerbic (Eds.), *Effective blended learning practices: Evidence-based perspectives in ICT-facilitated education* (pp. 144–162). Hershey, PA: Information Science Reference. doi:10.4018/978-1-60566-296-1.ch008

Thornton, J. (2010). Framing pedagogy, diminishing technology: Teachers experience of online learning software. In H. Song, & T. Kidd (Eds.), *Handbook of research on human performance and instructional technology* (pp. 263–283). Hershey, PA: Information Science Reference.

Thornton, K., & Yoong, P. (2010). The application of blended action learning to leadership development: A case study. In P. Yoong (Ed.), *Leadership in the digital enterprise: Issues and challenges* (pp. 163–180). Hershey, PA: Business Science Reference.

Ting, A., & Jones, P. D. (2010). Using free source eportfolios to empower ESL teachers in collaborative peer reflection. In J. Yamamoto, J. Kush, R. Lombard, & C. Hertzog (Eds.), *Technology implementation and teacher education: Reflective models* (pp. 93–107). Hershey, PA: Information Science Reference. doi:10.4018/978-1-61520-897-5.ch006

Tomei, L. A. (2008). The KARPE model revisited – An updated investigation for differentiating teaching and learning with technology in higher education. In L. Tomei (Ed.), *Adapting information and communication technologies for effective education* (pp. 30–40). Hershey, PA: Information Science Reference.

Torrisi-Steele, G. (2005). Toward effective use of multimedia technologies in education. In S. Mishra, & R. Sharma (Eds.), *Interactive multimedia in education and training* (pp. 25–46). Hershey, PA: IGI Publishing.

Torrisi-Steele, G. (2008). Toward effective use of multimedia technologies in education. In M. Syed (Ed.), *Multimedia technologies: Concepts, methodologies, tools, and applications* (pp. 1651–1667). Hershey, PA: Information Science Reference. doi:10.4018/978-1-59904-953-3.ch118

Trujillo, K. M., Wiburg, K., Savic, M., & McKee, K. (2013). Teachers learn how to effectively integrate mobile technology by teaching students using math snacks animations and games. In J. Keengwe (Ed.), *Pedagogical applications and social effects of mobile technology integration* (pp. 98–113). Hershey, PA: Information Science Reference. doi:10.4018/978-1-4666-2985-1.ch006

Tynan, B., & Barnes, C. (2010). Web 2.0 and professional development of academic staff. In M. Lee, & C. McLoughlin (Eds.), *Web 2.0-based e-learning: Applying social informatics for tertiary teaching* (pp. 365–379). Hershey, PA: Information Science Reference. doi:10.4018/978-1-60566-294-7.ch019

Related References

Tynan, B., & Barnes, C. (2012). Web 2.0 and professional development of academic staff. In *Virtual learning environments: Concepts, methodologies, tools and applications* (pp. 94–108). Hershey, PA: Information Science Reference. doi:10.4018/978-1-4666-0011-9.ch107

Uehara, D. L. (2007). Research in the Pacific: Utilizing technology to inform and improve teacher practice. In Y. Inoue (Ed.), *Technology and diversity in higher education: New challenges* (pp. 213–232). Hershey, PA: Information Science Publishing.

Velez-Solic, A., & Banas, J. R. (2013). Professional development for online educators: Problems, predictions, and best practices. In J. Keengwe, & L. Kyei-Blankson (Eds.), *Virtual mentoring for teachers: Online professional development practices* (pp. 204–226). Hershey, PA: Information Science Reference.

Venkatesh, V., Bures, E., Davidson, A., Wade, C. A., Lysenko, L., & Abrami, P. C. (2013). Electronic portfolio encouraging active and reflective learning: A case study in improving academic self-regulation through innovative use of educational technologies. In A. Ritzhaupt, & S. Kumar (Eds.), *Cases on educational technology implementation for facilitating learning* (pp. 341–376). Hershey, PA: Information Science Reference. doi:10.4018/978-1-4666-3676-7.ch019

Watson, C. E., Zaldivar, M., & Summers, T. (2010). ePortfolios for learning, assessment, and professional development. In R. Donnelly, J. Harvey, & K. O'Rourke (Eds.), Critical design and effective tools for e-learning in higher education: Theory into practice (pp. 157-175). Hershey, PA: Information Science Reference. doi: doi:10.4018/978-1-61520-879-1.ch010

Whitehouse, P., McCloskey, E., & Ketelhut, D. J. (2010). Online pedagogy design and development: New models for 21st century online teacher professional development. In J. Lindberg, & A. Olofsson (Eds.), *Online learning communities and teacher professional development: Methods for improved education delivery* (pp. 247–262). Hershey, PA: Information Science Reference.

Williams, I. M., & Olaniran, B. A. (2012). Professional development through web 2.0 collaborative applications. In V. Dennen, & J. Myers (Eds.), *Virtual professional development and informal learning via social networks* (pp. 1–24). Hershey, PA: Information Science Reference. doi:10.4018/978-1-4666-1815-2.ch001

Wilson, A., & Christie, D. (2010). Realising the potential of virtual environments: A challenge for Scottish teachers. In J. Lindberg, & A. Olofsson (Eds.), *Online learning communities and teacher professional development: Methods for improved education delivery* (pp. 96–113). Hershey, PA: Information Science Reference.

Wilson, G. (2009). Case studies of ICT-enhanced blended learning and implications for professional development. In E. Stacey, & P. Gerbic (Eds.), *Effective blended learning practices: Evidence-based perspectives in ICT-facilitated education* (pp. 239–258). Hershey, PA: Information Science Reference. doi:10.4018/978-1-60566-296-1.ch013

Witt, L. A., & Burke, L. A. (2003). Using cognitive ability and personality to select information technology professionals. In M. Mahmood (Ed.), *Advanced topics in end user computing* (Vol. 2, pp. 1–17). Hershey, PA: Idea Group Publishing. doi:10.4018/978-1-59140-065-3.ch001

Wynne, C. W. (2014). Cultivating leaders from within: Transforming workers into leaders. In S. Mukerji, & P. Tripathi (Eds.), *Handbook of research on transnational higher education* (pp. 42–58). Hershey, PA: Information Science Reference.

Yakavenka, H. (2012). Developing professional competencies through international peer learning communities. In V. Dennen, & J. Myers (Eds.), *Virtual professional development and informal learning via social networks* (pp. 134–154). Hershey, PA: Information Science Reference. doi:10.4018/978-1-4666-1815-2.ch008

Yamamoto, J., Linaberger, M., & Forbes, L. S. (2005). Mentoring and technology integration for teachers. In D. Carbonara (Ed.), *Technology literacy applications in learning environments* (pp. 161–170). Hershey, PA: Information Science Publishing. doi:10.4018/978-1-59140-479-8.ch012

Yukawa, J. (2011). Telementoring and project-based learning: An integrated model for 21st century skills. In D. Scigliano (Ed.), *Telementoring in the K-12 classroom: Online communication technologies for learning* (pp. 31–56). Hershey, PA: Information Science Reference.

Zellermayer, M., Mor, N., & Heilweil, I. (2009). The intersection of theory, tools and tasks in a postgraduate learning environment. In C. Payne (Ed.), *Information technology and constructivism in higher education: Progressive learning frameworks* (pp. 319–333). Hershey, PA: Information Science Reference. doi:10.4018/978-1-60566-654-9.ch021

Zuidema, L. A. (2008). Parawork. In P. Zemliansky, & K. St.Amant (Eds.), *Handbook of research on virtual workplaces and the new nature of business practices* (pp. 81–97). Hershey, PA: Information Science Reference. doi:10.4018/978-1-59904-893-2.ch007

Zygouris-Coe, V. I. (2013). A model for online instructor training, support, and professional development. In J. Keengwe, & L. Kyei-Blankson (Eds.), *Virtual mentoring for teachers: Online professional development practices* (pp. 97–121). Hershey, PA: Information Science Reference.

Zygouris-Coe, V. I., & Swan, B. (2010). Challenges of online teacher professional development communities: A statewide case study in the United States. In J. Lindberg, & A. Olofsson (Eds.), *Online learning communities and teacher professional development: Methods for improved education delivery* (pp. 114–133). Hershey, PA: Information Science Reference.

Compilation of References

Academy of Inquiry-based Learning. (n.d.). What is inquiry-based learning? *Retrieved from* http://www.inquirybasedlearning.org/?page=What_is_IBL

Akhras, F. N., & Self, A. J. (2000). System intelligence in constructivist learning. *International Journal of Artificial Intelligence in Education*, *11*(4), 344–376.

Alberta Learning. (2004). Focus on inquiry: A teacher's guide to implementing inquiry-based learning. Alberta, Canada: Alberta Learning. Retrieved from http://www.learning.gov.ab.ca/k_12/curriculum/bySubject/focusoninquiry.pdf

Albion, P. (2001). Some factors in the development of self-efficacy beliefs for computer use among teacher education students. *Journal of Technology and Teacher Education*, *9*(3), 321–347.

Albrecht, U. V., Behrends, M., Von Jan, U., & Folta-Schoofs, K. (2013). Effects of mobile augmented reality learning compared to textbook learning on medical students: Randomized controlled pilot study. *Journal of Medical Internet Research*, *15*(8). doi:10.2196/jmir.2497 PMID:23963306

Al-Daihani, S. (2010). Exploring the use of social software by master of library and information science students. *Library Review*, *59*(2), 117–131. doi:10.1108/00242531011023871

Alexander, B. (2004). Going nomadic: Moblile learning in higher education. *EDUCAUSE Review*, *39*(5), 28.

Alexander, L. T., & Davis, R. H. (1977). *Choosing instructional techniques*. East Lansing, MI: Michigan State University.

Al-Fahad, F. N. (2009). Students' attitudes and perceptions towards the effectiveness of mobile learning in King Saud University, Saudi Arabia. *The Turkish Online Journal of Educational Technology*, *8*(2), 111–119.

Al-Hmouz, A., Shen, J., Yan, J., & Al-Hmouz, R. (2010). Enhanced learner model for adaptive mobile learning. In *Proceedings of the 12th International Conference on Information Integration and Web-based Applications & Services - iiWAS 2010*, (pp. 783 – 786). iiWAS.

Ali, A., Ouda, A., & Capretz, L. F. (2012). A conceptual framework for measuring the quality aspects of mobile learning. *Bulletin of the IEEE Technical Committee on Learning Technology*, *14*(4), 31–34.

Allen, I. E., & Seaman, J. (2013). *Changing course: Then years of tracking online education in the United States*. Babson Survey Research Group and Quahog Research Group, LLC.

Ally, M. (2005). Using learning theories to design instruction for mobile learning devices. In J. Attewell & C. Savill-Smith (Eds.), Mobile learning anytime everywhere. A book of papers from MLEARN 2004 (pp. 5–8). Retrieved from http://stu.westga.edu/~bthibau1/MEDT%208484-%20Baylen/mLearn04_papers.pdf#page=14

Alnuaim, A., Caleb-Solly, P., & Perry, C. (2012). A mobile location-based situated learning framework for supporting critical thinking: A requirements analysis study. In *Proceedings of IADIS International Conference on Cognition and Exploratory Learning in Digital Age*, (pp. 163-170). IADIS.

Alyahya, S., & Gall, J. E. (2012). iPads in Education: A Qualitative Study of Students' Attitudes and Experiences. In *Proceedings of World Conference on Educational Multimedia, Hypermedia and Telecommunications* (Vol. 1, pp. 1266-1271). Academic Press.

Alzaza, N. S., & Zulkifli, A. N. (2007). Mobile Based Library Loan Service (MBLLS). In *Proceeding of the Rural ICT Development Conference*. Retrieved from http://citeseerx.ist.psu.edu/viewdoc/download?doi=10.1.1.97.7749&rep=rep1&type=pdf

Alzaza, N. S., & Yaakub, A. R. (2011). Students' awareness and requirements of mobile learning services in the higher education environment. *American Journal of Economics and Business Administration, 3*(1), 95–100. doi:10.3844/ajebasp.2011.95.100

Amador-Lankster, C., & Naffziger, L. (2013). Power of using iPads during clinical practice with teacher candidates. In R. McBride & M. Searson (Eds.), *Proceedings of Society for Information Technology & Teacher Education International Conference 2013* (pp. 2534-2539). Chesapeake, VA: AACE. Retrieved January 19, 2014 from http://www.editlib.org/p/48484

American Association of Colleges of Teacher Education (Ed.). (2008). *Handbook of technological pedagogical content knowledge (TPCK) for educators*. New York, NY: Routledge.

Anderson, T., & Dron, J. (2010). Three generations of distance education pedagogy. *International Review of Research in Open and Distance Learning, 12*(3), 80–97. Retrieved from http://www.irrodl.org/index.php/irrodl/article/view/890

Anderson, T., & Kanuka, H. (2003). *E-research: Methods, strategies and issues*. Boston, MA: Allyn and Bacon.

Angeli, C. (2005). Transforming a teacher education method course through technology: Effects on preservice teachers' technology competency. *Computers & Education, 45*(4), 383–398. doi:10.1016/j.compedu.2004.06.002

Ani, E. O. (2010). Internet access and use: A study of undergraduate students in three Nigerian universities. The Electronic Library, 28 (4), 555 – 567.

Archambault, L. M., & Barnett, J. H. (2010). Revisiting technological pedagogical content knowledge: Exploring the TPACK framework. *Computers & Education, 55*, 1656–1662. doi:10.1016/j.compedu.2010.07.009

Armellini, A., & Jones, S. (2008). Carpe Diem: seizing each day to foster change in e-learning design. *Reflecting Education, 4*(1), 17–29.

Armstrong, D. A. (2011). Students' perceptions of online learning and instructional tools: A qualitative study of undergraduate students use of online tools. *Turkish Online Journal of Educational Technology, 10*(3), 222–226.

Arnbak, E. (Ed.). (2003). *Faglig læsning*. Copenhagen, Denmark: Gyldendal.

Attewell, J., Savill-Smith, C., Douch, R., & Parker, G. (2010). *Modernising education and training: Mobilising technology for learning*. Available from http://www.talpalink.co.uk/resources/Modernising+education+and+training$2C+mobilising+technology+for+learning.pdf

Attewell, J. (2005). *Mobile technologies and learning: a technology update and m-learning project summary*. London: Learning and Skills Development Agency.

Attewell, J., & Savill-Smith, C. (2004). *Learning with mobile devices: research and development – a book of papers*. London: Learning and Skills Development Agency.

Aubusson, P., Schuck, S., & Burden, K. (2009). Mobile learning for teacher professional learning: Benefits, obstacles and issues. *ALT-J Research in Learning Technology, 17*(3), 233–247. doi:10.1080/09687760903247641

Azevedo, R. (2005). Using hypermedia as a metacognitive tool for enhancing student learning? The role of self-regulated learning. *Educational Psychologist, 40*(4), 199–209. doi:10.1207/s15326985ep4004_2

Bailey, G. D., & Powell, D. (1998). Technology staff development and support programs: Applying Abraham Maslow's hierarchy of need. *Leading and Learning with Technology, 26*(3), 47-51, 64.

Balsamo, A. (2011). *Designing Culture: The Technological Imagination at Work*. Duke University Press. doi:10.1215/9780822392149

Bandura, A. (1997). *Self-efficacy: The exercise of control*. New York, NY: W.H. Freeman and Company.

Barber, M., & Mourshed, M. (2007). *How the world's best-performing school systems come out on top*. London, UK: McKinsey & Company.

Barley, Z. A., & Brigham, N. (2008). Preparing teachers to teach in rural schools (Issues & Answers Report, REL 2008–No. 045). Washington, DC: U.S. Department of Education, Institute of Education Sciences, National Center for Education Evaluation and Regional Assistance, Regional Educational Laboratory Central. Retrieved from. Retrieved from http://ies.ed.gov/ncee/edlabs

Baron, N. (2013). Redefining Reading: The Impact of Digital Communication Media. *PMLA, 128*(1), 193–200. doi:10.1632/pmla.2013.128.1.193

Basham, J. D., & Marino, M. T. (2013). Understanding STEM Education and Supporting Students Through Universal Design for Learning. *Teaching Exceptional Children, 45*(4), 8–15.

Baskin, C., Barker, M., & Woods, P. (2005). When group work leaves the classroom does group skills development also go out the window? *British Journal of Educational Technology, 36*(1), 19–31. doi:10.1111/j.1467-8535.2005.00435.x

Bates, M. (2004). From knowledge to action and back again: Building a bridge. *Asia-Pacific Journal of Cooperative Education, 5*(1), 7–14.

Bauer, J., & Kenton, J. (2005). Toward technology integration in schools: Why it is not happening. *Journal of Technology and Teacher Education, 13*, 519–546.

Bawden, D., Robinson, L., Anderson, T., Bates, J., Rutkauskiene, U., & Vilar, P. (2007). Towards curriculum 2.0: library/information education for a Web 2.0 world. *Library and Information Research, 31*(99), 14–25.

Baya'a, N., & Daher, W. (2009). Learning mathematics in an authentic mobile environment: The perceptions of students. *International Journal of Interactive Mobile Technologies, 3*, 6–14.

Becker, H. J., & Ravitz, J. L. (2001). *Proceedings from the American Educational Research Association (AERA): Computer use by teachers: Are Cuban's predictions correct?* Retrieved from http://www.crito.uci.edu/tlc/findings/conferences-pdf/aera_2001.pdf

BenMoussa, C. (2003). *Workers on the move: New opportunities through mobile commerce*. Paper presented at the meeting of the Stockholm Mobility Roundtable. Stockholm, Sweden.

Berge, Z. L., & Muilenburg, L. (Eds.). (2013). *Handbook of mobile learning*. New York, NY: Routledge.

Bezemer, J., & Kress, G. (2008). Writing in multimodal texts: A social semiotic account of designs for learning. (Special Issue on Writing and New Media). *Written Communication, 25*(2), 166–195. doi:10.1177/0741088307313177

Bird, T. (2013). *Impact of University of Leicester Criminology iPad and Course App in distance learning*. Available at http://www.youtube.com/watch?v=iYspVOGs2zs

Black, P., Harrison, C., Lee, C., & Wiliam, D. (2003). *Assessment for learning: Putting it into practice*. New York, NY: Open University Press.

Blau, A. (2004). The future of independent media. *Deeper News, 10* (1). Retrieved February 3, 2008, from http://www.gbn.com/ArticleDisplayServlet.srv?aid=34045

Blok, H., Oostdam, R., Otter, M. E., & Overmaat, M. (2002). Computer-assisted instruction in support of beginning reading instruction: A review. *Review of Educational Research, 72*(1), 101–130. doi:10.3102/00346543072001101

Bonsignore, E., Quinn, A. J., Druin, A., & Bederson, B. (2013). Sharing Stories "in the Wild": A Mobile Storytelling Case Study Using StoryKit. *ACM Transactions on Computer-Human Interaction*, *20*(3), 18. doi:10.1145/2491500.2491506

Bora, U. J., & Ahmed, M. (2013). E-learning using cloud computing. *International Journal of Science and Modern Engineering*, *1*(2), 9–13.

Borko, H., & Putnam, R. (2000). What do new views of knowledge and thinking have to say about research on teacher learning. *Educational Researcher*, *29*, 4–15. doi:10.3102/0013189X029001004

Borrergo, M., Cutler, S., Prince, M., Henderson, C., & Froyd, J. E. (2013). Fidelity of implementation of research-based instructional strategies (RBIS) in engineering science courses. *Journal of Engineering Education*, *102*(3), 394–425. doi:10.1002/jee.20020

Boud, D., & Walker, D. (1998). Promoting reflection in professional courses: The challenge of context. *Studies in Higher Education*. Retrieved 7/12/13 from http://www.tandfonline.com/doi/abs/10.1080/03075079812331380384#.UvYlJGKSyuM

Boulware-Gooden, R., Carreker, S., Thornhill, A., & Joshi, R. M. (2007). Instruction of metacognitive strategies enhances reading comprehension and vocabulary achievement of third-grade students. *The Reading Teacher*, *61*(1), 70–77. doi:10.1598/RT.61.1.7

boyd, d. (2008). Why youth (heart) social network sites: The role of networked publics in teenage social life. In D. Buckingham (Ed.), *Youth, Identity, and Digital Media* (pp. 119-142). Cambridge, MA: MIT Press.

Boyd, D. J., Grossman, P. L., Lankford, H., Loeb, S., & Wyckoff, J. (2009). Teacher preparation and student achievement. *Educational Evaluation and Policy Analysis*, *31*(4), 416–440. doi:10.3102/0162373709353129

Brand, J., & Kinash, S. (2010). Pad-agogy: A quasi-experimental and ethnographic pilot test of the iPad in a blended mobile learning environment. The *Proceedings of the 27th Annual Conference of the Australian Society for Computers in Learning in Tertiary Education* (ASCILITE). Sydney, Australia: ASCILITE.

Brandsford, J. D., Pellegrino, J. W., & Donovan, S. (Eds.). (1999). *How people learn: Bridging research and practice*. Washington, D.C.: National Academy Press.

Bransford, J., Brown, A., & Cocking, R. (Eds.). (1999). *How people learn: Brain, mind, experience, and school*. Washington, DC: National Academy Press.

Brownell, M. T., Sindelar, P. T., Bishop, A. G., Langley, L. K., Seo, S., Rosenburg, M. S., & Bishop, L. (2005). *Growing and Improving the Special Education Teacher Workforce*. University of Florida.

Brown, T. H. (2005). Towards a model for m-learning in Africa. *International Journal on E-Learning*, *4*(3), 299–315.

Brundrett, M., & Silcock, P. (2002). Achieving competence, success and excellence in teaching. New York, NY: Routledge.

Bryant, T. (2006). Social software in academia. *EDUCAUSE Quarterly*, *2*, 61–64.

Bugeja, M. (2008, January-February). The Age of Distraction: The Professor or the Processor? *The Futurist*, *42*(1), 66.

Bullock, D. (2004). Moving from theory to practice: An examination of the factors that pre-service teachers encounter as the attempt to gain experience teaching with technology during field placement experiences. *Journal of Technology and Teacher Education*, *12*(2), 211–237.

Bull, S., & Reid, E. (2004). Individualized revision material for use on a handheld computer. In J. Attewell, & C. Savill-Smith (Eds.), *Learning with Mobile Devices Research and Development* (pp. 35–42). London: Learning with Mobile Devices, Learning and Skills Development Agency.

Bundsgaard, J. (2009). Skærmlæsning. In A. Mangen (Ed.), *Lesing på skjerm* (pp. 35–41). Stavanger, Norway: Lesesenteret, Universitetet i Stavanger.

Burgstahler, S. (2002). *Bridging the Digital Divide in Postsecondary Education: Technology access for youth with disabilities*. Minneapolis, MN: University of Minnesota.

Burkhardt, G., Monsour, M., Valdez, G., Gunn, C., Dawson, M., Lemke, C., et al. (2003). *21st century skills: Literacy in the digital age*. Retrieved January 29, 2008, from http://www.ncrel.org/engauge

Butoi, A., Tomai, N., & Mocean, L. (2013). Cloud-based mobile learning. *Informatica Economica*, *17*(2), 27–40. doi:10.12948/issn14531305/17.2.2013.03

Cahn, P. S., Benjamin, E. J., & Shanahan, C. W. (2013). Uncrunching time: Medical schools use of social media for faculty development. *Medical Education Online*, *18*, 20995. doi:10.3402/meo.v18i0.20995 PMID:23810170

California Commission on Teacher Credentialing. (2009). *Teacher Supply in California: A Report to the Legislature, Annual Report 2007-2008*. Sacramento, CA: Author.

California Department of Education. (2009). Educational Demographics Office – DataQuest. Sacramento, CA: Author.

California Department of Education. (2010). Educational Demographics Office – DataQuest. Sacramento, CA: Author.

Cardullo, V. (2013). *Eighth-grade students reading non-fiction literature on the iPad: An exploratory case study*. (Unpublished doctoral dissertation). University of Central Florida, Orlando, FL.

Cardullo, V., Zygouris-Coe, V., Wilson, N. S., Craneen, P., & Stafford, T. (2012). Exploring think-alouds and text coding for comprehension of digital-based text. *American Reading Forum Online Yearbook, 32*. Retrieved from http://www.americanreadingforum.org/yearbook/12_yearbook/volume12.htm

Carlson, S. (2005). The Net Generation goes to college. *The Chronicle of Higher Education, Section: Information Technology*, *52*(7), A34. Retrieved October 30, 2010 from http://www.msmc.la.edu/include/learning_resources/todays_learner/The_Net_Generation.pdf

CAST. (2011). *Universal Design for Learning Guidelines version 2.0*. Wakefield, MA: Author. Retrieved from http://www.udlcenter.org/aboutudl/udlguidelines

Cates, C. (2005). *Building a bridge between university and employment: Work-Integrated learning*. Brisbane, Australia: Research Publications and Resources Section.

Chamot, A. U., Barnhardt, S., El-Dinary, P. B., & Robbins, J. (1999). *The learning strategies handbook*. White Plains, USA: Addison Wesley Longman.

Chapelle, C. A. (2009). The relationship between second language acquisition theory and computer-assisted language learning. *Modern Language Journal*, *93*, 741–753. doi:10.1111/j.1540-4781.2009.00970.x

Chen, B., & Denoyelles, A. (2013). Exploring students' mobile learning practices in higher education. Boulder, CO: Educause Center for Applied Research. Retrieved from http://www.educause.edu/ero/article/exploring-students-mobile-learning-practices-higher-education

Chen, G. D., Chang, C. K., & Wang, C. Y. (2008). Ubiquitous learning website: Scaffold learners by mobile devices with information-aware techniques. *Computers & Education*, *50*, 77–90. doi:10.1016/j.compedu.2006.03.004

Cheng, Y. C. (2006). New paradigm of learning and teaching in a networked environment: Implications for ICT literacy. In L. T. Wee Han, & R. Subramaniam (Eds.), *Handbook of research on literacy in technology at the K-12 level*. Hershey, PA: IDEA Group, Inc. doi:10.4018/978-1-59140-494-1.ch001

Chen, N.S., & Hsieh, S.W., & Kinshuk. (2008). Effects of short-term memory and content representation type on mobile language learning. *Language Learning & Technology*, *12*, 93–113.

Cheon, J., Lee, S., Crooks, S. M., & Song, J. (2012). An investigation of mobile learning readiness in higher education based on the theory of planned behavior. *Computers & Education*, *59*(3), 1054–1064. doi:10.1016/j.compedu.2012.04.015

Cheung, A. C., & Slavin, R. E. (2012). How features of educational technology applications affect student reading outcomes: A meta-analysis. *Educational Research Review*, *7*(3), 198–215. doi:10.1016/j.edurev.2012.05.002

Chi, M., & Hausmann, R. (2003). Do radical discoveries require ontological shifts? In L. Shavinina, & R. Sternberg (Eds.), *International Handbook on Innovation* (Vol. 3, pp. 430–444). New York: Elsevier Science Ltd. doi:10.1016/B978-008044198-6/50030-9

Christie, A. (2007). Using GPS and geocaching engages, empowers & enlightens middle school teachers and students. *Meridian: A Middle School Computer Technologies Journal, 10*. Retrieved September 19, 2009, from http://ncsu.edu/meridian/win2007/gps/index.htm

Chu, H. C., Hwang, G. J., & Tsai, C. C. (2010). A knowledge engineering approach to developing mindtools for context-aware ubiquitous learning. *Computers & Education, 54*(1), 289–297. doi:10.1016/j.compedu.2009.08.023

Chun, D. M., & Plass, J. L. (1997). Research on text comprehension in multimedia environments. *Language Learning & Technology, 1*(1), 60–81.

Cisco (2012). *Cisco visual networking index: Global mobile data traffic forecast update, 2011-2016*. Retrieved from http://www.cisco.com/en/US/solutions/collateral/ns341/ns525/ns537/ns705/ns827/white_paper_c11-520862.html

Clinton, G., & Rieber, L. R. (2010). The Studio experience at the University of Georgia: An example of constructionist learning for adults. *Educational Technology Research and Development, 58*, 755–780. doi:10.1007/s11423-010-9165-2

Coates, H. (2007). A model of online and general campus-based student engagement. *Assessment & Evaluation in Higher Education, 32*(2), 121–141. doi:10.1080/02602930600801878

Cobb, P., Confrey, J., Lehrer, R., & Schauble, L. (2003). Design experiments in educational research. *Educational Researcher, 32*(1), 9–13. doi:10.3102/0013189X032001009

Cobcroft, R., Towers, S., Smith, J., & Bruns, A. (2006). Mobile learning in review: Opportunities and challenges for learners, teachers, and institutions. In *Proceedings of OLT 2006 Conference*. Queensland University of Technology.

Cochrane, T., & Antonczak, L. (2013a, September 18). *Mobile Social Media as a Catalyst For Creative Pedagogy*. Paper presented at the EC-TEL 2013 Eigth European conference on technology enhanced learning: Scaling up learning for sustained impact. Paphos, Cyprus.

Cochrane, T., & Antonczak, L. (2013b). Post Web 2.0 Media: Mobile Social Media. *QScience Proceedings, (3)*, 2.

Cochrane, T., & Bateman, R. (2010). Smartphones give you wings: Pedagogical affordances of mobile Web 2.0. *Australasian Journal of Educational Technology, 26*(1), 1-14.

Cochrane, T., & Withell, A. (2013). Augmenting design education with mobile social media: A transferable framework. *Journal of the NUS Teaching Academy, 3*(4), 150-168.

Cochrane, T., Antonczak, L., Guinibert, M., & Mulrennan, D. (2014). *Developing a mobile social media framework for creative pedagogies*. Paper presented at the 10th International Conference on Mobile Learning. Retrieved from http://www.mlearning-conf.org

Cochrane, T., Antonczak, L., Guinibert, M., Withell, A., Mulrennan, D., Mountfort, P., et al. (2013). *Collaboration unplugged: Herding a flock of MOAs*. Paper presented at the Electric Dreams: 30th Ascilite Conference. Sydney, Australia.

Cochrane, T., Munn, J., & Antonczak, L. (2013). *Design thinking for mlearning: Herding a flock of MOAs*. Paper presented at the 3rd Mobile Creativity and Innovation Symposium. Auckland, New Zealand.

Cochrane, T., Sissons, H., & Mulrennan, D. (2012). Journalism 2.0: Exploring the impact of Mobile and Social Media on Journalism Education. In I. A. Sánchez & P. Isaias (Eds.), *Proceedings of the IADIS International Conference on Mobile Learning 2012* (pp. 165-172). Berlin, Germany: IADIS International Association for Development of the Information Society.

Cochrane, T. (2013). Mlearning as a catalyst for pedagogical change. In Z. Berge, & L. Muilenburg (Eds.), *Handbook of mobile learning* (pp. 247–258). Routledge.

Cochrane, T. D. (2014). Critical success factors for transforming pedagogy with mobile Web 2.0. *British Journal of Educational Technology*, *45*(1), 65–82. doi:10.1111/j.1467-8535.2012.01384.x

Cochrane, T., & Rhodes, D. (2013). iArchi[tech]ture: Developing a mobile social media framework for pedagogical transformation. *Australasian Journal of Educational Technology*, *29*(3), 372–386.

Cochrane, T., Sissons, H., Mulrennan, D., & Pamatatau, R. (2013). Journalism 2.0: Exploring the impact of Mobile and Social Media on Journalism Education. *International Journal of Mobile and Blended Learning*, *5*(2), 22–38. doi:10.4018/jmbl.2013040102

Coiro, J., & Dobler, E. (2007). Exploring the online reading comprehension strategies used by sixth grade skilled readers to search for and locate information on the internet. *Reading Research Quarterly*, *42*, 214–257. doi:10.1598/RRQ.42.2.2

Colburn, A. (2000). An inquiry primer. *Science Scope*, *6*(23), 42–44.

Collins, L. J., & Liang, X. (2013). Task relevance in the design of online professional development for teachers of ELLS: A Q methodology study. *Professional Development in Education*, *39*(3), 441–443. doi:10.1080/19415257.2012.712752

Collison, C., & Parcell, G. (2001). *Learning to fly: Practical lessons from one of the world's leading knowledge companies*. Milford, CT: Capstone Pub.

Coll, R. K., & Zegwaard, K. E. (2006). Perceptions of desirable graduate competencies for science and technology new graduates. *Research in Science & Technological Education*, *24*(1), 29–58. doi:10.1080/02635140500485340

Colorado, J. (2012). Teaching 21st Century Learners with Mobile Devices. In *Proceedings of World Conference on Educational Multimedia, Hypermedia and Telecommunications* (Vol. 1, pp. 2247-2252). Academic Press.

Common Core Standards. (n.d.). Retrieved from https://itunes.apple.com/us/app/common-core-standards/id439424555?mt=8

Cooper, D. R., & Schindler, P. S. (2006). *Business research methods* (9th ed.). McGraw- Hill Companies, Inc.

Cordingley, P., Bell, M., Thomason, S., & Firth, A. (2005). The impact of collaborative continuing professional development (CPD) on classroom teaching and learning. Review: How do collaborative and sustained CPD and sustained but not collaborative CPD affect teaching and learning? In *Research Evidence in Education Library*. London, UK: EPPI-Centre, Social Science Research Unit, Institute of Education, University of London. Retrieved from www.eppi.ioe.ac.uk

Cordray, D., Harris, T., & Klein, S. (2009). A research synthesis of the effectiveness, replicability, and generality of the VaNTH challenge-based instructional modules in bioengineering. *Journal of Engineering Education*, *98*(4), 335–348. doi:10.1002/j.2168-9830.2009.tb01031.x

Costello, S. (2013). What are iPad Sales All Time? *About.com Website*. Retrieved from http://ipod.about.com/od/ipadmodelsandterms/f/ipad-sales-to-date.htm

Costly, C., & Armsby, P. (2007). Work-based learning assessed as a field or a mode of study. *Assessment & Evaluation in Higher Education*, *32*(1), 21–33. doi:10.1080/02602930600848267

Coyne-Smith, T. (2012, October 4). *5 Ways to Maximize Mobile Learning through Professional Development*. Retrieved from http://www.workforceanywhere.com/2012/10/04/5-ways-to-maximize-mobile-learning

Cranmer, S. (2006). Enhancing graduate employability: Best intentions and mixed outcomes. *Studies in Higher Education*, *31*(2), 169–184. doi:10.1080/03075070600572041

Crescente, M. L., & Lee, D. (2011). Critical issues of m-learning: Design models, adoption processes, and future trends. *Journal of the Chinese Institute of Industrial Engineers*, *28*(2), 111–123. doi:10.1080/10170669.2010.548856

Cross, K. (2010). *iPad replaces uni textbooks at University of Adelaide Science Faculty*. Retrieved from http://www.adelaidenow.com.au/news/ipad-replaces-uni-textbooks-at-university-ofadelaide-science-faculty/story-fn5jhv6y-1225918213032

Cummins, J. (2007). Rethinking monolingual instructional strategies in multilingual classrooms. *Canadian Journal of Applied Linguistics*, *10*(2), 221–240.

Cunningham, J. (2013). Between technology and teacher effectiveness: Professional development teaching and learning. Retrieved from http://www.teachlearning.com/print.aspx?articleid=41214

D'Orio, W. (2011). iPads in Class. *Scholastic Administrator Magazine*. Retrieved from http://www.scholastic.com/browse/article.jsp?id=3755865

Dahlstrom, E. (2012). ECAR study of undergraduate students and information technology. Louisville, CO: EDUCAUSE Center for Applied Research. Retrieved from http://www.educause.edu/library/resources/ecar-study-undergraduate-students-and-information-technology-2012

Dahlstrom, E., Walker, J. D., & Dziuban, C. (2013). ECAR Study of undergraduate students and information technology, 2013 (Research Report). Louisville, CO: EDUCAUSE Center for Analysis and Research; Available from http://www.educause.edu/ecar

Dahlstrom, E. (2012). *ECAR study of undergraduate students and information technology*. Boulder, CO: Educause Center for Applied Research.

Damon, W. (2005). Personality test: The dispositional dispute in teacher preparation today, and what to do about it. *Fwd: Thomas Fordham Foundation*, *2*(3), 1–5.

Danaher, P., Gururajan, R., & Hafeez-Baig, A. (2009). Transforming the practice of mobile learning: promoting pedagogical innovation through educational principles and strategies that work. In H. Ryu, & D. Parsons (Eds.), *Innovative mobile learning: Techniques and technologies* (pp. 21–46). Hershey, PA: IGI Global.

Dann, C. E., & Allen, B. (2013). Using mobile video technologies to enhance the assessment and learning of preservice teachers in Work Integrated Learning (WIL). In *Proceedings of the Society for Information Technology & Teacher Education International Conference AACE*. New Orleans, LA: AACE.

Day, C., Sammons, P., Kington, A., Gu, Q., & Stobart, G. (2006). Methodological synergy in a national project: The VITAE story. *Evaluation and Research in Education*, *19*(2), 102–125. doi:10.2167/eri422.0

de Groot, C., Fogleman, J., & Kern, D. (2013, November). *STEM student teachers' uses of iPads: Planning, teaching and managing, and reflecting*. Paper presented at the Annual meeting of the School Science and Mathematics Association. San Antonio, TX.

De Jong, T., Fuertes, A., Schmeits, T., Specht, M., & Koper, R. (2010). A contextualised multi-platform framework to support blended learning scenarios in learning networks. In T. T. Goh (Ed.), *Multiplatform E-Learning Systems and Technologies* (pp. 1–19). Hershey, PA: Information Sceince Reference.

Dehaan, R. L. (2005). The impending revolution in undergraduate science education. *Journal of Science Education and Technology*, *14*(2), 253–269. doi:10.1007/s10956-005-4425-3

De-Marcos, L., Hilera, J. R., Barchino, R., Jiménez, L., Martínez, J. J., & Gutiérrez, J. A. (2010). An experiment for improving students' performance in secondary and tertiary education by means of m-learning auto-assessment. *Computers & Education*, *55*(3), 1069–1079. doi:10.1016/j.compedu.2010.05.003

Desimone, L. M. (2009). Improving impact studies of teachers' professional development: Toward better conceptualization and measures. *Educational Researcher*, *38*(3), 181–199. doi:10.3102/0013189X08331140

Despotović-Zrakić, M., Simić, K., Labus, A., Milić, A., & Jovanić, B. (2013). Scaffolding environment for e-learning through cloud computing. *Journal of Educational Technology & Society*, *16*(3), 301–314.

Dispositon. (n.d.). In *Merriam-Webster online dictionary*. Retrieved from http://www.merriam-webster.com/dictionary/disposition

Dogan, B. (2012). Integration of IPad in Higher Education: A Pilot Project. Global Time, 1, 27-30.

Dolk, M. L. A. M. (1997). *Onmiddellijk onderwijsgedrag; over denken en handelen van leraren in onmiddellijke onderwijssituaties* [Immediate teaching behavior: About thinking and acting of teachers in immediate classroom situations]. Utrecht, The Netherlands: IVLOS, Utrecht University.

Doolittle, P., & Mariano, G. (2008). Working memory capacity and mobile multimedia learning environments: individual differences in learning while mobile. *Journal of Educational Multimedia and Hypermedia*, *17*(4), 511–530.

Driscoll, M. (2002). "Blended Learning: Let's get beyond the hype." IBM Global Services. Retrieved from https://www-07.ibm.com/services/pdf/blended_learning.pdf

Driscoll, M. P. (2005). *Psychology of learning for instruction*. New York, NY: Pearson Education.

Dropbox. (n.d.). Retrieved from http://www.dropbox.com

Duffy, G. G. (2005). Developing metacognitive teachers: Visioning and the expert's changing role in teacher education and professional development. In S. E. Israel, C. C. Block, K. L. Bauserman, & K. Kinnucan-Welsch (Eds.), *Metacognition in literacy learning: Theory, assessment, instruction, and professional development* (pp. 299–314). Mahwah, NJ: Lawrence Erlbaum.

Duffy, G. G., Miller, S. D., Parsons, S. A., & Meloth, M. (2009). Teachers as metacognitive professionals. In D. J. Hacker, J. Dunlosky, & A. C. Graesser (Eds.), *Handbook of metacognition in education* (pp. 240–256). New York, NY: Routledge.

Dufour, R. (2004). What is a professional learning community? *Educational Leadership*, *61*(8), 6–11.

Dunleavy, M., Dede, C., & Mitchell, R. (2009). Affordances and limitations of immersive participatory augmented reality simulations for teaching and learning. *Journal of Science Education and Technology*, *18*(1), 7–22. doi:10.1007/s10956-008-9119-1

Dunn, J. (2011). *How should Students Use Cell Phones In School?*. Retrieved from http://www.edudemic.com/phones-in-classroom/

Dyck, B. (2007, October 11). *VoiceThread*. Retrieved December 31, 2008, from Education World Web site: http://www.education-world.com/a_tech/columnists/dyck/dyck019.shtml

Dyson, L. E., Litchfield, A., Raban, R., & Tyler, J. (2009). Interactive classroom mLearning and the experiential transactions between students and lecturer. In R. J. Atkinson & C. McBeath (Eds.), *Same places, different spaces: Proceedings of ASCILITE Auckland 2009, 26th Annual ASCILITE International Conference* (pp. 233-242). Auckland, New Zealand: ASCILITE.

Eberly, J., Rand, M., & O'Conner, T. (2007). Analyzing teachers' dispositions towards diversity: Using adult development theory. *Multicultural Education*, *14*(4), 31–36.

Eco, U. (1996, November 12). *From Internet to Gutenberg*. Retrieved February 3, 2008 from, http://www.italianacademy.columbia.edu/pdfs/lectures/eco_internet_gutenberg.pdf

Edelson, D. C., Gordin, D. N., & Pea, R. D. (1999). Addressing the challenges of inquiry-based learning through technology and curriculum design. *Journal of the Learning Sciences*, *8*(3-4), 391–450. doi:10.1080/10508406.1999.9672075

Educational Broadcasting Corporation. (2004). Concept to classroom: What is inquiry-based learning. Retrieved from http://www.thirteen.org/edonline/concept2class/inquiry/index.html

Educreations. (n.d.). Retrieved from http://www.educreations.com

Egbunike, N. A. (2011). New Media and Health Communication: Communication Strategies in Malaria Control in Nigeria. In D. Ndirangu Wachanga (Ed.), Cultural Identity and New Communication Technologies (pp. 197-213). Hershey, PA: IGI Global.

Eisenberg, M., Heycox, K., & Hughes, L. (1996). Fear of the personal: Assessing students in practicum. *Australian Social Work*, *49*(4), 33–40. doi:10.1080/03124079608411186

Elbert, J., Code, J., & Irvine, V. (2013a). Integrating iPads: Perspectives and Possibilities in a High School ELA Context. In *Proceedings of World Conference on Educational Multimedia, Hypermedia and Telecommunications* (Vol. 1, pp. 1739-1742). Academic Press.

Elbert, J., Code, D. J., & Irvine, D. V. (2013b). iPads on Practicum: Perspective of a Student-Teacher. *The Arbutus Review, 4*(1), 1–18.

El-Bishouty, M. M., Ogata, H., Rahman, S., & Yano, Y. (2010). Social Knowledge Awareness Map for Computer Supported Ubiquitous Learning Environment. *Journal of Educational Technology & Society, 13*(4), 27–37.

E-Learning. (2013). *Introduction to mobile learning*. Retrieved from learning-india.com/E-learning-Articles/

El-Hussein, M. O. M., & Cronje, J. C. (2010). Defining mobile learning in the higher education landscape. *Journal of Educational Technology & Society, 13*(3), 12–21.

Elias, T. (2011). Universal instructional design principles for mobile learning. *International Review of Research in Open and Distance Learning, 12*(2), 143–156.

Ertmer, P. A., & Ottenbreit-Leftwich, A. (2010). Teacher technology change: How knowledge, confidence, beliefs, and culture intersect. *Journal of Research on Technology in Education, 42*(3), 255–284. doi:10.1080/15391523.2010.10782551

Ertmer, P. A., Ottenbreit-Leftwich, A., & York, C. (2006). Exemplary technology-using teachers: Perceptions of factors influencing success. *Journal of Computing in Teacher Education, 23*(2), 55–61.

European Commission. (2013). *Working Conditions - Employment, Social Affairs and Inclusion - European Commission*. Retrieved from http://ec.europa.eu/social/main.jsp?catId=706&langId=en&intPageId=205

Evans, C. (2008). The effectiveness of m-learning in the form of podcast revision lectures in higher education. *Computers & Education, 50*, 491–498. doi:10.1016/j.compedu.2007.09.016

Evans, N. J., Forney, D. S., Guido, F. M., Patton, L. D., & Renn, K. A. (2009). *Student development in college, theory research, and practice* (2nd ed.). San Francisco, CA: Jossey-Bass.

Evernote. (n.d.). Retrieved from https://evernote.com

Exploratorium Institute for Inquiry. (1996). A description of inquiry. Retrieved from http://www.exploratorium.edu/ifi/resources/inquirydesc.html#inquiry

Ferriter, W.M. (2010). *Digitally Speaking/Cell phones as Teaching Tools*. Retrieved from http://www.ascd.org/publications/educational-leadership/oct10/vol68

Feuer, G. (2011). Is social software really a "killer app" in the education of net generation students? Findings from a case study. *Library Hi Tech News, 28*(7), 14–17. doi:10.1108/07419051111184043

Fisher, M., Thompson, G. S., & Silverberg, D. A. (2004/2005). Effective group dynamics in e-learning: Case study. *Journal of Educational Technology Systems, 33*(3), 205–222. doi:10.2190/YTJ7-PLQB-VNDV-71UU

Flavell, J. H. (1979). Metacognition and cognitive monitoring: A new area of cognitive-developmental inquiry. *The American Psychologist, 34*, 906–911. doi:10.1037/0003-066X.34.10.906

Fogleman, J., de Groot, C., Kern, D., & Byrd, D. (2013). *Infusing tablet computers into the student teaching triad: Student teachers' use of iPads for planning, teaching, and reflection*. Paper presented at the annual meeting of the Association of Teacher Educators. Atlanta, GA.

Fogleman, J., de Groot, C., Kern, D., & Byrd, D. (2014). *Using Evernote to support preservice teachers' personal knowledge management*. Paper presented at the annual meeting of the Association of Teacher Educators. St. Louis, MO.

Foley, G. (2004). Introduction: The state of adult education and learning. In G. Foley (Ed.), *Dimensions of Adult Learning: Adult education and training in a global era* (pp. 3–19). Crows Nest, Australia: Allen & Unwin.

Fosnot, C. T. (2005). *Preface. In Constructivism: Theory, perspectives and practice* (pp. ix–xii). New York, NY: Teachers College Press.

Frank, K. A., Zhao, Y., & Borman, K. (2004). Social capital and the diffusion of innovations within organizations: Application to the implementation of computer technology in schools. *Sociology of Education, 77*(2), 148–171. doi:10.1177/003804070407700203

Franklin, T., & Van Harmelen, M. (2007). *Web 2.0 for content for learning and teaching in higher education.* Retrieved February 3, 2008, from http://www.jisc.ac.uk/media/documents/programmes/digital_repositories/web2-content-learning-and-teaching.pdf

Freire, P. (1998). *Pedagogy of the oppressed.* New York: Continuum.

Friend, M., & Cook, L. (2003). *Interactions: Collaboration skills for school professionals. (4th editon).* Boston, MA: Allyn and Bacon.

Fuegen, S. (2012). The impact of mobile technologies on distance education. *TechTrends, 56*(6), 49–53. doi:10.1007/s11528-012-0614-0

Garet, M. S., Porter, A. C., Desimone, L., Birman, B. F., & Yoon, K. S. (2001). What makes professional development effective? Results from a national sample of teachers. *American Educational Research Journal, 38*(4), 915–945. doi:10.3102/00028312038004915

Garret, J. L., & Dudt, K. (1998). Using video conferencing to supervise student teachers. *Technology and Teacher Education Annual,* 1084-1088.

Gathura, G. (2014, January 27). eHealth poses risks, says Kemri. The Standard.

Geddes, S. (2004). Mobile learning in the 21st century: Benefit for learners. *The Knowledge Tree: an e-Journal of Learning Innovation.*

Gegner, J. A., Mackay, D. H. J., & Mayer, R. E. (2009). Computer-supported aids to making sense of scientific articles: Cognitive, motivational, and attitudinal effects. *Educational Technology Research and Development, 57*(1), 79–97. doi:10.1007/s11423-008-9088-3

Geist, E. (2011). The game changer: Using iPads in college teacher education classes. *College Student Journal, 45*(4), 758–768.

George, P., Dumenco, L., Doyle, R., & Dollase, R. (2013). Incorporating iPads into a preclinical curriculum: A pilot study. *Medical Teacher. Informa Healthcare, 35*(3), 226–230.

Georgiev, T., Georgieva, E., & Smrikarov, A. (2004). M-learning: A new stage of e-learning. Retrieved from http://www.pttmedia.com/newmedia_knowhow/KnowHow_Design/Instructional%20Design/iMobile/mlearning.pdf

Georgieva, M. (2012). Learning in the Apps: Enabling A Student-Centered Approach to Learning with Mobile Technology. In *Proceedings of World Conference on Educational Multimedia, Hypermedia and Telecommunications* (Vol. 1, pp. 358-363). Academic Press.

Glenn, J. M. (2000). Teaching the Net Generation. *Business Education Forum, 54*(3), 6–14.

Goh, C. M. (1998). Strategic processing and metacognition in second language listening. *RELC Journal, 29*(2), 173–175.

Goh, C. M. (2000). A cognitive perspective on language learners' listening comprehension problems. *System, 28*(1), 55–75. doi:10.1016/S0346-251X(99)00060-3

Goh, T. T. (2010). *Multiplatform e-learning systems and technologies: Mobile devices for ubiquitous ICT-based education.* Hershey, PA: Information Science Reference.

Gould, E. (2003). *The university in a corporate culture.* New Haven, CT: Yale University Press.

Graham, C. R. (2011). Theoretical considerations for understanding technological pedagogical content knowledge (TPACK). *Computers & Education, 57*(3), 1953–1960. doi:10.1016/j.compedu.2011.04.010

Gronn, D., Romeo, G., McNamara, S., & Teo, Y. H. (2013). Web conferencing of pre-service teachers' practicum in remote schools. *Journal of Technology and Teacher Education, 21*(2), 247–271.

Guardian. (2013). *University Guide 2014: University League Table.* Retrieved from http://www.theguardian.com/education/table/2013/jun/03/university-league-table-2014

Gupta, M., & Manjrekar, P. (2012). Using mobile learning to enhance quality in higher education. *SIES Journal of Management, 8*(1), 23–30.

Guskey, T. R. (2002). Professional development and teacher change. *Teachers and Teaching: Theory and Practice, 8*(3/4), 381-391.

Guskey, T. (2000). *Evaluating Professional Development*. Thousand Oaks, CA: Corwin Press.

Guskey, T. R., & Yoon, K. S. (2009). What works in professional development? *Phi Delta Kappan, 90*(7), 495–500.

Guyton, E., & McIntyre, D. J. (1990). Student teaching and school experience. In W. R. Houston (Ed.), *Handbook of research on teacher education 7* (pp. 514–534). Thousand Oaks, CA: Corwin Press.

H.R. 4137--110th Congress: Higher Education Opportunity Act. (2007). In www.GovTrack.us. Retrieved December 28, 2013, from http://www.govtrack.us/congress/bills/110/hr4137

Haag, J. (2011). From eLearning to mLearning: The effectiveness of mobile course delivery. *The Interservice/Industry Training, Simulation and Education Conference*. National Training Systems Association. Retrieved from http://www.ww.adlnet.org/wp-content/uploads/2011/12/e_to_mLearning_paper.pdf

Hager, M. A., Wilson, S., Pollak, T. H., & Rooney, P. M. (2003). Response Rates for Mail Surveys of Nonprofit Organisations: A Review and Empirical Test. *Nonprofit and Voluntary Sector Quarterly, 32*(2), 252–267. doi:10.1177/0899764003032002005

Haigh, M., & Ell, F. (2013). And Mackisack, V. *Judging Teacher candidates' readiness to teach. Teaching and Teacher Education, 34,* 1–11. doi:10.1016/j.tate.2013.03.002

Hamel, C. (2012). Supervision of pre-service teacher: Using internet collaborative tools to support their return to their region of origin. *Canadian Journal of Education, 31*(2), 141–154.

Hancock, V. (2010) Essential, desirable or optional? Making distance e-learning courses available to those without internet access. *European Journal of Open, Distance and E-Learning, 11*. http://www.eurodl.org/materials/contrib/2010/Val_Hancock.pdf

Handal, B., El-Khoury, J., Campbell, C., & Cavanagh, M. (2013). *A framework for categorising mobile applications in mathematics education*. Retrieved from http://researchonline.nd.edu.au/cgi/viewcontent.cgi?article=1072&context=edu_conference

Han, J. H., & Finkelstein, A. (2013). Understanding the effects of professors' pedagogical development with clicker assessment and feedback technologies and the impact of students' engagement learning in higher education. *Computers & Education, 65,* 64–76. doi:10.1016/j.compedu.2013.02.002

Harris, J., Mishra, P., & Koehler, M. (2009). Teachers' technological pedagogical content knowledge and learning activity types: Curriculum-based technology integration reframed. *Journal of Research on Technology in Education, 41*(4), 393–416. doi:10.1080/15391523.2009.10782536

Hartnett, M., St. George, A., & Dron, J. (2011). Examining motivation in online distance learning environments: Complex, multifaceted and situation-dependent. *International Review of Research in Open and Distance Learning, 12*(6), 20–38. Retrieved from http://www.irrodl.org/index.php/irrodl/article/view/1030

Hase, S., & Kenyon, C. (2007). Heutagogy: A child of complexity theory. *Complicity: An International Journal of Complexity and Education, 4*(1), 111–118.

Hattie, J., & Clinton, J. (2001). The assessment of teachers. *Teaching Education, 12,* 279–300. doi:10.1080/10476210120096551

Hauck, M. (2005). Metacognitive knowledge, metacognitive strategies, and CALL. In J. L. Egbert, & G. Petrie (Eds.), *CALL research perspectives. ESL and applied linguistics professional series* (pp. 65–86). New Jersey, USA: Lawrence Erlbaum.

Hawley, W., & Valli, L. (1991). The essentials of effective professional development. In L. Darling-Hammond, & G. Sykes (Eds.), *Teaching as the Learning Profession: Handbook of Policy and Practice*. San Francisco, CA: Jossey Bass Publishers.

Hay, L. E. (2000). Educating the Net Generation. *School Administrator*, 57(54), 6–10.

Haythornthwaite, C. (2000). Online personal networks: Size, composition and media use among distance learners. *New Media & Society*, 2(2), 195–226. doi:10.1177/14614440022225779

Heinrich, P. (n.d.). *The iPad as a tool for education: A study of the introduction of iPads at Longfield Academy, Kent*. Naace and 9ine Consulting.

Hemabala, J., & Suresh, E. (2012). The frame work design of mobile learning management system. *International Journal of Computer and Information Technology*, 1(2), 179–184.

Henderson, R. G., & Chapman, B. F. (2012). Business educators' perceptions concerning mobile learning (M-Learning). *Delta Pi Epsilon Journal*, 54(1), 16–26.

Hendron, J. G. (2008). RSS for educators: blogs, newsfeeds, podcasts, and wikis in the classroom. Washington, DC: Academic Press.

Hennessy, S., Ruthven, K., & Brindley, S. (2005). Teacher perspectives on integrating ICT into subject teaching: Commitment, constraints, caution, and change. *Journal of Curriculum Studies*, 37, 155–192. doi:10.1080/0022027032000276961

Heritage, M., Kim, J., Vendlinski, T. P., & Herman, J. L. (2008). From Evidence to Action: A Seamless Process in Formative Assessment? (CRESST Report 741). National Centre for Research on Evaluation, Standards and Student Testing (CRESST). University o California.

Herrington, J., Mantei, J., Herrington, A., Olney, I., & Ferry, B. (2008). New technologies, new pedagogies: Mobile technologies and new ways of teaching and learning. In *Hello! Where are you in the landscape of educational technology? Proceedings ascilite Melbourne 2008*. Retrieved from http://www.ascilite.org.au/conferences/melbourne08/procs/herrington-j.pdf

Herrington, T., & Herrington, J. (2006). Authentic Learning Environments in Higher Education. Information Science Publishing.

Herrington, J., Herrington, A., Mantei, J., Olney, I., & Ferry, B. (Eds.). (2009). *New technologies, new pedagogies: Mobile learning in higher education*. Wollongong: Faculty of Education, University of Wollongong.

Herrington, J., Reeves, T. C., & Oliver, R. (2009). *A guide to authentic e-learning*. Routledge.

He, W., & Abdous, M. (2013). An online knowledge-centered framework for faculty support and service innovation. *VINE: The Journal of Information & Knowledge Management Systems*, 43(1), 96–110. doi:10.1108/03055721311302160

Hewson, C., Yule, P., Laurent, D., & Vogel, C. (2003). *Internet research methods*. London: Sage Publications.

Hine, N., Rentoul, R., & Specht, M. (2004). Collaboration and roles in remote field trips. In J. Attewell, & C. Savill-Smith (Eds.), *Learning with Mobile Devices Research and Development* (pp. 69–72). London: Learning and Skills Development Agency.

Hmelo-Silver, C. E., Duncan, R. G., & Chinn, C. A. (2007). Scaffolding and achievement in problem-based and inquiry learning: A response to Kirschner, Sweller and Clark (2006). *Educational Psychologist*, 42(2), 99–107. doi:10.1080/00461520701263368

Hobson, A. J., Malderez, A., Tracey, L., Homer, M., Mitchell, N., & Biddulph, M. ... Tomlinson, P. D. (2007). Newly qualified teachers' experiences of their first year of teaching: Findings from Phase III of the Becoming a Teacher project. Nottingham, UK: Department for Children, Schools and Families (9781847750204).

Hobson, A., Malderez, A., Tracey, L., Giannakaki, M. S., Pell, R. G., & Kerr, K. ... Roper, T. (2006). Becoming a teacher: Student teachers' experiences of initial teacher training in England (Research Report 744). Nottingham, UK: DfES Publications.

Hodges, D., Smith, B. W., & Jones, P. D. (2004). The assessment of cooperative education. In R. K. Cool, & C. Eames (Eds.), *International handbook for cooperative education: An international perspective of the theory, research and practice of work-integrated learning* (pp. 49–64). Boston, MA: World Association for Cooperative Education.

Hollins, E. R., & Torres Guzman, M. (2005). Research on preparing teachers for diverse population. In M. Cochran-Smith, & K. Zeichner (Eds.), *Studying teaching education: The report of the AERA Panel on Research and Teacher Education* (pp. 477–544). Mahwah, NJ: Lawrence Erlbaum.

Honey, M., & Moeller, B. (1990). *Teachers' beliefs and technology integration: Different values, different understandings* (Technical Report 6). Center For Technology in Education.

Honey, M., Mandinach, E., & McMillan, K. C. (2003). *A retrospective on twenty years of education technology policy*. Education Development Center, Center for Children and Technology, U.S. Department of Education, Office of Educational Technologies.

Hsiao, T., & Oxford, R. L. (2002). Comparing theories of language learning strategies: A confirmatory factor analysis. *Modern Language Journal*, *86*(3), 368–383. doi:10.1111/1540-4781.00155

Huang, C. J., Chen, H. X., & Chen, C. H. (2009). Developing argumentation processing agents for computer-supported collaborative learning. *Expert Systems with Applications*, *36*, 2615–2624. doi:10.1016/j.eswa.2008.01.036

Hudges, A. (2009). Higher education in a Web 2.0 world, General Publications. *JISC*. Retrieved August 7, 2012, from www.jisc.ac.uk/publications/generalpublications/2009/heweb2.aspx

Hughes, J. (2005). The role of teacher knowledge and learning experiences in forming technology-integrated pedagogy. *Journal of Technology and Teacher Education*, *13*, 277–302.

Hull, R., Reid, J., & Geelhoed, E. (2002). Creating experiences with wearable computing. *IEEE Pervasive Computing*, *1*(4), 56–61. doi:10.1109/MPRV.2002.1158279

Hurd, B. (2012). *The Shoah: 101 keys to understanding the Holocaust*. Little Falls, MN: Zoomable Media.

Hussin, S., Manap, M. R., Amir, Z., & Krish, P. (2012). Mobile learning readiness among Malaysian students at higher learning institutes. *Asian Social Science*, *8*(12), 276–283. doi:10.5539/ass.v8n12p276

Hwang, G.-J., Yang, T.-C., Tsai, C.-C., & Yang, S. J. H. (2009). A context-aware ubiquitous learning environment for conducting complex science experiments. *Computers & Education*, *53*(2), 402-413. http://dx.doi.org/10.1016/j.compedu.2009.02.016

Hwang, G., & Chang, H. (2011). A formative assessment-based mobile learning approach to improving the learning attitudes and achievements of students. *Computers & Education*, *56*(4), 1023–1031. doi:10.1016/j.compedu.2010.12.002

Ifenthaler, D., & Schweinbenz, V. (2013). The acceptance of tablet-PCs in classroom instruction: The teachers' perspectives. *Computers in Human Behavior*, *29*, 525–534. doi:10.1016/j.chb.2012.11.004

Ihanainen, P., & Gallagher, M. S. (2013). Pedagogy supporting the simultaneous learning processes of open education: Pedagogy of Simultaneity (PoS). In I. Garcilaso (Ed.), Open Education 2030. JRC-IPTS call for vision papers. (Seville, Spain: European Commission, Joint Research Centre, Institute for Prospective Technological Studies.

Ilgen, D. R., & Davis, C. A. (2000). Bearing Bad news: Reactions to negative performance feedback. *Applied Psychology: An International Review*, *49*(3), 550–565.

Ingerman, B. L., & Yang, C. (2010). Top-10 IT issues, 2010. *EDUCAUSE Review*, *45*(3), 46–60.

International Society for Technology in Education. (2007). *National educational technology standards for students: The next generation*. Retrieved January 18, 2008, from http://cnets.iste.org/NETS_S_standards-1-6.pdf

iPad App - MSc in Security, Conflict and International Development from the University of Leicester and KuKu Apps. (n.d.). Retrieved from https://itunes.apple.com/gb/app/scid-course/id503579966

Iraki, F. K. (2011). The Cultural, Economic and Political Implications of New Media: A Case Study on Mobile Telephony among University Students in Kenya. In D. Ndirangu Wachanga (Ed.), Cultural Identity and New Communication Technologies, (pp. 90-110). Hershey, PA: IGI Global.

Ito, M., Horst, H., Bittanti, M., boyd d., Herr-Stephenson, B., Lange, P.G., Pascoe, C.J., & Robinson, L. (2008). *Living and Learning with New Media: Summary of Findings from the Digital Youth Project*. Chicago: The MacArthur Foundation. Retrieved Dec 31, 2008, from http://www.macfound.org/atf/cf/%7BB0386CE3-8B29-4162-8098-E466FB856794%7D/DML_ETHNOG_WHITEPAPER.PDF

Jackson, C. (Kirabo), & Bruegmann, E. (2009). Teaching students and teaching each other: The importance of peer learning for teachers. *American Economic Journal: Applied Economics*, *1*(4), 85–108.

Jalali, A., Trottier, D., Tremblay, M., & Hincke, M. (2011). Administering a gross anatomy exam using mobile technology. *e-Learn Magazine*, *2*.

Jaworowski, S. (2011). Law professors and the iPad: A likely innovation? Global TIME, 1, 21-26.

Jeng, Y. L., Wu, T. T., Huang, Y. M., Tan, Q., & Yang, S. J. H. (2010). The add-on impact of mobile applications in learning strategies: A review study. *Journal of Educational Technology & Society*, *13*(3), 3–11.

Jenkins, H. (2006, October 20). *Confronting the challenges of participatory culture: Media education for the 21st century (part one)*. Retrieved March 20, 2008, from http://www.henryjenkins.org/2006/10/confronting_the_challenges_of.html

Jenkins, H., Purushotma, R., Clinton, K., Weigel, M., & Robinson, A. (2006). *Confronting the challenges of participatory culture: Media education for the 21st century*. Chicago, IL: The MacArthur Foundation. Retrieved from http://www.newmedialiteracies.org/wp-content/uploads/pdfs/NMLWhitePaper.pdf

Jewitt, C. (2013). Multimodality and digital technologies in the classroom. In I. de Saint-Georges, & J. J. Weber (Eds.), *Multilingualism and multimodality: Current challenges for educational studies* (pp. 141–152). Rotterdam, The Netherlands: Sense Publishers. doi:10.1007/978-94-6209-266-2_8

Johnson, L. F., Levine, A., Smith, R. S., & Haywood, K. (2010). Key emerging technologies for elementary and secondary education. *Education Digest*, *76*(1), 36–40.

Johnson, L., Adams Becker, S., Cummins, M., Estrada, V., Freeman, A., & Ludgate, H. (2013). *NMC Horizon Report: 2013 Higher Education Edition*. Austin, TX: The New Media Consortium.

Johnson, L., Adams, S., & Cummins, M. (2012). *The NMC Horizon Report: 2012 Higher Education Edition*. Austin, TX: The New Media Consortium.

Johnson, L., Levine, A., Smith, R., & Stone, S. (2010). *The 2010 horizon report*. Austin, TX: The New Media Consortium.

Johnson, S. D., & Daugherty, J. (2008). Quality and characteristics of recent research in technology education. *Journal of Technology Education*, *20*(1), 16–31.

Jonassen, D. (1992). What are cognitive tools? In P. A. Kommers, D. H. Jonassen, & J. T. Mayers (Eds.), *Cognitive tools for learning* (pp. 1–6). Berlin, Germany: Springer-Verlag NATO Scientific Affairs Division. doi:10.1007/978-3-642-77222-1_1

Jones, M., Jackson, J.T., Coiacetto, E., Budge, T., Cote, M., Steele, W., Gall, S., & Kennedy, M. (2009). *Generating academic standards in planning practice education: Final report to the Australian Learning and Teaching Council*. Retrieved from https://www.google.com.au/?gfe_rd=ctrl&ei=0x_2UuTZG6qN8Qey94G4Dw&gws_rd=cr#q=generating+academic+standards+in+planning+practice+education%3A+Final+report+to+the+australian+learning+nd+teaching+council

Jones, A. C., Scanlon, E., & Clough, G. (2013). Mobile learning: Two case studies of supporting inquiry learning in informal and semiformal settings. *Computers & Education, 61*, 21–32. doi:10.1016/j.compedu.2012.08.008

Jones, A., & Issroff, K. (2007). Motivation and mobile devices: Exploring the role of appropriation and coping strategies. *ALT-J. Research in Learning Technology, 15*, 247–258. doi:10.1080/09687760701673675

Jones, C., Ramanau, R., Cross, S., & Healing, G. (2010). Net generation or digital natives: Is there a distinct new generation entering university? *Computers & Education, 54*(3), 722–732. doi:10.1016/j.compedu.2009.09.022

Jones, M., Buchanan, G., & Thimbleby, H. (2003). Improving web search on small screen devices. *Interacting with Computers, 15*, 479–495. doi:10.1016/S0953-5438(03)00036-5

Jorgensen, D., & Howard, P. (2005). *Assessment practice for orientation education. (J. Goldson, Trans.)*. Rockhampton, Australia: Central Queensland University.

Judson, E. (2006). How teachers integrate technology and their beliefs about learning: Is there a connection? *Journal of Technology and Teacher Education, 14*(3), 581–597.

Jung, L. A., Galyon-Keramidas, C., Collins, B., & Ludlow, B. (2006). Distance Education Strategies to Support Practica in Rural Settings. *Rural Special Education Quarterly, 25*(2), 18–24.

Kadirire, J. (2009). Mobile Learning DeMystified. In R. Guy (Ed.), *The Evolution of Mobile Teaching and Learning*. California, USA: Informing Science Press.

Kahn, R., & Keller, D. (2007). Paulo Freire and Ivan Illich: Technology, politics and the reconstruction of education. *Policy Futures in Education, 5*(4), 431–448. doi:10.2304/pfie.2007.5.4.431

Kambourakis, G. (2013). Security and privacy in m-learning and beyond: Challenges and state-of-the-art. *International Journal of U- and E-Service. Science and Technology, 6*(3), 67–84.

Kanaya, T., Light, D., & Culp, K. M. (2005). Factors influencing outcomes from a technology-focused professional development program. *Journal of Research on Technology in Education, 37*, 313–329. doi:10.1080/15391523.2005.10782439

Kant, K. (2012). The future of higher education: M-learning. *Indian Streams Research Journal, 2*(11), 1–6.

Kearney, M., Schuck, S., Burden, K., & Aubusson, P. (2012). Viewing mobile learning from a pedagogical perspective. *Research In Learning Technology, 20*. doi:10.3402/rlt.v20i0.14406

Keengwe, J., Kidd, T., & Kyei-Blankson, L. (2009). Faculty and technology: Impact for faculty training and technology leadership. *Journal of Science Education and Technology, 18*(1), 23–28. doi:10.1007/s10956-008-9126-2

Kennedy, G. E., Dalgarno, B., Bennett, S., Gray, K., Waycott, J., Judd, T. S., et al. (2009). *Educating the Net Generation: A handbook of findings for practice and policy*. Retrieved from http://www.voced.edu.au/td/tnc_97.139

Kennedy, G., Dalgarno, B., Gray, K., Judd, T., Waycott, J., & Bennett, S. et al. (2007). The net generation are not big users of Web 2.0 technologies: Preliminary findings. In R. J. Atkinson, C. McBeath, S. K. A. Song, & C. Cheers (Eds.), *Proceedings of Ascilite 2007, ICT: Providing choices for learners and learning* (pp. 517–525). Singapore: Centre for Educational Development, Nanyang Technological University.

Kenya National Bureau of Statistics (2010). K*enya - National Information and Communication Technology Survey 2010*. KNE-KNBS-NICTS-2010-v01. Author.

Kern, D., Fogleman, J., & de Groot, C. (2013). *Hold hands and stick together: Using iPad technology to enhance teachers' planning, instruction and reflection*. Paper presented at the annual meeting of the Association of Literacy Educators and Researchers. Dallas, TX.

Kerpen, D. (2011). *Likeable social media: How to delight your customers, create an irresistible brand, and be generally amazing on Facebook*. New York, NY: McGraw-Hill.

Keskin, N. O., & Metcalf, D. (2011). The current perspectives, theories, and practices of mobile learning. *The Turkish Online Journal of Educational Technology*, *10*(2), 202–208.

Ketamo, H. (2003). xTask-an adaptable learning environment. *Journal of Computer Assisted Learning*, *19*, 360–370. doi:10.1046/j.0266-4909.2003.00037.x

Keys, C. W., & Bryan, L. A. (2001). Co-constructing inquiry-based science with teachers: Essential research for lasting reform. *Journal of Research in Science Teaching*, *38*(6), 631–645. doi:10.1002/tea.1023

Killilea, J. (2012). Leveraging mobile devices for asynchronous learning: Best practices. Retrieved from http://www.scs.org/upload/documents/conferences/autumnsim/2012/presentations/etms/4_Final_Submission.pdf

Kim, B. (2001). Social constructivism. In M. Orey (Ed.), Emerging perspectives on learning, teaching, and technology. Retrieved from http://epltt.coe.uga.edu/index.php?title=Social_Constructivism

Kinash, S., Brand, J., & Mathew, T. (2012). Challenging mobile learning discourse through research: Student perceptions of Blackboard mobile learn and iPads. *Australasian Journal of Educational Technology*, *28*(4), 639–655.

King, A. (1993). From sage on the stage to guide on the side. *College Teaching*, *41*(1), 30–35. doi:10.1080/87567555.1993.9926781

Kinshuk, Chang, M., Graf, S., & Yang, G. (2010). Adaptivity and personalization in mobile learning. *Technology, Instruction. Cognition and Learning*, *8*, 163–174.

Kjeldskov, J., & Graham, C. (2003). A review of mobile HCI research methods. Proceedings of Mobile HCI 2003, Springer-Verlag. *Lecture Notes in Computer Science*, *2795*, 317–335. doi:10.1007/978-3-540-45233-1_23

Koehler, M. (2013). *TPACK*. Retrieved from http://www.matt-koehler.com/tpack/using-the-tpack-image/

Koehler, M. J., Mishra, P., & Yahya, K. (2007). Tracing the development of teacher knowledge in a design seminar: Integrating content, pedagogy and technology. *Computers & Education*, *49*(3), 740–762. doi:10.1016/j.compedu.2005.11.012

Kolb, D. A., (1984). Experiential learning: Experience as the source of learning and development. Englewood Cliffs, NJ: Prentice Hall.

Koole, M. (2009). A model for framing mobile learning. In M. Ally (Ed.), Mobile learning: Transforming the delivery of education and training (pp. 25–47). Edmonton, AB: AU Press, Athabasca University. Retrieved from http://www.aupress.ca/index.php/books/120155

Koole, M. (2011, July 9). *Thoughts, writing & snippets. Mobile learning: Is the FRAME model still current?* [Web log comment]. Retrieved from http://kooleady.ca/thoughts/?p=619

Koole, M. L. (2009). A model for framing mobile learning. In M. Ally (Ed.), *Empowering learners and educators with mobile learning* (pp. 25–47). Athabasca, Canada: Athabasca University Press.

Korthagen, F. A. J., & Kessels, J. P. A. M. (1999). Linking theory and practice: Changing the pedagogy of teacher education. *Educational Researcher*, *28*(4), 4–17. doi:10.3102/0013189X028004004

Koschmann, T. (2001). Revisiting the paradigms of instructional technology. In G. Kennedy, M. Keppell, C. McNaught & T. Petrovic (Eds.), *Meeting at the Crossroads, Proceedings of the 18th Annual Conference of the Australian Society for Computers in Learning in Tertiary Education* (pp. 15-22). Melbourne: Biomedical Multimedia Unit, The University of Melbourne.

Koschmann, T. (1996). Paradigm shifts and instructional technology: an introduction. In T. Koschmann (Ed.), *CSCL: Theory and Practice of an Emerging Paradigm* (pp. 1–23). Mahwah, NJ: Lawrence Erlbaum.

Koster, B., & Korthagen, F. A. J. (1997). Opleiden in een snel veranderende samenleving: enkele aspecten van de professionalisering van lerarenopleiders.[Educating in a fast changing society: Several aspects of the professionalization of teacher educators.]. *PML-Nieuwsbrief*, *2*, 2–4.

Kothari, C. R. (2007). *Research methodology: Methods and techniques* (2nd ed.). India: New Age Publications.

Kozma, R. (2005). *ICT, education reform, and economic growth*. Chandler, AZ: Intel Corporation.

Kroop, S., Nussbaumer, A., & Fruhhman, K. (2010). *Motivating Collaborative Learning Activities by Using Existing Web 2.0 Tools.* Retrieved from http://mature-ip.eu/files/mate110/kroop.pdf

Kubitskey, M. E., Fishman, B. J., & Marx, R. W. (2003). *The relationship between professional development and student learning: Exploring the link through design research.* Paper presented at the annual meeting of the American Education Research Association. New Orleans, LA.

Kuhlthau, C., & Todd, R. (2012). *Guided inquiry.* Retrieved from http://ebookbrowsee.net/guided-inquiry-by-carol-kuhlthau-and-ross-todd-doc-d347681374

Kukulask-Hulme, A. (2007). Mobile usability in educational context: What have we learnt? *International Review of Research in Open and Distance Learning, 8*(2), 1–16.

Kukulska-Hulme, A. (2009). Will mobile learning change language learning? *ReCALL, 21,* 157–165. doi:10.1017/S0958344009000202

Kukulska-Hulme, A. (2010). Mobile learning as a catalyst for change. *Open Learning: The Journal of Open and Distance Learning, 25*(3), 181–185. doi:10.1080/02680513.2010.511945

Kukulska-Hulme, A., Sharples, M., Milrad, M., Arnedillo-Sánchez, I., & Vavoula, G. (2005). Innovation in Mobile Learning: a European Perspective. *International Journal of Mobile and Blended Learning, 1,* 1.

Kukulska-Hulme, A., & Traxler, J. (2005). *Mobile learning: A handbook for educators and trainers.* London: Routledge.

Kukulska-Hulme, A., & Traxler, J. (2007). Designed and user-generated activity in the mobile age. *Journal of Learning Design, 2*(1), 1–13. doi:10.5204/jld.v2i1.28

Kukulska-Hulme, A., & Traxler, J. (2013). Design principles for mobile learning. In H. Beetham, & R. Sharp (Eds.), *Rethinking Pedagogy for a Digital Age: Designing for 21st Century Learning* (pp. 244–257). New York, NY: Taylor and Francis.

Kuo, Y. H., Huang, Y. M., Liu, T. C., & Chang, M. (2008). Collaborative creation of authentic examples with location for u-learning. *Proc. e-Learning, 2,* 16–20.

Labaree, D. F. (2004). The trouble with Ed schools. New Haven, CT: Yale University Press.

Lahiri, M., & Moseley, J. L. (2012). Is mobile learning the future of 21st century education? Educational considerations from various perspectives. *Educational Technology,* (July-August): 3–13.

Lampert, M. (2001). *Teaching problems and the problems in teaching.* New Haven, CT: Yale University Press.

Land, S. M., & Hannafin, M. J. (2000). Student-centered learning environments. In D. H. Jonassen, & S. M. Land (Eds.), *Theoretical foundations of learning environments* (pp. 1–23). Mahwah, NJ: Erlbaum.

Lan, Y. F., & Sie, Y. S. (2010). Using RSS to support mobile learning based on media richness theory. *Computers & Education, 55*(2), 723–732. doi:10.1016/j.compedu.2010.03.005

Laouris, Y., & Eteokleous, N. (2005). *We need an educationally relevant definition of mobile learning.* Paper presented at mLearn 2005. Cape Town, South Africa.

Lapp, D., Fisher, D., & Grant, M. (2008). "You can read this text-I'll show you how": Interactive comprehension instruction. *Journal of Adolescent & Adult Literacy, 51*(5), 372–383. doi:10.1598/JAAL.51.5.1

Lary, L. M. (2004). Hide and seek: GPS and geocaching in the classroom. *Learning and Leading with Technology, 31*(6), 14–18.

Laurillard, D., Charlton, P., Craft, B., Dimakopoulos, D., Ljubojevic, D., Magoulas, G., et al. (2011). A constructionist learning environment for teachers to model learning designs. *Journal of Computer Assisted Learning, Pre-Publication.* Retrieved from. doi:10.1111/j.1365-2729.2011.00458.x

Laurillard, D. (2012). *Teaching as a design science: Building pedagogical patterns for learning and technology.* New York: Routledge.

Laurillard, D., & Pachler, N. (2007). Pedagogical forms of mobile learning: Framing research questions. In N. Pachler (Ed.), *Mobile learning: towards a research agenda* (pp. 33–54). London: WLE Centre, IOE.

Lave, J., & Wenger, E. (1991). *Situated learning: Legitimate peripheral participation*. New York: Cambridge University Press. doi:10.1017/CBO9780511815355

Leander, K., & Frank, A. (2006). The aesthetic production and distribution of image/subjects among online youth. *E-learning*, *3*(2), 185–206. doi:10.2304/elea.2006.3.2.185

Lee, V. S., & Greene, D. B., Odom, J., Schechter, E., & Slatta, R. W. (2004). What is inquiry-guided learning?. In V. S. Lee (Ed.), Teaching and learning through inquiry (pp. 3-16). Sterling, VA: Stylus.

Lee, Y. H., Waxman, H., Wu, J. Y., Michko, G., & Lin, G. (2013). Revisit the effect of teaching and learning with technology. *Journal of Educational Technology & Society*, *16*(1), 133–146.

Lehtinen, E. (2006). Teknologian kehitys ja oppimisen utopiat. In S. Järvelä, P. Häkkinen, & E. Lehtinen (Eds.), Oppimisen teoria ja teknologian opetuskäyttö (pp. 264-278). Porvoo: WSOY.

Leong, R., & Kavanagh, M. (2013). A work-integrated learning (WIL) framework to develop graduate skills and attributes in an Australian university's accounting program. *Asia-Pacific Journal of Cooperative Education*, *14*(1), 1–14.

Leu, D. J. (2000). Literacy and Technology: Deictic Consequences for Literacy Education in an Information Age. In M. L. Kamil, P. Mosenthal, P. D. Pearson, & R. Barr (Eds.), *Handbook of Reading Research* (Vol. III, pp. 743–771). Mahwah, US: Lawrence Erlbaum Associates Publishers.

Levinsen, K., & Sørensen, B. H. (2008). *It, faglig læring og pædagogisk videnledelse: Rapport vedr. projekt it læring 2006-2007*. København, Danmark: Danmarks Pædagogiske Universitetsforlag.

Levin, T., & Wadmany, R. (2005). Changes in educational beliefs and classroom practices of teachers and students in rich technology-based classrooms. *Technology, Pedagogy and Education*, *14*, 281–307. doi:10.1080/14759390500200208

Lévi-Strauss, C. (1998). *The savage mind*. London: Weidenfeld & Nicolson.

Lieberman, G. A., & Hoody, L. L. (1998). *Closing the achievement gap: Using the environment as an integrating context for learning*. San Diego, CA: State Education and Environment Roundtable.

Liestøl, G. (2011). *Learning through situated simulations: Exploring mobile augmented reality* (ECAR Research Bulletin 1). Boulder, CO: EDUCAUSE Center for Applied Research. Retrieved from http://www.educause.edu/ecar

Lin, J., & Tallman, J. (2006). A theoretical framework for online inquiry-based learning. In C. Crawford et al. (Eds.), *Proceedings of Society for Information Technology & Teacher Education International Conference* (pp. 967-974). Chesapeake, VA: AACE. Retrieved from http://editlib.org/p/22178/

Lin, X. D. (2001). Reflective adaptation of a technology artifact: A case study of classroom change. *Cognition and Instruction*, *19*, 395–440. doi:10.1207/S1532690XCI1904_1

Lin, X., Schwartz, D. L., & Hatano, G. (2005). Toward teachers' adaptive metacognition. *Educational Psychologist*, *40*(4), 245–255. doi:10.1207/s15326985ep4004_6

Little, J. W. (Chair), Lampert, M., Graziani, F., Borko, H., Clark, K. K., & Wong, N. (2007, April). *Conceptualizing and investigating the practice of facilitation in content-oriented teacher professional development*. Paper presented at the 2007 Annual Meeting of the American Educational Research Association. Chicago, IL.

Little, B. (2012). Effective and efficient mobile learning: issues and tips for developers. *Industrial and Commercial Training*, *44*(7), 402–407. doi:10.1108/00197851211267983

Little, B. (2013). Issues in mobile learning technology. *Human Resource Management International Digest*, *21*(3), 26–29. doi:10.1108/09670731311318361

Low, L., & O'Connell. (2006). Learner-centric design of digital mobile learning. *Proceedings of the OLT Conference*. Retrieved from: http://s3.amazonaws.com/academia.edu.documents/30832501/learner-centric-design-of-digital-mlearning-low-oconnell-2007.pdf?AWSAccessKeyId=AKIAIR6FSIMDFXPEERSA&Expires=1380491751&Signature=SX3KiZEbsd6eOrAc2Rp5TmWjmZ8%3D&response-content-disposition=inline

Luckin, R., Clark, W., Garnett, F., Whitworth, A., Akass, J., & Cook, J. et al. (2010). Learner-Generated Contexts: A Framework to Support the Effective Use of Technology for Learning. In M. Lee, & C. McLoughlin (Eds.), *Web 2.0-Based E-Learning: Applying Social Informatics for Tertiary Teaching* (pp. 70–84). Hershey, PA: IGI Global. doi:10.4018/978-1-60566-294-7.ch004

Ludlow, B. L., Conner, D., & Schechter, J. (2005). Low Incidence Disabilities and Personnel Preparation for Rural Areas: Current Status and Future Trends. *Rural Special Education Quarterly*, 24(3), 15–24.

Lu, M. (2008). Effectiveness of vocabulary learning via mobile phone. *Journal of Computer Assisted Learning*, 24, 515–525. doi:10.1111/j.1365-2729.2008.00289.x

Macaro, E. (2006). Strategies for language learning and for language use: Revising the theoretical framework. *Modern Language Journal*, 90(3), 320–337. doi:10.1111/j.1540-4781.2006.00425.x

Macaro, E., & Mutton, T. (2009). Developing reading achievement in primary learners of french: Inferencing strategies versus exposure to 'graded readers'. *Language Learning Journal*, 37(2), 165–182. doi:10.1080/09571730902928045

Mahaley, D. (2013, August 11). *iPad educator professional development - The three r's*. Retrieved from Emerging Ed Tech: http://www.emergingedtech.com/2013/08/ipad-educator-professional-development-the-three-rs/

Maher, D. (2013). *Pre-service primary teachers' use of iPads to support teaching: Implications for teacher education*. Retrieved from http://ersc.nmmu.ac.za/articles/Vol2No1_Maher_pp48-63_April_2013.pdf

Makoul, G., Zick, A. B., Aakhus, M., Neely, K. J., & Roemer, P. E. (2010). Using an online forum to encourage reflection about difficult conversations in medicine. *Patient Education and Counseling*, 79(1), 83–86. doi:10.1016/j.pec.2009.07.027 PMID:19717269

Mandinach, E., & Cline, H. (1992, April). *The impact of technological curriculum innovation on teaching and learning activities*. Paper presented at the Annual Conference of the American Educational Research Association. San Francisco, CA.

Mangen, A., Bente, R., & Brønnick, K. (2013). Reading linear texts on paper versus computer screen: Effects on reading comprehension. *International Journal of Educational Research*, 58, 61–68. doi:10.1016/j.ijer.2012.12.002

Manuguerra, M., & Petocz, P. (2011). Promoting student engagement by integrating new technology into tertiary education: The role of the iPad. *Asian Social Science*, 7(11), 61–65. doi:10.5539/ass.v7n11p61

Margaryan, A., Littlejohn, A., & Vojt, G. (2011). Are digital natives a myth or reality? University students' use of digital technologies. *Computers and Education*, 56 (2), 429-440.

Maria, M., & Muyinda, P. B. (2013). *A Ubiquitous Method for Sustainable Use of Mobile Learning in the Classroom*. Paper presented at the e-learning Innovations Conference & Expo. Nairobi, Kenya.

Martin, R., Ostashewski, N., & Dickinson-Delaporte, S. (2013). Creating authentic iPad activities to increase student engagement: A learning design approach. In *Proceedings of World Conference on Educational Multimedia, Hypermedia and Telecommunications* (Vol. 1, pp. 249-253). Academic Press.

Martin, F., & Ertzberger, J. (2013). Here and now mobile learning: An experimental study on the use of mobile technology. *Computers & Education*, 68, 76–85. doi:10.1016/j.compedu.2013.04.021

Martin, S., Diaz, G., Plaza, I., Larrocha, E. R., Castro, M., & Peire, J. (2011). State of the art of frameworks and middleware for facilitating mobile and ubiquitous learning development. *Journal of Systems and Software, 84*(11), 1883–1891. doi:10.1016/j.jss.2011.06.042

Mastascusa, E. J., Snyder, W. J., & Hoyt, B. S. (2011). *Effective instruction for STEM disciplines: From learning theory to college*. San Francisco, CA: John Wiley & Sons, Inc.

Masterman, L. (1985/2001). *Teaching the media*. New York, NY: Routledge. doi:10.4324/9780203359051

Masud, A. H., & Huang, X. (2012). An e-learning system architecture based on cloud computing. *World Academy of Science. Engineering and Technology, 62*, 74–78.

Matherson, L., Wright, V., Inman, C., & Wilson, E. (2008). Get up, get out with geocaching: Engaging technology for the social studies classroom. *Social Studies Research and Practice, 3*(3), 80-85. Retrieved from http://www.socstrp.org/issues/PDF/3.3.6.pdf

Mayer, R. E. (1997). Multimedia learning: Are we asking the right questions? *Educational Psychologist, 32*(1), 1–19. doi:10.1207/s15326985ep3201_1

Mayer, R. E. (2001). *Multimedia learning*. New York, USA: Cambridge University Press. doi:10.1017/CBO9781139164603

Mayer, R. E., & Moreno, R. (2003). Nine ways to reduce cognitive load in multimedia learning. *Educational Psychologist, 38*(1), 43–52. doi:10.1207/S15326985EP3801_6

Mazman, S. G., & Usluel, Y. K. (2009). The usage of social networks in educational context. World Academy of Science, Engineering and Technology, 49(1).

Mc Burney, D. H., & White, T. L. (2004). Research methods (6th ed.). Thomson: Wadsworth Publishing.

McClanahan, B. (2012). A breakthrough for Josh: How use of an iPad facilitated reading improvement. *TechTrends, 56*(3), 20–28. doi:10.1007/s11528-012-0572-6

McCombs, S., & Liu, Y. (2011). *Channeling the channel: Can iPad meet the needs of today's M-Learner*. Paper presented at the Society for Information Technology & Teacher Education International Conference 2011. Nashville, TN. Retrieved from http://www.editlib.org/p/36322

McConatha, D., Praul, M., & Lynch, M. J. (2008). Mobile learning in higher education: An empirical assessment of a new educational tool. *The Turkish Online Journal of Educational Technology, 7*(3), 15–21.

McDermott, R., Brindley, G., & Eccleston, G. (2010). Developing tools to encourage reflection in first year students blogs. In *Proceedings of the 15th Annual Conference on Innovation and Technology in Computer Science Education, ITiCSE'10*. Ankara, Turkey: ITiCSE.

McNamara, J. (2008, December). *The challenge of assessing student employability skills in legal internships*. Paper presented at the WACE Asia Pacific Conference. Sydney, Australia.

Mejias, U. (2006, June/July). Teaching social software with social software. *Journal of Online Education, 2*(5).

Mell, P., & Grance, T. (2011). The NIST definition of cloud computing.. *Communications of the ACM, 53*(6), 50.

Miles, M. B., & Huberman, A. M. (1994). *Qualitative data analysis: An expanded sourcebook*. Thousand Oaks, CA: Sage Publications.

Ministry of Nairobi Metropolitan Development. (2008). *Nairobi Metro 2030 A World Class African Metropolis*. Government of the Republic of Kenya. Retrieved from http://www.tatucity.com/DynamicData/Downloads/NM_Vision_2030.pdf

Minocha, S., et al. (2009). A study on the effective use of social software by further and higher education in the UK to support student learning and engagement: final report. *JISC*.

Mishra, P., & Koehler, M. (2006). Technological Pedagogical Content Knowledge: A framework for teacher knowledge. *Teachers College Record, 108*(6), 1017–1054. doi:10.1111/j.1467-9620.2006.00684.x

Mitra, S. (2011). *Can Mobile phones be used to Improve The Quality of Learning*. Retrieved from https://www.google.com/search?q=n+Mobile+Phones+Be+Used+To+Improve+The+Quality+Of+Learning++In+Open+Schooling%3F&ie=utf-8&oe=utf-8&aq=t&rls=org.mozilla:en-US:official&client=firefox-a

Mokhtari, K., & Reichard, C. (2002). Assessing students' metacognitive awareness of reading strategies. *Journal of Educational Psychology*, *94*(2), 249–259. doi:10.1037/0022-0663.94.2.249

Morita, M. (2003). The Mobile-Based Learning (MBL) in Japan. In *Proceedings of the First Conference on Creating, Connecting and Collaborating through Computing*. Retrieved from http://origin-www.computer.org/csdl/proceedings/c5/2003/1975/00/19750128.pdf

Motiwalla, L. F. (2007). Mobile learning: A framework and evaluation. *Computers & Education*, *49*(3), 581–596. doi:10.1016/j.compedu.2005.10.011

Mueller, J., Wood, E., Willoughby, T., Ross, C., & Specht, J. (2008). Identifying discriminating variables between teachers who fully integrate computers and teachers with limited integration. *Computers & Education*, *51*, 1523–1537. doi:10.1016/j.compedu.2008.02.003

Mugenda, A. G. (2008). *Social science research: Theory and principles*. Nairobi: Applied research and training services.

Mugenda, M. O., & Mugenda, G. A. (1999). *Research methods: Quantitative and qualitative approaches*. Nairobi, Kenya: ACTS press.

Mugenda, M. O., & Mugenda, G. A. (2003). *Research Methods Quantitative and Qualitative Approaches*. Nairobi, Kenya: ACTS press.

Munoz, C., & Sperling, G. (2013). *Bringing America's students into the digital age*. White House Blog. Retrieved October 1st, 2013, from http://www.whitehouse.gov/blog/2013/06/06/bringing-america-s-students-digital-age

Murawski, W. M., & Dieker, L. A. (2004). Tips and strategies for co-teaching at the secondary level. *Teaching Exceptional Children*, *35*(5), 52–58.

Murphy, G. D. (2011). Post-PC devices: A summary of early iPad technology adoption in tertiary environments. *e-Journal of Business Education & Scholarship of Teaching*, *5*(1), 18-32.

Murungi, C. G., & Gitonga, R. K. (2013). *Are lecturers and Students in Our Public Universities Interacting with Technology in the Blended/Hybrid Classes?*. Paper presented at the e-learning Innovations Conference & Expo. Nairobi, Kenya.

Naismith, L., Lonsdale, P., Vavoula, G., & Sharples, M. (2004). Literature review in mobile technologies and learning. Retrieved from http://telearn.archives-ouvertes.fr/docs/00/19/01/43/PDF/Naismith_2004.pdf

National Council for Accreditation of Teacher Education. (2010). *Glossary, Professional Dispositions*. Retrieved from http://www.ncate.org/Standards/UnitStandards/Glossary/tabid/477/Default.aspx#P

National Council for Accreditation of Teacher Education. (2010). Transforming teacher education through clinical practice: A national strategy to prepare effective teachers. Washington, DC: Author.

National Council for the Accreditation of Teacher Education. (2008). *Professional Standards for the Accreditation of Schools, Colleges, and Departments of Education*. Washington, DC: NCATE.

Ndume, V., Tilya, F. N., & Twaakyondo, H. (2008). Challenges of adaptive e-learning at higher learning institutions: a case study in Tanzania. *International Journal of Computing and ICT Research*, *2*(1), 47–59.

Nedungadi, P., & Raman, R. (2012). A new approach to personalization: Integrating e-learning and m-learning. *Educational Technology Research and Development*, *60*, 659–678. doi:10.1007/s11423-012-9250-9

Nespor, J. (1987). The role of beliefs in the practice of teaching. *Journal of Curriculum Studies*, *19*(4), 317–328. doi:10.1080/0022027870190403

New London Group. (2000). A pedagogy of multiliteracies: Designing social futures. In B. Cope, & M. Kalantzis (Eds.), *Multiliteracies: Literacy learning and the design of social futures* (pp. 9–38). London: Routledge.

Newby, T. J., Lehman, J., Russell, J., & Stepich, D. A. (2010). *Instructional Technology for Teaching and Learning: Designing Instruction, Integrating Computers, and Using Media* (4th ed.). Allyn & Bacon.

Newhouse, C. (2006). *Mobile education devices for pre-service teachers*. Australian Council for Computers in Education. Retrieved from http://acce.edu.au/sites/acce.edu.au/files/archived_papers/conf_P_288_newhouse_mobiles_fin.doc

Newman, D., & Gullie, K. (2009). *Using constructivist methods in technology-supported learning: Evidence of student impact*. Paper presented at the Annual Meeting of the American Educational Research Association. San Diego, CA.

Newman, D., Gullie, K., & Hunter, K. (2012). *Syracuse city school district urban natural science initiative*. Paper presented at the Math Science Partnership Regional Conference. New Orleans, LA.

Newman, D., Reinhard, D. E., & Clure, G. (2007). *Using constructivist methods in technology supported learning: Evidence of student impact*. Paper presented at the American Educational Research Association. Chicago, IL.

Newman, D., Clure, G., Morris Deyoe, M., & Connor, K. (2013). Using technology in a studio approach to learning: Results of a five year study of an innovative mobile teaching tool. In J. Keengwe (Ed.), *Pedagogical applications and social effects of mobile technology integration* (pp. 114–132). Hershey, PA: IGI Global. doi:10.4018/978-1-4666-2985-1.ch007

Newman, D., Coyle, V., & McKenna, L. (2013). Changing the face of ELA classrooms: A case study of TPACK in professional development. In J. Keengwe (Ed.), *Research perspectives and best practices in educational technology integration*. Hershey, PA: IGI Global.

Newman, D., Morris Deyoe, M., Connor, K., & Lamendola, J. (2014). Flipping STEM learning: Impact on students' process of learning and faculty instructional activities. In J. Keengwe, & G. Onchwari (Eds.), *Promoting active learning through a flipped classroom model*. Hershey, PA: IGI Global. doi:10.4018/978-1-4666-4987-3.ch006

Nie, M., Bird, T., Beck, A., Hayes, N., & Conole, G. (2013). *Adding Mobility to Distance Learning. Places Case Study*. Retrieved from: http://www.le.ac.uk/places-mlearn

Noon, D. (2007, June 14). Democracy 2.0. *Borderland*. Retrieved from http://borderland.northernattitude.org/2007/06/14/democracy-20

Notability. (n.d.). Retrieved from http://www.gingerlabs.com

NPD Group. (2013). *U.S. Commercial Channel Computing Device Sales Set to End 2013 with Double-Digit Growth, According to NPD*. Retrieved from https://www.npd.com/wps/portal/npd/us/news/press-releases/u-s-commercial-channel-computing-device-sales-set-to-end-2013-with-double-digit-growth-according-to-npd/

Nunan, D. (1997). Does learner strategy training make a difference? *Lenguas Modernas*, *24*, 123–142.

O'Connor, K. A., Good, A. J., & Greene, H. C. (2006). Lead by example: The impact of teleobservation on social studies methods courses. *Social Studies Research and Practice*, *1*(2), 165–178.

O'Donnell, C. L. (2008). Defining, conceptualizing, and measuring fidelity of implementation and its relationship to outcomes in K–12 curriculum intervention research. *Review of Educational Research*, *78*, 33–84. doi:10.3102/0034654307313793

O'Hara, S., Pritchard, R., Huang, C., & Pella, S. (2013). Learning to integrate new technologies into teaching and learning through a design-based model of professional development. *Journal of Technology and Teacher Education*, *21*(2), 203–223.

Oblinger, D. G. (2012). IT as a game changer. In D.G. Oblinger (Ed.), *Game changers: Education and information technologies*. EDUCAUSE. Available from http://www.educause.edu/research-and-publications/books

Oblinger, D. G., & Oblinger, J. L. (2005). *Educating the Net Generation*. In D. Oblinger & J. Oblinger (Eds), *Educating the Net generation* (pp. 2.1– 2.20). Boulder, CO: EDUCAUSE. Retrieved August 14, 2013 from http://net.educause.edu/ir/library/pdf/pub7101m.pdf

Oblinger, D., & Oblinger, J. L. (2005). *Educating the net generation*. Boulder, CO: EDUCAUSE.

Oldenburg, R. (1999). *The great good place: Cafes, coffee Shops, bookstores, bars, hair salons and other hangouts at the heart of a community* (2nd ed.). New York, NY: Marlowe& Company.

Oliver, R., Harper, B., Hedberg, J., Wills, S., & Agostinho, S. (2002). Formalising the description of learning designs. In A. Goody, J. Herrington, & M. Northcote (Eds.), *Quality Conversations: Research and Development in Higher Education* (Vol. 25, pp. 496–504). Jamison, Australia: HERDSA.

Olney, I., Herrington, J., & Verenikina, I. (2009). Digital story telling using iPods. In J. Herrington, A. Herrington, J. Mantei, I. Olney, & B. Ferry (Eds.), *New technologies, new pedagogies: Mobile learning in higher education* (pp. 36–44). Wollongong, Australia: University of Wollongong.

O'Malley, J. M., & Chamot, A. U. (1990). *Learning strategies in second language acquisition*. Cambridge, UK: Cambridge University Press. doi:10.1017/CBO9781139524490

Ormiston, M. (2013). *How to Use Cell Phones as Learning Tools*. Retrieved from http://www.teachhub.com/how-use-cell-phones-learning-tools

Orr, G. (2010). A review of literature in mobile learning: Affordances and constraints. In *Proceedings of the 6th IEEE International Conference on Wireless, Mobile, and Ubiquitous Technologies in Education*, (pp. 107–11). Kaohsiung, Taiwan: IEEE Computer Society Press.

Ostashewski, N., Reid, D., & Ostashewski, M. (2011). The iPad as mobile teaching device: multimedia database access in a classroom context. In *Proceedings of Global TIME 2011* (pp. 49–53). AACE.

Owen, M., Grant, L., Sayers, S., & Facer, K. (2006). Social software and learning. Futurelab. Retrieved from http://www.futurelab.org.uk/research/opening_education.htm

Owens, R., Hester, J. L., & Teale, W. H. (2002). Where do you want to go today? Inquiry-based learning and technology integration. *The Reading Teacher*, *55*(7), 616–625.

Oxford, R. L. (1990). *Language learning strategies: What every teacher should know*. Rowley, USA: Newbury House.

Oxford, R. L. (2011). *Teaching and researching language learning strategies*. Harlow, UK: Pearson Education.

Ozdamli, F., & Cavus, N. (2011). Basic elements of mobile learning. *Social and Behavioral Sciences Procedia*, *28*, 937–942. doi:10.1016/j.sbspro.2011.11.173

Pachler, N., Bachmair, B., & Cook, J. (2010). *Mobile learning: Structures, agency, practices*. London: Springer. doi:10.1007/978-1-4419-0585-7

Park, Y. (2011). A pedagogical framework for mobile learning: Categorizing educational applications of mobile technologies into four types. *International Review of Research in Open and Distance Learning*, *12*(2).

Parsons, D. (Ed.). (2013). *Innovations in Mobile Educational Technologies and Applications*. Hershey, PA: IGI Global.

Parsons, D., Ryu, H., & Cranshaw, M. (2007). A design requirements framework for mobile learning environments. *Journal of Computers*, *2*(4), 1–8. doi:10.4304/jcp.2.4.1-8

Partnership for 21st Century Skills. (2007, July 23). *Framework for 21st century learning*. Retrieved from http://www.21stcenturyskills.org/documents/framework-flyer_072307.pdf

Patrick, C. J., Peach, D., & Pocknee, C. (2009). The WIL (Work Integrated Learning) report: A national scoping study. Strawberry Hills, Australia: Australian Learning and Teaching Council in association with the Australian Collaborative Education Network.

Patrick, C. J., Peach, D., Pocknee, C., Webb, F., Fletcher, M., & Pretto, G. (2009). The WIL report: A national scoping study. Brisbane, Australia: Academic Press.

Patrick, R. (2013). *"Don't rock the boat": Conflicting mentor and pre-service teacher narratives of professional experience*. The Australian Association for Research in Education.

Patten, B., Arnedillo-Sánchez, I., & Tangney, B. (2006). Designing collaborative, constructionist and contextual applications for handheld devices. *Computers & Education*, *46*(3), 294–308. doi:10.1016/j.compedu.2005.11.011

Pea, R., & Maldonado, H. (2006). WILD for learning: Interacting through new computing devices anytime, anywhere. In R. K. Sawyer (Ed.), *The Cambridge handbook of the learning sciences* (pp. 427–441). Cambridge, UK: Cambridge University Press.

Pellerin, M. (2013). E-inclusion in Early French Immersion Classrooms: Using Technologies to Support Inclusive Practices That Meet the Needs of All Learners. *Canadian Journal of Education*, *36*(1), 44-70.

Peng, H., Su, Y., Chou, C., & Tsai, C. (2009). Ubiquitous knowledge construction: Mobile learning redefined and a conceptual framework. *Innovations in Education and Teaching International*, *46*(2), 171–183. doi:10.1080/14703290902843828

Pepper, N. (1996). Supervision: A positive learning experience or an anxiety provoking exercise? *Australian Social Work*, *49*(3), 55–64. doi:10.1080/03124079608415690

Perfetti, C., Landi, N., & Oakhill, J. (2005). The acquisition of reading comprehension skill. In M. Snowling, & C. Hulme (Eds.), *The science of reading* (pp. 227–247). Malden, USA: Blackwell. doi:10.1002/9780470757642.ch13

Perkins, S., Hamm, S., Pamplin, K., Morris, J., & McKelvain, R. (2011). Exploring learning with the iPad: ACU connected and the future of digital texts. In M. Koehler & P. Mishra (Eds.), *Proceedings of Society for Information Technology & Teacher Education International Conference 2011* (pp. 1640-1642). Chesapeake, VA: AACE.

Peters, K. (2007). M-learning: Positioning educators for a mobile, connected future. *International Journal of Research in Open and Distance Learning*, *8*(2), 1–17.

Pew Internet and American Life Project. (2007, December 19). *Teens and social media*. Retrieved from http://www.pewinternet.org/pdfs/PIP_Teens_Social_Media_Final.pdf

Pfeiffer, V. D. I., Gemballa, S., Jarodzka, H., Scheiter, K., & Gerjets, P. (2009). Situated learning in the mobile age: Mobile devices on a field trip to the sea. *ALT-J. Research in Learning Technology*, *17*(3), 187–199. doi:10.1080/09687760903247666

PollEverywhere. (n.d.). Retrieved from http://www.polleverywhere.com

Prensky, M. (2005). *Search vs. research. Or, the fear of The Wikipedia overcome by new understanding for a digital era*. Retrieved from http://www.marcprensky.com/writing/Prensky-Search_vs_Research-01.pdf

President's Commission on Excellence in Special Education. (2002). A New Era: Revitalizing special education for children and their families. Washington, DC: Department of Education, Office of Special Education and Rehabilitative Services.

Prince, M. J., & Felder, R. M. (2006). Inductive teaching and learning methods: Definitions, comparisons, and research bases. *Journal of Engineering Education*, *95*(2), 123–138. doi:10.1002/j.2168-9830.2006.tb00884.x

Project Pipeline. (2003). *Seeking Out Special Educators: An in-depth look at California's special education teacher shortage*. Sacramento, CA: Project Pipeline.

Puentedura, R. (2006). *Transformation, Technology, and Education*. Retrieved 18 February, 2013, from http://hippasus.com/resources/tte/puentedura_tte.pdf

Quinn, C. (2000). M-learning: Mobile, wireless, in-your-pocket learning. *Linezine: Learning in the new economy*. Retrieved from http://www.linezine.com/2.1/features/cqmmwiyp.htm

Quinn, C. (2013). Mobile Learning. In The Really Useful eLearning Instruction Manual: Your toolkit for putting elearning into practice. Chichester, UK: Wiley and Sons.

Ramanau, R., & Geng, F. (2009). Researching the use of Wiki's to facilitate group work. *Procedia Social and Behavioral Sciences*, *1*(1), 2620–2626. doi:10.1016/j.sbspro.2009.01.463

Reid, D., & Ostashewski, N. (2011). iPads in the Classroom–New Technologies, Old Issues: Are they worth the effort? In *Proceedings of World Conference on Educational Multimedia, Hypermedia and Telecommunications* (Vol. 1, pp. 1689-1694). Academic Press.

Rheingold, H. (2008, October) *Writing, Reading, and Social Media Literacy Writing, Reading, and Social Media Literacy*. Harvard Business Publishing: Retrieved from http://discussionleader.hbsp.com/now-new-next/2008/10/the-importance-of-social-media.html

Rice, M. L., & Wilson, E. K. (1999). How technology aids constructivism in the social studies classroom. *Social Studies*, *90*, 28–34. doi:10.1080/00377999909602388

Richardson, W. (2006). *Blogs, wikis, podcasts and other powerful web tools for classrooms*. Thousand Oaks, CA: Corwin Press.

Roach, J. H. L. (1976). The academic department chairperson: roles and responsibilities. *The Educational Record*, *57*(1), 13–23.

Robinson, K. (2009). *Transform Education? Yes, We Must*. Retrieved from http://www.huffingtonpost.com/sir-ken-robinson/transform-education-yes-w_b_157014.html

Robinson, K. (2009). *The elements: How finding your passion changes everything*. London, UK: Penguin.

Rockman., I., F. (2004). *Integrating Information Literacy into the Higher Education Curriculum; Practiccal Models for Transformation*. John Wiley Publishers.

Rogers, E. M. (2003). *Diffusion of innovations* (5th ed.). New York, NY: Free Press.

Ronfeldt, M. (2012). Where should student teachers learn to teach? Effects of field placement school characterstics on teacher retention and effectiveness. *Educational Evaluation and Policy Analysis*, *34*(1), 3–26. doi:10.3102/0162373711420865

Rossing, J. P., Miller, W. M., Cecil, A. K., & Stamper, S. E. (2012). iLearning: The future of higher education? Student perceptions on learning with mobile tablets. *Journal of the Scholarship of Teaching and Learning*, *12*(2), 1–26.

Rowntree, D. (1992). *Exploring open and distance learning*. London: Kogan Page.

Rule, A. C. (2006). The components of authentic learning. *Journal of Authentic Learning*, *3*(1), 1–10.

Rust, F. O'C. (1999). Professional conversations: New teachers explore teaching through conversation, story, and narrative. *Teaching and Teacher Education*, *15*(4), 367–380. doi:10.1016/S0742-051X(98)00049-3

Ryokai, K. (2012). Mobile learning with the engineering pathway digital library. *International Journal of Engineering Education*, *28*(5), 1119–1126.

Sachs, L., & Bull, P. (2012). Case study: Using iPad2 for a graduate practicum course. In *Proceedings of Society for Information Technology & Teacher Education International Conference* (Vol. 1, pp. 3054-3059). Academic Press.

Sadler, D. R. (1989). Formative assessment and the design of instructional systems. *Instructional Science*, *18*, 119–144. doi:10.1007/BF00117714

Salaway, G., Caruso, J. B., & Nelson, M. R. (2008). The ECAR study of undergraduate students and information technology, 2008 (Vol. Research Study, Vol. 8). Boulder, CO: EDUCAUSE Center for Applied Research.

Salaway, G., Caruso, J. B., & Nelson, M. R. (2007). *The ECAR study of undergraduate students and information technology, 2007*. Boulder, CO: EDUCAUSE Center for Applied Research.

Salmon, G. (2013). *E-tivities: The key to active online learning* (2nd ed.). London: Routledge.

Salmon, G., & Angood, R. (2013). Sleeping with the enemy. *British Journal of Educational Technology*, *44*(6), 916–925. doi:10.1111/bjet.12097

Sandholtz, J. H., Ringstaff, C., & Dwyer, D. C. (1997). *Teaching with technology: Creating student-centered classrooms*. New York, NY: Teachers College Press.

Sandoval, W. A., & Bell, P. (2004). Design-based research methods for studying learning in context: Introduction. *Educational Psychologist*, *39*(4), 199–201. doi:10.1207/s15326985ep3904_1

Saran, M. (2008). Use of Mobile Phones in Language Learning: Developing Effective Instructional Materials. In *Proceedings of Fifth IEEE International Conference on Wireless, Mobile, and Ubiquitous Technology in Education (wmute 2008)*, (pp. 39-43). IEEE.

Saunders, M., Lewis, P., & Thornhill, A. (2007). *Research Methods for Business Students* (4th ed.). Harlow: FT Prentice Hall.

Savery, J. R. (2006). Overview of problem-based learning: Definitions and distinctions. *Interdisciplinary Journal of Problem-based Learning*, *1*(1), 9–20. doi:10.7771/1541-5015.1002

Schlatter, B. E., & Hurd, A. R. (2005). Geocaching: 21st century hide and seek. *Journal of Physical Education, Recreation & Dance*, *76*(7), 28–32. doi:10.1080/07303084.2005.10609309

Schrum, L., Skeele, R., & Grant, M. (2002). One college of education's effort to infuse technology: A systemic approach to revisioning teaching and learning. *Journal of Research on Technology in Education*, *35*(2), 256–271. doi:10.1080/15391523.2002.10782385

Seagren, A. T., Wheeler, D. W., Creswell, J. W., Miller, M. T., & VanHorn-Grassmeyer, K. (1994). *Academic leadership in community colleges*. Lincoln, NE: University of Nebraska.

Segall, N., Doolen, T., & Porter, D. (2005). A usability comparison of PDA-based quizzes and paper-and-pencil quizzes. *Computers & Education*, *45*, 417–432. doi:10.1016/j.compedu.2004.05.004

Sekaran, U. (2003). *Research method of business: A skill Building Approach* (4th ed.). New York, NY: John Willey & Sons, Inc.

Seppala, P., Sariola, J., & Kynaslahti, H. (2002). Mobile learning in personnel training of university teachers. In *Proceeding of the IEEE International Workshop on Wireless and Mobile Technologies in Education* (pp. 136-139). IEEE.

Seppala, P., & Alamaki, H. (2003). Mobile learning in teacher training. *Journal of Computer Assisted Learning*, *19*, 330–335. doi:10.1046/j.0266-4909.2003.00034.x

Serdyuko, P., & Hill, R. (2007). Cultivating quality educators through innovative and comprehensive teacher preparation programs. *Journal of Research in Innovative Teaching*, *4*(1), 106-119.106-107.

Serdyukov, P., & Ferguson, B. F. (2011). Teacher dispositions: What kind of candidates do we have in a teacher preparation program, and how can we make them better? *Journal of Research in Innovative Teaching*, *4*(1), 106–119.

Serin, O. (2012). Mobile learning perceptions of the prospective teachers. *The Turkish Online Journal of Educational Technology*, *11*(3).

Shanmugapriya, M., & Tamilarasi, A. (2012). Developing a mobile adaptive test (MAT) in an m-learning environment for Android based 3G mobile devices. *International Journal on Computer Science and Engineering*, *4*(2), 153–161.

Sharples, M. (2009). *Learning at large*. Paper presented at the MLearn 2009: The 8th World Conference on Mobile and Contextual Learning, University of Central Florida, Institute for Simulation and Training. Orlando, FL.

Sharples, M., Taylor, J., & Vavoula, G. (2005). *Towards a theory of mobile learning*. Paper presented at mLearn 2005. Cape Town, South Africa.

Sharples, M. (2000). The design of personal mobile technologies for lifelong learning. *Computers & Education*, *34*, 177–193. doi:10.1016/S0360-1315(99)00044-5

Sharples, M. (2002). Disruptive devices: Mobile technology for conversational learning. *International Journal of Continuing Engineering Education and Lifelong Learning*, *12*(5/6), 504–520. doi:10.1504/IJCEELL.2002.002148

Sharples, M., Corlett, D., & Westmancott, O. (2002). The design and implementation of a mobile learning resource. *Personal and Ubiquitous Computing*, 6(3), 220–234. doi:10.1007/s007790200021

Sharples, M., Taylor, J., & Vavoula, G. (2007). A theory of learning for the mobile age. In R. Andrews, & C. Haythornthwaite (Eds.), *The Sage handbook of e-learning research* (pp. 221–247). London: Sage.

Shaughnessy, M. F., Vennemann, M. V. E., & Kleyn-Kennedy, C. (Eds.). (2008). *Meta-cognition: A recent review of research, theory, and perspectives*. New York, USA: Nova Science Publishers, Inc.

Shaunessy, E., & Page, C. (2006). Promoting inquiry in the gifted classroom through GPS and GIS technologies. *Gifted Child Today*, 29(4), 42–53.

Sheely, S. (2008). *Latour meets the digital natives: What do we really know*. Paper presented at the Hello! Where are you in the landscape of educational technology? ASCILITE 2008. Retrieved from http://www.ascilite.org.au/conferences/melbourne08/procs/sheely.pdf

Sheldon, P., & Thornthwaite, L. (2005). Employability skills and vocational education and training policy in Australia: An analysis of employer association agendas. *Asia-Pacific Journal Resources*, 43(3), 404–425. doi:10.1177/1038411105059100

Shen, L., & Shen, R. (2008). The pervasive learning platform of a Shanghai online college: A large-scale test-bed for hybrid learning. Lecture Notes in Computer Science, 5169, 178-189.

Shen, R., Wang, M., & Pan, X. (2008). Increasing interactivity in blended classrooms through a cutting-edge mobile learning system. *British Journal of Educational Technology*, 39(6), 1073–1086. doi:10.1111/j.1467-8535.2007.00778.x

Sheorey, R., & Mokhtari, K. (2001). Differences in the metacognitive awareness of reading strategies among native and non-native readers. *System*, 29(4), 431–449. doi:10.1016/S0346-251X(01)00039-2

Sheppard, D. (2011). Reading with iPads – The difference makes a difference. *Education Today*, 3, 12–15.

Shields, P., Esch, C., Humphrey, D., Wechsler, M., Chang-Ross, C., & Gallagher, H. et al. (2003). *The Status of the Teaching Profession*. Santa Cruz, CA: The Center for the Future of Teaching and Learning.

Shulman, L. S. (1986). Those who understand: Knowledge growth in teaching. *Educational Researcher*, 12(2), 4–14. doi:10.3102/0013189X015002004

Shurtz, S., Halling, T. D., & McKay, B. (2011). Assessing user preference to circulate iPads in an academic medical library. *Journal of Electronic Resources in Medical Libraries*, 8(4), 311–324. doi:10.1080/15424065.2011.626342

Simpson, O. (2003). *Student retention in Online, Open and Distance Learning*. London, UK: Kogan Page. doi:10.4324/9780203416563

Smith, S., & Caruso, J. (2010). *The ECAR study of undergraduate students and information technology, 2010 Key Findings* (Vol. 6, pp. 1–13). Boulder, CO: EDUCAUSE Center for Applied Research.

Smith, S., Salaway, G., & Caruso, J. B. (2009). *The ECAR study of undergraduate students and information technology, 2009*. Boulder, CO: EDUCAUSE Center for Applied Research.

Snoeyink, R., & Ertmer, P. A. (2001/2002). Thrust into technology: How veteran teachers respond. *Journal of Educational Technology Systems*, 30(1), 85–111. doi:10.2190/YDL7-XH09-RLJ6-MTP1

Soe, K., Koki, S., & Chang, J. M. (2000). *Effect of Computer-Assisted Instruction (CAI) on reading achievement: A meta-analysis*. Honolulu, HI: Pacific Resources for Education and Learning.

Somekh, B. (2008). Factors affecting teachers' pedagogical adoption of ICT. In J. Voogt, & G. Knezek (Eds.), *International handbook of information technology in primary and secondary education* (pp. 449–460). New York, NY: Springer. doi:10.1007/978-0-387-73315-9_27

Song, Y. (2011). Investigating undergraduate student mobile device use in context. A. Kitchenham (Ed.), Models for interdisciplinary mobile learning: Delivering information to students (pp. 120–136). Hershey, PA: IGI Global for publication.

Soukup, C. (2006). Computer-mediated communication as a virtual third place: Building Oldenburg's great good places on the World Wide Web. *New Media & Society, 8*, 421–440. doi:10.1177/1461444806061953

Spindler, G. (1963). *Education and Culture: Anthropological Approaches*. New York, NY: Holt, Rinehart and Wilson.

Spooner, F., Spooner, M., Algozzine, B., & Jordan, L. (1998). Distance Education and Special Education: Promises, practices, and potential pitfalls. *Teacher Education and Special Education, 22*(2), 97–109. doi:10.1177/088840649902200203

Sporn, B. (1999). *Adaptive university structures*. Philadelphia, PA: Kingsley Publishers.

Spotts, T. H. (1999). Discriminating factors in faculty use of instructional technology in higher education. *Journal of Educational Technology & Society, 2*(4), 92–99.

Srinivasan, R. (2006). Where information society and community voice intersect. *The Information Society, 22*(5), 355–365. doi:10.1080/01972240600904324

Stahl, G., Koschmann, T., & Suthers, D. (2006). Computer supported collaborative learning: An historical perspective. In R. K. Sawyer (Ed.), *Cambridge handbook of the learning sciences* (pp. 409-426). Cambridge, UK: Cambridge University Press. Retrieved from http://www.cis.drexel.edu/faculty/gerry/cscl/CSCL_English.pdf

Stanton, G., & Ophoff, J. (2013). Towards a method for mobile learning design. *Issues in Informing Science and Information Technology, 10*, 501–523.

Stebbins, R. A. (2001, May/June). Serious leisure. *Society*, 53–57. doi:10.1007/s12115-001-1023-8

Sternberg, R. J., Kaufman, J. C., & Pretz, J. E. (2002). *The creativity conundrum: A propulsion model of kinds of creative contributions*. Philadelphia: Psychology Press.

Stick Pick. (n.d.). Retrieved from https://itunes.apple.com/us/app/stick-pick/id436682059?mt=8

Stimson, B. (2007, October). *An Educator's Manifesto! Arise! You have nothing to lose but your chains!* Classroom 2.0. Retrieved from http://www.classroom20.com/forum/topics/649749:Topic:56987

Strømsø, H. I., & Bråten, I. (2008). Forståelse af digitale tekster - nye udfordringer. In I. Bråten (Ed.), Læseforståelse (pp. 201-224). Århus, Danmark: Klim.

Suki, N. M., & Suki, N. M. (2011). Using mobile device for learning: From students' perspective. *US-China Education Review*, 44-53.

Sultan, W. H., Woods, P. C., & Koo, A. (2011). A constructivist approach for digital learning: Malaysian schools case study. *Journal of Educational Technology & Society, 14*(4), 149–163.

Sung, E., & Mayer, R. E. (2013). Online multimedia learning with mobile devices and desktop computers: An experimental test of Clark's methods-not-media hypothesis. *Computers in Human Behavior, 29*, 639–647. doi:10.1016/j.chb.2012.10.022

Suter, V., Alexander, B., & Kaplan, P. (2005). Social software and the future of conferences— Right now. *EDUCAUSE Review, 40*(1).

Swanson, J. A. (2013). *Emerging adults: Analysis of learning patterns in collegiate classrooms*. (Unpublished doctoral dissertation). University at Albany, State University of New York, Albany, NY.

Swantz, M. L. (2008). Participatory Action Research as Practice. In P. Reason, & H. Bradbury (Eds.), *The SAGE Handbook of Action Research: Participative Inquiry and Practice* (2nd ed., pp. 31–48). London: SAGE Publications. doi:10.4135/9781848607934.d8

Swenson, P. W. (2011). iPad - The third hand. *National Social Science Technology Journal, 1*(3). Retrieved from http://www.nssa.us/tech_journal/volume_1-3/vol1-3_article_9.htm

Szalavitz, M. (2012, March 14). Do E-books make it harder to remember what you just read? *Time*. Retrieved from http://healthland.time.com/2012/03/14/do-e-books-impair-memory/

Tamim, R. M., Bernard, R. M., Borokhovski, E., Abrami, P. C., & Schmid, R. F. (2011). What forty years of research says about the impact of technology on learning a second-order meta-analysis and validation study. *Review of Educational Research, 81*(1), 4–28. doi:10.3102/0034654310393361

Tan, T.-H., Lin, M.-S., Chu, Y.-L., & Liu, T.-Y. (2012). Educational affordances of a ubiquitous learning environment in a natural science course. *Journal of Educational Technology & Society, 15*(2), 206–219.

Taylor, A. S., & Harper, R. (2002). *Age-old practices in the 'New World': A study of gift-giving between teenage mobile phone users*. Paper presented to the Conference on Human Factors in Computing Systems. Minneapolis, MN.

Teclehaimanot, B., Mentzer, G., & Hickman, T. (2011). A mixed methods comparison of teacher education faculty perceptions of the integration of technology into their courses and students feedback on technology proficiency. *Journal of Technology and Teacher Education, 19*(1), 5–21.

The Complete University Guide. (2013). *Top UK University League Tables and Rankings 2014*. Retrieved from: http://www.thecompleteuniversityguide.co.uk/league-tables/rankings

Thorton, P., & Houser, C. (2002). M-learning in transit. In P. Lewis (Ed.), *The changing face of CALL* (pp. 229–243). Lisse, The Netherlands: Swets and Zeitlinger.

Times Higher Education. (2013). *World University Rankings 2013-2014 - Times Higher Education*. Retrieved from http://www.timeshighereducation.co.uk/world-university-rankings/2013-14/world-ranking

Ting, Y. (2012). The pitfalls of mobile devices in learning: A different view and implications for pedagogical design. *Journal of Educational Computing Research, 46*(2), 119–134. doi:10.2190/EC.46.2.a

Totter, A., Stutz, D., & Grote, G. (2006). ICT and schools: Identification of factors influencing the use of new media in vocational training schools. *The Electronic Journal of e-Learning, 4*(1), 95-102. Retrieved from www.ejel.org

Traxler, J. (2005). *Defining mobile learning*. IADIS International Conference Mobile Learning 2005. Retrieved from http://www.marcosbarros.com.br/ead/file.php/10/200506C018.pdf

Traxler, J. (2011). Introduction. In J. Traxler & J. Wishart (Eds.), *Making mobile learning work: Case studies of practice* (pp. 4-12). Bristol, UK: ESCalate. Retrieved from http://www.leeds.ac.uk/educol/documents/201799.pdf

Traxler, J., & Bridges, N. (2004). Mobile learning: The ethical and legal challenges. Retrieved from http://www.mobilearn.org/download/events/mlearn_2004/presentations/Traxler.pdf

Traxler, J. (2007). Defining, discussing, and evaluating mobile learning: The moving finger writes and having writ..... *International Review of Research in Open and Distance Learning, 8*(2), 1–12.

Traxler, J. (2010). Students and mobile devices. *Research in Learning Technology, 18*(2). doi:10.3402/rlt.v18i2.10759

Traxler, J. (2010). Will student devices deliver innovation, inclusion, and transformation?[RCET]. *Journal of the Research Center for Educational Technology, 6*(1), 3–15.

Triantafillou, E., & Georgiadou, E., & Economides. (2008). The design and evaluation of a computerized adaptive test on mobile devices. *Computers & Education, 50*, 1319–1330. doi:10.1016/j.compedu.2006.12.005

Tucker, P. (2007, January-February). The over-mediated world. *The Futurist, 16*, 12–13.

Turney, C. S. M., Robinson, D., Lee, M., & Soutar, A. (2009). Using technology to direct learning in higher education: The way forward? *Active Learning in Higher Education, 10*(1), 71–83. doi:10.1177/1469787408100196

Tushnet, N. et al. (2002). *Independent Evaluation of the Beginning Teacher Support and Assessment (BTSA) System*. San Francisco, CA: WestEd.

Twitter. (n.d.). Retrieved from https://www.twitter.com

Tynjälä, P. (2012). Toward a 3-P Model of Workplace Learning: a Literature Review. *Vocations and Learning, 6*, 11 – 36.

U.S. Department of Education. (2008). *Personnel in Full Time Equivalency of Assignment Employed To Provide Special Education Programs. Data Analysis Systems (DANS)*. Washington, DC: Office of Special Education Programs.

Udell, C. (2012). *Learning everywhere: How mobile content strategies are transforming training*. Nashville, TN: RockBench Publishing.

UNESCO. (2012). *Turning on mobile learning: Global themes*. Paris, France: United Nations Educational, Scientific and Cultural Organization.

UNESCO. (2013). *The future of mobile learning: Implications for policy makers and planners*. Retrieved from http://unesdoc.unesco.org/images/0021/002196/219637E.pdf

United Nations Educational, Scientific and Cultural Organization (UNESCO). (2008). ICT competency standards for teachers: Policy framework (No. CI-2007/WS/21). UNESCO's Communication and Information Sector.

University of Leicester. (2013a). *Armed Conflict Learning shortlisted for national e-learning award*. Retrieved from http://www2.le.ac.uk/colleges/socsci/college%20news/armed-conflict-learning-shortlisted-for-national-e-learning-award

University of Leicester. (2013b). *Using Other Libraries—University of Leicester*. Retrieved from http://www2.le.ac.uk/library/services/otherlibraries/using-other-libraries

University of Leicester. (2013c). *Places: Adding Mobility to Distance Learning*. Retrieved from: http://www2.le.ac.uk/departments/beyond-distance-research-alliance/projects/places

University of Leicester. (2013d). *Our Achievements — University of Leicester*. Retrieved from http://www2.le.ac.uk/about/facts

University of Leicester. (2013e). *Times Higher Education Awards - University of Leicester*. Retrieved from http://www2.le.ac.uk/about/the-awards

Unsworth, L. (2008). Multiliteracies, e-literature and English teaching. *Language and Education: International Journal, 22* (1).

Unsworth, L. (Ed.). (2008). *New literacies and the English curriculum*. London, UK: Continuum.

Unterfrauner, E., & Marschalek, I. (2010). Appropriation of an online mobile community by marginalised young people: experiences from an Austrian case study. In M. Montebello, V. Camilleri & A. Dingli (Eds.), *Proceedings of MLearn 2010: The 9th International Conference on Mobile Learning* (pp. 276-281). Valletta, Malta: University of Malta.

Uzunboylu, H., Cavus, N., & Ercag, E. (2009). Using mobile learning to increase environmental awareness. *Computers & Education, 52*, 381–389. doi:10.1016/j.compedu.2008.09.008

Valtonen, T. (2011). *An Insight into Collaborative Learning with ICT: Teachers' and Students' Perspectives*. University of Eastern Finland.

Van Merrienboer, J. J. G., & de Bruin, A. B. H. (2014). Research paradigms and perspectives on learning. In M. Spector, D. Merrill, J. Elen, & M. Bishop (Eds.), *Handbook of research on educational communications and technology* (pp. 21–29). New York, NY: Springer. doi:10.1007/978-1-4614-3185-5_2

Vandergrift, L. (2004). Listening to learn or learning to listen. *Annual Review of Applied Linguistics, 24*, 3–25. doi:10.1017/S0267190504000017

Vavoula, G. N., & Sharples, M. (2008). Challenges in evaluating mobile informal learning. In *Proceedings of the m-Learn 2008 conference* (pp. 296–303). Wolverhampton.

Vavoula, G. N., Lefrere, P., O'Malley, C., & Sharples, M. (2004). *Producing guidelines for learning, teaching and tutoring in a mobile environment*. Paper presented at the 2nd IEEE International Workshop on Wireless and Mobile Technologies in Education (WMTE). Taoyuan, Taiwan.

Verezub, E., & Wang, H. (2008). The role of metacognitive reading strategies instructions and various types of links in comprehending hypertexts. In Hello! Where are you in the landscape of educational technology? Proceedings Ascilite Melbourne 2008. Retrieved from http://www.ascilite.org.au/conferences/melbourne08/procs/verezub.pdf

VirtualAbility. (2008). *Virtual Ability Our People*. Retrieved from Virtual Ability, Inc. Web site: http://virtualability.org/ourpeople.aspx

Vogt, F., & Rogalla, M. (2009). Developing adaptive teaching competency through coaching. *Teaching and Teacher Education, 25*, 1051–1060. doi:10.1016/j.tate.2009.04.002

Voss, J. F., & Post, T. A. (1988). On the solving of ill-structured problems. In M. T. H. Chi, R. Glaser, & M. J. Farr (Eds.), *The nature of expertise* (pp. 261–285). Hillsdale, NJ: Lawrence Erlbaum.

Vygotsky, L. S. (1962). *Thought and Language*. Cambridge, MA: MIT Press. doi:10.1037/11193-000

Vygotsky, L. S. (1978). *Mind and Society: The Development of Higher Mental Processes*. Cambridge, MA: Harvard University Press.

Waema, E. F. (2000). *The impact of introducing computers into library services: The case of the University of Dar es Salaam*. (MA dissertation). University of Dar es Salaam, Dar es Salaam, Tanzania.

Wahl, L., & Duffield, J. (2005). *Using flexible technology to meet the needs of diverse learners: What teachers can do*. Retrieved from http://www.wested.org/online_pubs/kn-05-01.pdf

Walker, K. (2006). Introduction: Mapping the landscape of mobile learning. In M. Sharples (Ed.), *Big issues in mobile learning: Report of a workshop by the kaleidoscope network of excellence mobile learning initiative*. University of Nottingham.

Wang, M., Shen, R., Novak, D., & Pan, X. (2009). The impact of mobile learning on students' learning behaviours and performance: Report from a large blended classroom. *British Journal of Educational Technology*, *40*(4), 673–695. doi:10.1111/j.1467-8535.2008.00846.x

Wang, R., Wiesemes, R., & Gibbons, C. (2012). Developing digital fluency through ubiquitous mobile devices: Findings from a small-scale study. *Computers & Education*, *58*(1), 570–578. doi:10.1016/j.compedu.2011.04.013

Wasicsko, M. (2004). The 20-minute hiring assessment. *School Administrator*, *61*(9), 40–42.

Wasko, C. (2013). What Teachers Need to Know About Augmented Reality Enhanced Learning Environments. *TechTrends: Linking Research & Practice to Improve Learning*, *57*(4), 17–21. doi:10.1007/s11528-013-0672-y

Waxman, H., Lin, M., & Michko, G. (2003). *A meta-analysis of the effectiveness of teaching and learning with technology on student outcomes*. Naperville, IL: Learning Point Associates.

Wedgwood, J. (2013). Blended Learning. In The Really Useful eLearning Instruction Manual: Your toolkit for putting elearning into practice. Chichester, UK: Wiley & Sons.

Wellington, P., Powell, T. I., & Clarke, B. (2002). Authentic assessment applied to engineering business undergraduate consulting teams. Melbourne, Australia: Department of Mechanical Engineering Monash University.

Wenden, A. L. (1998). Metacognitive knowledge and language learning. *Applied Linguistics*, *19*(4), 515–537. doi:10.1093/applin/19.4.515

Wenden, A., & Rubin, J. (Eds.). (1987). *Learner strategies in language learning*. Englewood Cliffs, NJ: Prentice Hall International.

Wesch, M. (2008b, October 21). *A Vision of Students Today (& What Teachers Must Do)*. Britannica Blog. Retrieved from http://www.britannica.com/blogs/2008/10/a-vision-of-students-today-what-teachers-must-do/

Wesch, M. (2008a). Anti-Teaching: Confronting the Crisis of Significance. *Education Canada*, *48*(2), 4–7.

Wheeler, S. (2013). *'Always on' learning*. Retrieved from http://steve-wheeler.blogspot.co.uk/2013/10/always-on-learning.html

White, C. (1995). Autonomy and strategy use in distance foreign language learning: Research findings. *System*, *23*(2), 207–221. doi:10.1016/0346-251X(95)00009-9

White, D. S., & Le Cornu, A. (2011). Visitors and residents: A new typology for inline engagement. *First Monday*, *16*(9). doi:10.5210/fm.v16i9.3171

Wiggins, G., & McTighe, J. (n.d.). *Understanding by design®* (2nd ed.). Alexandria, VA: Association for Supervision and Curriculum Development.

Wiliam, D., & Thompson, M. (2007). Integrating assessment with learning: What will it take to make it work? In C. A. Dwyer (Ed.), *The future of assessment: Shaping teaching and learning*. Mahwah, NJ: Lawrence Erlbaum Associates.

Williams, P. W. (2009). Assessing mobile learning effectiveness and acceptance. Retrieved from http://www.scribd.com/doc/95393980/Assessing-Mobile-Learning-Effectiveness-and-Acceptance

Williams, K. C., Morgan, K., & Cameron, B. A. (2011). How do students define their roles and responsibilities in online learning group projects? *Distance Education*, *32*(1), 49–62. doi:10.1080/01587919.2011.565498

Compilation of References

Wilson, N. S., Zygouris-Coe, V., & Cardullo, V. (2013). Trying to make sense of e-readers. *Journal of Reading Education*.

Wilson, N. S., Zygouris-Coe, V., Cardullo, V., & Fong, J. (2013). Pedagogical frameworks of mobile learning technologies in education. For publication. In S. Keengwe (Ed.), *Pedagogical applications and social effects of mobile technology integration* (pp. 1–24). doi:10.4018/978-1-4666-2985-1.ch001

Wilson, S. M., Floden, R. E., & Ferrini-Mundy, J. (2001). *Teacher preparation research: Current knowledge, gaps, and recommendations*. Seattle, WA: University of Washington.

Winters, N. (2006). What is mobile learning? In M. Sharples (Ed.), *Big issues in mobile learning: Report of a workshop by the kaleidoscope network of excellence mobile learning initiative*. University of Nottingham.

Witthaus, G., & Williamson, H. (2010). *OTTER Project Final Report*. Retrieved from http://www.jisc.ac.uk/media/documents/programmes/oer/otterfinalreport-t27april2010_v2 1.pdf

Wolf, M. (2010). *Our "deep reading" brain: Its digital evolution poses questions*. Retrieved on June 22, 2013, from http://www.nieman.harvard.edu/reports/article/102396/Our-Deep-Reading-Brain-Its-Digital-Evolution--Poses-Questions.aspx

Wong, L., Chin, C., Tan, C., & Liu, M. (2010). Students' personal and social meaning making in a Chinese idiom mobile learning environment. *Journal of Educational Technology & Society*, *13*(4), 15–26.

Wood, E., Zivcakova, L., Gentile, P., Archer, K., De Pasquale, D., & Nosko, A. (2011). Examining the impact of off-task multi-tasking with technology on real-time classroom learning. *Computers & Education*, *58*(1), 365–374. doi:10.1016/j.compedu.2011.08.029

Woodill, G. (2011). *The mobile learning edge: Tools and technologies for developing your teams*. New York: McGraw-Hill Professional.

Woodill, G. (2013). E-learning vs. m-learning: Same or different? *Chief Learning Officer*, *12*(3), 37.

Wozney, L., Venkatesh, V., & Abrami, P. C. (2006). Implementing computer technologies: Teachers' perceptions and practices. *Journal of Technology and Teacher Education*, *14*(1), 173–207.

Wright, S., & Parchoma, G. (2011). Technologies for learning? An actor-network theory critique of 'affordances' in research on mobile learning. *Research in learning. Technology (Elmsford, N.Y.)*, *19*(3), 247–258.

Wu, W. H., Wu, Y. C., Chen, C. Y., Kao, H. Y., Lin, C. H., & Huang, S. H. (2012). Review of trends from mobile learning studies: A meta-analysis. *Computers & Education*, *59*, 817–827. doi:10.1016/j.compedu.2012.03.016

Wycliff, O. (2013). *Developing Human Capital Through e-learning and Mobile Technologies*. Paper presented at the e-learning Innovations Conference & Expo. Nairobi, Kenya.

Xia, F. (2011). *Research on the Use of Mobile Devices in Distance EFL Learning*. Retrieved from http://link.springer.com/chapter/10.1007%2F978-3-642-23321-0_16#page-1

Yalçan, F. (2011). An international dimension of the student's attitudes towards the use of English in Web 2.0 technology. *The Turkish Online Journal of Educational Technology*, *10*(3), 63–68.

Yang, S. (2012). Exploring college students' attitudes and self-efficacy of mobile learning. *The Turkish Online Journal of Educational Technology*, *11*(4), 148–154.

Yau, J. Y-K, & Joy, M.S. (2010). Proposal of a mobile learning preferences model. *International Journal of Interactive Mobile Technologies*, *4*(4). Retrieved from: http://eprints.dcs.warwick.ac.uk/638/1/yau_joy_ijim_4.pdf

Yi, C. C., Liao, W. P., Huang, C. F., & Hwang, I. H. (2009). Acceptance of mobile learning: a respecification and validation of information system success. *Proceedings of World Academy of Science, Engineering and Technology*, *41*.

Yoo, S. J., & Huang, W.-H. D. (2011). Comparison of Web 2.0 Technology Acceptance Level based on Cultural Differences. *Journal of Educational Technology & Society*, *14*(4), 241–252.

Yousef, M. I. (2007). Effectiveness of mobile learning in distance education. *Turkish Online Journal of Distance Education*, *8*(4), 114–124.

Zeichner, K. (1990). Changing directions in the practicum: looking ahead in the 1990s. *Journal of Education for Teaching*, *16*(2), 105–132. doi:10.1080/0260747900160201

Zhang, K., & Bonk, C. J. (2008). Addressing diverse learner preferences and intelligences with emerging technologies: Matching models to online opportunities. *Canadian Journal of Learning and Technology*, *34*(2). Retrieved from http://www.cjlt.ca/index.php/cjlt/article/view/496/227

Zhang, D., & Adipat, B. (2005). Challenges, methodologies, and issues in the usability testing of mobile applications. *International Journal of Human-Computer Interaction*, *18*, 293–308. doi:10.1207/s15327590ijhc1803_3

Zohar, A. (2006). The nature and development of teachers' metastrategic knowledge in the context of teaching higher order thinking. *Journal of the Learning Sciences*, *15*(3), 331–377. doi:10.1207/s15327809jls1503_2

About the Contributors

Jared Keengwe is an Associate Professor at the University of North Dakota (UND), USA. Dr. Keengwe is the editor-in-chief of two IGI Global Book Series: *Advances in Higher Education and Professional Development* (AHEPD) and *Advances in Early Childhood and K-12 Education* (AECKE). He serves on the editorial review board of several international journals and is also the co-editor-in-chief of the *Journal of Education and Learning* (EduLearn). Dr. Keengwe's primary research interests focus on technology integration and constructivist pedagogy in teacher education. He has co-authored more than 65 journal articles and edited more than 10 scholarly textbooks with a focus on instructional technologies both in K-12 and in higher education. Dr. Keengwe's work in the classroom was honored with the 2011 McDermott Faculty Award for Excellence in Academic Advising. He was also a recipient of the 2010 North Dakota Spirit Faculty Achievement Award, and the 13th (2010) Annual Martin Luther King Jr. Award in recognition of significant contribution in scholarship and service respectively. At the national level, Dr. Keengwe was one of the 10 recipients selected to receive the 2010 American Educational Research Association (AERA) Division K – Teacher Education –Travel Award.

Marian B. Maxfield is an Assistant Professor at Ashland University, Ashland, Ohio, USA. Dr. Maxfield received a BAEd in Secondary Education English, psychology, and sociology from The University of Akron, Akron, Ohio USA. She holds an MEd in Instructional Technology and a PhD in Educational Psychology and Instructional Technology from Kent State University, Kent, Ohio, USA. Dr. Maxfield has over a decade of experience teaching online in K-20. She designed online K-12 curriculum for First Ladies National Library and taught technology to international teachers through the IREX grant. She was the chair of the AERA Division H dissertation awards committee in 2013. Dr. Maxfield's primary research interests are technology integration for pre-service teachers and K-20 professional development, mobile technologies, problem-based learning, electronic portfolios, discussion forums, and information literacy. Her scholarly work has won awards including 2012 AERA dissertation second place and appeared in multiple national and international peer-reviewed educational and medical journals, proceedings, and magazines.

* * *

Natalia Auer is a PhD student in the Institute of Learning Innovation at the University of Leicester. Her main research interests are technology-enhanced language learning, Spanish language learning as a foreign language, comprehension processes and strategies for reading digital texts. Her PhD research focuses on mobile assisted language learning (MALL) and how metacognitive reading strategies can be facilitated by mobile technologies. Natalia has taught "Foreign Language Acquisition and Pedagogy" to undergraduate and graduate students in the Department of English, Germanic, and Romance Studies at the University of Copenhagen. At present, she is a lecturer at Vestegnen HF and VUC, an Adult Education Centre in Albertslund, Denmark, where she is conducting her research besides her full-time job.

Ross Brannigan is a lecturer in Digital Media and Performance at the School of Communication Studies, Faculty of Design and Creative Technologies, and AUT University. Brannigan's research interests include: Intermediality, Cinematic Theatre and Theatrical Cinema, The Use of Digital Media in Live Theatre, Liminality, and Mobile devices in teaching performance.

Victoria M. Cardullo is an assistant professor of Reading in the College of Education and the Department of Curriculum and Teaching at Auburn University. She is actively involved in publications and presentations related to her research in digital literacies, specifically New Literacies. Her work has been published in *School-University Partnerships: The Journal of the National Association for Professional Development Schools, Journal of Reading Education,* and *American Reading Forum Annual Yearbook.* She is particularly interested in exploring how to support adolescent readers' reading and comprehension skills to prepare them for 21st century learning. She serves in several editorial roles, including associate editor of *Florida Educational Leadership Journal,* associate editor for *American Reading Forum* as well as a reviewer for *NAPDS National Association of Professional Development Schools, NAPDS Award Committee* and an invited reviewer for *ALER Association of Literacy Educators and Researchers.*

Thomas Cochrane is an Academic Advisor and Senior Lecturer in educational Technology at AUT University's Centre for Learning and Teaching (CfLAT). In 2011, he was awarded as an Ascilite Fellow. His research interests include mobile learning, web 2.0, and communities of practice. His PhD thesis was titled "Mobilizing Learning: Transforming pedagogy with mobile web 2.0." Thomas has managed and implemented over 45 mobile learning projects, with a recent focus upon Android and iOS smartphones and the iPad as catalysts to enable student-generated content and student-generated learning contexts, bridging formal and informal learning environments. He has over 100 peer reviewed publications, receiving best paper awards at Ascilite 2009, ALT-C 2011, and ALT-C 2012 and has been invited to keynote at several international educational technology conferences including: the 2012 Australian Moodle Moot, the 2012 m-Libraries conference in the UK, and the launch of UWS massive iPad project in February 2013.

Christopher Dann leads the creative and technical arm of the team. He is a lecturer in Education and research fellow at the University of the Sunshine Coast. Chris has worked as a principal and administrator in state schools for 18 years before moving to the higher education sector. He has been innovating in assessment since the late 80's and more recently has specialized in assessment and reporting in educational settings (Higher Ed, TAFE and Schools). While completing a masters degree in Internationalisation of Pre-service Teacher Education, Chris led the work-integrated unit at USC which was responsible for the placement and management of approximately 1000 students each year. In 2009, he led the writing of a four-year undergraduate degree in Pre-service Primary Teacher Education.

About the Contributors

Cornelis de Groot is an Associate Professor in the School of Education at the College of Human Science and Services at the University of Rhode Island, USA. Dr. de Groot is program coordinator for secondary mathematics education and teaches courses in educational measurement, mathematics methods, mathematics curriculum, and student teaching seminar. Dr. de Groot also supervises student teachers in secondary mathematics. His research interests are related to mobile technology in teacher education, realistic teacher education, teacher cognition, and the teaching and learning of mathematical structure. Dr. de Groot was awarded a Presidential Award of Excellence in Science and Mathematics Teaching for his work as a mathematics high school teacher. He has authored and co-authored over 45 publications, including books, refereed articles and conference papers.

Meghan Morris Deyoe is a senior evaluator at the Evaluation Consortium at the University at Albany/SUNY. She has assisted in the evaluation of both federally and state-funded grants and her major areas of study include evaluation practices in K-14 settings, the incorporation of technology in education, innovative instructional approaches, and emerging practices/trends in childhood development and in education for students with disabilities. She has a Master of Science in Literacy, B-6, is certified in Childhood Education (B-6) and Literacy Education (B-6), and has a Certificate of Advanced Study in Educational Research.

Sonia Dickinson-Delaporte is an Associate Professor in the School of Marketing, Curtin University, Western Australia. She lectures in Postgraduate marketing courses with a focus on marketing communications. In 2011, her contribution to student learning was recognized by the Australian Learning and Teaching Council (ALTC) where she was awarded a Citation for Outstanding Contribution to Student Learning. Her teaching excellence has also been recognized by Curtin Business School and Curtin University and she is the recipient of various teaching awards. Sonia has published in various highly ranked marketing journals including the European Journal of Marketing, Journal of Advertising Research (forthcoming), and the Journal of Marketing Management. Her areas of research interest include advertising self-regulation, message source effects in advertising, empowerment issues in social media and technology facilitated student engagement. Her supervision of Doctoral and Masters Research candidates also relates to these areas of research interest.

Tracey Dodman is a Senior Lecturer in the Department of Criminology at the University of Leicester, UK. Tracey is the course convenor for the Department's four distance learning masters programmes, and she also Chairs the Department's Academic Committee. Her research interests are mainly pedagogic. She has completed research in the effectiveness of feedback for distance learning students and has an ongoing interest in how technologies can be used to facilitate learning and student engagement (particularly amongst distance learning students). She is currently working on a collaborative research project looking into 'what goes on in guided independent study' establishing how students study, what students study and whether students know how to undertake successful independent study.

Cathi Draper Rodriguez is an Associate Professor and the Chair of the School of Education at California State University, Monterey Bay. Dr. Draper Rodriguez teaches curriculum, assessment and introduction to research in the Special Education and Masters programs. Since earning her doctorate from the University of Nevada, Las Vegas, she has focused her research on using technology with English learners with and without disabilities, the diagnosis of disabilities in English learners, assessment in education, and multicultural education. Dr. Draper Rodriguez is a Nationally Certified School Psychologist. Her previous work experience includes serving as a bilingual school psychologist in a public school setting and as an early interventionist providing services to young Latina mothers.

Carlos Ewing is a doctoral student in the Department of Instructional Systems and Workforce Development at Mississippi State University, where he teaches Computer Applications to undergraduate students. Previously, Mr. Ewing has taught or assisted teaching Records Management, Information Technology Project Management, Integrating Technology for Meaningful Learning, Computer Repair and Maintenance, and Designing Technology Training. He has presented at state and national conferences on various social media topics. His current research focuses on examining students' use of professional social networking sites, while his primary focus is on the use of immersive digital learning environments.

Jay Fogleman is an Associate Professor in the School of Education at the College of Human Science and Services at the University of Rhode Island, USA. Dr. Fogleman is program coordinator for secondary science education and teaches courses in educational foundations, science teaching methods, and student teaching seminar. Dr. Fogleman also supervises student teachers in secondary science. His research interests involve the use of digital tools by college learners, teacher learning, and the characteristics of effective professional development experiences. He previously taught high school physics and technology education. He has authored and co-authored over 45 publications, including books, refereed articles and conference papers.

Rhoda Karimi Gitonga completed her undergraduate work at Kenyatta University and received her Bachelor of Education (Science). She received her Masters of Science Degree in Information Management and completed her PhD degree in Curriculum and Instruction in 2013 from Egerton University. Her specific interest is in ICT integration and E-learning. She has worked in the university as a teaching staff member for 6 years. She has published two papers in 2013, *The Perceived extent of ICT Integration in Intra-University Communication among Kenyan Universities: doi: 10.11648/j.com.20130102.11, and The Perception of the Influence of ICT Integration on Quality of Student's Records Management in Kenyan Universities: ISSN: 2278-0211 (Online)*. Two other publications are in press: *Web 2.0 Technologies Use by Students in Higher Education: A Case of Kenyan Universities and Students Experiences of Using Wiki Spaces to Support Collaborative Learning in a Blended Classroom; A Case of Kenyatta and KCA Universities in Kenya.*

Kenda Grover is an assistant professor in the Adult and Lifelong Learning program. She earned her EdD in Adult Education from the University of Arkansas, an MS in Counseling Psychology, a BA in Psychology from Northeastern State University, and an AA in Journalism from Northeastern Oklahoma A&M College. She has been with the Department of Rehabilitation, Human Resources, and Communication Disorders since August of 2003. In addition to faculty responsibilities, she serves as the program coordinator for the ADLL MED program. She is a member of the American Association for Adult and Continuing Education, the Arkansas Association of Continuing and Adult Education, and the Eastern Educational Research Association. Dr. Grover's research interests include self-directed learning and community engagement (SDL), SDL as it relates to health, and serious leisure and communities of practice.

About the Contributors

Matthew Guinibert has been an educator for 8 years working in various roles as a lecturer, supervisor, consultant, curriculum writer, and course supervisor. He presently teaches visual communication and web technologies at AUT. His masters research involved producing interactive simulation software for teaching 3D computer graphics. He conducts research in the field of computer mediated learning, where he has been involved with projects such as writing interactive simulation software for learning computer graphics and m-learning projects exploring student collaboration. Presently, Matt is exploring the potential of mobile HUDs such as Google Glass as m-learning tools for learning visual literacy competencies through a PhD.

Josh Harrower is a professor in the Department of Teacher Education at California State University, Monterey Bay where he coordinates the Special Education Credential Programs and the university's certificate program in behavior analysis. Additionally, Dr. Harrower serves as the Principal Investigator and Director of Project STREAM, a grant funded by the Office of Special Education Programs to provide a professional development scholarship program utilizing technology and mentorship to support candidates pursuing a Moderate to Severe Special Education Credential. Dr. Harrower received his doctoral degree from the University of California, Santa Barbara and holds certification as a Board Certified Behavior Analyst-Doctoral. His primary areas of scholarly interest include positive behavior interventions and support, autism spectrum disorders, applied behavior analysis, pivotal response treatment, functional assessment, and behavior intervention.

David Hopkins is an experienced and respected Learning Technologist. His work and research centres around the use of appropriate technology for, and with, students online and on-campus. From a background in commercial Internet technologies and online communities, David has been able to apply knowledge and experience with online learning and support and bring effective and appropriate use of technology for learning. His current interests and research is based around the use of mobile devices for online learning (for both campus and distance learners) and the use of social media and social networks for effective communication and collaboration between staff, students, and his peers.

Kim A. Hosler is a graduate of the University of Northern Colorado and holds a doctorate in Educational Technology. She is also adjunct faculty for the University College at the University of Denver, as well as adjunct faculty for Regis University, in Denver, Colorado. Additionally, she works full time in faculty development for the Office of Teaching and Learning at the University of Denver. Dr. Hosler facilitates courses in research methods, adult learning theory, as well as graduate-level courses in organizational and professional communications. Her research focuses on several areas: supporting faculty who are new to the online and hybrid teaching environments, the intersection of mobile learning and instructional design, and establishing communities of inquiry in the classroom and online. Dr. Hosler has published her research in refereed journals, book chapters, and conference proceedings.

Abhishek Kala has worked in the digital media industry for over 11 years in various roles ranging from visual effects technical director for television shows to lead technical artist in game development studios. Currently, he is lecturing in Digital Media at AUT. His research interests include transmedia storytelling, gamification, and entertainment education. Currently, he is exploring frameworks for using transmedia storytelling and entertainment education to generate behaviour changes in targeted communities through a PhD.

Frederick Kang'ethe Iraki is a Professor of French at the United States International University in Nairobi, Kenya. He teaches French language and literature and enjoys writing short stories. His research areas include language and mind, culture, language, and technology. Dr. Iraki is also the founding editor of the *Journal of Language, Technology & Entrepreneurship in Africa* (JOLTE). He is a knight of the Order of Academic Palms (France).

Diane Kern is an Associate Professor in the School of Education at the University of Rhode Island, USA. She is program coordinator for secondary English language arts education and teaches courses in educational foundations, classroom management, content area literacy, English language arts methods and student teaching seminar. Dr. Kern also supervises student teachers in English language arts. Her research interests include comprehension strategy instruction, transformative pedagogies, and improving literacy teacher education. She has authored and co-authored approximately 35 publications, including books, refereed articles, standards for literacy professionals, and conference papers.

Jessica M. Lamendola is a doctoral student in Educational Psychology and Methodology and a project assistant at the Evaluation Consortium at the University at Albany/SUNY. Her major areas of interest include quantitative data analyses and the adaptation of innovative technology in classrooms. She has received a Masters of Science in Educational Psychology and Methodology.

Sang Joon Lee is an Assistant Professor in the Department of Instructional Systems and Workforce Development at Mississippi State University (MSU), where he teaches multimedia and web design courses for undergraduate and graduate students. Prior to joining MSU, he was an Instructional/Multimedia Developer at the Office of Educational Technology and Assessment in the College of Public Health and an Adjunct Faculty of Instructional Technology program at the University of South Florida. His research focus has been on improving students' learning experiences in constructivist, student-centered learning environments.

Romana Martin is a Senior Lecturer in the Curtin Learning Institute at Curtin University in Western Australia. Her qualifications include a MEd from Edith Cowan University and a PhD from Murdoch University in Western Australia. Her background is in the field of educational design, academic development and educational technology, and she has multidisciplinary qualifications in education, information technology, and educational multimedia. In her current role, she provides academic leadership and expertise in online and blended learning, teaching in collaborative learning spaces, and the application of new technologies to support student learning. She has led a wide range of teaching and learning initiatives and her research interests are in the field of online learning, mobile learning, student engagement, student-centered learning and new generation learning spaces.

Michael T. Miller is a Professor of Higher Education and Associate Dean for Academic Affairs in the College of Education and Health Professions at the University of Arkansas. He has served as president of two national associations and on the board of directors of five national associations. He has served as the editor of three different academic journals, and has been recognized for his research, winning the

About the Contributors

AIR Director's Paper Award and the Mortimer Award for Research on Shared Governance. Miller has published nearly 300 articles and chapters, has authored three books, and has edited eight books. His primary area of research has been aligned with participatory communities in higher education, related to both student and faculty involvement in institutional life. He has also served on the editorial boards of five different journals. He has authored over $2.5 million in externally funded grants and contracts.

Catherine Gakii Murungi is a Lecturer at Kenyatta University in the Department of Early Childhood Studies. She holds a PhD in Education, MEd and a Bachelors degree in Early Childhood Studies all from Kenyatta University. She is currently an editorial board member and peer reviewer to many international journals. Catherine is a mentor, academic advisor, e-learning trainer and facilitator, as well as a supervisor to several undergraduate and graduate students in the university. She is a passionate researcher in the field of developmental psychology and she is published widely. She has a keen interest on community education and development and in particular basic education. Besides being an academician, she is married and a proud mother of two adorable children, Ethan and Valerie.

Dianna L. Newman is a Professor in Educational Psychology and Methodology and Director of the Evaluation Consortium at the University at Albany/SUNY. Dr. Newman has served as principal evaluator for multiple federal and state-funded technology-based curriculum integration grants and is currently developing and piloting an innovative model of evaluation that will document systems changes resulting from technology-based curriculum integration into instructional settings. Dr. Newman is widely published in the area of technology innovation, K-12 curriculum and instructional practices, and higher education STEM technology support for learning. Her more recent publications include qualitative meta-analyses of evaluations documenting technology integration that supports hands-on and student-centered learning in K-12 and higher education classrooms.

Richard E. Newman is an assistant clinical professor of Educational Studies at the University of Arkansas. Previously, he served as a departmental chair of Physical Education and interim Athletic Director at Presbyterian College in South Carolina, and also spent nearly 30 years as a college football coach. Dr. Newman has served on the faculty at a number of different institutions of higher education, including California State University of Chico and the University of Mary. Recently, he was honored as an emeritus professor in Physical Education at Presbyterian College. He has written widely in the field of college athletic administration, college student-athletes, coaching education, and college faculty member performance. He is the author of over 50 articles and has made over 100 professional presentations.

Nathaniel M. Ostashewski is a Senior Lecturer and Academic Engagement Projects Developer for Curtin University, Western Australia. He holds a Canadian teaching license and has taught a complete range of K20 subjects. Nathaniel has been engaged in providing professional development related to technology use since 1996. In the past, he has worked as a teacher, media producer, academic consultant, instructional designer, social media researcher, and a dance choreographer. In Curtin University, Nathaniel has been supporting faculty in their use of learning technologies focusing on authentic student engagement through discussion and collaboration. Nathaniel also manages the Curtin MOOC portfolio as part of a strategic initiative in Curtin's Centre for Teaching and Learning. Over the past several years, Nathaniel has been designing networked learning and professional development courselets. His

Networked Learning Framework (http://www.editlib.org/p/39029/) is an instructional design model that utilizes media to support learner engagement, an approach common in MOOC design.

Susan Powers serves as Associate Vice President of Academic Affairs for Curriculum and Faculty at Indiana State University and is a Professor of Education Technology. Dr. Powers earned her doctorate at the University of Virginia. She has been involved with distance learning since 1997 and co-chaired Indiana State University's move to adopt a laptop requirement for all students. She has over 18 years of experience with teacher training grants for educational technologies, and has authored a book, papers, and presentations on the effective integration of technology for teaching and learning. She is also the author and co-chair of institutional and programmatic accreditation reports.

Tony Richardson is a tutor at the University of the Sunshine Coast and a teacher employed by the Department of Education and Training, Queensland, Australia. Currently, Tony is a Doctor of Philosophy student, at the University of the Sunshine Coast undertaking research in a quality teacher. His dissertation focuses on 'Early career teacher conceptions of a quality teacher – A Phenomenographic Study.'

Kristine Scharaldi is as an educational consultant with a specialty in the field of educational technology. She earned her Bachelors Degree in Sociology and Education at Rutgers University and Masters Degree in Computing and Education from Teachers College, Columbia University. She has worked as an elementary school teacher, computer teacher, and staff developer. She has been a workshop presenter and instructional coach at several institutions, including The Center for Mathematics, Science, and Computer Education at Rutgers University and the School for Global Education and Innovation at Kean University.

Clinton Simeti is a lecturer at AUT and facilitates courses on a diverse range of fields within the sphere of Digital Media scholarship. He has taught 3D modeling and animation, Motion Capture, interactivity, moving image compositing/editing and visual communication at an undergraduate and postgraduate level. His masters research explored notions of human identity as fluid, fragmented and decentered in the age of digital surveillance and the computer database. His is currently exploring the potential of eye-tracking techniques and augmented reality as media for non-linear storytelling.

Nance S. Wilson is an Associate Professor of literacy education at State University of New York at Cortland. Her research focuses on professional development, new literacies, comprehension, and adolescent literacy. Dr. Wilson's work has been published in the *Journal of Reading Education, Middle School Journal, Journal of Adolescent and Adult Literacy, Reading Horizons, Literacy, Metacognition and Learning, California Reader, Florida Educational Leadership Journal*, and *Florida Association of Teacher Educators* among others. She serves in several editorial roles, including *Reading and Writing Quarterly: Overcoming Reading Difficulties* and *Reading in the Middle*. She has served in leadership positions in the American Reading Forum and the Middle School Reading Special Interest Group of the International Reading Association.

Melda N. Yildiz is a global scholar and teacher educator in the School for Global Education and Innovation at Kean University and adjunct faculty in Master of Education in Technology in Education at Lesley University.Melda served as the first Fulbright Scholar in Turkmenistan from 2009-2010. Since